BASEBALL AMERICA'S 1997 DIRECTORY

Major And Minor League Names, Addresses, Schedules, Phone and FAX Numbers: Plus Detailed Information On International, College and Amateur Baseball

PUBLISHED BY
BASEBALL AMERICA

PUBLISHED BY
BASEBALL AMERICA

EDITOR
Allan Simpson
ASSOCIATE EDITOR
John Royster
ASSISTANT EDITORS
Stephen Borelli
John Manuel
Jeff Rosner

PRODUCTION SUPERVISOR
Jeff Brunk
PRODUCTION MANAGER
Valerie Holbert
PRODUCTION ASSISTANT
Casey Mansfield Thomas

BASEBALL AMERICA, INC.
PUBLISHER
Dave Chase
MANAGING EDITOR
Jim Callis
ASSISTANT EDITOR
Will Lingo

Distributed by Simon & Schuster

For additional copies, send $12.95 plus $5 shipping to:
Baseball America, P.O. Box 2089, Durham NC 27702.

1997 DIRECTORY
CONTENTS

MAJOR LEAGUES

MINOR LEAGUES

MISCELLANEOUS

1997-1998 CALENDAR

March, 1997

Sun	Mon	Tues	Wed	Thur	Fri	Sat
						1
2	3	4	5	6	7	8
9	10	11	12	13	14	15
16	17	18	19	20	21	22
23	24	25	26	27	28	29
30	31					

April, 1997

Sun	Mon	Tues	Wed	Thur	Fri	Sat
		1	2	3	4	5
6	7	8	9	10	11	12
13	14	15	16	17	18	19
20	21	22	23	24	25	26
27	28	29	30			

May, 1997

Sun	Mon	Tues	Wed	Thur	Fri	Sat
				1	2	3
4	5	6	7	8	9	10
11	12	13	14	15	16	17
18	19	20	21	22	23	24
25	26	27	28	29	30	31

June, 1997

Sun	Mon	Tues	Wed	Thur	Fri	Sat
1	2	3	4	5	6	7
8	9	10	11	12	13	14
15	16	17	18	19	20	21
22	23	24	25	26	27	28
29	30					

July, 1997

Sun	Mon	Tues	Wed	Thur	Fri	Sat
		1	2	3	4	5
6	7	8	9	10	11	12
13	14	15	16	17	18	19
20	21	22	23	24	25	26
27	28	29	30	31		

August, 1997

Sun	Mon	Tues	Wed	Thur	Fri	Sat
					1	2
3	4	5	6	7	8	9
10	11	12	13	14	15	16
17	18	19	20	21	22	23
24	25	26	27	28	29	30
31						

September, 1997

Sun	Mon	Tues	Wed	Thur	Fri	Sat
	1	2	3	4	5	6
7	8	9	10	11	12	13
14	15	16	17	18	19	20
21	22	23	24	25	26	27
28	29	30				

October, 1997

Sun	Mon	Tues	Wed	Thur	Fri	Sat
			1	2	3	4
5	6	7	8	9	10	11
12	13	14	15	16	17	18
19	20	21	22	23	24	25
26	27	28	29	30	31	

November, 1997

Sun	Mon	Tues	Wed	Thur	Fri	Sat
						1
2	3	4	5	6	7	8
9	10	11	12	13	14	15
16	17	18	19	20	21	22
23	24	25	26	27	28	29
30						

December, 1997

Sun	Mon	Tues	Wed	Thur	Fri	Sat
	1	2	3	4	5	6
7	8	9	10	11	12	13
14	15	16	17	18	19	20
21	22	23	24	25	26	27
28	29	30	31			

January, 1998

Sun	Mon	Tues	Wed	Thur	Fri	Sat
				1	2	3
4	5	6	7	8	9	10
11	12	13	14	15	16	17
18	19	20	21	22	23	24
25	26	27	28	29	30	31

February, 1998

Sun	Mon	Tues	Wed	Thur	Fri	Sat
1	2	3	4	5	6	7
8	9	10	11	12	13	14
15	16	17	18	19	20	21
22	23	24	25	26	27	28

March, 1998

Sun	Mon	Tues	Wed	Thur	Fri	Sat
1	2	3	4	5	6	7
8	9	10	11	12	13	14
15	16	17	18	19	20	21
22	23	24	25	26	27	28
29	30	31				

April, 1998

Sun	Mon	Tues	Wed	Thur	Fri	Sat
			1	2	3	4
5	6	7	8	9	10	11
12	13	14	15	16	17	18
19	20	21	22	23	24	25
26	27	28	29	30		

EVENTS CALENDAR

March 1997-February 1998

March 19—Opening Day: Mexican League.

March 31-April 3—National Classic High School Tournament at Orange County, Calif.

April 1—Opening Day: American League.

April 1—Opening Day: National League.

April 3—Opening Day: American Association, International League, Pacific Coast League, Eastern League, Southern League, Texas League, California League, Florida State League, South Atlantic League.

April 4—Opening Day: Carolina League, Midwest League.

May 22-25—NCAA Division I Regionals at campus sites.

May 23-29—NAIA World Series at Sioux City, Iowa.

May 24-28—NCAA Division III World Series at Salem, Va.

May 24-31—NCAA Division II World Series at Montgomery, Ala.

May 24-31—Junior College World Series at Grand Junction, Colo.

May 30-June 7—College World Series at Omaha.

June 1—Opening Day: Dominican Summer League.

June 3-5—Amateur free agent draft.

June 10-25—Team USA trials, site unavailable.

June 17—Opening Day: New York-Penn League, Northwest League. California League vs. Carolina League all-star game at Durham, N.C. Midwest League all-star game at Lansing, Mich. South Atlantic League all-star game at Augusta, Ga.

June 18—Opening Day: Appalachian League, Pioneer League.

June 20—Opening Day: Gulf Coast League.

June 20-29—USA Junior Olympic Championship at Fort Myers, Fla.

June 21—Florida State League all-star game at Kissimmee, Fla.

June 24—Opening Day: Arizona League.

June 24-28—Sunbelt Classic Baseball Series at Shawnee/Tecumseh, Okla.

June 26-29—Team One National Showcase at Sarasota, Fla.

June 26-July 1—National Amateur All-Star Baseball Tournament, site unavailable.

July 7—Double-A all-star game at San Antonio.

July 8—68th Major League All-Star Game at Jacobs Field, Cleveland.

July 9—Triple-A all-star game at Des Moines.

July 12-20—AA World Junior Championships at Taiwan.

July 21—Southern League all-star game vs. Seattle Mariners at Zebulon, N.C.

July 30—Texas League all-star game at Shreveport, La.

Aug. 1—End of major league trading period without waivers.

Aug. 1-10—Intercontinental Cup at Barcelona, Spain.

Aug. 1-15—National Baseball Congress World Series at Wichita, Kan.

Aug. 3—Hall of Fame induction ceremonies at Cooperstown, N.Y.

Aug. 4—Hall of Fame Game, Los Angeles Dodgers vs. San Diego Padres at Cooperstown, N.Y.

Aug. 6-9—Eastern U.S. Baseball Showcase at Chapel Hill, N.C.

Aug. 8-16—AAA World Youth Championship at Moncton, New Brunswick.

Aug. 9-16—Babe Ruth 16-18 World Series at Jamestown, N.Y.

Aug. 11-17—Area Code Games at San Diego.

Aug. 16-23—Babe Ruth 13-15 World Series at Longview, Wash.

Aug. 18-23—Little League World Series at Williamsport, Pa.

Aug. 20-31—World University Games at Palermo, Italy.

Aug. 21-26—American Legion World Series at Rapid City, S.D.

Aug. 31—Postseason major league roster eligibility frozen.

Sept. 1—Major league roster limits expanded from 25 to 40.

Sept. 28—Major league season ends.

Sept. 30—Major league playoffs begin.

Oct. 7—Major League Championship Series begin.

Oct. 18—World Series begins at home of National League champion.

Nov. TBD—Major league expansion draft: Arizona, Tampa Bay

Nov. 20—Forty-man major league winter rosters must be filed.

Dec. 5-7—National High School Baseball Coaches Association convention at Louisville.

Dec. 12-16—95th annual Winter Meetings at New Orleans.

Dec. 15—Rule 5 draft.

Dec. 21-28—Goodwill Series XIII at Adelaide, Australia.

Jan. 2-5—American Baseball Coaches Association convention at San Diego.

Feb. 3-8—Caribbean World Series at Puerto la Cruz, Venezuela.

BASEBALL AMERICA

ESTABLISHED 1981

PUBLISHER: Dave Chase

EDITOR: Allan Simpson

PRODUCTION SUPERVISOR: Jeff Brunk

MANAGING EDITOR: Jim Callis
SENIOR ASSOCIATE EDITOR: John Royster
ASSOCIATE EDITOR: Will Lingo
ASSISTANT EDITOR: Stephen Borelli
ASSISTANT EDITOR: John Manuel
NATIONAL WRITER: Alan Schwarz
EDITORIAL INTERN: Jeff Rosner

PRODUCTION MANAGER: Valerie Holbert

PRODUCTION ASSISTANT: Casey Mansfield Thomas

CUSTOMER SERVICE: Ronnie McCabe, Maxine Tillman

ADVERTISING SALES
Kris Howard, Advertising Manager
Carole Budd, Marketplace Manager
P.O. Box 2089, Durham, NC 27702
Phone (800) 845-2726; FAX: 919-682-2880
Michael Applegate, Southeast Representative
3132 Paces Station Ridge, Atlanta, GA 30339
Phone (770) 805-0949
NATIONAL NEWSSTAND CONSULTANT
John Blassingame, Linden, NJ

BASEBALL AMERICA, Inc.
PRESIDENT: Miles Wolff
P.O. Box 2089, Durham, NC 27702
Street Address: 600 S. Duke St., Durham, NC 27701
Phone: (919) 682-9635
Toll-Free: (800) 845-2726
FAX: (919) 682-2880
E-mail: ba@interpath.com

TOLL FREE PHONE NUMBERS

Airlines

Aero Mexico	800-237-6639
Air Canada	800-776-3000
Alaska Airlines	800-426-0333
Aloha Airlines	800-227-4900
America West	800-235-9292
American Airlines	800-433-7300
Continental Airlines	800-525-0280
Delta Airlines	800-221-1212
Northwest Airlines	800-225-2525
Olympic Airways	800-223-1226
Qantas Airways	800-227-4500
Southwest Airlines	800-435-9792
Trans World Airlines	800-221-2000
United Airlines	800-631-1500
U.S. Air	800-428-4322

Car Rentals

Alamo (national)	800-327-9633
Alamo (international)	800-522-9696
Avis	800-331-1212
Avis International	800-331-1084
Budget	800-527-0700
Dollar	800-800-4000
Enterprise	800-325-8007
Hertz	800-654-3131
Hertz International	800-654-3001
National	800-227-7368
Thrifty	800-367-2277

Hotels/Motels

Best Western	800-528-1234
Choice Hotels	800-424-6423
Courtyard by Marriott	800-321-2211
Days Inn	800-325-2525
Doubletree Hotels/Guest Suites	800-424-2900
Embassy Suites	800-362-2779
Hampton Inns	800-426-7866
Hilton Hotels	800-445-8667
Holiday Inns	800-465-4329
Howard Johnsons Motor Lodges	800-654-2000
Hyatt Hotels	800-228-9000
La Quinta	800-531-5900
Marriott Hotels	800-228-9290
Omni Hotels	800-843-6664
Radisson Hotels	800-333-3333
Ramada Inns	800-228-2828
Red Roof Inns	800-843-7663
Sheraton Hotels	800-325-3535
Renaissance Hotels	800-468-3571
TraveLodge	800-578-7878
Westin Hotels	800-228-3000

Rail

Amtrak	800-872-7245

OFFICE OF THE COMMISSIONER

Bud Selig

Mailing Address: 350 Park Ave., 17th Floor, New York, NY 10022. **Telephone:** (212) 339-7800. **FAX:** (212) 758-8660.

Commissioner: Vacant.

Chairman, Executive Council: Allan H. "Bud" Selig.

Officers and Directors

President, Chief Executive Officer: Greg Murphy. **Vice President, Chief Information Officer:** James Inasterson.

Executive Director, Baseball Operations: Bill Murray. **Director:** Roy Krasik. **Supervisor:** George Pfister. **Administrator:** Jeff Pfeifer. **Records Coordinator:** George Moreira. **Administrative Assistant:** Jean Coen.

Executive Director, Minor League Operations: Jimmie Lee Solomon.

Executive Director, Public Relations: Richard Levin. **Managers:** Carole Coleman, Pat Courtney. **Baseball Information Systems:** Rob Doelger. **Administrator, Community Relations:** Wally Weibel. **Supervisor, Public Relations:** Kathleen Fineout. **Administrator, Media Relations:** Denise Michaels.

Executive Director, Security/Facility Management: Kevin Hallinan.

Chief Financial Officer: Jeffrey White. **Controller:** Robert Clark.

General Counsel: Thomas Ostertag.

Executive Director, Market Development and MLB Charities: Kathy Francis.

Director of Human Resources: Wendy Lewis.

Director of Broadcasting: Leslie Sullivan.

Director, Special Events: Carolyn Taylor.

1997 Major League All-Star Game: July 8 at Jacobs Field, Cleveland.

MAJOR LEAGUE BASEBALL PLAYER RELATIONS COMMITTEE

Mailing Address: 350 Park Ave., New York, NY 10022. **Telephone:** (212) 339-7400. **FAX:** (212) 371-2242.

Chief Labor Negotiator: Randy Levine.

Associate Counsel: John Westhoff, Louis Melendez.

Contract Administrator: John Ricco.

MAJOR LEAGUE BASEBALL PROPERTIES

Mailing Address: 350 Park Ave., New York, NY 10022. **Telephone:** (212) 339-7900. **FAX:** (212) 339-7628.

President: Bob Gamgort.

Vice President, Business Development and New Ventures: Michael Bernstein. **Vice President, Creative Design and Marketing Services:** Anne Occi. **Vice President, Finance and Royalty Administration:** Tom Duffy.

MAJOR LEAGUE BASEBALL INTERNATIONAL

Mailing Address: 350 Park Ave., 22nd Floor, New York, NY 10022. **Telephone:** (212) 350-8300. **FAX:** (212) 826-2230.

Chief Operating Officer: Tim Brosnan.

Vice President, Market Development: Steve Baker. **Vice President, Corporate Sponsorship:** Paul Archey. **Vice President, Operations and Television Production:** Russell Gabay.

Director, European Operations: Clive Russell. **Director, Australia:** Peter Carton. **Game Development Coordinator, Latin America:** George Santiago.

Associate Director, Broadcasting: Margie O'Neill. **Associate Director, Client Services:** Sara Fernandez.

AMERICAN LEAGUE

AMERICAN LEAGUE

Gene Budig

Mailing Address: 350 Park Ave., 18th Floor, New York, NY 10022.

Telephone: (212) 339-7600. **FAX:** (212) 593-7138.

Years League Active: 1901-.

Board of Directors: Anaheim, Baltimore, Milwaukee, New York, Oakland, Texas.

President: Gene Budig.

Vice President: Gene Autry.

Executive Director, Umpiring: Marty Springstead. **Coordinator, Umpire Operations:** Philip Janssen. **Administrator, Umpire Travel:** Tess Basta.

Vice President, Administration and Media Affairs: Phyllis Merhige.

Vice President, Finance: Derek Irwin.

Director of Waiver and Player Records: Kim Ng.

Administrative Assistant, Secretary to the President: Carolyn Coen.

Receptionist: Nancy Perez.

1997 Opening Date: April 1. **Closing Date:** Sept. 28.

No. of Games: 162.

Division Structure: East--Baltimore, Boston, Detroit, New York, Toronto. **Central**—Chicago, Cleveland, Kansas City, Milwaukee, Minnesota. **West**—Anaheim, Oakland, Seattle, Texas. **NOTE:** Tampa Bay will begin league play in 1998.

Roster Limit: 25, through Aug. 31 when rosters expanded to 40.

Umpires: Larry Barnett (Prospect, OH), Joe Brinkman (Cocoa, FL), Gary Cedarstrom (Minot, ND), Al Clark (Williamsburg, VA), Drew Coble (Graham, NC), Derryl Cousins (Hermosa Beach, CA), Terry Craft (Sarasota, FL), Don Denkinger (Waterloo, IA), Jim Evans (Castle Rock, CO), Dale Ford (Jonesboro, TN), Rich Garcia (Clearwater, FL), Ted Hendry (Scottsdale, AZ), John Hirschbeck (Poland, OH), Mark Johnson (Honolulu, HI), Jim Joyce (Beaverton, OR), Ken Kaiser (Pompano Beach, FL), Greg Kosc (Medina, OH), Tim McClelland (West Des Moines, IA), Larry McCoy (Greenway, AR), Jim McKean (St. Petersburg, FL), Chuck Meriwether (Nashville, TN), Durwood Merrill (Hooks, TX), Dan Morrison (Largo, FL), Dave Phillips (Lake St. Louis, MO), Rick Reed (Rochester Hills, MI), Mike Reilly (Battle Creek, MI), Rocky Roe (Milford, MI), Dale Scott (Portland, OR), John Shulock (Vero Beach, FL), Tim Tschida (Turtle Lake, WI), Tim Welke (Kalamazoo, MI), Larry Young (Roscoe, IL).

1996 Standings

East	W	L	Pct.	GB
New York	92	70	.568	—
Baltimore	88	74	.543	4
Boston	85	77	.525	7
Toronto	74	88	.457	18
Detroit	53	109	.327	39

West	W	L	Pct.	GB
Texas	90	72	.556	—
Seattle	85	76	.528	4½

Central	W	L	Pct.	GB
Cleveland	99	62	.615	—
Chicago	85	77	.525	14½
Milwaukee	80	82	.494	19½
Minnesota	78	84	.481	21½
Kansas City	75	86	.466	24

West	W	L	Pct.	GB
Oakland	78	84	.481	12
California	70	91	.435	19½

Stadium Information

		Dimensions				
City	Stadium	LF	CF	RF	Capacity	'96 Att.
Anaheim*	Anaheim Stadium	333	404	333	33,851	1,820,532
Baltimore	Camden Yards	333	410	318	48,876	3,646,950
Boston	Fenway Park	310	390	302	33,871	2,315,233
Chicago	Comiskey Park	347	400	347	44,321	1,676,416
Cleveland	Jacobs Field	325	405	325	42,865	3,318,174
Detroit	Tiger Stadium	340	440	325	46,945	1,168,610
Kansas City	Kauffman Stadium	330	400	330	40,625	1,436,007
Milwaukee	County Stadium	315	402	315	53,192	1,327,155
Minnesota	Humphrey Metrodome	343	408	327	48,678	1,437,352
New York	Yankee Stadium	318	408	314	57,545	2,250,124
Oakland	Alameda County	330	400	330	43,012	1,148,382
Seattle	Kingdome	331	405	312	58,801	2,722,054
Texas	Ballpark in Arlington	334	400	325	49,166	2,888,920
Toronto	SkyDome	328	400	328	50,516	2,559,563

*Known as California in 1996

ANAHEIM

Telephone, Address

Office Address: Anaheim Stadium, 2000 Gene Autry Way, Anaheim, CA 92806. **Mailing Address:** P.O. Box 2000, Anaheim, CA 92803. **Telephone:** (714) 940-2000. **FAX:** (714) 940-2205.

Ownership

Operated by: Anaheim Sports, Inc.

Principal Owners: Gene Autry, Anaheim Sports, Inc. **Chairman/Chief Excecutive Officer:** Michael Eisner.

President: Tony Tavares. **Administrative Assistant to the President:** Jennifer Mitchell.

BUSINESS OPERATIONS

Vice President of Finance/Administration: Andy Roundtree.

Vice President of Business Affairs: Kevin Gilmore. **Administrative Assistant, Business Affairs:** Tia Wood. **Manager, Business Operations:** Larry Cohen.

Manager, Human Resources: Jenny Price. **Administrative Assistant, Human Resources:** Cindy Williams. **Manager, Information Services:** Andy Roe. **Office Manager:** Barbara Potts.

Finance

Director of Finance: Martin Greenspun. **Controller:** Jon Sullivan. **Assistant Controllers:** Cristina Fisher, Melody Martin.

Marketing, Sales

Director of Marketing: Bill Holford. **Director of Advertising and Broadcast Sales:** Bob Wagner. **Manager, Promotions and Sponsorship Services:** Sue O'Shea. **Manager, Group Sales:** Andy Silverman. **Manager, Ticket Sales:** Lisa Manning.

Advertising Sales Managers: John Covarrubias, Richard McClemmy, Dave Severson. **Sales Coordinator:** Debbie Nielander. **Marketing Associate:** Tony Reagins.

Director of Entertainment: Charlie Messerly.

Public Relations, Communications

Telephone: (714) 940-2000. **FAX:** (714) 940-2205.

Director of Communications: Bill Robertson.

Manager, Media Services: Larry Babcock. **Manager, Publications:** Doug Ward. **Manager, Civic Affairs:** Tory Whittingham. **Manager, Community Relations:** Marie Moreno. **Media Relations Coordinator:** Marc Simon. **Assistant, Media Relations:** Carolyn LaPierre.

Speakers Bureau: Clyde Wright.

Stadium Operations

Director, Stadium Operations: Kevin Uhlich. **Administrative Assistant:** Leslie Flammini. **Manager, Facility Services:** Mike McKay. **Event Supervisor:** John Drum.

Manager, Field/Ground Maintenance: Barney Lopas.

PA Announcer: David Courtney. **Official Scorer:** Ed Munson.

Ticketing

Manager, Ticket Operations: Don Boudreau. **Assistant Ticket Manager:** Susan Weiss.

Travel, Clubhouse

Equipment Manager: Ken Higdon. **Visiting Clubhouse:** Brian Harkins. **Senior Video Coordinator:** Diego Lopez.

Radio, TV, Media

Radio Announcers: Mario Impemba, Bob Starr. **Flagship Station:** KMPC 710-AM.

TV Announcers: Steve Physioc, Sparky Anderson (cable); Steve Physioc, Jerry Reuss (local). **Flagship Stations:** KCAL Channel 9, Fox Sports West (regional cable).

NEWSPAPERS, Daily Coverage: Los Angeles Times, Orange County Register, Long Beach Press-Telegram, Riverside Press Enterprise, San Bernandino Sun, La Opinion.

General Information

Hometown Dugout: Third Base. **Playing Surface:** Grass.

Stadium Location: Highway 57 (Orange Freeway) to Katella Ave. exit, west on Katella, stadium on west side of Orange Freeway.

Standard Game Times: 7:05 p.m., Wed. 7:35, Sun. 1:05.

Player Representative: Tim Salmon.

ANGELS

BASEBALL OPERATIONS

Bill Bavasi

Vice President, General Manager: Bill Bavasi.

Assistant General Manager: Tim Mead. **Special Assistants to General Manager:** Preston Gomez, Bob Harrison. **Adminsistrative Assistant to President:** Jennifer Mitchell. **Administrative Assistant to General Manager:** Cathy Carey.

Legal Counsel/Contract Negotiations: Mark Rosenthal.

Major League Staff

Manager: Terry Collins.

Coaches: Bench—Joe Maddon; Pitching—Marcel Lachemann; Batting—Rod Carew; First Base—Dave Parker; Third Base—Larry Bowa; Bullpen—Joe Coleman; Bullpen Coordinator—Mick Billmeyer.

Medical, Training

Medical Director: Dr. Lewis Yocum. **Team Physician:** Dr. Craig Milhouse.

Terry Collins

Trainers: Ned Bergert, Rick Smith. **Strength and Conditioning:** Tom Wilson. **Sports Psychologist:** Ken Ravizza. **Physical Therapy Consultant:** Bick Harmon. **Administrative Assistant:** Chris Titchenal.

Minor Leagues

Director, Player Development: Ken Forsch. **Manager, Baseball Operations:** Jeff Parker. **Administrative Assistants:** Janet German, Lisa Harryman.

Field Coordinator: Eddie Rodriguez.

Roving Instructors: Bob Clear (special assignments), Mike Couchee (pitching), John McNamara (catching), Gene Richards (hitting).

Farm System

Class	Farm Team	Manager	Coach	Pitching Coach
AAA	Vancouver	Bruce Hines	Leon Durham	Howie Gershberg
AA	Midland	Mitch Seoane	Orlando Mercado	Greg Minton
A	Lake Elsinore	Don Long	Tyrone Boykin	Jim Bennett
A	Cedar Rapids	Mario Mendoza	Todd Claus	Rick Wise
A	Boise	Tom Kotchman	Unavailable	Zeke Zimmerman
Rookie	Butte	Bill Lachemann	Charlie Romero	Kernan Ronan

Scouting

Bob Fontaine

Director, Scouting: Bob Fontaine Jr.

Administrative Assistant, Scouting: Lisa Harryman.

Special Assistant to Scouting/Player Personnel: Rich Schlenker (Walnut Creek, CA).

Advance Scout: Matt Keough (Cota de Caza, CA).

Major League Scouts: Dave Garcia (El Cajon, CA), Jay Hankins (Greenwood, MO), Bob Harrison (Long Beach, CA), Nick Kamzic (Evergreen Park, IL), Joe McDonald (Lakeland, FL), Tom Romenesko (Santee, CA), Moose Stubing (Villa Park, CA), Dale Sutherland (La Crescenta, CA).

Free-Agent Supervisors: John Burden (Fairfield, OH), Tom Burns (Harrisburg, PA), Pete Coachman (Cottonwood, AL), Tom Davis (Auburn, CA), Red Gaskill (La Marque, TX), Steve Gruwell (West Covina, CA), Rick Ingalls (Anaheim Hills, CA), Hal Keller (Issaquah, WA), Tim Kelly (Carlsbad, CA), Kris Kline (Fort Worth, TX), Tom Kotchman (Seminole, FL), Tony La Cava (Oakmont, PA), Ron Marigny (Lake Charles, LA), Jim McLaughlin (Yonkers, NY), Darrell Miller (Yorba Linda, CA), Jon Neiderer (Pittsburgh, PA), Tom Osowski (Milwaukee, WI), Paul Robinson (Fort Worth, TX), Jerry Streeter (Modesto, CA), Rip Tutor (Lenoir, NC), Jack Uhey (Vancouver, WA), Dick Wilson (Sun Valley, NV).

Director, International Scouting: Ta Honda (Osaka, Japan). **International Scouts:** Marco Davalillo (Venezuela), Pompeyo Davalillo (Venezuela), Jose Gomez (Dominican Republic), Eusebio Perez (Mexico).

BALTIMORE

Telephone, Address

Office Address: 333 West Camden St., Baltimore, MD 21201. **Telephone:** (410) 685-9800. **FAX:** (410) 547-6272.

Ownership

Operated by: The Home Team Limited Partnership.

Chairman of the Board, Chief Executive Officer: Peter Angelos.

Vice Chairman/Community Projects and Public Affairs: Tom Clancy.

Peter Angelos

BUSINESS OPERATIONS

Executive Vice President, Business and Finance: Joe Foss.

Chief Administrative/Executive Officer: Walt Gutowski. **General Counsel:** George Stamas.

Director of Human Resources: Martena Clinton.

Finance

Vice President, Finance: Robert Ames.

Marketing, Sales

Executive Director, Marketing and Broadcasting: Michael Lehr. **Director of Marketing and Advertising:** Scott Nickle. **Corporate Marketing Managers:** Nan Rehfield, Jim Hawes. **Advertising and Promotions Manager:** Jim Brylcwski. **Administrative Assistant, Marketing and Broadcasting:** Kristen Kepplo. **Marketing Coordinator:** Kathy Case.

Public Relations, Communications

Telephone: (410) 547-6150. **FAX:** (410) 547-6272.

Director of Public Relations: John Maroon. **Assistant Director, Public Relations:** Bill Stetka. **Administrative Assistant:** Heather Tilles. **Director, Publications:** Stephanie Parrillo.

Director of Community Relations: Julie Wagner. **Assistant Director:** Stacy Beckwith. **Administrative Assistant:** Jennifer Steier.

Stadium Operations

Director, Stadium Operations: Roy Summerhof. **Assistant Director, Stadium Operations:** Mike Rogers. **Director of Field Maintenance, Head Groundskeeper:** Paul Zwaska.

PA Announcer: Rex Barney. **Official Scorer:** Marc Jacobson.

Ticketing

Telephone: (410) 685-9800. **FAX:** (410) 547-6270.

Director, Ticket Operations: Audrey Brown. **Assistant Director:** Denise Addicks. **Operations Manager, Ticket Services/Box Office Manager:** Steve Kowalski.

Travel, Clubhouse

Traveling Secretary: Phil Itzoe.

Equipment Manager, Home: Jim Tyler. **Equipment Manager, Visitors:** Fred Tyler.

Radio, TV, Media

Radio Announcers: Jim Hunter, Fred Manfra, Chuck Thompson. **Flagship Station:** WBAL 1090-AM. **No. of Network Stations:** 25.

TV Announcers: Unavailable. **Flagship Stations:** WJZ Channel 13, Home Team Sports (regional cable).

NEWSPAPERS, Daily Coverage: Baltimore Sun, Washington Post, York (Pa.) Daily Record.

General Information

Team Colors: Orange and black.

Hometown Dugout: First Base. **Playing Surface:** Grass.

Stadium Location: I-95 to exit 52 or 53.

Standard Games Times: 7:35 p.m., Sat. 1:05, Sun. 1:35.

Player Representative: Mike Mussina.

ORIOLES

BASEBALL OPERATIONS

General Manager: Pat Gillick.

Assistant General Manager: Kevin Malone. **Administrative Assistant, Baseball Operations:** Ellen Harrigan.

Pat Gillick

Major League Staff

Manager: Davey Johnson.

Coaches: Dugout—Andy Etchebarren; Pitching—Ray Miller; Batting—Rick Down; First Base—John Stearns; Third Base—Sam Perlozzo; Bullpen—Elrod Hendricks.

Medical, Training

Club Physician: Dr. William Goldiner.

Head Trainer: Richie Bancells. **Assistant Trainer:** Brian Ebel. **Strength and Conditioning Director:** Tim Bishop.

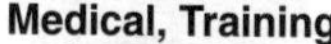

Davey Johnson

Minor Leagues

Telephone: (410) 547-6120. **FAX:** (410) 547-6298.

Director of Player Development: Syd Thrift. **Assistant Director of Player Development:** Don Buford.

Coordinator of Instruction: Tom Trebelhorn. **Minor League Camp Coordinator:** Lenny Johnston.

Roving Instructors: Bobby Dickerson (infield), Moe Drabowsky (pitching), Mike Easler (hitting), David Stockstill (hitting), Joe Tanner (bunting).

Medical Coordinator: Brian Ebel. **Strength and Conditioning:** Pat Hedge. **Groundskeeper:** Jaime Rodriguez.

Farm System

Class	Farm Team	Manager	Coach	Pitching Coach
AAA	Rochester	Marv Foley	Dave Cash	Fred Dallimore
AA	Bowie	Joe Ferguson	Bien Figueroa	Larry McCall
A	Frederick	Dave Hilton	None	Jeff Morris
A	Delmarva	Tommy Shields	None	Larry Jaster
Rookie	Bluefield	Bobby Dickerson	None	Charlie Puleo
Rookie	Sarasota	Butch Davis	Jesus Alfaro	John O'Donoghue

Scouting

Telephone: (410) 547-6133. **FAX:** (410) 547-6298.

Director of Scouting: Gary Nickels.

Scouting Administrator: Matt Slater. **Computer Services Assistant:** Marcy Zerhusen.

Advance Scout: Deacon Jones (Sugar Land, TX).

Major League Scouts: Curt Motton (Woodstock, MD), Fred Uhlman Sr. (Baltimore, MD), Don Welke (Louisville, KY).

National Crosschecker: Mike Ledna (Buffalo Grove, IL).

Gary Nickels

Scouting Supervisors: West—Logan White (Phoenix, AZ); Midwest—Earl Winn (Bowling Green, KY); East—John Stokoe (Alexandria, NH).

Scouts: Rick Arnold (Murrieta, CA), Dean DeCillis (Tamarac, FL), Lane Decker (Piedmont, OK), John Green (Phoenix, AZ), Jim Howard (Clifton Park, NY), Gil Kubski (Huntington Beach, CA), Lamar North (Rossville, GA), Fred Petersen (Lisle, IL), Jim Robinson (Mansfield, TX), Harry Shelton (Ocoee, FL), Ed Sprague (Lodi, CA), Marc Trabouta (Germantown, MD), Mike Tullier (New Orleans, LA), Marc Ziegler (Bowling Green, KY), Jerry Zimmerman (Neskowin, OR).

International Supervisor: Manny Estrada (Brandon, FL).

International Scouts: Carlos Bernhardt (Dominican Republic), Patrick Guerrero (Dominican Republic), Jesus Halabi (Aruba), Ubaldo Heredia (Venezuela), Arturo Sanchez (Venezuela), Brett Ward (Australia).

BOSTON

Telephone, Address

Office Address: Fenway Park, 4 Yawkey Way, Boston, MA 02215. **Telephone:** (617) 267-9440. **FAX:** (617) 236-6797.

E-Mail Address: www.redsox.com

Ownership

Operated by: Boston Red Sox Baseball Club.

General Partner: Jean R. Yawkey Trust (Trustees: John Harrington, William Gutfarb). **Limited Partners:** ARAMARK Corp (Chairman: Joseph Neubauer).; Dexter Group (Principal: Harold Alfond); Jean R. Yawkey Trust; Dr. Arthur Pappas; Samuel Tamposi Trust; Thomas DiBenedetto; John Harrington; John Kaneb.

John Harrington

Chief Executive Officer: John Harrington.

BUSINESS OPERATIONS

Executive Vice President, Administration: John Buckley.

Finance

Vice President, Chief Financial Officer: Robert Furbush.

Controller: Stanley Tran. **Staff Accountant:** Robin Yeingst.

Marketing, Sales

Vice President, Marketing/Sales: Larry Cancro.

Director of Sales: Robert Capilli. **Director of Advertising and Sponsorship:** Jeff Goldenberg. **Promotions and Special Events Manager:** Susan Salerno. **Group Sales Manager:** Tim Dalton.

Vice President, Broadcasting/Information Technology: James Healey. **Broadcasting Manager:** James Shannahan.

Public Affairs, Communications

Telephone: (617) 236-6715. **FAX:** (617) 236-6797.

Vice President, Public Affairs: Dick Bresciani.

Publications Manager: Debra Matson. **Community Relations Manager:** Ron Burton. **Customer Relations Manager:** Ann Marie Starzyk. **Public Afffairs Administrator:** Mary Jane Ryan.

Executive Consultant, Public Affairs: Lou Gorman.

Stadium Operations

Vice President, Stadium Operations: Joe McDermott.

Director of Facilities Management: Tom Queenan. **Superintendent of Grounds and Maintenance:** Joe Mooney. **Ground Crew Manager:** Casey Erven. **Property Maintenance Manager:** John Caron. **Director of Food Services:** Patricia Flanagan.

PA Announcer: Leslie Sterling. **Official Scorers:** Charlie Scoggins, Ben Ells.

Ticketing

Telephone: (617) 267-1700. **FAX:** (617) 236-6640.

Director of Ticket Operations: Joe Helyar. **Box Office Manager:** Richard Beaton. **Telephone Sales Manager:** Jeff Connors.

Travel, Clubhouse

Traveling Secretary: John McCormick.

Equipment Manager/Clubhouse Operations: Joe Cochran. **Visiting Clubhouse Operations:** Tom McLaughlin.

Radio, TV, Media

Radio Announcers: Joe Castiglione, Jerry Trupiano. **Flagship Station:** WEEI 590-AM. **No. of Network Stations:** 65.

TV Announcers: WABU—Sean McDonough, Jerry Remy. NESN—Bob Kurtz, Jerry Remy. **Flagship Stations:** WABU, New England Sports Network (regional cable).

NEWSPAPERS, Daily Coverage: Boston Globe, Boston Herald, Patriot Ledger, Providence Journal, Worcester Telegram, Hartford Courant.

General Information

Hometown Dugout: First Base. **Playing Surface:** Grass.

Standard Games Times: Day—1:05 p.m. Night—7:05.

Directions to Stadium: Massachusetts Turnpike (I-90) to Prudential exit (stay left), right at first set of lights, right on Dalton Street, left on Boylston Street, right on Ipswich Street.

Player Representative: Unavailable.

RED SOX

BASEBALL OPERATIONS

Dan Duquette

Telephone: (617) 267-9440. **FAX:** (617) 236-6649.

Executive Vice President, General Manager: Dan Duquette.

Vice President, Baseball Operations: Mike Port. **Assistant General Manager, Legal Counsel:** Elaine W. Steward. **Director of Major League Administration:** Steve August. **Coordinator of Baseball Development and Administration:** Kent Qualls. **Baseball Operations Assistant:** Thomas Moore.

Director of Communications and Baseball Information: Kevin Shea. **Baseball Information Manager:** Fred Seymour. **Credentials Administrator:** Kathleen Gordon.

Jimy Williams

Major League Staff

Manager: Jimy Williams.

Coaches: Dugout—Grady Little; Pitching—Joe Kerrigan; Batting—Jim Rice; First Base—Dave Jauss; Third Base—Wendell Kim; Bullpen—Herm Starrette.

Medical, Training

Medical Director: Dr. Arthur Pappas.

Head Trainer: James Rowe Jr. **Strength and Conditioning Coordinator:** B.J. Baker. **Physical Therapist:** Richard Zawacki.

Minor Leagues

Telephone: (617) 267-9440. **FAX:** (617) 236-6695.

Director of Player Development: Bob Schaefer. **Director of Affiliate Operations:** Ed Kenney. **Special Assistant, Player Development:** Johnny Pesky.

Assistant Field Coordinator: Dick Berardino. **Pitching Coordinator:** Sammy Ellis. **Hitting Coordinator:** Steve Braun. **Rehab Coordinator:** Chris Correnti.

Roving Instructors: Tommy Barrett (infield), Bob Geren (catching), Bobby Mitchell (outfield, baserunning).

Coordinator, Latin American Instruction: Felix Maldonado.

Special Instructors: Eddie Popowski, Charlie Wagner, Carl Yastrzemski.

Farm System

Class	Farm Team	Manager	Coach	Pitching Coach
AAA	Pawtucket	Ken Macha	Rico Petrocelli	John Cumberland
AA	Trenton	DeMarlo Hale	Dave Gallagher	Al Nipper
A	Sarasota	Rob Derksen	Victor Rodriguez	Jeff Gray
A	Michigan	Bill Gardner	Gerald Perry	Dan Gakeler
A	Lowell	Dick Berardino	Rafael Santana	Larry Pierson
Rookie	Fort Myers	Luis Aguayo	Gomer Hodge	Ralph Treuel
Rookie	DSL	Nelson Norman	None	Milciades Olivo

Scouting

Wayne Britton

Scouting Director: Wayne Britton (Staunton, VA).

Assistant Director, Scouting: Erwin Bryant.

Advance Scout: Buddy Bailey (Madison Heights, VA).

Special Assignment Scouts: Eddie Haas (Paducah, KY), Frank Malzone (Needham, MA).

National Crosschecker: Lenny Strelitz (Temple City, CA).

Scouts: Ray Blanco (Miami, FL), Buzz Bowers (Wayland, MA), Kevin Burrell (Sharpsburg, GA), Ray Crone Jr. (Waxahachie, TX), Ray Fagnant (Chicopee, MA), Butch Hobson (Fairhope, AL), Steve McAllister (Chillicothe, IL), Gary Rajsich (Lake Oswego, OR), Mike Rizzo (Rolling Meadows, IL), Phil Rossi (Archbald, PA), Alex Scott (Mobile, AL), Matt Scezesny (Deer Park, NY), Harry Smith (Oceanside, CA), Jerry Stephenson (Fullerton, CA), Fay Thompson (Vallejo, CA), Luke Wrenn (Lakeland, FL), Jeff Zona (Mechanicsville, VA).

Executive Director, International Baseball Operations: Ray Poitevint.

International Scouts: John Candelaria (Dominican Republic), Luis Delgado (Puerto Rico), Adrian Meagher (Australia), Levy Ochoa (Venezuela).

CHICAGO

Jerry Reinsdorf

Telephone, Address

Office Address: 333 W. 35th St., Chicago, IL 60616. **Telephone:** (312) 674-1000. **FAX:** (312) 674-5116. **E-Mail Address:** www.chisox.com.

Ownership

Operated by: Chicago White Sox, Ltd.

Chairman: Jerry Reinsdorf. **Vice Chairman:** Eddie Einhorn.

Board of Directors: Fred Brzozowski, Jack Gould, Robert Judelson, Judd Malkin, Robert Mazer, Allan Muchin, Jay Pinsky, Larry Pogofsky, Lee Stern, Sanford Takiff, Burton Ury, Charles Walsh.

General Counsel: Allan Muchin.

BUSINESS OPERATIONS

Executive Vice President: Howard Pizer.

Director of Information Services: Don Brown. **Director of Human Resources:** Moira Foy.

Special Assistant to the Chairman/Director of Minor League Operations: Ken Williams. **Assistant to the Chairman:** Anita Fasano.

Finance

Vice President, Finance: Tim Buzard.

Controller: Bill Waters. **Accounting Manager:** Julie O'Shea.

Marketing, Sales

Senior Vice President, Marketing and Broadcasting: Rob Gallas.

Director of Marketing and Broadcasting: Bob Grim. **Manager of Promotions and Marketing Services:** Sharon Sreniawski. **Manager of Scoreboard Operations and Production:** Jeff Szynal. **Manager of Sponsorship Sales and Broadcast Operations:** John Browne. **Manager of Marketing Communications and Services:** Dan Polvere. **Marketing Account Executives:** Jim Biegalski, Ty Harvey, Pam Walsh. **Coordinator of Promotions and Marketing Services:** Jo Simmons.

Communications

Telephone: (312) 674-5300. **FAX:** (312) 674-5116.

Director of Communications: Eric Webb. **Assistant Director:** Scott Reifert. **Coordinator of Publicity:** Bob Beghtol.

Secretary and Credentials Coordinator: Mary Dosek.

Manager, Publications: Suzanne Reichart.

Director of Community Relations: Christine Makowski. **Coordinator of Community Relations:** Brian East. **Coordinator of Charitable Programs:** Dionne Smith.

Stadium Operations

Vice President, Stadium Operations: Terry Savarise.

Director of Park Operations: David Schaffer. **Director of Guest Services/Diamond Suite Operations:** Julie Taylor.

Head Groundskeeper: Roger Bossard.

PA Announcer: Gene Honda. **Official Scorer:** Bob Rosenberg.

Ticketing

Telephone: (312) 674-1000. **FAX:** (312) 674-5102.

Director of Ticket Sales: Jim Muno.

Director of Ticket Operations: Bob Devoy. **Ticket Manager:** Ed Cassin.

Travel, Clubhouse

Traveling Secretary: Glen Rosenbaum.

Equipment Manager/Clubhouse Operations: Willie Thompson. **Visiting Clubhouse:** Gabe Morell. **Umpires Clubhouse:** Vince Fresso.

Radio, TV, Media

Radio Announcers: John Rooney, Ed Farmer. **Flagship Station:** WMVP 1000-AM. **No. of Network Stations:** 25.

TV Announcers: Ken Harrelson, Tom Paciorek. **Flagship Stations:** WGN TV-9, SportsChannel Chicago (regional cable).

NEWSPAPERS, Daily Coverage: Chicago Sun-Times, Chicago Tribune, Arlington Heights Daily Herald, Daily Southtown.

General Information

Hometown Dugout: Third Base. **Playing Surface:** Grass.

Standard Game Times: 7:05 p.m., Sat. 6:05, Sun. 1:05.

Stadium Location: 35th Street exit off Dan Ryan Expressway (I-90/94).

Player Representative: Lyle Mouton.

WHITE SOX

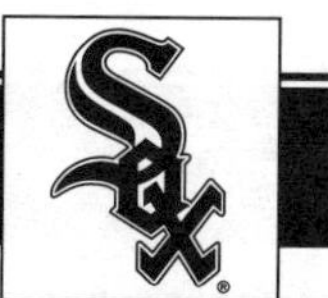

BASEBALL OPERATIONS

Ron Schueler

Senior Vice President, Major League Operations: Ron Schueler. **Senior Vice President, Baseball:** Jack Gould.

Assistant General Manager: Dan Evans. **Major League Computer Scouting Analyst:** Mike Maziarka. **Technical Director:** Joe Inzerillo. **Video Coordinator:** Andrew Pinter.

Major League Staff

Manager: Terry Bevington.

Coaches: Dugout—Joe Nossek; Pitching—Mike Pazik; Batting—Bill Buckner; First Base—Ron Jackson; Third Base—Doug Rader; Bullpen—Art Kusyner.

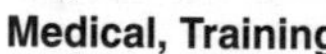

Medical, Training

Senior Team Physician: Dr. James Boscardin.

Head Trainer: Herm Schneider. **Assistant Trainer:** Mark Anderson. **Director of Conditioning:** Steve Odgers.

Minor Leagues

Telephone: (312) 674-1000. **FAX:** (312) 674-5015.

Minor League Development Complex: 1090 N. Euclid Ave., Sarasota, FL 34237. **Telephone:** (941) 366-8451. **FAX:** (941) 366-6615.

Terry Bevington

Vice President, Player Development: Ken Williams. **Director of Minor League Administration:** Steve Noworyta. **Coordinator of Cultural Development and Minor League Administration:** Sal Artiaga. **Minor League Administrator:** Glynis Wilkins. **Clubhouse and Equipment Manager:** Mark Brown.

Director of Instruction: Jim Snyder. **Conditioning Coordinator:** Trung Cao.

Roving Instructors: Don Cooper (pitching), Mike Gellinger (infield), Bryan Little (general), Mike Lum (hitting), Gary Pettis (outfield, baserunning), Tommy Thompson (catching).

Farm System

Class	Farm Team	Manager	Coach	Pitching Coach
AAA	Nashville	Tom Spencer	Von Joshua	Kirk Champion
AA	Birmingham	Dave Huppert	Rance Mulliniks	Steve Renko
A	Win.-Salem	Mike Heath	Mark Haley	Curt Hasler
A	Hickory	Chris Cron	Dallas Williams	Sean Snedeker
Rookie	Bristol	Nick Capra	Gregg Ritchie	J.R. Perdue
Rookie	Sarasota	Roly de Armas	Mike Barnett	Luis Tiant

Scouting

Duane Shaffer

Telephone: (312) 674-1000. **FAX:** (312) 451-5105.

Vice President, Free Agent and Major League Scouting: Larry Monroe.

Director of Scouting: Duane Shaffer.

Assistant to the Director of Scouting/Minor League Administration: Grace Guerrero Zwit. **Assistant to the Director of Scouting/Minor League Operations:** Dan Fabian.

Advance Scout: Mark Weidemaier (Tierra Verde, FL).

Special Assignment Scouts: Ed Brinkman (Cincinnati, OH), Dave Yoakum (Orlando, FL).

National Crosschecker: George Bradley (Tampa, FL).

Scouting Supervisors: East—Doug Laumann (Florence, KY); West—Ed Pebley (Hillsborough, CA).

Full-Time Scouts: Joseph Butler (East Rancho Dominguez, CA), Scott Cerny (Davis, CA), Rico Cortes (Tampa, FL), Alex Cosmidis (Raleigh, NC), Ed Crosby (Garden Grove, CA), Nathan Durst (Elmhurst, IL), Larry Grefer (Park Hills, KY), Jack Hubbard (Safety Harbor, FL), Warren Hughes (Mobile, AL), Joe Karp (Bothell, WA), John Kazanas (Phoenix, AZ), Reggie Lewis (Elkton, MD), Jose Ortega (Hialeah, FL), Gary Pellant (Chandler, AZ), Paul Provas (Shawnee Mission, KS), Mike Sgobba (Yorba Linda, CA), Ken Stauffer (Katy, TX), John Tumminia (Newburgh, NY).

International Scouts: Juan Bernhardt (Dominican Republic), Warren Hughes (Australia), Miguel Ibarra (Panama), Hector Rincones (Venezuela), Mike Sgobba (Latin American coordinator), Jun Teramoto (Far East).

CLEVELAND

Richard Jacobs

Telephone, Address

Office Address: Jacobs Field, 2401 Ontario St., Cleveland, OH 44115. **Telephone:** (216) 420-4200. **FAX:** (216) 420-4396.

Ownership

Operated by: Richard E. Jacobs Group.

Chairman of the Board, Chief Executive Officer: Richard Jacobs.

Board of Directors: Richard Jacobs, Martin Cleary, Gary Bryenton.

BUSINESS OPERATIONS

Executive Vice President, Business: Dennis Lehman.

Manager, Spring Training: Jerry Crabb. **Human Resource Manager:** Mary Terrell. **Administrative Assistant, Business:** Jacqueline Stetter.

Finance

Vice President, Finance: Ken Stefanov.

Controller: Ron McQuate. **Director, Information Systems:** Dave Powell. **Manager, Compensation and Benefits:** Lisa Ostry. **Senior Accountant:** Karen Menzing.

Marketing, Sales

Vice President, Marketing and Communications: Jeff Overton.

Director, Corporate Marketing and Sales: Jon Starrett. **Manager, Corporate Marketing:** Chris Previte.

Director, Advertising/Publications: Valerie Arcuri. **Manager, Advertising/Publications:** Kim Jarrell.

Public Relations, Communications

Telephone: (216) 420-4350. **FAX:** (216) 420-4396.

Vice President, Public Relations: Bob DiBiasio.

Director, Community Relations: Allen Davis. **Coordinator, Community Relations:** Melissa Zapanta.

Manager, Media Relations: Bart Swain. **Assistant Director, Media Relations:** Susie Gharrity. **Media Relations Assistant:** Joel Gunderson.

Manager, Broadcasting: Nadine Glinski. **Manager, Broadcast Operations:** Steve Warren. **Coordinator, Broadcasting:** Dan Foust.

Stadium Operations

Director of Ballpark Operations: Jim Folk. **Manager, Field Maintenance:** Brandon Koehnke. **Manager, Building Maintenance:** Chris Donahoe. **Assistant Manager, Field Maintenance:** Tony Walley.

PA Announcer: Mark Tromba. **Official Scorers:** Hank Kosloski, Rick Rembielak.

Ticketing

Director, Ticket Services: John Schulze. **Box Office Manager:** Gail Leibenguth. **Box Office Controller:** Jim Harrah.

Director, Ticket Sales: Scott Sterneckert. **Manager, Ticket Sales:** Larry Abel. **Senior Account Executive:** Dick Sapara.

Travel, Clubhouse

Director, Team Travel: Mike Seghi.

Home Clubhouse/Equipment Manager: Ted Walsh. **Visiting Clubhouse Manager:** Cy Buynak. **Manager, Equipment Acquisitions:** Jeff Sipos. **Baseball Video Operations:** Bob Chester, Joe Catalioti.

Radio, TV, Media

Radio Announcers: Tom Hamilton, Herb Score. **Flagship Station:** WKNR 1220-AM. **No. of Network Stations:** 34.

TV Announcers: WUAB—Jack Corrigan, Mike Hegan; SportsChannel—Rick Manning, John Sanders. **Flagship Stations:** WUAB Channel 43, SportsChannel Ohio (regional cable).

NEWSPAPERS, Daily Coverage: Cleveland Plain Dealer, Lake County News-Herald, Akron Beacon-Journal.

General Information

Hometown Dugout: Third Base. **Playing Surface:** Grass.

Standard Game Times: 7:05 p.m.; Weekends—1:05.

Stadium Location: From south—I-77 North to East 9th St. exit, to Ontario Street; From east—I-90/Rt. 2 west to downtown, remain on Rt. 2 to East 9th St., left to stadium.

Player Representative: Charles Nagy.

INDIANS

BASEBALL OPERATIONS

John Hart

Executive Vice President, General Manager: John Hart.

Director of Baseball Operations/Assistant General Manager: Dan O'Dowd. **Administrator, Player Personnel:** Wendy Hoppel. **Executive Administrative Assistant, Baseball Operations:** Ethel LaRue. **Assistant, Baseball Operations:** Paul DePodesta. **Administative Assistant, Baseball Operations:** Barbara Lessman.

Special Assistant, Baseball Operations: Bud Black.

Major League Staff

Manager: Mike Hargrove.

Coaches: Pitching—Mark Wiley; Batting—Charlie Manuel; Infield—John Goryl; First Base—Dave Nelson; Third Base—Jeff Newman; Bullpen—Luis Isaac, Dan Williams.

Medical, Training

Medical Director: Dr. William Wilder.

Mike Hargrove

Head Trainer: Paul Spicuzza. **Assistant Trainer:** Jim Warfield. **Strength and Conditioning Coach:** Fernando Montes.

Minor Leagues

Telephone: (216) 420-4200. **FAX:** (216) 420-4321.

Director, Minor League Operations: Mark Shapiro. **Assistant, Minor League Operations:** Gordy Gutowsky. **Administrative Assistant:** Joan Pachinger.

Coordinator of Instruction: Boyd Coffie.

Roving Instructors: Mike Brown (pitching), Trent Clark (strength and conditioning), Brian Graham (defense), Gordie MacKenzie (general), Dr. Charles Maher (sports psychologist), Harry Spilman (hitting).

Farm System

Class	Farm Team	Manager	Coach	Pitching Coach
AAA	Buffalo	Brian Graham	Dave Keller	Gary Ruby
AA	Akron	Jeff Datz	Minnie Mendoza	Tony Arnold
A	Kinston	Joel Skinner	Boots Day	Ken Rowe
A	Columbus	Jack Mull	Mike Sarbaugh	Fred Gladding
A	Watertown	Ted Kubiak	Billy Williams	Carl Willis
Rookie	Burlington	Harry Spilman	Joe Mikulik	Dave Miller
Rookie	DSL	Alex Taveras	Virgilio Veras	Juan Jimenez

Scouting

Lee MacPhail

Telephone: (216) 420-4309. **FAX:** (216) 420-4321.

Director of Scouting: Lee MacPhail.

Assistant Director of Scouting: Josh Byrnes. **Assistant, Scouting:** Brad Grant.

Major League/Special Assignment Scouts: Dan Carnevale (Buffalo, NY), Dom Chiti (Pulaski, VA), Tom Giordano (Amityville, NY), Jay Robertson (Citrus Heights, CA), Ted Simmons (Chesterfield, MO), Bill Werle (San Mateo, CA).

National Crosschecker: Bill Schmidt (Garden Grove, CA).

Free Agent Supervisors: Jesse Flores (Sacramento, CA), Jerry Jordan (Wise, VA), Bob Mayer (Somerset, PA).

Full-Time Area Scouts: Steve Avila (Olympia, WA), Doug Baker (Encinitas, CA), Keith Boeck (Phoenix, AZ), Ted Brzenk (Waukesha, WI), Paul Cogan (Sacramento, CA), Phil Cook (Dayton, OH), Jay Franklin (Shawnee, KS), Jim Gabella (Deltona, FL), Rene Gayo (Galveston, TX), Mark Germann (Chattanooga, TN), Chris Jefts (Agoura, CA), Guy Mader (Tewksbury, MA), Kasey McKeon (Burlington, NC), Jim Moran (Davenport, FL), Max Semler (Collierville, TN), Jim Stevenson (Miami, OK), Mike Toomey (Hyattsville, MD).

Latin America Supervisors: Luis Aponte (Venezuela), Winston Llenas (Domincan Republic).

DETROIT

Telephone, Address

Office Address: Tiger Stadium, 2121 Trumbull Ave., Detroit, MI 48216. **Telephone:** (313) 962-4000. **FAX:** (313) 965-2138.

John McHale Jr.

Ownership

Operated by: Detroit Tigers, Inc.

Principal Owners: Mike Ilitch, Marian Ilitch.

Chairman of the Board: Mike Ilitch.

Board of Directors: Marian Ilitch, Charles Jones, Jay Bielfield, Denise Ilitch Lites, Ronald Ilitch, Mike Ilitch Jr., Lisa Ilitch Murray, Atanas Ilitch, Christopher Ilitch, Carole Ilitch Trepeck.

President, Chief Executive Officer: John McHale Jr. **Assistant to the President:** Margaret Gramlich.

BUSINESS OPERATIONS

Vice President, Business Operations: David Glazier. **Assistant to Vice President, Business Operations:** Andrea Dohring.

Finance

Controller: Scott Fisher.

Marketing, Sales, Merchandising

Senior Director, Marketing and Operations: Michael Dietz. **Assistants to the Senior Director, Marketing and Operations:** Liz McCausland, Jill Ulle. **Marketing Manager:** Christine Lauts.

Senior Director, Corporate Sales: Gary Vitto. **Director of Corporate Sales:** Martin Pawlusiak.

Director of Merchandise: Kayla French. **Merchandising Manager:** Dave Szewczul.

Media, Community Relations

Telephone: (313) 965-2113. **FAX:** (313) 965-2138.

Director of Public Relations: Tyler Barnes. **Assistant Director of Public Relations:** David Matheson. **Manager, Community Relations:** Celia Bobrowsky. **Coordinator, Public Relations:** Giovanni Loria. **Administrative Assistant, Public Relations:** Connie Bell.

Director of Broadcasting: Amy Goan.

Stadium Operations

Director of Stadium Operations: Tom Folk.

Head Groundskeeper: Frank Feneck. **Stadium Services Supervisor:** Ed Goward. **Guest Services Manager:** Jodi Schroeder.

PA Announcer: Jimmy Barrett. **Official Scorers:** Chuck Klonke, Rich Shook.

Ticketing

Telephone: (313) 962-4000. **FAX:** (313) 962-4600.

Director of Ticket Services: Ken Marchetti. **Assistant Director of Ticket Services:** James Cleary.

Group Sales Manager: Bob Palmisano. **Season Ticket Manager:** Kevin Marcy.

Travel, Clubhouse

Traveling Secretary: Bill Brown.

Manager, Tiger Clubhouse: Jim Schmakel. **Assistant Manager, Visitors Clubhouse:** John Nelson.

Radio, TV, Media

Radio Announcers: Frank Beckmann, Lary Sorensen. **Flagship Station:** WJR 760-AM. **No. of Stations on Network:** 30.

TV Announcers: Al Kaline, George Kell, Jim Price. **Flagship Stations:** WKBD UPN 50, PASS (regional cable).

NEWSPAPERS, Daily Coverage: Detroit Free Press, The Detroit News, The Oakland Press, Booth Newspaper Group.

General Information

Hometown Dugout: Third Base. **Playing Surface:** Grass.

Standard Game Times: Day—1:05 p.m. Night—7:05.

Stadium Directions: From north, I-75 South to exit 49A, or I-96 East to the Lodge Freeway (US 10), to Rosa Parks Blvd. exit; From south, I-75 North to exit 49A; From east, I-94 West to exit 215A, to the Lodge Freeway (US 10), to I-75 South, to Trumbull Ave., exit; From west, I-94 East to exit 213B, to the Lodge Freeway (US 10), to Rosa Parks Blvd.

Player Representative: Travis Fryman.

TIGERS

BASEBALL OPERATIONS

Telephone: (313) 965-2098. **FAX:** (313) 965-2099.

Vice President of Baseball Operations/General Manager: Randy Smith.

Assistant General Manager: Steve Lubratich. **Special Assistants to General Manager:** Al Hargesheimer, Randy Johnson. **Assistant to the General Manager:** Gwen Keating.

Randy Smith

Major League Staff

Manager: Buddy Bell.

Coaches: Dugout—Larry Parrish; Pitching—Rick Adair; Batting—Larry Herndon; First Base—Jerry White; Third Base—Perry Hill; Bullpen—Fred Kendall.

Medical, Training

Team Physicians: Dr. Clarence Livingood, Dr. David Collon, Dr. Terry Lock, Dr. Louis Saco (Florida).

Head Trainer: Russ Miller. **Assistant Trainer:** Steve Carter. **Strength and Conditioning Coach:** Brad Andress.

Buddy Bell

Minor Leagues

Telephone: (313) 965-2096. **FAX:** (313) 965-2099.

Director of Minor League Operations: Dave Miller. **Administrative Assistant, Minor Leagues:** Audrey Zielinski.

Coordinator of Instruction: Steve Boros.

Roving Instructors: Toby Harrah (hitting), Marty Martinez (infield), Jon Matlack (pitching), Gene Roof (outfield).

Farm System

Class	Farm Team	Manager	Coach	Pitching Coach
AAA	Toledo	Glenn Ezell	Gary Green	Jeff Jones
AA	Jacksonville	Dave Anderson	Tim Torricelli	Rich Bombard
A	Lakeland	Mark Meleski	None	Joe Georger
A	Fayetteville	Bruce Fields	Skeeter Barnes	Brian Allard
A	Jamestown	Dwight Lowry	None	Steve McCatty
Rookie	Lakeland	Kevin Bradshaw	Basilio Cabrera	Hector Berrios
Rookie	DSL	Felix Nivar	Liliano Castro	None

Scouting

Telephone: (313) 965-2098. **FAX:** (313) 965-2099.

Director of Scouting: Greg Smith.

Administrative Assistant, Scouting: Gwen Keating.

Advance Scout: Tom Runnells (Sylvania, OH).

Special Assignment Scouts: Larry Bearnarth (Seminole, FL), Al Hargesheimer (Arlington Heights, IL), Randy Johnson (Detroit, MI).

Regional Crosscheckers: Central—Dave Owen (Arlington, TX); Northeast—Rob Guzik (Latrobe, PA); Southeast—John Mirabelli (Cary, NC); West—Jeff Malinoff (Lopez, WA).

Scouts: Rick Bennett (Birmingham, AL), Bill Buck (Manassas, VA), Jack Hays (Portland, OR), Ray Hayward (Oklahoma City, OK), Mike Humphreys (Cedar Hill, TX), Lou Laslo (Pemberville, OH), Steve Lemke (Lincolnshire, IL), Dennis Lieberthal (Westlake, CA), Mark Monahan (Ann Arbor, MI), Dave Roberts (Portland, OR), Mike Stafford (Auburn, IN), Chuck Stone (Long Beach, CA), Clyde Weir (Mt. Pleasant, MI), Jeff Wetherby (Tampa, FL), Rob Wilfong (West Covina, CA), Gary York (Rome, GA).

Latin American Coordinator: Ramon Pena (New York, NY).

KANSAS CITY

Telephone, Address

Office Address: One Royal Way, Kansas City, MO 64129. **Mailing Address:** P.O. Box 419969, Kansas City, MO 64141. **Telephone:** (816) 921-2200. **FAX:** (816) 921-5775.

Ownership

Operated by: Kansas City Royals Baseball Club, Inc.

Principal Owner: Greater Kansas City Community Foundation.

Chairman of the Board/Chief Executive Officer: David Glass. **President:** Michael Herman.

David Glass

Board of Directors: David Glass, Richard Green, Michael Herman, Larry Kauffman, Janice Kreamer, Joe McGuff, Louis Smith.

General Counsel: Jennings Newcom.

BUSINESS OPERATIONS

Vice President, Administration/Development: Dennis Cryder.

Director of Administration: John Johnson. **Director of Human Resources:** Lauris Hawthorne.

Finance

Vice President, Finance: Dale Rohr.

Controller: Patrick Fleischmann. **Director of Information Systems:** Jim Edwards. **Director of Compensation:** Tom Pfannenstiel. **Director of Royal Lancers Program:** Chris Muehlbach.

Marketing, Sales

Vice President, Marketing/Communications: Mike Levy.

Director of Marketing and Sales: Mike Behymer. **Manager, Corporate Sales and Promotions:** Vernice Givens. **Assistant Director, Marketing and Promotions:** Jill Fencl. **Account Executives:** Jeff Foster, Chris Freshour. **Marketing Coordinator:** Tonya Mangris. **Director of Season Ticket Sales:** Joe Grigoli. **Manager of Group Sales:** Michele Kammerer. **Group Sales Coordinator:** Jacque Tschirhart.

Media Relations, Communications

Telephone: (816) 921-8154. **FAX:** (816) 921-5775.

Director, Media Relations: Steve Fink. **Administrative Assistant, Media Relations:** Chris Stathos. **Administrative Assistant, Communications:** Cindy Hamilton.

Director, Community Relations: Jim Lachimia. **Manager, Community Relations:** Barry Holmes.

Stadium Operations

Manager, Stadium Operations: Rodney Lewallen.

Assistant Director, Stadium Operations: Rey Chavez.

Head Groundskeeper: Trevor Vance.

PA Announcer: Dan Hurst. **Official Scorers:** Del Black, Sid Bordman.

Ticketing

Director of Ticket Operations: John Walker. **Manager, Ticket Office:** Christine Burgeson. **Ticket Office Associate:** Betty Bax.

Travel, Clubhouse

Director, Team Travel: Dave Witty. **Equipment Manager:** Mike Burkhalter. **Visiting Clubhouse Manager:** Chuck Hawke.

Radio, TV, Media

Radio Announcers: Denny Matthews, Fred White, Paul Splittorf, John Wathan. **Flagship Stations:** WIBW 580-AM, Topeka. **No. of Stations on Network:** 106.

TV Announcers: Unavailable. **Flagship Station:** KCWB-TV, Fox Sports Rocky Mountain (regional cable).

NEWSPAPERS, Daily Coverage: Kansas City Star, Topeka Capital Journal.

General Information

Team Colors: Royal blue and white.

Hometown Dugout: First Base. **Playing Surface:** Grass.

Standard Game Times: 7:05, Sun. 1:05.

Stadium Location: From north or south, take I-435 to stadium exits. From east or west, take I-70 to stadium exits.

Player Representative: Jeff Montgomery.

ROYALS

BASEBALL OPERATIONS

Executive Vice President/General Manager: Herk Robinson.

Vice President, Baseball Operations: George Brett.

Assistant General Manager: Jay Hinrichs.

Director, Player Personnel: Larry Doughty.

Assistant Director, Player Personnel: Dan Glass.

Administrative Assistant, Baseball Operations: Joanne Snow.

Herk Robinson

Major League Staff

Manager: Bob Boone.

Coaches: Bench—Jamie Quirk; Pitching—Bruce Kison; Batting—Greg Luzinski; First Base—Mitchell Page; Third Base—Rich Dauer; Bullpen—Guy Hansen.

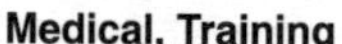

Medical, Training

Team Physician: Dr. Steve Joyce.

Associate Physicians: Dr. Mark Bernhardt, Dr. Dan Gurba, Dr. Thomas Phillips, Dr. Charles Rhoades.

Bob Boone

Head Trainer: Nick Swartz. **Assistant Trainer:** Steve Morrow. **Strength and Conditioning Coordinator:** Kevin Barr.

Minor Leagues

Telephone: (816) 921-2200. **FAX:** (816) 924-0347.

Director, Minor League Operations: Bob Hegman. **Assistant Director, Scouting/Player Development:** Muzzy Jackson. **Secretary, Baseball Operations:** Mindy Walker.

Coordinator of Instruction: Jimmy Johnson.

Roving Instructors: Jerry Cram (pitching), Brian Poldberg (catching), Tom Poquette (hitting).

Farm System

Class	Farm Team	Manager	Coach	Pitching Coach
AAA	Omaha	Mike Jirschele	U.L. Washington	Mike Alvarez
AA	Wichita	Ron Johnson	Sixto Lezcano	Gary Lance
A	Wilmington	John Mizerock	Keith Hughes	Buster Keeton
A	Lansing	Bob Herold	Curtis Wilkerson	Mike Mason
A	Spokane	Jeff Garber	Greg Smith	Steve Crawford
Rookie	Fort Myers	Al Pedrique	Jose Tartabull	Unavailable
Rookie	DSL	Fausto Sosa	Unavailable	Oscar Martinez

Scouting

Telephone: (816) 921-2200. **FAX:** (816) 924-0347.

Director of Scouting: Art Stewart.

Administrative Assistant: Karol Kyte.

Special Assignment Scouts: Bill Schudlich (Detroit, MI), Dick Wiencek (Rancho Mirage, CA).

National Crosscheckers: Allard Baird (Pembroke Pines, FL), Steve Flores (Temecula, CA), Terry Wetzel (Sugar Land, TX).

Art Stewart

Scouts: Frank Baez (Los Angeles, CA), Bob Bishop (San Dimas, CA), Carl Blando (Overland Park, KS), Bob Carter (Chambersburg, PA), Balos Davis (Charlotte, NC), Albert Gonzalez (Pembroke Pines, FL), Dave Herrera (Danville, CA), Ray Jackson (Windsor, CT), Gary Johnson (Costa Mesa, CA), Tony Levato (Peotone, IL), Tom McDevitt (Charleston, IL), Jeff McKay (Springfield, OR), Cliff Pastornicky (Venice, FL) Bill Price (Austin, TX), Wil Rutenschroer (Cincinnati, OH), Jerry Stephens (West Bloomfield, MI), Dennis Woody (Mobile, AL).

Latin American Supervisor: Luis Silverio (Dominican Republic). **International Scouts:** Johnny Ramos (Puerto Rico), Graciano Ravelo (Venezuela), Oadro Salas (Panama).

MILWAUKEE

Bud Selig

Telephone, Address

Office Address: County Stadium, 201 South 46th St., Milwaukee, WI 53214. **Mailing Address:** P.O. Box 3099, Milwaukee, WI 53201. **Telephone:** (414) 933-4114. **FAX:** (414) 933-7323.

E-Mail Address: www.milwaukeebrewers.com.

Ownership

Operated by: Milwaukee Brewers Baseball Club.

President, Chief Executive Officer: Allan (Bud) Selig.

Board of Directors: Allan (Bud) Selig, Everett Smith, Charles Krause, Bernard Kubale.

Vice President, General Counsel: Wendy Selig-Prieb.

BUSINESS OPERATIONS

Vice President, Administration and Human Resources: Tom Gausden.

Assistant General Counsel: Eugene Randolph.

Administrative Assistant, Legal and Human Resources: Mary Burns.

Finance

Director, Finance: Paul Baniel. **Director, Management Information Systems:** Dan Krautkramer.

Corporate Affairs, Marketing

Vice President, Corporate Affairs: Laurel Prieb. **Director, Corporate Sales:** Dean Rennicke. **Managers, Corporate Sales:** Steve Malliet, Amy Welch. **Corporate Sales Coordinator:** Cathy Bradley. **Corporate Sales Associate:** Nicole Clark.

Vice President, Broadcast Operations: Bill Haig.

Director, Radio Sales: Cathy Dailey. **Manager, Television Sales:** Rik DeGrave. **Manager, Radio Network and Merchandising Services:** Stephanie Schmidt. **Manager, Television Operations:** Tim Van Wagoner.

Public Relations, Communications

Telephone: (414) 933-6975. **FAX:** (414) 933-3251.

Director, Media Relations: Jon Greenberg. **Manager, Baseball Information:** Steve Gilbert. **Media Relations Associate:** Dan Larrea.

Director, Publications: Mario Ziino. **Director, Community Relations:** Mike Downs. **Assistant, Community Relations:** Marquette Baylor.

Stadium Operations

Director, Stadium Administration: Terry Ann Peterson. **Director, Grounds:** Gary VandenBerg. **Assistant Director, Grounds:** David Mellor.

PA Announcer: Bob Betts. **Official Scorers:** Tim O'Driscoll, Wayne Franke.

Ticketing

Telephone: (414) 933-9000. **FAX:** (414) 933-3547.

Vice President, Ticket Sales: Bob Voight.

Director, Ticket Operations: John Barnes. **Assistant Director, Ticket Operations:** Nancy Dressel. **Operations Manager:** Jeff Gittins.

Manager, Brewers Gold Club: Geoff Campion. **Manager, Ticket Sales Development:** Jim Bathey. **Manager, Account Services:** Matt Groniger.

Travel, Clubhouse

Traveling Secretary: Steve Ethier.

Equipment Manager/Home Clubhouse: Tony Migliaccio. **Visitors Clubhouse:** Jim Ksicinski.

Radio, TV, Media

Radio Announcers: Jim Powell, Bob Uecker. **Flagship Station:** WTMJ 620-AM. **No. of Network Stations:** 55.

TV Announcers: Unavailable, Bill Schroeder. **Flagship Station:** WVTV Channel 18, Wisconsin Sports Network (regional cable).

NEWSPAPERS, Daily Coverage: Milwaukee Journal, Milwaukee Sentinel.

General Information

Hometown Dugout: First Base. **Playing Surface:** Grass.

Standard Game Times: 7:05 p.m., (April) 6:05; Day, Sun. 1:05.

Stadium Location: From airport/south, I-94 West to Madison exit, to stadium.

Player Representative: Matt Mieske.

BREWERS

BASEBALL OPERATIONS

Senior Vice President, Baseball Operations: Sal Bando.

Assistant General Manager/Baseball Operations: Fred Stanley. **Senior Consultant to the Vice President, Baseball Operations:** Dee Fondy (Redlands, CA). **Special Assistants, Baseball Operations:** Larry Haney (Barboursville, VA), Chuck Tanner (New Castle, PA).

Administrator, Baseball Operations: Barb Stark. **Administrative Assistant, Baseball Operations:** Kate Geenen.

Sal Bando

Major League Staff

Manager: Phil Garner.

Coaches: Pitching—Don Rowe; Batting—Lamar Johnson; First Base—Jim Gantner; Third Base—Chris Bando; Bullpen—Bill Castro.

Phil Garner

Medical, Training

Medical Director: Dr. Dennis Sullivan.

Head Trainer: John Adam. **Assistant Trainer:** Al Price. **Strength and Conditioning Coach:** John Rewolinski.

Minor Leagues

Telelphone: (414) 933-4114. **FAX:** (414) 933-4655.

Director of Player Development: Cecil Cooper. **Administrator, Minor League Operations:** Barb Stark.

Field Coordinator: Bob Humphreys. **Roving Instructors:** Bill Campbell (pitching), Ralph Dickenson (hitting), Ed Romero (infield, bunting), Ed Sedar (outfield).

Farm System

Class	Farm Team	Manager	Coach	Pitching Coach
AAA	Tucson	Tim Ireland	Bob Mariano	Mark Littell
AA	El Paso	Dave Machemer	Jon Pont	Mike Caldwell
A	Stockton	Greg Mahlberg	Theron Todd	Randy St. Claire
A	Beloit	Luis Salazar	John Mallee	Jaime Garcia
Rookie	Helena	Alex Morales	Javier Gonzalez	Jim Merrick
Rookie	Ogden	Bernie Moncallo	Tom Houk	Steve Cline
Rookie	DSL	Mike Guerrero	None	Andy Araujo

Scouting

Telephone: (414) 933-4114. **FAX:** (414) 933-4655.

Director, Scouting: Ken Califano.

Assistant Director, Scouting: Scott Martens. **Administrative Assistant, Scouting:** Kate Geenen.

Pro Scouting: Harry Dunlop (Elk Grove, CA).

Special Assignment Scouts: Felix Delgado (Rio Piedras, PR), Paul Tretiak (Hannibal, MO), Walter Youse (Sykesville, MD).

National Crosscheckers: East—Ron Rizzi (Joppa, MD), West—Lou Snipp (Galveston, TX).

Ken Califano

Scouting Supervisors: Midwest—Fred Beene (Oakhurst, TX), East Coast—Russ Bove (Apopka, FL), West Coast—Kevin Christman (Calabasas, CA).

Scouts: Jeff Brookens (Chambersburg, PA), Rich Chiles (Davis, CA), Ramon Conde (Juana Diaz, PR), Felix Delgado (Rio Piedras, PR), Bill Foley (Columbia, SC), Dick Foster (Otis, OR), Danny Garcia (Jericho, NY), Mike Gibbons (West Chester, OH), Ken Houp (Long Beach, CA), Harvey Kuenn Jr. (New Berlin, WI), Demie Mainieri (Tamarac, FL), Alex Morales (Boynton Beach, FL), Mike Powers (Galveston, TX), Corey Rodriguez (Sherman Oaks, CA), Bob Sloan (Amarillo, TX), Jonathan Story (Oxford, MS), Red Whitsett (Villa Rica, GA), Ric Wilson (Chandler, AZ), David Young (Kountze, TX).

International Supervisor: Epy Guerrero (Santo Domingo, DR).

International Scouts: Domingo Carrasquel (Venezuela), Elvio Jimenez (Dominican Republic), John Viney (Australia).

MINNESOTA

Carl Pohlad

Telephone, Address

Office Address: 34 Kirby Puckett Place, Minneapolis, MN 55415. **Telephone:** (612) 375-1366. **E-Mail Address:** www.mntwins.com.

Ownership

Operated by: The Minnesota Twins.

Owner: Carl Pohlad. **Chairman of Executive Committee:** Howard Fox.

Board of Directors: Jerry Bell, Donald Benson, Chris Clouser, Carl Pohlad, Eloise Pohlad, James Pohlad, Robert Pohlad, William Pohlad, Kirby Puckett.

President: Jerry Bell.

BUSINESS OPERATIONS

Vice President, Operations: Matt Hoy.

Administrative Assistant to President/Office Manager: Joan Boeser.

Finance

Director of Human Resources: Raenell Dorn. **Controller:** Kip Elliott. **Accounting Manager:** Beth Ungar. **Human Resources Coordinator:** Lori Beasley. **Accountant:** Jerry McLaughlin.

Marketing, Promotions

Telephone: (612) 375-1366. **FAX, Sales:** (612) 375-7522. **FAX, Marketing/Promotions:** (612) 375-7480.

Sales and Marketing Consultant: Pat Forceia.

Director of Sales: Phil Huebner. **Sales Manager:** Jon Arends. **Senior Account Sales Executive:** Scott O'Connell. **Account Sales Executives:** Jack Blesi, Stacey Bjorklund, Chris Malek, John Neppl, Mike Roslansky. **Sales Coordinator:** Beth Vail. **Telemarketing Manager:** Jim Pounian.

Director of Corporate Sales: Laura Day. **Corporate Sales Executives:** Jeff Jurgella, Dick Schultz. **Director of Communications:** Dave St. Peter. **Community Affairs Manager:** Sue Hanson.

Media Relations

Telephone: (612) 375-1366. **FAX:** (612) 375-7473.

Manager of Media Relations: Sean Harlin. **Administrative Assistant:** Wendie Erickson.

Stadium Operations

Stadium Operations Manager: Ric Johnson. **Assistant Manager:** Dave Horsman. **Operations Coordinator:** Heidi Sammon.

Security Manager: Doug Wills. **Managers, Pro Shop:** Mike Pitzen, Dave Strobel. **Office Services Coordinator:** Rod Collins.

Head Groundskeeper: Dick Ericson.

PA Announcer: Bob Casey. **Official Scorers:** Tom Mee, Barry Fritz.

Ticketing

Telephone: (612) 33TWINS. **FAX:** (612) 375-7522.

Ticket Manager: Paul Froehle. **Assistant Ticket Manager:** Mike Stiles. **Ticket Office Supervisor:** Tracy Nordall.

Travel, Clubhouse

Traveling Secretary: Remzi Kiratli.

Equipment/Clubhouse Manager: Jim Dunn. **Visitors Clubhouse:** Rick Pollack.

Internal Video Specialist: Nyal Peterson.

Radio, TV, Media

Radio Announcers: Herb Carneal, John Gordon. **Flagship Station:** WCCO 830-AM. **No. of Network Stations:** 66.

TV Announcers: Bert Blyleven, Dick Bremer, Ryan Lefebvre. **Flagship Stations:** WCCO Channel 4, Midwest SportsChannel (regional cable).

NEWSPAPERS, Daily Coverage: Minneapolis Star-Tribune, St. Paul Pioneer Press.

General Information

Hometown Dugout: Third Base. **Playing Surface:** Astroturf.

Standard Game Times: Day—12:15 p.m., 1:05 (Sunday). Night—7:05.

Stadium Directions: I-35W south to Washington Ave. exit or I-35W north to 3rd Street exit. I-94 East to I-35W north to 3rd Street exit or I-94 West to 5th Street exit.

Player Representative: Frank Rodriguez.

TWINS

BASEBALL OPERATIONS

Telephone: (612) 375-1366. **FAX:** (612) 375-7417.

Vice President, General Manager: Terry Ryan.

Executive Vice President, Baseball: Kirby Puckett. **Vice President, Assistant General Manager:** Bill Smith. **Administrative Assistant, Major League Operations:** Ann Waara.

Director of Baseball Operations: Rob Antony. **Assistant, Baseball Operations:** Brad Smith.

Terry Ryan

Major League Staff

Manager: Tom Kelly.

Coaches: Pitching—Dick Such; Batting—Terry Crowley; First Base—Scott Ullger; Third Base—Ron Gardenhire; Bullpen—Rick Stelmaszek.

Tom Kelly

Medical, Training

Club Physicians: Dr. L.J. Michienzi, Dr. John Steubs.

Trainer: Dick Martin. **Assistant Trainer:** Jim Kahmann.

Minor Leagues

Telephone: (612) 375-7486. **FAX:** (612) 375-7417.

Director of Minor Leagues: Jim Rantz. **Administrative Assistant:** Colleen Schroeder.

Minor League Field Coordinator: Larry Corrigan.

Roving Instructors: Jim Dwyer (hitting), Rick Knapp (pitching).

Farm System

Class	Farm Team	Manager	Coach	Pitching Coach
AAA	Salt Lake	Phil Roof	Bill Springman	Rick Anderson
AA	New Britain	Al Newman	Jose Baez	Gorman Heimueller
A	Fort Myers	John Russell	Jon Mathews	Eric Rasmussen
A	Fort Wayne	Mike Boulanger	Jeff Carter	Stu Cliburn
Rookie	Elizabethton	Jose Marzan	Ray Smith	Jim Shellenback
Rookie	Fort Myers	Steve Liddle	Unavailable	Unavailable

Scouting

Telephone: (612) 375-7474. **FAX:** (612) 375-7417.

Scouting Director: Mike Radcliff.

Administrative Assistant: Alison Walk.

Advance Scout: Ray Coley (Ponte Vedra Beach, FL).

Special Assignment Scouts: Ellsworth Brown (Beason, IL), Cal Ermer (Chattanooga, TN), Bill Harford (Chicago, IL), Wayne Krivsky (Arlington, TX), Eddie Robinson (Fort Worth, TX).

Scouting Supervisors: West Coast—Vern Followell (Lakewood, CA); Midwest—Mike Ruth (Lee's Summit, MO); East—Earl Frishman (Tampa, FL).

Mike Radcliff

Full-Time Scouts: Gene DeBoer (Brandon, WI), Marty Esposito (Hewitt, TX), Scott Groot (Mission Viejo, CA), Deron Johnson (Daly City, CA), John Leavitt (Norman, OK), Joel Lepel (Plato, MN), Bill Lohr (Centralia, WA), Bill Milos (South Holland, IL), Kevin Murphy (Studio City, CA), Tim O'Neil (Lexington, KY), Mark Quimuyog (Lynn Haven, FL), Clair Rierson (Gilbert, AZ), Ricky Taylor (Hickory, NC), Brad Weitzel (Haines City, FL), John Wilson (West Paterson, NJ).

International Scouts: Enrique Brito (Venezuela), Howard Norsetter (Australia, Canada), Johnny Sierra (Dominican Republic).

NEW YORK

Telephone, Address

Office Address: Yankee Stadium, 161st Street and River Avenue, Bronx, NY 10451. **Telephone:** (718) 293-4300. **FAX:** (718) 293-8431.

Ownership

Operated by: New York Yankees.

Principal Owner: George Steinbrenner. **General Partners:** Joseph Molloy, Harold Steinbrenner.

George Steinbrenner

Limited Partners: Harold Bowman, Daniel Crown, James Crown, Lester Crown, Michael Friedman, Marvin Goldklang, Barry Halper, John Henry, Harvey Leighton, Daniel McCarthy, Jessica Molloy, Harry Nederlander, James Nederlander, Robert Nederlander, William Rose Sr., Edward Rosenthal, Jack Satter, Harold Steinbrenner, Henry Steinbrenner, Joan Steinbrenner, Jennifer Swindell, Charlotte Witkind, Richard Witkind.

BUSINESS OPERATIONS

Executive Vice President, General Counsel: David Sussman. **Vice President:** Ed Weaver. **Vice President, Business Development:** Derek Schiller. **Director of Office Administration and Services:** Harvey Winston.

Finance

Vice President, Chief Financial Officer: Barry Pincus.

Director of Internal Audit: Mike Macaluso. **Controller:** Robert Brown.

Marketing, Public Relations

Director of Marketing: Deborah Tymon.

Director of Community Relations: Brian Smith. **Director of Public and Community Affairs, Tampa:** John Szponar.

Manager, Public Relations and Special Events: Annette Guardabascio. **Director of Entertainment:** Stanley Kay.

Media Relations, Publications

Telephone: (718) 293-4300. **FAX:** (718) 293-8414.

Special Advisor/Consultant: Arthur Richman.

Director of Media Relations: Rick Cerrone. **Assistant Director of Media Relations:** John Thursby. **Director of Publications:** Tim Wood. **Assistant Director, Publications:** Kara McGovern.

Stadium Operations

Director of Stadium Operations: Sonny Hight. **Manager of Stadium Operations:** Kirk Randazzo. **Director of Customer Services:** Joel White. **Assistant Director, Customer Services:** David Bernstein.

Director of Broadcasting and Video Operations: Mayra Jimenez. **Assistant Director, Broadcasting:** Jennifer Giandalone.

PA Announcer: Bob Sheppard. **Official Scorers:** Bill Shannon, Red Foley.

Ticketing

Telephone: (718) 293-6000. **FAX:** (718) 293-4841.

Executive Director of Ticket Operations: Jeff Kline. **Ticket Director:** Ken Skrypek.

Travel, Clubhouse

Traveling Secretary: David Szen.

Equipment Manager: Nick Priore. **Home Clubhouse:** Rob Cucuzza. **Visiting Clubhouse:** Lou Cucuzza.

Radio, TV, Media

Radio Announcers: John Sterling, Michael Kay. **Flagship Station:** Unavailable.

TV Announcers: Unavailable. **Flagship Station:** Madison Square Garden Network (regional cable).

NEWSPAPERS, Daily Coverage: New York Daily News, New York Post, New York Times, Newark Star-Ledger, The Bergen Record, Newsday, Hartford Courant.

General Information

Hometown Dugout: First Base. **Playing Surface:** Grass.

Standard Game Times: 7:35 p.m.; weekends—1:35 p.m.

Stadium Directions: From I-95, exit 1C to Major Deegan South exit G for the stadium; I-87 North to 149th or 155th Streets; I-87 South to 161st Street.

Player Representative: David Cone.

YANKEES

BASEBALL OPERATIONS

Vice President, General Manager: Bob Watson.

Assistant General Manager: Brian Cashman. **Major League Administrator:** Tom May. **Assistant, Baseball Operations:** Gene Keohane. **Administrative Assistant, Baseball Operations:** Mary Pellino.

Special Advisor to Owner: Reggie Jackson.

Major League Staff

Manager: Joe Torre.

Coaches: Dugout—Don Zimmer. Pitching—Mel Stottlemyre; Batting—Chris Chambliss; First Base/Outfield—Jose Cardenal; Third Base/Infield—Willie Randolph; Bullpen—Tony Cloninger.

Bob Watson

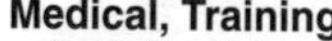

Medical, Training

Team Physician: Dr. Stuart Hershon.

Head Trainer: Gene Monahan. **Assistant Trainer:** Steve Donohue. **Strength and Conditioning Coach:** Paul Mastropasqua.

Minor Leagues

Florida Complex: 3102 N. Himes Ave., Tampa, FL 33607. **Telephone:** (813) 875-7753. **FAX:** (813) 877-8505.

Vice President, Player Development and Scouting: Mark Newman.

Assistant Director of Player Development: Rigo Garcia. **Administrative Assistant, Player Development and Scouting:** Dan Matheson. **Secretary, Player Development:** Jackie Williams.

Coordinator of Latin America Player Development: Ken Dominguez. **Special Advisor, Latin America Affairs:** Ray Negron.

Minor League Pitching Coordinator: Billy Connors.

Clubhouse Coordinator/Equipment Manager: Dave Hays. **Clubhouse Manager:** Eric Sims. **Video Coordinator:** Mark Ferrar. **Facilities Manager:** Eddie Robinson III.

Joe Torre

Head Trainer, Minor Leagues: Mark Littlefield. **Strength and Conditioning Coach:** Shawn Powell.

Farm System

Class	Farm Team	Manager	Coach	Pitching Coach
AAA	Columbus	Stump Merrill	Rob Thomson	Oscar Acosta
AA	Norwich	Trey Hillman	Tony Perezchica	Rick Tomlin
A	Tampa	Lee Mazzilli	Dave Howard	Mark Shifflett
A	Greensboro	Tom Nieto	Ramon Ortiz	Tom Filer
A	Oneonta	Gary Tuck	Bobby DeJardin	Steve Webber
Rookie	Tampa	Ken Dominguez	Hector Lopez	Hoyt Wilhelm

Scouting

Telephone: (813) 875-7569. **FAX:** (813) 348-9198.

Director of Scouting: Lin Garrett. **Assistant Director of Scouting:** Joe Caro. **Scouting Secretary:** Debbie Gallagher.

Advance Scout: Bob Didier (Seattle, WA).

Major League Scouts: Ron Brand, Ron Hansen, Wade Taylor, Stan Williams.

Special Assignment Scouts: Ket Barber (Ocala, FL), Bill Emslie (Safety Harbor, FL), Bobby DeJardin (Hidden Hills, CA).

National Crosscheckers: West Coast—John Cox (Redlands, CA); Midwest—Damon Oppenheimer (Phoenix, AZ); East Coast—Don Rowland (Orlando, FL).

Scouts: Rich Arena (Coral Springs, FL), Joe Arnold (Gainesville, FL), Mike Baker (Cave Creek, AZ), Mark Batchko (Arlington, TX), Lee Elder (Martinez, GA), Tim Kelly (New Lenox, IL), Greg Orr (Sacramento, CA), Scott Pleis (St. Charles, MO), Cesar Presbott (Bronx, NY), Joe Robison (Dayton, TX), Reggie Waller (El Cajon, CA), Steve Webber (Watkinsville, GA), Roy White (Oradell, NJ), Leon Wurth (Nashville, TN), Bill Young (Long Beach, CA).

Director of Player Personnel/International Operations: Gordon Blakeley (Gilbert, AZ). **Coordinator, Canadian Scouting:** Dick Groch (Marysville, MI). **Supervisors, Latin America Scouting:** Richard Heron (Panama), Vic Mata (Dominican Republic), Jorge Oquendo (Puerto Rico), Raul Ortega (Venezuela).

OAKLAND

Telephone, Address

Office Address: 7677 Oakport St., Suite 200, Oakland, CA 94621. **Telephone:** (510) 638-4900. **FAX:** (510) 568-3770. **E-Mail Address:** www.oaklandathletics.com.

Ownership

Operated by: Athletics Investment Group LLC.

Co-Owner/Managing Partner: Steve Schott. **Partner/Owner:** Ken Hofmann.

Strategic Planning Advisor: David Nasaw. **Executive Secretary:** Erin Buckert.

Steve Schott

BUSINESS OPERATIONS

Director of Customer, Ticket and Information Services: David Lozow. **Director of Human Resources:** Eleanor Yee.

Finance

Chief Financial Officer: Goy Fuller. **Controller:** Paul Wong.

Marketing, Sales

Senior Director, Sales and Marketing: David Alioto.

Director of Corporate Advertising Sales: Mark Sowinski.

Director, Promotions and Special Events: Susan Bress. **Manager, Promotions and Special Events:** Ross Hatamlya. **Manager, Group Promotions:** Barbara Reilly. **Director, Ticket Sales:** Paul Solby. **Manager, Ticket Sales:** Dennis Murphy.

Director of Purchasing and Merchandising: Drew Bruno.

Spring Training Marketing and Operations Manager: Travis Dray.

Public Relations, Communications

Telephone: (510) 563-2207. **FAX:** (510) 562-1633.

Senior Director, Broadcasting and Communications: Ken Pries. **Assistant Director, Broadcasting and Communications:** Ann Luke.

Director of Marketing Communications: Jim Bloom.

Baseball Information Manager: Mike Selleck. **Public Relations Manager:** Eric Carrington. **Broadcasting and Public Relations Coordinator:** Robert Buan. **Administrative Assistant, Public and Community Relations:** Debbie Kenney.

Special Projects and Publications Manager: Audrey Minagawa.

Stadium Operations

Senior Director, Stadium Operations: David Rinetti. **Manager, Stadium Operations:** Robert Zuniga.

Head Groundskeeper: Clay Wood.

Ticketing

Ticket/Customer Service Manager: Mike Ono. **Ticket Operations Manager:** Gary Phillips. **Ticket Projects Manager:** Jennie Costa.

Travel, Clubhouse

Director of Team Travel: Mickey Morabito.

Equipment Manager: Steve Vucinich. **Visiting Clubhouse Manager:** Mike Thalblum. **Assistant Clubhouse Manager:** Brian Davis.

Radio, TV, Media

Radio Announcers: Bill King, Ray Fosse, Ken Korach. **Flagship Station:** KFRC 610-AM.

TV Announcers: Ray Fosse, Greg Papa, Ken Wilson. **Flagship Stations:** KRON Channel 4, SportsChannel Pacific (regional cable).

NEWSPAPERS, Daily Coverage: San Francisco Chronicle, Oakland Tribune, Contra Costa Times, Sacramento Bee, San Francisco Examiner, San Jose Mercury-News, Hayward Daily Review.

General Information

Hometown Dugout: Third Base. **Playing Surface:** Grass.

Standard Game Times: Weekday—1:05 p.m., 7:05, 7:35. Weekend—1:05.

Stadium Location: From San Jose—north on I-880 to Oakland, exit at 66th Ave.; From San Francisco—east on Bay Bridge to I-580 toward Hayward, to downtown Oakland and I-880 south, exit at 66th Avenue; From Sacramento—I-80 west to Oakland, I-580 toward Hayward and I-980 to downtown Oakland, then I-880 South, exit at 66th Avenue.

Player Representative: Scott Brosius.

ATHLETICS

BASEBALL OPERATIONS

General Manager: Sandy Alderson.

Assistant General Manager: Billy Beane. **Special Assistant to the General Manager:** Bill Rigney.

Sandy Alderson

Director of Baseball Administration: Pamela Pitts. **Administrative Assistant, Baseball Operations:** Betty Shinoda.

Major League Staff

Manager: Art Howe.

Coaches: Dugout—Duffy Dyer; Pitching—Bob Cluck; Batting—Denny Walling; First Base—Brad Fischer; Third Base—Ron Washington; Bullpen—Bob Alejo.

Medical, Training

Team Physician: Dr. Allan Pont. **Team Orthopedist:** Dr. Jerrald Goldman. **Arizona Team Physician:** Dr. Robert Flores.

Trainers: Barry Weinberg, Larry Davis. **Conditioning Coach:** Bob Alejo.

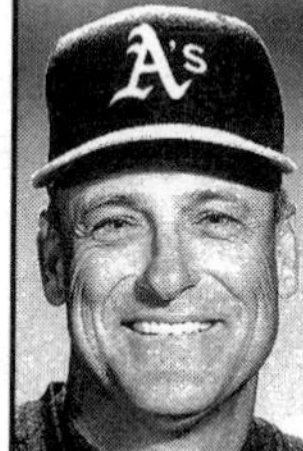
Art Howe

Minor Leagues

Telephone, Oakland (510) 638-4900. **FAX:** (510) 563-2376.

Arizona Complex: Papago Park Baseball Complex, 1802 North 64th St., Phoenix, AZ 85008. **Telephone:** (602) 949-5951. **FAX:** (602) 945-0557.

Director, Player Development: Keith Lieppman. **Assistant Director, Player Development:** Dave Hudgens.

Director, Arizona Operations: Ted Polakowski.

Roving Instructor: Ron Plaza. **Minor League Medical, Strength and Conditioning Coordinator:** Greg Hauck.

Farm System

Class	Farm Team	Manager	Coach	Pitching Coach
AAA	Edmonton	Gary Jones	Orv Franchuk	Pete Richert
AA	Huntsville	Mike Quade	Gil Lopez	Bert Bradley
A	Modesto	Jeffrey Leonard	Dave Joppie	Rick Rodriguez
A	Visalia	Tony DeFrancesco	Greg Sparks	Glenn Abbott
A	So. Oregon	John Kuehl	Randy Elliott	Steve Bowden
Rookie	Scottsdale	Juan Navarrete	Ruben Escalera	Curt Young
Rookie	DSL I	Evaristo Lantigua	Tomas Silverio	Nasusel Cabrera
Rookie	DSL II	Luis Gomez	Luis Martinez	Unavailable

Scouting

Telephone: (510) 638-4900, ext. 2369. **FAX:** (510) 563-2376.

Director of Scouting: Grady Fuson (Stockton, CA).

Assistant Director of Scouting: David Seifert (Castro Valley, CA).

Advance/Major League Scout: Bob Johnson (Rockaway, NJ).

Special Assignment Scouts: Dick Bogard (La Palma, CA), J.P. Ricciardi (West Boylston, MA).

National Crosschecker: Ron Hopkins (Seattle, WA).

Grady Fuson

Scouts: Steve Bowden (Houston, TX), Tom Clark (Worcester, MA), Ron Elam (Richmond, VA), Tim Holt (Dallas, TX), Ruben Escalera (Villa Carolina, PR), Tim Holt (Dallas, TX), John Kuehl (Fountain Hills, AZ), Rick Magnante (Van Nuys, CA), Gary McGraw (Newberg, OR), Chris Pittaro (Hamilton Township, NJ), John Poloni (Tarpon Springs, FL), Joe Robinson (Burlington, IA), Will Schock (Oakland, CA), Mike Soper (Miami, FL), Rich Sparks (Sterling Heights, MI), Ron Vaughn (Corona, CA).

Latin American Coordinator: Miguel Machado (Miami, FL). **Pacific Rim Coordinator:** Eric Kubota (Oakland, CA).

International Scouts: Angel Eusebio (Dominican Republic), Julio Franco (Venezuela), Santiago Villalona (Dominican Republic).

SEATTLE

Telephone, Address

Office Address: 83 South King St., Seattle, WA 98104. **Telephone:** (206) 628-3555. **FAX:** (206) 628-3340. **E-Mail Address:** http://www.mariners.org.

Chuck Armstrong

Ownership

Operated by: Baseball Club of Seattle, LP.

Board of Directors: Minoru Arakawa, John Ellis, Chris Larson, Howard Lincoln, John McCaw, Frank Shrontz, Craig Watjen.

Chairman, Chief Executive Officer: John Ellis. **President, Chief Operating Officer:** Chuck Armstrong.

BUSINESS OPERATIONS

Vice President, Business Development: Paul Isaki. **Vice President, Ballpark Planning and Development:** John Palmer.

Director, Human Resources: Katherine Kummerow. **Director, Strategic Planning:** Tim Kornegay.

Executive Assistant, Ownership/Business Development: Janet O'Brien.

Finance

Vice President, Finance and Administration: Kevin Mather.

Controller: Denise Podosek. **Assistant Controller:** Karen Vaughn.

Marketing, Sales

Director, Marketing: Kevin Martinez. **Director, Regional Marketing:** David Venneri. **Manager, Regional Marketing:** Jonathan Gesinger. **Assistant Director, Corporate Marketing:** Robin Karr.

Director, Sales: Beth Wojcik. **Assistant Director, Ticket Sales:** Ron Babes. **Senior Account Executive/Ticket Sales:** Moose Clausen.

Director, Merchandising: Todd Vecchio.

Public Relations, Communications

Telephone: (206) 628-3555. **FAX:** (206) 628-3340.

Vice President, Communications: Randy Adamack.

Director, Public Relations: Dave Aust. **Assistant Director, Public Relations:** Tim Hevly. **Public Relations Assistant:** Eric Radovich. **Administrative Assistant, Public Relations:** Kelly Gluth.

Director, Community Relations: Joe Chard. **Coordinator, Community Projects:** Sean Grindley.

Director, Public Affairs: Todd Myers. **Associate, Public Affairs:** Krista Bunch. **Manager, Publications:** Allison Mauck.

Coordinator, Promotions and Special Events: Gina Syre.

Ticketing

Telephone: (206) 343-4600. **FAX:** (206) 628-2911.

Director, Ticket Services: Kristin Fortier. **Manager, Season Ticket Services:** Joan Moeller. **Manager, Ticket Operations:** Connie McKay. **Supervisor, Ticket Operations:** Rob Brautigam.

Stadium Operations

Director, Stadium Operations: Tony Pereira. **Assistant Director:** Kameron Durham. **Manager, Game Operations:** Ray Eldridge.

Maintenance and Operations Manager: Randy Shores. **Head Groundskeeper:** Wilber Loo.

PA Announcer: Tom Hutyler. **Official Scorer:** Harland Beery.

Travel, Clubhouse

Director, Team Travel: Craig Detwiler.

Clubhouse Manager/Equipment: Scott Gilbert. **Visiting Clubhouse Manager:** Henry Genzale. **Video Coordinator:** Carl Hamilton.

Radio, TV, Media

Radio Announcers: Dave Niehaus, Ron Fairly, Rick Rizzs. **Flagship Station:** KIRO 710-AM.

TV Announcers: Dave Niehaus, Ron Fairly, Rick Rizzs. **Flagship Station:** KIRO Channel 7, Prime Sports Northwest (regional cable).

NEWSPAPERS, Daily Coverage: Seattle Times, Seattle Post-Intelligencer, Tacoma News Tribune.

General Information

Hometown Dugout: Third Base. **Playing Surface:** Artificial turf.

Standard Game Times: 7:05 p.m., Sun. 1:35.

Stadium Location: I-5 or I-90 to Fourth Ave. South exit.

Player Representative: Dan Wilson.

MARINERS

BASEBALL OPERATIONS

Vice President, Baseball Operations: Woody Woodward.

Senior Director, Baseball Administration: Lee Pelekoudas. **Assistant to Vice President, Baseball Operations:** George Zuraw. **Administrator, Baseball Operations:** Debbie Larsen.

Major League Staff

Manager: Lou Piniella.

Coaches: Dugout—Steve Smith; Pitching—Nardi Contreras; Batting—Lee Elia; First Base—Sam Mejias; Third Base—John McLaren; Bullpen—Matt Sinatro.

Woody Woodward

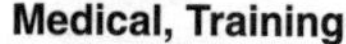

Medical, Training

Club Physicians: Dr. Larry Pedegana, Dr. Mitch Storey.

Head Trainer: Rick Griffin. **Assistant Trainer:** Tom Newberg. **Strength and Conditioning Coach:** Allen Wirtala.

Lou Piniella

Minor Leagues

Telephone: (206) 628-3555. **FAX:** (206) 682-4292.

Vice President, Scouting and Player Development: Roger Jongewaard.

Director, Player Development: Larry Beinfest. **Assistant Director, Player Development:** Greg Hunter. **Administrative Assistant:** Emily Sinclair-Leer.

Coordinator of Instruction: Mike Goff. **Player Education Coordinator:** Al Coons. **Employeee and Player Assistance Program Coordinator:** Gary Mack. **Roving Instructors:** Roger Hansen (catching), Ron Romanick (pitching).

Farm System

Class	Farm Team	Manager	Coach	Pitching Coach
AAA	Tacoma	Dave Myers	Henry Cotto	Jeff Andrews
AA	Memphis	Dave Brundage	Dan Rohn	Bryan Price
A	Lancaster	Rick Burleson	Dana Williams	Jim Slaton
A	Wisconsin	Gary Varsho	Omer Munoz	Pat Rice
A	Everett	Orlando Gomez	Andy Bottin	Steve Peck
Rookie	Peoria	Darrin Garner	Tommy Cruz	Gary Wheelock
Rookie	DSL	R. de los Santos	Maximo Alverez	Roberto Valdez

Scouting

Telephone: (206) 628-3555. **FAX:** (206) 682-4292.

Director, Scouting: Roger Jongewaard. **Administrator, Scouting:** Hallie Larson.

Major League/Special Assignment Scouts: Ken Compton (Cypress, CA), Bill Kearns (Milton, MA).

National Supervisor/Special Assignment Scout: Benny Looper (Ada, OK).

Scouting Supervisors: West—Frank Mattox (Los Angeles, CA); East—Steve Pope (Asheville, NC); Midwest—Carroll Sembera (Shiner, TX).

Roger Jongewaard

Area Scouts: Dave Alexander (Lafayette, IN), Fernando Arguelles (Miami, FL), Rodney Davis (Chandler, AZ), Curtis Dishman (Allen, TX), Larry Harper (Redwood Shores, CA), John McMichen (Treasure Island, FL), Tom McNamara (Nanuet, NY), Billy Merkel (Columbia, TN), Don Poplin (Norwood, NC), Alex Smith (Bel Air, MD), Chris Smith (The Woodlands, TX), Craig Weissmann (San Diego, CA), Darren Wittcke (Portland, OR).

Director, Pacific Rim Operations: Jim Colborn (Ventura, CA). **Supervisor, Latin America:** Fernando Arguelles (Miami, FL). **Supervisor, Canada:** Ken Madeja (Novi, MI).

International Scout: Ramon de los Santos (Dominican Republic).

TAMPA BAY

(Scheduled to begin league play in 1998)

Vince Naimoli

Telephone, Address

Office Address: Tropicana Field, One Tropicana Dr., St. Petersburg, FL 33705. **Telephone:** (813) 825-3137. **FAX:** (813) 825-3300.

Ownership

Operated by: Tampa Bay Devil Rays, Ltd.

Managing General Partner: Vincent Naimoli.

BUSINESS OPERATIONS

Vice President/General Counsel: John Higgins.

Executive Assistant to the Managing General Partner: Cass Halpin.

Finance

Senior Vice President, Chief Financial Officer: Raymond Naimoli.

Accountant: Sheryl Evans. **Office Administrator:** Bill Wiener.

Marketing, Sales

Vice President, Sales and Marketing: Robert Aylward. **Director of Marketing/Sales:** David Auker. **Marketing Coordinator:** Noel Beaulieu.

Public Relations, Communications

Telephone: (813) 825-3242. **FAX:** (813) 825-3300.

Vice President, Public Relations: Rick Vaughn. **Assistant, Public Relations:** Steve Matesich. **Administrative Assistant, Public Relations:** Carmen Molina.

Director, Community Relations: Orestes Destrade.

Stadium Operations

Vice President, Stadia Operations and Facilities: Rick Nafe. **Administrative Assistant:** Meredith Cernuda.

Ticketing

Telephone: (813) 825-3250. **FAX:** (813) 825-3111.

Director of Ticket Operations: Robert Bennett. **Ticket Coordinators:** Jim Cook, Liz Lauck.

Radio, TV, Media

Radio Announcers: Unavailable. **Flagship Station:** WFLA 970-AM.

TV Announcers: Unavailable, **Flagship Stations:** WWWB Channel 32, WRSP Channel 10, SportsChannel Florida (regional cable).

NEWSPAPERS: St. Petersburg Times, Tampa Tribune.

DEVIL RAYS

BASEBALL OPERATIONS

Chuck LaMar

Telephone: (813) 825-3137. **FAX:** (813) 825-3365.

Senior Vice President, Baseball Operations/General Manager: Chuck LaMar.

Assistant General Managers: Bart Braun (baseball operations), Scott Proefrock (administration). **Special Assistants to the General Manager:** Bill Geivett, Bart Johnson, Mickey White. **Executive Assistant:** Debbie Bent.

Medical, Training

Medical Director: Dr. James Andrews. **Team Physicians:** Dr. William Carson, Dr. Mike Reilly, Dr. Koco Eaton.

Head Trainer: Jamie Reed. **Strength and Conditioning Coordinator:** Ken Crenshaw.

Minor Leagues

Telephone: (813) 825-3137. **FAX:** (813) 825-3365.

Director of Player Personnel: Bill Livesey. **Director of Minor League Operations:** Tom Foley. **Assistant, Player Development and Scouting:** Michael Hill. **Administrative Assistant:** Denise Vega.

Coordinator of Instruction: Bill Geivett. **Pitching Coordinator:** Jackie Brown. **Hitting Coordinator:** Steve Henderson. **Outfield/Baserunning Coordinator:** Milt Thompson.

Minor League Medical and Rehab Coordinator: Ron Porterfield. **Minor League Equipment Manager:** Guy Gallagher.

Farm System

Class	Farm Team	Manager	Coach	Pitching Coach
A	St. Petersburg	Bill Evers	Billy Hatcher	Chuck Hernandez
A	Charleston, S.C.	Scott Fletcher	Unavailable	Dennis Rasmussen
A	Hudson Valley	Julio Garcia	Steve Livesey	Greg Harris
Rookie	Princeton	Charlie Montoyo	Mike Tosar	Milt Hill
Rookie	St. Petersburg	Bobby Ramos	Edwin Rodriguez	Mitch Lukevics
Rookie	DSL	Ruben Rodriguez	Jose Perez	Rafael DeLeon

Scouting

Dan Jennings

Telephone: (813) 825-3137. **FAX:** (813) 825-3365.

Director of Scouting: Dan Jennings. **Administrative Assistant, Scouting:** LaRonda Graham.

Major League Scouts: Jerry Gardner (Los Alamitos, CA), Al LaMacchia (San Antonio, TX), Don Lindeberg (Anaheim, CA), Don Williams (Paragould, AR).

National Crosscheckers: Jack Gillis (Sarasota, FL), Stan Meek (Norman, OK).

Regional Crosscheckers: East—Shawn Pender (Drexel Hill, PA). West—R.J. Harrison (Phoenix, AZ).

Area Scouts: Fernando Arango (Oklahoma City, OK), Skip Bundy (Birmingham, AL), Tim Corcoran (La Verne, CA), Matt Dodd (Middlebury, CT), Kevin Elfering (Lutz, FL), Paul Faulk (Raleigh, NC), Doug Gassaway (Blum, TX), Matt Kinzer (Fort Wayne, IN), Paul Kirsch (Tigard, OR), Blaise Kozeniewski (Somerdale, NJ), Fred Mazuca (Tustin, CA), Mark McKnight (Atlanta, GA), Pat O'Neil (Covington, IN), Nelson Rood (Scottsdale, AZ), Charles Scott (San Rafael, CA).

Director of Latin American Operations: Rudy Santin (Miami, FL). **International Scouts:** Philip Elhage (Netherlands Antilles), Jose Perez (Dominican Republic), Carlos Ramirez (Dominican Republic), Edwin Rodriguez (Puerto Rico), Freddy Torres (Venezuela).

TEXAS

Tom Schieffer

Telephone, Address

Office Address: 1000 Ballpark Way, Arlington, TX 76011. **Mailing Address:** P.O. Box 90111, Arlington, TX 76004. **Telephone:** (817) 273-5222. **FAX:** (817) 273-5206.

E-Mail Address: www.texasrangers.com.

Ownership

Operated by: Texas Rangers, Ltd.

General Partners: Edward "Rusty" Rose, Thomas Schieffer.

President: Thomas Schieffer. **Assistant to the President:** Nolan Ryan.

BUSINESS OPERATIONS

Vice President, Business Operations/Treasurer: John McMichael.

Vice President, Legal Affairs: Bill Miller. **Vice President, Human Resources:** Kimberly Smith. **Vice President, Information Technology:** Steve McNeill. **General Counsel:** Gerald Haddock.

Finance

Assistant Vice President/Controller: Charles Sawicki. **Assistant Controller:** Susan Capps.

Marketing, Sales

Vice President, Marketing: Charles Seraphin.

Director, Corporate Relations: Dave Fendrick. **Director, Corporate Sales:** Mike Phillips. **Director, In-Park Entertainment:** Chuck Morgan. **Director, Merchandising:** Nancy Hill. **Director, Sales:** Ross Scott. **Promotions Manager:** Sherry Flow.

Public Relations, Communications

Telephone: (817) 273-5203. **FAX:** (817) 273-5206.

Vice President, Public Relations: John Blake.

Vice President, Community Development: Norman Lyons.

Assistant Director, Public Relations: Charley Green. **Assistant Director, Public Relations/Community/Ballpark Relations:** Lydia Martin. **Administrative Assistant, Public Relations:** Michelle Baugh.

Director, Publications: Eric Kolb. **Assistant Director, Publications:** Michelle Lancaster. **Director, Player Relations:** Taunee Taylor. **Assistant Director, Player Relations:** Dana Wilcox. **Director, Spanish Broadcasting/Latin America Liasion:** Luis Mayoral.

Stadium Operations

Assistant Vice President, Facilities: Billy Ray Johnson.

Director, Ballpark Operations: Kevin Jimison. **Director, Grounds:** Tom Burns. **Major League Groundskeeper:** Brad Richards. **Youth Ballpark Groundskeeper:** Andrew Gulley.

PA Announcer: Chuck Morgan. **Official Scorer:** Kurt Iverson.

Ticketing

Telephone: (817) 273-5100. **FAX:** (817) 273-5190.

Director, Ticket Operations: Marty Schueren. **Assistant Director, Ticket Operations:** Tracie Gregory. **Ticket Operations:** Ranae Lewis.

Group/Season Ticket Manager: Michael Wood. **Group Sales Coordinator:** Scott Faris.

Travel, Clubhouse

Traveling Secretary: Dan Schimek.

Equipment Manager: Zack Minasian. **Visiting Clubhouse:** Joe Macko.

Radio, TV, Media

Radio Announcers: Eric Nadel, Brad Sham. **Flagship Station:** KRLD 1080-AM. **No. of Network Stations:** 52.

TV Announcers: Mark Holtz, Tom Grieve. **Flagship Stations:** KXAS, KXTX, Fox Sports Southwest (regional cable).

NEWSPAPERS, Daily Coverage: Dallas Morning News, Fort Worth Star-Telegram, Arlington Morning News.

General Information

Hometown Dugout: First Base. **Playing Surface:** Grass.

Game Times: 7:35 p.m.; Sun. (April-May, Sept.) 2:05, (June-Aug.) 7:05.

Directions to Stadium: From I-30, take Ballpark Way exit, south on Ballpark Way; From Route 360, take Randol Mill exit, west on Randol Mill.

Player Representative: Will Clark

RANGERS

BASEBALL OPERATIONS

Telephone: (817) 273-5226. **FAX:** (817) 273-5285.

Executive Vice President/General Manager: Doug Melvin.

Assistant General Manager: Dan O'Brien Jr.

Director, Major League Administration: Judy Johns.

Doug Melvin

Major League Staff

Manager: Johnny Oates.

Coaches: Dugout—Bucky Dent; Pitching—Dick Bosman; Batting—Rudy Jaramillo; First Base—Ed Napoleon; Third Base—Jerry Narron; Bullpen—Larry Hardy.

Medical, Training

Johnny Oates

Medical Director: Dr. Mike Mycoskie. **Club Physician:** Dr. John Conway.

Head Trainer: Danny Wheat. **Assistant Trainer:** Ray Ramirez. **Strength and Conditioning Coordinator:** Tim Lang.

Minor Leagues

Telephone: (817) 273-5228. **FAX:** (817) 273-5285.

Director, Player Development: Reid Nichols. **Assistant to Director, Player Development:** Alex Smith.

Field Coordinator: Bob Miscik. **Roving Instructors:** Jesse Barfield (hitting), Steve Luebber (pitching), Don Reynolds (outfield, baserunning).

Farm System

Class	Farm Team	Manager	Coach	Pitching Coach
AAA	Oklahoma City	Greg Biagini	Bump Wills	Tom Brown
AA	Tulsa	Bobby Jones	None	Brad Arnsberg
A	Charlotte	Butch Wynegar	None	Steve Foucault
Rookie	Pulaski	Julio Cruz	None	Unavailable
Rookie	Port Charlotte	James Byrd	Victor Ramirez	Unavailable

Scouting

Telephone: (817) 273-5277. **FAX:** (817) 273-5206.

Director, Amateur Scouting: Chuck McMichael. **Assistant to Director, Amateur Scouting:** Linda Smith.

Director, Professional/International Scouting: Omar Minaya (West New York, NJ). **Assistant Director, Professional/International Scouting:** Monty Clegg.

Advance Scout: Mike Paul (Tucson, AZ).

Professional Scouts: Larry D'Amato (Tualatin, OR), Toney Howell (Downers Grove, IL), Brian Lambe (Massapequa, NY), Bob Reasonover (Clearwater, FL), Richard Seko (Irvine, CA), Rudy Terrassas (Pasadena, TX).

Chuck McMichael

National Crosscheckers: Tim Hallgren (Clarkston, WA), Dave Klipstein (Eupora, MS), Jeff Taylor (Newark, DE).

Full-Time Area Scouts: Manny Batista (Vega Alta, PR), Dave Birecki (Peoria, AZ), Joe Branzell (Silver Spring, MD), Mike Cadahia (Miami, FL), Mike Daughtry (Elgin, IL), Kip Fagg (Manteca, CA), Jim Fairey (Clemson, SC), Mark Giegler (Fenton, MI), Joel Grampietro (Shrewsbury, MA), Mike Grouse (Independence, MO), Todd Guggiana (Garden Grove, CA), Doug Harris (Carlisle, PA), Bob Heck (Tallahassee, FL), Larry Izzo (Deer Park, NY), Jim Lentine (Rancho San Clemente, CA), Pat Rigby (Katy, TX), Greg Whitworth (Dillon, MT).

International Scouts: Hector Acevedo (Dominican Republic), Roney Calderon (Venezuela), Cornelio Pena (Dominican Republic), Danilo Troncoso (Dominican Republic).

TORONTO

Paul Beeston

Telephone, Address

Office Address: 300 Bremner Blvd, Gate 9, SkyDome, Toronto, Ontario M5V 1J1. **Mailing Address:** One Blue Jays Way, Ste. 3200, Toronto, Ontario M5V 1J1. **Telephone:** (416) 341-1000. **FAX:** (416) 341-1250.

E-Mail Address: bluejays@bluejays.ca.

Ownership

Operated by: Toronto Blue Jays Baseball Club.

Principal Owner: John Labatt Ltd (Interbrew SA).

Board of Directors: Paul Beeston, Allan Chapin, Luc Missorten, Hugo Powell, George Radford, George Taylor.

Chairman: Sam Pollock.

President, Chief Executive Officer: Paul Beeston.

BUSINESS OPERATIONS

Vice President, Business: Bob Nicholson.

Vice President, Development: Christine Legein.

Executive Administrative Assistant: Sue Cannell.

Finance

Director, Finance: Susan Quigley. **Manager, Accounting:** Cathy McNamara. **Manager, Information Systems:** Bart MacNeil. **Manager, Employee Compensation:** Perry Nicoletta.

Marketing, Sales

Director, Marketing/Sales: Paul Markle.

Manager, Promotions and Advertising: Rick Amos. **Coordinator, Community Relations:** Laurel Overland.

Public Relations, Communications

Telephone: (416) 341-1303. **FAX:** (416) 341-1250.

Director, Public Relations: Howard Starkman. **Assistant Director, Public Relations:** Jay Stenhouse. **Manager, Public Relations:** Janis Davidson Pressick. **Public Relations Assistant:** Laura Ammendolia.

Stadium Operations

Director, Stadium Operations: George Holm. **Head Groundskeeper:** Tom Farrell.

PA Announcer: Murray Eldon. **Official Scorers:** Neil MacCarl, Louis Cauz, Doug Hobbs, Joe Sawchuk.

Ticketing

Telephone: (416) 341-1280. **FAX:** (416) 341-1177.

Assistant Director of Ticket Operations, Box Office Manager: Randy Low. **Manager, Group Sales:** Maureen Haffey. **Manager, Ticket Vault Services:** Paul Goodyear. **Manager, Subscriber Services:** Doug Barr. **Manager, Mail Order Services:** Sandra Wilbur.

Travel, Clubhouse

Director of Team Travel: John Brioux.

Equipment Manager: Jeff Ross. **Clubhouse Operations:** Kevin Malloy. **Visitors Clubhouse:** Len Frejlich.

Radio, TV, Media

Radio Announcers: Tom Cheek, Jerry Howarth. **Flagship Station:** THE FAN 590-AM.

TV Announcers: TSN—Buck Martinez, Dan Shulman, Brian Williams. **Flagship Stations:** The Sports Network (national cable—Canada).

NEWSPAPERS, Daily Coverage: Toronto Sun, Toronto Star, Globe and Mail, Hamilton Spectator.

General Information

Hometown Dugout: Third Base. **Playing Surface:** Artificial turf.

Standard Game Times: 7:35 p.m.; Sat. 1:05 or 4:05; Sun. 1:05.

Stadium Location: From the west, take the QEW/Gardiner Expressway eastbound and exit at Spadina Ave., go north on Spadina one block, right on Blue Jays Way. From the east, take the Gardiner Expressway westbound and exit at Spadina Ave., north on Spadina one block, right on Blue Jays Way.

Player Representative: Shawn Green.

BLUE JAYS

BASEBALL OPERATIONS

Telephone: (416) 341-1000. **FAX:** (416) 341-1245.

Vice President, General Manager: Gord Ash.

Vice President, Baseball Operations: Bob Mattick.

Assistant General Manager, Player Personnel: Bob Engle. **Assistant General Manager:** Tim McCleary. **Special Assistants to General Manager:** Gordon Lakey, Moose Johnson, Al Widmar.

Administrative Assistant, Baseball: Fran Brown.

Gord Ash

Major League Staff

Manager: Cito Gaston.

Coaches: Pitching—Mel Queen; Batting—Willie Upshaw; First Base—Alfredo Griffin; Third Base—Nick Leyva; Bullpen—Gene Tenace. General—Jim Lett.

Cito Gaston

Medical, Training

Team Physician: Dr. Ron Taylor.

Trainer: Tommy Craig. **Assistant Trainer:** Brent Andrews. **Strength and Conditioning Coordinator:** Geoff Horne.

Minor Leagues

Telephone: (416) 341-1228. **FAX:** (416) 341-1245.

Director, Player Development: Karl Kuehl. **Director, Baseball Administration:** Bob Nelson. **Administrative Assistants:** Heather Connolly, Trina Hiscock.

Roving Instructors: Larry Hisle (hitting), Jim Hoff (infield), Rick Peterson (pitching), Ernie Whitt (catching).

Farm System

Class	Farm Team	Manager	Coach	Pitching Coach
AAA	Syracuse	Garth Iorg	Willie Wilson	Scott Breeden
AA	Knoxville	Omar Malave	Paul Elliott	Rick Langford
A	Dunedin	Dennis Holmberg	Hector Torres	Darren Balsley
A	Hagerstown	J.J. Cannon	Marty Pevey	Bruce Walton
A	St. Catharines	Rocket Wheeler	Lloyd Moseby	Bill Monbouquette
Rookie	Medicine Hat	Marty Pevey	Rolando Pino	Neil Allen
Rookie	DSL	Unavailable	None	Unavailable

Scouting

Telephone: (813) 734-5784. **FAX:** (813) 734-0117.

Director of Scouting: Tim Wilken.

Administrative Assistant, Scouting: Donna Kuzoff.

Advance Scout: Sal Butera.

Special Assignment Scouts: Chris Buckley (Temple Terrace, FL), Tom Hinkle (Atascadero, CA), Duane Larson (Harrisburg, NC).

Scouting Supervisors: Tony Arias (Miami Lakes, FL), David Blume (Elk Grove, CA), Chris Bourjos (Scottsdale, AZ), Bus Campbell (Littleton, CO), John Cole (Lake Forest, CA), Ellis Dungan (Pensacola, FL), Jim Hughes (Prosper, TX), Ted Lekas (Worcester, MA), Ben McLure (Palmyra, PA), Marty Miller (Chicago, IL), Bill Moore (Alta Loma, CA), Alvin Rittman (Memphis, TN), Jorge Rivera (Puerto Nuevo, PR), Joe Siers (Lexington, KY), Mark Snipp (Fort Worth, TX), Ron Tostenson (Issaquah, WA), Steve Williams (Raleigh, NC).

Scouts: Joe Ford (Yukon, OK), Don Hara (Long Beach, CA), Tim Hewes (Bakersfield, CA), Andy Pienovi (Portland, OR), Jerry Sobeck (Milpitas, CA)

Director, International Scouting: Wayne Morgan (Morgan Hill, CA). **International Scouts:** Wayne Durbidge (Australia), Paul Elliott (Australia), John Galloway (Australia), Bob Goodin (Australia), Cees Herkemij (The Netherlands), Greg Wade (Australia).

Director, Latin American Operations: Herb Raybourn. **Latin American Scouts:** Pedro Avila (Venezuela), Emilio Carrasquel (Venezuela), Juan Luis Joa (Dominican Republic), Geovany Miranda (Panama), Ramon Perez (Dominican Republic), Carlos Riera (Venezuela), Robert Rowley (Panama).

Director, Canadian Scouting: Bill Byckowski.

NATIONAL LEAGUE

NATIONAL LEAGUE

Mailing Address: 350 Park Ave., New York, NY 10022. **Telephone:** (212) 339-7700. **FAX:** (212) 935-5069.

Years League Active: 1876-.

Executive Committee: John Allen (Cincinnati), Bill Bartholomay (Atlanta), Peter Magowan (San Francisco).

President: Leonard Coleman.

Senior Vice President, Secretary: Katy Feeney.

Director of Umpire Supervision: Ed Vargo. **Administrative Assistant/Umpires:** Cathy Davis.

Executive Director, Public Relations: Ricky Clemons.

Executive Secretary: Rita Aughavin. **Executive Director, Player Records and Assistant Secretary:** Nancy Crofts. **Assistant, Media Relations and Player Records:** Glenn Wilburn.

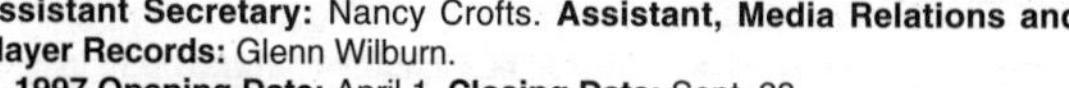

Leonard Coleman

1997 Opening Date: April 1. **Closing Date:** Sept. 28.

No. of Games: 162.

Division Structure: East—Atlanta, Florida, Montreal, New York, Philadelphia. **Central**—Chicago, Cincinnati, Houston, Pittsburgh, St. Louis. **West**—Colorado, Los Angeles, San Diego, San Francisco. **NOTE:** Arizona will begin league play in 1998.

Roster Limit: 25, until Aug. 31 when roster can be expanded to 40.

Umpires: Wally Bell (Canfield, OH), Greg Bonin (Broussard, LA), Gerry Crawford (Havertown, PA), Gary Darling (Phoenix, AZ), Bob Davidson (Littleton, CO), Gerry Davis (Appleton, WI), Dana DeMuth (Gilbert, AZ), Bruce Froemming (Vero Beach, FL), Brian Gorman (Camarillo, CA), Eric Gregg (Philadelphia, PA), Tom Hallion (Louisville, KY), Angel Hernandez (Hollywood, FL), Mark Hirschbeck (Stratford, CT), Bill Hohn (Collegeville, PA), Jeff Kellogg (Ypsilanti Township, MI), Jerry Layne (Winter Haven, FL), Randy Marsh (Edgewood, KY), Ed Montague (San Mateo, CA), Larry Poncino (Tucson, AZ), Frank Pulli (Palm Harbor, FL), Jim Quick (Scottsdale, AZ), Ed Rapuano (North Haven, CT), Charlie Reliford (Tampa, FL), Rich Rieker (St. Louis, MO), Steve Rippley (Seminole, FL), Paul Runge (El Cajon, CA), Terry Tata (Cheshire, CT), Larry Vanover (Antioch, TN), Harry Wendelstedt (Ormond Beach, FL), Joe West (Kilby Island, NC), Charlie Williams (Chicago, IL), Mike Winters (Poway, CA).

1996 Standings

East	W	L	Pct.	GB
Atlanta	96	66	.593	—
Montreal	88	74	.543	8
Florida	80	82	.494	16
New York	71	91	.438	25
Philadelphia	67	95	.414	29

West	W	L	Pct.	GB
San Diego	91	71	.562	—
Los Angeles	90	72	.556	1

Central	W	L	Pct.	GB
St. Louis	88	74	.543	—
Houston	82	80	.506	6
Cincinnati	81	81	.500	7
Chicago	76	86	.469	12
Pittsburgh	73	89	.451	15

West	W	L	Pct.	GB
Colorado	83	79	.512	8
San Francisco	68	94	.420	23

Stadium Information

		Dimensions				
City	Stadium	LF	CF	RF	Capacity	'96 Att.
Atlanta	Turner Field	335	401	330	50,528	2,901,242
Chicago	Wrigley Field	355	400	353	38,884	2,219,110
Cincinnati	Cinergy Field	330	404	330	52,952	1,861,428
Colorado	Coors Field	347	415	350	50,200	3,891,014
Florida	Pro Player Park	335	410	345	40,585	1,746,757
Houston	Astrodome	325	400	325	54,370	1,975,888
Los Angeles	Dodger	330	395	330	56,000	3,188,454
Montreal	Olympic	325	404	325	46,500	1,618,573
New York	Shea	338	410	338	55,777	1,588,323
Philadelphia	Veterans	330	408	330	62,136	1,801,677
Pittsburgh	Three Rivers	335	400	335	48,044	1,332,150
St. Louis	Busch	330	402	330	49,676	2,659,251
San Diego	SD Jack Murphy	327	405	327	48,639	2,187,884
San Francisco	3Com Park	335	400	328	63,000	1,413,687

ARIZONA

(Scheduled to begin league play in 1998)

Jerry Colangelo

Telephone, Address

Office Address: 400 North Fifth St., Suite 1100, Phoenix, AZ 85004. **Mailing Address:** P.O. Box 2095, Phoenix, AZ 85001. **Telephone:** (602) 514-8500. **FAX:** (602) 514-8599. **E-Mail Address:** www.azdiamondbacks.com.

Ownership

Operated by: AZPB, Limited Partnership.

Chairman of the Board: Jerry Colangelo.

Advisory Committee: George Getz, Dale Jensen, David Moore, Jerry Moyes, Rich Stephan.

President: Richard Dozer.

BUSINESS OPERATIONS

Assistant to the President: Michelle Avella.

Finance

Vice President, Finance: Tom Harris.

Controller: Larry White. **Director, Management Information Systems:** Bill Bolt. **Staff Accountant:** Polly Rassi. **Administrative Assistant:** Pat Perez.

Marketing, Sales

Vice President, Marketing and Sales: Scott Brubaker.

Director, Sales and Marketing: Blake Edwards. **Director of Hispanic Marketing:** Richard Saenz. **Assistant, Marketing:** Kelly Wilson.

Public Relations, Communications

Telephone: (602) 514-8528. **FAX:** (602) 514-8599.

Media Relations Manager: Bob Crawford. **Community Relations Manager:** Gina Giallonardo. **Editor, Diamondbacks Quarterly:** Joel Horn.

Stadium Operations

Project Manager: John Wasson. **Assistant Project Manager:** Ed Brisson. **Administrative Assistant:** Toni Zody.

Ticketing

Telephone: (602) 514-8400. **FAX:** (602) 514-8699.

Vice President, Tickets and Special Services: Dianne Aguilar.

Sales Manager: Rob Klese. **Broadcast Services Manager:** Leo Gilmartin. **Administrative Assistants:** Julie Graham, Maxine Royer.

Radio, TV, Media

Radio Announcers: Thom Brennaman, Greg Schulte. **Flagship Station:** KTAR 620-AM.

TV Announcers: Thom Brennaman, Greg Schulte. **Flagship Stations:** KTVK-TV Channel 3, FOX Sports Arizona (regional cable).

NEWSPAPERS, Daily Coverage: Arizona Republic, Tribune Newspapers.

DIAMONDBACKS

BASEBALL OPERATIONS

Telephone: (602) 514-8500. **FAX:** (602) 514-8599.

Vice President, General Manager: Joe Garagiola Jr.

Senior Executive Vice President, Baseball Operations: Roland Hemond. **Director, Pacific Rim Operations:** Jim Marshall. **Expansion Draft Coordinator:** Ralph Nelson.

Assistant to the General Manager: Laure Trimmer. **Administrative Assistant, Baseball Operations:** Melissa Grinker.

Joe Garagiola Jr.

Major League Staff

Manager: Buck Showalter.

Buck Showalter

Medical, Training

Club Physician: Dr. David Zeman.

Minor Leagues

Telephone: (602) 514-8500. **FAX:** (602) 514-8599.

Director, Player Development: Mel Didier. **Director, Field Operations:** Tommy Jones. **Spring Training Coordinator:** Ethan Blackaby. **Administrative Assistant:** Valerie Dietrich.

Roving Instructors: Mark Connor (pitching), Jeff Forney (strength and conditioning), Gil Patterson (pitching), Glenn Sherlock (catching).

Farm System

Class	Farm Team	Manager	Coach	Pitching Coach
A	High Desert	Chris Speier	Dwayne Murphy	Chuck Kniffin
A	South Bend	Dickie Scott	Jim Presley	Dennis Lewallyn
Rookie	Lethbridge	Rod Allen	Ty Van Burkleo	Mike Parrott
Rookie	Phoenix	Brian Butterfield	Don Wakamatsu	Marcos Garcia
Rookie	DSL	Julio Paula	None	Pablo Frias

Scouting

Telephone: (602) 514-8520. **FAX:** (602) 514-8547.

Director, Scouting: Don Mitchell.

Assistant Director, Scouting: Edwin Hartwell. **Administrative Assistant:** Lisa Ventresca.

National Coordinator: Kendall Carter. **Coordinator of Professional Scouting:** Ed Durkin.

Major League Scouts: Doc Edwards (Vero Beach, FL), Ron Hassey (Tucson, AZ), Sandy Johnson (Arlington, TX), Ted Uhlaender (Parshall, CO).

Don Mitchell

National Crosscheckers: Mack Babitt (Richmond, CA), Brannon Bonifay (Okeechobee, FL), Clay Daniel (Keller, TX).

Area Supervisors: Tony Arango (Stamford, CT), Ray Corbett (College Station, TX), Bill Earnhart (Point Clear, AL), Jesse Flores (Post Falls, ID), Brian Guinn (Richmond, CA), Scott Jaster (Midland, MI), Jim Johnson (Rancho Cucamonga, CA), Chris Knabenshue (Edmond, OK), Greg Lonigro (Connellsville, PA), David May (Newark, DE), Howard McCullough (Greenville, NC), Luis Medina (Phoenix, AZ), Mike Piatnik (Winter Haven, FL), Steve Springer (Huntington Beach, CA), Steve Swail (Macon, GA), Brad Vaughn (Griffithville, AR), Harold Zonder (Louisville, KY).

Scouts: Pete Carmona (Laredo, TX), Scott Jamieson (Denver, CO), James Keller (Long Beach, CA), Hal Kurtzman (Van Nuys, CA), George Lopez (Glendale, AZ), John Wright (Chantilly, VA).

Latin American Coordinator: Junior Noboa (Santo Domingo, DR). **International Scouts:** Oswaldo Alvarez (Mexico), Rogel Andrade (Venezuela), Arnold Cochran (Puerto Rico), Gary Davenport (Italy), Juan Escobar (Venezuela), Cesar Gomez (Mexico), Elias Lugo (Venezuela), Rafael Mena (Dominican Republic), Jose Perez (Panama), Carlos Porte (Venezuela), Tomas Santana (Dominican Republic), John Wadsworth (Australia).

ATLANTA

Telephone, Address

Office Address: 755 Hank Aaron Dr., Atlanta, GA 30312. **Mailing Address:** P.O. Box 4064, Atlanta, GA 30302. **Telephone:** (404) 522-7630. **FAX:** (404) 614-1391.

Stan Kasten

Ownership

Operated by: Atlanta National Baseball Club, Inc.

Principal Owner: Ted Turner. **Chairman of the Board:** Bill Bartholomay.

Board of Directors: Henry Aaron, Bill Bartholomay, Bobby Cox, Stan Kasten, Rubye Lucas, Terry McGuirk, John Schuerholz, M.B. Seretean, Ted Turner.

President: Stan Kasten.

Senior Vice President, Assistant to the President: Hank Aaron.

BUSINESS OPERATIONS

Senior Vice President, Administration: Bob Wolfe. **Team Counsel:** David Payne. **Director of Human Resources:** Lisa Stricklin.

Finance

Controller: Chip Moore.

Marketing, Sales

Vice President, Marketing and Broadcasting: Wayne Long.

Senior Director, Promotions and Civic Affairs: Miles McRea. **Director, Ticket Sales:** Paul Adams. **Director, Advertising:** Amy Richter. **Director, Community Relations/Fan Development:** Dexter Santos. **Director, Braves Foundation:** Danny Goodwin.

Public Relations, Communications

Telephone: (404) 614-1302. **FAX:** (404) 614-1391.

Director, Public Relations: Jim Schultz.

Media Relations Managers: Thurman Brooks, Glen Serra. **Administrative Assistant, Public Relations:** Joan Hicks.

Stadium Operations

Director, Stadium Operations and Security: Larry Bowman. **Field Director:** Ed Mangan.

PA Announcer: Unavailable. **Official Scorers:** Mark Frederickson, Scott McGregor. **Director, Audio-Visual Operations:** Jennifer Berger.

Ticketing

Telephone: (800) 326-4000. **FAX:** (404) 614-1391.

Director, Ticket Operations: Ed Newman. **Assistant Director, Ticket Operations:** Sam Williams.

Director, Ticket Sales: Paul Adams.

Travel, Clubhouse

Director of Team Travel/Equipment Manager: Bill Acree. **Assistant Clubhouse Manager:** Casey Stevenson. **Visiting Clubhouse Manager:** John Holland.

Radio, TV, Media

Radio Announcers: Skip Caray, Don Sutton, Joe Simpson, Pete Van Wieren. **Flagship Station:** WSB 750-AM. **No. of Network Stations:** 200.

TV Announcers: WTBS—Skip Caray, Pete Van Wieren, Don Sutton, Joe Simpson; SportSouth— Ernie Johnson, Bob Rathbun. **Flagship Stations:** WTBS Channel 17, Fox SportSouth (regional cable).

NEWSPAPERS, Daily Coverage: Atlanta Journal-Constitution, Morris News Service.

General Information

Hometown Dugout: First Base. **Playing Surface:** Grass.

Standard Game Times: 7:40 p.m.; Sat. 7:10, Sun. 1:10.

Directions to Stadium: I-75/85 northbound, take exit 91; I-75/85 southbound, take exit 91; I-20 westbound, take exit 24; I-20 eastbound, take exit 22, right on Windsor Street, left on Fulton Street.

Player Representative: Tom Glavine.

BRAVES

BASEBALL OPERATIONS

Telephone: (404) 522-7630. **FAX:** (404) 523-3962.

Executive Vice President, General Manager: John Schuerholz.

John Schuerholz

Assistant General Manager: Dean Taylor. **Special Assistants to General Manager:** Bill Lajoie, Brian Murphy. **Special Assistant to GM/Player Development:** Jose Martinez. **Executive Assistant, Baseball Operations:** June Cornillaud.

Major League Staff

Manager: Bobby Cox.

Coaches: Dugout—Jim Beauchamp; Pitching—Leo Mazzone; Batting—Clarence Jones; First Base—Pat Corrales; Third Base—Bobby Dews; Bullpen—Ned Yost.

Medical, Training

Team Physician: Dr. David Watson.

Trainer: Dave Pursley. **Assistant Trainer:** Jeff Porter. **Strength and Conditioning Coach:** Frank Fultz.

Bobby Cox

Minor Leagues

Telephone: (404) 522-7630. **FAX:** (404) 614-1350.

Director, Scouting and Player Development: Paul Snyder. **Director, Minor League Operations:** Deric Ladnier. **Assistant, Baseball Operations:** Tyrone Brooks. **Administrative Assistants, Minor Leagues:** Lena Burney, Bobbie Cranford.

Minor League Field Coordinator: Jeff Cox.

Roving Instructors: Chino Cadahia (catching), Leon Roberts (hitting), Dave Tomchek (strength and conditioning), David Tomlin (pitching).

Farm System

Class	Farm Team	Manager	Coach	Pitching Coach
AAA	Richmond	Bill Dancy	Max Venable	Bill Fischer
AA	Greenville	Randy Ingle	Mel Roberts	Bruce Dal Canton
A	Durham	Paul Runge	Wallace Johnson	Bill Slack
A	Macon	Brian Snitker	Glenn Hubbard	Mark Rose
A	Eugene	Jim Saul	Bobby Moore	Jerry Nyman
Rookie	Danville	Rick Albert	Franklin Stubbs	Kent Willis
Rookie	West Palm	Frank Howard	Ed Renteria	Eddie Watt
Rookie	DSL	Pedro Gonzalez	Dario Paulino	Andres Mena

Scouting

Telephone: (404) 614-1354.

Director, Scouting: Paul Snyder. **Assistant Director, Scouting:** Dayton Moore.

Advance Scout: Bobby Wine (Norristown, PA).

Major League Scouts: Scott Nethery (Houston, TX), Fred Shaffer (New Castle, PA), Bill Wight (Carmichael, CA).

National Crosscheckers: Roy Clark (Martinsville, VA), Bob Wadsworth (Westminster, CA).

Regional Supervisors: Hep Cronin (Cincinnati, OH); John Flannery (Austin, TX); Butch Baccala (Windsor, CA).

Paul Snyder

Area Scouts: Matt Anderson (Atchison, KS), Stu Cann (Bradley, IL), Sherard Clinkscales (Indianapolis, IN), Tom Ealy (Mesa, AZ), Rob English (Duluth, GA), Rene Francisco (Lake Worth, FL), Ralph Garr (Missouri City, TX), Rod Gilbreath (Lilburn, GA), John Hagemann (Staten Island, NY), Marcus Harrison (Vancouver, WA), Brian Kohlscheen (Norman, OK), Scott Littlefield (Valrico, FL), Jim Martz (Lima, OH), Marco Paddy (Columbus, GA), Julian Perez (Levittown, PR), John Ramey (Murrietta, CA), Alan Regier (Castro Valley, CA), John Stewart (Granville, NY), Junior Vizcaino (Durham, NC).

Scouts: Mike Baker (Phoenix, AZ), Steve Bishop (Atlanta, GA), Jim Buchert (Melrose, MA), Joe Caputo (Royersford, PA), Bob Dunning (Phoenix, AZ), Bob Irwin (Seal Beach, CA), Al Kubski (San Diego), Bill Marcot (Encino, CA), Ernie Pedersen (Tinley Park, IL), Charlie Smith (Austin, TX), Bob Turzilli (Kinnelon, NJ).

International Supervisor: Bill Clark (Columbia, MO).

CHICAGO

Telephone, Address

Office Address: Wrigley Field, 1060 West Addison St., Chicago, IL 60613. **Telephone:** (773) 404-2827. **FAX:** (773) 404-4129.

Ownership

Operated by: Chicago National League Ball Club, Inc. **Owner:** Tribune Company.

Board of Directors: James Dowdle, Andy MacPhail, Andrew McKenna.

President/Chief Executive Officer: Andy MacPhail.

Andy MacPhail

BUSINESS OPERATIONS

Executive Vice President, Business Operations: Mark McGuire.

Manager, Information Systems: Carl Rice.

Senior Legal Counsel/Corporate Secretary: Crane Kenney. **Executive Secretary, Business Operations:** Annette Hannah.

Director, Human Resources: Jenifer Surma.

Finance

Controller: Jodi Norman. **Manager, Accounting:** Cathy Bax. **Senior Accountants:** Terri Lynn, Vanessa Smith.

Marketing, Sales

Vice President, Marketing and Broadcasting: John McDonough.

Director, Promotions and Advertising: Jay Blunk. **Manager, Cubs Care/Community Relations:** Rebecca Polihronis. **Senior Account Executive:** Susan Otolski. **Account Executive:** Mary Therese Kraft. **Marketing Administration Coordinator:** Maria Torres.

Media Relations, Publications

Telephone: (773) 404-4191. **FAX:** (773) 404-4129.

Director, Media Relations: Sharon Pannozzo. **Media Information Coordinator:** Chuck Wasserstrom. **Media Relations Assistant:** Wanda Taylor.

Director of Publications/Special Projects: Ernie Roth. **Manager, Publications:** Lena McDonagh. **Publications Editorial Specialists:** Jim McArdle, Jay Rand. **Publications Project Specialist:** Patricia Mora-Gonzalez. **Photographer:** Stephen Green.

Stadium Operations

Director, Stadium Operations: Tom Cooper. **Assistant Director, Stadium Operations:** Paul Rathje.

Manager, Event Operations/Security: Mike Hill. **Facility Supervisor:** Frank Capparelli. **Assistant Facility Supervisors:** Roger Baird, Bill Scott. **Office Services Coordinator:** Randy Skocz.

PA Announcer: Paul Friedman. **Official Scorers:** Bob Rosenberg, Don Friske.

Ticketing

Telephone: (773) 404-2827. **FAX:** (773) 404-4014.

Director, Ticket Operations: Frank Maloney. **Assistant Director, Ticket Sales:** Jim Coffey. **Assistant Director, Ticket Services:** Joe Kirchen.

Travel, Clubhouse

Traveling Secretary: Jimmy Bank.

Equipment Manager: Yosh Kawano. **Assistant Equipment Manager:** Dana Noeltner. **Visiting Clubhouse Manager:** Tom Hellmann.

Radio, TV, Media

Radio Announcers: Pat Hughes, Ron Santo. **Flagship Station:** WGN 720-AM.

TV Announcers: Harry Caray, Josh Lewin, Steve Stone. **Flagship Stations:** WGN Channel 9, ChicagoLand (regional cable).

NEWSPAPERS, Daily Coverage: Chicago Sun-Times, Chicago Tribune, Arlington Heights Daily Herald.

General Information

Hometown Dugout: Third Base. **Playing Surface:** Grass.

Standard Game Times: Day—1:20 p.m. Night—7:05.

Stadium Location: Five miles along Addison Street East exit off I-90/I-94.

Player Representative: Scott Servais.

CUBS

BASEBALL OPERATIONS

Telephone: (773) 404-2827. **FAX:** (773) 404-4111.

General Manager: Ed Lynch.

Director, Baseball Administration: Scott Nelson.

Special Assistants to General Manager: Larry Himes (Mesa, AZ), Ken Kravec (Sarasota, FL). **Special Player Consultant:** Hugh Alexander (Brooksville, FL).

Executive Assistant to President and General Manager: Arlene Gill. **Baseball Operations Assistant:** Michelle Blanco.

Ed Lynch

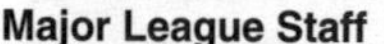

Major League Staff

Manager: Jim Riggleman.

Coaches: Bench—Billy Williams; Pitching—Phil Regan; Hitting—Tony Muser; First Base—Mako Oliveras; Third Base—Dan Radison; Bullpen—Dave Bialas.

Jim Riggleman

Medical, Training

Team Physicians: Dr. John Marquardt, Dr. Michael Schafer.

Head Trainer: David Tumbas. **Assistant Trainer:** Brian McCann. **Strength Coordinator:** Bruce Hammel.

Minor Leagues

Telephone: (773) 404-2827. **FAX:** (773) 404-4147.

Director, Minor Leagues: David Wilder. **Director, Minor League Business Operations:** Connie Kowal. **Assistant, Minor League Operations:** Patti Kargakis.

Equipment Manager: Michael Burkhart.

Coordinator of Instruction: Tom Gamboa.

Roving Instructors: Sandy Alomar Sr. (infield), Bruce Hammel (strength/conditioning), Gary Matthews (hitting), Jimmy Piersall (outfield), Lester Strode (pitching).

Farm System

Class	Farm Team	Manager	Coach	Pitching Coach
AAA	Iowa	Tim Johnson	Glenn Adams	Marty DeMerritt
AA	Orlando	Dave Trembley	Manny Trillo	Stan Kyles
A	Daytona	Steve Roadcap	Richie Zisk	Alan Dunn
A	Rockford	Ruben Amaro	Moe Hill	Unavailable
A	Williamsport	Bob Ralston	Tack Wilson	Charlie Greene
Rookie	Mesa	Terry Kennedy	John Pierson	Rick Tronerud
Rookie	DSL	Julio Valdez	Leo Hernandez	Unavailable

Scouting

Telephone: (773) 404-4039. **FAX:** (773) 404-4147.

Director, Scouting: Jim Hendry.

Administrative Assistant: Patricia Honzik.

Major League Advance Scout: Keith Champion (Ballwin, MO).

Regional Supervisors: Central—John Stockstill (Overland Park, KS); East—Tony DeMacio (Columbia, MD); West—Larry Maxie (Upland, CA).

Jim Hendry

Full-Time Scouts: Mark Adair (Flordell Hills, MO), Billy Blitzer (Brooklyn, NY), Tom Bourque (Cambridge, MA), Bill Capps (Arlington, TX), Jim Crawford (Chattanooga, TN), Frank DeMoss (Fairmont, WV), Oneri Fleita (Newnan, GA), Steve Fuller (Brea, CA), Al Geddes (Canby, OR), John Gracio (Chandler, AZ), Gene Handley (Huntington Beach, CA), Joe Housey (Hollywood, FL), Spider Jorgensen (Cucamonga, CA), Buzzy Keller (Seguin, TX), Brad Kelley (Fremont, CA), Jose Lugo (Ponce, PR), Scott May (Arlington Heights, IL), Brian Milner (Arlington, TX), Marc Russo (Charlotte, NC), Mark Servais (La Crosse, WI), Billy Swoope (Richmond, VA).

International Supervisors: Tom Bourque (Canada), Oneri Fleita (Latin America). **International Scouts:** Alberto Rondon (Venezuela), Jose Serra (Dominican Republic).

CINCINNATI

Telephone, Address

Office Address: 100 Cinergy Field, Cincinnati, OH 45202. **Telephone:** (513) 421-4510. **FAX:** (513) 421-7342.

Ownership

Operated by: The Cincinnati Reds, Inc.

President, Chief Executive Officer: Marge Schott.

Board of Directors: Frisch's Restaurants, Inc.; Gannett; Carl Kroch; Carl Lindner; Mrs. Louis Nippert; William Reik Jr.; George Strike.

Managing Executive: John Allen.

Marge Schott

BUSINESS OPERATIONS

General Counsel: Robert Martin.

Chief Administrative Assistant: Joyce Pfarr. **Administrative Assistant, Business:** Ginny Kamp.

Finance

Controller: Anthony Ward. **Internal Auditor:** Mike Chumbley. **Payroll Supervisor:** Cathy Secor. **Accounts Payable Superviser:** Cheri White. **Administrative Assistant:** Lois Wingo.

Marketing, Sales

Director of Marketing: Chip Baker. **Director of Season Ticket Sales:** Pat McCaffrey. **Director of Group Sales:** Barbara McManus. **Administrative Assistant/Marketing:** Kathy Schwab. **Group Sales Assistants:** Brad Callahan, Lisa Washnock. **Season Ticket Sales Assistants:** Beth Gladura, Cindy Strzynski.

Public Relations, Communications

Telephone: (513) 421-2990. **FAX:** (513) 421-7342.

Director of Media Relations: Rob Butcher.

Director, Public Relations and Publications: Mike Ringering. **Assistant, Publicity:** Charles Henderson. **Administrative Assistant:** Kelly Lippincott.

Stadium Operations

Director of Stadium Operations: Jody Pettyjohn. **Administrative Assistant, Stadium Operations:** Melissa James.

Head Groundskeeper: Howard Alford.

PA Announcer: John Walton. **Official Scorer:** Glenn Sample.

Ticketing

Telephone: (800) 829-5353, (513) 752-REDS. **FAX:** (513) 421-7342.

Director, Ticket Department: John O'Brien. **Assistant Ticket Director:** Ken Ayer. **Cashier:** Josh Logan. **Ticket Office Assistants:** Hallie Kinney, Amy Siefke.

Travel, Clubhouse

Traveling Secretary: Gary Wahoff.

Equipment Manager/Clubhouse Operations: Bernie Stowe. **Home Clubhouse:** Mark Stowe, Rick Stowe. **Visitors Clubhouse:** Ernie Britton.

Radio, TV, Media

Radio Announcers: Marty Brennaman, Joe Nuxhall. **Flagship Station:** WLW 700-AM. **No. of Network Stations:** 57.

TV Announcers: Marty Brennaman, George Grande, Chris Welsh. **Flagship Stations:** WSTR Channel 64, SportsChannel Ohio (regional cable).

NEWSPAPERS, Daily Coverage: Cincinnati Enquirer, Cincinnati Post, Dayton Daily News, Columbus Dispatch.

General Information

Hometown Dugout: First Base. **Playing Surface:** Artificial turf.

Standard Game Times: 7:35 p.m.; Sat. 7:05; Sun. 2:15.

Stadium Location: From north, take I-75 South and exit at I-71, follow downtown signs and exit on Pete Rose Way; From north, take I-71 South and exit at Elm Street/Third Street, right on Third Street, right on Race Street to Pete Rose Way. From Kentucky, take I-75/I-71 North, follow north I-71 sign to Pete Rose Way.

Player Representative: Hal Morris.

REDS

BASEBALL OPERATIONS

Telephone: (513) 421-4510, ext. 239. **FAX:** (513) 421-7342.

Jim Bowden

General Manager: Jim Bowden.

Assistant General Manager: Darrell "Doc" Rodgers.

Special Assistant to General Manager: Gene Bennett. **Senior Advisor/Player Personnel:** Jack McKeon. **Senior Advisors/Baseball Operations:** Larry Barton Jr., Bob Zuk.

Administrative Assistant, Baseball Operations: Brad Kullman. **Executive Assistant, Baseball Operations:** Lois Schneider.

Major League Staff

Manager: Ray Knight.

Coaches: Batting—Denis Menke; Pitching—Don Gullett; First Base—Ken Griffey Sr.; Third Base—Joel Youngblood; Bullpen—Tom Hume; Infield—Ron Oester.

Ray Knight

Medical, Training

Club Physician: Dr. Tim Kremchek. **Senior Consultant/Orthopedics:** Dr. James Andrews. **Consultants/Orthopedics:** Dr. Robert Burger, Dr. Scott Jolson.

Head Trainer: Greg Lynn. **Assistant Trainer:** Mark Mann.

Minor Leagues

Telephone: (513) 421-4510, ext. 244. **FAX:** (513) 421-7342.

Senior Director of Scouting and Player Development: Al Goldis. **Director of Player Development:** Chief Bender. **Administrative Assistant:** Lois Hudson.

Field Coordinator: Donnie Scott.

Roving Instructors: Bill Doran (infield, baserunning), George Foster (hitting, outfield), Mike Griffin (pitching), Jim Hickman (hitting, outfield), Lance Sewell (strength and conditioning).

Farm System

Class	Farm Team	Manager	Coach	Pitching Coach
AAA	Indianapolis	Dave Miley	Jim Thrift	Grant Jackson
AA	Chattanooga	Mark Berry	Mark Wagner	Mack Jenkins
A	Burlington	Phillip Wellman	None	Derek Botelho
A	Charleston, W.Va.	Barry Lyons	None	Andre Rabouin
Rookie	Billings	Derrel Thomas	None	Terry Abbott

Scouting

Telephone: (513) 421-4510, ext. 243. **FAX:** (513) 421-7342.

Julian Mock

Director, Scouting: Julian Mock (Peachtree City, GA).

Administrative Assistant, Scouting: Wilma Mann.

National Crosscheckers: Jeff Barton (Gilbert, AZ), Hank Sargent (Lakeland, FL), Thomas Wilson (Tuscaloosa, AL).

Scouting Supervisors: Johnny Almaraz (Spring Branch, TX), Ray Bellino (Jersey City, NJ), George Brill (Tigard, OR), Robert Filotei (Wilmer, AL), Jerry Flowers (Dolton, IL), Chris Gill (Tustin, CA), Jimmy Gonzales (San Antonio, TX), Robbie Guzik (South Hadley, MA), Les Houser (Gilbert, AZ), David Jennings (St. Charles, MO), Robert Koontz (McConnellsburg, PA), Steve Kring (Charlotte, NC), Mike LaCoss (Lemon Cove, CA), Mike Mangan (Clermont, FL), Tom Severtson (Denver, CO), Bob Szymkowski (Dyer, IN), Marion Trumbo (Bluemont, VA), Mike Wallace (Escondido, CA).

Scouts: Fred Blair (Springfield, OH), Jim Grief (Paducah, KY), Don Gust (West Jordan, UT), Fred Hayes (Battle Creek, MI), Don Hill (Kingsville, OH), Fred Leone (Pelham Manor, NY), Dion Lowe (Decatur, GA), Armando Morales (Levittown, PR), Denny Nagel (Cincinnati, OH), Jerry Raddatz (Winona, MN), Doug Stuart (Brentwood, TN), Marlon Styles (Cincinnati, OH), Lee Toole (Council Bluffs, IA), John Walsh (Windsor, CT), Fate Young (Rosamond, CA).

International Scouts: Tomas Herrera (Mexico), Jose Moreno (Dominican Republic), Murray Zuk (Canada).

COLORADO

Telephone, Address

Office Address: 2001 Blake St., Denver, CO 80205. **Mailing Address:** P.O. Box 120, Denver, CO 80201. **Telephone:** (303) 292-0200. **FAX:** (303) 312-2319.

Ownership

Operated by: Colorado Baseball Partnership 1993 Ltd.

Chairman, President and Chief Executive Officer: Jerry McMorris. **Vice Chairmen:** Oren Benton, Charles Monfort.

Jerry McMorris

BUSINESS OPERATIONS

Senior Vice President, Business Operations: Keli McGregor. **Senior Vice President, Corporate Counsel:** Clark Weaver.

Director, Personnel and Administration: Elizabeth Stecklein. **Director, Information Systems:** Mary Burns.

Finance

Senior Vice President, Chief Financial Officer: Hal Roth. **Vice President, Finance:** Michael Kent.

Director, Accounting: Gary Lawrence.

Marketing, Sales

Vice President, Sales and Marketing: Greg Feasel.

Assistant to Vice President, Sales and Marketing: Marcia McGovern. **Director, Corporate Sales:** Marcy English. **Assistant Director, Sales and Marketing:** Dave Madsen.

Director, Promotions and Special Events: Alan Bossart. **Promotions Coordinator:** Kris Morton.

Director, Broadcasting: Eric Brummond. **Manager, Broadcasting:** Angie Greene.

Director, Merchandising: Jim Kellogg.

Public Relations, Communications

Telephone: (303) 312-2325. **FAX:** (303) 312-2319.

Director, Public Relations: Mike Swanson. **Assistant Director, Public Relations:** Brandy Lay. **Staff Assistant, Public Relations:** John Kohl. **Media Coordinator, Public Relations:** Carey Brandt.

Director, Publications: Jimmy Oldham.

Director, Community Affairs: Roger Kinney. **Manager, Community Affairs:** Sean McGraw.

Stadium Operations

Director, Stadium Services: Kevin Kahn. **Manager, Facilities:** Stephen Mikolajczak. **Head Groundskeeper:** Mark Razum.

PA Announcer: Kelly Burnham. **Official Scorers:** Frank Haraway, Dave Einspar, Jack Rose.

Ticketing

Telephone: (303) ROCKIES. **FAX:** (303) 312-2115.

Vice President, Ticket Operations and Sales: Sue Ann McClaren.

Director, Ticket Operations: Chuck Javernick. **Assistant Director, Ticket Operations:** Claire Grover. **Director, Ticket Sales:** Kevin Fenton.

Travel, Clubhouse

Director, Team Travel: Peter Durso. **Assistant to Director, Team Travel:** Adele Armagost.

Clubhouse and Equipment Manager: Dan McGinn. **Visiting Clubhouse Manager:** Keith Schulz.

Radio, TV, Media

Radio Announcers: Wayne Hagin, Jeff Kingery. **Flagship Station:** KOA 850-AM. **No. of Network Stations:** 52.

TV Announcers: Dave Campbell, Dave Armstrong. **Flagship Station:** KWGN Channel 2.

NEWSPAPERS, Daily Coverage: Rocky Mountain News, Denver Post, Colorado Springs Gazette Telegraph, Boulder Daily Camera.

General Information

Hometown Dugout: First Base. **Playing Surface:** Grass.

Standard Game Times: 7:05 p.m., 3:05; Sat. 2:05, 6:05; Sun. 1:05.

Stadium Location: From I-70 East/West, to I-25 South to exit 213 (Park Avenue) or 212C (20th Street).

Player Representative: Walt Weiss.

ROCKIES

BASEBALL OPERATIONS

Telephone: (303) 312-2366. **FAX:** (303) 312-2320.

Executive Vice President, General Manager: Bob Gebhard.

Assistant General Manager: Tony Siegle. **Assistant to the General Manager:** Stacie Flores.

Bob Gebhard

Major League Staff

Manager: Don Baylor.

Coaches: Dugout—Jackie Moore; Pitching—Frank Funk; Batting/First Base—Clint Hurdle; Third Base—Gene Glynn; Bullpen—P.J. Carey.

Medical, Training

Don Baylor

Club Physicians: Dr. Wayne Gersoff, Dr. Allen Schreiber.

Head Trainer: Dave Cilladi. **Assistant Trainer:** Tom Probst. **Strength and Conditioning Coordinator:** Mark Wilbert.

Minor Leagues

Telephone: (303) 312-2312. **FAX:** (303) 312-2320.

Vice President, Player Personnel: Dick Balderson. **Assistant Director, Player Personnel:** Paul Egins. **Administrative Assistant:** Chris Rice.

Roving Instructors: Greg Gross (hitting), Rick Mathews (pitching).

Farm System

Class	Farm Team	Manager	Coach	Pitching Coach
AAA	Colo. Springs	Paul Zuvella	Tony Torchia	Sonny Seibert
AA	New Haven	Bill Hayes	Jay Loviglio	Jim Wright
A	Salem	Bill McGuire	Stu Cole	Bryn Smith
A	Asheville	Ron Gideon	Billy White	Jack Lamabe
A	Portland	Jim Eppard	Al Bleser	Tom Edens
Rookie	Chandler	Tim Blackwell	Rolando Fernandez	Cam Walker
Rookie	DSL	Rodolfo Rosario	Dario Arias	Herminio Troibio

Scouting

Telephone: (303) 292-0200. **FAX:** (303) 312-2320.

Vice President, Scouting: Pat Daugherty.

Assistant Director, Scouting: Jay Darnell. **Administrative Assistant:** Penny Biever.

Advance Scout: Dan Gladden.

Major League Scouts: Jack Bloomfield (McAllen, TX), Jim Fanning (Pointe Claire, Quebec), Larry High (Mesa, AZ), Bill Wood (Coppell, TX).

National Crosscheckers: Jeff Schugel (Winter Haven, FL), Dave Holliday (Coalgate, OK).

Regional Crosscheckers: West—Bruce Andrew (Northridge, CA); Midwest—Bill Gayton (Houston, TX), East—Robyn Lynch (Safety Harbor, FL).

Pat Daugherty

Full-Time Scouts: Ty Coslow (Louisville, KY), Dar Cox (Red Oak, TX), Mike Ericson (Glendale, AZ), Abe Flores (Huntington Beach, CA), Mike Garlatti (Edison, NJ), Bert Holt (Visalia, CA), Greg Hopkins (Portland, OR), Bill Hughes (Sherman Oaks, CA), Damon Iannelli (Brandon, MI), Pat Jones (Davie, FL), Bill MacKenzie (Ottawa, Ontario), Danny Montgomery (Charlotte, NC), Lance Nichols (Dodge City, KS), Steve Payne (Smyrna, GA), Art Pontarelli (Cranston, RI), Ed Santa (Columbus, OH), Nick Venuto (Crown Point, IN), Tom Wheeler (Pleasant Hill, CA).

International Scouts: Phil Allen (Australia), Dario Arias (Dominican Republic), Rolando Gamez (Venezuela), Cristobal Giron (Panama), Jim Hovorka (Holland), Brian McRobie (Canada), Amilcar Medina (Venezuela), Enrique Melendez (Puerto Rico), Atanacio Mendez (Venezuela), Jimmy Moreno (Puerto Rico), Jorge Posada (Puerto Rico), Rodolfo Rosario (Puerto Rico), Reed Spencer (Canada), Ron Steele (Canada), Herminio Toribio (Dominican Republic).

FLORIDA

Telephone, Address

Office Address: Pro Player Stadium, 2267 NW 199th St., Miami, FL 33056. **Telephone:** (305) 626-7400. **FAX:** (305) 626-7428. **E-Mail Address:** http://www.flamarlins.com

Ownership

Operated by: Florida Marlins Baseball Club, Inc.

Principal Owner/Chairman: Wayne Huizenga.

Partners: Steven Berrard, Harris Hudson, Harry Huizenga, Wayne Huizenga Jr.

President: Don Smiley.

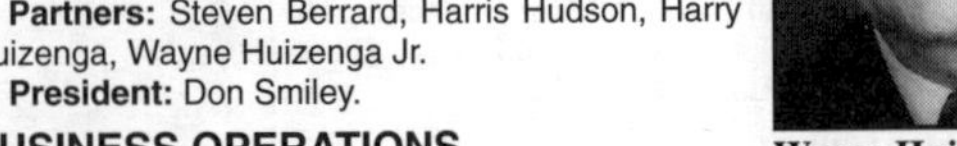

Wayne Huizenga

BUSINESS OPERATIONS

Finance

Vice President, Finance and Administration: Jonathan Mariner.

Director, Finance/Controller: Susan Jaison. **Director, Information Systems:** David Hunter. **Senior Staff Accountant:** Nancy Hernandez. **Executive Secretary, Finance and Administration:** Miranda Aly.

Marketing, Sales

Vice President, Sales and Marketing: James Ross.

Director, Marketing Partnerships: Ben Creed. **Director, In-Game Entertainment and Marketing Coordination:** Susan Budd. **Director of Season/Group Ticket Sales:** Lou DePaoli. **Director of Hispanic Marketing:** Jorge Plasencia.

Public Relations, Communications

Telephone: (305) 626-7304. **FAX:** (305) 626-7302.

Director of Baseball Information and Publicity: Ron Colangelo. **Assistant Director, Baseball Information and Publicity:** Julio Sarmiento. **Coordinator, Baseball Information and Publicity:** Margo Malone. **Assistant Coordinator, Baseball Information and Publicity:** Sandra van Meek.

Director, Communications: Mark Geddis. **Director, Creative Services:** Leslie Riguero. **Manager, Community Affairs:** Nancy Olson. **Manager, Foundation and Community Affairs:** Alan Brown. **Manager, Speakers Bureau and Player Relations:** Brian Randolf.

Stadium Operations

Vice President/General Manager, Stadium Operations: Bruce Schulze. **Director, Event Operations:** Todd Ellzey. **Head Groundskeeper:** Alan Sigwardt.

PA Announcer: Jay Rokeach. **Official Scorers:** Harvey Greene, Sonny Hirsch, Doug Pett.

Ticketing

Telephone: (305) 930-4487. **FAX:** (305) 626-7432.

Vice President/Ticket Operations: Bill Galante. **Managers, Ticket Operations:** Daniel Katz, Andy Major, Mitch Tormala.

Travel, Clubhouse

Director, Team Travel: Bill Beck.

Equipment Manager: Mike Wallace. **Assistant Equipment Manager:** Matt Rosenthal. **Visitors Clubhouse:** Carlos Ledezma.

Radio, TV, Media

Radio Announcers: Joe Angel, Dave O'Brien. **Flagship Stations:** WQAM 560-AM.

TV Announcers: Joe Angel, Dave O'Brien, Tommy Hutton. **Flagship Stations:** WBFS UPN 33, Sports Channel/Sunshine Network (regional cable).

NEWSPAPERS, Daily Coverage: Miami Herald, Fort Lauderdale Sun-Sentinel, Palm Beach Post, Florida Today. Spanish—El Nuevo Herald.

General Information

Hometown Dugout: First Base. **Playing Surface:** Grass.

Standard Game Times: 7:05 p.m.; Sun. 4:35.

Stadium Location: From south, Florida Turnpike extension to stadium exit; From north, I-95 to I-595 West to Florida Turnpike to stadium exit; From west, I-75 to I-595 to Florida Turnpike to stadium exit; From east, Highway 826 West to NW 27th Ave., north to 199th St., right to stadium.

Player Representative: Al Leiter.

MARLINS

BASEBALL OPERATIONS

Telephone: (305) 626-7434. **FAX:** (305) 626-7433.

Executive Vice President, General Manager: Dave Dombrowski.

Vice President, Assistant General Manager: Frank Wren. **Special Assistant to General Manager:** Tony Perez.

Vice President, Player Personnel: Gary Hughes. **Senior Advisor, Player Personnel:** Whitey Lockman. **Assistant, Baseball Operations:** DeJon Watson.

Director, Latin American Operations: Al Avila. **Assistant, Latin American Operations:** Louis Eljaua.

Dave Dombrowski

Major League Staff

Manager: Jim Leyland.

Coaches: Dugout—Jerry Manuel; Pitching—Larry Rothschild; Batting—Milt May; First Base—Tommy Sandt; Third Base—Rich Donnelly; Bullpen—Bruce Kimm.

Jim Leyland

Medical, Training

Club Physician: Dr. Dan Kanell.

Head Trainer: Larry Starr. **Assistant Trainer:** Kevin Rand. **Strength and Conditioning Director:** Rick Slate.

Minor Leagues

Telephone: (407) 633-8119. **FAX:** (407) 633-9216.

Vice President, Player Development: John Boles. **Director, Minor League Administration:** Dan Lunetta. **Administrative Assistants:** Kim-Lee Carkeek, Mike Parkinson.

Field Coordinator: Rob Leary. **Roving Instructors:** Joe Breeden (catching), Rich Dubee (pitching), Rusty Kuntz (outfield, baserunning), Jack Maloof (hitting), Tony Taylor (infield). **Coordinator, Trainers/Equipment:** John Spinosa. **Coordinator, Strength/Fitness:** Toby Oldham.

Farm System

Class	Farm Team	Manager	Coach	Pitching Coach
AAA	Charlotte	Carlos Tosca	Adrian Garrett	Rick Williams
AA	Portland	Fredi Gonzalez	Sal Rende	Britt Burns
A	Brevard	Lorenzo Bundy	Jose Castro	Randy Hennis
A	Kane County	Lynn Jones	Matt Winters	Brian Peterson
A	Utica	Juan Bustabad	Ken Joyce	Larry Pardo
Rookie	Melbourne	Jon Deeble	Manny Crespo	Euclides Rojas
Rookie	DSL	Nelson Silverio	Carlos de la Cruz	Jose Duran

Scouting

Telephone: (305) 626-7217. **FAX:** (305) 626-7433.

Director, Scouting: Orrin Freeman. **Administrative Assistant, Scouting:** Cheryl Evans.

Major League Scouts: Gary Hughes (Aptos, CA), Whitey Lockman (Scottsdale, AZ), Scott Reid (Phoeniz, AZ). **Coordinator of Video and Advance Scouting:** Mike Carr (Pembroke Pines, FL).

Special Assignment Scouts: Stan Saleski (Dayton, OH), DeJon Watson (Hollywood, FL).

National Crosscheckers: Murray Cook (Sarasota, FL), Dick Egan (Phoenix, AZ), Jax Robertson (Cary, NC), Greg Zunino (Cape Coral, FL).

Orrin Freeman

Full-Time Scouts: Rich Bordi (Rohnert Park, CA), Ty Brown (Ruther Glen, VA), John Castleberry (High Point, NC), David Chadd (Wichita, KS), Brad Del Barba (Taylor Mill, KY), Louis Eljaua (Pembroke Pines, FL), David Finley (San Diego, CA), Will George (Merchantville, NJ), Matt King (Aptos, CA), Bob Laurie (Plano, TX), Steve McFarland (Scottsdale, AZ), Steve Minor (Long Beach, CA), Cucho Rodriguez (San Juan, PR), Mike Russell (Pensacola, FL), Bill Scherrer (Buffalo, NY), Bill Singer (Costa Mesa, CA), Keith Snider (Stockton, CA), Wally Walker (Reno, NV), Jeff Wren (St. Petersburg, FL), Stan Zielinski (Winfield, IL).

Pacific Rim Supervisor: Bill Singer. **International Crosschecker:** Tim Schmidt (San Bernardino, CA). **International Scouts:** Jon Deeble (Australia).

HOUSTON

Telephone, Address

Office Address: 8400 Kirby Dr., Houston, TX 77054. **Mailing Address:** P.O. Box 288, Houston, TX 77001. **Telephone:** (713) 799-9500. **FAX:** (713) 799-9562. **E-Mail Address:** www.astros.com.

Ownership

Operated by: McLane Group, LP.

Principal Owner, Chairman: Drayton McLane Jr.

Board of Directors: Drayton McLane Jr., Sandy Sanford, Bob McClaren.

President: Tal Smith.

Drayton McLane

BUSINESS OPERATIONS

Senior Vice President, Business Operations: Bob McClaren.

General Counsel: Frank Rynd.

Director, Human Resources: Mike Anders.

Finance

Vice President, Finance: Webb Stickney.

Controller: Robert McBurnett. **Director of Management Information Systems:** Jeff Pascal.

Marketing, Sales

Director, Marketing: Pam Gardner. **Assistant Director, Marketing:** Erin Skelley.

Promotions Coordinator: Marian Harper. **Director, Season Ticket Sales:** John Sorrentino. **Director, Broadcast Operations and Promotions:** Jamie Hildreth. **Engineer:** Mike Cannon. **Assistant Director, Advertising Sales/Promotions:** Jim Ballweg. **Youth Programs Coordinator:** Heather Cox.

Public Relations, Communications

Telephone: (713) 799-9600. **FAX:** (713) 799-9881.

Director, Media Relations: Rob Matwick. **Assistant Director, Media Relations:** Darrell Simon. **Assistant, Media Relations:** Sandy Beck. **Coordinator, Publications:** Alyson Footer.

Director, Community Development: Gene Pemberton. **Community Outreach:** Robert Reid.

Stadium Operations

Director, Stadium Operations: Gary Cavey. **Assistant Director:** Greg Golightly.

Head Groundskeeper: Willie Berry.

PA Announcer: Bob Ford. **Official Scorers:** Rick Blount, Fred Duckett, Ivy McLemore. **Scoreboard Operations:** Doug Swan.

Ticketing

Telephone: (713) 799-9567. **FAX:** (713) 799-9812.

Director, Ticket Operations: Mike Mall. **Manager, Ticket Sales:** Tina Cash.

Travel, Clubhouse

Traveling Secretary: Barry Waters.

Equipment Manager/Home Clubhouse: Dennis Liborio. **Visiting Clubhouse Manager:** Steve Perry. **Assistant Equipment Manager:** Dan O'Rourke.

Radio, TV, Media

Radio Announcers: Milo Hamilton, Vince Cotroneo. Spanish—Francisco Ruiz, Alex Trevino. **Flagship Station:** KILT 610-AM, Spanish—KXYZ 1320-AM. **No. of Network Stations:** 70.

TV Announcers: Bill Brown, Jim Deshaies. **Flagship Stations:** UPN Channel 20, Fox Sports Southwest (regional cable).

NEWSPAPERS, Daily Coverage: Houston Chronicle.

General Information

Hometown Dugout: First Base. **Playing Surface:** Artificial turf.

Standard Game Times: 7:05 p.m., Sun. 1:35.

Stadium Location: From Loop 610 South, take Kirby Drive exit, right on Kirby Drive, enter Murworth Gate.

Player Representative: Unavailable.

ASTROS

BASEBALL OPERATIONS

Telephone: (713) 799-9611. **FAX:** (713) 799-9562.

General Manager: Gerry Hunsicker.

Assistant to General Manager: Tim Purpura. **Special Assistant to the General Manager:** Matt Galante. **Director of Baseball Administration:** Barry Waters. **Administrative Assistant, Major Leagues:** Beverly Rains.

Gerry Hunsicker

Major League Staff

Manager: Larry Dierker.

Coaches: Dugout—Bill Virdon; Pitching—Vern Ruhle; Batting—Tom McCraw; First Base—Jose Cruz Sr.; Third Base—Mike Cubbage; Bullpen—Alan Ashby.

Medical, Training

Medical Director: Dr. Bill Bryan. **Team Physicians:** Dr. Mike Feltovich, Dr. David Lintner, Dr. Tom Mehlhoff.

Larry Dierker

Head Trainer: Dave Labossiere. **Assistant Trainer:** Rex Jones. **Strength and Conditioning Coach:** Dr. Gene Coleman.

Minor Leagues

Office Address: 1000 Bill Beck Blvd., Kissimmee, FL 34744. **Mailing Address:** P.O. Box 422229, Kissimmee, FL 34742. **Telephone:** (407) 847-5443. **FAX:** (407) 847-4901.

Director, Player Development: Jim Duquette. **Administrative Assistants, Minor Leagues:** Jay Edmiston, Carol Wogsland.

Roving Instructors: Dave Engle (hitting), Chuck Hiller (infield), Dewey Robinson (pitching), Dickie Thon (infield, baserunning).

Farm System

Class	Farm Team	Manager	Coach	Pitching Coach
AAA	New Orleans	Steve Swisher	Jimmy Wynn	Craig McMurtry
AA	Jackson	Gary Allenson	Unavailable	Jim Hickey
A	Kissimmee	John Tamargo	Ivan DeJesus	Jack Billingham
A	Quad City	Manny Acta	Jorge Orta	Charley Taylor
A	Auburn	Mike Rojas	Sidney Holland	Bill Ballou
Rookie	Kissimmee	Julio Linares	Cesar Cedeno	Lyle Yates
Rookie	DSL	Unavailable	Unavailable	Rick Aponte

Scouting

Telephone: (713) 799-9616. **FAX:** (713) 799-9562.

Director, Scouting: David Lakey (Austin, TX).

Assistant Director, Scouting: David Rawnsley. **Administrative Assistant:** Traci Franklin.

Advance Scout: Tom Wiedenbauer (Ormond Beach, FL).

Professional Scouts: Joe Pittman (Columbus, GA), Larry Slusser (Carlisle, PA), Scipio Spinks (Houston, TX), Lynwood Stallings (Kingsport, TN), Tim Tolman (Tucson, AZ).

Major League Scouts: Stan Benjamin (Port Charlotte, FL), Fred Nelson (Richmond, TX), Bob Skinner (San Diego, CA), Paul Weaver (Phoenix, AZ).

National Supervisor: Bill Kelso (Grapevine, TX).

Regional Supervisors: West—Bob King (LaMesa, CA); East—Gerry Craft (St. Clairsville, OH); Central—Tad Slowik (Niles, IL).

Area Scouts: Bob Blair (Commack, NY), Stan Boroski (Kissimmee, FL), Ralph Bratton (Dripping Springs, TX), Doug Deutsch (Costa Mesa, CA), James Farrar (Shreveport, LA), Brian Granger (Dickson, TN), Dan Huston (Bellevue, WA), Mark Johnson (Englewood, CO), Brian Keegan (Charlotte, NC), Mike Maggart (Penn Yan, NY), Walt Matthews (Texarkana, TX), Tom Mooney (Pittsfield, MA), Jim Pransky (Davenport, IA), Deron Rombach (Escondido, CA), Rick Schroeder (San Jose, CA), Steve Smith (Marietta, GA), Kevin Stein (Blacklick, OH), Frankie Thon (Guaynabo, PR), Gene Wellman (Danville, CA).

International Scouts: Rick Aponte (Dominican Republic), Jesus Aristimuno (Venezuela), Ruben Cabrera (Venezuela), Rafael Cariel (Venezuela), Alexis Corro (Venezuela), Julio Linares (Dominican Republic), Domingo Mercedes (Dominican Republic), Andres Reiner (Venezuela), Anibal Relux (Panama), Adriano Rodriguez (Dominican Republic), Pablo Torrealba (Venezuela), Grant Weir (Australia).

LOS ANGELES

Peter O'Malley

Telephone, Address

Office Address: 1000 Elysian Park Ave., Los Angeles, CA 90012. **Telephone:** (213) 224-1500. **FAX:** (213) 224-1269.

Ownership

Operated by: Los Angeles Dodgers, Inc.

Principal Owner/Chairman: Peter O'Malley.

Board of Directors: Peter O'Malley, Roland Seidler, Terry Seidler.

Vice President: Tommy Lasorda. **Vice President, Campo las Palmas complex** (Dominican Republic): Ralph Avila.

BUSINESS OPERATIONS

General Counsel: Sam Fernandez.

Director, Human Resources: Irene Tanji. **Supervisor, Administrative Services:** Linda Cohen. **Managing Director, Dodgertown:** Craig Callan.

Finance

Vice President, Finance: Bob Graziano.

Director, Accounting and Finance: Bill Foltz. **Director, Management Information Services:** Mike Mularky.

Marketing, Sales

Vice President, Marketing: Barry Stockhamer. **Director, Advertising and Special Events:** Paul Kalil. **Manager, Marketing Services:** Monique LaVeau-Brennan. **Corporate Account Manager:** Greg Ashlock. **Manager, Youth Marketing:** Tom Seidler. **Manager, Group Events:** Steve Everett. **Supervisor, Ticket Sales:** Jerry Stipo.

Public Relations, Communications

Telephone: (213) 224-1301. **FAX:** (213) 224-1459.

Vice President, Communications: Tommy Hawkins.

Director, Publicity: Derrick Hall. **Assistant Director, Publicity:** Shaun Rechau. **Administrative Assistant, Publicity:** Barbara Conway. **Assistant, Baseball Information:** David Tuttle. **Archivist:** John Olguin.

Director, Broadcast and Publications: Brent Shyer. **Supervisor, Broadcast and Publications:** Paul Gomez.

Director, Community Relations: Don Newcombe. **Director, Community Affairs:** Monique Brandon.

Stadium Operations

Director, Stadium Operations: Doug Duennes. **Assistant Director, Stadium Operations:** Chris Fighera. **Head Groundskeeper:** Al Myers.

PA Announcer: Mike Carlucci. **Official Scorers:** Terry Bales, Larry Kahn, Ira Kaze.

Ticketing

Telephone: (213) 224-1471. **FAX:** (213) 224-2609..

Director, Ticket Operations: Debra Duncan. **Assistant Director, Ticket Operations:** Billy Hunter.

Travel, Clubhouse

Traveling Secretary: Billy DeLury.

Equipment Manager/Dodger Clubhouse Manager: David Wright. **Visiting Clubhouse Manager:** Jerry Turner.

Radio, TV, Media

Radio Announcers: English—Vin Scully, Rick Monday, Ross Porter. Spanish—Jaime Jarrin, Rene Cardenas. **Flagship Stations:** English—KABC 790-AM. Spanish—KWKW 1330-AM.

TV Announcers: Vin Scully, Ross Porter. **Flagship Station:** KTLA Channel 5, Fox Sports West (regional cable).

NEWSPAPERS, Daily Coverage: Los Angeles Times, South Bay Daily Breeze, Los Angeles Daily News, Long Beach Press-Telegram, Pasadena Star News, Orange County Register, San Bernardino Sun.

General Information

Hometown Dugout: Third Base. **Playing Surface:** Grass.

Stadium Location: I-5 to Stadium Way exit, left on Stadium Way, right on Academy Road, left to Stadium Way to Elysian Park Ave., left to stadium; I-110 to Dodger Stadium exit, left on Stadium Way, right on Elysian Park Ave.; U.S. 101 to Alvarado exit, right on Sunset, left on Elysian Park Ave.

Standard Game Times: 7:05 p.m., Wed. 7:35, Sun. 1:05.

Player Representatives: Billy Ashley, Todd Hollandsworth.

DODGERS

BASEBALL OPERATIONS

Telephone: (213) 224-1306. **FAX:** (213) 224-1269.

Executive Vice President, General Manager: Fred Claire.

Fred Claire

Administrator, Baseball Operations: Robert Schweppe. **Administrative Assistant:** Rosalyn Gutierrez.

Major League Staff

Manager: Bill Russell.

Coaches: Dugout—Mike Scioscia; Pitching—Dave Wallace; Batting/Third Base—Reggie Smith; First Base—Joe Amalfitano; Bullpen—Mark Cresse.

Medical, Training

Team Physicians: Dr. Frank Jobe, Dr. Michael Mellman.

Bill Russell

Head Trainer: Charlie Strasser. **Assistant Trainer:** Stan Johnston. **Physical Therapist:** Pat Screnar.

Minor Leagues

Telephone: (213) 224-1431. **FAX:** (213) 224-1359.

Vice President, Minor League Operations: Charlie Blaney. **Administrative Assistant, Minor Leagues:** Luchy Guerra. **Secretary:** Tana Bertaux.

Coordinator of Instruction: Glenn Hoffman.

Roving Instructors: Tom Beyers (hitting), Chico Fernandez (infield), Goose Gregson (pitching), Dick McLaughlin (outfield/bunting), Joe Vavra (baserunning).

Farm System

Class	Farm Team	Manager	Coach	Pitching Coach
AAA	Albuquerque	Glenn Hoffman	Jon Debus	Claude Osteen
AA	San Antonio	Ron Roenicke	Lance Parrish	Guy Conti
A	San Bernardino	Del Crandall	Dino Ebel	Charlie Hough
A	Vero Beach	John Shoemaker	Tony Harris	Edwin Correa
A	Savannah	John Shelby	Travis Barbary	Mark Brewer
A	Yakima	Joe Vavra	Mitch Webster	Unavailable
Rookie	Great Falls	Mickey Hatcher	Tom Thomas	Joe Almaraz
Rookie	DSL I	Teddy Martinez	Algona Read	Eleodoro Arias
Rookie	DSL II	Tony Bautista	Pedro Mega	Luis Barreiro

Scouting

Telephone: (213) 224-1437. **FAX:** (213) 224-1359.

Director, Scouting: Terry Reynolds.

Advance Scout: John VanOrnum (Base Lake, CA).

Coordinator of Professional Scouting: Gary Sutherland (Monrovia, CA).

Major League Scout: Eddie Bane (Phoenix, AZ). **Special Assignment Scout:** Tim Thompson (Lewistown, PA).

National Crosschecker: Tommy Mixon (Macon, GA).

Terry Reynolds

Regional Supervisors: West Coast—Gib Bodet (San Clemente, CA); Midwest—John Keenan (Great Bend, KS); East—Gary LaRocque (Greensboro, NC).

Scouts: Bill Barkley (Waco, TX), Joe Campbell (Leeds, AL), Bobby Darwin (Cerritos, CA), Joe Ferrone (Sherman Oaks, CA), Mike Hankins (Lee's Summit, MO), Dennis Haren (San Diego, CA), Hank Jones (Vancouver, WA), Lon Joyce (Spartanburg, SC), Gene Kerns (Hagerstown, MD), John Kosciak (Milford, MA), Mike Leuzinger (Grand Prairie, TX), Carl Loewenstine (Hamilton, OH), Dale McReynolds (Walworth, WI), Bill Pleis (Parrish, FL), Eddie Rodriguez (Anasco, PR), Ross Sapp (Moreno Valley, CA), Mark Sheehy (Sacramento, CA), Tom Thomas (Phoenix, AZ), Glen VanProyen (West Chicago, IL).

International Supervisor: Jim Stoeckel (Vero Beach, FL). **Supervisor, Mexico and Central America:** Mike Brito (Los Angeles). **Supervisor, Venezuela and Puerto Rico:** Camilo Pascual (Miami, FL).

MONTREAL

Claude Brochu

Telephone, Address

Office Address: 4549 Pierre-de-Coubertin Ave., Montreal, Quebec H1V 3N7. **Mailing Address:** P.O. Box 500, Station M, Montreal, Quebec H1V 3P2. **Telephone:** (514) 253-3434. **FAX:** (514) 253-8282.

Ownership

Operated by: Montreal Baseball Club, Inc.

President and General Partner: Claude Brochu.

Chairman of the Partnership Committee: Jacques Menard. **Vice Chairmen of the Partnership Committee:** Claude Blanchet, Jocelyn Proteau, Louis Tanguay.

BUSINESS OPERATIONS

Finance

Vice President, Finance: Laurier Carpentier.

Director, Financial Planning and Administration: Michel Bussiere. **Manager, Accounting Services:** Francois Lalonde.

Marketing, Sales

Vice President, Marketing and Communications: Richard Morency.

Directors, Advertising Sales: Luigi Carola, John Di Terlizzi, Danielle La Roche. **Director, Advertising:** Johanne Heroux.

Coordinator, Promotions: Marc Griffin. **Coordinator, Special Events:** Gina Hackl.

Public Relations, Communications

Director, Media Services: Monique Giroux. **Director, Media Relations:** P.J. Loyello.

Stadium Operations

Vice President, Stadium Operations: Claude Delorme.

Director, Operations: Pierre Touzin. **Director, Merchandising and Licensing:** Susan LeBlanc.

Ticketing

Vice President, Sales: Lucien Baril.

Director, Season Ticket Sales: Gilles Beauregard. **Director, Group Sales:** Jean Cyr.

Director, Ticket Office: Chantal Dalpe. **Assistant Director, Ticket Office:** Hubert Richard.

Travel, Clubhouse

Traveling Secretary: Sean Cunningham.

Equipment Manager: John Silverman. **Visiting Clubhouse:** Bryan Greenberg.

Radio, TV, Media

Radio Announcers: CKAC/French—Jacques Doucet, Rodger Brulotte, Alain Chantelois. CIQC/English—Dave Van Horne, Elliott Price, Gary Carter, Joe Cannon. **Flagship Stations:** French—CKAC 730-AM. English—CIQC 600-AM.

TV Announcers: SRC/French—Rene Pothier, Claude Raymond. TQS/French—Michel Villeneuve, Marc Griffin. RDS/French—Denis Casavant, Rodger Brulotte. TSN/English—Dave Van Horne, Ken Singleton. **Flagship Stations:** French—Societe Radio Canada. English—The Sports Network (national cable).

NEWSPAPERS, Daily Coverage: French—La Presse, Le Journal de Montreal, La Presse Canadienne. English—Montreal Gazette.

General Information

Hometown Dugout: First Base. **Playing Surface:** Artificial turf.

Standard Game Times: Day—1:35 p.m.; Night—7:35 p.m.

Stadium Location: From New England, take I-87 North from Vermont to Quebec Highway 15 to the Jacques Cartier Bridge, exit left, right on Sherbrooke. From upstate New York, take I-81 North to Trans Canada Highway 401, east to Quebec Highway 20, north to Highway 40 to the Boulevard Pie IX exit south to stadium. Access by subway from downtown Montreal to Pie IX Metro station.

Player Representative: Unavailable.

EXPOS

BASEBALL OPERATIONS

Vice President, General Manager: Jim Beattie.

Vice President, Baseball Operations: Bill Stoneman.

Jim Beattie

Major League Staff

Manager: Felipe Alou.

Coaches: Dugout—Jim Tracy; Pitching—Bobby Cuellar; Batting/First Base—Tommy Harper; Third Base—Pete Mackanin; Bullpen—Pierre Arsenault.

Medical, Training

Team Physician: Dr. Mike Thomassin. **Team Orthopedist:** Dr. Larry Coughlin.

Head Trainer: Ron McClain. **Assistant Trainer:** Mike Kozak. **Strength and Conditioning Director:** Sean Cunningham.

Felipe Alou

Minor Leagues

Office Address: Municipal Stadium, 715 Hank Aaron Dr., West Palm Beach, FL 33401. **Telephone:** (561) 684-6801, ex. 254. **FAX:** (561) 681-4876.

Director, Player Development: David Littlefield. **Assistant Director, Player Development:** Neal Huntington. **Administrative Assistant, Minor Leagues:** Patricia Lobato.

Clubhouse Manager, Equipment Supervisor: Chris Westmoreland.

Minor League Coordinators: Jim Benedict (pitching), Paul Fournier (conditioning), Pat Roessler (hitting).

Farm System

Class	Farm Team	Manager	Coach	Pitching Coach
AAA	Ottawa	Pat Kelly	Frank Kremblas	Bo McLaughlin
AA	Harrisburg	Rick Sofield	Jeff Livesey	Dean Treanor
A	West Palm	Doug Sisson	Rodney McCray	Dennis Burtt
A	Cape Fear	Phil Stephenson	Kash Beauchamp	Bryan Kelly
A	Vermont	Kevin Higgins	Unavailable	Unavailable
Rookie	West Palm	Luis Dorante	Troy Buckley	Wayne Rosenthal
Rookie	DSL	Arturo DeFreites	Unavailable	Jose Zapata

Scouting

Office Address: Expos Minor League Development Center, 6850 Lawrence Rd., Lantana, FL 33462. **Mailing Address:** P.O. 6808, Lake Worth, FL 33466. **Telephone:** (561) 433-1990. **FAX:** (561) 433-3481.

Director, Scouting: Ed Creech (Moultrie, GA).

Assistant Director, Scouting: Gregg Leonard. **Secretary:** Jennifer Ruffa.

Advance Scout: Phil Favia (Apache Junction, AZ).

National Crosschecker: Jim Fleming (Purcell, OK).

Regional Supervisors: East—Jim Lester (Columbus, GA), West—Dave Malpass (Huntington Beach, CA).

Ed Creech

Scouts: Alex Agostino (St. Bruno, Quebec), Mark Baca (Tustin Ranch, CA), Mike Berger (Pittsburgh, PA), Dennis Cardoza (Norman, OK), Doug Carpenter (Boca Raton, FL), Robby Corsaro (Adelanto, CA), Marc Delpiano (Auburn, NY), Greg Evans (Cleveland, MS), Dan Freed (Bloomington, IL), Scott Goldby (Vancouver, WA), John Hughes (Walnut Creek, CA), Joe Jordan (Blanchard, OK), Mark Leavitt (Centreville, VA), Roy McMillan (Bonham, TX), Scott Stanley (Peoria, AZ), Dennis Weeks (Sewanee, TN).

Director, International Operations: Fred Ferreira (Fort Lauderdale, FL). **International Scouts:** Carlos Acosta (Venezuela), Arturo DeFreites (Dominican Republic), Juan Loyola (Puerto Rico), Carlos Moreno (Venezuela), Rene Picota (Panama).

NEW YORK

Telephone, Address

Office Address: 123-01 Roosevelt Ave., Flushing, NY 11368. **Telephone:** (718) 507-6387. **FAX:** (718) 565-6395.

Ownership

Operated by: Sterling Doubleday.

Chairman of the Board: Nelson Doubleday. **President:** Fred Wilpon.

Board of Directors: Nelson Doubleday, Fred Wilpon, Saul Katz, Joe McIlvaine, Marvin Tepper, Richard Cummins.

Fred Wilpon

BUSINESS OPERATIONS

Chief Executive Officer: Fred Wilpon.

Vice President, Business Affairs Secretary and General Counsel: David Howard. **Legal Counsel:** David Cohen.

Director of Human Relations: Raymond Scott. **Director of Administration and Data Processing:** Russ Richardson.

Finance

Senior Vice President, Treasurer: Harry O'Shaughnessy.

Controller: Leonard Labita. **Chief Accountant:** Alan Kindler.

Marketing, Sales

Vice President, Marketing and Broadcasting: Mark Bingham.

Manager, Corporate Sales: Paul Danforth. **Director of Promotions:** James Plummer. **Season Ticket Manager:** Marie Melluso. **Director of Group Sales:** Tom Fersch.

Public Relations, Communications

Telephone: (718) 565-4330. **FAX:** (718) 639-3619.

Director of Media Relations: Jay Horwitz. **Administrative Assistants:** Shannon Dalton, Stella Fiore.

Director of Community Relations: Jill Knee. **Assistant Director:** Jonathan Rosenberg. **Video Production:** Tim Gunkel, Vito Vitiello.

Stadium Operations

Vice President, Stadium Operations: Bob Mandt.

Stadium Manager: Kevin McCarthy. **Head Groundskeeper:** Pete Flynn. **PA Announcer:** Del Demontreaux. **Official Scorers:** Joe Donnelly, Red Foley, Bill Shannon.

Ticketing

Telephone: (718) 507-8499. **FAX:** (718) 507-6396.

Vice President, Ticket Sales and Services: Bill Ianniciello.

Director, Ticket Operations: Dan DeMato.

Travel, Clubhouse

Traveling Secretary: Jay Horwitz, Charlie Samuels.

Equipment Manager/Clubhouse Operations: Charlie Samuels. **Assistant Equipment Manager:** Vinny Greco. **Visiting Clubhouse Manager:** Tony Carullo.

Radio, TV, Media

Radio Announcers: Bob Murphy, Gary Cohen. **Flagship Station:** WFAN 660-AM. **No. of Stations on Network:** 2.

TV Announcers: WWOR—Ralph Kiner, Tim McCarver, Gary Thorne. SportsChannel—Fran Healy, Howie Rose. **Flagship Stations:** WWOR Channel 9, SportsChannel America (regional cable).

NEWSPAPERS, Daily Coverage: New York Times, New York Daily News, New York Post, Newsday, Newark Star-Ledger, The Bergen Record, Gannett-Westchester.

General Information

Hometown Dugout: First Base. **Playing Surface:** Grass.

Standard Game Times: Day—1:40 p.m. Night—7:40; Sat., 7:10.

Stadium Location: From the Bronx and Westchester, take the Cross Bronx Expressway to the Bronx-Whitestone Bridge, then take the bridge to the Whitestone Expressway to the Northern Boulevard/Shea Stadium exit. From Brooklyn, take the Eastbound BQE to the Eastbound Grand Central Parkway. From Long Island, take either the Northern State Parkway or LIE to the Westbound Grand Central Parkway. From Northern New Jersey, take the George Washington Bridge to the Cross Bronx Expressway. **By subway**—Take the #7 and exit at the Willets Point/Shea Stadium stop.

Player Representative: Tim Bogar.

METS

BASEBALL OPERATIONS

Telephone: (718) 507-6387. **FAX:** (718) 507-6391.

Executive Vice President, Baseball Operations: Joe McIlvaine.

Assistant General Manager: Steve Phillips. **Executive Assistant to the General Manager:** Maureen Cooke. **Secretary:** Lynne Daly-DeJoseph.

Special Assistants to the General Manager: Carmen Fusco (Camp Hill, PA), Harry Minor (Long Beach, CA).

Joe McIlvaine

Major League Staff

Manager: Bobby Valentine.

Coaches: Batting—Tom Robson; Pitching—Bob Apodaca; First Base—Mookie Wilson; Third Base—Cookie Rojas; Bullpen—Randy Niemann; Catching—Bruce Benedict.

Bobby Valentine

Medical, Training

Team Physician: Dr. David Altchek. **Consulting Physician:** Dr. John O'Lichney.

Trainer: Fred Hina. **Assistant Trainer:** Scott Lawrenson. **Fitness Coordinator:** Barry Heyden.

Minor Leagues

Office Address: 525 NW Peacock Blvd., Port St. Lucie, FL 34986. **Telephone:** (561) 871-2132. **FAX:** (561) 871-2181.

Director, Minor League Operations: Jack Zduriencik. **Administrative Assistant:** Tom Hutchinson. **Administrator:** Sally Schlegel. **Latin America Coordinator:** Felix Millan.

Field Coordinator: Bobby Floyd. **Coordinators:** Mickey Brantley (assistant hitting), Al Jackson (pitching), Rick Miller (outfield, baserunning) Jeff Pentland (hitting).

Training and Fitness Coordinator: Mike Herbst. **Minor League Equipment Manager:** Joe Tarnowski.

Farm System

Class	Farm Team	Manager	Coach	Pitching Coach
AAA	Norfolk	Rick Dempsey	Tom Lawless	Ray Rippelmeyer
AA	Binghamton	Rick Sweet	Howie Freiling	Billy Champion
A	St. Lucie	John Gibbons	Doug Flynn	Rick Waits
A	Columbia	Doug Mansolino	Tim Leiper	Dave Jorn
A	Pittsfield	Doug Davis	Juan Lopez	Bob Stanley
Rookie	Kingsport	Ken Berry	Gary Ward	Buzz Capra
Rookie	Port St. Lucie	John Stephenson	Felix Millan	Mickey Weston
Rookie	DSL	Luis Natera	Zoilo Sanchez	Jesus Hernaiz

Scouting

Office Address: 525 NW Peacock Blvd., Port St. Lucie, FL 34986. **Telephone:** (561) 871-2100. **FAX:** (561) 871-2181.

Director of Scouting: John Barr.

Administrative Assistant, Scouting: Brian Bark. **Administrator:** Stephanie Morgan.

Special Assignment Scouts: Darrell Johnson (Suisun, CA), Buddy Kerr (Oradell, NJ).

Major League Scouts: Dick Gernert (Reading, PA), Roland Johnson (Newington, CT), Bill Latham (Trussville, AL)

John Barr

National Crosscheckers: Paul Fryer (Calabassas, CA), Paul Ricciarini (Pittsfield, MA).

Regional Scouting Supervisors: South—Joe Mason (Millbrook, AL); West—Bob Minor (Garden Grove, CA).

Area Supervisors: Tom Allison (Laguna Niguel, CA), Paul Baretta (Kensington, CT), Kevin Blankenship (Roseville, CA), Larry Chase (Pearcy, AR), Clark Crist (Tucson, AZ), Joe DelliCarri (Longwood, FL), Chuck Hensley Jr. (Bakersfield, CA), Dave Lottsfeldt (Garland, TX), Lee May Jr. (Cincinnati, OH), Marlin McPhail (Irmo, SC), Randy Milligan (Owings Mills, MD), Joe Nigro (Staten Island, NY), Jim Reeves (Camas, WA), Bob Rossi (Baton Rouge, LA), Terry Tripp (Harrisburg, IL), Greg Tubbs (Cookeville, TN).

International Supervisors: Carlos Pascual (Miami, FL), Junior Roman (Puerto Rico), Eddy Toledo (Dominican Republic).

PHILADELPHIA

Bill Giles

Telephone, Address

Office Address: Veterans Stadium, 3501 South Broad St., Philadelphia, PA 19148. **Mailing Address:** P.O. Box 7575, Philadelphia, PA 19101. **Telephone:** (215) 463-6000. **FAX:** (215) 389-3050.

Ownership

Operated by: The Phillies.

Managing General Partner: Bill Giles. **Co-General Partner:** David Montgomery.

Partners: Claire Betz, Fitz Eugene Dixon Jr., Bill Giles, David Montgomery, Double Play, Inc. (Herbert Middleton Jr.), Tri-Play Associates (Alexander Buck, J. Mahlon Buck Jr., William Buck).

BUSINESS OPERATIONS

President, Chief Executive Officer: Bill Giles. **Executive Vice President, Chief Operating Officer:** David Montgomery.

Secretary and General Counsel: Bill Webb. **Executive Administrator:** Nancy Nolan. **Administrator:** Bettyanne Robb. **Director, Business Development:** Joseph Giles.

Finance

Senior Vice President, Finance and Planning: Jerry Clothier.

Executive Secretary/Benefits Administrator: JoAnn Marano. **Controller:** Lou Perez.

Marketing, Promotions

Vice President, Marketing: Dennis Mannion. **Assistant to the Vice President, Marketing:** Debbie Nocito. **Director, Events:** Kurt Funk.

Director, Advertising Sales: Dave Buck. **Manager, Advertising and Broadcasting:** JoAnne Levy-Lamoreaux. **Manager, Promotions:** John Brazer. **Manager, Entertainment:** Chris Legault.

Public Relations, Communications

Telephone: (215) 463-6000, 755-9321. **FAX:** (215) 389-3050.

Vice President, Public Relations: Larry Shenk.

Manager, Print/Creative Services: Tina Urban. **Manager, Publicity:** Leigh Tobin. **Manager, Media Relations:** Gene Dias.

Director, Community Relations: Regina Castellani.

Stadium Operations

Director, Stadium Operations: Mike DiMuzio. **Assistant Director, Stadium Operations:** Eric Tobin.

Supervisor, Field and Maintenance Operations: Ralph Frangipani.

PA Announcer: Dan Baker.

Ticketing

Telephone: (215) 463-1000. **FAX:** (215) 463-9878.

Vice President, Ticket Operations: Richard Deats.

Director, Sales: Rory McNeil. **Director, Ticket Department:** Dan Goroff. **Director, Sales Operations:** John Weber. **Director, Group Sales:** Kathy Killian.

Travel, Clubhouse

Traveling Secretary: Eddie Ferenz.

Manager, Equipment and Home Clubhouse: Frank Coppenbarger. **Assistant Equipment Manager:** Joe Dunn. **Manager, Visiting Clubhouse:** Kevin Steinhour. **Assistant, Home Clubhouse:** Pete Cera.

Radio, TV, Media

Radio Announcers: Harry Kalas, Rich Ashburn, Andy Musser, Chris Wheeler. **Flagship Station:** WPHT 1210-AM. **No. of Network Stations:** 18.

Television Announcers: Harry Kalas, Rich Ashburn, Andy Musser, Kent Tekulve, Chris Wheeler. **Flagship Stations:** WB Channel 17, PRISM, SportsChannel Philadelphia (regional cable).

NEWSPAPERS, Daily Coverage: Philadelphia Inquirer, Philadelphia Daily News, Camden County Courier Post, Delaware County Daily Times, Wilmington News-Journal, Trenton Times.

General Information

Hometown Dugout: First Base. **Playing Surface:** Astroturf.

Game Times: Night—7:05 (April, May, September), 7:35 (June, July, August); Sat. 7:05; Sun. 1:35.

Stadium Location: I-95 or I-76 West to Broad Street exit.

Player Representative: Curt Schilling.

PHILLIES

BASEBALL OPERATIONS

Telephone: (215) 463-6000. **Fax:** (215) 755-9324.

Senior Vice President, General Manager: Lee Thomas.

Lee Thomas

Assistant General Manager: Ed Wade. **Assistant to the President:** Paul Owens.

Administrator, Baseball Operations: Susan Ingersoll.

Major League Staff

Manager: Terry Francona.

Coaches: Dugout—Chuck Cottier; Pitching—Galen Cisco; Batting—Hal McRae; First Base—Brad Mills; Third Base—John Vukovich; Bullpen—Joe Rigoli.

Terry Francona

Medical, Training

Team Physician: Dr. Phillip Marone.

Head Trainer: Jeff Cooper. **Assistant Trainer:** Mark Andersen. **Strength and Conditioning Coordinator:** Scott Hoffman.

Minor Leagues

Telephone: (215) 952-8225. **FAX:** (215) 755-9324.

Director, Player Development: Del Unser. **Administrative Assistant, Minor Leagues and Scouting:** Maryann Skedzielewski. **Computer Analyst:** Jay McLaughlin.

Director of Florida Operations: John Timberlake. **Business Manager:** Dianne Gonzalez.

Coordinator of Instruction: Don Blasingame.

Roving Instructors: Ramon Aviles (infield), George Culver (pitching), Bill DeMars (hitting), Jerry Martin (hitting), Don McCormack (catching), Tony Scott (outfield).

Farm System

Class	Farm Team	Manager	Coach	Pitching Coach
AAA	Scranton/W-B	Marc Bombard	Bill Robinson	Larry Andersen
AA	Reading	Al LeBoeuf	Ramon Henderson	Ross Grimsley
A	Clearwater	Roy Majtyka	Glenn Brummer	Darold Knowles
A	Piedmont	Ken Oberkfell	Floyd Rayford	John Martin
A	Batavia	Greg Legg	Unavailable	Ken Westray
Rookie	Martinsville	Kelly Heath	Tony Scott	Carlos Arroyo
Rookie	DSL	Alberto Fana	Unavailable	Unavailable

Scouting

Telephone: (215) 952-8225. **FAX:** (215) 755-9324.

Director, Scouting: Mike Arbuckle.

Advance Scout: Hank King (Limerick, PA).

Major League Coverage: Jimmy Stewart (Odessa, FL).

Professional Coverage: Bing Devine (St. Louis, MO), Larry Rojas (Clearwater, FL), Steve Schryver (Lake Geneva, WI).

National Crosschecker: Marti Wolever (Papillon, NE).

Mike Arbuckle

Regional Supervisors: Central—Sonny Bowers (Waco, TX); East—Dick Lawlor (Windsor, CT); Western—Dean Jongewaard (Fountain Valley, CA).

Scouts: Sal Agostinelli (Nesconset, NY), Emil Belich (West Allis, WI), Tommie Ferguson (Santa Ana, CA), Jim Fregosi Jr. (Murrieta, CA), Eli Grba (Elkmont, AL), Bill Harper (Corvallis, OR), Ken Hultzapple (Newport, PA), Jerry Lafferty (Trenton, MO), George Lauzerique (West Palm Beach, FL), Terry Logan (Brenham, TX), Leon McGraw (Baton Rouge, LA), Lloyd Merritt (Lexington, KY), Art Parrack (Goldenrod, FL), Bob Poole (Redwood City, CA), Mark Ralston (Chatsworth, CA), Mitch Sokol (Phoenix, AZ), Roy Tanner (Charleston, SC), Scott Trcka (Hobart, IN).

Latin American Supervisor: George Lauzerique (West Palm Beach, FL).

International Scouts: Allan Lewis (Panama), Willie Montanez (Puerto Rico), Wilfredo Tejada (Dominican Republic).

PITTSBURGH

Telephone, Address

Office Address: 600 Stadium Circle, Pittsburgh, PA 15212. **Mailing Address:** P.O. Box 7000, Pittsburgh, PA 15212. **Telephone:** (412) 323-5000. **FAX:** (412) 323-9133.

Ownership

Operated by: Pittsburgh Pirates Acquisition, Inc.

Board of Directors: Don Beaver, Frank Brenner, Floyd Gnassi Jr., Kevin McClatchy, Ogden Nutting, Kenneth Pollock, William Springer.

Principal Owner: Kevin McClatchy.

Kevin McClatchy

BUSINESS OPERATIONS

Chief Operating Officer: Dick Freeman. **Director of Human Resources:** Linda Zwergel.

Finance

Vice President, Finance: James Plake.

Director of Finance: Patti Mistick. **Director of Management Information Systems:** Dale Dressler.

Marketing, Sales, Broadcasting

Vice President, Marketing/Public Relations: Steven Greenberg.

Director of Marketing/Sales: Gary Remlinger. **Account Executives:** Jim Alexander, Greg Barckhoff, Charlene Cheroke, Chris Cronin, Shawn Gaertner.

Director of Group Sales: Christine Antone.

Promotions Coordinator: Christiol Stevens. **Director of Broadcast Operations:** Marc Garda.

Public Relations, Communications

Telephone: (412) 323-5018. **FAX:** (412) 323-9133.

Director, Public Relations: Michael Gordon. **Assistant, Public Relations:** Sherry Rusiski. **Assistant, Public and Media Relations:** Christine Serkoch.

Director, Media Relations: Jim Trdinich. **Director, Player Relations:** Kathy Guy.

Director, Corporate Relations: Nelson Briles. **Director, Community Sales:** Al Gordon.

Stadium Operations

Director, Stadium Operations: Dennis DaPra. **Administrative Assistants:** Chris Hunter, Patty Mihalics.

Director, In-Game Entertainment: Eric Wolff.

PA Announcer: Tim DeBacco.

Ticketing

Telephone: (412) 321-2827. **FAX:** (412) 323-9133.

Director, Ticket Operations: David Wysocki. **Manager, Ticket Operations:** Jeff Smith. **Ticket Office Staff:** Mike Krachkowski.

Travel, Clubhouse

Traveling Secretary: Greg Johnson.

Equipment Manager/Home Clubhouse Operations: Roger Wilson. **Visitors Clubhouse Operations:** John Bucci.

Radio, TV, Media

Radio Announcers: Lanny Frattare, Steve Blass, Greg Brown, Bob Walk. **Flagship Station:** KDKA 1020-AM. **TV Announcers:** Steve Blass, Greg Brown, Bob Walk. **Flagship Station:** Fox Sports Pittsburgh (regional cable).

NEWSPAPERS, Daily Coverage: Pittsburgh Post-Gazette, Pittsburgh Tribune-Review, Beaver County Times.

General Information

Hometown Dugout: First base. **Playing Surface:** Artificial turf.

Standard Game Times: 7:05 p.m. (April, May, September); 7:35 (June, July, August); Sat. 7:05, Sun. 1:35.

Stadium Directions: From south—I-279 through Fort Pitt Tunnel, make left off bridge to Fort Duquesne Bridge, cross Fort Duquesne Bridge, follow signs to Three Rivers Stadium, make left to stadium parking at light. From north—I-279 to Three Rivers Stadium exit (exit 12, left lane), follow directions to parking.

Player Representative: Al Martin.

PIRATES

BASEBALL OPERATIONS

Senior Vice President, General Manager: Cam Bonifay.

Assistant General Manager: John Sirignano. **Assistant to the General Manager:** Willie Stargell. **Administrative Assistant:** Jeannie Donatelli.

Special Assistants to General Manager: Chet Montgomery, Ken Parker, Lenny Yochim.

Cam Bonifay

Major League Staff

Manager: Gene Lamont.

Coaches: Bench—Rich Renick; Pitching—Pete Vuckovich; Batting—Lloyd McClendon; First Base—Joe Jones; Third Base—Jack Lind; Bullpen—Spin Williams.

Medical, Training

Gene Lamont

Team Physicians: Dr. Joe Coroso, Dr. Jack Failla.

Head Trainer: Kent Biggerstaff. **Assistant Trainer:** Bill Henry. **Strength and Conditioning Coach:** Dr. Warren Sipp.

Minor Leagues

Telephone: (412) 323-5045. **FAX:** (412) 323-5024.

Director of Player Development: Paul Tinnell. **Assistant Director:** Bill Bryk. **Administrative Assistant, Minor Leagues:** Diane Grimaldi.

Coordinator of Instruction: Steve Demeter. **Roving Instructors:** Tom Dettore (pitching), Joe Lonnett (catching), Bobby Meacham (infield), Gary Redus (baserunning, outfield).

Farm System

Class	Farm Team	Manager	Coach	Pitching Coach
AAA	Calgary	Trent Jewett	Ben Oglivie	Dave Rajsich
AA	Carolina	Marc Hill	Tracy Woodson	Bruce Tanner
A	Lynchburg	Jeff Banister	Richie Hebner	Jim Bibby
A	Augusta	Jeff Richardson	Scott Little	Scott Lovekamp
A	Erie	Marty Brown	None	Chris Lein
Rookie	Bradenton	Woody Huyke	Doc Watson	Larry Smith
Rookie	DSL	Ramon Zapata	None	Miguel Bonilla

Scouting

Telephone: (412) 323-5035. **FAX:** (412) 323-5024.

Director, Scouting: Leland Maddox.

Administrative Assistant, Scouting: Sandy Deutsch.

Special Assignment Scouts: Angel Figueroa (Los Angeles, CA), Jim Guinn (Fairfield, CA), Boyd Odom (Cumming, GA), Roy Smith (Phoenix, AZ).

National Coordinators: Central—Tom Barnard (Houston, TX); East—Fred Wright (Charlotte, NC); West—Ron King (Sacramento, CA).

Scouts: Russell Bowen (Charlotte, NC), Grant Brittain (Oklahoma City, OK), Dana Brown (Somerset, NJ), Steve Fleming (Matoaca, VA), Duane Gustavson (Schererville, IN), James House (Sacramento, CA), Craig Kornfeld (Durham, NC), Greg McClain (Emeryville, CA), Jack Powell (Sweetwater, TN), Steve Riha (Houston, TX), Ed Roebuck (Lakewood, CA), Delvy Santiago (Vega Alta, PR), Bruce Seid (Columbus, OH), Rob Sidwell (Windermere, FL), George Swain (Raleigh, NC), Douglas Takaragawa (Fountain Valley, CA), Mike Williams (Oakland, CA).

Latin American Coordinators: Pablo Cruz (Dominican Republic), Jose Luna (Miami, FL).

International Scouts: Marciano Alvarez (Dominican Republic), Rafel Castro (Dominican Republic), Ismael Cruz (Colombia), Osmin Melendez (Venezuela), Pastor Melendez (Venezuela), Rudiy Rico (Dominican Republic), Alex Zapata (Panama).

ST. LOUIS

Mark Lamping

Telephone, Address

Office Address: 250 Stadium Plaza, St. Louis, MO 63102. **Telephone:** (314) 421-3060. **FAX:** (314) 425-0640. **E-Mail Address:** www.stlcardinals.com.

Ownership

Chairman of the Board/General Partner: William DeWitt Jr. **Chairman:** Fred Hanser. **Secretary-Treasurer:** Andrew Baur.

BUSINESS OPERATIONS

President: Mark Lamping. **Senior Administrative Assistants:** Grace Hale, Julie Laningham.

Director, Human Resources and Office Services: Marian Rhodes. **Contract Coordinator and Office Services Assistant:** Karen Brown.

Finance

Controller: Brad Wood. **Administrative Assistant:** Beverly Finger.

Director, Accounting: Deborah Pfaff. **Director, Management Information Systems:** Sally Lemons. **Senior Accountant:** Natalie Boyd.

Marketing, Sales

Vice President, Corporate Sales: Dan Farrell. **Administrative Assistant, Corporate Sales:** Gail Ruhling. **Corporate Sales Assistants:** Mike Ball, Theron Morgan, Tony Simokaitis, Kevin Stretch.

Vice President, Community Relations: Marty Hendin. **Administrative Assistant, Community Relations:** Mary Ellen Edmiston.

Director, Promotions: Thane van Breusegen. **Director, Target Marketing:** Ted Savage.

Director, Group Sales: Joe Strohm. **Account Executives, Group Sales:** Mary Clare Bena, Linda Burnside, Mark Murray.

Director of Merchandising: Bill DeWitt III.

Public Relations, Communications

Telephone: (314) 425-0626. **FAX:** (314) 982-7399.

Director, Media Relations: Brian Bartow. **Assistants, Media Relations:** Mary Ford, Shawn Bertani.

Director, Publications: Steve Zesch.

Stadium Operations

Vice President, Stadium Operations: Joe Abernathy.

Director, Stadium Operations: Mike Bertani. **Director, Food and Beverage:** Vicki Bryant. **Director, Security and Special Services:** Joe Walsh. **Director, Quality Assurance and Guest Services:** Pat Breihan.

Head Groundskeeper: Steve Peeler.

Ticketing

Telephone: (314) 421-2400. **FAX:** (314) 425-0649.

Director, Ticket Operations: Josie Arnold. **Manager, Customer Service/Telephone Operations:** Patti McCormick. **Customer Service Supervisor:** Angie Patterson.

Group Director, Sales: Kevin Wade. **Manager, Season Sales:** Chris Scherting. **Account Executive, Ticket Sales:** Dennis Dolan.

Travel, Clubhouse

Traveling Secretary: C.J. Cherre.

Equipment Manager: Buddy Bates. **Assistant Equipment Manager:** Rip Rowan. **Visiting Clubhouse Manager:** Jerry Risch. **Video Coordinator:** Chad Blair.

Radio, TV, Media

Radio Announcers: Jack Buck, Joe Buck, Mike Shannon. **Flagship Station:** KMOX 1120-AM.

TV Announcers: Unavailable. **Flagship Station:** KPLR Channel 11.

NEWSPAPER, Daily Coverage: St. Louis Post-Dispatch.

General Information

Hometown Dugout: First Base. **Playing Surface:** Grass.

Standard Game Times: Weekdays—7:05 p.m.; Sat.—12:15, 7:05 p.m., Sun.—1:15 p.m.

Stadium Directions: From Illinois, take I-55 South, I-64 West, I-70 West or US 40 West across the Mississippi River (Poplar Street Bridge) to Busch Stadium exit. In Missouri, take I-55 North, I-64 East, I-70 East, I-44 East or US 40 East to downtown St. Louis and Busch Stadium exit.

Player Representative: Tom Pagnozzi.

CARDINALS

BASEBALL OPERATIONS

Telephone: (314) 425-0687. **FAX:** (314) 425-0648.

Vice President, General Manager: Walt Jocketty.

Vice President, Player Personnel: Jerry Walker. **Senior Executive Assistant to General Manager**: Judy Carpenter-Barada.

Walt Jocketty

Major League Staff

Manager: Tony La Russa.

Coaches: Dugout—Carney Lansford; Pitching—Dave Duncan; Batting—George Hendrick; First Base—Dave McKay; Third Base—Rene Lachemann; Bullpen—Mark DeJohn.

Instructors: Lou Brock, Bob Gibson, Red Schoendienst.

Medical, Training

Club Physician: Dr. Stan London.

Head Trainer: Gene Geiselmann. **Assistant Trainer:** Brad Henderson.

Tony La Russa

Minor Leagues

Telephone: (314) 425-0627, 425-0628. **FAX:** (314) 425-0638.

Director, Player Development: Mike Jorgensen. **Manager, Business Operations:** Scott Smulczenski. **Assistant, Player Development:** John Vuch. **Administrative Assistant:** Judy Francis.

Senior Field Coordinator: George Kissell. **Field Coordinator:** Joe Pettini. **Roving Instructors:** John Lewis (hitting), Dyar Miller (pitching), Dave Ricketts (catching), Mark Riggins (pitching), Jose Oquendo (infield).

Farm System

Class	Farm Team	Manager	Coach	Pitching Coach
AAA	Louisville	Gaylen Pitts	Chris Maloney	Marty Mason
AA	Arkansas	Rick Mahler	Luis Melendez	Rich Folkers
A	Prince William	Roy Silver	None	Ray Searage
A	Peoria	Joe Cunningham	None	Gary Buckels
A	New Jersey	Jeff Shireman	None	Mark Grater
Rookie	Johnson City	Steve Turco	None	Mike Snyder
Rookie	DSL	Bobby Diaz	Manny Espinosa	Jose Sosa

Scouting

Telephone: (314) 421-3060. **FAX:** (314) 425-0638.

Director, Scouting: Marty Maier (Oakland, CA). **Assistant Director, Scouting:** John Mozeliak.

Special Assignment Scouts: Fred McAlister (Clearwater, FL), Jeff Scott (Bourbonnais, IL), Joe Sparks (Phoenix, AZ), Mike Squires (Kalamazoo, MI).

National Crosscheckers: Marty Keough (Irvine, CA), Mike Roberts (Kansas City, MO).

Marty Maier

Scouts: Jim Belz (Springfield, IL), Randy Benson (Salisbury, NC), Tim Conroy (Victorville, CA), John DiPuglia (Miami, FL), Chuck Fick (Newbury Park, CA), Steve Grilli (Baldwinsville, NY), Manny Guerra (North Las Vegas, NV), Dave Karaff (Kansas City, MO), Tom McCormack (University City, MO), Scott Melvin (Springfield, IL), Joe Morlan (New Albany, OH), Scott Nichols, Jay North (Vacaville, CA), Hal Smith (Hilltop Lakes, TX), Roger Smith (Eastman, GA).

Coordinator, International Scouting: Tim Hanser. **International Supervisor:** Roberto Diaz (Dominican Republic).

SAN DIEGO

Larry Lucchino

Telephone, Address

Office Address: 8880 Rio San Diego Dr., San Diego, CA 92108. **Mailing Address:** P.O. Box 2000, San Diego, CA 92112. **Telephone:** (619) 881-6500. **FAX:** (619) 497-5454.

Ownership

Operated by: Padres, LP.

Principal Owners: John Moores, Larry Lucchino. **Board of Directors:** Larry Lucchino, John Moores (chairman), Charles Noell (vice chairman), John Watson, Tom Werner, George Will.

President, Chief Executive Officer: Larry Lucchino.

BUSINESS OPERATIONS

Executive Vice President, Business Operations: Bill Adams.

General Counsel: Alan Ostfield.

Assistant to the Vice President/Chief Executive Officer: Rosemary Pohl. **Special Assistant to the President/Fan Services:** Tim Katzman. **Special Assistant to the President/Ballpark Planning:** Erik Judson.

Director, Administrative Services: Lucy Freeman.

Finance

Vice President, Finance and Administration: Bob Wells.

Controller: Steve Fitch. **Director, Accounting:** Flo Borromeo.

Marketing, Sales

Vice President, Marketing: Don Johnson.

Director, Corporate Development: Mike Dee. **Senior Manager, Promotions and Sponsorships:** Cheryl Smith. **Account Executives:** Chip Bowers, Sam Kennedy. **Coordinator, Corporate Development:** Barrie Nettles.

Director, Multicultural Marketing: Enrique Morones. **Marketing Manager:** Darbi Gaunt.

Director, Sales: Louie Ruvane. **Assistant Director, Sales:** Ron Bumgarner.

Public, Community Relations

Telephone: (619) 881-6500. **FAX:** (619) 497-5454.

Senior Vice President, Public Affairs: Charles Steinberg. **Assistant to Vice President, Public Affairs:** Dayle Boyd.

Director, Media Relations: Ken Nigro. **Assistant Director, Media Relations:** Glenn Geffner. **Manager, Media Relations:** Theo Epstein. **Director, Entertainment:** Tim Young.

Director, Community Relations: Michele Anderson. **Assistant Director, Community Relations:** Beatriz Palomino.

Stadium Operations

Director, Stadium Operations: Mark Guglielmo. **Manager, Stadium Operations:** David Born.

Ticketing

Telephone: (619) 283-4494. **FAX:** (619) 280-6239.

Director, Ticket Operations and Services: Dave Gilmore. **Assistant Director, Ticket Operations:** Jim Kiersnowski. **Assistant Director, Ticket Services:** Bill Risser. **Manager, Ticket Operations:** George Stieren. **Manager Ticket Services:** Chandra George.

Radio, TV, Media

Radio Announcers: Jerry Coleman, Ted Leitner, Bob Chandler. **Flagship Stations:** KFMB 760-AM.

TV Announcers: Mel Proctor, Rick Sutcliffe, Mark Grant. **Flagship Stations:** KUSI Channel 51, Cox Channel 4 (regional cable).

NEWSPAPERS, Daily Coverage: San Diego Union-Tribune, North County Times.

General Information

Hometown Dugout: First Base. **Playing Surface:** Grass.

Standard Game Times: 7:05 p.m.; Sun. 1:05.

Stadium Location: From downtown—take Rt. 163 North to Friars Road, east to stadium. From north—take I-15 South to Friars Road, west to stadium, or I-805 South to Rt. 163 South to Friars Road, west to stadium. From east—take I-8 West to I-15 North to Friars Road, west to stadium. From west—take I-8 East to Rt. 163 North to Friars Road, east to stadium.

Player Representative: Archi Cianfrocco.

PADRES

BASEBALL OPERATIONS

Telephone: (619) 881-6500. **FAX:** (619) 497-5338.

Kevin Towers

Senior Vice President, General Manager: Kevin Towers.

Assistant General Manager: Fred Uhlman Jr. **Special Assistant to the General Manager:** Dave Stewart. **Director, Baseball Operations:** Eddie Epstein. **Director, Major League Administration/ Team Travel:** Roger Riley. **Assistant, Baseball Operations:** Chris Martin. **Secretary, Baseball Operations:** Alison Aboody.

Major League Staff

Manager: Bruce Bochy.

Coaches: Dugout—Rob Picciolo; Pitching—Dan Warthen; Batting—Merv Rettenmund; First Base—Davey Lopes; Third Base—Tim Flannery; Bullpen—Greg Booker.

Bruce Bochy

Medical, Training

Club Physician: Scripps Clinic Medical Staff.

Head Trainer: Larry Duensing. **Assistant Trainer:** Todd Hutcheson. **Strength and Conditioning Director:** Sam Gannelli.

Minor Leagues

Telephone: (619) 881-6500. **FAX:** (619) 497-5338.

Director, Player Development: Jim Skaalen. **Director, Minor League Operations:** Priscilla Oppenheimer. **Administrative Assistant, Minor Leagues:** Earleen Bender.

International Baseball Consultant: Tom House.

Coordinator of Minor League Instruction: Tye Waller. **Roving Instructors:** Eric Bullock (outfield, baserunning), Duane Espy (hitting), Tony Franklin (infield), Brent Strom (pitching), Dan Werner (catching).

Farm System

Class	Farm Team	Manager	Coach	Pitching Coach
AAA	Las Vegas	Jerry Royster	None	Sid Monge
AA	Mobile	Mike Ramsey	None	Don Alexander
A	Rancho Cuca.	Mike Basso	Jason McLeod	Dave Smith
A	Clinton	Tom LeVasseur	Dan Simonds	Darrel Akerfelds
Rookie	Idaho Falls	Don Werner	Mark Wasinger	Rick Sutcliffe
Rookie	Peoria	Randy Whisler	Angel Morris	Saul Soltero

Scouting

Telephone: (619) 881-6500. **FAX:** (619) 497-5338.

Director, Scouting: Brad Sloan.

Assistant Director, Scouting: Rene Mons. **Adminstrative Assistant, Scouting:** Herta Bingham.

Major League Scouts: Ken Bracey (Morton, IL), Ray Crone (Waxahachie, TX).

Advance Scout: Jeff Gardner (Newport Beach, CA).

National Supervisor: Bob Cummings (Oaklawn, IL).

Regional Supervisors: East—Andy Hancock (Tryon, NC); West—Jim Woodward (La Mirada, CA).

Professional Scouts: Charles Bolton (San Diego, CA), Gary Roenicke (Nevada City, CA), Gene Watson (Temple, TX).

Full-Time Scouts: Howard Bowens (Tacoma, WA), Bob Buob (Fanwood, NJ), Eddie Dixon (Leesburg, GA), Jimmy Dreyer (Euless, TX), Denny Galehouse (Doylestown, OH), Robert Gutierrez (Carol City, FL), Rich Hacker (Belleville, IL), Gary Kendall (Baltimore, MD), William Killian (Stanwood, MI), Steve Leavitt (Huntington Beach, CA), Don Lyle (Sacramento, CA), Tim McWilliam (San Diego, CA), Bill Mele (El Segundo, CA), Darryl Milne (Denver, CO), Rene Mons (Manchester, NH), Pat Murtaugh (Lexington, KY), Steve Nichols (Augusta, GA), Chuck Pierce (Bakersfield, CA), Van Smith (Belleville, IL), Gene Thompson (Scottsdale AZ), Mark Wasinger (El Paso, TX).

International Scouts: Cesar Berroteran (Venezuela), Julio Coronado (Dominican Republic), Ronquito Garcia (Puerto Rico), Tim Harkness (Canada), Juan Melo (Dominican Republic).

SAN FRANCISCO

Telephone, Address

Office Address: 3Com Park at Candlestick Point, San Francisco, CA 94124. **Telephone:** (415) 468-3700. **FAX:** (415) 467-0485. **E-Mail Address:** www.sfgiants.com.

Ownership

Operated by: San Francisco Baseball Associates, LP.

President, Managing General Partner: Peter Magowan. **Senior General Partner:** Harmon Burns.

Special Assistant to the President: Willie Mays.

Peter Magowan

BUSINESS OPERATIONS

Executive Vice President, Chief Operating Officer: Larry Baer. **Senior Vice President, Business Operations:** Pat Gallagher. **Vice President, General Counsel:** Jack Bair.

Director of Public Affairs: Staci Walters. **Legal and Public Affairs Coordinator:** Alfonso Felder. **Human Resources Manager:** Joyce Thomas.

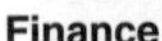

Finance

Senior Vice President, Chief Financial Officer: John Yee.

Director of Finance: Robert J. Quinn. **Financial Reporting Manager:** Lawrence Dodd. **Accounting Manager:** Norma Edar.

Director, Information Systems: Jerry Drobny.

Marketing, Sales

Vice President, Marketing and Sales: Mario Alioto. **Vice President, Marketing and Sales/China Basin Ballpark Company:** Tom McDonald.

Corporate Sponsorship Manager: Jason Pearl. **Corporate Sponsorship Coordinator:** Danny Dann.

Promotions Manager: Valerie McGuire.

General Manager, Retail/Internet: Connie Kullberg. **Director, Retail Operations:** Derik Landry.

Public Relations, Communications

Telephone: (415) 330-2448. **FAX:** (415) 467-0485.

Vice President, Communications: Bob Rose.

Media Relations Manager: Jim Moorehead. **Media Services/ Broadcast Coordinator:** Maria Jacinto. **Media Relations Assistant:** Blake Rhodes. **Director, Publications:** Nancy Donati. **Assistant, Publications:** Ivania Barraza.

Community Development Manager: Larry Chew. **Executive Assistant, Giants Community Fund:** Sue Petersen.

Stadium Operations

Vice President, Stadium Operations/Security: Jorge Costa.

Director, Stadium Operations: Gene Telucci. **Supervisor, Stadium Operations:** Bob DeAntoni. **Director, Guest Services:** Deborah Houston.

Ticketing

Telephone: (415) 467-8000. **FAX:** (415) 467-3803.

Vice President, Ticket Services: Russ Stanley. **Assistant Director, Ticket Services:** Shelley Landeros. **Ticket Operations Manager:** Anita Sprinkles. **Ticket Services Manager:** Bob Bisio. **Vice President, Ticket Sales:** Mark Norelli. **Director of Inside Sales:** Frank Vega.

Travel, Clubhouse

Director of Travel: Reggie Younger Jr.

Clubhouse Manager: Miguel Murphy. **Visitors Clubhouse:** Harvey Hodgerney. **Clubhouse Assistants:** David Loewenstein, Dennis Parry.

Radio, TV, Media

Radio Announcers: Jon Miller, Mike Krukow, Ted Robinson, Duane Kuiper, Lon Simmons. **Flagship Station:** KNBR 680-AM. **No. of Network Stations:** 4.

TV Announcers: Same as radio. **Flagship Stations:** KTVU, SportsChannel Pacific (regional cable).

NEWSPAPERS, Daily Coverage: San Francisco Chronicle, San Francisco Examiner, San Jose Mercury News, Contra Costa Times, Sacramento Bee, Oakland Tribune.

General Information

Hometown Dugout: First Base. **Playing Surface:** Grass.

Standard Game Times: Day—12:35 p.m., 1:05. Night—7:05, 7:35.

Stadium Location: Highway 101 to 3Com Park exit.

Player Representative: Jim Poole.

GIANTS

BASEBALL OPERATIONS

Telephone: (415) 330-2507. **FAX:** (415) 467-0485.

Senior Vice President, General Manager: Brian Sabean.

Vice President, Senior Advisor: Bob Quinn. **Assistant General Manager:** Ned Colletti. **Director of Player Personnel:** Dick Tidrow.

Executive Assistant to General Manager: Jamie Gaines. **Administrative Assistant, Baseball Operations:** Jeremy Shelley.

Brian Sabean

Major League Staff

Manager: Dusty Baker.

Coaches: Dugout—Ron Perranoski; Pitching—Dick Pole; Batting—Gene Clines; First Base—Carlos Alfonso. Third Base—Sonny Jackson; Bullpen—Juan Lopez.

Dusty Baker

Medical, Training

Team Physicians: Dr. Gordon Campbell, Dr. Warren King, Dr. Charles Pascal, Dr. William Straw.

Head Trainer: Mark Letendre. **Assistant Trainer:** Barney Nugent. **Strength and Rehabilitation Coordinator:** Stan Conte.

Minor Leagues

Director, Player Development: Jack Hiatt. **Assistant Director, Player Development:** Bobby Evans.

Coordinator of Instruction: Keith Bodie. **Coordinator of Pitching:** Todd Oakes. **Coordinator of Hitting:** Joe Lefebvre. **Roving Instrctor:** Jim Davenport.

Rehabilitation Coordinator: Bill Carpine. **Equipment Manager:** Phil Garcia.

Farm System

Class	Farm Team	Manager	Coach	Pitching Coach
AAA	Phoenix	Ron Wotus	Joe Lefebvre	Joel Horlen
AA	Shreveport	Carlos Lezcano	Mike Hart	Frank Reberger
A	San Jose	Frank Cacciatore	None	Keith Comstock
A	Bakersfield	Glenn Tufts	None	Bryan Hickerson
A	Salem-Keizer	Shane Turner	Joe Strain	Shawn Barton
Rookie	DSL	Ozzie Virgil Sr.	Victor Feliciano	Robert Lopez

Scouting

Telephone: (415) 330-2538. **FAX:** (415) 330-2691.

Coordinator of Scouting: Bob Hartsfield. **Assistant Coordinator of Scouting:** Matt Nerland. **Administrative Assistant, Scouting and Player Personnel:** Karen Sweeney.

Major League Scouts: Joe DiCarlo (Ringwood, NJ), Pat Dobson (Cape Coral, FL), Cal Emery (Lake Forest, CA).

Special Assignment Scout: Jim Fregosi.

National Crosschecker: Randy Waddill (Brandon, FL).

Regional Crosscheckers/Special Assignment Scouts: North—Jack Bowen (Bethel Park, PA); West—Doug Mapson (Phoenix, AZ); South—Larry Osborne (Woodstock, GA); East—Paul Turco (Sarasota, FL),

Area Scouts: Dick Cole (Costa Mesa, CA), Bob Gardner (Oviedo, FL), Mike Keenan (Chicago, IL), Tom Korenek (Houston, TX), Alan Marr (Bellmore, NY), Doug McMillan (Shingle Springs, CA), Tony Michalak (Fairfield, OH), Bobby Myrick (Colonial Heights, VA), Rick Ragazzo (Tustin, CA), John Shafer (Portland, OR), Joe Strain (Englewood, CO), Todd Thomas (St. Louis, MO), Elanis Westbrooks (Birmingham, AL), Tom Zimmer (St. Petersburg, FL).

Coordinator of International Operations: Rick Ragazzo. **Coordinator of Latin American Operations:** Luis Rosa (Laquillo, PR).

International Scouts: Claudio Brito (Dominican Republic), Jose Cassino (Panama), Diego Herrera (Venezuela), Abraham Martinez (Puerto Rico), Hector Rivera (Puerto Rico), Jorge Urribarri (Venezuela).

MAJOR LEAGUE SCHEDULES

AMERICAN LEAGUE

ANAHEIM ANGELS
Anaheim Stadium

APRIL
2-3......................Boston
4-5-**6**..............Cleveland
7-8-9................Yankees
11-12-13.... at Cleveland
14-15...........at Yankees
16-**17** ....at Minnesota
19-20.......at Kansas City
21-22-23 ....Toronto
25-26-**27** ....Detroit
29-30...............at Boston

MAY
1......................at Boston
2-3-**4** ....at White Sox
5-6-7 ....at Baltimore
9-**10-11**..... at Milwaukee
12-13 .... White Sox
14-15...............Baltimore
16-17-**18**........Milwaukee
19-20-21 ....Seattle
23-**24-25** ....at Toronto
26-27 ....at Detroit
28-**29** ....at Oakland
30-31 ....Minnesota

JUNE
1 ....Minnesota
3-4..............Kansas City
5-6-7-**8**.......at Minnesota
9-10-**11** .. at Kansas City
12-13...........*San Diego
14-15 .....*San Francisco
17-18.....*at Los Angeles
19-20-21-**22** ......Oakland
23-24-**25**..........at Texas
26-27-28-**29** ....at Seattle
30 .... *at Colorado

JULY
1 .... *at Colorado
2-3........... *Los Angeles
4-5-**6** ....Seattle
10-11-**12-13** . at Oakland
14-15 ....Texas
16-17 ....Detroit
18-19-**20** ....Toronto
22-**23**-24..... at Yankees
25-**26-27** ....at Boston
28-29-30.... at Cleveland
31..................White Sox

AUGUST
1-**2-3** ....White Sox
4-5-**6**............ Milwaukee
8-9-**10** ....Baltimore
12-13 ....at White Sox
14-15.........at Milwaukee
16-**17**-18 .....at Baltimore
19-20-21..........Yankees
22-23-**24** ....Boston
26-27............ Cleveland
28-29 ...... *at San Diego
30-31 .*at San Francisco

SEPTEMBER
1-2..................*Colorado
4-5-**6-7**............at Detroit
8-9 .... at Toronto
11-12-**13-14**........... K.C.
15-16 .... Minnesota
17-**18** ....Oakland
19-20-**21** ....at Texas
23-24............. at Seattle
25-26-27-**28**.........Texas

BALTIMORE ORIOLES
Oriole Park at Camden Yards

APRIL
1-3............. Kansas City
4-5-**6**............... at Texas
7-9-10 .... at Kansas City
11-**12-13**............. Texas
14-15 .... Minnesota
16-17 .... at White Sox
18-**19-20-21** ... at Boston
22-23 .... White Sox
24-25-**26-27** .... Boston
29-30 .... at Minnesota

MAY
1 .... at Minnesota
2-**3-4** .... Oakland
5-6-7 .... Anaheim
8-9-**10-11** .... Seattle
12-**13** .... at Oakland
14-15...........at Anaheim
16-17-**18** ....at Seattle
20-**21** .... Detroit
23-**24-25**.... at Cleveland
26-27.......... at Yankees
28-**29** .... at Detroit
30-**31** ....Cleveland

JUNE
1-2................ Cleveland
3-4.................. Yankees
6-**7-8-9**...... at White Sox
10-11.............. at Boston
13-**14**-15 ...... *at Atlanta
16-17-**18** .... *Montreal
20-**21-22** .... at Toronto
23-24-**25**... at Milwaukee
26-27-28-**29**...... Toronto
30 .... *Philadelphia

JULY
1-**2** .... Philadelphia
3-4-5-**6**........... at Detroit
11-12-**13**....... Milwaukee
14-15 ....Toronto
16-17.................. Boston
18-**19-20** .... White Sox
21-22-23......... at Texas
25-26-**27** ... at Minnesota
29-**30** .... Texas
31.................at Oakland

AUGUST
1-**2-3** .... at Oakland
5-6.................. at Seattle
8-9-**10** .... at Anaheim
12-13 .... Oakland
14-15................. Seattle
16-**17**-18 .... Anaheim
19-20-21 at Kansas City
22-23-**24** .... Minnesota
26-27-**28** .... Kansas City
29-**30-31** .... *Mets

SEPTEMBER
1-2-3 .... *at Florida
4-5-6-**7** .... at Yankees
8-9............ at Cleveland
11-12-**13**-14 .... Yankees
15-16............ Cleveland
17-18........... Milwaukee
19-**20-21**-22........ Detroit
23-24-25 .... at Toronto
26-27-**28**... at Milwaukee

NOTE: Dates in **bold** indicate afternoon games.
* Interleague Series

BOSTON RED SOX
Fenway Park

APRIL
2-3 at Anaheim
4-5-**6** at Seattle
7-8-**9** at Oakland
11-12-**13** Seattle
14-15 Oakland
16-17 Cleveland
18-**19-20-21** Baltimore
22-**23** at Cleveland
24-25-**26-27** at Baltimore
29-30 Anaheim

MAY
1 Anaheim
2-3-**4** at Texas
5-6 Kansas City
7-8 Minnesota
9-**10-11** Texas
13-14 at Kansas City
16-17-**18** at Minnesota
20-21 at White Sox
22-23-**24**-25 at Yankees
26-27 Milwaukee
28-29 White Sox
30-**31** Yankees

JUNE
1-2 Yankees
3-4-**5** at Milwaukee
6-**7-8** Cleveland
10-11 Baltimore
13-**14**-15 *at Mets
16-17-18 *Philadelphia
20-21-**22** at Detroit
23-24-25 at Toronto
26-27-**28-29** Detroit
30 *Florida

JULY
1-2 *Florida
3-4-5-**6** at White Sox
10-**11-12-13** Toronto
14-15 Detroit
16-17 at Baltimore
18-**19-20**-21 at Cleveland
22-23-24 Oakland
25-**26-27** Anaheim
29-**30** Seattle
31 at Kansas City

AUGUST
1-**2-3** at Kansas City
4-5 at Texas
6-7 at Minnesota
8-9-10 Kansas City
11-12-13 Texas
14-15-**16-17** Minnesota
19-20-**21** at Oakland
22-23-**24** at Anaheim
25-26-**27** at Seattle
29-**30**-31 *Atlanta

SEPTEMBER
1-2-3 *at Montreal
5-**6-7** Milwaukee
9-10 Yankees
12-13-**14** at Milwaukee
15-16 at Yankees
17-18 Toronto
19-**20-21** White Sox
23-24-**25** at Detroit
26-**27-28** at Toronto

CHICAGO WHITE SOX
Comiskey Park

APRIL
1-2 at Toronto
4-5-6 Detroit
8-9-**10** Toronto
11-12-13 at Detroit
14-15 at Texas
16-17 Baltimore
18-**19-20-21** Yankees
22-23 at Baltimore
25-**26-27** at Yankees
29-30 Texas

MAY
2-3-**4** Anaheim
6-7 Seattle
8-9-10-**11** Oakland
12-13 at Anaheim
14-**15** at Seattle
16-**17-18** at Oakland
20-21 Boston
23-24-**25** Milwaukee
26-27 Cleveland
28-29 at Boston
30-31 at Milwaukee

JUNE
1-2 at Milwaukee
3-4-5 at Cleveland
6-**7-8**-9 Baltimore
10-11 at Yankees
13-**14-15** *at Cincinnati
16-17-18 *Cubs
20-21-**22** Minnesota
23-24-**25** Kansas City
26-27-28-**29** at Minn.
30 *at Pittsburgh

JULY
1-2 *at Pittsburgh
3-**4-5-6** Boston
10-11-12-**13** at K.C.
14-15 at Minnesota
16-17 Yankees
18-**19-20** at Baltimore
21-22-**23** at Detroit
24-25-**26-27** Texas
29-**30** Detroit
31 at Anaheim

AUGUST
1-**2-3** at Anaheim
5-6 at Oakland
7-8-**9-10** at Seattle
12-13 Anaheim
14-15 Oakland
16-17-18 Seattle
19-20-**21** Toronto
22-23-24 at Texas
26-27-**28** at Toronto
29-30-**31** *Houston

SEPTEMBER
1-2-3 *at St. Louis
5-**6-7** at Cleveland
8-9-10 Milwaukee
11-12-13-**14** Cleveland
15-16 at Milwaukee
17-18 at Kansas City
19-**20-21** at Boston
23-24-25 Minnesota
26-27-**28** Kansas City

CLEVELAND INDIANS
Jacobs Field

APRIL
2-**3** at Oakland
4-5-**6** at Anaheim
7-8-9 at Seattle
11-12-13 Anaheim
14-15 Seattle
16-17 at Boston
18-**19-20** Milwaukee
22-**23** Boston
24-25-26-**27** at Milwaukee
29-30 Oakland

MAY
1 Oakland
2-**3-4** Detroit
5-6 Texas
7-8 Toronto
9-**10-11** at Detroit
12-13-14 at Texas
16-**17-18** at Toronto
20-21-**22** Kansas City
23-**24-25** Baltimore
26-27 at White Sox
28-29 at Kansas City
30-**31** at Baltimore

JUNE
1-2 at Baltimore
3-4-5 White Sox
6-**7-8** at Boston
10-11-12 Milwaukee
13-**14-15** *at St.Louis
16-17-18 *Cincinnati
20-**21-22** Yankees
23-24-25 Minnesota
27-**28-29** at Yankees
30 *at Houston

JULY
1-2 *at Houston
4-**5-6** Kansas City
10-11-12-**13** at Minn.
14-**15** at Yankees
16-17 at Milwaukee
18-**19-20**-21 Boston
22-23-24 Seattle
25-**26-27** Oakland
28-29-30 Anaheim

AUGUST
1-2-3 at Texas
4-**5** at Detroit
6-7 at Toronto
8-**9-10** Texas
12-13-14 Detroit
15-**16-17-18** Toronto
19-20-21 at Seattle
22-23-**24** at Oakland
26-27 at Anaheim
29-**30-31** *Cubs

SEPTEMBER
1-2-3 *at Pittsburgh
5-**6**-7 White Sox
8-9 Baltimore
11-12-13-**14** at W. Sox
15-16 at Baltimore
17-18 at Minnesota
19-20-**21**-22 at K.C.
23-24-25 Yankees
26-**27-28** Minnesota

DETROIT TIGERS
Tiger Stadium

APRIL
1-2-3 .... at Minnesota
4-5-6 .... at White Sox
7-9-10 .... Minnesota
11-12-13 .... White Sox
14-**15** .... at Milwaukee
16-**17** .... Seattle
18-**19-20** .... Oakland
21-23-**24** .... at Texas
25-26-**27** ..... at Anaheim
29-**30** .... Milwaukee
MAY
2-**3-4** .... at Cleveland
5-6 .... at Toronto
7-**8** .... Kansas City
9-**10-11** .... Cleveland
13-**14** .... Toronto
15-16-17-**18** .... at K.C.
20-**21** .... at Baltimore
23-24-**25** .... Texas
26-27 .... Anaheim
28-**29** .... Baltimore
30-31 .... at Seattle
JUNE
1 .... at Seattle
2-**3** .... at Oakland
5-6-**7-8** .... Seattle
10-**11** .... Oakland
13-14-**15** .... *at Montreal
16-17-**18** .... *Florida
20-21-**22** .... Boston
23-24-**25** .... Yankees
26-27-**28-29** ... at Boston
30 .... *Mets
JULY
1-**2** .... *Mets
3-4-5-**6** .... Baltimore
10-11-**12-13** at Yankees
14-15 .... at Boston
16-17 .... at Anaheim
18-19-20 .... at Texas
21-22-**23** .... White Sox
25-26-**27** .... Milwaukee
29-**30** .... at White Sox
31 .... Toronto
AUGUST
1-2-**3** .... Toronto
4-**5** .... Cleveland
6-**7** .... at Kansas City
8-**9-10**-11 ...... at Toronto
12-13-14.... at Cleveland
15-16-**17** .... Kansas City
19-**20** .... Minnesota
21-22-23-**24** at Milwaukee
25-26-27 ... at Minnesota
29-30-**31** ... *Philadelphia
SEPTEMBER
1-2-**3** .... *at Atlanta
4-5-**6-7** .... Anaheim
8-**9** .... Texas
10-11 .... at Seattle
12-**13-14**-15 . at Oakland
17-18 .... at Yankees
19-20-21-22 at Baltimore
23-24-**25** .... Boston
26-**27-28** .... Yankees

KANSAS CITY ROYALS
Kauffman Stadium

APRIL
1-3 .... at Baltimore
4-5-**6** .... at Minnesota
7-9-10 .... Baltimore
11-**12-13** ...... Minnesota
14-15 .... at Toronto
16-17 .... Texas
19-20 .... Anaheim
21-22-23 .... at Seattle
25-**26-27** ...... at Oakland
29-30 .... Toronto
MAY
1 .... Toronto
2-3-**4** .... Yankees
5-6 .... at Boston
7-**8** .... at Detroit
9-**10-11** .... at Yankees
13-14 .... Boston
15-16-17-**18** .... Detroit
20-21-**22** .... at Cleveland
23-24-**25** .... Seattle
26-27 .... Oakland
28-29 .... Cleveland
30-31 .... at Texas
JUNE
1 .... at Texas
3-4 .... at Anaheim
5-6-**7-8** .... Texas
9-10-**11** .... Anaheim
13-14-**15** .. *at Pittsburgh
16-17-18 .... *Houston
20-21-**22** ... at Milwaukee
23-24-**25** ... at White Sox
26-27-28-**29** . Milwaukee
30 .... *at Cubs
JULY
1-2 .... *at Cubs
4-**5-6** .... at Cleveland
10-11-12-**13** .. White Sox
14-15 .... Milwaukee
16-**17** .... at Oakland
18-19-**20** .... at Seattle
22-23-**24** ... at Minnesota
25-**26-27** .... at Toronto
28-29-30 .... Minnesota
31 .... Boston
AUGUST
1-**2-3** .... Boston
4-5 .... Yankees
6-**7** .... Detroit
8-**9-10** .... at Boston
12-**13**-14 ..... at Yankees
15-16-**17** .... at Detroit
19-20-21 .... Baltimore
22-23-**24** .... Toronto
26-27-**28** .... at Baltimore
29-30-**31** .... *St. Louis
SEPTEMBER
1-2-3 .... *at Cincinnati
4-5-6-7 .... Oakland
8-9 .... Seattle
11-12-**13-14** at Anaheim
15-16 .... at Texas
17-18 .... White Sox
19-20-**21**-22 .. Cleveland
23-24-**25** ... at Milwaukee
26-27-**28** ... at White Sox

MILWAUKEE BREWERS
County Stadium

APRIL
1-3 .... at Texas
4-5-6 .... at Toronto
7-9-10 .... Texas
11-**12-13** .... Toronto
14-**15** .... Detroit
16-**17** .... Yankees
18-**19-20** .... at Cleveland
22-**23** ....at Yankees
24-25-26-**27** .. Cleveland
29-**30** .... at Detroit
MAY
2-3-**4** .... at Seattle
5-6-**7** .... Oakland
9-**10-11** .... Anaheim
12-**13** .... Seattle
14-15 .... at Oakland
16-17-**18** ..... at Anaheim
20-**21** .... Minnesota
23-24-**25** ... at White Sox
26-27 .... at Boston
28-**29** .... at Minnesota
30-31 .... White Sox
JUNE
1-2 .... White Sox
3-4-**5** .... Boston
6-**7-8** .... at Yankees
10-11-12.... at Cleveland
13-14-15 .... *at Cubs
16-17-18 .... *St. Louis
20-21-**22** .... Kansas City
23-24-**25** .... Baltimore
26-27-28-**29** .... at K.C.
30 ....at *Cincinnati
JULY
1-2 .... *at Cincinnati
3-4-5-6 .... Minnesota
11-12-**13** .... at Baltimore
14-15...... at Kansas City
16-17 .... Cleveland
18-19-20-21 .... Yankees
22-23-24 .... at Toronto
25-26-**27** .... at Detroit
28-**29** .... Toronto
31 .... Seattle
AUGUST
1-2-**3** .... Seattle
4-5-**6** .... at Anaheim
7-8-9-10 .... at Oakland
11-**12** .... at Seattle
14-15 .... Anaheim
16-**17** .... Oakland
18-19-20 .... at Texas
21-22-23-**24** .... Detroit
25-26-**27** .... Texas
29-30-**31** .... Pittsburgh
SEPTEMBER
1-2-3 .... at Houston
5-**6-7** .... at Boston
8-9-10 .... at White Sox
12-13-**14** .... Boston
15-16 .... White Sox
17-18 .... at Baltimore
19-20-**21**-22 .... at Minn.
23-24-**25** .... Kansas City
26-27-**28** .... Baltimore

MINNESOTA TWINS
Hubert H. Humphrey Metrodome

APRIL
1-2-3 .... Detroit
4-5-**6** .... Kansas City
7-9-10 .... at Detroit
11-**12-13** at Kansas City
14-15 .... at Baltimore
16-**17** .... Anaheim
18-19-**20** .... at Seattle
22-23-**24** .... at Oakland
25-26-**27** .... Texas
29-30 .... Baltimore
MAY
1 .... Baltimore
2-**3-4** .... at Toronto
5-6 .... at Yankees
7-8 .... at Boston
9-10-11-12 .... Toronto
13-**14** .... Yankees
16-17-**18** .... Boston
20-**21** .... at Milwaukee
23-24-**25** .... Oakland
26-27 .... Seattle
28-**29** .... Milwaukee
30-31 .... at Anaheim
JUNE
1 .... at Anaheim
2-3 .... at Texas
5-6-7-**8** .... Anaheim
10-11 .... Texas
13-14-**15** ..... *at Houston
16-17-**18** ...... *Pittsburgh
20-21-**22** ... at White Sox
23-24-25 .... at Cleveland
26-27-28-**29** .. White Sox
30 .... *at St. Louis
JULY
1-2 .... *at St. Louis
3-4-5-**6** ..... at Milwaukee
10-11-12-**13** .. Cleveland
14-15 .... White Sox
16-17 .... at Seattle
18-**19-20** ...... at Oakland
22-23-**24** .... Kansas City
25-26-**27** .... Baltimore
28-29-30 at Kansas City
AUGUST
1-**2-3** .... at Yankees
4-5 .... Toronto
6-7 .... Boston
8-9-**10**-11 .... Yankees
12-13 .... at Toronto
14-15-**16-17** ... at Boston
19-**20** .... at Detroit
22-23-**24** .... at Baltimore
25-26-27 .... Detroit
29-30-**31** ...... *Cincinnati
SEPTEMBER
1-2-**3** .... *at Cubs
4-5-6-**7** .... Seattle
8-**9** .... Oakland
11-12-13-**14** ..... at Texas
15-16 .... at Anaheim
17-18 .... Cleveland
19-20-**21**-22 . Milwaukee
23-24-25 ... at White Sox
26-**27-28** .... at Cleveland

NEW YORK YANKEES
Yankee Stadium

APRIL
1-2 .... at Seattle
4-**5-6** .... at Oakland
7-8-9 .... at Anaheim
11-12-13 .... Oakland
14-15 .... Anaheim
16-**17** .... at Milwaukee
18-**19-20**-21 at White Sox
22-**23** .... Milwaukee
25-**26-27** .... White Sox
28-29-30 .... Seattle
MAY
2-3-4 ...... at Kansas City
5-6 .... Minnesota
7-8 .... Texas
9-**10-11** ...... Kansas City
13-**14** .... at Minnesota
15-16-17-**18** ..... at Texas
20-21 .... Toronto
22-23-**24**-25 .... Boston
26-27 .... Baltimore
28-**29** .... at Toronto
30-**31** .... at Boston
JUNE
1-2 .... at Boston
3-4 .... at Baltimore
6-**7-8** .... Milwaukee
10-11 .... White Sox
13-14-**15** .... *at Florida
16-17-**18** .... *Mets
20-**21-22** .... at Cleveland
23-24-**25** .... at Detroit
27-**28-29** .... Cleveland
30 .... *Atlanta
JULY
1-2 .... *Atlanta
3-4-**5-6** .... at Toronto
10-11-**12-13** .... Detroit
14-**15** .... Cleveland
16-17 .... at White Sox
18-19-20-21 at Milwaukee
22-**23**-24 .... Anaheim
25-**26-27** .... Seattle
28-29-**30** .... Oakland
AUGUST
1-**2-3** .... Minnesota
4-5 .... at Kansas City
6-7 .... at Texas
8-9-**10**-11 .. at Minnesota
12-**13**-14 .... Kansas City
15-**16-17** .... Texas
19-20-21 ..... at Anaheim
22-**23-24** .... at Seattle
26-27 .... at Oakland
29-**30-31** .... *Montreal
SEPTEMBER
1-2-3..... *at Philadelphia
4-5-**6-7** .... Baltimore
9-10 .... at Boston
11-12-**13**-14 .... at Balt.
15-16 .... Boston
17-18 .... Detroit
19-**20-21**-22 ...... Toronto
23-24-25 .... at Cleveland
26-**27-28** .... at Detroit

OAKLAND ATHLETICS
Oakland-Alameda County Coliseum

APRIL
2-**3** .... Cleveland
4-**5-6** .... Yankees
7-8-**9** .... Boston
11-12-13 ...... at Yankees
14-15 .... at Boston
16-**17** .... at Toronto
18-**19-20** .... at Detroit
22-23-**24** .... Minnesota
25-**26-27** .... Kansas City
29-30 .... at Cleveland
MAY
1 .... at Cleveland
2-**3-4** .... at Baltimore
5-6-**7** .... at Milwaukee
8-9-10-**11** .. at White Sox
12-**13** .... Baltimore
14-15 .... Milwaukee
16-**17-18** .... White Sox
20-21-**22** .... at Texas
23-24-**25** ... at Minnesota
26-27 ...... at Kansas City
28-**29** .... Anaheim
30-**31** .... Toronto
JUNE
1 .... Toronto
2-**3** .... Detroit
5-6-**7-8** .... at Toronto
10-**11** .... at Detroit
12-13 .... *Los Angeles
14-15 .... *Colorado
17-18 .... *at San Diego
19-20-21-**22** at Anaheim
23-24-25 .... at Seattle
26-27-**28-29** .... Texas
30 .... *San Diego
JULY
1 .... *San Diego
2-3 ... *at San Francisco
4-5-6 .... at Texas
10-11-**12-13** ... Anaheim
14-**15** .... Seattle
16-**17** .... Kansas City
18-**19-20** .... Minnesota
22-23-24 .... at Boston
25-**26-27** .... at Cleveland
28-29-**30** ...... at Yankees
31 .... Baltimore
AUGUST
1-**2-3** .... Baltimore
5-6 .... White Sox
7-8-**9-10** .... Milwaukee
12-13 .... at Baltimore
14-15 .... at White Sox
16-**17** .... at Milwaukee
19-20-**21** .... Boston
22-23-**24** .... Cleveland
26-**27** .... Yankees
28-29 .... *at Los Angeles
30-**31** .... *at Colorado
SEPTEMBER
1-3 .... *San Francisco
4-5-6-**7** ... at Kansas City
8-**9** .... at Minnesota
10-**11** .... Toronto
12-**13-14**-15 .... Detroit
17-**18** .... at Anaheim
19-**20-21**-22 .... Seattle
23-**24** .... Texas
26-**27-28** .... at Seattle

SEATTLE MARINERS
Kingdome

APRIL
- **1**-2 Yankees
- 4-5-**6** Boston
- 7-8-**9** Cleveland
- **11**-12-**13** at Boston
- 14-15 at Cleveland
- 16-**17** at Detroit
- 18-19-**20** Minnesota
- 21-22-23 Kansas City
- 25-**26**-**27** at Toronto
- 28-29-30 at Yankees

MAY
- 2-3-**4** Milwaukee
- 6-7 at White Sox
- 8-9-**10**-**11** at Baltimore
- 12-**13** at Milwaukee
- 14-**15** White Sox
- 16-17-**18** Baltimore
- 19-20-21 at Anaheim
- 23-24-**25** at Kansas City
- **26**-27 at Minnesota
- 28-29 Texas
- 30-31 Detroit

JUNE
- **1** Detroit
- 2-**3** Toronto
- 5-6-7-**8** at Detroit
- 10-**11** at Toronto
- 12-13 *Colorado
- **14**-**15** *Los Angeles
- 17-**18** *at San Francisco
- 19-20-21-22 at Texas
- 23-24-25 Oakland
- 26-27-28-**29** Anaheim
- 30 *San Francisco

JULY
- **1** *San Francisco
- 2-3 *at San Diego
- 4-5-**6** at Anaheim
- 10-11-**12**-**13** Texas
- **14**-**15** at Oakland
- 16-17 Minnesota
- 18-19-**20** Kansas City
- 22-23-24 at Cleveland
- 25-**26**-**27** at Yankees
- 29-**30** at Boston
- 31 at Milwaukee

AUGUST
- 1-2-**3** at Milwaukee
- 5-6 Baltimore
- 7-8-**9**-**10** White Sox
- 11-**12** Milwaukee
- 14-15 at Baltimore
- **16**-**17**-18 at White Sox
- 19-20-21 Cleveland
- 22-**23**-**24** Yankees
- 25-26-**27** Boston
- 28-29 *at Colorado
- **30**-**31** *at Los Angeles

SEPTEMBER
- **1**-3 *San Diego
- 4-5-6-**7** at Minnesota
- 8-9 at Kansas City
- 10-11 Detroit
- 12-13-**14**-15 Toronto
- 17-18 at Texas
- 19-**20**-**21**-22 at Oakland
- 23-24 Anaheim
- 26-**27**-**28** Oakland

TEXAS RANGERS
Ballpark in Arlington

APRIL
- **1**-3 Milwaukee
- 4-5-**6** Baltimore
- **7**-**9**-**10** at Milwaukee
- 11-**12**-**13** at Baltimore
- 14-15 White Sox
- 16-17 at Kansas City
- 18-19-**20** Toronto
- 21-23-**24** Detroit
- 25-26-**27** at Minnesota
- 29-30 at White Sox

MAY
- 2-3-**4** Boston
- 5-6 at Cleveland
- 7-8 at Yankees
- 9-**10**-**11** at Boston
- 12-13-14 Cleveland
- 15-16-17-**18** Yankees
- 20-21-**22** Oakland
- 23-24-**25** at Detroit
- 26-27 at Toronto
- 28-29 at Seattle
- 30-31 Kansas City

JUNE
- **1** Kansas City
- 2-3 Minnesota
- 5-6-**7**-**8** at Kansas City
- 10-11 at Minnesota
- 12-13 *San Francisco
- 14-15 *San Diego
- 17-**18** *at Colorado
- 19-20-21-22 Seattle
- 23-24-**25** Anaheim
- 26-27-28-**29** at Oakland
- 30 *at Los Angeles

JULY
- 1 *at Los Angeles
- 2-3 *Colorado
- 4-5-6 Oakland
- 10-11-**12**-**13** at Seattle
- 14-15 at Anaheim
- 16-17 Toronto
- 18-19-20 Detroit
- 21-22-23 Baltimore
- 24-25-**26**-27 at White Sox
- 29-**30** at Baltimore

AUGUST
- 1-2-3 Cleveland
- 4-5 Boston
- 6-7 Yankees
- **8**-**9**-**10** at Cleveland
- 11-12-13 at Boston
- 15-**16**-**17** at Yankees
- 18-19-20 Milwaukee
- 22-23-24 White Sox
- 25-26-**27** at Milwaukee
- 28-29 *at San Francisco
- 30-**31** *at San Diego

SEPTEMBER
- 2-3 *Los Angeles
- 4-5-**6**-**7** at Toronto
- 8-**9** at Detroit
- 11-12-13-**14** Minnesota
- 15-16 Kansas City
- 17-18 Seattle
- 19-20-**21** Anaheim
- 23-**24** at Oakland
- 25-26-27-**28** at Anaheim

TORONTO BLUE JAYS
SkyDome

APRIL
- **1**-2 White Sox
- 4-**5**-**6** Milwaukee
- 8-9-**10** at White Sox
- 11-**12**-**13** at Milwaukee
- 14-15 Kansas City
- 16-**17** Oakland
- 18-19-**20** at Texas
- 21-22-23 at Anaheim
- 25-**26**-**27** Seattle
- 29-30 at Kansas City

MAY
- 1 at Kansas City
- 2-**3**-**4** Minnesota
- 5-6 Detroit
- 7-8 at Cleveland
- 9-10-**11**-12 at Minn.
- 13-**14** at Detroit
- 16-**17**-**18** Cleveland
- 20-21 at Yankees
- 23-**24**-**25** Anaheim
- 26-27 Texas
- 28-**29** Yankees
- 30-**31** at Oakland

JUNE
- **1** at Oakland
- 2-**3** at Seattle
- 5-6-**7**-**8** Oakland
- 10-11 Seattle
- 13-14-**15** *at Phil.
- 16-17-18 *Atlanta
- 20-**21**-**22** Baltimore
- 23-24-25 Boston
- 26-27-28-**29** at Baltimore
- 30 *Montreal

JULY
- **1**-2 *Montreal
- 3-4-**5**-**6** Yankees
- 10-11-**12**-**13** at Boston
- 14-15 at Baltimore
- 16-17 at Texas
- 18-19-**20** at Anaheim
- 22-23-24 Milwaukee
- 25-**26**-**27** Kansas City
- 28-**29** at Milwaukee
- 31 at Detroit

AUGUST
- 1-2-**3** at Detroit
- **4**-**5** at Minnesota
- 6-7 Cleveland
- **8**-**9**-**10**-11 Detroit
- 12-13 Minnesota
- 15-**16**-**17**-**18** at Cleveland
- 19-20-**21** at White Sox
- 22-23-**24** at Kansas City
- 26-27-**28** White Sox
- 29-**30**-**31** *Florida

SEPTEMBER
- **1**-2-3 *at Mets
- 4-5-**6**-**7** Texas
- 8-9 Anaheim
- 10-**11** at Oakland
- 12-13-**14**-15 at Seattle
- 17-18 at Boston
- 19-**20**-**21**-22 at Yankees
- 23-24-25 Baltimore
- 26-**27**-**28** Boston

NATIONAL LEAGUE

ATLANTA BRAVES
Turner Field

APRIL

1-2-3 ... at Houston
4-5-**6** ... Cubs
8-9-10 ... Houston
11-12-13 ... at Cubs
14-15-**16** ... Cincinnati
18-**19-20** ... at Colorado
22-**23** .. at San Francisco
25-26-**27** ... San Diego
28-29 ... Los Angeles
30 ... at Cincinnati

MAY

1 ... at Cincinnati
2-3-**4** ... Pittsburgh
5-6 ... at St. Louis
7-8 ... at Florida
9-10-**11**-12 at Pittsburgh
13-14 ... Florida
16-17-**18**-19 ... St. Louis
20-**21** ... Montreal
23-24-**25** at Los Angeles
26-27 ... at San Diego
28-29-30 .. San Francisco

JUNE

1 ... San Francisco
2-3 ... San Diego
4-**5** ... at Montreal
6-**7-8** ... at San Francisco
9-10-**11** ... at Colorado
13-**14-15** ... Baltimore
16-17-18 ... at Toronto
20-21-**22** at Philadelphia
23-24-**25** ... at Mets
26-27-28-**29** ... Phil.
30 ... at Yankees

JULY

1-**2** ... *at Yankees
3-4-5-**6** ... at Montreal
10-11-12-**13** ... Mets
14-15 ... Philadelphia
16-17 ... Colorado
18-19-**20-21** ... L.A.
22-23 ... at Cubs
25-**26-27** ... at Cincinnati
28-29-30 ... Cubs
31 ... at Florida

AUGUST

1-2-**3** ... at Florida
4-5 ... at Pittsburgh
6-7 ... St. Louis
8-**9-10**-11 ... Florida
12-13 ... Pittsburgh
15-**16-17** ... at St. Louis
19-20 ... at Houston
22-**23-24** ... Cincinnati
26-27-28 ... Houston
29-**30-31** ... at Boston

SEPTEMBER

1-2-**3** ... Detroit
4-5-6-7 ... at San Diego
9-10 ... at Los Angeles
12-13-**14** ... Colorado
15-**16** ... San Francisco
17-18 ... Mets
19-20-**21**-22 ... Montreal
23-24-25 at Philadelphia
26-**27-28** ... at Mets

CHICAGO CUBS
Wrigley Field

APRIL

1-2-3 ... at Florida
4-5-**6** ... at Atlanta
8-10 ... Florida
11-12-13 ... Atlanta
15-16 ... Colorado
18-19-20-21 ... at Mets
22-23 ... at Montreal
24-25-26-27 .. Pittsburgh
28-29 ... Montreal
30 ... at Colorado

MAY

1 ... at Colorado
2-3-**4** ... at Los Angeles
6-7-**8** ... at San Diego
9-**10-11** at San Francisco
13-**14** ... Los Angeles
15-16 ... San Diego
17-**18-19**. San Francisco
20-**21** ... Philadelphia
23-24-**25** ... at Cincinnati
26-27-28 ... at Pittsburgh
29-**30-31** ... Cincinnati

JUNE

1 ... Cincinnati
2-3 ... Pittsburgh
4-5 ... at Philadelphia
6-7-**8**-9 ... at Montreal
10-**11** ... Mets
13-14-15 ... Milwakee
16-17-18 ... at White Sox
20-**21-22** ... at Houston
23-24-25 ... at St. Louis
26-**27-28-29** ... Houston
30 ... Kansas City

JULY

1-2 ... Kansas City
3-4-5-6 ... at Philadelphia
10-11-12-13 ... St. Louis
14-**15** ... Houston
16-**17** ... at Mets
18-19-20 ... Colorado
22-23 ... Atlanta
24-25-26-**27** at Colorado
28-29-30 ... at Atlanta
30 ... Los Angeles

AUGUST

1-2-3 ... Los Angeles
5-**6-7** ... San Francisco
8-9-10 ... San Diego
11-12 ... at Los Angeles
13-14 .. at San Francisco
15-16-**17** ... at San Diego
19-20 ... at Florida
22-23-24 ... Montreal
25-26-**27-28** ... Florida
29-**30-31** .. *at Cleveland

SEPTEMBER

1-2-3 ... *Minnesota
5-6-7 ... Mets
8-9-10 ... at Cincinnati
12-13-**14** ... at Pittsburgh
15-16 ... Cincinnati
17-18 ... St. Louis
19-20-21 ... Philadelphia
23-24-25 ... at Houston
26-**27-28** ... at St. Louis

NOTE: Dates in **bold** indicate afternoon games.
*Interleague series

CINCINNATI REDS
Cinergy Field

APRIL
1-2-**3** .... Colorado
4-5-**6**.............. at Florida
7-9-10 .... at Colorado
11-**12-13**............ Florida
14-15-**16** .... at Atlanta
17-18-**19-20** at Pittsburgh
22-23 .... at Mets
25-**26-27**.... Philadelphia
28-29..................... Mets
30......................... Atlanta
MAY
1......................... Atlanta
2-**3-4**... at San Francisco
5-6-7...... at Los Angeles
9-10-**11**..... at San Diego
13-14...... San Francisco
15-16........ Los Angeles
17-18-19....... San Diego
20-21 .... at Houston
23-**24-25** .... Cubs
26-27-28.... Philadelphia
29-**30-31** ....at Cubs
JUNE
1........................ at Cubs
2-3 .... at Philadelphia
4-5 .... Houston
6-**7-8**...................... Mets
10-11.............. Pittsburgh
13-**14-15**...... *White Sox
16-17-18 .. *at Cleveland
20-21-**22**........ at St. Louis
23-24-**25**...... at Montreal
26-27-**28-29** .... St. Louis
30............... *Milwaukee
JULY
1-**2** .... *Milwaukee
3-4-5-**6**......... at Houston
11-12-**13**......... Montreal
14-15.................. St. Louis
16-17........ at Pittsburgh
18-**19-20-21**....... at Mets
22-23.................. Florida
25-**26-27** .... Atlanta
28-29-30......... at Florida
AUGUST
1-**2-3**-4 ... San Francisco
5-6-7............ San Diego
8-9-**10**........ Los Angeles
11-**12**.. at San Francisco
13-**14**........ at San Diego
15-16-17 at Los Angeles
19-**20** .... Colorado
22-**23-24** .... at Atlanta
25-26-**27**..... at Colorado
29-30-**31**.. *at Minnesota
SEPTEMBER
1-2-3........ *Kansas City
4-5-**6-7** .... Pittsburgh
8-9-**10** .... Cubs
12-**13-14** at Philadelphia
15-16 .... at Cubs
17-18................ Montreal
19-**20-21-22**..... Houston
23-24-25...... at St. Louis
26-27-**28**...... at Montreal

COLORADO ROCKIES
Coors Field

APRIL
1-2-**3**......... at Cincinnati
4-**5-6**........... at Montreal
7-9-10........... Cincinnati
11-12-13......... Montreal
15-16 .... at Cubs
18-**19-20** .... Atlanta
22-**23**................. Florida
25-**26-27**...... at St. Louis
28-**29** .... at Houston
30......................... Cubs
MAY
1........................... Cubs
2-**3-4**......... Philadelphia
5-**6**......................... Mets
7-**8**................ Pittsburgh
9-10-**11**-12 .... at Phil.
14-15......... at Pittsburgh
16-**17-18-19**...... at Mets
20-**21-22**........... at S. F.
23-**24-25** .... Houston
26-27.............. St. Louis
29-30-31......... at Florida
JUNE
1 .... at Florida
2-**3**.............. at St. Louis
4-**5** .... San Diego
6-7-8................... Florida
9-10-**11** .... Atlanta
12-13 .... *at Seattle
14-15 .... *at Oakland
17-**18**................. *Texas
19-20-21-**22** .... at S.D.
23-24-25 .... at L.A.
26-27-28-**29**........... S.F.
30 .... *Anaheim
JULY
1 .... *Anaheim
2-3................. *at Texas
4-**5-6**... at San Francisco
10-11-**12-13**.. San Diego
14-**15**........ Los Angeles
16-17............. at Atlanta
18-19-20 .... at Cubs
21-22.......... at Montreal
24-25-26-**27** .... Cubs
28-29-**30**......... Montreal
31 .... at Pittsburgh
AUGUST
1-2-**3** .... at Pittsburgh
4-5 .... at Philadelphia
6-**7** .... at Mets
8-**9-10** .... Pittsburgh
12-**13** .... Philadelphia
15-16-**17**............... Mets
19-**20**......... at Cincinnati
21-22-**23-24**. at Houston
25-26-**27**........ Cincinnati
28-29 .... *Seattle
30-**31** .... *Oakland
SEPTEMBER
1-2 .... *at Anaheim
4-5-**6-7** .... St. Louis
9-**10** .... Houston
12-13-**14** .... at Atlanta
15-16................ at Florida
17-**18**........ at San Diego
19-20-21 at Los Angeles
23-**24**...... San Francisco
25-26-**27-28** .... L.A.

FLORIDA MARLINS
Pro Player Stadium

APRIL
1-2-3 .... Cubs
4-5-**6**............. Cincinnati
8-10 .... at Cubs
11-**12-13**.... at Cincinnati
15-16-**17**......... St. Louis
18-**19-20** .... at S.F.
22-**23** .... at Colorado
25-26-27.... Los Angeles
28-29........... San Diego
30 .... at St. Louis
MAY
1 .... at St. Louis
2-3-4 .... at Houston
5-6................. Pittsburgh
7-8...................... Atlanta
9-10-**11**-12....... Houston
13-14............. at Atlanta
16-17-**18** ... at Pittsburgh
20-21 .... Mets
23-24-**25**... at San Diego
26-27..... at Los Angeles
29-30-**31** .... Colorado
JUNE
1 .... Colorado
2-**3**......... San Francisco
4-**5** .... at Mets
6-7-8 .... at Colorado
9-**10-11** .... at S.F.
13-14-**15** .... *Yankees
16-17-**18**........ *at Detroit
20-**21-22**...... at Montreal
23-24-**25**............. at Phil.
26-27-28-**29** .... Montreal
30 .... *at Boston
JULY
1-2 .... *at Boston
3-4-**5-6**............... at Mets
10-11-12-**13** .... Phil.
14-15................. Montreal
16-17......... Los Angeles
18-19-**20-21**.. San Diego
22-23......... at Cincinnati
25-**26-27**...... at St. Louis
28-29-30........ Cincinnati
31....................... Atlanta
AUGUST
1-2-**3** .... Atlanta
4-5 .... Houston
6-**7**............ at Pittsburgh
8-**9-10**-11 .... at Atlanta
12-13 .... at Houston
15-16-**17**-18 .. Pittsburgh
19-20 .... Cubs
22-23-**24**.......... St. Louis
25-26-**27-28**...... at Cubs
29-**30-31**...... *at Toronto
SEPTEMBER
1-2-3............ *Baltimore
5-**6-7**-8... at Los Angeles
9-10.......... at San Diego
12-**13-14**. San Francisco
15-16 .... Colorado
17-**18** .... Philadelphia
19-20-**21**-22........... Mets
23-24-25...... at Montreal
26-27-**28** at Philadelphia

HOUSTON ASTROS
Astrodome

APRIL
1-2-3 ... Atlanta
4-5-**6** ... St. Louis
8-9-10 ... at Atlanta
11-**12-13-14** at St. Louis
15-16 ... Montreal
18-19-**20** at Los Angeles
22-23 ... at San Diego
25-26-**27**. San Francisco
28-29 ... Colorado
30 ... at Montreal

MAY
1 ... at Montreal
2-3-4 ... Florida
5-6 ... Philadelphia
7-**8** ... Mets
9-10-**11**-12 ... at Florida
13-14 ... at Mets
16-17-**18-19** ... at Phil.
20-21 ... Cincinnati
23-**24-25** ... at Colorado
26-27.. at San Francisco
29-30-31 ... San Diego

JUNE
1 ... San Diego
2-**3** ... Los Angeles
4-**5** ... at Cincinnati
6-7-**8** ... at San Diego
9-10-11 .. at Los Angeles
13-14-**15** ... *Minnesota
16-17-18 *at Kansas City
20-**21-22** ... Cubs
23-24-**25** ... Pittsburgh
26-**27-28-29** ... at Cubs
30 ... *Cleveland

JULY
1-2 ... *Cleveland
3-4-5-**6** ... Cincinnati
10-11-12-**13** ... at Pitt.
14-**15** ... at Cubs
16-**17** ... San Francisco
18-19-**20** ... at Montreal
22-23 ... at St. Louis
24-25-26-**27** .... Montreal
28-29-30 ... St. Louis

AUGUST
1-**2-3** ... Mets
4-5 ... at Florida
6-**7** ... at Philadelphia
8-9-**10**-11 ... at Mets
12-13 ... Florida
15-**16-17** .... Philadelphia
19-20 ... Atlanta
21-22-**23-24** .... Colorado
26-27-28 ... at Atlanta
29-30-**31** .. *at White Sox

SEPTEMBER
1-2-3 ... *Milwaukee
4-5-**6-7** ... at S.F.
9-**10** ... at Colorado
12-13-**14** .... Los Angeles
15-**16** ... San Diego
17-18 ... at Pittsburgh
19-**20-21-22** ... at Cinc.
23-24-25 ... Cubs
26-27-**28** ... Pittsburgh

LOS ANGELES DODGERS
Dodger Stadium

APRIL
1-2-3 ... Philadelphia
4-5-**6** ... Pittsburgh
7-8-9 ... Mets
11-**12-13** ... at Pittsburgh
15-**16** ... at Mets
18-19-**20** ... Houston
22-23 ... St. Louis
25-26-27 ... at Florida
28-29 ... at Atlanta
30 ... at Philadelphia

MAY
1 ... at Philadelphia
2-3-**4** ... Cubs
5-6-7 ... Cincinnati
9-10-**11** ... Montreal
13-**14** ... at Cubs
15-16 ... at Cincinnati
17-**18-19** ... at Montreal
20-21-**22** ... at San Diego
23-24-**25** ... Atlanta
26-27 ... Florida
29-30-**31** ... at St. Louis

JUNE
1 ... at St. Louis
2-**3** ... at Houston
4-5 ... San Francisco
6-7-**8** ... St. Louis
9-10-11 ... Houston
12-13 ... *at Oakland
14-**15** ... *at Seattle
17-18 ... *Anaheim
19-20-**21**-22 ... at S.F.
23-24-25 ... Colorado
26-27-**28-29**.. San Diego
30 ... *Texas

JULY
1 ... *Texas
2-3 ... *at Anaheim
4-**5-6** ... at San Diego
10-11-12-**13** ... S.F.
14-**15** ... at Colorado
16-17 ... at Florida
18-19-**20-21** ... at Atlanta
22-23-24 ... Mets
25-26-**27** .... Philadelphia
28-**29** ... Pittsburgh
31 ... at Cubs

AUGUST
1-2-3 ... at Cubs
5-6-7 ... at Montreal
8-9-**10** ... at Cincinnati
11-12 ... Cubs
13-**14** ... Montreal
15-16-17 ... Cincinnati
19-20-21 ... at Mets
22-23-**24** at Philadelphia
25-26-**27** ... at Pittsburgh
28-29 ... *Oakland
30-31 ... *Seattle

SEPTEMBER
2-3 ... *at Texas
5-**6-7**-8 ... Florida
9-10 ... Atlanta
12-13-**14** ... at Houston
15-16 ... at St. Louis
17-**18**.. at San Francisco
19-20-21 ... Colorado
23-24 ... San Diego
25-26-**27-28** at Colorado

MONTREAL EXPOS
Olympic Stadium

APRIL
1-2-3 ... St. Louis
4-**5-6** ... Colorado
8-**10** ... at St. Louis
11-12-13 ... at Colorado
15-16 ... at Houston
17-18-19-**20** ... at Phil.
22-23 ... Cubs
25-**26-27** ... Mets
28-**29** ... at Cubs
30 ... Houston

MAY
1 ... Houston
2-3-**4** ... at San Diego
5-6-**7**... at San Francisco
9-10-**11**.. at Los Angeles
13-**14** ... San Diego
15-16 ... San Francisco
17-**18-19** .... Los Angeles
20-**21** ... at Atlanta
22-23-24-**25** .. Pittsburgh
26-27-28 ... Mets
30-31 ... at Pittsburgh

JUNE
1 ... at Pittsburgh
2-3 ... at Mets
4-**5** ... Atlanta
6-7-**8**-9 ... Cubs
10-11 ... Philadelphia
13-14-**15** ... *Detroit
16-17-**18** ... *at Baltimore
20-**21-22** ... Florida
23-24-25 ... Cincinnati
26-27-28-**29** ... at Florida
30 ... *at Toronto

JULY
1-2 ... *at Toronto
3-4-5-**6** ... Atlanta
11-12-**13** .... at Cincinnati
14-15 ... at Florida
16-17 ... at Philadelphia
18-19-**20** ... Houston
21-22 ... Colorado
24-25-26-**27**. at Houston
28-29-**30** ... at Colorado
31 ... San Diego

AUGUST
1-2-**3** ... San Diego
4-5-6-**7** ... Los Angeles
8-9-**10** ... San Francisco
11-12 ... at San Diego
13-**14** ... at Los Angeles
15-**16-17** ... at S.F.
19-20-**21** ... St, Louis
22-23-24 ... at Cubs
26-27-28 ... at St. Louis
29-**30-31** .... *at Yankees

SEPTEMBER
1-2-3 ... *Boston
4-5-6-**7** ... Philadelphia
9-10 ... Pittsburgh
11-12-**13-14** ... at Mets
15-16 ... at Pittsburgh
17-18 ... at Cincinnati
19-20-**21**-22 ... at Atlanta
23-24-25 ... Florida
26-27-**28** ... Cincinnati

NEW YORK METS
Shea Stadium

APRIL
1-2-**3** ... at San Diego
4-**5**-**6** ... at San Francisco
7-8-9 ... at Los Angeles
12-**13**-14. San Francisco
15-**16** ... Los Angeles
18-**19**-**20**-**21** ... Cubs
22-**23** ... Cincinnati
25-**26**-**27** ... at Montreal
28-29 ... at Cincinnati
30 ... San Diego

MAY
1 ... San Diego
2-**3**-**4** ... St. Louis
5-**6** ... at Colorado
7-**8** ... at Houston
9-10-**11** ... at St. Louis
13-14 ... Houston
16-**17**-**18**-**19** ... Colorado
20-21 ... at Florida
22-23-24-**25** ... at Phil.
26-27-28 ... at Montreal
30-31 ... Philadelphia

JUNE
1 ... Philadelphia
2-3 ... Montreal
4-**5** ... Florida
6-**7**-**8** ... at Cincinnati
10-**11** ... at Cubs
13-**14**-15 ... *Boston
16-17-**18** ... *at Yankees
19-20-**21**-**22** .. Pittsburgh
23-24-**25** ... Atlanta
27-28-**29** ... at Pittsburgh
30 ... *at Detroit

JULY
1-**2** ... *at Detroit
3-4-**5**-**6** ... Florida
10-11-**12**-13 ... at Atlanta
14-15 ... at Pittsburgh
16-**17** ... Cubs
18-**19**-**20**-**21** ... Cincinnati
22-23-24 at Los Angeles
25-26-**27** ... at San Diego
29-30 .. at San Francisco

AUGUST
1-**2**-**3** ... at Houston
4-5 ... St. Louis
6-**7** ... Colorado
8-**9**-**10**-11 ... Houston
12-13-14 ... at St. Louis
15-16-**17** ... at Colorado
19-20-21 ... Los Angeles
22-23-**24** ... San Diego
25-26-**27** San Francisco
29-**30**-**31** ... *at Baltimore

SEPTEMBER
1-2-3 ... *Toronto
5-**6**-**7** ... at Cubs
8-9-**10** ... Philadelphia
11-12-**13**-**14** ... Montreal
15-16 ... at Philadelphia
17-18 ... at Atlanta
19-20-**21**-22 ... at Florida
23-24 ... Pittsburgh
26-**27**-**28** ... Atlanta

PHILADELPHIA PHILLIES
Veterans Stadium

APRIL
1-2-3 ... at Los Angeles
4-5-**6** ... at San Diego
7-**8**-**9** ... at San Francisco
11-12-**13** ... San Diego
15-16 ... San Francisco
17-18-19-**20** ... Montreal
21-23 ... at Pittsburgh
25-**26**-**27** ... at Cincinnati
28-29 ... Pittsburgh
30 ... Los Angeles

MAY
1 ... Los Angeles
2-**3**-**4** ... at Colorado
5-6 ... at Houston
7-**8** ... at St. Louis
9-10-**11**-12 ... Colorado
13-14 ... St. Louis
16-17-**18**-19 ... Houston
20-**21** ... at Cubs
22-23-24-**25** ... Mets
26-27-28 ... at Cincinnati
30-31 ... at Mets

JUNE
1 ... at Mets
2-3 ... Cincinnati
4-5 ... Cubs
6-7-**8** ... at Pittsburgh
10-11 ... at Montreal
13-14-**15** ... *Toronto
16-17-18 ... *at Boston
20-21-**22** ... Atlanta
23-24-**25** ... Florida
26-27-28-**29** ... at Atlanta
30 ... *at Baltimore

JULY
1-**2** ... *at Baltimore
3-4-5-**6** ... Cubs
10-11-12-**13** ... at Florida
14-15 ... at Atlanta
16-17 ... Montreal
18-**19**-**20**-**21** .. Pittsburgh
22-**23**-**24** ... at S.F.
25-26-**27** at Los Angeles
28-29 ... at San Diego
31 ... St. Louis

AUGUST
1-**2**-**3** ... St. Louis
4-5 ... Colorado
6-**7** ... Houston
8-9-**10** ... at St. Louis
12-**13** ... at Colorado
15-**16**-**17** ... at Houston
18-19-20. San Francisco
22-23-**24** ... Los Angeles
25-26-**27** ... San Diego
29-30-**31** ... *at Detroit

SEPTEMBER
1-2-3 ... *Yankees
4-5-6-**7** ... at Montreal
8-9-10 ... at Mets
12-**13**-**14** ... Cincinnati
15-16 ... Mets
17-**18** ... at Florida
19-**20**-**21** ... at Cubs
23-24-25 ... Atlanta
26-27-**28** ... Florida

PITTSBURGH PIRATES
Three Rivers Stadium

APRIL
1-3 ... at San Francisco
4-5-**6** ... at Los Angeles
7-8-9 ... at San Diego
11-**12**-**13** ... Los Angeles
15-16 ... San Diego
17-18-**19**-**20** ... Cincinnati
21-23 ... Philadelphia
24-**25**-**26**-**27** ... at Cubs
28-29 ... at Philadelphia
30 ... San Francisco

MAY
1 ... San Francisco
2-3-**4** ... at Atlanta
5-6 ... at Florida
7-**8** ... at Colorado
9-10-**11**-12 ... Atlanta
14-15 ... Colorado
16-17-**18** ... Florida
20-**21** ... at St. Louis
22-23-24-**25** at Montreal
26-27-28 ... Cubs
30-31 ... Montreal

JUNE
1 ... Montreal
2-**3** ... at Cubs
4-**5** ... St. Louis
6-7-**8** ... Philadelphia
10-11 ... at Cincinnati
13-14-**15** ... *Kansas City
16-17-**18** .. *at Minnesota
19-20-**21**-**22** ... at Mets
23-24-**25** ... at Houston
27-28-**29** ... Mets
30 ... *White Sox

JULY
1-2 ... *White Sox
3-**4**-**5**-**6** ... at St. Louis
10-11-12-**13** ... Houston
14-15 ... Mets
16-17 ... Cincinnati
18-**19**-**20**-**21** ... at Phil.
22-23-**24** ... at San Diego
25-**26**-**27**-**27** ... at S.F.
28-**29** ... at Los Angeles
31 ... Colorado

AUGUST
1-2-**3** ... Colorado
4-5 ... Atlanta
6-**7** ... Florida
8-**9**-**10** ... at Colorado
12-13 ... at Atlanta
15-16-**17**-18 ... at Florida
19-20-21 ... San Diego
22-23-**24**. San Francisco
25-26-**27** ... Los Angeles
29-30-**31** . *at Milwaukee

SEPTEMBER
1-2-3 ... *Cleveland
4-5-**6**-**7** ... at Cincinnati
9-10 ... at Montreal
12-13-**14** ... Cubs
15-16 ... Montreal
17-18 ... Houston
19-**20**-**21**-**22** ... St. Louis
23-24 ... at Mets
26-27-**28** ... at Houston

ST. LOUIS CARDINALS
Busch Stadium

APRIL

1-2-3 ... at Montreal
4-5-**6** ... at Houston
8-**10** ... Montreal
11-**12-13-14** ... Houston
15-16-**17** ... at Florida
18-19-20 ... at San Diego
22-23 ... at Los Angeles
25-**26-27** ... Colorado
28-29 ... San Francisco
30 ... Florida

MAY

1 ... Florida
2-**3-4** ... at Mets
5-6 ... Atlanta
7-**8** ... Philadelphia
9-10-**11** ... Mets
13-14 ... at Philadelphia
16-**17**-18-19 ... at Atlanta
20-**21** ... Pittsburgh
23-**24-25** ... at S.F.
26-27 ... at Colorado
29-30-**31** ... Los Angeles

JUNE

1 ... Los Angeles
2-**3** ... Colorado
4-**5** ... at Pittsburgh
6-7-**8** ... at Los Angeles
9-10-11 ... at San Diego
13-**14-15** ... *Cleveland
16-17-18 ... *at Milwaukee
20-21-**22** ... Cincinnati
23-24-25 ... Cubs
26-27-**28-29** at Cincinnati
30 ... *Minnesota

JULY

1-2 ... *Minnesota
3-**4-5-6** ... Pittsburgh
10-11-12-13 ... at Cubs
14-**15** ... at Cincinnati
16-17 ... San Diego
18-19-**20**-21 ... S.F.
22-23 ... Houston
25-**26-27** ... Florida
28-29-30 ... at Houston
31 ... at Philadelphia

AUGUST

1-**2-3** ... at Philadelphia
4-5 ... at Mets
6-7 ... at Atlanta
8-9-**10** ... Philadelphia
12-13-14 ... Mets
15-**16**-17 ... Atlanta
19-20-**21** ... at Montreal
22-23-**24** ... at Florida
26-27-28 ... Montreal
29-30-**31** *at Kansas City

SEPTEMBER

1-2-3 ... *White Sox
4-5-**6-7** ... at Colorado
9-**10** ... at San Francisco
12-**13-14** ... San Diego
15-16 ... Los Angeles
17-18 ... at Cubs
19-20-**21**-22 ... at Pitt.
23-24-25 ... Cincinnati
26-**27-28** ... Cubs

SAN DIEGO PADRES
Jack Murphy Stadium

APRIL

1-2-**3** ... Mets
4-5-**6** ... Philadelphia
7-8-9 ... Pittsburgh
11-12-**13** at Philadelphia
15-16 ... at Pittsburgh
18-19-20 ... St. Louis
22-23 ... Houston
25-26-**27** ... at Atlanta
28-29 ... at Florida
30 ... at Mets

MAY

1 ... at Mets
2-3-**4** ... Montreal
6-7-**8** ... Cubs
9-10-**11** ... Cincinnati
13-**14** ... at Montreal
15-16 ... at Cubs
17-18-19 ... at Cincinnati
20-21-**22** ... Los Angeles
23-24-**25** ... Florida
26-27 ... Atlanta
29-30-31 ... at Houston

JUNE

1 ... at Houston
2-3 ... at Atlanta
4-5 ... at Colorado
6-7-**8** ... Houston
9-10-11 ... St. Louis
12-13 ... *at Anaheim
14-15 ... *at Texas
17-18 ... *Oakland
19-20-21-**22** ... Colorado
23-**24-25** ... at S.F.
26-27-**28-29** ... at L.A.
30 ... *at Oakland

JULY

1 ... *at Oakland
2-3 ... *Seattle
4-**5-6** ... Los Angeles
10-11-**12-13** at Colorado
14-15 ... San Francisco
16-17 ... at St. Louis
18-19-**20-21** ... at Florida
22-23-**24** ... Pittsburgh
25-**26-27-27** ... Mets
28-29 ... Philadelphia
31 ... at Montreal

AUGUST

1-2-**3** ... at Montreal
5-6-7 ... at Cincinnati
8-9-10 ... at Cubs
11-12 ... Montreal
13-**14** ... Cincinnati
15-16-**17** ... Cubs
19-20-21 ... at Pittsburgh
22-23-**24** ... at Mets
25-26-**27** at Philadelphia
28-29 ... *Anaheim
30-**31** ... *Texas

SEPTEMBER

1-3 ... *at Seattle
4-5-6-**7** ... Atlanta
9-10 ... Florida
12-**13-14** ... at St. Louis
15-**16** ... at Houston
17-**18** ... Colorado
19-20-**21**-22 ... S.F.
23-24 ... at Los Angeles
26-**27-28** ... at S.F.

SAN FRANCISCO GIANTS
Candlestick Park

APRIL

1-3 ... Pittsburgh
4-**5-6** ... Mets
7-**8-9** ... Philadelphia
12-13-14 ... at Mets
15-16 ... at Philadelphia
18-**19-20** ... Florida
22-**23** ... Atlanta
25-26-**27** ... at Houston
28-29 ... at St. Louis
30 ... at Pittsburgh

MAY

1 ... at Pittsburgh
2-**3-4** ... Cincinnati
5-6-7 ... Montreal
9-**10-11** ... Cubs
13-14 ... at Cincinnati
15-16 ... at Montreal
17-**18-19** ... at Cubs
20-**21-22** ... Colorado
23-**24-25** ... St. Louis
26-27 ... Houston
29-30-31 ... at Atlanta

JUNE

1 ... at Atlanta
2-**3** ... at Florida
4-5 ... at Los Angeles
6-7-8 ... Atlanta
9-**10-11** ... Florida
12-13 ... *at Texas
14-**15** ... *at Anaheim
17-**18** ... *Seattle
19-20-**21**-22 ... L.A.
23-**24-25** ... San Diego
26-27-28-**29** at Colorado
30 ... *at Seattle

JULY

1 ... *at Seattle
2-3 ... *Oakland
4-5-6 ... Colorado
10-11-12-**13** ... at L.A.
14-15 ... at San Diego
16-**17** ... at Houston
18-19-**20**-21 at St. Louis
22-**23-24** ... Philadelphia
25-**26-27** ... Pitt.
29-**30** ... Mets

AUGUST

1-**2-3**-4 ... at Cincinnati
5-**6-7** ... at Cubs
8-9-**10** ... at Montreal
11-**12** ... Cincinnati
13-14 ... Cubs
15-**16-17** ... Montreal
18-19-20 at Philadelphia
22-23-**24** ... at Pittsburgh
25-26-**27** ... at Mets
28-29 ... *Texas
30-31 ... *Anaheim

SEPTEMBER

1-3 ... *at Oakland
4-5-**6-7** ... Houston
9-**10** ... St. Louis
12-**13-14** ... at Florida
15-**16** ... at Atlanta
17-**18** ... Los Angeles
19-20-**21-22** at San Diego
23-**24** ... at Colorado
26-**27-28** ... San Diego

INTERLEAGUE SCHEDULE

JUNE 12

Los Angeles at Oakland
San Diego at Anaheim
San Francisco at Texas
Colorado at Seattle

JUNE 13

Baltimore at Atlanta
Boston at Mets
Cleveland at St. Louis
Colorado at Seattle
Detroit at Montreal
Kansas City at Pittsburgh
Los Angeles at Oakland
Milwaukee at Cubs*
Minnesota at Houston
San Diego at Anaheim
San Francisco at Texas
Toronto at Philadelphia
White Sox at Cincinnati
Yankees at Florida

JUNE 14

Detroit at Montreal
Kansas City at Pittsburgh
Los Angeles at Seattle
Milwaukee at Cubs*
Minnesota at Houston
San Diego at Texas
Cleveland at St. Louis
San Francisco at Anaheim
Toronto at Philadelphia
White Sox at Cincinnati*
Yankees at Florida
Colorado at Oakland*
Baltimore at Atlanta*
Boston at Mets*

JUNE 15

Baltimore at Atlanta*
Boston at Mets
Cleveland at St. Louis*
Colorado at Oakland*
Detroit at Montreal*
Kansas City at Pittsburgh*
Los Angeles at Seattle*
Milwaukee at Cubs*
Minnesota at Houston*
San Diego at Texas
San Francisco at Anaheim*
Toronto at Philadelphia*
White Sox at Cincinnati*
Yankees at Florida*

JUNE 16

Atlanta at Toronto
Cincinnati at Cleveland
Cubs at White Sox*
Florida at Detroit
Houston at Kansas City
Mets at Yankees
Montreal at Baltimore
Philadelphia at Boston
Pittsburgh at Minnesota
St. Louis at Milwaukee

JUNE 17

Anaheim at Los Angeles
Atlanta at Toronto
Cincinnati at Cleveland
Cubs at White Sox*
Florida at Detroit
Houston at Kansas City
Mets at Yankees
Montreal at Baltimore
Oakland at San Diego
Philadelphia at Boston
Pittsburgh at Minnesota
St. Louis at Milwaukee
Seattle at San Francisco
Texas at Colorado

JUNE 18

Anaheim at Los Angeles
Atlanta at Toronto
Cincinnati at Cleveland
Cubs at White Sox
Florida at Detroit*
Houston at Kansas City
Mets at Yankees*
Montreal at Baltimore*
Oakland at San Diego
Philadelphia at Boston
Pittsburgh at Minnesota*
St. Louis at Milwaukee
Seattle at San Francisco*
Texas at Colorado*

JUNE 30

Anaheim at Colorado
Atlanta at Yankees
Cleveland at Houston
Florida at Boston
Kansas City at Cubs*
Mets at Detroit
Milwaukee at Cincinnati
Minnesota at St. Louis
Montreal at Toronto
Philadelphia at Baltimore
San Diego at Oakland
San Francisco at Seattle
Texas at Los Angeles
White Sox at Pittsburgh

JULY 1

Anaheim at Colorado*
Atlanta at Yankees
Cleveland at Houston
Florida at Boston
Kansas City at Cubs*
Mets at Detroit
Milwaukee at Cincinnati
Minnesota at St. Louis
Montreal at Toronto*
Philadelphia at Baltimore
San Diego at Oakland*
San Francisco at Seattle*
Texas at Los Angeles
White Sox at Pittsburgh

JULY 2

Atlanta at Yankees*
Cleveland at Houston
Colorado at Texas
Florida at Boston
Kansas City at Cubs*
Los Angeles at Anaheim
Mets at Detroit*
Milwaukee at Cincinnati*
Minnesota at St. Louis
Montreal at Toronto
Oakland at San Francisco*
Philadelphia at Baltimore*
Seattle at San Diego
White Sox at Pittsburgh

JULY 3

Colorado at Texas
Los Angeles at Anaheim
Oakland at San Francisco
Seattle at San Diego

AUGUST 28

Anaheim at San Diego*
Oakland at Los Angeles
Seattle at Colorado
Texas at San Francisco

AUGUST 29

Anaheim at San Diego
Atlanta at Boston
Cincinnati at Minnesota
Cubs at Cleveland
Florida at Toronto
Houston at White Sox
Mets at Baltimore
Montreal at Yankees
Oakland at Los Angeles
Philadelphia at Detroit
Pittsburgh at Milwaukee
St. Louis at Kansas City
Seattle at Colorado
Texas at San Francisco

AUGUST 30

Anaheim at San Francisco*
Atlanta at Boston*
Cincinnati at Minnesota
Cubs at Cleveland*
Florida at Toronto*
Houston at White Sox
Mets at Baltimore
Montreal at Yankees*
Oakland at Colorado
Philadelphia at Detroit
Pittsburgh at Milwaukee
St. Louis at Kansas City
Seattle at Los Angeles
Texas at San Diego

AUGUST 31

Anaheim at San Francisco*
Atlanta at Boston*
Cincinnati at Minnesota*
Cubs at Cleveland*
Florida at Toronto*
Houston at White Sox*
Mets at Baltimore*
Montreal at Yankees*
Oakland at Colorado*
Philadelphia at Detroit*
Pittsburgh at Milwaukee*
St. Louis at Kansas City*
Seattle at Los Angeles*
Texas at San Diego*

SEPTEMBER 1

Baltimore at Florida*
Boston at Montreal
Colorado at Anaheim
Cleveland at Pittsburgh*
Detroit at Atlanta
Kansas City at Cincinnati*
Milwaukee at Houston*
Minnesota at Cubs*
San Diego at Seattle*
San Francisco at Oakland*
Toronto at Mets*
White Sox at St. Louis*
Yankees at Philadelphia*

SEPTEMBER 2

Baltimore at Florida
Boston at Montreal
Colorado at Anaheim
Cleveland at Pittsburgh
Detroit at Atlanta
Kansas City at Cincinnati
Los Angeles at Texas
Milwaukee at Houston
Minnesota at Cubs
Toronto at Mets
White Sox at St. Louis
Yankees at Philadelphia

SEPTEMBER 3

Baltimore at Florida
Boston at Montreal
Cleveland at Pittsburgh
Detroit at Atlanta*
Kansas City at Cincinnati
Los Angeles at Texas
Milwaukee at Houston
Minnesota at Cubs*
San Diego at Seattle*
San Francisco at Oakland
Toronto at Mets
White Sox at St. Louis
Yankees at Philadelphia

*Day games

SPRING TRAINING

AMERICAN LEAGUE

ANAHEIM ANGELS

Major League Club

Hotel Address: Fiesta Inn, 2100 South Priest Dr., Tempe, AZ 85282. Telephone: (602) 967-1441. **Complex Address:** Tempe Diablo Stadium, 2200 West Alameda, Tempe, AZ 85282. Telephone: (602) 438-4300.

Minor League Clubs

Hotel Address: None. **Complex Address:** Gene Autry Park, 4125 E. McKellips, Mesa, AZ 85205. Telephone: (602) 830-4137.

BALTIMORE ORIOLES

Major League Club

Hotel Address: Doubletree Suites Hotel, 555 NW 62nd St., Fort Lauderdale, FL 33309. Telephone: (954) 772-5400. **Complex Address:** Fort Lauderdale Stadium, 5301 NW 12th Ave., Fort Lauderdale, FL 33309. Telephone: (954) 776-1921.

Minor League Clubs

Hotel Address: Unavailable. **Complex Address:** Twin Lakes Park, 6700 Clark Road, Sarasota, FL 34243. Telephone: (941) 923-1996.

BOSTON RED SOX

Major League Club

Hotel Address: Sheraton Harborplace, 2500 Edwards Dr., Fort Myers, FL 33901. Telephone: (941) 337-0300. **Complex Address:** City of Palms Park, 2201 Edison Ave., Fort Myers, FL 33901. Telephone: (941) 334-4700.

Minor League Clubs

Hotel Address: Same as major league club. **Complex Address:** Red Sox Minor League Complex, 4301 Edison Ave., Fort Myers, FL 33916. Telephone: (813) 332-8106. FAX: (813) 332-8107.

CHICAGO WHITE SOX

Major League Club

Hotel Address: Sleep Inn, 900 University Parkway, Sarasota, FL 34234. Telephone: (941) 359-8558. **Complex Address:** Ed Smith Stadium, 1090 North Euclid Ave., Sarasota, FL 34237. Telephone: (941) 366-8451.

Minor League Clubs

Hotel Address: Quality Inn Suites, 2303 First St. East (U.S. 41), Bradenton, FL 34208. Telephone: (941) 747-6465. **Complex Address:** Same as major league club.

CLEVELAND INDIANS

Major League Club

Hotel Address: Holiday Inn, 1150 Third St. SW, Winter Haven, FL 33880. Telephone: (941) 294-4451. **Complex Address:** Chain of Lakes Park, Cypress Gardens Blvd. and US 17, Winter Haven, FL 33880. Telephone: 941) 291-5803. FAX: (941) 299-4491.

Minor League Clubs

Hotel, Complex Address: Same as major league club.

DETROIT TIGERS

Major League Club

Hotel Address: Hoilday Inn South, 3405 South Florida Ave., Lakeland, FL 33803. Telephone: (941) 646-5731. **Complex Address:** Tigertown, P.O. Box 90187, Lakeland, FL 33804. Telephone: (941) 686-8075. FAX: (941) 688-9589.

Minor League Clubs

Hotel, Complex Address: Tigertown, P.O. Box 90187, Lakeland, FL 33804. Telephone: (941) 686-8075. FAX: (941) 688-9589.

KANSAS CITY ROYALS

Major League Club

Hotel Address: Ramada Limited, 4825 Hwy. 27 North, Davenport, FL 33837. Telephone: (941) 424-2211. **Complex Address:** Baseball City Stadium, 300 Stadium Way, Davenport, FL 33837. Telephone: (941) 424-7211.

Minor League Clubs

Hotel Address: Same as major league club. **Complex Address:** Minor league building, 300 Stadium Way, Davenport, FL 33837. Telephone: (941) 424-7272. FAX: (941) 424-3094.

MILWAUKEE BREWERS

Major League Club

Hotel Address: The Dobson Ranch Inn, 1666 South Dobson Road,

Chandler, AZ 85248. Telephone: (602) 831-7000. **Complex Address:** Compadre Stadium, 4001 South Alma School Road, Chandler, AZ 85248. Telephone: (602) 895-6000. FAX: (602) 895-2649.

Minor League Clubs

Hotel Address: Quality Inn Phoenix Southeast, 5121 East La Puente Ave., Phoenix, AZ 85044. Telephone: (602) 893-3900. **Complex Address:** Chandler Complex, 4500 South Alma School Road, Chandler, AZ 85248. Telephone: (602) 895-1412. FAX: (602) 895-1414.

MINNESOTA TWINS

Major League Club

Hotel Address: Holiday Inn Select, 13051 Bell Tower Dr., Fort Myers, FL 33907. Telephone: (941) 482-2900. **Complex Address:** Lee County Sports Complex/Hammond Stadium, 14100 Six Mile Cypress Pkwy., Fort Myers, FL 33912. Telephone: (941) 768-4200. FAX: (941) 768-4207.

Minor League Clubs

Hotel Address: Radisson Hotel,12635 Cleveland Ave. (US 41), Fort Myers, FL 33907. Telephone: (941) 936-4300. **Complex Address:** Lee County Sports Complex, 14200 Six Mile Cypress Pkwy., Fort Myers, FL 33912. Telephone: (941) 768-4280.

NEW YORK YANKEES

Major League Club

Hotel Address: Radisson Bay Harbor Inn, 770 Courtney Campbell Causeway, Tampa, FL 33607. Telephone: (813) 281-8900. **Complex Address:** Legends Field, 3802 West Dr. Martin Luther King Blvd., Tampa, FL, 33614. Telephone: (813) 875-7753. FAX: (813) 673-3199.

Minor League Clubs

Hotel Address: Same as major league club. **Complex Address:** Yankees Minor League Complex, 3102 North Himes Ave., Tampa, FL 33607. Telephone: (813) 875-7753.

OAKLAND ATHLETICS

Major League Club

Hotel Address: Airport Hilton, 2435 S. 47th St., Phoenix, AZ 85034. Telephone: (602) 894-1600. **Complex Address:** Phoenix Municipal Stadium, 5999 East Van Buren, Phoenix, AZ 85008. Telephone: (602) 225-9400. FAX: (602) 225-9473.

Minor League Clubs

Hotel Address: Unavailable. **Complex Address:** Papago Park Baseball Complex, 1802 North 64th St., Phoenix, AZ 85004. Telephone: (602) 949-5951. FAX: (602) 945-0557.

SEATTLE MARINERS

Major League Club

Hotel Address: Wyndham Hotel, 10220 N. Metro Parkway East, Phoenix, AZ 85051. Telephone: (602) 997-5900. **Complex Address:** Peoria Sports Complex, 15707 N. 83rd Ave., Peoria, AZ 85382. Telephone: (602) 412-9000. FAX: (602) 412-9002.

Minor League Clubs

Hotel Address: Comfort Inn, 1711 W. Bell Rd., Phoenix, AZ 85023. Telephone: (602) 866-2089. **Complex Address:** Same as major league club.

TAMPA BAY DEVIL RAYS

Minor Legue Clubs

Hotel Address: St. Petersburg Bayfront Hilton, 333 1st St. South, St. Petersburg, FL 33701. Telephone: (813) 894-5000. **Stadium Address:** Huggins-Stengel Field, 1320 5th St. North, St. Petersburg, FL 33705. Telephone: (813) 825-3260. FAX: (813) 825-3262.

TEXAS RANGERS

Major League Club

Hotel Address: Days Inn, 1941 Tamiami Trail, Murdock, FL 33938. Telephone: (941) 627-8900. **Stadium Address:** Charlotte County Stadium, 3609 El Jobean Road, Port Charlotte, FL 33948. Telephone: (941) 625-9500. FAX: (941) 624-5168.

Minor League Clubs

Hotel, Complex Address: Same as major league club.

TORONTO BLUE JAYS

Major League Club

Hotel: None. **Stadium Addresses:** Englebert Complex, 1700 Solon Ave., Dunedin, FL 34697. Telephone: (813) 733-3339. FAX: (813) 734-3862; Dunedin Stadium, 373 Douglas Ave., Dunedin, FL 34697. Telephone: (813) 733-9302. FAX: (813) 734-2382.

Minor League Clubs

Hotel Address: Comfort Inn, 2890 U.S. 19 North, Clearwater, FL 34698. Telephone: (813) 796-0135. **Complex Address:** Englebert Complex, 1700 Solon Ave., Dunedin, FL 34697. Telephone: (813) 733-3339. FAX: (813) 734-3862.

NATIONAL LEAGUE

ARIZONA DIAMONDBACKS

Minor League Clubs

Hotel Address: Inn Suites, 1450 Castle Dome Ave., Yuma, AZ 85365. Telephone: (520) 783-8341. **Complex Address:** Ray Kroc Baseball Complex, Desert Sun Stadium, 1280 Desert Sun Dr., Yuma, AZ 85365. Telephone: Unavailable.

ATLANTA BRAVES

Major League Club

Hotel Address: Palm Beach Gardens Marriott, 4000 RCA Blvd., Palm Beach Gardens, FL 33410. Telephone: (561) 622-8888. **Stadium Address:** Municipal Stadium, 715 Hank Aaron Dr., West Palm Beach, FL 33402. Telephone: (561) 683-6100. FAX: (561) 471-3647.

Minor League Clubs

Hotel Address: Unavailable. **Complex Address:** Municipal Stadium, 715 Hank Aaron Dr., West Palm Beach, FL 33401. Telephone: (561) 471-3620. FAX: (561) 471-3645.

CHICAGO CUBS

Major League Club

Hotel Address: Mezona Motor Inn, 250 West Main St., Mesa, AZ 85201. Telephone: (602) 834-9233. **Complex Address:** HoHoKam Park, 1235 North Center St., Mesa, AZ 85201. Telephone: (602) 668-0500.

Minor League Clubs

Hotel Address: Motel 6, 630 West Main St., Mesa, AZ 85201. Telephone: (602) 969-8111. **Complex Address:** Fitch Park, 6th and Center Streets, Mesa, AZ 85201. Telephone: (602) 668-0500.

CINCINNATI REDS

Major League Club

Hotel Address: Ramada Inn, Route 39 at I-4, Plant City, FL 33566. Telephone: (813) 752-1878. **Complex Address:** Plant City Stadium, 1900 South Park Road, Plant City, FL 33566. Telephone: (813) 752-1878. FAX: (813) 757-6351.

Minor League Clubs

Hotel, Complex Address: Same as major league club.

COLORADO ROCKIES

Major League Club

Hotel Address: Viscount Suites, 4855 East Broadway, Tucson, AZ 85711. Telephone: (520) 745-6500. **Complex Address:** Hi Corbett Field, 3400 East Camino Campestre, Tucson, AZ 85716. Telephone: (520) 322-4549. FAX: (520) 322-4545.

Minor League Clubs

Hotel Address: Holiday Inn-Palo Verde, 4550 South Palo Verde Blvd., Tucson, AZ 85711. Telephone: (520) 746-1161. **Complex Address:** Same as major league club.

FLORIDA MARLINS

Major League Club

Hotel Address: Airport Hilton, 200 Rialto Place, Viera, FL 32940. Telephone: (407) 633-9200. **Complex Address:** Space Coast Stadium, 5800 Stadium Pkwy., Melbourne, FL 32940. Telephone: (407) 633-9200. FAX: (407) 633-9210.

Minor League Clubs

Hotel Address: Holiday Inn Cocoa Beach Resort, 1300 North Atlantic Ave., Cocoa Beach, FL 32931. Telephone: (407) 783-2271. **Complex Address:** Carl Barger Baseball Complex, 5600 Stadium Pkwy., Melbourne, FL 32940. Telephone: (407) 633-8119. Telephone: (407) 633-9216.

HOUSTON ASTROS

Major League Club

Hotel Address: Renaissance Orlando Hotel Airport, 5445 Forbes Place, Orlando, FL 32812. Telephone: (407) 240-1000. **Complex Address:** Osceola County Stadium, 1000 Bill Beck Blvd., Kissimmee, FL 34744. Telephone: (407) 933-6500. FAX: (407) 847-4901.

Minor League Clubs

Hotel Address: Holiday Inn-Kissimmee, 2009 West Vine St. (US 192), Kissimmee, FL 34741. Telephone: (407) 846-2713. FAX: (407) 846-8695. **Complex Address:** Same as major league club. Telephone: (407) 846-2713. FAX: (407) 846-8695.

LOS ANGELES DODGERS

Major League Club

Hotel/Complex Address: Dodgertown, 4001 26th St., Vero Beach, FL 32961. Telephone: (561) 569-4900. FAX: (561) 569-4900.

Minor League Clubs

Hotel, Complex Address: Same as major league club.

MONTREAL EXPOS

Major League Club

Hotel Address: Holiday Inn-Airport, 1301 Belvedere Road, West Palm Beach, FL 33405. **Telephone:** (561) 659-3880. **Complex Address:** West Palm Beach Municpal Stadium, 715 Hank Aaron Dr., West Palm Beach, FL 33401. Telephone: (561) 684-6801. FAX: (561) 681-4876.

Minor League Clubs

Hotel Address: Comfort Inn, 1901 Palm Beach Lakes Blvd., West Palm Beach, FL 33409. Telephone: (561) 689-6100. **Complex Address:** Expos Minor League Development Center, Santaluces High School, 6850 Lawrence Road, Lantana, FL 33462. Telephone: (561) 433-1990. FAX: (561) 433-3481.

NEW YORK METS

Major League Club

Hotel Address: Holiday Inn, 10120 South Federal Hwy., Port St. Lucie, FL 34952. Telephone: (561) 337-2200. FAX: (561) 335-7872. **Complex Address:** St. Lucie County Sports Complex, 525 NW Peacock Blvd., Port St. Lucie, FL 34986. Telephone: (561) 871-2100. FAX: (561) 878-2181.

Minor League Clubs

Hotel Address: Same as major league club. **Complex Address:** Mets Minor League Complex, 525 NW Peacock Blvd., Port St. Lucie, FL 34986. Telephone: (407) 871-2132. FAX: (407) 871-2181.

PHILADELPHIA PHILLIES

Major League Club

Hotel: None. **Complex Address:** Jack Russell Memorial Stadium, 800 Phillies Dr., Clearwater, FL 34615. Telephone: (813) 441-9943. FAX: (813) 461-7768.

Minor League Clubs

Hotel Address: Unavailable. **Complex Address:** Carpenter Complex, 651 Old Coachman Road, Clearwater, FL 34625. Telephone: (813) 799-0503. FAX: (813) 447-3924.

PITTSBURGH PIRATES

Major League Club

Hotel Address: Pirate City, 1701 Roberto Clemente Memorial Dr. (27th St. East), Bradenton, FL 34208. Telephone: (941) 747-3031. FAX: (941) 747-9549. **Complex Address:** McKechnie Field, 17th Ave. West and 9th St. West, Bradenton, FL 34208. Telephone: (941) 748-4610.

Minor League Clubs

Hotel, Complex Address: Same as major league club.

ST. LOUIS CARDINALS

Major League Club

Hotel Address: St. Petersburg Hilton and Towers, 333 First St. South, St. Petersburg, FL 33701. Telephone: (813) 894-5000. **Complex Address:** Al Lang Stadium, 180 Second Ave. SE, St. Petersburg, FL 33701. Telephone: (813) 896-4641. FAX: (813) 822-2843.

Minor League Clubs

Hotel Address: Best Western Mirage, 5005 34th St. North, St. Petersburg, FL 33714. Telephone: (813) 894-5000. **Complex Address:** Busch Complex, 7901 30th Ave. North, St. Petersburg, FL 33733. Telephone: (813) 345-5300. FAX: (813) 345-4279.

SAN DIEGO PADRES

Major League Club

Hotel Address: Premier Inns, 10402 Black Canyon Hwy., Phoenix, AZ 85051. Telephone: (602) 943-2371. **Complex Address:** Peoria Sports Complex, 8131 West Paradise Lane, Peoria, AZ 85382. Telephone: (602) 486-7000. FAX: (602) 486-9341.

Minor League Clubs

Hotel Address: Premier Inn at Metro Center, 10402 Black Canyon Highway, Phoenix, AZ 85051. Telephone: (602) 943-2371. **Complex Address:** Same as major league club. Telephone: (602) 486-7000. FAX: (602) 486-7154.

SAN FRANCISCO GIANTS

Major League Club

Hotel Address: Scottsdale Plaza Resort, 7200 North Scottsdale Rd., Scottsdale, AZ 85253. Telephone: (602) 948-5000. **Complex Address:** Scottsdale Stadium, 7408 East Osborn Rd., Scottsdale, AZ 85251. Telephone: (602) 990-7972. FAX: (602) 990-2643.

Minor League Clubs

Hotel Address: Days Inn, 4710 North Scottsdale Rd., Scottsdale, AZ 85351. Telephone: (602) 947-5411. **Complex Address:** Indian School Park, 4289 North Hayden Road at Camelback Road, Scottsdale, AZ 85251. Telephone: (602) 990-0052.

GENERAL INFORMATION

Major Leagues

MAJOR LEAGUE BASEBALL PRODUCTIONS

THE PHOENIX COMMUNICATIONS GROUP, INC.

Mailing Address: 3 Empire Blvd., South Hackensack, NJ 07606. **Telephone:** (201) 807-0888. **FAX:** (201) 807-0272.

Chairman: Joe Podesta. **President:** James Holland. **Senior Vice President, Executive Producer:** Geoff Belinfante. **Vice President, Sales and Marketing:** Rich Domich. **Vice President, Program Development:** Jim Scott. **Director, Marketing and Home Video:** Chris Brande.

MAJOR LEAGUE PLAYERS ASSOCIATION

Mailing Address: 12 East 49th St., 24th Floor, New York, NY 10017. **Telephone:** (212) 826-0808. **FAX:** (212) 752-3649.

Year Founded: 1966.

Executive Director, General Counsel: Donald Fehr.

Special Assistants: Mark Belanger, Tony Bernazard.

Associate General Counsel: Eugene Orza. **Assistant General Counsel:** Lauren Rich, Doyle Pryor, Michael Weiner. **Counsel:** Robert Lenaghan, Arthur Schack.

Director of Licensing: Judy Heeter. **Manager, Marketing Services:** Allyne Price. **Manager, Retail Licensing:** Tina Morris. **Director of Communications:** Richard Weiss.

Executive Board: Player representatives of the 28 major league clubs.

League Representatives: American League—David Cone; **National League**—Tom Glavine.

MAJOR LEAGUE SCOUTING BUREAU

Mailing Address: 23712 Birtcher Dr., Suite A, Lake Forest, CA 92630. **Telephone:** (714) 458-7600. **FAX:** (714) 458-9454.

Year Founded: 1974.

Director: Don Pries.

Assistant Director: Frank Marcos. **Administrator:** RoseMary Durgin. **Secretary:** Rease Leverenz.

Board of Directors: Bill Murray, chairman; Bill Bavasi (Angels), Dan Duquette (Red Sox), Bob Gebhard (Rockies), Roland Hemond (Diamondbacks), Joe Klein (Tigers), Joe McIlvaine (Mets), Don Pries, Randy Smith (Tigers), Art Stewart (Royals).

Scouts: Mike Childers (Lexington, KY), Dick Colpaert (Utica, MI), Jeff Cornell (Lee's Summit, MO), Dan Dixon (Temecula, CA), Art Gardner (Walnut Grove, MS), Rusty Gerhardt (New London, TX), Mike Hamilton (Arlington, TX), Doug Horning (Schereville, IN), Don Jacoby (Winter Haven, FL), Brad Kohler (Bethlehem, PA), Don Kohler (North Plainfield, NJ), Mike Larson (Waseca, MN), Jethro McIntyre (Pittsburg, CA), Lenny Merullo (Reading, MA), Paul Mirocke (Lutz, FL), Carl Moesche (Gresham, OR), Rick Oliver (La Verne, CA), Tim Osborne (Marietta, GA), Buddy Pritchard (Fullerton, CA), Gary Randall (Rock Hill, SC), Al Ronning (Sunnyvale, CA), Kevin Saucier (Pensacola, FL), Pat Shortt (Rockville Centre, NY), Craig Smajstrla (Pearland, TX), Ed Sukla (Irvine, CA), Marv Thompson (Glendale, AZ), Tom Valcke (Fresno, CA), Jim Walton (Shattuck, OK).

Canadian Scouts: Walt Burrows (Brentwood Bay, B.C.), supervisor; Jim Baba (Saskatoon, Saskatchewan), Curtis Bailey (Red Deer, Alberta), Kevin Bly (North York, Ontario), Bob Cohen (North York, Ontario), Gerry Falk (Carman, Manitoba), Bill Green (Vancouver, B.C.), Sean Gulliver (St. John's, Newfoundland), Lowell Hodges (Sidney, B.C.), Ian Jordan (Chomedey, Quebec), Jay Lapp (London, Ontario), Ken Lenihan (Bedford, N.S.), Dave McConnell (Kelowna, B.C.), Dave McManus (Hanwell, N.B.), Jean Marc Mercier (Charlesbourg, Quebec).

Puerto Rican Scout: Pepito Centeno (Bayamon), supervisor.

MAJOR LEAGUE UMPIRES ASSOCIATION

Mailing Address: 1735 Market St., Suite 3420, Philadelphia, PA 19103. **Telephone:** (215) 979-3200. **FAX:** (215) 979-3201.

Year Founded: 1967.

General Counsel: Richie Phillips. **Associate General Counsel:** Pat Campbell.

MLB UMPIRE DEVELOPMENT PROGRAM

Mailing Address: P.O. Box A, St. Petersburg, FL 33731. **Telephone:** (813) 823-1286. **FAX:** (813) 823-7212.

Year Founded: 1965.

Executive Director: Edwin Lawrence.

Administrative Secretary: Vickie Jones. **Bookkeeper:** Lillian Patterson.

Director of Field Supervision: Mike Fitzpatrick (Kalamazoo, MI).

Evaluators/Instructors: Dennis Cregg (Webster, MA), Tom Lepperd (Des Moines, IA), Dick Nelson (Enfield, CT).

Area Observer: Joe Linsalata (Hollywood, FL).

UMPIRE DEVELOPMENT SCHOOLS

Harry Wendelstedt Umpire School

Mailing Address: 88 South St. Andrews Drive, Ormond Beach, FL 32174. **Telephone:** (904) 672-4879.

Operator: Harry Wendelstedt.

Brinkman-Froemming Umpiring School

Mailing Address: 1021 Indian River Drive, Cocoa, FL 32922. **Telephone:** (407) 639-1515. **FAX:** (407) 633-7018.

Owner/Director: Joe Brinkman.

Academy of Professional Umpiring

Mailing Address: 12885 Research Blvd., Suite 107, Austin, TX 78750. **Telephone:** (512) 335-5959. **FAX:** (512) 335-5411.

Operator: Jim Evans.

PROFESSIONAL BASEBALL ATHLETIC TRAINERS SOCIETY

Mailing Address: P.O. Box 386, Atlanta, GA 30361. **Telephone:** (404) 875-4000. **FAX:** (404) 892-8560.

Year Founded: 1983.

President: Kent Biggerstaff (Pittsburgh Pirates). **American League Representative:** John Adam (Milwaukee Brewers). **National League Representative:** Gene Gieselmann (St. Louis Cardinals). **Secretary:** Dave Labossiere (Houston Astros).

General Counsel: Rollin Mallernee.

NATIONAL BASEBALL HALL OF FAME AND MUSEUM

Office Address: 25 Main St., Cooperstown, NY 13326. **Mailing Address:** P.O. Box 590, Cooperstown, NY 13326. **Telephone:** (607) 547-7200. **FAX:** (607) 547-2044.

Year Founded: 1939.

Chairman: Ed Stack. **President:** Don Marr. **Vice President:** Frank Simio. **Controller:** Fran Althiser. **Registrar:** Peter Clark. **Director of Public Relations:** Jeff Idelson. **Assistant Director of Public Relations:** John Ralph. **Director of Retail Marketing:** Barbara Shinn. **Curator:** Ted Spencer. **Librarian:** Jim Gates.

1997 Hall of Fame Induction Ceremonies: Aug. 3, 2:30 p.m., Cooperstown, NY. **Hall of Fame Game:** Aug. 4, Los Angeles vs. San Diego, 3:30 p.m.

NEGRO LEAGUES BASEBALL MUSEUM

Mailing Address: 1601 East 18th St., Suite 110, Kansas City, MO 64108. **Telephone:** (816) 221-1920. **FAX:** (816) 221-8424.

Year Founded: 1990.

Chairman: Buck O'Neil. **President:** Randall Ferguson.

Executive Director: Don Motley. **Curator:** Raymond Doswell.

ALUMNI ASSOCIATIONS

MLB Players Alumni Association

Mailing Address, National Headquarters: 3637 4th St. North, Suite 480, St. Petersburg, FL 33704. **Telephone:** (813) 822-3399. **FAX:** (813) 822-6300.

Mailing Address, Corporate Marketing: 381 Mansfield Ave., Suite 115, Pittsburgh, PA 15220. **Telephone:** (412) 928-0885. **FAX:** (412) 928-9720.

Year Founded: 1988.

President: Brooks Robinson.

Vice Presidents: Bobby Bonds, Bob Boone, George Brett, Carl Erskine, Mike Hegan, Chuck Hinton, Al Kaline, Rusty Staub, Robin Yount.

Secretary/Treasurer: Fred Valentine.

Board of Directors: Nelson Briles, Darrel Chaney, Denny Doyle, Jim "Mudcat" Grant, Rich Hand, Jim Hannan, Jerry Moses, Ken Sanders, Fred Valentine.

Executive Vice President: Carl Foster. **General Counsel:** Sam Moore. **Membership Coordinator:** Chandra Van Nostrand. **Director of Special Events:** Chris Torgusen. **Special Events Coordinators:** Drew Cloud, Mike Morey, Toby O'Brien.

Association of Professional Baseball Players of America

Mailing Address: 12062 Valley View St., Suite 211, Garden Grove, CA

92845. **Telephone:** (714) 892-9900. **FAX:** (714) 897-0233.

Year Founded: 1924.

President: John McHale.

1st Vice President: Joe DiMaggio. **2nd Vice President:** Arthur Richman. **3rd Vice President:** Bob Kennedy.

Advisory Council: Calvin Griffith, Eddie Sawyer.

Secretary-Treasurer: Chuck Stevens.

Baseball Assistance Team (BAT)

Mailing Address: 350 Park Ave., New York, NY 10022. **Telephone:** (212) 339-7884. **FAX:** (212) 888-8632.

Year Founded: 1986.

Chairman: Ralph Branca. **President:** Joe Garagiola. **Vice Presidents:** Joe Black, Earl Wilson. **Secretary:** Tom Ostertag. **Treasurer:** Jeff White.

Executive Director: Frank Slocum. **Administrator:** Eleanor Mieszerski. **Consultant:** Sam McDowell.

BASEBALL CHAPEL

Mailing Address: 21755 West Ravine Road, Forest Lake, IL 60047. **Telephone:** (847) 438-0978. **FAX:** (847) 438-6554.

Year Founded: 1972.

President: Gary Carter. **Vice President:** Tim Burke.

Executive Director: Vince Nauss.

Media Information

BASEBALL STATISTICS, RESEARCH

ELIAS SPORTS BUREAU, INC.

Official Major League Statistician

Mailing Address: 500 Fifth Ave., New York, NY 10110. **Telephone:** (212) 869-1530. **FAX:** (212) 354-0980.

General Manager: Seymour Siwoff.

HOWE SPORTSDATA INTERNATIONAL, INC.

Official Minor League Statistician

Mailing Address: Boston Fish Pier, West Bldg. #2, Suite 306, Boston, MA 02210. **Telephone:** (617) 951-0070. **Stats Service:** (617) 951-1379. **FAX:** (617) 737-9960.

President: Jay Virshbo. **Executive Vice President:** Jim Keller. **Vice President/Records and Administration:** Mike Walczak. **Vice President/Client Services:** Tom Graham. **Operations Manager:** Chris Pollari. **Communications Manager:** John Foley. **Data Processing Manager:** Wally Kent. **Managing Editor:** Vin Vitro. **Manager, Night Operations:** Paul LaRocca. **Assistant Manager, Night Operations:** Brian Joura. **Statisticians:** Bob Chaban, Bob Correia, Dan Landesman, Marshall Wright.

West Coast Office: P.O. Box 5061, San Mateo, CA 94402. **Telephone:** (415) 345-2907. **FAX:** (415) 571-1217. **Historical Consultant:** Bill Weiss.

STATS, Inc.

Mailing Address: 8131 Monticello Ave., Skokie, IL 60076. **Telephone:** (847) 676-3322. **FAX:** (847) 676-0821.

President: John Dewan. **Vice Presidents/Systems:** Arthur Ashley, Susan Dewan. **Vice President/Finance, Administration and Human Resources:** Bob Meyerhoff. **Vice President/Publications:** Don Zminda. **Vice President/National Sales:** Jim Capuano. **Director/Major League Operations:** Craig Wright. **Director/Sports Operations:** Doug Abel. **Assistant Director/Systems:** Mike Canter. **Senior Analyst/Systems:** David Pinto. **Statisticians:** Jeff Chernow, Jason Kinsey, Jim Osborne, John Sasman, Matt Senter, Allan Spear, Peter Woelflein.

SOCIETY FOR AMERICAN BASEBALL RESEARCH

Mailing Address: P.O. Box 93183, Cleveland, OH 44101. **Telephone:** (216) 575-0500. **FAX:** (216) 575-0502.

Year Founded: 1971.

President: David Pietrusza (Scotia, NY). **Vice President:** Dick Beverage (Placentia, CA). **Secretary:** Norman Macht (Baltimore, MD). **Treasurer:** Paul Andresen (Corvallis, OR). **Directors:** Larry Gerlach, James Riley, Rick Salamon, David Vincent.

Executive Director: Morris Eckhouse. **Manager, Membership Services:** John Zajc.

Publications Director: Mark Alvarez.

TELEVISION NETWORKS

ESPN

Mailing Address: Connecticut Office—ESPN Plaza, Bristol, CT 06010. **Telephone:** (860) 585-2000. **FAX:** (860) 585-2400. **New York**

Office—605 Third Ave., New York, NY 10158. **Telephone:** (212) 916-9200. **FAX:** (212) 916-9312.

President, Chief Executive Officer: Steve Bornstein. **Executive Vice President, Administration:** Ed Durso.

Executive Vice President, Production: Howard Katz. **Senior Vice President, Programming:** John Wildhack. **Senior Vice President, Managing Director:** David Zucker. **Senior Vice President, Executive Editor:** John Walsh. **Vice President, Remote Production:** Jed Drake. **Vice President, Managing Editor, Studio Programs:** Bob Eaton. **Assistant Vice President and News Director, Studio Programs:** Vince Doria. **Vice President, Programming:** Steve Risser. **Senior Coordinating Producer, Baseball Tonight/Studio:** Bob Rauscher. **Coordinating Producer, Remote Production:** Tim Scanlan. **Coordinating Producer, Baseball Tonight/Studio:** Jeff Schneider.

Managers, Communications: Diane Lamb, Rob Tobias.

Sunday Night Telecasts: Play-by-play—Jon Miller. Analyst—Joe Morgan.

Studio Hosts: Chris Berman, Gary Miller, Karl Ravech. **Studio Analysts:** Peter Gammons, Harold Reynolds.

Play-by-Play Announcers: Chris Berman, Bob Carpenter, Joel Meyers, Dan Shulman, DeWayne Staats. **Analysts:** Dave Campbell, Buck Martinez, Jim Rooker.

FOX SPORTS

Mailing Address, Los Angeles: Sunset Building, 2nd Floor, 5746 Sunset Blvd., Los Angeles, CA 90028. **Telephone:** (213) 856-1234. **FAX:** (213) 462-5931. **Mailing Address, New York:** 1211 Avenue of the Americas, 2nd Floor, New York, NY 10036. **Telephone:** (212) 556-2500. **FAX:** (212) 354-6902.

President: David Hill. **Executive Producer:** Ed Goren. **Coordinating Producer, Baseball:** John Fillipelli. **Vice President, Public Relations:** Vince Wladika. **Director, Media Relations:** Lou D'Ermilio. **Publicist, Media Relations:** Dan Bell.

Play-by-Play Announcers (Analysts): Thom Brennaman (Bob Brenly), Joe Buck (Tim McCarver), John Rooney (Jeff Torborg), Josh Lewin (Ken Singleton).

NBC SPORTS

Mailing Address: 30 Rockefeller Plaza, Suite 1445, New York, NY 10112. **Telephone:** (212) 664-4444. **FAX:** (212) 664-3602.

President, NBC Sports: Dick Ebersol.

Vice President, Sports Information and Special Projects: Ed Markey. **Play-by-Play Announcers:** Bob Costas, Greg Gumbel. **Analysts:** Joe Morgan, Bob Uecker.

ABC SPORTS

Mailing Address: 47 West 66th St., New York, NY 10023. **Telephone:** (212) 456-7777. **FAX:** (212) 456-2930.

President, ABC Sports: Steve Bornstein. **Senior Vice President, Programming:** David Downs. **Senior Vice President, Production:** Steve Anderson. **Director of Media Relations:** Mark Mandel.

CBS SPORTS

Mailing Address: 51 W. 52nd St., New York, NY 10019. **Telephone:** (212) 975-5230. **FAX:** (212) 975-4074.

President, CBS Sports: Sean McManus. **Director of Communications:** Leslie Anne Wade.

CNN/SI

Mailing Address: One CNN Center, Atlanta, GA 30303. **Telephone:** (404) 878-1600. **FAX:** (404) 878-1601.

Managing Editor: Steve Robinson. **Coordinating Producer:** Greg Agvent. **Assignment Editor:** Tony Lamb. **Public Relations Coordinator:** Erskine McDaniel.

CTV (Canada)

Mailing Address: 250 Yonge St., Suite 1800, Toronto, Ontario M5B 2N8. **Telephone:** (416) 595-4100. **FAX:** (416) 595-0559.

Vice President, Sports: Doug Beeforth.

THE SPORTS NETWORK (Canada)

Mailing Address: 2225 Sheppard Ave. East, Suite 100, North York, Ontario M2J 5C2. **Telephone:** (416) 494-1212. **FAX:** (416) 490-7010.

Executive Vice President, General Manager: Rick Brace. **Supervising Producer, Baseball:** Rick Briggs. **Supervising Producer, News and Information:** Mike Day. **Manager, Public Relations:** Rosemary Pitfield.

Play-by-Play Announcers: Dan Shulman (Blue Jays), Dave Van Horne (Expos). **Analysts:** Buck Martinez (Blue Jays).

Baseball Today Tonight: Paul Romanuk (host), Pat Tabler (analyst).

SUPERSTATIONS

WGN, Chicago (Chicago Cubs, Chicago White Sox)

Mailing Address: 2501 Bradley Place, Chicago, IL 60618. **Telephone:** (773) 528-2311.

WTBS, Atlanta (Atlanta Braves)

Mailing Address: One CNN Center, P.O. Box 105366, Atlanta, GA 30348. **Telephone:** (404) 827-1700. **FAX:** (404) 827-1593.

Executive Producer: Glenn Diamond.

WWOR, New York (New York Mets)

Mailing Address: 9 Broadcast Plaza, Secaucus, NJ 07096. **Telephone:** (201) 330-2246. **FAX:** (201) 330-3844.

RADIO NETWORKS

ESPN SPORTS RADIO

Mailing Address: ESPN Plaza, Bristol, CT 06010. **Telephone:** (860) 585-2661. **FAX:** (860) 589-5523.

General Manager: Drew Hayes. **Executive Producer:** John Martin. **Program Director:** Len Weiner.

CBS

Mailing Address: 51 W. 52nd St., New York, NY 10019. **Telephone:** (212) 975-4321. **FAX:** (212) 975-3515.

Vice President, Executive Producer: Frank Murphy. **Director, Sports and Features:** David Kurman. **Vice President, Communications:** Helene Blieberg. **Manager, Communications:** Sina DeVito.

AP NETWORK SPORTS

Mailing Address: 1825 K St. NW, Washington, D.C. 20006. **Telephone:** (202) 736-9540.

Sports Director: Dave Lubeski.

PRESS ASSOCIATIONS

ASSOCIATED PRESS

Mailing Address: 50 Rockefeller Plaza, New York, NY 10020. **Telephone:** (212) 621-1630. **FAX:** (212) 621-1639.

Sports Editor: Terry Taylor. **Deputy Sports Editor:** Brian Friedman. **Agate Editor:** Paul Montella. **Sports Photo Editor:** Brian Horton. **Baseball Writers:** Ron Blum, Ben Walker, Tom Withers.

SPORTSTICKER

Mailing Address: Harborside Financial Center, 600 Plaza Two, 8th floor, Jersey City, NJ 07311. **Telephone:** (201) 309-1200. **FAX:** (800) 336-0383, (201) 860-9742.

Vice President, General Manager: Rick Alessandri. **Executive Director, News:** Jim Morganthaler. **General Manager, News:** John Mastroberardino. **Managing Editor:** Doug Mitler. **Director, Marketing Services:** Lou Monaco.

CANADIAN PRESS

Mailing Address: 36 King St. East, Toronto, Ontario M5C 2L9. **Telephone:** (416) 594-2154.

General Sports Editor: Neil Davidson. **Baseball Writer:** Doug Smith.

BASEBALL WRITERS ASSOCIATION OF AMERICA

Mailing Address: 78 Olive St., Lake Grove, NY 11755. **Telephone:** (516) 981-7938. **FAX:** (516) 585-4669.

President: Hal McCoy (Dayton, Ohio, Daily News). **Vice President:** Jim Street (Seattle Post-Intelligencer).

Board of Directors: Jerome Holtzman (Chicago Tribune), Rick Hummel (St. Louis Post-Dispatch), Paul Meyer (Pittsburgh Post-Gazette), Marty Noble (Newsday), Ray Ratto (San Francisco Examiner),

Secretary-Treasurer: Jack O'Connell (Hartford Courant). **Assistant Secretary:** Jack Lang (Sportsticker).

NATIONAL ASSOCIATION OF BASEBALL WRITERS AND BROADCASTERS

Mailing Address: P.O. Box A, St. Petersburg, FL 33731. **Telephone:** (813) 822-6937. **FAX:** (813) 821-5819.

Secretary-Treasurer: Jim Ferguson (National Association).

NATIONAL COLLEGIATE BASEBALL WRITERS ASSOCIATION

Mailing Address: 35 East Wacker Dr., Suite 650, Chicago, IL 60601. **Telephone:** (312) 553-0483. **FAX:** (312) 553-0495.

Board of Directors: Bo Carter (Big 12 Conference), Bob Bradley (Clemson), Tom Price (South Carolina).

President: Rod Commons (Washington State). **First Vice President:** Alan Cannon (Texas A&M). **Secretary-Treasurer:** Russ Anderson (Conference USA).

Newsletter Editor: John Askins, Sports Media Group, 1255 Florida Road, Suite 5, Durango, CO 81301.

NEWSPAPERS/PERIODICALS

USA TODAY

Mailing Address: 1000 Wilson Blvd., Arlington, VA 22229. **Telephone/Baseball Desk:** (703) 276-3731, 276-3725. **FAX:** (703) 558-3988.

Baseball Editors: John Porter, Denise Tom. **Baseball Columnist:** Hal Bodley. **Major League Beat Writers:** Rod Beaton (National Leage), Mel Antonen (American League). **Baseball Reporters:** Chuck Johnson, Mike Dodd. **Agate Editor:** Matt Seaman.

USA TODAY BASEBALL WEEKLY

Mailing Address: 1000 Wilson Blvd., 21st floor, Arlington, VA 22229. **Telephone:** (703) 558-5630. **FAX:** (703) 558-4678.

Publisher: Keith Cutler. **Executive Editor:** Lee Ivory. **Editor:** Paul White. **National Advertising Manager:** Jim Schiekofer. **Classified Advertising Manager:** Lynn Busby.

THE SPORTING NEWS

Mailing Address: 10176 Corporate Square Dr., Suite 200, St. Louis, MO 63132. **Telephone:** (314) 997-7111. **FAX:** (314) 997-0765.

Editor: John Rawlings. **Executive Editor:** Steve Meyerhoff. **Managing Editors:** Mike Nahrstedt, Bob Hille. **Senior Writers:** Michael Knisley, Steve Marantz.

SPORTS ILLUSTRATED

Mailing Address: Time & Life Building, 1271 Avenue of the Americas, New York, NY 10020. **Telephone:** (212) 522-1212. **FAX, Editorial:** (212) 522-4543. **FAX, Public Relations:** (212) 522-4832.

Managing Editor: Bill Colson. **Senior Editor, Baseball:** Paul Fichtenbaum. **Senior Writers:** Gerry Callahan, Tim Kurkjian, Tom Verducci.

Director of Communications: Art Berke. **Publicity Director:** Dave Mingey.

INSIDE SPORTS

Mailing Address: 990 Grove St., Evanston, IL 60201. **Telephone:** (847) 491-6440. **FAX:** (847) 491-0867.

President, Chief Executive Officer: Norman Jacobs. **Executive Vice President, Publisher:** Jerry Croft. **Editor:** Ken Leiker. **Photo Editor:** Steve Levin.

BASEBALL DIGEST

Mailing Address: 990 Grove St., Evanston, IL 60201. **Telephone:** (847) 491-6440. **FAX:** (847) 491-0867.

Editor: John Kuenster. **Managing Editor:** Bob Kuenster.

ATHLON'S BASEBALL

Mailing Address: 220 25th Ave. North, Suite 200, Nashville, TN 37203. **Telephone:** (615) 327-0747. **FAX:** (615) 327-1149.

Chief Executive Officer: Roger DiSilvestro. **Managing Editor:** Charlie Miller. **Senior Editor:** George Leonard. **Associate Managing Editor:** Suzanne Boggs.

STREET AND SMITH'S BASEBALL

Mailing Address: 342 Madison Ave., New York, NY 10017. **Telephone:** (212) 880-8698. **FAX:** (212) 880-4347.

Publisher: Sal Schiliro. **Editor:** Gerard Kavanagh.

SPRING TRAINING BASEBALL YEARBOOK

Mailing Address: Vanguard Sports Publications, P.O. Box 667, Chapel Hill, NC 27514. **Telephone:** (919) 967-2420. **FAX:** (919) 967-6294.

Publisher: Merle Thorpe. **Editor:** Myles Friedman.

COLLEGIATE BASEBALL

Mailing Address: P.O. Box 50566, Tucson, AZ 85703. **Telephone:** (520) 623-4530. **FAX:** (520) 624-5501.

Publisher: Lou Pavlovich. **Editor:** Lou Pavlovich Jr.

HIGH SCHOOL BASEBALL USA

Mailing Address: P.O. Box 8943, Cincinnati, OH 45208. **Telephone/FAX:** (606) 291-4463.

Editor: Jeff Spelman.

INTERNATIONAL BASEBALL RUNDOWN

Mailing Address: P.O. Box 608, Glen Ellyn, IL 60138. **Telephone:** (630) 790-3087. **FAX:** (630) 790-3182.

Editor: Jeff Elijah.

TOTAL BASEBALL

Mailing Address: 205 Main St., Westport, CT 06880. **Telephone:** (203) 454-2451. **FAX:** (203) 454-8761.

Partners: Mike Gershman, John Thorn. **Statistician:** Pete Palmer. **Managing Editor:** David Pietrusza.

HOBBY PUBLICATIONS

BECKETT PUBLICATIONS

Mailing Address: 15850 Dallas Parkway, Dallas, TX 75248. **Telephone:** (972) 991-6657. **FAX:** (972) 991-8930.

Managing Editor: Mike Payne. **Associate Editor, Beckett Baseball Card Monthly:** Tracy Hackler. **Beckett Preview '97:** Tim Polzer, senior editor.

KRAUSE PUBLICATIONS

Mailing Address: 700 East State St., Iola, WI 54990. **Telephone:** (715) 445-2214. **FAX:** (715) 445-4087.

Publisher: Hugh McAloon.

Editor, Fantasy Baseball/Sports Cards Magazine: Greg Ambrosius. **Editor, Sports Collectors Digest:** Tom Mortenson.

TEAM PUBLICATIONS

COMAN PUBLISHING, INC.

(Atlanta Braves, Boston Red Sox, New York Mets)

Mailing Address: P.O. Box 2331, Durham, NC 27702. **Telephone:** (800) 421-7751; (919) 688-0218. **FAX:** (919) 682-1532.

Publisher: Stuart Coman.

Editor, Tomahawk (Atlanta Braves): Bill Ballew. **Managing Editor, New York Mets Inside Pitch**: Todd McGee. **Editor, Diehard** (Boston Red Sox): George Whitney.

PHILLIES REPORT

(Philadelphia Phillies)

Mailing Address: P.O. Box 157, Springfield, PA 19064. **Telephone:** (610) 543-4077. **Editor:** Rich Westcott.

VINE LINE

(Chicago Cubs)

Mailing Address: 1060 W. Addison St., Chicago, IL 60613. **Telephone:** (773) 404-2827. **Managing Editor:** Ernie Roth. **Editor:** Jay Rand.

YANKEES MAGAZINE

(New York Yankees)

Mailing Address: Yankee Stadium, Bronx, NY 10451. **Telephone:** (718) 579-4495. **Publisher:** Tim Wood. **Editor:** Pat McEvoy.

JET MEDIA

(Indians Ink)

Mailing Address: P.O. Box 539, Mentor, OH 44061. **Telephone:** (216) 953-2200. **FAX:** (216) 953-2202. **Editor:** Frank Derry.

OUTSIDE PITCH

(Baltimore Orioles)

Mailing Address: P.O. Box 27143, Baltimore, MD 21230. **Telephone:** (410)234-8888. **FAX:** (410) 234-1029. **Publisher:** David Simone. **Editor:** David Hill.

REDS REPORT

(Cincinnati Reds)

Mailing Address: Columbus Sports Publications, P.O. Box 12453, Columbus, OH 43212. **Telephone:** (614) 486-2202. **FAX:** (614) 486-3650. **Publisher:** Frank Moskowitz. **Editor:** Steve Helwagon.

BASEBALL CARD MANUFACTURERS

SCORE BOARD

Mailing Address: 1951 Old Cuthbert Rd., Cherry Hill, NJ 08034. **Telephone:** (609) 354-9000. **FAX:** (609) 427-3565.

DONRUSS TRADING CARD CO.

Mailing Address: 907 Avenue R, Grand Prairie, TX 75050. **Telephone:** (972) 975-0022. **FAX:** (972) 975-0077.

FLEER/SKYBOX INTERNATIONAL

Mailing Address: Executive Plaza, 1120 Route 73, Suite 300, Mt. Laurel, NJ 08054. **Telephone:** (609) 231-6200. **FAX:** (609) 727-9460.

PINNACLE BRANDS

Mailing Address: 1845 Wooddall Rodgers Freeway, Suite 1300, Dallas, TX 75201. **Telephone:** (214) 981-8100. **FAX:** (214) 981-8200.

TOPPS

Mailing Address: One Whitehall St., New York, NY 10004. **Telephone:** (212) 376-0300. **FAX:** (212) 376-0573.

UPPER DECK

Mailing Address: 5909 Sea Otter Place, Carlsbad, CA 92008. **Telephone:** (619) 929-6500. **FAX:** (619) 929-6548.

Other Leagues/Organizations

COLORADO SILVER BULLETS

Mailing Address: 1575 Sheridan Rd. NE, Suite 200, Atlanta, GA 30324. **Telephone:** (404) 636-8200. **FAX:** (404) 636-0530.

Operated by: Hope-Beckham, Inc.

President: Bob Hope. **Chairman of the Board:** Paul Beckham. **Vice President, Finance:** Randal Greene.

Director, Player Development: Bruce Crabbe. **Director, Marketing:** Kimberly Sacco. **Director, Merchandise:** Michael King. **Manager, Merchandise:** Tom Lucas. **Director, Business Development:** Jeff Lamkin. **Publicist:** Ashley Swadel. **Public Relations Assistant:** Allison Overton. **Administrator:** Molly Leonard. **Director, Baseball Operations:** Kevin Lewis.

Manager: Phil Niekro. **Coaches:** Bruce Crabbe, John Niekro, Joe Szekely.

ATHLETES IN ACTION

Mailing Address: 3802 Ehrlich Road, Suite 110, Tampa, FL 33624. **Telephone:** (813) 968-7400. **FAX:** (813) 968-7515.

Director, Baseball: Jason Lester. **Director, Recruiting:** Scott Shepherd.

SENIOR LEAGUES

MEN'S SENIOR BASEBALL LEAGUE

(30 and Over, 40 and Over)

Mailing Address: One Huntington Quadrangle, Suite 3NO7, Mellville, NY 11747. **Telephone:** (516) 753-6725. **FAX:** (516) 753-4031.

President: Steve Sigler. **Vice President:** Gary D'Ambrisi.

1997 World Series: Oct. 27-Nov. 8, Phoenix, AZ; Nov. 3-8, St. Petersburg, FL.

MEN'S ADULT BASEBALL LEAGUE

(18 and Over)

Mailing Address: One Huntington Quadrangle, Suite 3NO7, Mellville, NY 11747. **Telephone:** (516) 753-6725. **FAX:** (516) 753-4031.

President: Steve Sigler. **Vice President:** Gary D'Ambrisi.

1997 World Series: Oct. 23-26, Phoenix, AZ; Nov. 1-4, St. Petersburg, FL.

NATIONAL ADULT BASEBALL ASSOCIATION

(18-65)

Mailing Address: 3900 East Mexico Ave., Suite 330, Denver, CO 80201. **Telephone:** (303) 639-9955. **FAX:** (303) 753-6804.

President: Brad Coldiron.

ROY HOBBS BASEBALL

(Open, 30 and Over, 40 and Over, 48 and Over)

Mailing Address: 1864 Deepwood Dr., Akron, OH 44313. **Telephone:** (330) 940-2008. **FAX:** (330) 940-2008.

President: Tom Giffen. **Vice President:** Ellen Giffen.

1997 National Championship: 30 and Over (A, B, C divisions)—Nov. 1-8, Fort Myers, FL. 40 and Over (A division)—Nov. 1-8, Fort Myers, FL. 40 and Over (B, C divisions)—Nov. 8-15, Fort Myers, FL. Masters (48 and over)—Nov. 8-15, Fort Myers, FL

TRADE, EMPLOYMENT

THE BASEBALL TRADE SHOW

Mailing Address: P.O. Box A, St. Petersburg, FL 33731. **Telephone:** (813) 822-6937. **FAX:** (813) 821-5819.

Show Director: Kecia Tillman.

1997 Convention: Dec. 12-15 at New Orleans, LA.

SPORTS EVENT MANAGEMENT

Mailing Address: P.O. Box 948, Doylestown, PA 18901. **Telephone:** (215) 230-8333. **FAX:** (215) 345-6692.

President, Event Development: Stephen Cook. **President, Marketing and Administration:** Michael Ivankovich.

PROFESSIONAL BASEBALL EMPLOYMENT OPPORTUNITIES

Mailing Address: P.O. Box 310, Old Fort, NC 28762. **Telephone:** (800) 842-5618. **FAX:** (704) 668-4762.

Director: Ann Perkins.

MINOR LEAGUES

NATIONAL ASSOCIATION

Mike Moore

Office Address: 201 Bayshore Dr. SE, St. Petersburg, FL 33701. **Mailing Address:** P.O. Box A, St. Petersburg, FL 33731. **Telephone:** (813) 822-6937. **FAX:** (813) 821-5819.

Year Founded: 1901.

President: Mike Moore. **Assistant to the President:** Carolyn Ashe.

Vice President: Stan Brand (Washington, DC). **Vice President, Administration:** Pat O'Conner.

Chief Operating Officer: Rob Dlugozima. **Assistant to the COO:** Kelly Butler.

Director of Operations: Tim Brunswick. **Director of Business and Finance:** Eric Krupa. **Director of Licensing:** Misann Ellmaker. **Assistant Director of Licensing:** Brian Earle. **Assistant to Director of Licensing:** Steve Densa. **Licensing and Trademark Assistant:** Rich Arnold. **Director of Media Relations:** Jim Ferguson. **Assistant to Director of Media Relations:** Sandra Dean. **Assistant Directors of Marketing:** Michelle Montgomery, Dale Coxe. **Director, Trade Show:** Kecia Tillman.

General Counsel: Ben Hayes

1997 WINTER MEETINGS: Dec. 12-16, New Orleans, LA.

Affiliated Members/Council of League Presidents

Class AAA

League	President	Telephone	FAX Number
American Assn.	Branch Rickey	(513) 271-4800	(513) 271-7887
International	Randy Mobley	(614) 791-9300	(614) 791-9009
Mexican	Pedro Treto Cisneros	(525) 557-1007	(525) 395-2454
Pacific Coast	Bill Cutler	(602) 838-2171	(602) 838-2741

Class AA

League	President	Telephone	FAX Number
Eastern	Bill Troubh	(207) 761-2700	(207) 761-7064
Southern	Arnold Fielkow	(770) 428-4749	(770) 428-4849
Texas	Tom Kayser	(210) 545-5297	(210) 545-5298

Class A Advanced

League	President	Telephone	FAX Number
California	Joe Gagliardi	(408) 369-8038	(408) 369-1409
Carolina	John Hopkins	(910) 691-9030	(910) 691-9070
Florida State	Chuck Murphy	(904) 252-7479	(904) 252-7495

Class A

League	President	Telephone	FAX Number
Midwest	George Spelius	(608) 364-1188	(608) 364-1913
South Atlantic	John Moss	(704) 739-3466	(704) 739-1974

Short-Season Class A

League	President	Telephone	FAX Number
New York-Penn	Bob Julian	(315) 733-8036	(315) 797-7403
Northwest	Bob Richmond	(541) 686-5412	(541) 484-7672

Rookie Advanced

League	President	Telephone	FAX Number
Appalachian	Lee Landers	(704) 873-5300	(704) 873-4333
Pioneer	Jim McCurdy	(509) 456-7615	(509) 456-0136

Rookie

League	President	Telephone	FAX Number
Arizona	Bob Richmond	(602) 483-8224	(602) 443-3450
Dominican Summer	Freddy Jana	(809) 563-3233	(809) 563-2455
Gulf Coast	Tom Saffell	(941) 966-6407	(941) 966-6872

National Association Board of Trustees

American Association—Dan Ulmer, chairman (Louisville). **International League**—Mike Tamburro (Pawtucket). **Pacific Coast League**—Richard Holtzman (Tucson). **Eastern League**—Joe Finley (Trenton). **Southern League**—Steve Bryant (Carolina). **Texas League**—Miles Prentice, vice chairman (Midland). **California League**—Hank Stickney (Rancho Cucamonga). **Carolina League**—Calvin Falwell (Lynchburg). **Florida State League**—Ken Carson, secretary (Dunedin). **Midwest League**—Dave Walker (Burlington). **South Atlantic League**—Winston Blenckstone (Hagerstown). **New York-Penn League**—Sam Nader (Oneonta). **Northwest League**—Bob Beban (Eugene). **Appalachian League**—Bill Smith (Elizabethton). **Pioneer League**—Bob Wilson (Billings). **Gulf Coast League**—Cam Bonifay (Pirates).

AMERICAN ASSOCIATION

Class AAA

Office Address: 6801 Miami Ave., Suite 3, Cincinnati, OH 45243. **Telephone:** (513) 271-4800. **FAX:** (513) 271-7887.

Years League Active: 1902-1962, 1969-.

President/Treasurer: Branch B. Rickey.

Vice President: Ken Grandquist. **Corporate Secretary:** Max Schumacher.

Directors: Joe Adams (Omaha), Clay Bennett (Oklahoma City), Rob Couhig (New Orleans), Ken Grandquist (Iowa), Robert Rich Jr. (Buffalo), Max Schumacher (Indianapolis), Dan Ulmer (Louisville); Nashville unavailable.

Administrative Assistants: Diane Rickey, Jennifer Garula.

1997 Opening Date: April 3. **Closing Date:** Sept. 1.

Branch Rickey

Regular Season: 144 games.

Division Structure: East—Buffalo, Indianapolis, Louisville, Nashville. **West**—Iowa, New Orleans, Oklahoma City, Omaha.

Playoff Format: Top two teams in each division meet in best-of-5 semifinals. Winners meet in best-of-5 series for league championship.

All-Star Game: July 9 at Des Moines (joint Triple-A game).

Roster Limit: 23 active, until midnight Aug. 10 when rosters can be expanded to 25. **Player Eligibility Rule:** No restrictions.

Brand of Baseball: Rawlings ROM.

Statistician: Howe Sportsdata International, Boston Fish Pier, West Bldg. #2, Suite 306, Boston MA 02210.

Umpires: Mark Barron (Lawrenceville, GA), Fred Cannon (Brookhaven, MS), Eric Cooper (Des Moines, IA), John Dezelan (Imperial, PA), Bruce Dreckman (Marcus, IA), Martin Foster (Beloit, WI), Matt Hughes (Louisville, KY), Chris Jarboe (Baltimore, MD), Jeff Kowalczyk (Bloomington, IL), Jeff Nelson (Cottage Grove, MN), Kraig Sanders (Little Rock, AR), Paul Schrieber (Louisville, KY), Mitch Schwark (Battle Creek, MI), Scott Simonides (Lakeland, FL).

1996 Standings (Overall)

Club (Affiliate)	W	L	Pct.	GB	'96 Manager
#Buffalo (Indians)	84	60	.583	—	Brian Graham
#Omaha (Royals)	79	65	.549	5	Mike Jirschele
Indianapolis (Reds)	78	66	.542	6	Dave Miley
Nashville (White Sox)	77	67	.535	7	Rick Renick
*Oklahoma City (Rangers)	74	70	.514	10	Greg Biagini
Iowa (Cubs)	64	78	.451	19	Ron Clark
Louisville (Cardinals)	60	84	.417	24	Joe Pettini
New Orleans (Brewers)	58	84	.408	25	Tim Ireland

*Won playoffs. #Won division title.

Stadium Information

Club	Stadium	Dimensions LF	CF	RF	Capacity	'96 Att.
Buffalo	North AmeriCare Park	325	404	325	21,050	825,530
Indianapolis	Victory Field	320	402	320	15,250	529,238
Iowa	Sec Taylor	335	400	335	10,800	453,630
Louisville	Cardinal*	360	405	312	33,600	494,929
Nashville	Herschel Greer	327	400	327	15,500	353,302
New Orleans	Zephyr Field	332	407	333	10,000	180,485
Okla. City	All Sports	340	415	340	12,000	267,784
Omaha	Rosenblatt	332	408	332	22,000	427,482

*Artificial turf playing surface

BUFFALO
BISONS

Office Address: 275 Washington St., Buffalo, NY 14203. **Mailing Address:** P.O. Box 450, Buffalo, NY 14205. **Telephone:** (716) 846-2000. **FAX:** (716) 852-6530.

Affiliation (first year): Cleveland Indians (1995). **Years in League:** 1985-.

Ownership, Management

Operated by: Rich Products Corporation.

Principal Owner/President: Robert E. Rich Jr.

Chairman of the Board: Robert E. Rich Sr.

Executive Vice Presidents: Melinda Rich, Jon Dandes. **Vice President/Treasurer:** David Rich. **Vice President/Secretary:** William Gisel Jr. **Vice President/Sales and Marketing:** Marta Hiczewski.

General Manager: Mike Buczkowski. **Controller:** John Dougherty. **Senior Account Representatives:** Leigh Balcom, Ted Rich, Pete Sinagra. **Director of Public Relations:** Tom Burns. **Director of Promotions:** Rick Orienza. **Director of Ticket Sales:** Jim Mack. **Director of Community Relations:** John Wiedeman. **Director of Merchandising:** Nancy Martin. **Director of Food Services:** Eric Nelson. **Office Manager:** Margaret Russo. **Head Groundskeeper:** Jim Hornung. **Director of Clubhouse Operations:** Ronald Krauza.

Field Staff

Manager: Brian Graham. **Coach:** Dave Keller. **Pitching Coach:** Gary Ruby. **Trainer:** Lee Kuntz.

Game Information

Radio Announcer: Jim Rosenhaus. **No. of Games Broadcast:** Home-72, Away-72. **Flagship Station:** WGR 550-AM.

PA Announcer: Unavailable. **Official Scorers:** Mike Kelly, Duke McGuire.

Stadium Name (year opened): North AmeriCare Park (1988). **Location:** From north/south, take I-190 to Elm Street exit, left onto Swan Street. From east, take I-90 West, exit 51 (Route 33) to end, exit at Oak Street, right onto Swan Street. From west, take I-90 East, exit 53 to I-190 North, exit at Elm Street, left onto Swan Street. **Standard Game Times:** 7:05 p.m.; Wed 1:05, Sat. 2:05 and 7:05, Sun 2:05.

Visiting Club Hotel: Holiday Inn Downtown, 620 Delaware Ave., Buffalo, NY 14202. Telephone: (716) 886-2121.

INDIANAPOLIS
INDIANS

Office Address: 501 W. Maryland St., Indianapolis, IN 46225. **Telephone:** (317) 269-3545. **FAX:** (317) 269-3541. **E-Mail Address:** indians@indyindians.com.

Affiliation (first year): Cincinnati Reds (1993). **Years in League:** 1902-62, 1969-.

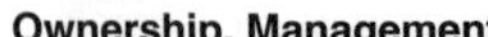

Ownership, Management

Operated by: Indianapolis Indians, Inc.

Chairman of the Board: Henry Warren.

President/General Manager: Max Schumacher. **Assistant General Manager:** Cal Burleson. **Director of Business Operations**: Dan Madden. **Director of Stadium Operations:** Belinda Kinch. **Head Groundskeeper:** Gary Shepherd. **Director of Media/Public Relations:** Mark Walpole. **Director of Publications:** Tim Harms. **Director of Broadcasting:** Howard Kellman. **Director of Community Relations:** Chris Herndon. **Director of Promotions:** Daryle Keith. **Director of Ticket Sales:** Mike Schneider. **Assistant Director of Ticket Sales:** Randy Lewandowski. **Director of Merchandising:** Mark Schumacher. **Director of Special Projects:** Bruce Schumacher. **Office Manager:** Brad Morris.

Field Staff

Manager: Dave Miley. **Coach:** Jim Thrift. **Pitching Coach:** Grant Jackson. **Trainer:** John Young.

Game Information

Radio Announcers: Howard Kellman, Brian Giffin. **No. of Games Broadcast:** Home-72, Away-72. **Flagship Stations:** WNDE 1260-AM, WIRE 100.9-FM.

PA Announcer: Bruce Schumacher. **Official Scorer:** Kim Rogers.

Stadium Name (year opened): Victory Field (1996). **Location:** From I-

70—West St. exit, then north on Missouri/West St. to Washington St.; west on Washington St. .2 mile to crossover to Victory Field. From I-65—Martin Luther King exit, then south on MLK/West St. to Washington St. **Standard Game Times:** 7 p.m.; Sun. (April-June) 2, (July-August) 6.

Visiting Club Hotel: Ramada East Indianapolis, 7701 E. 42nd St., Indianapolis, IN 46226. Telephone: (317) 897-4000.

IOWA *CUBS*

Office Address: 350 SW 1st St., Des Moines, IA 50309. **Telephone:** (515) 243-6111. **FAX:** (515) 243-5152.

Affiliation (first year): Chicago Cubs (1981). **Years in League:** 1969-.

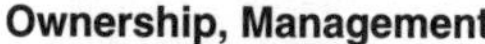

Ownership, Management

Operated by: Greater Des Moines Baseball Co., Inc.

Principal Owners: Ken Grandquist, Dick Easter.

Chairman of the Board: Dick Easter. **President:** Ken Grandquist.

General Manager: Sam Bernabe. **Assistant General Manager/ Director of Media Relations:** Rick Rungaitis. **Controller:** Sue Tollefson. **Director of Stadium Operations:** Boyd Davis. **Sales/Marketing:** Mike Rickard. **Director of Broadcasting:** Deene Ehlis. **Director of Ticket Sales:** Jim Nahas. **Director of Food Services**: Frank Brown. **Director of Group Sales:** Nick Willey. **Head Groundskeeper:** Luke Yoder. **Office Manager:** Stacy Butcher.

Field Staff

Manager: Tim Johnson. **Coach:** Glenn Adams. **Pitching Coach:** Marty DeMerritt. **Trainer:** Bob Grimes.

Game Information

Radio Announcer: Deene Ehlis. **No. of Games Broadcast:** Home-72, Away-72. **Flagship Station:** KXTK 940-AM.

PA Announcers: Lee Githens, Chuck Shockley. **Official Scorers:** Dick McDonald, Dirk Brinkmeyer.

Stadium Name (year opened): Sec Taylor Stadium (1992). **Location:** I-235 to 3rd Street exit, south on 3rd Street to Tuttle St., left on Tuttle. **Standard Game Times:** 7:15 p.m.; Sun. 2:05.

Visiting Club Hotel: Savery Hotel, 401 Locust St., Des Moines, IA 50309. Telephone: (515) 244-2151.

LOUISVILLE *REDBIRDS*

Office Address: Cardinal Stadium, Phillips Lane and Freedom Way, Louisville, KY 40209. **Mailing Address:** P.O. Box 36407, Louisville, KY 40233. **Telephone:** (502) 367-9121. **FAX:** (502) 368-5120.

Affiliation (first year): St. Louis Cardinals (1982). **Years in League:** 1902-62, 1982-.

Ownership, Management

Operated by: Louisville Baseball Club, Inc.

Owners: Dan Ulmer, John Hillerich III, Dale Owens, Ed Glasscock, Ken Huber, Jim Morrissey, Tom Musselman, Bob Stallings, Gary Ulmer.

Chairman of the Board: Dan Ulmer. **Corporation President:** John Hillerich III. **Club President:** Gary Ulmer. **Vice President/Treasurer:** Ed Glasscock.

Vice President/General Manager: Dale Owens. **Assistant General Manager, Marketing and Public Relations:** Tab Brockman. **Assistant General Manager, Sales:** Greg Galiette. **Director of Baseball Operations:** Mary Barney. **Bookkeeper:** Michele Anderson. **Director of Broadcasting:** Jim Kelch. **Director of Group Sales:** Dave Arnold. **Director of Stadium Operations:** Scott Shoemaker. **Director of Stadium Promotions:** Dave Allen. **Public Relations Coordinator:** Shawn Howe. **Ticket Manager:** George Veith. **Community Events Coordinator:** Stacie Douglas. **Sales Representative:** Scott Barton.

Field Staff

Manager: Gaylen Pitts. **Coach:** Chris Maloney. **Pitching Coach:** Marty Mason. **Trainer:** Mark O'Neal.

Game Information

Radio Announcers: Jim Kelch, Dave Wilson. **No. of Games Broadcast:** Home-72, Away-72. **Flagship Station:** WKJK 1080-AM.

PA Announcer: Charles Gazaway. **Official Scorer:** Ed Peak.

Stadium Name (year opened): Cardinal Stadium (1957). **Location:** Intersection of I-65 and I-264 at Kentucky Fair and Expo Center. **Standard**

Game Times: 7:05 p.m.; Thur. 12:05, Sun. 1:30.

Visiting Club Hotels: Executive Inn, 978 Phillips Lane, Louisville, KY 40209. Telephone: (502) 367-9121; Days Hotel, 101 E. Jefferson St., Louisville, KY 40202. Telephone: (502) 585-2200.

NASHVILLE *SOUNDS*

Office Address: 534 Chestnut St., Nashville, TN 37203. **Mailing Address:** P.O. Box 23290, Nashville, TN 37202. **Telephone:** (615) 242-4371. **FAX:** (615) 256-5684.

Affiliation (first year): Chicago White Sox (1993). **Years in League:** 1985-.

Ownership, Management

Principal Owners: Al Gordon, Mike Murtaugh, Mike Woleben.

General Manager: Bill Larson. **Director of Sales/Marketing, Business Operations:** Ron Schmittou. **Director of Stadium Operations:** Brad Dennis. **Assistant Director of Stadium Operations:** Greg Harvey. **Head Groundskeeper:** Dave Nasypany. **Director of Media Relations:** Robbie Bohren. **Director of Promotions:** Mike Schmittou. **Director of Ticket Sales:** Dot Cloud. **Director of Group Sales:** Delmar Smith. **Director of Food Services:** Walt Mehlenbacher. **Office Manager:** Sharon Carson.

Field Staff

Manager: Tom Spencer. **Coach:** Von Joshua. **Pitching Coach:** Kirk Champion. **Trainer:** Greg Latta.

Game Information

Radio Announcer: Steve Selby. **No. of Games Broadcast:** Home-72, Away-72. **Flagship Station:** WAMB 1160-AM.

PA Announcer: Unavailable. **Official Scorer:** Unavailable.

Stadium Name (year opened): Herschel Greer Stadium (1978). **Location:** I-65 to Wedgewood exit. **Standard Game Times:** 7:15 p.m.

Visiting Club Hotel: Unavailable.

NEW ORLEANS *ZEPHYRS*

Office Address: 6000 Airline Highway, Metairie, LA 70003. **Telephone:** (504) 734-5155. **FAX:** (504) 734-5118.

Affiliation (first year): Houston Astros (1997). **Years in League:** 1977, 1993-.

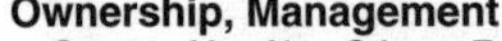

Ownership, Management

Operated by: New Orleans Zephyrs Baseball Club, LLC.

Principal Owners: Rob Couhig, Don Beaver. **President:** Rob Couhig.

General Manager: Jay Miller. **Assistant General Manager:** Dan Hanrahan. **Director of Stadium Operations:** Rick Sneed. **Director of Media/Public Relations:** Les East. **Account Executives:** Terry Alario, Josh Danzig. **Corporate Sales:** Dale Duronselet. **Community Relations/Group Sales:** Aaron Lombard. **Director of Promotions:** Derrick Grubbs. **Director of Ticket Operations:** Randy Habluetzel. **Director of Group Sales:** Scott Sidwell. **Director of Merchandising:** Heather Woods-Menendez. **Director of Corporate Sales:** Dawn Mentel. **Director of Customer Relations:** Sue Denny. **Office Manager:** Christina Bridges. **Accounting Clerk:** Shawn Kelly.

Field Staff

Manager: Steve Swisher. **Coach:** Jim Wynn. **Pitching Coach:** Craig McMurtry. **Trainer:** Mike Freer.

Game Information

Radio Announcers: Ken Trahan, Ron Swoboda. **No. of Games Broadcast:** Home-72, Away-72. **Flagship Stations:** WWL 870-AM, WSMB 1350-AM.

PA Announcer: Derrick Grubbs. **Official Scorer:** J.L. Vangilder.

Stadium Name (year opened): Zephyr Field (1997). **Location:** I-10 to Clearview South, right on Airline Highway (Route 61). **Standard Game Times:** 7:05 p.m.; Sun. 6:05.

Visiting Club Hotel: Landmark, 2601 Severn Ave., Metairie, LA 70002. Telephone: (504) 888-9500.

OKLAHOMA CITY
89ers

Office Address: 820 89er Drive, Oklahoma City, OK 73107. **Mailing Address:** P.O. Box 75089, Oklahoma City, OK 73147. **Telephone:** (405) 946-8989. **FAX:** (405) 942-4198. **E-Mail Address:** 89ers@mail.icnet.net

Affiliation (first year): Texas Rangers (1983). **Years in League:** 1962, 1969-.

Ownership, Management

Operated by: OKC Athletic Club, LP.

President: Clayton Bennett.

Vice President/General Manager: David Vance. **Assistant General Manager:** Andy Thiem. **Director of Marketing:** Darla Hall. **Director of Sales:** Brad Tammen. **Director of Finance:** Matt Davies. **Director of Media Relations/Promotions:** John Allgood. **Ticket Manager:** Donny Frissell. **Manager of Groups and Special Events:** Nancy Mullins. **Account Executives:** Amy Clelland, Geren Steiner, Skip Wallace. **Operations Managaer:** Tim Gorman. **Head Groundskeeper:** Monty McCoy. **Concessions Manager:** Milton Neal. **Retail Manager:** Mike Prange. **Clubhouse Manager:** Jeff Brown.

Field Staff

Manager: Greg Biagini. **Coach:** Bump Wills. **Pitching Coach:** Tom Brown. **Trainer:** Greg Harrel.

Game Information

Radio Announcer: Jack Damrill. **Flagship Station:** WKY 930-AM.

PA Announcer: Unavailable. **Official Scorer:** Pat Petree.

Stadium Name (year opened): All Sports Stadium (1961). **Location:** I-44 West to NW 10th Street, east to 89er Drive on the State Fairgrounds. **Standard Game Times:** 7:05; Sun. (April-May) 2:05, (June-August) 7:05.

Visiting Club Hotel: Unavailable.

OMAHA
ROYALS

Office Address: Rosenblatt Stadium, 1202 Bert Murphy Dr., Omaha, NE 68107. **Mailing Address:** P.O. Box 3665, Omaha, NE 68103. **Telephone:** (402) 734-2550. **FAX:** (402) 734-7166. **E-Mail Address:** mmashanic@earthlink.net.

Affiliation (first year): Kansas City Royals (1969). **Years in League:** 1955-59, 1961-62, 1969-.

Ownership, Management

Operated by: Omaha Royals, LP.

Principal Owners: Union Pacific Railroad, Warren Buffett, Walter Scott.

President: Joe Adams.

Vice President/General Manager: Bill Gorman. **Assistant General Manager/Director of Corporate Sales:** Terry Wendlandt. **Director of Media Relations:** Mike Mashanic. **Ticket Office Manager:** Joe Volquartsen. **Controller:** Jessica Graner. **Stadium Superintendent:** Jesse Cuevas. **Director of Marketing:** Mike Stephens. **Broadcast Sales Representative:** Kevin McNabb. **Corporate Sales Representatives:** Tony Duffek, Christy Frank, Andy Lewis, Joe Matuella. **Manager, Concessions:** Rick Bronwell. **Administrative Assistants:** Kay Besta, Lisa Meinzer. **Ticket Office Assistants:** Marlene Lee, Joe Pane. **Comptroller:** Sue Nicholson.

Field Staff

Manager: Mike Jirschele. **Coach:** U.L. Washington. **Pitching Coach:** Mike Alvarez. **Trainer:** Mark Farnsworth.

Game Information

Radio Announcers: Frank Adkisson, Kevin McNabb. **No. of Games Broadcast:** Home-72, Away-72. **Flagship Station:** KOSR 1490-AM.

PA Announcer: Bill Jensen. **Official Scorer:** Steve Pivovar.

Stadium Name (year opened): Rosenblatt Stadium (1948). **Location:** I-80 to 13th Street South exit, south one block. **Standard Game Times:** 7:05 p.m., Wed. 12:05, Sun. 1:35.

Visiting Club Hotel: Ramada Hotel Central, 7007 Grover St., Omaha, NE 68106. Telephone: (402) 397-7030.

INTERNATIONAL LEAGUE

Class AAA

Office Address: 55 S. High St., Suite 202, Dublin, OH 43017. **Telephone:** (614) 791-9300. **FAX:** (614) 791-9009.

E-mail Address: www.ilbaseball.com

Years League Active: 1884-.

President/Treasurer: Randy Mobley.

Vice Presidents: Harold Cooper, Dave Rosenfield, Tex Simone, George Sisler.

Corporate Secretary: Richard Davis.

Directors: Bruce Baldwin (Richmond), Gene Cook (Toledo), Howard Darwin (Ottawa), Dave Rosenfield (Norfolk), Sam Russo (Charlotte), Ken Schnacke (Columbus), Naomi Silver (Rochester), John Simone (Syracuse), Mike Tamburro (Pawtucket), Bill Terlecky (Scranton/Wilkes-Barre).

Randy Mobley

Office Secretary: Marcia Willison.

Administrative Intern: Nathan Blackmon.

1997 Opening Date: April 3. **Closing Date:** Sept. 1.

Regular Season: 142 games.

Division Structure: East—Ottawa, Pawtucket, Rochester, Scranton/Wilkes-Barre, Syracuse. **West**—Charlotte, Columbus, Norfolk, Richmond, Toledo.

Playoff Format: First-place teams in each division play second-place teams in best-of-5 series. Winners meet in best-of-5 series for Governors' Cup championship.

All-Star Game: July 9 at Des Moines (joint Triple-A game).

Roster Limit: 23 active, until midnight Aug. 10 when roster can expand to 25. **Player Eligibility Rule:** No restrictions.

Brand of Baseball: Rawlings ROM-INT.

Statistician: Howe Sportsdata International, Boston Fish Pier, West Bldg. #2—Suite 306, Boston MA 02210.

Umpires: C.B. Bucknor (Brooklyn, NY), Pat Connors (Berlin, WI), Field Culbreth (Inman, SC), Kerwin Danley (Chandler, AZ), Lazaro Diaz (Opa Locka, FL), Mark Facto (Ellicott City, MD), Brain Gibbons (South Bend, IN), Greg Gibson (Catlettsburg, KY), Ed Hickox (Deland, FL), Sam Holbrook (Lexington, KY), Gerald Meals (Salem, OH), Paul Nauert (Lawrenceville, GA), Brian O'Nora (Youngstown, OH), Scott Potter (Daytona Beach, FL), Jeff Schrupp (Birmingham, AL), Tim Timmons (Columbus, OH), Hunter Wendelstedt (Ormond Beach, FL).

1996 Standings (Overall)

Club (Affiliate)	W	L	Pct.	GB	'96 Manager
*#Columbus (Yankees)	85	57	.599	—	Stump Merrill
Norfolk (Mets)	82	59	.582	2½	Valentine/Benedict
#Pawtucket (Red Sox)	78	64	.549	7	Buddy Bailey
Rochester (Orioles)	72	69	.511	12½	Marv Foley
Toledo (Tigers)	70	72	.493	15	Tom Runnells
Scranton/W-B (Phillies)	70	72	.493	15	Hobson/Aviles
Syracuse (Blue Jays)	67	75	.472	18	Rich Hebner
Richmond (Braves)	62	79	.440	22½	Bill Dancy
Charlotte (Marlins)	62	79	.440	22½	Sal Rende
*Ottawa (Expos)	60	82	.423	25	Pete Mackanin

*Won playoffs #Won division title.

Stadium Information

Club	Stadium	Dimensions LF	CF	RF	Capacity	'96 Att.
Charlotte	Knights Castle	325	400	325	10,000	326,761
Columbus	Cooper*	355	400	330	15,000	533,012
Norfolk	Harbor Park	333	410	338	12,059	510,130
Ottawa	Ottawa	325	404	325	10,332	347,050
Pawtucket	McCoy	325	380	325	7,002	367,754
Richmond	The Diamond	330	402	330	12,146	500,035
Rochester	Frontier	330	400	322	10,600	375,781
Scranton	Lackawanna County*	330	408	330	10,832	458,033
Syracuse	P&C*	328	400	328	8,416	300,903
Toledo	Ned Skeldon	325	410	325	10,025	316,126

*Artificial turf playing surface.

CHARLOTTE
KNIGHTS

Office Address: 2280 Deerfield Dr., Fort Mill, SC 29715. **Mailing Address:** P.O. Box 1207, Fort Mill, SC 29716. **Telephone:** (704) 357-8071, (803) 548-8050. **FAX:** (704) 329-6255, (803) 548-8055. **E-Mail address:** http://www.aaaknights.com/

Affiliation (first year): Florida Marlins (1995). **Years in League:** 1993-.

Ownership, Management

Operated by: Charlotte Knights Baseball Club, Shinn Enterprises.

Principal Owner: George Shinn. **Vice President of Operations:** Sam Russo.

General Manager: Pete Moore. **Assistant General Manager:** Chris Carroll. **Accounting Manager:** Amy Johnson. **Director of Stadium Operations:** Marc Farha. **Head Groundskeeper:** Larry Rhodes. **Director of Marketing/Sponsor Services:** Julie Sigmon. **Director of Media/Public Relations:** Melissa Booker. **Director of Promotions:** Lisa Chico Hanselman. **Assistant Ticket Manager:** Jamie Hall. **Ticket Sales Manager:** Scott Graham. **Clubhouse Operations:** Jay Barnhouse. **Executive Assistant:** Vicki Miller. **Ticket Sales Representatives:** Ajay Boyd, Olivia Kaylor, Anthony DeNino. **Receptionist:** Jennifer Grieves. **Assistant Facility Manager:** Ed Hrynkow. **Events Operation Manager:** Jon Percival. **Building Operations:** Dean Henry.

Field Staff

Manager: Carlos Tosca. **Coach:** Adrian Garrett. **Pitching Coach:** Rick Williams. **Trainer:** Mike Leon.

Game Information

Radio Announcer: Bob Licht. **No. of Games Broadcast:** Home-71, Away-71. **Flagship Station:** Unavailable.

PA Announcer: Ken Gunther. **Official Scorer:** Ed Walton.

Stadium Name (year opened): Knights Castle (1990). **Location:** Exit 88 off I-77, east on Gold Hill Road for ⅛ mile. Entrance on right. **Standard Game Times:** 7:30 p.m., Sun. 2 (April-May), 7 (June-September).

Visiting Club Hotel: Radisson Grand Resort, 9700 Regent Parkway., Fort Mill, SC 29716. Telephone: (803) 548-7800.

COLUMBUS
CLIPPERS

Office Address: 1155 West Mound St., Columbus, OH 43223. **Telephone:** (614) 462-5250. **FAX:** (614) 462-3271. **E-Mail Address:** clippers@earthlink.net.

Affiliation (first year): New York Yankees (1979). **Years in League:** 1955-70, 1977-.

Ownership, Management

Operated by: Columbus Baseball Team, Inc.

Principal Owner: Franklin County, Ohio.

Chairman: Donald Borror. **President:** Richard Smith.

General Manager: Ken Schnacke. **Assistant General Manager:** Mark Warren. **Assistant General Manager/Park Supervisor:** Dick Fitzpatrick. **Director of Stadium Operations:** Steve Dalin. **Director of Ticket Sales:** Scott Ziegler. **Director of Media Relations:** Gregg Kaye. **Director of Sales:** Mark Galuska. **Director of Marketing:** David Echols. **Director of Merchandising:** Jim Coverstone. **Director of Advertising:** Keif Fetch. **Director of Finance:** Chris Burleson. **Director of Publications:** Chris Daugherty. **Directory of Community Relations:** Danny Mummey. **Assistant to General Manager:** Judi Timmons. **Secretary:** Monica Schemrich. **Receptionist:** Lisa Miller.

Field Staff

Manager: Stump Merrill. **Coaches:** Hop Cassady, Arnie Beyeler, Rob Thomson. **Pitching Coach:** Oscar Acosta. **Trainer:** Darren London.

Game Information

Radio Announcers: Terry Smith, Brooks Melchior. **No. of Games Broadcast:** Home-71, Away-71. **Flagship Station:** WBNS 1460-AM.

PA Announcers: John Ross, Dr. Robert Lewis. **Official Scorers:** Chuck Emmerling, Kris Hutchins, Randy Parker, Jeff Rapp, Joe Santry.

Stadium Name (year opened): Cooper Stadium (1977). **Location:** From north/south, I-71 to I-70 West, exit at Mound Street. From west, I-70 East, exit at Broad Street, east to Glenwood, south to Mound Street. **Standard Game Times:** 7:15 p.m.; Sat. 6:15, 7:15; Sun. 2:15, 6:15.

Visiting Club Hotel: Best Western-Columbus North, 888 East Dublin-Granville Rd., Columbus, OH 43229. Telephone: (614) 888-8230.

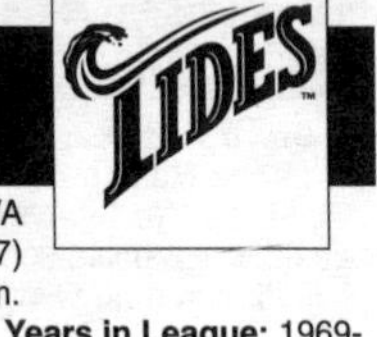

NORFOLK
TIDES

Office Address: 150 Park Ave., Norfolk, VA 23510. **Telephone:** (757) 622-2222. **FAX:** (757) 624-9090. **E-Mail Address:** info@norfolktides.com.

Affiliation (first year): New York Mets (1969). **Years in League:** 1969-.

Ownership, Management

Operated by: Tides Baseball Club, LP.

President: Ken Young.

General Manager: Dave Rosenfield. **Director of Sales/Broadcasting:** Jack Ankerson. **Director of Stadium Operations:** Joe Gorza. **Director of Media Relations:** Shon Sbarra. **Director of Ticket Operations:** Glenn Riggs. **Ticket Manager:** Linda Waisanen. **Promotions/Merchandise Coordinator:** Jay Richardson. **Business Manager:** David Hall. **Accounting Manager:** Lew Schwartz. **Group Sales:** Dave Harrah. **Director of Community Relations:** Susan Pinckney. **Administrative Assistant:** Isaac Ravizee. **Receptionist:** Judy Dennis. **Equipment/Clubhouse Manager:** Kevin Kierst. **Head Groundskeeper:** Ken Magner. **Assistant Groundskeeper:** Keith Collins.

Field Staff

Manager: Rick Dempsey **Coach:** Tom Lawless **Pitching Coach:** Ray Rippelmeyer. **Trainer:** Joe Hawkins.

Game Information

Radio Announcers: Jack Ankerson, Rob Evans. **No. of Games Broadcast:** Home-71, Away-71. **Flagship Station:** WTAR 790-AM.

PA Announcer: Frank Bennett. **Official Scorers:** Charlie Denn, Dave Lewis, Bob Moskowitz.

Stadium Name (year opened): Harbor Park (1993). **Location:** Exit 9, 11A or 11B off I-264, adjacent to the Elizabeth River in downtown Norfolk. **Standard Game Times:** 7:15 p.m.; Sun. (April-June) 1:15, (July-Sept.) 6:15.

Visiting Club Hotel: Omni Norfolk, 777 Waterside Dr., Norfolk, VA 23510. Telephone: (757) 622-6664; Doubletree Club Hotel, 880 N. Military Hwy., Norfolk, VA 23502. Telephone: (757) 461-9192.

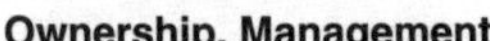

OTTAWA
LYNX

Office Address: 300 Coventry Road, Ottawa, Ontario K1K 4P5. **Telephone:** (613) 747-5969. **FAX:** (613) 747-0003. **E-Mail Address:** lynx@magi.com

Affiliation (first year): Montreal Expos (1993). **Years in League:** 1993-.

Ownership, Management

Operated By: Ottawa Lynx Baseball Club.

Principal Owner/President: Howard Darwin.

Director, Baseball Operations: Joe Bohringer. **Controller:** Ruth Saunders. **Director, Stadium Operations:** Jack Darwin. **Head Groundskeeper:** Jamie Whelan. **Director of Media/Public Relations:** Morgan Quarry. **Sales Manager:** Mark Russet. **Sales Directors:** Wendy Berg, Peter Leyser. **Director of Promotions/Marketing:** Ron Lemaire. **Ticket Manager:** Joe Fagan. **Merchandise Manager:** Nancy Darwin. **Clubhouse Manager:** John Bryk. **Receptionist:** Lorraine Charrette. **Administrative Assistant:** Heather Gale. **Director of Publications:** Mark McKenna. **Administrative Manager:** Rupert Darwin.

Field Staff

Manager: Pat Kelly. **Coach:** Frank Kremblas. **Pitching Coach:** Bo McLaughlin. **Trainer:** Alex Ochoa.

Game Information

Radio: Unavailable.

PA Announcer: Gord Breen. **Official Scorer:** Randy Fix.

Stadium Name (year opened): Ottawa Stadium (1993). **Location:** From Queensway eastbound/westbound, take Vanier exit, right on Coventry to stadium. **Standard Game Times:** 7:05 p.m., Sat.-Sun. 2:05.

Visiting Club Hotel: Chimo Inn Hotel, 1199 Joseph Cyr St., Ottawa, Ontario K1J 7T4. Telephone: (613) 744-1060.

PAWTUCKET
RED SOX

Office Address: One Columbus Ave., Pawtucket, RI 02860. **Mailing Address:** P.O. Box 2365, Pawtucket, RI 02861. **Telephone:** (401) 724-7300. **FAX:** (401) 724-2140. **E-Mail Address:** pawsox@world.net

Affiliation (first year): Boston Red Sox (1973). **Years in League:** 1973-.

Ownership, Management

Operated by: Pawtucket Red Sox Baseball Club, Inc.

Principal Owner, Chairman: Ben Mondor. **President:** Mike Tamburro.

General Manager: Lou Schwechheimer. **Vice President, Treasurer:** Kathy Crowley. **Vice President, Sales and Marketing:** Michael Gwynn. **Vice President, Stadium Operations:** Mick Tedesco. **Vice President, Public Relations:** Bill Wanless. **Office Manager:** Kathy Davenport. **Director of Community Relations/Broadcaster:** Don Orsillo. **Director of Ticket Sales:** Ed Brock. **Account Executives:** Daryl Jasper, Larry Tocci, Jeff Dooley, Keith Kuceris. **Director of Hospitality:** Kathy Walsh. **Stadium Services Manager:** Derek Molhan. **Clubhouse Managers:** Dave Johnson (visitor), Chris Parent (home). **Head Groundskeeper:** Larry Devito. **Office Assistant:** Sandi Browne.

Field Staff

Manager: Ken Macha. **Coach:** Rico Petrocelli. **Pitching Coach:** John Cumberland. **Trainer:** Jim Young.

Game Information

Radio Announcer: Don Orsillo, Jack LeFaivre. **No. of Games Broadcast:** Home-71, Away-71. **Flagship Station:** WLKW 790-AM

PA Announcer: Jim Martin. **Official Scorer:** Bruce Guindon.

Stadium Name (year opened): McCoy Stadium (1942). **Location:** I-95 North to exit 28 (School Street); I-95 South to exit 2A (Newport Avenue). **Standard Game Times:** 6 p.m. (April-May), 7 (June-Sept.); Sat. 1 (April), 7 (May-Sept.); Sun. 1.

Visiting Club Hotel: Comfort Inn, 2 George St., Pawtucket, RI 02860. Telephone: (401) 723-6700.

RICHMOND
BRAVES

Office Address: The Diamond, 3001 N. Boulevard, Richmond, VA 23230. **Mailing Address:** P.O. Box 6667, Richmond, VA 23230. **Telephone:** (804) 359-4444. **FAX:** (804) 359-0731. **E-Mail Address:** rbraves@bznet.com.

Affiliation (first year): Atlanta Braves (1966). **Years in League:** 1884, 1915-17, 1954-64, 1966-.

Ownership, Management

Operated by: Atlanta National League Baseball, Inc.

Principal Owner: Ted Turner.

General Manager: Bruce Baldwin. **Assistant General Manager:** Ken Clary. **Controller:** Chip Moore. **Director of Stadium Operations:** Nate Doughty. **Head Groundskeeper:** Tim Estensen. **Director of Media/Public Relations:** Robert Gahagan. **Director of Sales/Marketing:** Colleen Standiford. **Senior Account Representative:** Corey Bowdre. **Director of Community Relations:** Janet Zimmerman. **Director of Promotions:** Dan Saggese. **Director of Ticket Sales:** Debra Lynch. **Director of Group Sales:** Tom Smeltzer. **Director of Merchandising:** John Balmain. **Director of Food Services:** Jerome Bill. **Clubhouse Operations:** Scott Donovan. **Office Manager:** Joanne Curnutt.

Field Staff

Manager: Bill Dancy. **Coach:** Max Venable. **Pitching Coach:** Bill Fischer. **Trainer:** Jim Lovell.

Game Information

Radio Announcers: Robert Fish. **No. of Games Broadcast:** Home-71, Away-71. **Flagship Station:** WRVH 910-AM.

PA Announcer: Mike Blacker. **Official Scorer:** Leonard Alley.

Stadium Name (year opened): The Diamond (1985). **Location:** Exit 78 (Boulevard) at junction of I-64 and I-95, follow signs to park. **Standard Game Times:** 7 p.m., Sun. 2.

Visiting Club Hotel: Holiday Inn I-64 and West Broad, 6531 W. Broad St., Richmond, VA 23230. Telephone: (804) 285-9951.

ROCHESTER *RED WINGS*

Office Address: One Morrie Silver Way, Rochester, NY 14608. **Telephone:** (716) 454-1001. **FAX:** (716) 454-1056. **E-Mail Address:** red wings@frontiernet.net.

Affiliation (first year): Baltimore Orioles (1961). **Years in League:** 1885-89, 1891-92, 1895-.

Ownership, Management

Operated by: Rochester Community Baseball, Inc.

Chairman of the Board: Fred Strauss. **President:** Elliot Curwin.

Chief Operating Officer: Naomi Silver. **General Manager:** Dan Mason. **Assistant General Manager:** Will Rumbold. **Controller:** Darlene Giardina. **Head Groundskeeper:** Gene Buonomo. **Director of Media/Public Relations:** Joe Castellano. **Director of Marketing:** Joe Altobelli. **Director of Community Relations:** Chuck Hinkel. **Director of Promotions:** Steve Salluzzo. **Director of Ticket Sales:** Dave Wheat. **Ticket Office Manager:** Dave Welker. **Director of Group Sales:** Russ Ruter. **Director of Merchandising:** Wendy Morrissette. **Director of Food Services:** Tom Sadtler. **Clubhouse Operations:** Kenny Slough. **Executive Secretary:** Paula LoVerde. **Executive Assistant:** Jennifer Waldow. **Administrative Assistants:** Dave Bills, Joe Ferrigno.

Field Staff

Manager: Marv Foley. **Coach:** Dave Cash. **Pitching Coach:** Fred Dallimore. **Trainer:** Guido Van Ryssegem.

Game Information

Radio Announcer: Joe Castellano. **No. of Games Broadcast:** Home-71, Away-71. **Flagship Station:** WHTK 1280-AM.

PA Announcer: Kevin Spears. **Official Scorer:** Len Lustik.

Stadium Name (year opened): Frontier Field (1997). **Location:** Visible and accesible from I-490. NYS Thruway connects with I-490 at exit 45 east of Rochester and exit 47 west of Rochester. When in downtown area, use Plymouth Ave exit to access field. **Standard Game Times:** 7:15 p.m.; Sun. 2:15.

Visiting Club Hotel: Four Points Sheraton, 120 E. Main St., Rochester, NY 14604. Telephone: (716) 546-6400.

SCRANTON/W-B *RED BARONS*

Office Address: 235 Montage Mountain Rd., Moosic, PA 18507. **Mailing Address:** P.O. Box 3449, Scranton, PA 18505. **Telephone:** (717) 969-2255. **FAX:** (717) 963-6564. **E-Mail Address:** barons@epix.net

Affiliation (first year): Philadelphia Phillies (1989). **Years in League:** 1989-.

Ownership, Management

Operated by: Multi-purpose Stadium Authority.

Principal Owner: Lackawanna County.

General Manager: Bill Terlecky. **Assistant General Manager:** Rick Muntean. **Controller:** Tom Durkin. **Director of Media/Public Relations:** Mike Cummings. **Director of Stadium Operations:** Ray Nick. **Head Groundskeeper:** Bill Casterline. **Director of Community Relations:** Kelly Byron. **Director of Ticket Sales:** Cathy Kacer. **Director of Group Sales:** Ron Prislupski. **Director of Food Services:** Rich Sweeney. **Director of Special Projects:** Karen Healy. **Clubhouse Operations:** Frank Worsnick. **Office Manager:** Donna McDonald. **Box Office Manager:** Todd Peters.

Field Staff

Manager: Marc Bombard. **Coach:** Bill Robinson. **Pitching Coach:** Larry Andersen. **Trainer:** Craig Strobel.

Game Information

Radio Announcer: Kent Westling. **No. of Games Broadcast:** Home-71; Away-71. **Flagship Station:** WILK 910/960/980/1300-AM.

PA Announcer: John Davies. **Official Scorer:** Bob McGoff.

Stadium Name (year opened): Lackawanna County Stadium (1989). **Location:** I-81 to exit 51 (Davis Street). **Standard Game Times:** 7:30 p.m., Sun. 6.

Visiting Club Hotel: Radisson, 700 Lackawanna Ave., Scranton, PA 18503. Telephone: (717) 342-8300.

SYRACUSE
SKYCHIEFS

Office Address: P&C Stadium, Syracuse, NY 13208. **Telephone:** (315) 474-7833. **FAX:** (315) 474-2658. **E-Mail Address:** chiefs@dreamscape.com

Affiliation (first year): Toronto Blue Jays (1978). **Years in League:** 1885-89, 1891-92, 1894-1901, 1918, 1920-27, 1934-55, 1961-.

Ownership, Management

Operated by: Community Owned Baseball Club of Central New York, Inc.

Chairman of the Board: Richard Ryan. **President:** Donald Waful.

Executive Vice President/Chief Operating Officer: Anthony "Tex" Simone. **General Manager:** John Simone. **Assistant General Manager:** Tom Van Schaak. **Director of Stadium Operations:** Brian Honeyager. **Assistant, Stadium Operations:** Pat Adorante. **Director of Community Relations and Event Staff Personnel:** Jeff Emmi. **Director of Ticket Sales:** Brian Huebsch. **Director of Group Sales:** Vic Gallucci. **Director of Merchandising:** Mark Hills. **Director of Food Services:** Mark Johnson. **Clubhouse Operations:** Mike Maser, Ryan Abbott. **Administrative Assistant:** Brian Ippolitto. **Assistant Director of Ticket Sales:** H.J. Refici.

Field Staff

Manager: Garth Iorg. **Coach:** Willie Wilson. **Pitching Coach:** Scott Breeden. **Trainer:** Jon Woodworth.

Game Information

Radio Announcer: Ted Deluca, Steve Hyder. **No. of Games Broadcast:** Home-71, Away-71. **Flagship Station:** WHEN 620-AM.

PA Announcer: Unavailable. **Official Scorer:** Joel Marieniss.

Stadium Name (year opened): P&C Stadium (1997). **Location:** NYS Thruway exit 36 to I-81 South, to 7th North St exit, make left on 7th North, right on Hiawatha Boulevard. **Standard Game Times:** 7 p.m., Sun. 6.

Visiting Club Hotel: Ramada Inn, 1305 Buckley Rd., Syracuse, NY 13212. Telephone: (315) 457-8670.

TOLEDO
MUD HENS

Office Address: 2901 Key St., Maumee, OH 43537. **Mailing Address:** P.O. Box 6212, Toledo, OH 43614. **Telephone:** (419) 893-9483. **FAX:** (419) 893-5847. **E-Mail Address:** mudhens@aol.com.

Affiliation (first year): Detroit Tigers (1987). **Years in League:** 1889, 1965-.

Ownership, Management

Operated by: Toledo Mud Hens Baseball Club, Inc.

Principal Owner: Lucas County.

President: Edwin Bergsmark.

General Manager: Gene Cook. **Assistant General Manager, Community Relations:** Jeff Condon. **Assistant General Manager, Public Relations:** Jim Konecny. **Executive Director, Baseball Operations** Joe Napoli. **Marketing and Entertainment Director:** Scott Jeffer. **Marketing and Promotions Director:** Neil Neukam. **Business Manager:** Dorothy Welniak. **Office Manager:** Carol Hamilton. **Group Sales and Marketing:** Erik Ibsen. **Ticket Sales and Marketing:** Kerri White.

Field Staff

Manager: Glenn Ezell. **Coach:** Gary Green. **Pitching Coach:** Jeff Jones. **Trainer:** Lon Pinhey.

Game Information

Radio Announcers: Frank Gilhooley, Jim Weber. **No. of Games Broadcast:** Home-71, Away-71. **Flagship Station:** WMTR 96.1-FM, WFRO 900-AM/99.1-FM.

PA Announcer: John Keller. **Official Scorer:** John Wagner.

Stadium Name (year opened): Ned Skeldon Stadium (1965). **Location:** From Ohio Turnpike, exit 4, north to Toledo, onto Reynolds, right onto Heatherdowns, right onto Key Street. From Detroit, I-75 South to exit 201A (Route 25), right onto Key Street. From Ann Arbor, Route 23 South to Route 475 South, exit 6, left at stoplight, follow Dussel to stadium. From Dayton, I-75 via Route 475 to Maumee exit (Route 24), left onto Key Street. **Standard Game Times:** 7 p.m., Sun. 2.

Visiting Club Hotel: Holiday Inn West, 2340 South Reynolds Rd., Toledo, OH, 43614. Telephone: (419) 865-1361.

PACIFIC COAST LEAGUE

Class AAA

Mailing Address: 2345 South Alma School Road, Suite 110, Mesa, AZ 85210. **Telephone:** (602) 838-2171. **FAX:** (602) 838-2741.

Years League Active: 1903-.

President/Secretary-Treasurer: Bill Cutler.

Vice President: Pat McKernan.

Directors: Joe Buzas (Salt Lake), George Foster (Tacoma), Bob Goughan (Colorado Springs), Richard Holtzman (Tucson), Brent Imlach (Vancouver), Mel Kowalchuk (Edmonton), Pat McKernan (Albuquerque), Russ Parker (Calgary), Craig Pletenik (Phoenix), Hank Stickney (Las Vegas).

Office Secretary: Jeannie Bordes.

Bill Cutler

1997 Opening Date: April 3. **Closing Date:** Sept. 1.

Regular Season: 144 games (split-schedule).

Division Structure: North—Calgary, Edmonton, Salt Lake, Tacoma, Vancouver. **South**—Albuquerque, Colorado Springs, Las Vegas, Phoenix, Tucson.

Playoff Format: First-half division winners play second-half division winners in best-of-5 series. Division playoff winners meet in best-of-5 series for league championship.

All-Star Game: July 9 at Des Moines, IA (joint Triple-A game).

Roster Limit: 23 active, until midnight Aug. 10 when roster can be expanded to 25. **Player Eligibility Rule:** No restrictions.

Brand of Baseball: Rawlings.

Umpires: Ron Barnes (Tucson AZ), Ted Barrett (Mesa, AZ), Robert Brooks (Mesa, AZ), Mike DiMuro (Chandler, AZ), Ray DiMuro (Chandler, AZ), Doug Eddings (Las Cruces, NM), Mark Erramouspe (Rock Springs, WY), Mike Everitt (Chandler, AZ), Joel Fincher (Fort Worth, TX), Andrew Fletcher (Memphis, TN), Heath Jones (Hawthorne, CA), Travis Katzenmeier (Liberal, KS), Ian Lamplugh (Victoria, British Columbia), Bill Miller (Auburn, CA), Scott Nance (Novi, MI), Jeff Patterson (Imperial Beach, CA), Anthony Randazzo (Las Cruces, NM), Don Rea (Las Vegas, NV).

1996 Standings

Club (Affiliate)	W	L	Pct.	GB	'96 Manager
*#Edmonton (Athletics)	84	58	.592	—	Gary Jones
Salt Lake (Twins)	78	66	.542	7	Phil Roof
#Las Vegas (Padres)	73	67	.521	10	Jerry Royster
Calgary (Pirates)	74	68	.521	10	Trent Jewett
Vancouver (Angels)	68	70	.493	14	Don Long
Tucson (Astros)	70	74	.486	15	Tim Tolman
Tacoma (Mariners)	69	73	.486	15	Dave Myers
#Phoenix (Giants)	69	75	.479	16	Ron Wotus
Albuquerque (Dodgers)	67	76	.469	17½	Phil Regan
Colorado Springs (Rockies)	58	83	.411	25½	Brad Mills

*Won playoffs. #Won split-season pennant.

Stadium Information

		Dimensions				
Club	Stadium	LF	CF	RF	Capacity	'96 Att.
Albuquerque	Albuquerque Sports	360	410	340	10,510	307,445
Calgary	Burns	325	400	325	8,000	273,545
Colo. Springs	Sky Sox	350	400	350	9,000	237,826
Edmonton	*TELUS	340	420	320	9,200	463,684
Las Vegas	Cashman Field	328	433	328	9,334	313,212
Phoenix	Scottsdale	360	430	340	10,000	267,649
Salt Lake	Franklin Quest	345	420	315	15,500	621,027
Tacoma	Cheney	325	425	325	9,600	338,500
Tucson	Hi Corbett Field	366	392	348	8,000	307,091
Vancouver	Nat Bailey	335	395	335	6,500	334,800

*Artificial-turf infield

ALBUQUERQUE
DUKES

Office Address: 1601 Stadium Blvd. SE, Albuquerque, NM 87106. **Telephone:** (505) 243-1791. **FAX:** (505) 842-0561. **E-Mail Address:** http://www.fanlink.com/ALBQ DUKES.

Affiliation (first year): Los Angeles Dodgers (1972). **Years in League:** 1972-.

Ownership, Management

Operated by: Albuquerque Professional Baseball, Inc.

Principal Owner, Chairman of the Board: Bob Lozinak.

President, General Manager: Pat McKernan. **Director of Media Relations:** David Sheriff. **Director of Accounting:** Dawnene Shoup. **Director of Administration/General Counsel:** Scott Jacobson. **Director of Sales:** Jim Guscott. **Director of Merchandising/Food Services:** Patrick J. McKernan. **Director of Stadium Operations**: Mick Byers. **Director of Ticket Operations:** Mark Spencer. **Director of Marketing/ Entertainment:** Kip Whittemore. **Director of Business Operations:** Pat Fachet.

Field Staff

Manager: Glenn Hoffman. **Coach:** Jon Debus. **Pitching Coach:** Claude Osteen. **Trainer:** Matt Wilson.

Game Information

Radio Announcers: Mike Roberts, Russ Langer. **No. of Games Broadcast:** Home-72, Away-72. **Flagship Station:** KHTL 920-AM, KNML 1050-AM.

PA Announcer: David Sheriff. **Official Scorer:** Gary Herron.

Stadium Name (year opened): Albuquerque Sports Stadium (1969). **Location:** I-25 to Stadium Blvd. exit, east on Stadium Blvd. to stadium. **Standard Game Times:** 7 p.m., Sun. 1.

Visiting Club Hotel: Plaza Inn Albuquerque, 900 Medical Arts NE, Albuquerque, NM 87106. Telephone: (505) 243-5693.

CALGARY
CANNONS

Office Address: Burns Stadium, 2255 Crowchild Trail NW, Calgary, Alberta T2M 4S7. **Telephone:** (403) 284-1111. **FAX:** (403) 284-4343. **E-Mail Address:** cannons@cadvision.com.

Affiliation (first year): Pittsburgh Pirates (1995). **Years in League:** 1985-.

Ownership, Management

Operated by: Braken Holdings Ltd.

Principal Owners: Russ Parker, Diane Parker.

President: Russ Parker. **Secretary/Tresurer:** Diane Parker.

Directors: Brent Parker, Blake Parker, Darren Parker, Bill Clapham.

Vice President, Baseball Operations: John Traub. **Vice President, Marketing:** Karen Connellan. **Vice President, Finance:** Chris Poffenroth. **Director of Ticketing:** Greg Winthers. **Director of Events and Community Relations:** Darren Parker. **Public Relations Assistant:** Craig Burak. **Marketing and Promotions:** Mike Kaban, Chris Artibello. **Account Executive:** Jason MacAskill. **Food Service Managers:** Murray Drope, Pat Fehr. **Administrative Assistant:** Joan Sherlock. **Clubhouse Managers:** Blair McAusland (visitors), Brian Miettinen (home). **Head Groundskeeper:** Rob Foliot.

Field Staff

Manager: Trent Jewett. **Coach:** Ben Oglivie. **Pitching Coach:** Dave Rajsich. **Trainer:** Sandy Krum.

Game Information

Radio: Unavailable.

PA Announcer: Bill Clapham. **Official Scorer:** Fred Collins.

Stadium Name (year opened): Burns Stadium (1966). **Location:** Crowchild Trail NW to 24th Avenue. **Standard Game Times:** 6:05 p.m. (April), 7:05 (May-August); Sat. 1:35 (April-May), 7:05 (June-August); Sun. 1:35.

Visiting Club Hotel: Sandman Hotel, 888 7th Ave. SW, Calgary. Telephone: (403) 237-8626.

COLORADO SPRINGS
SKY SOX

Office Address: 4385 Tutt Blvd., Colorado Springs, CO 80922. **Telephone:** (719) 597-1449. **FAX:** (719) 597-2491. **E-Mail Address:** info@skysox.com

Affiliation (first year): Colorado Rockies (1993). **Years in League:** 1988-.

Ownership, Management

Operated by: Colorado Springs Sky Sox, Inc.

Principal Owners: David Elmore, D.G. Elmore.

President/General Manager: Bob Goughan. **Senior Vice President, Administration:** Sam Polizzi. **Senior Vice President, Finance:** Carrol Payne. **Vice President, Operations:** Dwight Hall. **Vice President, Marketing:** Rai Henniger. **Vice President, Stadium Operations:** Mark Leasure. **Assistant General Manager, Public Relations:** Chris Costello. **Assistant General Manager, Corporate Development:** Chad Starbuck. **Assistant General Manager, Advertising:** Nick Sciarratta. **Director, Broadcast Operations:** Dan Karcher. **Director, Group Sales:** Brien Smith. **Director, Merchandising:** Robert Stein. **Clubhouse Managers:** Brian Ochsie, Murlin Whitten. **Director, Community Relations:** Michael Hirsch.

Field Staff

Manager: Paul Zuvella. **Coach:** Tony Torchia. **Pitching Coach:** Sonny Siebert. **Trainer:** Keith Dugger.

Game Information

Radio Announcers: Dick Chase, Dan Karcher. **No. of Games Bradcast:** Home-72, Away-72. **Flagship Station:** KRDO 1240-AM.

PA Announcer: Unavailable. **Official Scorers:** Marty Grantz, Dave Toller.

Stadium Name (year opened): Sky Sox Stadium (1988). **Location:** I-25 South to Woodmen Road exit, east on Woodmen to Powers Blvd., right on Powers to Barnes Road. **Standard Game Times:** 6:35 p.m. (April-June 4), 7:05 (June 10-Aug.); Sat.-Sun. 1:35 (April-June 22).

Visiting Club Hotel: LeBaron Hotel, 314 West Bijou St., Colorado Springs, CO 80905. Telephone: (719) 471-8680.

EDMONTON
TRAPPERS

Office Address: 10233 96th Ave., Edmonton, Alberta T5K 0A5. **Telephone:** (403) 429-2934. **FAX:** (403) 426-5640. **E-Mail Address:** trappers@planet.eon.net.

Affiliation (first year): Oakland Athletics (1995). **Years in League:** 1981-.

Ownership, Management

Operated by: Trappers Baseball Corp.

Principal Owner: Peter Pocklington.

President/General Manager: Mel Kowalchuk. **Assistant General Manager:** Dennis Henke. **Accountant:** Gabrielle Hampel. **Stadium Manager:** Reuben Konnik. **Baseball Information Manager:** Gary Tater. **Sales Manager:** Rob McGillis. **Senior Account Representative:** Ken Charuk. **Community Relations/Marketing Manager:** Lauri Holomis. **Ticket Manager:** Barb Little. **Group Sales Manager:** Susan Jackson. **Clubhouse Operations:** Ian Rose. **Director of Broadcasting:** Al Coates. **Office Manager:** Nancy Yeo.

Field Staff

Manager: Gary Jones. **Coach:** Orv Franchuk. **Pitching Coach:** Pete Richert. **Trainer:** Walt Horn.

Game Information

Radio Announcer: Al Coates. **No. of Games Broadcast:** Unavailable. **Flagship Station:** Unavailable.

PA Announcer: Dean Parthenis. **Official Scorer:** Al Coates.

Stadium Name (year opened): TELUS Field (1995). **Location:** From north, 101st St. to 96th Ave., left on 96th, one block east; From south, take Calgary Trail North to Queen Elizabeth hill, turn right across Walterdale Bridge, right on 96th Ave. **Standard Game Times:** 7:05; Sun. 2:05.

Visiting Club Hotel: Edmonton Hilton, 10235 101st St., Edmonton, Alberta P5J 3E9. Telephone: (403) 428-7111.

LAS VEGAS
STARS

Office Address: 850 Las Vegas Blvd. N., Las Vegas, NV 89101. **Telephone:** (702) 386-7200. **FAX:** (702) 386-7214. **E-Mail Address:** lvstars@earthlink.com.

Affiliation (first year): San Diego Padres (1982). **Years in League:** 1982-.

Ownership, Management

Operated by: Mandalay Sports Enterprises.

Principal Owners: Hank Stickney, Ken Stickney, Peter Guber, Paul Schaeffer.

General Manager: Don Logan. **Assistant General Manager:** Mark Grenier. **Senior Administrative Assistant:** Robert Blum. **Vice President, Business Operations:** Robert Murphy. **Controller:** Allen Taylor. **Accounting:** Cindy Goodwyn. **Sales Manager:** Steve Moser. **Operations Manager:** Nick Fitzenreider. **Director of Ticket Operations:** Marie Schenk. **Manager of Ticket Administration:** Robin Anderson. **Ticketing Coordinator:** Richard Funke. **Director of Public Relations/Marketing:** Lisa Talley. **Public Relations Managers:** D.J. Allen, Jim Anderson. **Marketing Coordinator/Community Relations:** Karin Tomcik. **Director of Merchandising:** Eric Deutsch. **Special Projects Coordinator:** Meredith Breen. **Account Executives:** Eric Carrington, Eric Dornak, Chuck Johnson, Jon Sandler. **Group Sales Representatives:** Greg Dye, Melissa Freeland, Darren Smith, Laurie Wanser. **Administrative Services Manager:** Mary McConnell.

Field Staff

Manager: Jerry Royster. **Pitching Coach:** Sid Monge. **Trainer:** Steve Sayles.

Game Information

Radio Announcers: Jon Sandler, Tim Neverett. **No. of Games Broadcast:** Home-72, Away-72. **Flagship Station:** KORK 920-AM.

PA Announcer: Unavailable. **Official Scorer:** Jim Gemma.

Stadium Name (year opened): Cashman Field (1983). **Location:** I-15 to U.S. 95 (exit downtown), east on 95 to Las Vegas Blvd. North exit, north on Las Vegas Boulevard. **Standard Game Times:** 7:05 p.m.; Sun. 1:05 (April-May), 7:05 (June-September).

Visiting Club Hotel: Las Vegas Club Hotel and Casino, 18 E. Fremont St., Las Vegas, NV 89101. Telephone: (702) 385-1664.

PHOENIX
FIREBIRDS

Office Address: 7408 E. Osborn Road, Scottsdale, AZ 85251. **Mailing Address:** P.O. Box 8528, Scottsdale, AZ 85252. **Telephone:** (602) 275-0500. **FAX:** (602) 990-8987. **E-Mail Address:** firebird@primenet.com

Affiliation (first year): San Francisco Giants (1966). **Years in League:** 1958-59, 1966-.

Ownership, Management

Operated by: Professional Sports, Inc.

Principal Owner/Chairman: Martin Stone. **President:** Larry Yount.

General Manager: Craig Pletenik. **Assistant General Manager:** Bill Gatlin. **Controller:** Mary Jo Balthasar. **Director of Media/Public Relations:** George King. **Director of Sales/Marketing:** Bill Sandillo. **Senior Account Representative:** Becky Larsen. **Director of Promotions:** Tom FitzSimons. **Director of Ticket Sales/Merchandising:** Craig Bradley. **Assistant Director of Merchandise:** Mort Bloomberg. **Clubhouse Operations:** Phil Garcia (home), Mike Murray (visitors). **Office Manager:** Jamie Jeffries.

Field Staff

Manager: Ron Wotus. **Coach:** Joe Lefebvre. **Pitching Coach:** Joel Horlen. **Trainer:** Donna Papangellin.

Game Information

Radio Announcers: Kent Derdivanis, Nick Simonetta, Jim Lefebvre. **No. of Games Broadcast:** Home-72, Away-72. **Flagship Station:** KUPD2 1060-AM.

PA Announcer: Bob Baker. **Official Scorer:** Dale Messmer.

Stadium Name (year opened): Scottsdale Stadium (1992). **Location:** From I-10 (I-17 South), take Broadway Road East exit to Scottsdale Road, left on Scottsdale, right on Osborn Road. **Standard Game Times:** 7:05

p.m.; Sun. 6:05.

Visiting Club Hotel: Days Inn-Scottsdale, 4710 N. Scottsdale Road, Scottsdale, AZ 85251. Telephone: (602) 947-9511.

SALT LAKE
BUZZ

Office Address: 77 W. 1300, Salt Lake City, UT 84115. **Mailing Address:** P.O. Box 4108, Salt Lake City, UT 84110. **Telephone:** (801) 485-3800. **FAX:** (801) 485-6818. **E-mail Address:** slbuzz@ix.netcom.com

Affiliation (first year): Minnesota Twins (1994). **Years in League:** 1915-25, 1958-65, 1970-84, 1994-.

Ownership, Management

Operated by: Buzas Baseball, Inc.

Principal Owners: Joe Buzas, Penny Buzas.

President/General Manager: Joe Buzas. **Assistant General Managers:** Dorsena Picknell, Rob White. **Director of Media/Public Relations:** Kent Haslam. **Director of Marketing:** Brett Hullinger. **Business Manager:** Jackie Riley. **Marketingl/Sales Manager:** Dennis Wansor. **Ticket Manager:** Meg Madson. **Senior Account Executives:** Jim Hochstrasser, David Kemper.

Field Staff

Manager: Phil Roof. **Coach:** Bill Springman. **Pitching Coach:** Rick Anderson. **Trainer:** Rick McWane.

Game Information

Radio Announcer: Steve Klauke. **No. of Games Broadcast:** Home-72, Away-72. **Flagship Station:** KFAN 1320-AM.

PA Announcer: Jeff Reeves. **Official Scorers:** Howard Nakagama, Bruce Hilton.

Stadium Name (year opened): Franklin Quest Field (1994). **Location:** From I-15/I-80, east at 1300 South exit to corner of 1300 South and West Temple. **Standard Game Times:** 7 p.m.; Sun. 2 (April), 5 (May-September).

Visiting Club Hotel: Holiday Inn-Downtown, 999 S. Main St., Salt Lake City, UT 84111. Telephone: (801) 359-8600.

TACOMA
RAINIERS

Office Address: 2502 S. Tyler, Tacoma, WA 98405. **Mailing Address:** P.O. Box 11087, Tacoma, WA 98411. **Telephone:** (206) 752-7707. **FAX:** (206) 752-7135. **E-Mail Address:** TacomaPCL@aol.com

Affiliation (first year): Seattle Mariners (1995). **Years in League:** 1904-05, 1960-.

Ownership, Management

Operated by: George's Pastime, Inc.

Principal Owners: George Foster, Sue Foster.

President: George Foster. **Board of Directors:** Sue Foster, Jack Pless, Carl Dowdy.

Director of Sales/Marketing: Mel Taylor. **Director of Stadium Operations:** Bob Christofferson. **Director of Media/Public Relations:** Kevin Kalal. **Executive Assistant:** Jan Plein. **Financial Manager:** Gene Boggio. **Accounting:** Tara Duncan, Cindi Yee. **Director of Promotions:** Colleen Sullivan. **Director of Group Sales:** Dave Lewis. **Director of Food Services:** Frank Maryott. **Director of Ticket Sales:** John Pesch. **Director of Merchandising:** Jeanette Collett. **Director of Media/Advertising:** Renee Waltz. **Account Representatives:** Connie Littlejohn-Rivers, Andy Hanson. **Groundskeepers:** Tim Silcott, Dave Sterbick.

Field Staff

Manager: Dave Myers. **Coach:** Henry Cotto. **Pitching Coach:** Jeff Andrews. **Trainer:** Randy Roetter.

Game Information

Radio Announcer: Bob Robertson. **No. of Games Broadcast:** Home-72, Away-72. **Flagship Stations:** KH20 850-AM.

PA Announcer: Jeff Randall. **Official Scorers:** Kevin Kalal, Darin Padur, Mark Johnston.

Stadium Name (year opened): Cheney Stadium (1960). **Location:** From I-5 North/South, take exit 132 (Highway 16 West) for two miles, 19th Avenue East exit, right on Tyler Street. **Standard Game Times:** 7:05 p.m.,

Sun. 1:35.

Visiting Club Hotel: Days Inn, 6802 Tacoma Mall Blvd., Tacoma, WA 98409. Telephone: (206) 475-5900.

TUCSON
TOROS

Office Address: 3400 E. Camino Campestre, Tucson, AZ 85716. **Mailing Address:** P.O. Box 27045, Tucson, AZ 85726. **Telephone:** (520) 325-2621. **FAX:** (520) 327-2371. **E-Mail Address:** toros@azstarnet.com.

Affiliation (first year): Milwaukee Brewers (1997). **Years in League:** 1969-.

Ownership, Management

Operated by: Tucson Toros, Inc.

Principal Owner/President: Richard Holtzman. **Chairman of the Board:** John Henry.

General Manager: Mike Feder. **Assistant General Manager:** Diane Ronstadt. **Director of Business Operations:** Pattie Feder. **Director of Media/Public Relations:** David Brady. **Director of Community Relations:** Eric May. **Director of Ticket Sales:** Doug Leary. **Director of Merchandising:** Matt Halverson. **Account Executive/In-Game Operations:** Kristin Taylor. **Head Groundskeeper:** Rick Horscht.

Field Staff

Manager: Tim Ireland. **Coach:** Bob Mariano. **Pitching Coach:** Mark Littell. **Trainer:** Peter Kolb.

Game Information

Radio Announcer: Dave Brady. **No. of Games Broadcast:** Home-72, Away-72. **Flagship Station:** KTKT 990-AM.

PA Announcers: Anthony DeFazio, Bill Roemer. **Official Scorer:** Irwin Fletcher.

Stadium Name (year opened): Hi Corbett Field (1937). **Location:** I-10 to Broadway exit, east to Randolph Way, south one mile. **Standard Games Times:** 7:30 p.m.; Sun. 6 (April-May), 7 (June-August).

Visiting Club Hotel: Ramada Inn-Foothills, 6944 E. Tanque Verde, Tucson, AZ 85715. Telephone: (520) 886-9595.

VANCOUVER
CANADIANS

Office Address: 4601 Ontario St., Vancouver, B.C. V5V 3H4. **Telephone:** (604) 872-5232. **FAX:** (604) 872-1714.

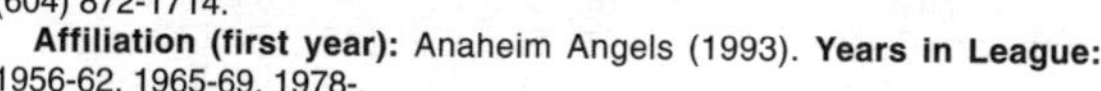

Affiliation (first year): Anaheim Angels (1993). **Years in League:** 1956-62, 1965-69, 1978-.

Ownership, Management

Operated by: Japan Sports Systems, Inc.

President: John McHale.

Vice President/General Manager: Brent Imlach. **Vice President:** Gary Arthur. **Manager, Accounting/Administration:** Harry Chan. **Manager, Marketing Services/Game Promotions:** Ken Cooper. **Manager, Marketing Services/Souvenir Operations:** Torchy Pechet. **Manager, Team Operations:** Peter Daubaras. **Manager, Media Relations:** Steve Hoem. **Manager, Stadium/Field Operations:** Bill Posthumus.

Field Staff

Manager: Bruce Hines. **Coach:** Leon Durham. **Pitching Coach:** Howie Gersberg. **Trainer:** Don McGann.

Game Information

Radio Announcer: Brook Ward. **No. of Games Broadcast:** All night games. **Flagship Station:** CKMA 850-AM.

PA Announcer: Jerry Landa. **Official Scorer:** Pat Karl.

Stadium Name (year opened): Nat Bailey Stadium (1952). **Location:** From downtown—Cambie Street Bridge, left on East 33rd St., left on Clancy Loringer Way, right to stadium. From south—Highway 99 to Oak Street, right on 41st Ave., left on Ontario. **Standard Game Times:** 7:05 p.m.; Wed. 12:15, Sun. 1:30.

Visiting Club Hotel: Unavailable.

EASTERN LEAGUE

Class AA

Office Address: 511 Congress, Portland, ME 04104. **Mailing Address:** P.O. Box 9711, Portland, ME 04104. **Telephone:** (207) 761-2700. **FAX:** (207) 761-7064.

Years League Active: 1923-.

President: Bill Troubh.

Vice President: Greg Agganis. **Corporate Secretary:** Gerry Berthiaume.

Directors: Greg Agganis (Akron), Joe Buzas (New Britain), Charles Eshbach (Portland), Barry Gordon (Norwich), Peter Kirk (Bowie), Ed Massey (New Haven), Steve Resnick (Harrisburg), Dick Stanley (Trenton), Craig Stein (Reading), Mike Urda (Binghamton).

Bill Troubh

1997 Opening Date: April 3. **Closing Date:** Sept. 1.

Regular Season: 142 games.

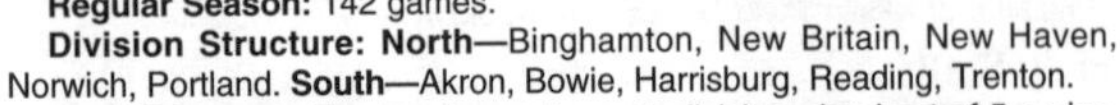

Division Structure: North—Binghamton, New Britain, New Haven, Norwich, Portland. **South**—Akron, Bowie, Harrisburg, Reading, Trenton.

Playoff Format: Top two teams in each division play best-of-5 series. Division playoff winners meet in best-of-5 series for league championship.

All-Star Game: July 7 at San Antonio (joint Double-A game).

Roster Limit: 23 active, until midnight Aug. 10 when roster can be expanded to 25. **Player Eligibility Rule:** No restrictions.

Brand of Baseball: Rawlings ROM-EL.

Statistician: Howe Sportsdata International, Boston Fish Pier, West Bldg. #2—Suite 306, Boston MA 02210.

Umpires: Jorge Bauza (San Juan, PR), Troy Blades (Clark's Harbour, Nova Scotia), Chris Boberg (South Grafton, MA), Robert Cook (Gahanna, OH), John Creek (Kalamazoo, MI), Robert Drake (Mesa, AZ), Paul Emmel (Sanford, MI), Michael Fichter (Lansing, IL), Dan Gnadt (Moorhead, MN), Pat McGinnis (Joliet, IL), Tim Pasch (Plant City, FL), Pat Spieler (Omaha, NE), Mike Van Vleet (Battle Creek, MI), Mark Wegner (Lakeland, FL), Bill Welke (Coldwater, MI).

1996 Standings

Club (Affiliate)	W	L	Pct.	GB	'96 Manager
#Trenton (Red Sox)	86	56	.606	—	Ken Macha
#Portland (Marlins)	83	58	.589	2½	Carlos Tosca
Binghamton (Mets)	76	66	.535	10	John Tamargo
*Harrisburg (Expos)	74	68	.521	12	Pat Kelly
Norwich (Yankees)	71	70	.504	14½	Jim Essian
Canton-Akron (Indians)	71	71	.500	15	Jeff Datz
New Haven (Rockies)	66	75	.468	19½	Bill Hayes
Reading (Phillies)	66	75	.468	19½	Bill Robinson
Hardware City (Twins)	61	81	.430	25	Al Newman
Bowie (Orioles)	54	88	.380	32	B.Miscik/T.Blackwell

*Won playoffs #Won division pennant

Stadium Information

Club	Stadium	Dimensions LF	CF	RF	Capacity	'96 Att.
Akron*	Canal Park	332	400	337	10,000	213,278
Binghamton	Binghamton Municipal	330	400	330	6,042	202,461
Bowie	Prince George's	309	405	309	10,000	396,086
Harrisburg	RiverSide	335	400	335	6,200	230,744
New Britain#	New Britain	325	400	325	6,125	160,765
New Haven	Yale Field	345	405	315	5,900	254,084
Norwich	Thomas J. Dodd	309	401	309	6,200	269,022
Portland	Hadlock Field	315	400	325	6,860	408,503
Reading	Municipal Memorial	330	400	330	8,000	375,326
Trenton	Mercer County	330	407	330	6,341	437,396

*Franchise operated in Canton in 1996
#Known as Hardware City in 1996

AKRON
AEROS

(Franchise operated in Canton, Ohio, in 1996)

Office Address: 300 S. Main St., Akron, OH 44308. **Telephone:** (330) 253-5151. **FAX:** (330) 253-3300.

Affiliation (first year): Cleveland Indians (1989). **Years in League:** 1989-.

Ownership, Management

Operated by: Akron Professional Baseball, Inc.

Principal Owners: Mike Agganis, Greg Agganis.

Chief Executive Officer: Mike Agganis. **President:** Greg Agganis.

Vice President, General Manager: Jeff Auman. **Assistant General Manager, Marketing and Communications:** Vinny Maculaitis. **Assistant General Manager, Ticket Operations:** Drew Cooke. **Assistant General Manager, Finance:** Bob Larkins. **Director, Community Relations:** Katie Dannemiller. **Director, Media Relations/Broadcasting:** Scot Berggren. **Director, Advertising/Publications:** Alyson Footer. **Director, Ticket Sales:** Kurt Landes. **Director, Group Sales:** Jim Draper. **Assistant Director, Group Sales:** Ben Tochinsky. **Director, Season Ticket/Loge Services:** Dan Bailey. **Account Representatives, Group Sales:** Thomas Craven, Mike Swope. **Director, Merchandising:** Kris Roukey. **Director, Field Maintenance:** Dan Schrier. **Director, Stadium Operations:** Steve Buso. **Director, Player Facilities:** Fletcher Wilkes.

Field Staff

Manager: Jeff Datz. **Coach:** Minnie Mendoza. **Pitching Coach:** Tony Arnold. **Trainer:** Dan DeVoe.

Game Information

Radio Announcers: Jim Clark, Scott Berggren. **No. of Games Broadcast:** Home-71, Away-71. **Flagship Station:** WHLO 640-AM.

PA Announcer: Joe Dunn. **Official Scorer:** Dick Ziegler.

Stadium Name (year opened): Canal Park (1997). **Location:** From I-76 East or I-77 South, exit onto Route 59 North, exit at Exchange/Cedar and turn right onto Cedar, left onto Main, ballpark is on left. From I-76 West or I-77 North, exit at Broadway/Main, follow Broadway and turn left onto State, left onto Main, ballpark is on right. **Standard Game Times:** 7:05 p.m.; Sat. (April) 2:05; Sun. 2:05.

Visiting Club Hotel: Ramada Plaza, 20 W. Mill St., Akron, OH 44308. Telephone: (330) 384-1500.

BINGHAMTON
METS

Office Address: 211 Henry St., Binghamton, NY 13901. **Mailing Address:** P.O. Box 598, Binghamton, NY 13902. **Telephone:** (607) 723-6387. **FAX:** (607) 723-7779. **E-Mail Address:** bmets@spectra.net.

Affiliation (first year): New York Mets (1992). **Years in League:** 1923-37, 1940-63, 1966-68, 1992-.

Ownership, Management

Operated by: Binghamton Mets Baseball Club, Inc.

Principal Owners: David Maines, William Maines, R.C. Reuteman, George Scherer, Christopher Urda, Michael Urda.

President: Michael Urda.

General Manager: R.C. Reuteman. **Assistant General Manager:** Tim Lyons. **Director of Business Operations:** Jim Weed. **Director of Stadium Operations:** Richard Tylicki. **Head Groundskeeper:** Craig Evans. **Director of Group Sales:** Mitti Daniel. **Director of Merchanding:** Domenic Ruffa. **Director of Food and Beverage:** Pete Brotherton. **Clubhouse Operations:** Tony Cleary. **Bookkeeper:** Karen Micalizzi. **Administrative Assistant:** Sally Subik.

Field Staff

Manager: Rick Sweet. **Coach:** Howie Freiling. **Pitching Coach:** Billy Champion. **Trainer:** Jeff Weems.

Game Information

Radio Announcer: Dave Schultz. **No. of Games Broadcast:** Home-71, Away-71. **Flagship Station:** WNBF 1290-AM.

PA Announcer: Roger Neel. **Official Scorer:** Steve Kraly.

Stadium Name (year opened): Binghamton Municipal (1992). **Location:** I-81 to exit 4S (Binghamton), Route 11 exit to Henry Street.

Standard Game Times: 7 p.m.; Sat. (April-May 24) 1:30, (June 7-Sept.) 7; Sun. 1:30.

Visiting Club Hotel: Holiday Inn Arena, 2-8 Hawley St., Binghamton, NY 13901. Telephone: (607) 722-1212.

BOWIE
BAYSOX

Office Address: 4101 NE Crain Highway, Bowie, MD 20716. **Mailing Address:** P.O. Box 1661, Bowie, MD 20717. **Telephone:** (301) 805-6000. **FAX:** (301) 805-6008.

Affiliation (first year): Baltimore Orioles (1993). **Years In League:** 1993-.

Ownership, Management

Operated by: Maryland Baseball, LP.

Principal Owners: Peter Kirk, Pete Simmons, Hugh Schindel, Frank Perdue, John Daskalakis.

Chairman of the Board, Chief Executive Officer: Peter Kirk. **President:** Pete Simmons.

General Manager: Jon Danos. **Assistant General Manager:** Mike Munter. **Controller:** Matt Ball. **Director of Stadium Operations:** Will Gardner. **Head Groundskeeper:** Jimmy Juergens. **Director of Public Relations and Broadcasting:** Dave Collins. **Account Representatives:** Jeff Basgin, Mark Calvert, Dave Funk, Eric Landseadel. **Director of Ticket Sales:** Matt Ruddo. **Director of Group Sales:** Brenda Berger. **Director of Merchandising:** Belinda Corken. **Merchandising Manager:** Jack Roberts. **Director of Special Projects:** Kia Dean. **Clubhouse Operations:** Dave Dolney. **Office Manager:** Margo Carpenter. **Administrative Assistant:** Becci Velasco. **Director of Mini-Plan Sales:** Stanley Cohen. **Assistant Director, Group Sales:** Laurie Norman.

Field Staff

Manager: Joe Ferguson. **Coach:** Bien Figueroa. **Pitching Coach:** Larry McCall. **Trainer:** Mitch Bibb.

Game Information

Radio Announcer: Dave Collins. **No. of Games Broadcast:** Home-71; Away-71. **Flagship Station:** WNAV 1430-AM.

PA Announcer: Bud Freeman. **Official Scorer:** Jeff Hertz.

Stadium Name (year opened): Prince George's Stadium (1994). **Location:** U.S. 50 to U.S. 301 South, left at second light into stadium.

Standard Game Times: 7:05 p.m., Sun. 1:05.

Visiting Club Hotel: Days Inn-Historic Annapolis, 2520 Riva Rd., Annapolis, MD 21401. Telephone: (410) 224-2800.

HARRISBURG
SENATORS

Office Address: RiverSide Stadium, City Island, Harrisburg, PA 17101. **Mailing Address:** P.O. Box 15757, Harrisburg, PA 17105. **Telephone:** (717) 231-4444. **FAX:** (717) 231-4445. **E-Mail Address:** www.fanlink.com/hburgsenators/

Affiliation (first year): Montreal Expos (1991). **Years in League:** 1924-35, 1987-.

Ownership, Management

Operated by: Harrisburg Civic Baseball Club, Inc.

Chairman of the Board: Greg Martini.

General Manager: Todd Vander Woude. **Business Manager:** Steve Resnick. **Assistant General Manager, Baseball Operations:** Mark Mattern. **Assistant General Manager, Business Operations:** Mark Clarke. **Director, Broadcasting:** Brad Sparesus. **Facilities Manager:** Tim Foreman. **Concessions Manager:** Steve Leininger. **Ticket Manager:** Paul Seeley. **Group Sales:** Brian Egli, Mickey Graham. **Picnic Operations:** Carol Baker. **Groundskeeper:** Joe Bialek. **Ticket Sales:** Tom Wess.

Field Staff

Manager: Rick Sofield. **Coach:** Jeff Livesey. **Pitching Coach:** Dean Treanor. **Trainer:** Jeff Barnes.

Game Information

Radio Announcers: Brad Sparesus, Mark Mattern. **No. of Games Broadcast:** Home-71, Away-71. **Flagship Station:** WKBO 1230-AM.

PA Announcer: Bob Morgan. **Official Scorer:** Unavailable.

Stadium Name (year opened): RiverSide Stadium (1987). **Location:** I-

83, exit 23 (Second Street) to Market Street, bridge to City Island. **Standard Game Times:** 7:05 p.m.; Sun. 1:05.

Visiting Club Hotel: Hilton Hotel, One 2nd St., Harrisburg, PA 17101. Telephone: (717) 233-6000.

NEW BRITAIN *ROCK CATS*

Office Address: New Britain Stadium, South Main Street, New Britain, CT 06051. **Mailing Address:** P.O. Box 1718, New Britain, CT 06050. **Telephone:** (860) 224-8383. **FAX:** (860) 225-6267.

Affiliation (first year): Minnesota Twins (1995). **Years in League:** 1983-.

Ownership, Management

Operated by: Buzas Enterprises, Inc.

Principal Owner, Chairman: Joe Buzas. **President:** Hilary Buzas-Drammis.

General Manager: Gerald Berthiaume. **Assistant General Manager:** Mark Mogul. **Director of Stadium Operations:** Jeremy Gibson. **Director of Media/Public Relations:** Robin Wentz. **Director of Ticket Sales:** Sebastian Thomas. **Director of Group Sales:** Ryan Donahue. **Director of Food Services:** Donna Mogul.

Field Staff

Manager: Al Newman. **Coach:** Jose Baez. **Pitching Coach:** Gorman Heimueller. **Trainer:** Lanning Tucker.

Game Information

Radio: None.

PA Announcer: Roy Zurell. **Official Scorer:** Unavailable.

Stadium Name (year opened): New Britain Stadium (1996). **Location:** I-84 to 72 East (exit 35) to Ellis St. (exit 25), left at light, left on South Main St., stadium one mile on right. **Standard Game Times:** 7 p.m., 6 April, Sun. 2.

Visiting Club Hotel: Ramada Hotel, 65 Columbus Blvd., New Britain, CT 06051. Telephone: (860) 224-9161.

NEW HAVEN *RAVENS*

Office Address: 252 Derby Ave., West Haven, CT 06516. **Telephone:** (203) 782-3140. **FAX:** (203) 782-3150. **E-Mail Address:** ravens@connix.com.

Affiliation (first year): Colorado Rockies (1994). **Years in League:** 1916-32, 1994-.

Ownership, Management

Operated by: New Haven Ravens Baseball, LP.

Principal Owner: Ed Massey.

General Manager: Charlie Dowd. **Assistant General Manager:** Joe Zajac. **Director of Operations:** Chris Canetti. **Director of Marketing:** Mark Tomey. **Accounting:** Tamaia Nolan. **Director of Ticket Sales:** Mark Calabro. **Director of Group Sales:** Nancy Gorman. **Director of Merchandising:** Tom McManus. **Director of Food Services:** Bill Brown. **Office Manager:** Lori McCarthy. **Director of Broadcasting:** Matt Devlin. **Facility Manager:** Roy Kirchner. **Assistant Accounting Manager:** Barbara Preto.

Field Staff

Manager: Bill Hayes. **Coach:** Jay Loviglio. **Pitching Coach:** Jim Wright. **Trainer:** Marc Gustafson.

Game Information

Radio Announcer: Matt Devlin. **No. of Games Broadcast:** Home-71, Away-71. **Flagship Station:** WAVZ 1300-AM.

PA Announcer: Unavailable. **Official Scorer:** Unavailable.

Stadium Name (year opened): Yale Field (1927). **Location:** From I-95, take eastbound exit 44 or westbound exit 45 to Route 10 and follow the Yale Bowl signs. From Merritt Parkway, take exit 57, follow 34 East. **Standard Game Times:** 7:05 p.m., Sun. 2:05.

Visiting Club Hotel: Days Hotel, 490 Saw Mill Road, West Haven, CT 06516. Telephone: (203) 933-0344.

NORWICH
NAVIGATORS

Office Address: 14 Stott Ave., Norwich, CT 06360. **Mailing Address:** P.O. Box 6003, Yantic, CT 06389. **Telephone:** (860) 887-7962. **FAX:** (860) 886-5996. **E-Mail Address:** www.gators.com.

Affiliation (first year): New York Yankees (1995). **Years in League:** 1995-.

Ownership, Management

Operated by: Minor League Sports Enterprises, LP.

Principal Owners: Bob Friedman, Neil Goldman, Barry Gordon, Marc Klee, Hank Smith.

Chairman of the Board: Barry Gordon. **President:** Hank Smith.

General Manager: Brian Mahoney. **Director of Stadium Operations:** Geoff Brown. **Director of Sales/Marketing:** Tom Hinsch. **Controller:** Richard Darling. **Head Groundskeeper:** Will Schnell. **Director of Media/Public Relations:** Shawn Holliday. **Ticket Sales Managers:** Jon Aronson, Chris Fritz. **Group Sales Managers:** John Clark, Keith O'Brien. **Director of Merchandising:** Mike Landeen. **Director of Food Services:** Matt Perachi.

Field Staff

Manager: Trey Hillman. **Coach:** Tony Perezchica. **Pitching Coach:** Rick Tomlin. **Trainer:** Greg Spratt.

Game Information

Radio Announcers: Shawn Holliday, Matt Provence. **No. of Games Broadcast:** Home-71, Away-71. **Flagship Station:** WSVB 980-AM.

PA Announcer: Sean Boardman. **Official Scorer:** Gene Gumbs.

Stadium Name (year opened): Senator Thomas J. Dodd Stadium (1995). **Location:** I-395 to exit 82, follow signs to Norwich Industrial Park, stadium is in back of industrial park. **Standard Game Times:** 7:05 p.m.; (April-May) 6:35; Sat. (April-May) 2:05; Sun. 2:05.

Visiting Club Hotel: Niantic Days Inn, 265 Flanders Road, Niantic, CT 06357. Telephone: (860) 739-6921.

PORTLAND
SEA DOGS

Office Address: 271 Park Ave., Portland, ME 04102. **Mailing Address:** P.O. Box 636, Portland, ME 04104. **Telephone:** (207) 874-9300. **FAX:** (207) 780-0317.

Affiliation (first year): Florida Marlins (1994). **Years in League:** 1994-.

Ownership, Management

Operated by: Portland, Maine Baseball, Inc.

Principal Owner, Chairman of the Board: Daniel Burke.

President, General Manager: Charles Eshbach. **Assistant General Manager:** John Kameisha. **Director of Business Operations:** Jim Heffley. **Director of Stadium Operations:** Mike Fagerson. **Head Groundskeeper:** Rick Anderson. **Director of Sales/Marketing:** Mike Gillogly. **Director of Ticket Sales:** Bill Connolly. **Assistant Director of Ticket Sales:** Jim Beaudoin. **Director of Merchandising:** Murray Roberts. **Assistant Director of Merchandising:** Elliott Barry. **Director of Food Services:** Matt Drivas. **Office Manager:** Judy Bray.

Field Staff

Manager: Fredi Gonzalez. **Coach:** Sal Rende. **Pitching Coach:** Britt Burns. **Trainer:** Tim Abraham.

Game Information

Radio Announcer: Andy Young. **No. of Games Broadcast:** Home-71, Away-71. **Flagship Station:** WZAN 970-AM.

PA Announcer: Dean Rogers. **Official Scorer:** Leroy Rand.

Stadium Name (year opened): Hadlock Field (1994). **Location:** From south—I-295 to exit 5A, merge onto Congress Street, left at St. John Street, merge right onto Park Avenue; From north—I-295 to exit 6A, right on Park Avenue. **Standard Game Times:** 6 p.m. (April-May), 7 (June-August); Sat. 1 (April-May), 7 (June-August); Sun.: 1 (April-June), 4 (June-August).

Visiting Club Hotel: Radisson Eastland Plaza, 157 High St., Portland, ME 04101. Telephone: (207) 775-5411.

READING *PHILLIES*

Office Address: Rt. 61/South Centre Ave., Reading, PA 19605. **Mailing Address:** P.O. Box 15050, Reading, PA 19612. **Telephone:** (610) 375-8469. **FAX:** (610) 373-5868. **E-Mail address:** rphils@voicenet.com

Affiliation (first year): Philadelphia Phillies (1967). **Years in League:** 1933-35, 1952-61, 1963-65, 1967-.

Ownership, Management

Operated by: E&J Baseball Club, Inc.

Principal Owner/President: Craig Stein.

General Manager: Chuck Domino. **Director of Sales and Marketing:** Scott Hunsicker. **Director of Stadium and Food Operations:** Andy Bortz. **Director of Media/Community Relations:** Mark Wallace. **Director of Ticket Operations:** Zach Conen. **Director of Business Development and Game Operations:** Troy Potthoff. **Business Manager:** Denise Haage. **Director of Group Sales:** Jeff Tagliaferro. **Director of Stadium Grounds:** Dan Douglas. **Assistant Director of Operations:** Jamie Keitsock. **Assistant Directors of Group Sales:** Joe Pew, Kevin Sklenarik.

Field Staff

Manager: Al LeBoeuf. **Coach:** Ramon Henderson. **Pitching Coach:** Ross Grimsley. **Trainer:** Troy Hoffert.

Game Information

Radio Announcer: Steve Degler. **No. of Games Broadcast:** Home-71, Away-71. **Flagship Station:** WRAW 1340-AM.

PA Announcer: Dave Bauman. **Official Scorer:** Ernie Adams.

Stadium Name (year opened): Reading Municipal Memorial Stadium (1950). **Location:** From Pennsylvania Turnpike, Route 222 North to 422 West to Rt. 61 South. From I-78, Rt. 61 South about 20 miles, stadium on right. **Standard Game Times:** 7:05; Sun. 1:05.

Visiting Club Hotel: Wellesley Inn, 910 Woodland Ave., Reading, PA 19610. Telephone: (610) 374-1500.

TRENTON *THUNDER*

Office Address: One Thunder Rd., Trenton, NJ 08611. **Telephone:** (609) 394-3300. **FAX:** (609) 394-9666. **E-Mail Address:** www.trentonthunder.com

Affiliation (first year): Boston Red Sox (1995). **Years in League:** 1994-.

Ownership, Management

Operated by: Garden State Baseball, LP.

General Manager, Chief Operating Officer: Wayne Hodes. **Assistant General Manager:** Tom McCarthy. **Director of Business Operations:** Todd Pae. **Controller:** John Coletta. **Director of Marketing/Merchandising:** Eric Lipsman. **Director of Public Relations:** Rick Brenner. **Director of Ticket Sales:** John Fierko. **Director of Group Sales:** Adam Palant. **Director of Community Relations:** Andrea Bunney. **Ticket Manager:** Scott Gross. **Group Sales Manager:** Annie Warms. **Director of Broadcasting:** Andy Freed. **Clubhouse Manager:** Kent Brown. **Office Manager:** Sue Chassen. **Head Groundskeeper:** Jeff Migliaccio.

Field Staff

Manager: DeMarlo Hale. **Coach:** Dave Gallagher. **Pitching Coach:** Al Nipper. **Trainer:** Ric Moreno.

Game Information

Radio Announcers: Andy Freed, Tom McCarthy. **No. of Games Broadcast:** Home-71, Away-71. **Flagship Station:** WTTM 920-AM.

PA Announcer: Brandon Hardison. **Official Scorers:** Jay Dunn, Jerry Price, David Rosenfeld.

Stadium Name (year opened): Mercer County Waterfront Park (1994). **Location:** Route129 North to Cass St., left onto Cass Street to ballpark. **Standard Game Times:** 7:05 p.m.; Sat. (April-June) 1:05, (July-Aug.) 7:05; Sun. 1:05.

Visiting Club Hotel: The McIntosh Inn, 3270 Brunswick Pike, Lawrenceville, NJ 08648. Telephone: (609) 896-3700.

SOUTHERN LEAGUE

Class AA

Mailing Address: One Depot St., Suite 300, Marietta, GA 30060. **Telephone:** (770) 428-4749. **FAX:** (770) 428-4849.

Years League Active: 1964-.

President/Secretary-Treasuer: Arnold Fielkow.

Vice President: Bill Hardekopf.

Directors: Don Beaver (Knoxville), Peter Bragan Sr. (Jacksonville), Steve Bryant (Carolina), Frank Burke (Chattanooga), Steve DeSalvo (Greenville), Bill Hardekopf (Birmingham), David Hersh (Memphis), John Higgins (Orlando), Eric Margenau (Mobile), Don Mincher (Huntsville).

Director of Business Development/ Marketing: Melissa Hill. **Executive Assistant:** Lori Webb.

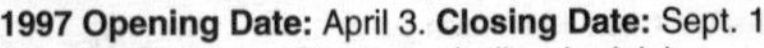

Arnold Fielkow

1997 Opening Date: April 3. **Closing Date:** Sept. 1.

Regular Season: 140 games (split-schedule).

Division Structure: East—Carolina, Greenville, Jacksonville, Knoxville, Orlando. **West**—Birmingham, Chattanooga, Huntsville, Memphis, Mobile.

Playoff Format: First-half division winners play second-half division winners in best-of-5 series. Division playoff winners meet in best-of-5 series for league championship.

All-Star Games: July 21 vs. Seattle Mariners at Carolina, July 7 at San Antonio (joint Double-A game).

Roster Limit: 23 active, until midnight Aug. 10 when roster can be expanded to 24. **Player Eligibility Rule:** No restrictions.

Brand of Baseball: Rawlings.

Statistician: Howe Sportsdata International, Boston Fish Pier, West Bldg. #2—Suite 306, Boston MA 02210.

Umpires: Mike Alvarado (Moses Lake, WA), Lance Barksdale (Jackson, MS), Mike Billings (Pembroke Pines, FL), Mark Carlson (Chicago, IL), Cory Erickson (St. Petersburg, FL), Daryn Frederickson (Louisville, KY), Jeff Head (Jasper, AL), Morris Hodges (Helena, AL), Marvin Hudson (Washington, GA), Alfonso Marquez (Anaheim, CA), Ken Page (Phoenix, AZ), Ray Parrish (Lakeland, FL), Alan Paternoster (Melbourne Beach, FL), Jim Reynolds (Wethersfield, CT), Stu Robertson (Gretna, VA).

1996 Standings (Overall)

Club (Affiliate)	W	L	Pct.	GB	'96 Manager
#Memphis (Padres)	81	58	.583	—	Ed Romero
#Chattanooga (Reds)	81	59	.579	½	Mark Berry
*#Jacksonville (Tigers)	75	63	.543	5½	B. Plummer/L. Parrish
Knoxville (Blue Jays)	75	65	.536	6½	Omar Malave
Birmingham (White Sox)	74	65	.532	7	Mike Heath
Carolina (Pirates)	70	69	.504	11	Marc Hill
Huntsville (Athletics)	66	74	.471	15½	Dick Scott
Orlando (Cubs)	60	78	.439	20½	Bruce Kimm
Greenville (Braves)	58	82	.414	23½	Jeff Cox
Port City (Mariners)	56	84	.400	25½	Orlando Gomez

*Won playoffs #Won split-season pennant

Stadium Information

		Dimensions				
Club	Stadium	LF	CF	RF	Capacity	'96 Att.
Birmingham	Hoover Metro.	340	405	340	10,800	296,131
Carolina	Five County	330	400	330	6,000	278,361
Chattanooga	Engel	325	471	318	7,500	227,885
Greenville	Greenville Municipal	335	405	335	7,027	230,124
Huntsville	Davis Municipal	345	405	330	10,000	255,139
Jacksonville	Wolfson Park	320	390	320	8,200	219,947
Knoxville	Bill Meyer	330	400	330	6,412	142,537
Memphis	Tim McCarver*	323	398	325	10,000	197,084
Mobile#	Hank Aaron	325	400	310	6,000	—
Orlando	Tinker Field	340	425	320	5,104	175,399

*Artificial turf infield

#Franchise operated in Wilmington, N.C., in 1996

BIRMINGHAM
BARONS

Office Address: 100 Ben Chapman Dr., Birmingham, AL 35244. **Mailing Address:** P.O. Box 360007, Birmingham, AL 35236. **Telephone:** (205) 988-3200. **FAX:** (205) 988-9698. **E-Mail Address:** barons@quicklink.net

Affiliation (first year): Chicago White Sox (1986). **Years in League:** 1964-65, 1967-75, 1981-.

Ownership, Management

Operated by: Elmore Sports Group, Ltd.

Chairman of the Board: Dave Elmore.

President/General Manager: Bill Hardekopf. **Vice President:** Tony Ensor. **Directors, Stadium Operations:** Brad Chandler, Tim Wilding. **Head Groundskeeper:** Steve Horne. **Director of Media Relations:** David Lee. **Group Sales Managers:** Christy Culpepper, Jonathan Nelson. **Director of Public Relations:** Richard Flight. **Director of Ticket Operations:** Joe Drake. **Director of Food Services:** Dan Beaulieu. **Office Manager:** Norma Rosebrough. **Accounting Clerk:** Kecia Arnold. **Catering Manager:** Jeanne Holmes. **Assistant Groundskeeper:** Mike Zullo. **Administrative Assistants:** Joe Dorolek, Mack Elliot, Lisa Flores, Chris Jenkins, Melanie McCullough.

Field Staff

Manager: Dave Huppert. **Coaches:** Sam Hairston, Rance Mulliniks. **Pitching Coach:** Steve Renko. **Trainer:** Scott Johnson.

Game Information

Radio Announcer: Curt Bloom. **No. of Games Broadcast:** Home-70, Away-70. **Flagship Station:** WAPI 1070-AM.

PA Announcer: Derek Scudder. **Official Scorer:** Bill Graham.

Stadium Name (year opened): Hoover Metropolitan Stadium (1988). **Location:** I-459 to Highway 150 (exit 10) in Hoover. **Standard Game Times:** 7 p.m., 6, 12:30; Sat 6, 7; Sun. 2, 7.

Visiting Club Hotel: Riverchase Inn-Galleria, 1800 Riverchase Dr., Birmingham, AL 35244. Telephone: (205) 985-7500.

CAROLINA
MUDCATS

Office Address: 1501 N.C. Highway 39, Zebulon, NC 27597. **Mailing Address:** P.O. Drawer 1218, Zebulon, NC 27597. **Telephone:** (919) 269-2287. **FAX:** (919) 269-4910.

Affiliation (first year): Pittsburgh Pirates (1991). **Years in League:** 1991-.

Ownership, Management

Operated by: Carolina Mudcats Professional Baseball Club, Inc.

Principal Owner/President: Steve Bryant.

General Manager: Joe Kremer. **Assistant General Manager:** Joe Chatman. **Director of Stadium Operations/Concessions:** Brian Becknell. **Head Groundskeeper:** Bill Riggan. **Director of Media Relations:** David Smith. **Director of Sales/Marketing:** Duke Sanders. **Director of Broadcasting:** Pete Schopen. **Director of Community Relations:** Kelly Edwards. **Community Relations:** James Miller. **Director of Ticket Sales:** Steven Weydig. **Director of Group Sales:** Fred Hilker. **Director of Merchandising:** Dan Trimbur. **Assistant Director of Food Services:** Mark Reardon. **Director of Special Projects:** Steve Sophis. **Office Manager:** Jackie DiPrimo.

Field Staff

Manager: Marc Hill. **Coach:** Tracy Woodson. **Pitching Coach:** Bruce Tanner. **Trainer:** Mike Sandoval.

Game Information

Radio Announcers: Pete Schopen, David Smith. **No. of Games Broadcast:** Home-70, Away-70. **Flagship Station:** Unavailable.

PA Announcer: Duke Sanders. **Official Scorer:** Unavailable.

Stadium Name (year opened): Five County Stadium (1991). **Location:** From Raleigh, I-64 East to 264 East, exit at Hwy. 39 in Zebulon. **Standard Game Times:** 7:30 p.m.; Sun. (April-May) 2:05, (June-Sept.) 5:05.

Visiting Club Hotel: Unavailable.

CHATTANOOGA
LOOKOUTS

Office Address: 1130 East Third St., Chattanooga, TN 37403. **Mailing Address:** P.O. Box 11002, Chattanooga, TN 37401. **Telephone:** (423) 267-2208. **FAX:** (423) 267-4258.

Affiliation (first year): Cincinnati Reds (1988). **Years in League:** 1964-65, 1976-.

Ownership, Management

Operated by: Engel Stadium Corporation.

Principal Owners: Frank Burke, Daniel Burke, Charles Eshbach.

President, General Manager: Frank Burke. **Assistant General Manager:** Rich Mozingo. **Director of Broadcasting:** Larry Ward. **Director of Promotions/Marketing:** Vickey Race. **Director of Stadium Operations:** Greg Grall. **Director of Public Relations/Administration:** Curt Hansen. **Director of Group Sales and Telemarketing:** Brian Harper. **Director of Concessions:** Tony DaSilveira. **Director of Ticket Operations:** Brad Smith. **Director of Corporate Group Sales:** Teri Warner. **Director of Field Operations:** Lee Batten. **Administrative Assistant:** Dena Newberry.

Field Staff

Manager: Mark Berry. **Coach:** Mark Wagner. **Pitching Coach:** Mack Jenkins. **Trainer:** Jim Knudtson.

Game Information

Radio Announcers: Larry Ward, Todd Agne. **No. of Games Broadcast:** Home-70, Away-70. **Flagship Station:** WSGC 101.9-FM.

PA Announcer: Chris Goforth. **Official Scorer:** Wirt Gammon Jr.

Stadium Name (year opened): Engel Stadium (1929). **Location:** I-24 to I-27 North to 4th St. exit, 1¾ miles to O'Neal Street, right on O'Neal. **Standard Game Times:** 7 p.m.; Wed. 12:30, Sun. 2.

Visiting Club Hotel: Holiday Inn SE, 6700 Ringgold Rd., Chattanooga, TN 37412. Telephone: (423) 892-8100.

GREENVILLE
BRAVES

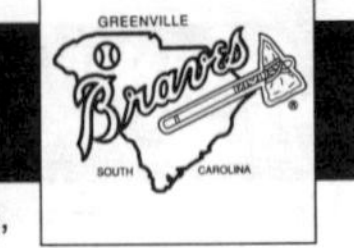

Office Address: One Braves Ave., Greenville, SC 29607. **Mailing Address:** P.O. Box 16683, Greenville, SC 29606. **Telephone:** (864) 299-3456. **FAX:** (864) 277-7369.

Affiliation (first year): Atlanta Braves (1984). **Years in League:** 1984-.

Ownership, Management

Operated by: Atlanta National League Baseball Club, Inc.

Principal Owner: Ted Turner. **Chairman of the Board:** Bill Bartholomay. **President:** Stan Kasten.

General Manager: Steve DeSalvo. **Assistant General Manager:** Jim Bishop. **Director of Ticket Sales:** Jimmy Moore. **Director of Food Services:** Vernon Sprouse. **Director of Broadcasting:** Mark Hauser. **Head Groundskeeper:** Matt Taylor.

Field Staff

Manager: Randy Ingle **Coach:** Mel Roberts. **Pitching Coach:** Bruce Dal Canton. **Trainer:** Jay Williams.

Game Information

Radio Announcer: Mark Hauser. **No. of Games Broadcast:** Home-70, Away-70. **Flagship Station:** WPCI 1490-AM.

PA Announcer: Tim Worley. **Official Scorer:** Jimmy Moore.

Stadium Name (year opened): Greenville Municipal Stadium (1984). **Location:** I-85 to exit 46 (Mauldin Road), east two miles. **Standard Game Times:** 7:15 p.m.; Sun. 2.

Visiting Club Hotel: Quality Inn, 50 Orchard Park Dr., Greenville, SC 29615. Telephone: (864) 297-9000.

HUNTSVILLE *STARS*

Office Address: 3125 Leeman Ferry Rd., Huntsville, AL 35801. **Mailing Address:** P.O. Box 2769, Huntsville, AL 35804. **Telephone:** (205) 882-2562. **FAX:** (205) 880-0801. **E-Mail Address:** STARS@traveller.com.

Affiliation (first year): Oakland Athletics (1985). **Years In League:** 1985-.

Ownership, Management

Operated by: Huntsville Stars Baseball, LLC.

President/General Manager: Don Mincher.

Assistant General Manager: Patrick Nichol. **Director of Operations:** Bryan Dingo. **Head Groundskeeper:** Tom McAfee. **Director of Promotions/Public Relations:** Marvin Julich. **Ticket Manager:** Cynthia Giles. **Director of Group Sales:** Karen Reish. **Director of Merchandising:** Devin Rose. **Concessions Manager:** Gregg Corbin. **Operations Assistant:** Mark Gorenc.

Field Staff

Manager: Mike Quade. **Coach:** Gil Lopez. **Pitching Coach:** Bert Bradley. **Trainer:** Brian Thorson.

Game Information

Radio Announcer: Steve Kornya. **No. of Games Broadcast:** Home-70, Away-70. **Flagship Station:** WTKI 1450-AM.

PA Announcer: Tommy Hayes. **Official Scorer:** Larry Smith.

Stadium Name (year opened): Joe W. Davis Municipal Stadium (1985). **Location:** I-65 to I-565 East, south on Memorial Parkway to Drake Ave. exit. **Standard Game Times:** 7:05 p.m.; Sun. (April-June) 2:05, (July-Sept.) 7:05.

Visiting Club Hotel: La Quinta, 3141 University Dr., Huntsville, AL 35816. Telephone: (205) 533-0756.

JACKSONVILLE *SUNS*

Office Address: 1201 East Duval St., Jacksonville, FL 32202. **Mailing Address:** P.O. Box 4756, Jacksonville, FL 32201. **Telephone:** (904) 358-2846. **FAX:** (904) 358-2845.

Affiliation (first year): Detroit Tigers (1995). **Years in League:** 1970-.

Ownership, Management

Operated by: Baseball Jax, Inc.

Principal Owner/President: Peter Bragan Sr.

Vice President/General Manager: Peter Bragan Jr. **Assistant to the President:** Jerry LeMoine. **Assistant General Manager/Operations:** Jay Grider. **Assistant General Manager/Marketing and Public Relations:** Todd Budnick. **Head Groundskeeper:** Mark Clay. **Director of Ticket Sales:** Christine Meyers. **Administrative Assistants:** Dean Miller, Ryan Valerius. **Office Manager:** Cathy Wiggins.

Field Staff

Manager: Dave Anderson. **Coach:** Tim Torricelli. **Pitching Coach:** Rich Bombard. **Trainer:** Matt Lewis.

Game Information

Radio Announcer: Chuck Valenches. **No. of Games Broadcast:** Home-70, Away-70. **Flagship Station:** Unavailable.

PA Announcer: John Leard. **Official Scorer:** Lou Eliopolus.

Stadium Name (year opened): Wolfson Park (1955). **Location:** From I-95 North to 20th Street East exit, take to end, turn right before Jacksonville Municipal Stadium; From I-95 South to Emerson St exit, take right to Hart Bridge, take Sports Complex exit, left at light to stop sign, take right and quick left; From Mathews Bridge, take A. Phillip Randolph exit, right off ramp, right at stop sign, left at second light to stadium. **Standard Game Times:** 7:35 p.m, 12:15.; Sun. 3:05, 6:05.

Visiting Club Hotels: La Quinta-Orange Park, 8555 Blanding Blvd., Jacksonville, FL 32244. Telephone: (904) 778-9539.

KNOXVILLE
SMOKIES

Office Address: 633 Jessamine St., Knoxville, TN 37917. **Telephone:** (423) 637-9494. **FAX:** (423) 523-9913. **E-Mail Address:** Smokies@1stresource.com

Affiliation (first year): Toronto Blue Jays (1980). **Years in League:** 1964-67, 1972-.

Ownership, Management

Operated by: Knoxville Smokies Baseball, Inc.

Principal Owner/Chairman/President: Don Beaver.

General Manager: Dan Rajkowski. **Assistant General Manager:** Brian Cox. **Director of Media/Public Relations:** Ed Beach. **Director of Sales/Marketing:** Mark Seaman. **Director of Community Relations:** Eric Booth. **Director of Group Sales:** Jeff Shoaf. **Head Groundskeeper:** Bob Shoemaker. **Office Manager:** Melissa Reinhard. **Operations Assistant:** Robby Sherman.

Field Staff

Manager: Omar Malave. **Coach:** Paul Elliot. **Pitching Coach:** Rick Langford. **Trainer:** Scott Shannon.

Game Information

Radio Announcer: Ed Beach. **No. of Games Broadcast:** Home-70, Away-70. **Flagship Station:** WQLA 104.9-FM.

PA Announcer: Unavailable. **Official Scorer:** Jack Tate.

Stadium Name (year opened): Bill Meyer Stadium (1955). **Location:** I-40 to Business Loop, right onto Summit Hill Drive, right on Central Ave., right on Willow Ave to park. **Standard Game Times:** 7:15 p.m., Wed 12, Sat 7:15, Sun. 5.

Visiting Club Hotel: Best Western, 118 Merchants Dr., Knoxville, TN 37912. Telephone: (423) 688-3141.

MEMPHIS
CHICKS

Office Address: 800 Home Run Lane, Memphis, TN 38104. **Telephone:** (901) 272-1687. **FAX:** (901) 278-3354.

Affiliation (first year): Seattle Mariners (1997). **Years In League:** 1978-.

Ownership, Management

Operated by: Professional Sports and Entertainment of Tennessee, Inc.

President/General Manager: David Hersh.

Assistant General Manager: Jarrod Coates. **Director of Stadium Operations:** Ed Collins. **Controller:** Susan Seelbinder. **Director of Media/Public Relations:** Jonathon Fuller. **Director of Promotions:** Daniel Dilella. **Director of Ticket Sales:** Chad Hullett. **Executive Secretary:** Patty Haynes.

Field Staff

Manager: Dave Brundage. **Coach:** Dan Rohn. **Pitching Coach:** Bryan Price. **Trainer:** Rob Nodine.

Game Information

Radio Announcer: Tom Stocker. **No. of Games Broadcast:** Home-70, Away-70. **Flagship Station:** WREC 600-AM.

PA Announcer: Mark Bialek. **Official Scorer:** John Guinozzo.

Stadium Name (year opened): Tim McCarver Stadium (1968). **Location:** I-240 South to Sam Cooper Blvd., left on E. Parkway, left on Central, right on Early Maxwell. In State Fairgrounds complex next to Liberty Bowl. **Standard Game Times:** 7:05 p.m.; Sun. 2:05.

Visiting Club Hotel: La Quinta, 2745 Airways Blvd., Memphis, TN 38132. Telephone: (901) 396-1000.

MOBILE
BAYBEARS

(Franchise operated in Wilmington, N.C., in 1996)

Office Address: Satchel Paige Ave., Mobile, AL. **Mailing Address:** P.O. Box 161663, Mobile, AL 36616. **Telephone:** (334) 479-2327. **FAX:** (334) 476-1147.

Affiliation (first year): San Diego Padres (1997). **Years in League:** 1997.

Ownership, Management

Operated by: United Sports Ventures.

Principal Owner: Eric Margenau.

Vice President/General Manager: Bill Shanahan. **Executive Director:** Matthew Riley. **Assistant General Manager/Finance:** Mark Ruckwardt. **Assistant General Manager/Tickets and Merchandising:** Lesley Kellison. **Assistant General Manager/Groups:** Dan Zusman. **Director of Broadcasting:** Tom Nichols. **Director of Ticket Sales:** Angelo Mazzella. **Director of Merchandising:** Anthony Holman. **Director of Facility Maintenance:** Pat White. **Director of Office Operations:** Monica Cooper. **Corporate Sales:** Travis Toth. **Community Relations Coordinator:** Chris Morgan. **Media Relations Coordinator:** William Younce. **Ticket Sales/Operations:** Lloyd Hebert, Freddie Parce. **Customer Service:** Allen Jernigan.

Field Staff

Manager: Mike Ramsey. **Pitching Coach:** Don Alexander. **Trainer:** George Poulis.

Game Information

Radio Announcer: Tom Nichols. **No. of Games Broadcast:** Home-70, Away-70. **Flagship Station:** WNSP 105.5-FM.

PA Announcer: Unavailable. **Official Scorer:** Unavailable.

Stadium Name (year opened): Hank Aaron Stadium (1997). **Location:** I-65 to Highway 90 East, go right at McVay, Satchel Paige Avenue is on right. **Standard Game Times:** 7:05 p.m.; Sun. 6:05.

Visiting Club Hotel: Holiday Inn-Downtown, 301 Government St., Mobile, AL 36602. Telephone (334) 694-0100.

ORLANDO
RAYS

Office Address: 287 Tampa Ave. S., Orlando, FL 32805. **Telephone:** (407) 649-7297. **FAX:** (407) 649-1637. **E-Mail Address:** orays@aol.com

Affiliation (first year): Chicago Cubs (1993). **Years in League:** 1973-.

Ownership, Management

Operated by: Orlando Rays Baseball, Inc.

President: Vincent Naimoli.

General Manager: Roger Wexelberg. **Director of Business Development:** Thomas Ramsberger. **Assistant General Manager:** John Cody. **Head Groundskeeper:** Doug Lopas. **Director of Media/Public Relations:** Pat Hernan. **Director of Sales/Marketing:** Tom Albano. **Director of Community Relations:** Kevin Holtz. **Director of Ticket Sales:** Lynn Barnette. **Director of Group Sales:** Diane Russo. **Director of Merchandising:** Mack Powell.

Field Staff

Manager: Dave Trembley. **Coach:** Manny Trillo. **Pitching Coach:** Stan Kyles. **Trainer:** Steve Melendez.

Game Information

Radio: None.

PA Announcer: Tom Peters. **Official Scorers:** Bill Smith, Jim Wilkening.

Stadium Name (year opened): Tinker Field (1964). **Location:** I-4 to Colonial Drive (State Road 50), west to Tampa Ave., left on Tampa Ave. **Standard Game Times:** 7 p.m.; Sun. (April-May) 2, (June-August.) 6.

Visiting Club Hotel: Comfort Inn, 830 Lee Rd., Orlando, FL 32810. Telephone: (407) 629-4000.

TEXAS LEAGUE

Class AA

Mailing Address: 2442 Facet Oak, San Antonio, TX 78232. **Telephone:** (210) 545-5297. **FAX:** (210) 545-5298. **E-Mail Address:** tkayser@texasleague.com.

Tom Kayser

Years League Active: 1888-1890, 1892, 1895-1899, 1902-1942, 1946-.

President/Treasurer: Tom Kayser.

Vice President: Steve Shaad. **Corporate Secretary:** Chuck Lamson.

Directors: Bill Blackwell (Jackson), Chuck Lamson (Tulsa), Taylor Moore (Shreveport), Jim Paul (El Paso), Miles Prentice (Midland), Steve Shaad (Wichita), Bill Valentine (Arkansas), Burl Yarbrough (San Antonio).

Administrative Assistant: Philip Cowan.

1997 Opening Date: April 3. **Closing Date:** Aug. 30.

Regular Season: 140 games (split-schedule).

Division Structure: East—Arkansas, Jackson, Shreveport, Tulsa. **West**—El Paso, Midland, San Antonio, Wichita.

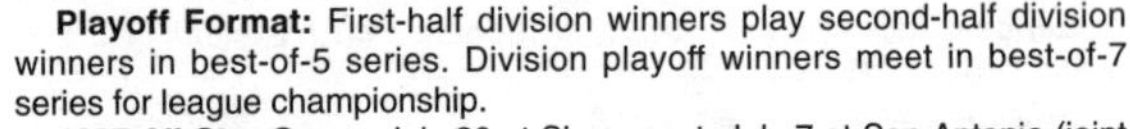

Playoff Format: First-half division winners play second-half division winners in best-of-5 series. Division playoff winners meet in best-of-7 series for league championship.

1997 All-Star Game: July 30 at Shreveport; July 7 at San Antonio (joint Double-A game).

Roster Limit: 23 active, until midnight Aug. 10 when roster can be expanded to 24. **Player Eligibility Rule:** No restrictions.

Brand of Baseball: Rawlings.

Statistician: Howe Sportsdata International, Boston Fish Pier, West Bldg. #2—Suite 306, Boston, MA 02210.

Umpires: David Aschwege (Lincoln, NE), David Baldwin (Reno, NV), David Brandt (Mission, KS), Scott Gasaway (Tulsa, OK), Scott Higgins (Keizer, OR), Dan Iassogna (Smyrna, GA), Wayne Kraus (Louisville, KY), Ron Kulpa (Florissant, MO), Jeff Powell (Arlington, TX), Steve Rackley (Springfield, MO), Jack Samuels (Orange, CA), Christian Taylor (Kansas City, MO).

1996 Standings

Club (Affiliate)	W	L	Pct.	GB	'96 Manager
#El Paso (Brewers)	76	63	.547	—	Dave Machemer
#Tulsa (Rangers)	75	64	.540	1	Bobby Jones
Shreveport (Giants)	73	66	.525	3	Frank Cacciatore
#Wichita (Royals)	70	70	.500	6½	Ron Johnson
*#Jackson (Astros)	70	70	.500	6½	Dave Engle
San Antonio (Dodgers)	69	70	.496	7	John Shelby
Arkansas (Cardinals)	67	73	.479	9½	Rick Mahler
Midland (Angels)	58	82	.414	18½	Mario Mendoza

*Won playoffs. #Won split-season pennant

Stadium Information

		Dimensions				
Club	Stadium	LF	CF	RF	Capacity	'96 Att.
Arkansas	Ray Winder Field	330	390	345	6,083	209,535
El Paso	Cohen	340	410	340	10,000	292,074
Jackson	Smith-Wills	330	400	330	5,200	179,423
Midland	Christensen	333	398	333	5,000	203,011
San Antonio	Wolff Municipal	310	402	340	8,300	381,001
Shreveport	Fair Grounds Field	330	400	330	6,200	179,584
Tulsa	Drillers	335	390	340	10,842	343,196
Wichita	Lawrence-Dumont*	344	401	312	6,058	186,084

*Artificial turf infield

ARKANSAS
TRAVELERS

Office Address: War Memorial Park, Little Rock, AR 72205. **Mailing Address:** P.O. Box 55066, Little Rock, AR 72215. **Telephone:** (501) 664-1555. **FAX:** (501) 664-1834. **E-mail Address:** www.travs.com

Affiliation (first year): St. Louis Cardinals (1966). **Years in League:** 1966-.

Ownership, Management

Operated by: Arkansas Travelers Baseball Club, Inc.

President: Bert Parke.

Executive Vice President/General Manager: Bill Valentine. **Assistant General Manager/Concessions:** John Evans. **Promotions Director:** Jason George. **Assistant GM/Stadium Operations:** Hap Seliga. **Sales Manager:** Barry Wells. **Park Superintendent/Head Groundskeeper:** Greg Johnston. **Clubhouse Operations:** Ernie Moore.

Field Staff

Manager: Rick Mahler. **Coach:** Luis Melendez. **Pitching Coach:** Rich Folkers. **Trainer:** Pete Fagan.

Game Information

Radio Announcer: Taylor Carr. **No. of Games Broadcast:** Home-70. **Flagship Station:** KARK 920-AM.

PA Announcer: Bill Downs. **Official Scorer:** George Avery.

Stadium Name (year opened): Ray Winder Field (1932). **Location:** I-630 at Fair Park Boulevard exit. **Standard Game Time:** 7:30 p.m.

Visiting Club Hotel: Holiday Inn-City Center, 617 S. Broadway, Little Rock, AR 72201. Telephone: (501) 376-4000.

EL PASO
DIABLOS

Office Address: 9700 Gateway North Blvd., El Paso, TX 79924. **Mailing Address:** P.O. Drawer 4797, El Paso, TX 79914. **Telephone:** (915) 755-2000. **FAX:** (915) 757-0671.

Affiliation (first year): Milwaukee Brewers (1981). **Years in League:** 1962-70, 1972-.

Ownership, Management

Operated by: El Paso Baseball Club, LLC.

Principal Owners: Bill Pereira, Peter Gray.

President: Jim Paul.

General Manager: Rick Parr. **Director of Stadium Operations:** Rob Sesich. **Head Groundskeeper:** Alan Beshears. **Director of Media/Public Relations:** Matt Hicks. **Director of Marketing:** Ken Schrom. **Director of Ticket Sales:** Bret Beer. **Director of Group Sales:** Beverly Mowad. **Director of Food Services:** Jerry McClelland. **Clubhouse Operations:** Dan Wallin. **Office Manager:** Heather Smith. **Ticket Office Manager:** Tim Kelly. **Ticket Account Executives:** Cori Vasquez, Jodi Thompson. **Receptionist:** Mary Hill.

Field Staff

Manager: Dave Machemer. **Coach:** Jon Pont. **Pitching Coach:** Mike Caldwell. **Trainer:** Richard Stark.

Game Information

Radio Announcers, English: Matt Hicks, Dave Popkin. **No. of Games Broadcast:** Home-70, Away-70. **Flagship Station:** KROD 600-AM. **Radio Announcers, Spanish:** Pancho Gonzalez, Raul Oscar Gomez. **No. of Games Broadcast:** Home-70, Away-70. **Flagship Station:** KSVE 1150-AM.

PA Announcer: Tony Bravo. **Official Scorer:** Bernie Olivas.

Stadium Name (year opened): Cohen Stadium (1990). **Location:** I-10 to U.S. 54 (Patriot Freeway), east to Diana exit to Gateway North Boulevard. **Standard Game Times:** April-May 6:45 p.m., June-August 7:15; Sun. 6:45.

Visiting Club Hotel: Quality Inn, 6201 Gateway West Blvd., El Paso, TX 79925. Telephone: (915) 778-6611.

JACKSON
GENERALS

Office Address: 1200 Lakeland Dr., Jackson, MS 39216. **Mailing Address:** P.O. Box 4209, Jackson, MS 39296. **Telephone:** (601) 981-4664. **FAX:** (601) 981-4669.

Affiliation (first year): Houston Astros (1991). **Years in League:** 1975-.

Ownership, Management

Operated by: Cowboy Maloney Supply Co., Inc.

Principal Owner/Chairman: Con Maloney. **President:** Eddie Maloney.

General Manager: Bill Blackwell. **Assistant General Manager/Concessions:** Frank Buccieri. **Assistant General Manager/Operations:** Adam Hathorn. **Head Groundskeeper:** Joe Whipps. **Director of Broadcasting:** Bill Walberg. **Director of Group Sales:** Tim Attel. **Clubhouse Operations:** Pete Phillips. **Office Manager:** Judy Blackwell. **Maintenance Supervisor:** Charles Owens.

Field Staff

Manager: Gary Allenson. **Pitching Coach:** Jim Hickey. **Trainer:** Mike Ra.

Game Information

Radio Announcer: Bill Walberg. **No. of Games Broadcast:** Home-70, Away-70. **Flagship Station:** WJDS 620-AM.

PA Announcer: Glen Waddle. **Official Scorer:** Unavailable.

Stadium Name (year opened): Smith-Wills Stadium (1975). **Location:** I-55 to Lakeland Drive exit. **Standard Game Times:** 7 p.m.; Sun. 2:30 (April-May), 6 (June-August).

Visiting Club Hotel: Holiday Inn-Southwest, 2649 Highway 80 West, Jackson, MS 39204. Telephone: (601) 355-3472.

MIDLAND
ANGELS

Office Address: 4300 N. Lamesa Rd., Midland, TX 79705. **Mailing Address:** P.O. Box 51187, Midland, TX 79710. **Telephone:** (915) 683-4251. **FAX:** (915) 683-0994. **E-Mail Address:** angels@iglobal.net.

Affiliation (first year): Anaheim Angels (1985). **Years in League:** 1972-.

Ownership, Management

Operated by: Midland Sports, Inc.

Principal Owners: Miles Prentice, Bob Richmond.

President: Miles Prentice. **Executive Vice President:** Bob Richmond.

General Manager: Monty Hoppel. **Assistant General Manager:** Rick Carden. **Director of Business Operations:** Eloisa Robledo. **Head Groundskeeper:** Lee Velarde. **Director of Broadcasting/Media Relations:** Bob Hards. **Director of Sales/Corporate Development:** Harold Fuller. **Sales and Marketing Representatives:** Bill Levy, Kevin Carney. **Director of Community Relations:** Andy Alvarez. **Director of Group Sales:** Rob Flannery. **Director of Merchandising:** Ray Fieldhouse. **Director of Concessions/Operations:** Jeff Von Holle. **Assistant Director of Concessions/Operations:** Jeff Corbett. **Clubhouse Operations:** Brad Haynes (home), Dave Weidner (vistitors). **Office Manager:** Christie Reaves. **Customer Service Manager:** Jamie Richardson. **Administrative Assistant:** Pat Kerin. **Odessa Office Manager:** Claudia Jaquez.

Field Staff

Manager: Mitch Seoane. **Coach:** Orlando Mercado. **Pitching Coach:** Greg Minton. **Trainer:** Scott Sowell.

Game Information

Radio Announcer: Bob Hards. **No. of Games Broadcast:** Home-70, Away-70. **Flagship Station:** KCRS 550-AM.

PA Announcer: Barry Sykes. **Official Scorer:** Bobby Dunn.

Stadium Name (year opened): Christensen Stadium (1972). **Location:** Big Spring exit off Rankin Highway to Loop 250, exit right on Lamesa Road. **Standard Game Times:** 7 p.m.; Sun. 6.

Visiting Club Hotel: Plaza Inn, 4108 N. Big Spring, Midland, TX 79705. Telephone: (915) 686-8733.

SAN ANTONIO *MISSIONS*

Office Address: Nelson W. Wolff Stadium, 5757 Highway 90 West, San Antonio, TX 78227. **Telephone:** (210) 675-7275. **FAX:** (210) 670-0001. **E-mail Address:** samissions.com

Affiliation (first year): Los Angeles Dodgers (1977). **Years In League:** 1888, 1892, 1895-99, 1907-42, 1946-64, 1967-.

Ownership, Management

Operated by: San Antonio Missions Baseball Club, Inc.

Principal Owner: Elmore Sports Group, Ltd. **President:** David Elmore. **Vice President**: Bob Beban.

General Manager: Burl Yarbrough. **Assistant General Manager:** David Oldham. **Director of Public Relations:** Bryan Beban. **Director of Sales:** Jimi Olsen. **Director of Marketing:** Dave Gasaway. **Director of Stadium Operations:** Jeff Long. **Director of Ticket Sales:** Ben Rivers. **Director of Group Sales:** Jeff Windle. **Director of Community Relations:** Mario Garcia. **Director of Merchandising:** Bill Gerlt. **Account Executives:** Jason Becking, Shannon Walsh, Joe Maldonado. **President, Diamond Concessions:** Doug Campbell. **Concessions Coordinator:** Candy Pena. **Business Manager:** Marc Frey. **Office Manager:** Delia Rodriguez. **Clubhouse Manager:** Dan Cardenas. **Head Groundskeeper:** Mike Pankey.

Field Staff

Manager: Ron Roenicke. **Coach:** Lance Parrish. **Pitching Coach:** Guy Conti. **Trainer:** Mike Collins.

Game Information

Radio Announcers: Roy Acuff, Brian Anderson. **No. of Games Broadcast:** Home-70, Away-70. **Flagship Station:** KKYX 680-AM.

PA Announcer: Stan Kelly. **Official Scorer:** David Humphrey.

Stadium Name (year opened): Nelson Wolff Municipal Stadium (1994). **Location:** From I-10, I-35 or I-37, take U.S. Hwy. 90 West to Callaghan Road exit. **Standard Game Times:** 7:05 p.m., Sun. 6:05.

Visiting Club Hotel: Thrifty Inn, 9806 I-10 West, San Antonio, TX 78230. Telephone: (210) 696-0810.

SHREVEPORT *CAPTAINS*

Office Address: 2901 Pershing Blvd., Shreveport, LA 71109. **Mailing Address:** P.O. Box 3448, Shreveport, LA 71133. **Telephone:** (318) 636-5555. **FAX:** (318) 636-5670. **E-Mail Address:** shycaps@iamerican.net

Affiliation (first year): San Francisco Giants (1979). **Years in League:** 1895, 1908-10, 1915-32, 1938-42, 1946-57, 1968-.

Ownership, Management

Operated by: Shreveport Baseball, Inc.

Principal Owner/President: Taylor Moore.

General Manager: Gilbert Little. **Assistant General Manager:** Terri Sipes. **Director of Sales/Marketing:** Michael Beasley. **Director of Media/Public Relations:** Dave Nitz. **Director of Group Sales:** Dan Robinson. **Director of Stadium Operations:** Kevin Stone. **Sales Associates:** Brian Dulin, Gabriel Fuller. **Clubhouse Operations:** J.J. Lewis. **Director of Food Services:** Leroy Beasley. **Administrative Assistant:** Sheila Martin. **Head Groundskeeper:** Steve Bange.

Field Staff

Manager: Carlos Lezcano. **Coach:** Mike Hart. **Pitching Coach:** Frank Reberger. **Trainer:** Ben Potenziano.

Game Information

Radio Announcer: Dave Nitz. **No. of Games Broadcast:** Home-70, Away-70. **Flagship Station:** KWKH 1130-AM.

PA Announcer: Unavailable. **Official Scorer:** Jim Dawson.

Stadium Name (year opened): Fair Grounds Field (1986). **Location:** Hearne Ave. (U.S. 171) exit off I-20 at Louisiana State Fairgrounds. **Standard Game Times:** April-May 7:05 p.m., June-Aug. 7:35; Sat. 7:35; Sun. 6:05.

Visiting Club Hotel: Ramada Inn-Airport, 5116 Monkhouse Dr., Shreveport, LA 71109. Telephone (318) 635-7531.

TULSA
DRILLERS

Office Address: 4802 E. 15th St., Tulsa, OK 74112. **Mailing Address:** P.O. Box 4448, Tulsa, OK 74159. **Telephone:** (918) 744-5998. **FAX:** (918) 747-3267.

Affiliation (first year): Texas Rangers (1977). **Years in League:** 1933-42, 1946-65, 1977-.

Ownership, Management

Operated by: Tulsa Baseball, Inc.

Principal Owner/President: Went Hubbard.

Executive Vice President/General Manager: Chuck Lamson. **Associate General Manager:** Chris Pound. **Assistant General Manager/ Director of Promotions:** Paul Birutis. **Director of Media/Public Relations:** Brian Carroll. **Director of Ticket Sales:** Debbie Jones. **Director of Food Services:** Mike Melega. **Director of Stadium Operations:** Mark Hilliard. **Head Groundskeeper:** Sam Clay. **Director of Broadcasting:** Mark Neely. **Office Manager:** Pam Mowery.

Field Staff

Manager: Bobby Jones. **Pitching Coach:** Brad Arnsberg. **Trainer:** Mike Quinn.

Game Information

Radio Announcer: Mark Neely. **No. of Games Broadcast:** Home-70, Road-70. **Flagship Station:** KQLL 1430-AM.

PA Announcer: Kirk McAnany. **Official Scorer:** Jeff Brucculeri.

Stadium Name (year opened): Drillers Stadium (1981). **Location:** Three miles north of I-44 and 1½ miles south of I-244 at 15th Street and Yale Avenue. **Standard Game Times:** Mon.-Thurs. (April-May, August) 7:05; (June-July) 7:35; Fri.-Sat. 7:35; Sun. (April-May) 2:05, (June-August) 6:05.

Visiting Club Hotel: Trade Winds Central, 3141 E. Skelly Dr., Tulsa, OK 74105. Telephone: (918) 749-5561.

WICHITA
WRANGLERS

Office Address: 300 S. Sycamore, Wichita, KS 67213. **Mailing Address:** P.O. Box 1420, Wichita, KS 67201. **Telephone:** (316) 267-3372. **FAX:** (316) 267-3382. **E-Mail Address:** wranglers@feist.com.

Affiliation (first year): Kansas City Royals (1995). **Years in League:** 1987-.

Ownership, Management

Operated by: Wichita Baseball, Inc.

Principal Owner: Rich Products Corp.

Chairman: Robert Rich Sr. **President:** Robert Rich Jr.

General Manager: Lance Deckinger. **Vice President/Wichita Baseball Inc.:** Steve Shaad. **Assistant General Manager/Sales and Marketing:** Gary Clifton. **Director of Advertising and Promotional Sales:** Tom Davis. **Marketing Manager:** Chris Overholser. **Stadium Manager:** Rich Zizek. **Business Manager:** Chris Taylor. **Ticket Sales Coordinators:** Erik Jordan, Tara Avery, Haze Clifford. **Media Relations Assistant:** Mike Drury. **Assistant Stadium Manager:** Dan Turner. **Account Executive:** Derrick Morgan. **Office Coordinator:** Shelly Meier. **Merchandise Coordinator:** Doug Renner. **Marketing Associate:** Natasha Frazier. **Sales Associates:** Shirley Cramer, Angela Haar. **Stadium Operations Assistant:** Neil Farthing. **Business Associate:** Cody Arnold.

Field Staff

Manager: Ron Johnson. **Coach:** Sixto Lezcano. **Pitching Coach:** Gary Lance. **Trainer:** Frank Kyte.

Game Information

Radio Announcer: Dennis Higgins. **No. of Games Broadcast:** Home-70, Away-70. **Flagship Station:** KFH 1330-AM.

PA Announcer: Unavailable. **Official Scorer:** Ted Woodward.

Stadium Name (year opened): Lawrence-Dumont Stadium (1934). **Location:** I-135 to Kellogg Ave. West, north on Broadway, west on Lewis. **Standard Game Times:** 7:15 p.m.; Sun. (April-May) 2:15, (June-August) 6:15.

Visiting Club Hotel: Harvey Hotel, 549 S. Rock, Wichita, KS 67207 Telephone: (316) 686-7131.

CALIFORNIA LEAGUE

Class A Advanced

Office Address: 2380 S. Bascom Ave., Suite 200, Campbell, CA 95008. **Telephone:** (408) 369-8038. **FAX:** (408) 369-1409.

Years League Active: 1941-1942, 1946-.

President/Treasurer: Joe Gagliardi.

Vice President: Harry Stavrenos. **Corporate Secretary:** Bill Weiss

Directors: Fred Anderson (Modesto), Bobby Brett (High Desert), Mike Ellis (Lancaster), Acey Kohrogi (Visalia), Pat Patton (Bakersfield), Dick Phelps (Stockton), Harry Stavrenos (San Jose), Hank Stickney (Rancho Cucamonga), Ken Stickney (Lake Elsinore), Donna Tuttle (San Bernardino).

Executive Assistant: Jim McCue.

Joe Gagliardi

1997 Opening Date: April 3. **Closing Date:** Aug. 31.

Regular Season: 140 games (split-schedule).

Division Structure: Freeway—Bakersfield, Lake Elsinore, Rancho Cucamonga, San Bernardino, Visalia. **Valley**—High Desert, Lancaster, Modesto, San Jose, Stockton.

Playoff Format: Six teams. Split-season winners in each division with best overall record earn first-round bye; other division split-season winner meets wild card with next best overall record in best-of-3 quarterfinals. Winners meet teams which earned first-round byes in best-of-5 semifinals. Winners meet in best-of-5 series for league championship.

All-Star Game: June 17 at Durham, N.C. (California League vs. Carolina League).

Roster Limit: 25 active. **Player Eligibility Rule:** No more than two players and one player-coach on active list may have more than six years experience.

Brand of Baseball: Rawlings ROM.

Statistician: Howe Sportsdata International, Boston Fish Pier, West Bldg. #2—Suite 306, Boston MA 02210; P.O. Box 5061, San Mateo, CA 94402.

1996 Standings

Club (Affiliate)	W	L	Pct.	GB	'96 Manager
#San Jose (Giants)	89	51	.636	—	Carlos Lezcano
Modesto (Athletics)	82	58	.586	7	Jim Colborn
Stockton (Brewers)	79	61	.564	10	Greg Mahlberg
#High Desert (Orioles)	76	64	.543	13	Joe Ferguson
*Lake Elsinore (Angels)	75	65	.536	14	Mitch Seoane
Lancaster (Mariners)	71	69	.507	18	Dave Brundage
San Bernardino (Dodgers)	70	70	.500	19	Del Crandall
#Rancho Cucamonga (Padres)	69	71	.493	20	Mike Basso
Visalia Oaks (Co-op)	50	90	.357	39	Tim Torricelli
Bakersfield (Co-op)	39	101	.279	50	Graig Nettles

*Won playoffs. #Won split-season pennant

Stadium Information

Club	Stadium	Dimensions LF	CF	RF	Capacity	'96 Att.
Bakersfield	Sam Lynn Ballpark	328	354	328	4,600	83,246
High Desert	Mavericks	340	410	340	3,808	143,852
Lake Elsinore	Lake Elsinore Diamond	330	400	310	7,866	360,393
Lancaster	Lancaster Municipal	350	410	350	4,500	316,390
Modesto	Thurman Field	345	365	340	2,500	98,795
R. Cucamonga	Epicenter	330	400	330	6,631	410,214
San Bernardino	The Ranch	330	410	330	5,000	148,363
San Jose	Municipal	340	400	340	4,200	144,782
Stockton	Billy Hebert Field	325	392	335	3,500	101,555
Visalia	Recreation Park	320	405	320	1,800	67,798

BAKERSFIELD
BLAZE

Office Address: 4009 Chester Ave., Bakersfield, CA 93301. **Mailing Address:** P.O. Box 10031, Bakersfield, CA 93389. **Telephone:** (805) 322-1363. **FAX:** (805) 322-6199. **E-Mail Address:** blaze1@lightspeed.net.

Affiliation (first year): San Francisco Giants (1997). **Years In League:** 1941-42, 1946-75, 1978-79, 1982-.

Ownership, Management

Principal Owner/President: Pat Patton.

Vice President/General Manager: Jack Patton. **Assistant General Managers:** Jim Gregovich, Susan Wells. **Director of Stadium Operations:** Craig Noren. **Head Groundskeeper:** Leon Williams. **Director of Community Relations:** Paul Sheldon. **Director of Ticket Sales:** Cricket Whitaker. **Administrative Assistant:** Dan Shanyfelt. **Account Executives:** Kent Bowersox, Kelly Sweatmon.

Field Staff

Manager: Glenn Tufts. **Pitching Coach:** Bryan Hickerson. **Trainer:** Rick Fuhriman.

Game Information

Radio Announcers: Mark Roberts, Dale Parsons. **No. of Games Broadcast:** Home-70, Away-70. **Flagship Station:** KGEO 1230-AM.

PA Announcer: Matt Kieke. **Official Scorer:** Tim Wheeler.

Stadium Name (year opened): Sam Lynn Ballpark (1941). **Location:** Highway 99 to California Avenue, east three miles to Chester Avenue, north two miles to stadium. **Standard Game Times:** 7:30 p.m..

Visiting Club Hotel: Travelodge Hotel, 818 Real Road, Bakersfield, CA 93309. Telephone: (805) 324-6666.

HIGH DESERT
MAVERICKS

Office Address: 12000 Stadium Way, Adelanto, CA 92301. **Telephone:** (619) 246-6287. **FAX:** (619) 246-3197.

Affiliation (first year): Arizona Diamondbacks (1997). **Years in League:** 1991-.

Ownership, Management

Operated by: High Desert Mavericks, Inc.

President: Bobby Brett.

Vice President/General Manager: Steve Pastorino. **Assistant General Managers:** Pete Thuresson, Kurt Wise. **Assistant General Manager/ Director of Ticket Sales:** Michael Guarini. **Director of Guest Services:** Kiyomi Endo. **Director of Group Sales** Mike Thompson. **Director of Concessions:** Mike Fleming. **Account Executives:** Justin Kozubal, Betsy Smoot. **Fan Services Manager:** Kaye Allen. **Director of Broadcasting:** Johnny Doskow. **Head Groundskeeper:** Tino Gonzalez.

Field Staff

Manager: Chris Speier. **Coach:** Dwayne Murphy. **Pitching Coach:** Chuck Kniffin. **Trainer:** Dave Edwards.

Game Information

Radio Announcer: Johnny Doskow. **No. of Games Broadcast:** Unavailable. **Flagship Station:** Unavailable.

PA Announcer: Unavailable. **Official Scorer:** Unavailable.

Stadium Name (year opened): Mavericks Stadium (1991). **Location:** I-15 to Highway 395 to Adelanto Road. **Standard Game Times:** 7:05 p.m.; Sun. (April-May) 2:05, (June-Sept.) 5:05.

Visiting Club Hotel: Holiday Inn-Victorville, 15494 Palmdale Road, Victorville, CA 92393 Telephone: (619) 241-1577.

LAKE ELSINORE
STORM

Office Address: 500 Diamond Drive, Lake Elsinore, CA 92530. **Mailing Address:** P.O. Box 535, Lake Elsinore, CA 92531. **Telephone:** (909) 245-4487. **FAX:** (909) 245-0305. **E-Mail Address:** lestorm@pe.net.

Affiliation (first year): Anaheim Angels (1994). **Years in League:** 1994-.

Ownership, Management

Operated by: Mandalay Sports Enterprises, Inc.

Principal Owner/President: Ken Stickney.

General Manager: Kevin Haughian. **Assistant General Manager:** Chris Hill. **Director, Media/Public Relations:** Wayne Teats. **Director of Telemarketing:** Mark Ottinger. **Director of Ticket Operations:** Mike Rigano. **Director of Operations:** Brent Boznanski. **Assistant Sales Director:** Darrin Gross. **Group Sales Director:** Kathy Davis. **Group Sales Assistant:** Cindy Molina. **Director of Merchandising:** Jennifer Bock. **Director of Broadcasting:** Sean McCall. **Accounting Administrator:** Yvonne Hunneman. **Office Manager:** Jo Equila.

Field Staff

Manager: Don Long. **Coach:** Tyrone Boykin. **Pitching Coach:** Jim Bennett. **Trainer:** Alan Russell.

Game Information

Radio Announcer: Sean McCall. **No. of Games Broadcast:** Home-70, Away-70. **Flagship Station:** Unavailable.

PA Announcer: Joe Martinez. **Official Scorer:** Dennis Bricker.

Stadium Name (year opened): Lake Elsinore Diamond (1994). **Location:** From I-15, take Diamond Drive exit, west on Diamond Drive to stadium. **Standard Game Times:** 7:05 p.m.; Sun. (April-May) 2:05, (June - Aug.) 5:05.

Visiting Club Hotel: Lake View Inn, 31808 Casino Drive, Lake Elsinore, CA 92530. Telephone: (909) 674-9694.

LANCASTER
JETHAWKS

Office Address: 2400 West Ave., Lancaster, CA 93536. **Mailing Address:** 45116 Valley Central Way, Lancaster, CA 93536. **Telephone:** (805) 726-5400. **FAX:** (805) 726-5406.

Affiliation (first year): Seattle Mariners (1996). **Years in League:** 1996-.

Ownership, Management

Operated by: Clutch Play Baseball, LLC.

Chairman of the Board: Horn Chen. **President:** Michael Ellis.

General Manager: Matt Ellis. **Assistant General Manager:** Wayne Berry. **Director of Stadium Operations:** Kyle Fisher. **Director of Sales:** Eileen Garcia. **Director of Ticket Sales:** Kevin Younkin. **Director of Finance:** Michele Ellis. **Office Manager:** Phyllis Fisher. **Public Relations Manager:** Melinda Mayne. **Group Sales Manager:** Chris Hale. **Special Projects Assistant:** John Laferney.

Field Staff

Manager: Rick Burleson. **Coach:** Dana Williams. **Pitching Coach:** Jim Slaton. **Trainer:** Troy McIntosh.

Game Information

Radio Announcer: Unavailable. **No. of Games Broadcast:** Home-70, Away-70. **Flagship Station:** Unavailable.

PA Announcer: Larry Thornhill. **Official Scorer:** David Guenther.

Stadium Name (year opened): Lancaster Municipal Stadium (1996). **Location:** 14 Freeway North to Avenue I exit, left under the bridge, go to first stop light and go left. **Standard Game Times:** 7:15 p.m.; Sun. (April-May) 2, (June-September) 5.

Visiting Club Hotel: Antelope Valley Inn, 44055 N. Sierra Highway, Lancaster, CA 93534. Telephone: (805) 948-4651.

MODESTO
A's

Office Address: 501 Neece Dr., Modesto, CA 95351. **Mailing Address:** P.O. Box 883, Modesto, CA 95353. **Telephone:** (209) 572-4487. **FAX:** (209) 572-4490. **E-Mail Address:** fun@modestoathletics.

Affiliation (first year): Oakland A's (1975). **Years in League:** 1946-64, 1966-.

Ownership, Management

Operated by: Modesto A's Professional Baseball Club, Inc.

Principal Owners: Fred Anderson, Kevin McClatchy.

Vice President/General Manager: Tim Marting. **Assistant General Manager:** David Gottfried. **Director of Sales:** Kevin Korn. **Director of Ticket Sales:** Jeff Titus. **Director of Telemarketing:** Gary Hutchings. **Groundskeeper:** Walter Woodley. **Director of Merchandise:** Jeff Colville.

Field Staff

Manager: Jeffrey Leonard. **Coach:** Dave Joppie. **Pitching Coach:** Rick Rodriguez. **Trainer:** Rich Ramirez.

Game Information

Radio: Unavailable.

PA Announcer: Unavailable. **Official Scorer:** Robert Tennant.

Stadium Name (year opened): John Thurman Stadium (1952). **Location:** Highway 99 to Tuolomne Blvd. exit, turn right and go one block to Neece Drive, left 1/4 mile to ballpark. **Standard Game Times:** 7:15 p.m.; Sun. (April-May) 1:15, (June-Aug.) 6:15.

Visiting Club Hotels: Vagabond Inn, 1525 McHenry Ave., Modesto, CA 95350. Telephone: (209) 521-6340.

RANCHO CUCAMONGA
QUAKES

Office Address: 8408 Rochester Ave., Rancho Cucamonga, CA 91730. **Mailing Address:** P.O. Box 4139, Rancho Cucamonga, CA 91729. **Telephone:** (909) 481-5000. **FAX:** (909) 481-5005. **E-Mail Address:** rcquakes@aol.com.

Affiliation (first year): San Diego Padres (1993). **Years In League:** 1993-.

Ownership, Management

Operated by: Valley Baseball Club, Inc.

President/General Manager: Hank Stickney.

Executive Vice President: Tom Henderson. **Vice President, Finance:** Jay Middleton. **Director of Ticket Operations:** Dennis O'Connor. **Director of Sales:** Bob Teixeira. **Senior Account Executive:** Brant Ringler. **Account Executive:** Janet Beard. **Director of Marketing/Community Relations:** Patti Geye. **Director of Broadcasting/Media Relations:** Michael Curto. **Director of Merchandising/Promotions:** Victor Rojas. **Operations Manager:** C.B. Stueland. **Client Sales Service Representative:** Gretchen Rojas. **Ticket Office Manager:** Kelli Pickwith. **Group Sales Manaer:** Scott Bull. **Direct Sales Manager:** Donna Greer. **Group Sales Representatives:** Connie Hernandez, Mike Junga. **Office Manager:** Frances Kolarz. **Head Groundskeeper:** Rex Whitney.

Field Staff

Manager: Mike Basso. **Coach:** Jason McLeod. **Pitching Coach:** Dave Smith **Trainer:** Jim Daniel.

Game Information

Radio Announcers: Michael Curto (English), Paco Chavez (Spanish). **No. of Games Broadcast:** Home-70, Away-70 (English), Home-11 (Spanish). **Flagship Station:** KCKC 1350-AM (English), KNSE 1510-AM (Spanish).

PA Announcer: David Achord. **Official Scorer:** Larry Kavanaugh.

Stadium Name (year opened): The Epicenter (1993). **Location:** I-10 to I-15 North, to Foothill Boulevard, exit left to Rochester Avenue, left to Stadium Way. **Standard Game Times:** 7:15 p.m.; Sun. (April-June) 2:15, (July-September) 5:15.

Visiting Club Hotel: Best Western Heritage Inn, 8179 Spruce Ave., Rancho Cucamonga, CA 91730. Telephone: (909) 466-1111.

SAN BERNARDINO
STAMPEDE

Office Address: 280 South E Street, San Bernardino, CA 92401. **Mailing Address:** P.O. Box 1806, San Bernardino, CA 92402. **Telephone:** (909) 888-9922. **FAX:** (909) 888-5251.

Affiliation (first year): Los Angeles Dodgers (1995). **Years in League:** 1941, 1987-.

Ownership, Management

Chairman of the Board: David Elmore. **President:** Donna Tuttle.

General Manager: Jason Watson. **Assistant General Manager:** Blake Inman. **Chief Financial Officer:** Kathleen Hightower. **Director of Stadium Operations:** Greg Cozzo. **Head Groundskeeper:** Jerry Brown. **Director of Community Relations:** J'Leen Manning. **Director of Promotions:** Stan Waite. **Director of Ticket Sales:** Mike Jermain. **Director of Group Sales:** Lisa Mueller. **Director of Merchandising:** Stephanie Reed. **Director of Food Services:** Matt Testrake. **Office Manager:** Krisie Moody. **Account Executives:** Jason Cavanagh, Chris Harman, Melissa Olds, Jason Pates.

Field Staff

Manager: Del Crandall. **Coach:** Dino Ebel. **Pitching Coach:** Charlie Hough. **Trainer:** Jim Cranmer.

Game Information

Radio Announcer: Michael Seager. **No. of Games Broadcast:** Home-70, Away-70. **Flagship Station:** KMEN 1290-AM.

PA Announcer: Unavailable. **Official Scorer:** Unavailable.

Stadium Name (year opened): The Ranch (1996). **Location:** From I-15 North, exit 2nd Street, right on 2nd, right on G. **Standard Game Times:** 7:05 p.m.; Sun. 2:05.

Visiting Club Hotel: Radisson, 295 North E Street, San Bernardino, CA 92401. Telephone: (909) 381-2091.

SAN JOSE
GIANTS

Office Address: 588 E. Alma Ave., San Jose, CA 95112. **Mailing Address:** P.O. Box 21727, San Jose, CA 95151. **Telephone:** (408) 297-1435. **FAX:** (408) 297-1453. **E-Mail Address:** www.sjgiants.com

Affiliation (first year): San Francisco Giants (1988). **Years in League:** 1942, 1947-58, 1962-76, 1979-.

Ownership, Management

Operated by: Progress Sports Management.

Chairman: Richard Beahrs.

President: Harry Stavrenos.

General Manager: Mark Wilson. **Assistant General Manager:** Steve Fields. **Director of Sales:** Linda Pereira. **Director of Public Relations:** Dave Moudry. **Group Sales:** Dave Guard. **Groundskeeper:** Hector Gonzales.

Field Staff

Manager: Frank Cacciatore. **Pitching Coach:** Keith Comstock. **Trainer:** Dave Groescher.

Game Information

Radio Announcer: Chris Towsen. **No. of Games Broadcast:** Home-20, Away-20. **Flagship Station:** KSJS 90.5-FM.

PA Announcer: Jim Chapman. **Official Scorers:** John Pletsch, Steve Iaconis.

Stadium Name (year opened): Municipal Stadium (1942). **Location:** From I-280—10th Street exit to Alma, left on Alma, stadium on right. From US 101—Tully Road exit to Senter, right on Senter, left on Alma, stadium on left. **Standard Game Times:** 7:15 p.m.; Sat. 5; Sun. (April-June) 1, (July-August) 5.

Visiting Club Hotel: Gateway Inn, 2585 Seaboard Ave., San Jose, CA 95131. Telephone: (408) 435-8800.

STOCKTON *PORTS*

Office Address: Billy Hebert Field, Alpine and Sutter Streets, Stockton, CA 95204. **Mailing Address:** P.O. Box 8550, Stockton, CA 95208. **Telephone:** (209) 944-5943. **FAX:** (209) 463-4937.

Affiliation (first year): Milwaukee Brewers (1979). **Years in League:** 1941, 1946-72, 1978-.

Ownership, Management

Operated by: Joy in Mudville, Inc.

Principal Owner: Richard Phelps.

General Manager: Dan Chapman. **Assistant General Manager:** Alfred Spear. **Director of Stadium Operations:** Chris Justen. **Director of Merchandising:** John Schaars. **Office Manager:** Molly Rogers. **Bookkeeper:** Nancy Nocks.

Field Staff

Manager: Greg Mahlberg. **Coach:** Theron Todd. **Pitching Coach:** Randy St. Claire. **Trainer:** Paul Anderson.

Game Information

Radio: None.

PA Announcer: Johnny Milford. **Official Scorer:** Tim Ankcorn.

Stadium Name (year opened): Billy Hebert Field (1950). **Location:** From I-5—March Lane exit east, south on Pacific Ave., east on Alpine Ave. From Hwy. 99—Wilson Way exit west to Alpine Avenue, west on Alpine. **Standard Game Times:** 7:05 p.m.; Sun. 5.

Visiting Club Hotel: Best Western Stockton Inn, 4219 E. Waterloo Rd., Stockton, CA 95215. Telephone: (209) 931-3131.

VISALIA *OAKS*

Office Address: 440 N. Giddings Ave., Visalia, CA 93291. **Mailing Address:** P.O. Box 48, Visalia, CA 93279. **Telephone:** (209) 625-0480. **FAX:** (209) 739-7732.

Affiliation (first-year): Oakland Athletics (1997). **Years in League:** 1946-62, 1968-75, 1977-.

Ownership, Management

Operated by: JSS/USA, Inc.

Chairman of the Board: Keiichi Tsukamoto. **President:** John McHale Sr.

General Manager: Andrew Bettencourt. **Assistant General Manager:** Bob Flanagan. **Director of Public Relations:** Harry Kargenian. **Director of Sales/Marketing:** Jason Matlock. **Director of Ticket Sales:** Kathy Elick. **Head Groundskeeper:** Darren Holt.

Field Staff

Manager: Tony DeFrancesco. **Coach:** Greg Sparks. **Pitching Coach:** Glenn Abbott. **Trainer:** Jeremy Loe.

Game Information

Radio Announcers: Bob Flanagan, Jason Matlock. **No. of Games Broadcast:** Away-21. **Flagship Station:** KJUG 1270-AM.

PA Announcer/Official Scorer: Harry Kargenian.

Stadium Name (year opened): Recreation Park (1946). **Location:** From Highway 198 east, take Mooney Boulevard exit, straight from exit to Giddings Avenue, left on Giddings. **Standard Game Times:** 7:05 p.m.

Visiting Club Hotel: Holiday Inn-Visalia, 9000 W. Airport Drive., Visalia, CA 93291. Telephone: (209) 651-5000.

CAROLINA LEAGUE

Class A Advanced

Office Address: 1806 Pembroke Rd., Greensboro, NC 27408. **Mailing Address:** P.O. Box 9503, Greensboro, NC 27429. **Telephone:** (910) 691-9030. **FAX:** (910) 691-9070.

Years League Active: 1945-.

President/Treasurer: John Hopkins.

Vice Presidents: Kelvin Bowles, Calvin Falwell. **Corporate Secretary:** Peter Kirk.

Directors: Don Beaver (Winston-Salem), Kelvin Bowles (Salem), Calvin Falwell (Lynchburg), Jim Goodmon (Durham), North Johnson (Kinston), Peter Kirk (Frederick), Matt Minker (Wilmington), Art Silber (Prince William)

Administrative Assistant: Marnee Larkins. **Legal Counsel:** Winburne King. **Accountant:** John Schwarz.

John Hopkins

1997 Opening Date: April 4. **Closing Date:** Aug 30.

Regular Season: 140 games (split-schedule).

Division Structure: Northern—Frederick, Lynchburg, Prince William, Wilmington. **Southern**—Durham, Kinston, Salem, Winston-Salem.

Playoff Format: First-half division winners play second-half division winners in best-of-3 series. Division playoff winners meet in best-of-5 series for Mills Cup.

All-Star Game: June 17 at Durham, N.C. (California League vs. Carolina League).

Roster Limit: 25 active. **Player Eligibility Rule:** No age limit. No more than two players and one player-coach on active list may have six or more years of prior minor league service.

Brand of Baseball: Rawlings.

Statistician: Howe Sportsdata International, Boston Fish Pier, West Bldg. #2—Suite 306, Boston MA 02210.

1996 Standings (Overall)

Club (Affiliate)	W	L	Pct.	GB	'96 Manager
*#Wilmington (Royals)	80	60	.571	—	John Mizerock
#Kinston (Indians)	76	62	.551	3	Jack Mull
Winston-Salem (Reds)	74	65	.532	5½	Phillip Wellman
#Durham (Braves)	73	66	.525	6½	Randy Ingle
Frederick (Orioles)	67	72	.482	12½	Tim Blackwell
Lynchburg (Pirates)	65	74	.468	14½	Jeff Banister
Salem (Rockies)	62	76	.449	17	Bill McGuire
Prince William (White Sox)	58	80	.420	21	Dave Huppert

*Won playoffs #Won split-season pennant

Stadium Information

Club	Stadium	Dimensions LF	CF	RF	Capacity	'96 Att.
Durham	Athletic Park	305	400	327	9,033	365,445
Frederick	Grove	325	400	325	5,400	258,427
Kinston	Grainger	335	390	335	4,100	145,493
Lynchburg	City	325	390	325	4,000	100,016
Prince William	Pfitzner	315	400	315	6,000	190,065
Salem	Salem Memorial	325	401	325	6,300	173,702
Wilmington	Frawley	325	400	325	5,911	335,309
Winston-Salem	Ernie Shore	325	400	325	6,280	154,132

DURHAM
BULLS

Office Address: 409 Blackwell St., Durham, NC 27701. **Mailing Address:** P.O. Box 507, Durham, NC 27702. **Telephone:** (919) 687-6500. **FAX:** (919) 687-6560.

Affiliation (first year): Atlanta Braves (1980). **Years in League:** 1945-71, 1980-.

Ownership, Management

Operated by: Capitol Broadcasting Co., Inc.

Principal Owner/President: James Goodmon.

Vice President/General Manager: Peter Anlyan. **Assistant General Manager:** Gillian Zucker. **Director of Sales/Marketing:** Rod Meadows. **Director of Ticket Sales:** Mike Snee. **Director of Group Sales:** Barry Gibson. **Head Groundskeeper:** Mike Boekholder. **Office Manager:** Andrea Harris. **Director of Promotions:** Kelly Pratt. **Public Relations Coordinator:** Scott Stephens. **Sales Assistant:** Latonya Raines. **Senior Account Representatives:** Mike Davis, Chip Hutchinson, Matt West. **Ticket Sales Assistants:** Doug Augis, Mitch Mann, Glenn Williford. **Group Sales Representatives:** Shelley Holmes, Tammy Weis. **Stadium Assistant:** Ed Kovalesky. **Trainees:** Ryan Fay, Brad Sims.

Field Staff

Manager: Paul Runge. **Coach:** Wallace Johnson. **Pitching Coach:** Bill Slack. **Trainer:** Willy Johnson.

Game Information

Radio Announcer: Steve Barnes. **No. of Games Broadcast:** Home-70, Away-70. **Flagship Station:** WDNC 620-AM.

PA Announcer: Bill Law. **Official Scorer:** Brent Belvin.

Stadium Name (year opened): Durham Bulls Athletic Park (1995). **Location:** From Raleigh—I-40 West to Hwy. 147 North, exit 12B to Willard, two blocks on Willard to stadium. From I-85—Gregson Street exit to downtown, left on Chapel Hill Street, right on Mangum Street. **Standard Game Times:** 7 p.m.; Sun. 6:05.

Visiting Club Hotel: Red Roof Inn, I-85 at Guess Road, Durham, NC 27705. Telephone: (919) 471-9882.

FREDERICK
KEYS

Office Address: 6201 New Design Road., Frederick, MD 21702. **Mailing Address:** P.O. Box 3169, Frederick, MD 21705. **Telephone:** (301) 662-0013. **FAX:** (301) 662-0018. **E-Mail Address:** fredkeys@aol.com.

Affiliation (first year): Baltimore Orioles (1989). **Years In League:** 1989-.

Ownership, Management

Operated by: Maryland Baseball, LP.

Principal Owners: Peter Kirk, Hugh Schindel, Pete Simmons, Frank Perdue, John Daskalakis.

Chairman: Peter Kirk. **President:** Pete Simmons.

General Manager: Joe Preseren. **Controller:** Sharon Hoffman. **Head Groundskeeper:** Tommy Long. **Director of Media/Public Relations:** Ernie Stepoulos. **Director of Sales:** Joe Pinto. **Director of Community Relations:** Shaun O'Neal. **Director of Group Sales:** Gina Little. **Director of Merchandising:** Kent Hornbrook. **Director of Food Services:** Chris Inouye. **Clubhouse Operations:** George Bell, Danny Benn. **Receptionist:** Laura Springer. **Assistants, Group Sales:** Debbie Beall, Heather Claybaugh. **Account Representative:** Karen Demeza. **Media Relations Assistant:** Robert Baker.

Field Staff

Manager: Dave Hilton. **Pitching Coach:** Jeff Morris. **Trainer:** Dave Walker.

Game Information

Radio Announcer: Matt Noble. **No. of Games Broadcast:** Home-70, Away-70. **Flagship Station:** WXTR 820-AM.

PA Announcer: Rick McCaushin. **Official Scorer:** Bryan Hissey.

Stadium Name (year opened): Harry Grove Stadium (1990). **Location:** From I-70, take exit 54 (Market Street) to Route 355 North. **Standard Game Times:** 7:05 p.m.; Sun. 1:05.

Visiting Club Hotel: Comfort Inn, 420 Prospect Blvd., Frederick, MD 21701. Telephone: (301) 695-6200.

KINSTON
INDIANS

Office Address: 400 East Grainger Ave., Kinston, NC 28501. **Mailing Address:** P.O. Box 3542, Kinston, NC 28502. **Telephone:** (919) 527-9111. **FAX:** (919) 527-2328. **E-Mail Address:** Indians@interpath.com.

Affiliation (first year): Cleveland Indians (1987). **Years in League:** 1956-57, 1962-74, 1978-.

Ownership, Management

Operated by: Slugger Partners, LP

Principal Owners: North Johnson, Cam McRae.

Chairman: Cam McRae. **President/General Manager:** North Johnson.

Assistant General Manager: Randy Shreiner. **Head Groundskeeper:** Tommy Walston. **Director of Merchandising:** John Purvis. **Clubhouse Operations:** Chris Ball. **Director of Broadcasting:** Josh Whetzel.

Field Staff

Manager: Joel Skinner. **Coach:** Boots Day. **Pitching Coach:** Ken Rowe. **Trainer:** Teddy Blackwell.

Game Information

Radio Announcer: Josh Whetzel. **No. of Games Broadcast:** Home-70, Away-70. **Flagship Station:** Unavailable.

PA Announcer: Unavailable. **Official Scorer:** Unavailable.

Stadium Name (year opened): Grainger Stadium (1949). **Location:** U.S. Route 70 Business to Vernon Avenue, left on East Street. **Standard Game Times:** 7 p.m.; Sun. (first half) 3, (second half) 7.

Visiting Club Hotel: Holiday Inn, Highway 70 Bypass, Kinston, NC 28501. Telephone: (919) 527-4155.

LYNCHBURG
HILLCATS

Office Address: City Stadium, 3176 Fort Ave., Lynchburg, VA 24501. **Mailing Address:** P.O. Box 10213, Lynchburg, VA 24506. **Telephone:** (804) 528-1144. **FAX:** (804) 846-0768. **E-Mail Address:** hillcats@interpath.com.

Affiliation (first year): Pittsburgh Pirates (1995). **Years in League:** 1966-.

Ownership, Management

Operated by: Lynchburg Baseball Corp.

President: Calvin Falwell.

General Manager: Paul Sunwall. **Assistant General Manager:** Ronnie Roberts. **Head Groundskeeper/Sales:** Darren Johnson. **Director of Group Sales:** Mike Ranelli. **Clubhouse Operations:** Chuck Watson, Lou Watson. **Director of Broadcasting:** John Miller. **Office Manager:** Karen East.

Field Staff

Manager: Jeff Banister. **Coach:** Richie Hebner. **Pitching Coach:** Jim Bibby. **Trainer:** Bryan Butz.

Game Information

Radio Announcer: John Miller. **No. of Games Broadcast:** Home-70, Away-70. **Flagship Station:** Unavailable.

PA Announcers: Sam Stutts, Chuck Young. **Official Scorers:** Malcolm Haley, Chuck Young.

Stadium Name (year opened): City Stadium (1939). **Location:** U.S. 29 South to City Stadium exit; U.S. 29 North to Lynchburg College exit. **Standard Game Times:** 7:05 p.m.; Sun. (April-June 8) 2:05, (June 22-August.) 6:05.

Visiting Club Hotel: Best Western, 2815 Candlers Mountain Road, Lynchburg, VA 24502. Telephone: (804) 237-2986.

PRINCE WILLIAM
CANNONS

Office Address: 7 County Complex Court, Woodbridge, VA 22193. **Mailing Address:** P.O. Box 2148, Woodbridge, VA 22192. **Telephone:** (703) 590-2311. **FAX:** (703) 590-5716. **E-Mail Address:** pwcannons@aol.com.

Affiliation (first year): St. Louis Cardinals (1997). **Years in League:**

1978-.

Ownership, Management

Operated by: Prince William Professional Baseball Club, Inc.

Principal Owner/President: Art Silber.

Board of Directors: Lani Silber, Seth Silber.

Vice President/General Manager: Pat Filippone. **Director of Food Services:** David John. **Director of Ticket Operations:** Gerard McKearney. **Ticket Manager:** Richard Girardo. **Director of Group Sales:** Matthew Louck. **Group Sales Manager:** Tucker Walsh. **Director of Marketing:** Darran Miner. **Director of Stadium Operations/Merchandising:** Max Baker. **Stadium Operations Manager:** Mike Sylvester. **Director of Broadcasting/Media Relations:** Bob McElligott. **Assistant Director of Broadcasting/Media Relations:** Mike Antonellis. **Director of Finance:** Dean Sisco. **Director of Community Relations:** Allison Tobin. **Special Projects Manager:** Darryl Walls. **Outside Sales Representative:** Don Wallace.

Field Staff

Manager: Roy Silver. **Pitching Coach:** Ray Searage. **Trainer:** B.J. Maack.

Game Information

Radio Announcer: Bob McElligott, Mike Antonellis. **No. of Games Broadcast:** Home-70; Away-70. **Flagship Station:** WAGE 1200-AM.

PA Announcer: Trip Morgan. **Official Scorer:** John Oravec, David Vincent.

Stadium Name (year opened): G. Richard Pfitzner Stadium (1984). **Location:** From I-95, Exit 158B, continue on Prince William Parkway for about five miles, right into County Complex Court. **Standard Game Times:** 7:30 p.m.; Sat. 7; Sun. (April-June 22) 1:30, (June 22-Sept.) 6.

Visiting Club Hotel: Days Inn-Potomac Mills, 14619 Potomac Mills Rd., Woodbridge, VA 22192. Telephone: (703) 494-4433.

SALEM
AVALANCHE

Office Address: 1004 Texas St., Salem, VA 24153. **Mailing Address:** P.O. Box 842, Salem, VA 24153. **Telephone:** (540) 389-3333. **FAX:** (540) 389-9710. **E-Mail Address:** avalanch@roanoke.info.net

Affiliation (first year): Colorado Rockies (1995). **Years In League:** 1968-.

Ownership, Management

Operated by: Salem Professional Baseball Club, Inc.

Principal Owner/President: Kelvin Bowles.

General Manager: Dave Oster. **Director of Business Operations:** Ross Vecchio. **Director of Stadium Operations/Head Groundskeeper:** Stan Macko. **Director of Broadcasting/Media Relations:** Mark Aucutt. **Director of Sales/Marketing:** Christian Carlson. **Assistant Director of Marketing:** Tracy Beskid. **Director of Public Relations:** Bruce Reynolds. **Director of Group Sales:** Deron Marchant. **Director of Merchandising:** Sue Lazzaro. **Director of Computer and Office Operations:** Brian Bowles. **Assistant Director of Ticket Operations:** Ethan Frank-Collins. **Assistant Directors of Operations:** Brian Fentress, Darin Strong.

Field Staff

Manager: Bill McGuire. **Coach:** Stu Cole. **Pitching Coach:** Bryn Smith. **Trainer:** Bill Borowski.

Game Information

Radio Announcer: Mark Aucutt. **No. of Games Broadcast:** Home-70, Away-70. **Flagship Stations:** WROV 1240-AM, WXCF 103.9-FM/1230-AM.

PA Announcers: Slam Duncan, Bruce Reynolds. **Official Scorer:** Brian Hoffman.

Stadium Name (year opened): Salem Memorial Baseball Stadium (1995). **Location:** I-81 exits to Salem Civic Center complex. **Standard Game Times:** 7 p.m.; Sun. (April-June) 2, (July-Aug.) 6.

Visiting Club Hotel: Days Inn-Airport, 8118 Plantation Rd., Roanoke, VA 24019. Telephone: (540) 366-0341.

WILMINGTON
BLUE ROCKS

Office Address: 801 South Madison St., Wilmington, DE 19801. **Telephone:** (302) 888-2015. **FAX:** (302) 888-2032. **E-Mail Address:** info@bluerocks.com.

Affiliation (first year): Kansas City Royals (1993). **Years in League:** 1993-.

Ownership, Management

Operated by: Wilmington Blue Rocks Baseball, LP.

Principal Owner/President: Matt Minker.

Vice President/Baseball Administration: Ken Shepard.

General Manager/Director of Community Relations: Chris Kemple. **Director of Finance:** Craig Bailey. **Director of Stadium Operations:** Andrew Layman. **Head Groundskeeper:** Steve Gold. **Director of Broadcasting/Media Relations:** Mark Nasser. **Director of Sales/ Marketing:** Douglas Stewart. **Assistant Director of Marketing:** Jim Beck. **Director of Ticket Sales:** Marla Chalfie. **Director of Merchandising:** Paul Siegwarth. **Director of Food Services:** Tom Brady. **Office Manager:** Monica King. **Assistant Director of Broadcasting/Media Relations:** Karl Schalk. **Assistant Director of Ticket Operations and Group Sales:** Lori Kresho. **Assistant Director of Merchandising:** Chris Parise. **Ticket Managers:** Chris Francis, Mark Porch, Jason Zahor. **Clubhouse Operations:** Scott Lesher.

Field Staff

Manager: John Mizerock. **Coach:** Keith Hughes. **Pitching Coach:** Buster Keeton. **Trainer:** John Finley.

Game Information

Radio Announcers: Mark Nasser, Karl Schalk. **No. of Games Broadcast:** Home-70, Away-70. **Flagship Station:** WJBR 1290-AM.

PA Announcers: John McAdams. **Official Scorers:** E.J. Casey, David Sannino.

Stadium Name (year opened): Judy Johnson Field at Daniel S. Frawley Stadium (1993). **Location:** I-95 North to Maryland Ave. (exit 6), right onto Maryland Ave., right on Read Street, right on South Madison Street to ballpark; I-95 South to Maryland Ave. (exit 6), left at Martin Luther King Blvd., right on South Madison Street. **Game Times:** 7:05 p.m.; Sat. (April-May) 2:05, (June-August) 7:05; Sun. 2:05.

Visiting Club Hotel: Quality Inn-Skyways, 147 N. DuPont Highway, New Castle, DE 19720. Telephone: (302) 328-6666.

WINSTON-SALEM
WARTHOGS

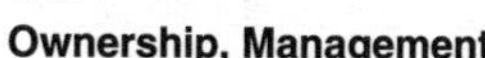

Office Address: 401 Deacon Blvd., Winston-Salem, NC 27105. **Mailing Address:** P.O. Box 4488, Winston-Salem, NC 27115. **Telephone:** (910) 759-2233. **FAX:** (910) 759-2042. **E-Mail Address:** warthogs@warthogs.com

Affiliation (first year): Chicago White Sox (1997). **Years in League:** 1945-.

Ownership, Management

Operated by: Beaver Sports, Inc.

Principal Owner/President: Donald Beaver.

Vice President: Marty Steele.

General Manager: Peter Fisch. **Assistant General Manager:** David Martin. **Director of Community Relations:** Donna Poyant. **Director of Broadcasting/Media Relations:** Tim Grubbs. **Director of Stadium Operations:** Chris Semmens. **Director of Food Services:** Jason Stacherski. **Ticket/Office Manager:** Liesa Ellis. **Head Groundskeeper:** Eddie Busque. **Merchandise:** Frank Burns. **Account Executives:** Mike Belton, Matt Diehl. **Special Assistant to the General Manager:** David Beal. **Clubhouse Operations:** Charles Royals.

Field Staff

Manager: Mike Heath. **Coach:** Mark Haley. **Pitching Coach:** Curt Hasler. **Trainer:** Scott Takao.

Game Information

Radio Announcer: Tim Grubbs. **No. of Games Broadcast:** Home-70, Away-70. **Flagship Station:** WTOB 1380-AM.

PA Announcer: Unavailable. **Official Scorer:** Charlie Cobb.

Stadium Name (year opened): Ernie Shore Field (1956). **Location:** I-40 Business to Cherry Street exit, north through downtown to Deacon Blvd., right to park. **Standard Game Times:** 7:15 p.m.; Sun. 3:05.

Visiting Club Hotel: Holiday Inn-North, 3050 University Parkway, Winston-Salem, NC 27105. Telephone: (910) 723-2911.

FLORIDA STATE LEAGUE

Class A Advanced

Chuck Murphy

Street Address: 103 E. Orange Ave., Daytona Beach, FL 32114. **Mailing Address:** P.O. Box 349, Daytona Beach, FL 32115. **Telephone:** (904) 252-7479. **FAX:** (904) 252-7495.

Years League Active: 1919-1927, 1936-1941, 1946-.

President/Treasurer: Chuck Murphy.

Vice Presidents: Ken Carson, Tom Simmons. **Corporate Secretary:** David Monaco.

Directors: Scott Brown (St. Lucie), Ken Carson (Dunedin), Tony Flores (St. Petersburg), Marvin Goldklang (Fort Myers), Chris Hammond (West Palm Beach), Woody Hicks (Lakeland), Scott Kelyman (Tampa), Edward Kenney (Sarasota), Jordan Kobritz (Daytona), Ken Lehner (Brevard County), Ken Mallory (Charlotte), Jeff Mercer (Kissimmee), Tom Simmons (Vero Beach), John Timberlake (Clearwater).

Office Secretary: Peggy Catigano.

1997 Opening Date: April 3. **Closing Date:** August 31.

Regular Season: 140 games (split-schedule).

Division Structure: East—Brevard County, Daytona, Kissimmee, St. Lucie, Vero Beach, West Palm Beach. **West**—Charlotte, Clearwater, Dunedin, Fort Myers, Lakeland, St. Petersburg, Sarasota, Tampa.

Playoff Format: First-half division winners play second-half division winners in best-of-3 series. Division playoff winners meet in best-of-5 series for league championship.

All-Star Game: June 21 at Kissimmee.

Roster Limit: 25. **Player Eligibility Rule:** No age limit. No more than two players and one player-coach on the active list may have six or more years of prior minor league service.

Brand of Baseball: Rawlings.

Statistician: Howe Sportsdata International, Boston Fish Pier, West Bldg. #2—Suite 306, Boston, MA 02210.

1996 Standings

Club (Affiliate)	W	L	Pct.	GB	'96 Manager
#Tampa (Yankees)	84	50	.627	—	Trey Hillman
Fort Myers (Twins)	79	58	.577	6½	John Russel
#Clearwater (Phillies)	75	62	.547	10½	Al LeBoeuf
St. Petersburg (Cardinals)	75	63	.543	11	Chris Maloney
*#St. Lucie (Mets)	71	62	.534	12½	John Gibbons
Daytona (Cubs)	71	66	.518	14½	Dave Trembley
West Palm Beach (Expos)	68	67	.504	16½	Rick Sofield
#Vero Beach (Dodgers)	65	66	.496	17½	Jon Debus
Sarasota (Red Sox)	67	69	.493	18	DeMarlo Hale
Dunedin (Blue Jays)	67	70	.489	18½	Dennis Holmberg
Charlotte (Rangers)	63	76	.453	23½	Butch Wynegar
Kissimmee (Astros)	60	75	.444	24½	Alan Ashby
Lakeland (Tigers)	61	77	.442	25	Dave Anderson
Brevard County (Marlins)	47	92	.338	39½	Fredi Gonzalez

*Won playoffs #Won split-season pennant

Stadium Information

		Dimensions				
Club	Stadium	LF	CF	RF	Cap.	'96 Att.
Brevard Co.	Space Coast	340	404	340	8,100	140,724
Charlotte	Charlotte County	340	410	340	6,011	70,941
Clearwater	Jack Russell Memorial	340	400	340	6,917	75,118
Daytona	Jackie Robinson Ballpark	315	400	325	4,200	97,098
Dunedin	Dunedin	330	400	315	6,200	66,567
Fort Myers	Bill Hammond	335	405	335	7,500	77,181
Kissimmee	Osceola County	330	410	330	5,180	29,482
Lakeland	Joker Marchant	340	420	340	7,100	24,165
St. Lucie	Thomas J. White	338	410	338	7,347	74,728
St. Petersburg	Al Lang	330	410	330	7,004	124,174
Sarasota	Ed Smith	340	400	340	7,500	69,487
Tampa	Legends Field	314	408	311	10,386	124,619
Vero Beach	Holman	340	400	340	6,500	76,196
W. Palm Beach	Municipal	330	405	330	4,404	76,172

BREVARD COUNTY
MANATEES

Office Address: 5800 Stadium Pkwy., Melbourne, FL 32940. **Telephone:** (407) 633-9200. **FAX:** (407) 633-9210.

Affiliation (first year): Florida Marlins (1994). **Years in League:** 1994-.

Ownership, Management

Operated by: Florida Marlins of Brevard, Ltd.

Principal Owner: Wayne Huizenga.

President: Don Smiley.

General Manager: Ken Lehner. **Office Manager/Bookkeeper:** Debbie Uher. **Facility Maintenance:** Harvey Wheeler. **Head Groundskeeper:** Jose Soto. **Director of Media Relations/Publications:** Mike Caires. **Account Executive:** Jason Camp. **Corporate Sales:** Jeannie Stephan. **Ticket Manager:** Keith Ford. **Account Executive, Group Sales:** Joe Waddy. **President, Brevard Concessions:** Roy Lake. **Receptionist:** Marty Depew.

Field Staff

Manager: Lorenzo Bundy. **Coach:** Jose Castro. **Pitching Coach:** Randy Hennis. **Trainer:** Mike McGowan.

Game Information

Radio: None.

PA Announcers: Chuck Bennett, Gary Henderson. **Official Scorer:** Ron Jernick.

Stadium Name (year opened): Space Coast Stadium (1994). **Location:** I-95 North to Wickham Road (exit 73), left onto Wickham, right onto Lake Andrew Drive, left onto St. Johns, right onto Stadium Parkway; I-95 South to Fiske Blvd. (exit 74), left onto Fiske, follow Fiske/Stadium Parkway. **Standard Game Times:** 7:05 p.m., Sun. 1:35.

Visiting Club Hotel: Melbourne Airport Hilton, 200 Rialto Place, Melbourne, FL 32901. Telephone: (407) 768-0200.

CHARLOTTE
RANGERS

Office Address: 2300 El Jobean Road, Port Charlotte, FL 33948. **Telephone:** (941) 625-9500. **FAX:** (941) 624-5168.

Affiliation (first year): Texas Rangers (1987). **Years in League:** 1987-.

Ownership, Management

Operated by: Texas Rangers Baseball Club, Ltd.

President: Tom Schieffer.

General Manager: Ken Mallory. **Director of Business Development:** Jim Herlihy. **Director of Ticketing and Merchandising:** Chris Snyder. **Head Groundskeeper:** Tom Vido. **Office Manager:** Pam Munz. **Sales Associates:** Shane Johnston, Mickey McCracken, Scott Robb. **Assistant Field Superintendent:** Joe Sonderfer.

Field Staff

Manager: Butch Wynegar. **Pitching Coach:** Steve Foucault. **Trainer:** Frank Velasquez.

Game Information

Radio: None.

PA Announcer: Unavailable. **Official Scorer:** Pete Dulk.

Stadium Name (year opened): Charlotte County Stadium (1987). **Location:** I-75 South to exit 32, follow Toledo Blade Blvd. west for seven miles to stop sign at SR 776, right on 776 for one mile. **Standard Game Times:** 7 p.m., Sun. 6.

Visiting Club Hotel: Days Inn, 1941 Tamiami Trail, Murdock, FL 33948. Telephone: (941) 627-8900.

CLEARWATER
PHILLIES

Office Address: 800 Phillies Dr., Clearwater, FL 34615. **Mailing Address:** P.O. Box 10336, Clearwater, FL 34617. **Telephone:** (813) 441-8638. **FAX:** (813) 447-3924.

Affiliation (first year): Philadelphia Phillies (1985). **Years in League:** 1985-.

Ownership, Management

Operated by: The Philadelphia Phillies.

Principal Owner: Bill Giles.

General Manager: Lee McDaniel. **Director of Sales:** Dan McDonough. **Director of Public Relations/Marketing:** Andy Shenk. **Director of Tickets:** Lauren Fortier. **Concessions Manager:** Larry Hawkins.

Field Staff

Manager: Roy Majtyka. **Coach:** Glenn Brummer. **Pitching Coach:** Darold Knowles. **Trainer:** Clete Sigwart.

Game Information

Radio: None.

PA Announcer: Don Guckian. **Official Scorer:** J. Daniel.

Stadium Name (year opened): Jack Russell Memorial Stadium (1955). **Location:** U.S. 19 north to Drew St., west to Greenwood Avenue, north to Seminole Street, right to park. **Standard Game Times:** 7 p.m., Sun. 2.

Visiting Club Hotels: Howard Johnson, 21030 U.S. 19 North, Clearwater, FL 34625. Telephone: (813) 797-8173.

DAYTONA
CUBS

Office Address: 105 East Orange Ave., Daytona Beach, FL 32114. **Mailing Address:** P.O. Box 15080, Daytona Beach, FL 32115. **Telephone:** (904) 257-3172. **FAX:** (904) 257-3382.

Affiliation (first year): Chicago Cubs (1993). **Years in League:** 1920-24, 1928, 1936-41, 1946-73, 1977-87, 1993-.

Ownership, Management

Operated by: Florida Professional Sports, Inc.

Principal Owner/President: Jordan Kobritz.

General Manager: Debbie Berg. **Senior Account Representative:** Bryan Wentworth. **Clubhouse Operations:** Patrick Silke.

Field Staff

Manager: Steve Roadcap. **Coach:** Richie Zisk. **Pitching Coach:** Alan Dunn. **Trainer:** Eric Sugarman.

Game Information

Radio: None.

PA Announcer: Unavailable. **Official Scorer:** Lyle Fox.

Stadium Name (year opened): Jackie Robinson Ballpark (1930). **Location:** I-95 to International Speedway Blvd. exit (Route 92), east to Beach Street, south to Orange Ave., east to ballpark; A1A North/South to Orange Ave., west to ballpark. **Standard Game Times:** 7 p.m.; Sun.1.

Visiting Club Hotel: Clarion, 905 S. Atlantic Ave., Daytona Beach, FL 32118. Telephone: (904) 255-5432.

DUNEDIN
BLUE JAYS

Office Address: Dunedin Stadium, 373 Douglas Ave., Dunedin, FL 34698. **Mailing Address:** P.O. Box 957, Dunedin, FL 34697. **Telephone:** (813) 733-9302. **FAX:** (813) 734-7661.

Affiliation (first year): Toronto Blue Jays (1987). **Years in League:** 1978-79, 1987-.

Ownership, Management

Operated by: Toronto Blue Jays.

Director of Florida Operations: Ken Carson.

General Manager: Gary Rigley. **Sales/Marketing Coordinator:** Chris Applegate. **Sales/Promotions Coordinator:** Ed Vonnes. **Administrative Assistant:** Pat Smith. **Secretary:** Kim Hamill. **Clubhouse Operations:** Darren Englemeier.

Field Staff

Manager: Dennis Holmberg. **Coach:** Hector Torres. **Pitching Coach:** Darren Balsley. **Trainer:** Mike Wirsta.

Game Information

Radio: None.

PA Announcers: Jim Henderson, Ed Groth. **Official Scorer:** Larry Wiederecht.

Stadium Name (year opened): Dunedin Stadium at Grant Field (1990). **Location:** From North—U.S. 19 to SR 580, west on 580 to Douglas

Avenue, south on Douglas ½ mile to stadium. From South—U.S. 19 to Sunset Point Road, west on Sunset Point, north on Douglas Avenue. **Standard Game Times:** 7 p.m.; Sun. 5.

Visiting Club Hotel: Comfort Inn, 27988 U.S. 19 North, Clearwater, FL 34621. Telephone: (813) 796-0135.

FORT MYERS
MIRACLE

Office Address: 14400 Six Mile Cypress Pkwy., Fort Myers, FL 33912. **Telephone:** (941) 768-4210. **FAX:** (941) 768-4211. **E-Mail Address:** miracle@miraclebaseball.com.

Affiliation: Minnesota Twins (1993). **Years in League:** 1978-87, 1992-.

Ownership, Management

Operated by: Greater Miami Baseball Club, LP.

Principal Owner/Chairman: Marvin Goldklang. **President:** Mike Veeck.

General Manager: Derek Sharrer. **Director of Stadium Operations:** David Burke. **Director of Sales/Marketing:** Linda McNabb. **Director of Business Operations:** Suzanne Reaves. **Director of Media/Public Relations:** Rob Malec. **Director of Promotions:** Andrew Seymour. **Director of Ticket/Group Sales:** Tom Cooper. **Director of Community Relations:** Lou Slack. **Senior Account Representative:** Mark Rich. **Groundskeepers:** Scott Swenson, Terry Slausen.

Field Staff

Manager: John Russell. **Coach:** Jon Mathews. **Pitching Coach:** Eric Rasmussen. **Trainer:** Dave Pruemer.

Game Information

Radio Announcer: Rob Malec. **No. of Games Broadcast:** Away-70. **Flagship Station:** WWCN 770-AM.

PA Announcer: Ted Fitzgeorge. **Official Scorer:** Scott Peterson.

Stadium Name (year opened): Bill Hammond Stadium (1991). **Location:** Exit 21 off I-75, west on Daniels Parkway, left on Six Mile Cypress Parkway. **Standard Game Times:** 7:05 p.m.; Sun 5.

Visiting Club Hotel: Wellesley Inn Suites, 4400 Ford St. Extension, Fort Myers, FL 33909. Telephone: (941) 278-3949.

KISSIMMEE
COBRAS

Office Address: 1000 Bill Beck Blvd., Kissimmee, FL 34744. **Mailing Address:** P.O. Box 422229, Kissimmee, FL 34742. **Telephone:** (407) 933-5500. **FAX:** (407) 847-6237.

Affiliation (first year): Houston Astros (1985). **Years In League:** 1985-.

Ownership, Management

Operated by: Houston Astros (McLane Group).

President: Tal Smith

General Manager: Jeff Mercer. **Assistant General Manager:** Jeff Kuenzli. **Head Groundskeeper:** Rick Raasch. **Office Manager:** Olga Torres.

Field Staff

Manager: John Tamargo. **Coach:** Ivan DeJesus. **Pitching Coach:** Jack Billingham. **Trainer:** Shawn Moffit.

Game Information

Radio: None.

PA Announcer: Norm Allen. **Official Scorer:** Bert Kidwell.

Stadium Name (year opened): Osceola County Stadium (1985). **Location:** Florida Turnpike exit 244, west on U.S. 192, right on Bill Beck Blvd.; I-4 exit onto 192 East, proceed 12 miles, stadium on left; 17-92 South to U.S. 192, left for 3 miles. **Standard Game Times:** 7:05 p.m.; Sun. 2:05.

Visiting Club Hotel: Stadium Inn, 2039 E. Irlo Bronson Hwy., Kissimmee, FL 34744. Telephone: (407) 846-7814.

LAKELAND
TIGERS

Office Address: 2125 N. Lake Ave., Lakeland, FL 33805. **Mailing Address:** P.O. Box 90187, Lakeland, FL 33804. **Telephone:** (941) 688-7911. **FAX:** (941) 688-9589.

Affiliation (first year): Detroit Tigers (1967). **Years in League:** 1919-26, 1953-55, 1960, 1962-64, 1967-.

Ownership, Management

Operated by: Detroit Tigers, Inc.

President: John McHale Jr.

General Manager: Woody Hicks. **Assistant General Manager:** Tripp Norton. **Director of Sales/Communtiy Relations:** Patti Sarano. **Director of Merchandising:** Kay Lalonde. **Director of Food Services:** Roosevelt Clay. **Clubhouse Operations:** Dan Price.

Field Staff

Manager: Mark Meleski. **Pitching Coach:** Joe Georger. **Trainer:** Mark Gruesbeck.

Game Information

Radio: None.

PA Announcer: Unavailable. **Official Scorer:** Sandy Shaw.

Stadium Name (year opened): Joker Marchant Stadium (1960). **Location:** Exit 19 on I-4 to Lakeland Hills Blvd., left 1½ miles. **Standard Game Times:** 7 p.m.; Sun. (April-June) 2, (July-August) 6.

Visiting Club Hotel: Unavailable.

ST. LUCIE
METS

Office Address: 525 NW Peacock Blvd., Port St. Lucie, FL 34986. **Telephone:** (561) 871-2100. **FAX:** (561) 878-9802.

Affiliation (first year): New York Mets (1988). **Years in League:** 1988-.

Ownership, Management

Operated by: New York Mets.

General Manager: Scott Brown. **Assistant General Manager:** Kevin Mahoney. **Director of Media/Public Relations:** George McClelland. **Director of Ticket Sales:** Grace Benway. **Director of Food Services:** Dave Offhaus. **Office Manager:** Kristen Sherwin.

Field Staff

Manager: John Gibbons. **Coach:** Doug Flynn. **Pitching Coach:** Rick Waits. **Trainer:** Brandon Sheppard.

Game Information

Radio: None.

PA Announcer: Unavailable. **Official Scorer:** George McClelland.

Stadium Name (year opened): Thomas J. White Stadium (1988). **Location:** Exit 63C (St. Lucie West Blvd.) off I-95, east ½ mile to NW Peacock, left on NW Peacock. **Standard Game Times:** 7 p.m., Sun. 2.

Visiting Club Hotel: Holiday Inn, 10120 S. Federal Hwy., Port St. Lucie, FL 34952. Telephone: (561) 337-2200.

ST. PETERSBURG
DEVIL RAYS

Office Address: 180 2nd Ave. SE, St. Petersburg, FL 33701. **Mailing Address:** P.O. Box 12557, St. Petersburg, FL 33733. **Telephone:** (813) 822-3384. **FAX:** (813) 895-1556.

Affiliation (first year): Tampa Bay Devil Rays (1997). **Years In League:** 1920-27, 1955-.

Ownership, Management

Operated by: Naimoli Baseball Enterprises, Inc.

Principal Owner/President: Vincent Naimoli.

General Manager: Tony Flores. **Assistant General Manager:** Steve Cohen. **Head Groundskeeper:** John O'Brien. **Director of Media/Public Relations:** Lee Rohrlich. **Director of Sales/Marketing:** Pete Decaro. **Director of Community Relations:** Kristin Kovalcik. **Director of**

Promotions: Mark Hoover. **Director of Group Sales:** John McGraw. **Clubhouse Operations:** Jeff Harrell.

Field Staff

Manager: Bill Evers. **Coach:** Billy Hatcher. **Pitching Coach:** Chuck Hernandez. **Trainer:** Paul Harker.

Game Information

Radio: None.

PA Announcer: Bill Couch. **Official Scorer:** Richard Martin.

Stadium Name (year opened): Al Lang Stadium (1966). **Location:** I-275 to exit 9, left 1st Street South. **Standard Game Times:** 7:05 p.m.; Sun. 5.

Visiting Club Hotel: St. Petersburg Hilton, 333 1st St. S., St. Petersburg, FL 33701. Telephone: (813) 894-5000.

SARASOTA
RED SOX

Office Address: 2700 12th St., Sarasota, FL 34237. **Mailing Address:** P.O. Box 2816, Sarasota, FL 34230. **Telephone:** (941) 365-4460, ext. 230. **FAX:** (941) 365-4217.

Affiliation (first year): Boston Red Sox (1994). **Years in League:** 1966-67, 1969-.

Ownership, Management

Operated by: Red Sox of Florida, Inc.

Principal Owner: Boston Red Sox.

General Manager: Kevin Cummings. **Ticket Manager:** Tommy Larsen. **Group Sales Manager:** Jeff Floerke. **Office Manager:** JoAnn Krohn.

Field Staff

Manager: Rob Derksen. **Coach:** Victor Rodriguez. **Pitching Coach:** Jeff Gray. **Trainer:** Bryan Jaquette.

Game Information

Radio: None.

PA Announcer: Todd Merickel. **Official Scorer:** Walter Jacobus.

Stadium Name (year opened): Ed Smith Stadium (1988). **Location:** I-75 to exit 39, three miles west to Tuttle Ave., right on Tuttle ½ mile to 12th St., stadium on left. **Standard Game Times:** 7 p.m., Sun. 5.

Visiting Club Hotel: Wellesley Inn, 1803 N. Tamiami Trail, Sarasota, FL 34234. Telephone: (941) 366-5128.

TAMPA
YANKEES

Office Address: 3802 W. Dr. Martin Luther King Blvd., Tampa, FL 33614. **Telephone:** (813) 875-7753. **FAX:** (813) 673-3174.

Affiliation (first year): New York Yankees (1994). **Years in League:** 1919-27, 1957-1988, 1994-.

Ownership, Management

Operated by: New York Yankees, LP.

Principal Owner: George Steinbrenner.

General Manager: Scott Kelyman. **Assistant General Manager:** Sam Arena. **Head Groundskeeper:** Mike Hurd. **Director of Sales/Marketing:** Howard Grosswirth. **Director of Ticket Sales:** Vance Smith.

Field Staff

Manager: Lee Mazzilli. **Coach:** Dave Howard. **Pitching Coach:** Mark Shiflett. **Trainer:** Unavailable.

Game Information

Radio: None.

PA Announcer: Todd Wright. **Official Scorer:** J.J. Pizio Jr.

Stadium Name (year opened): Legends Field (1996). **Location:** I-275 to Dale Mabry North, north for 2 miles. **Standard Game Times:** 7 p.m., Sun. 1.

Visiting Club Hotel: Holiday Inn Express, 4732 North Dale Mabry Hwy., Tampa, FL 33614. Telephone: (813) 877-6061.

VERO BEACH
DODGERS

Office Address: 4101 26th St., Vero Beach, FL 32960. **Mailing Address:** P.O. Box 2887, Vero Beach, FL 32961. **Telephone:** (561) 569-4900, ext. 305. **FAX:** (561) 567-0819. **E-Mail Address:** bomalt@vero.com

Affiliation (first year): Los Angeles Dodgers (1980). **Years in League:** 1980-.

Ownership, Management

Operated by: Los Angeles Dodgers, Inc.

Principal Owner/President: Peter O'Malley.

General Manager: Tom Simmons. **Assistant General Manager:** Jeff Maultsby. **Controller:** Link Stanton. **Head Groundskeeper:** John Yencho. **Director of Ticket Sales:** Louise Boissy. **Director of Group Sales:** Rob Croll. **Director of Food Services:** Bruce Callahan. **Clubhouse Operations:** Mike Parrish. **Administrative Assistants:** Chris Haydock, Christian Callan.

Field Staff

Manager: John Shoemaker. **Coach:** Tony Harris. **Pitching Coach:** Edwin Correa. **Trainer:** Rob Giesecke.

Game Information

Radio Announcer: Pete Michaud. **No. of Games Broadcast:** Home-70, Away-70. **Flagship Station:** WAXE 1370-AM.

PA Announcer: Dave Peterson. **Official Scorer:** Randy Phillips.

Stadium Name (year opened): Holman Stadium (1953). **Location:** Exit I-95 at Route 60 East, to 43rd Ave, north to Aviation Blvd., east one block. **Standard Game Times:** 7 p.m., Sun. (April) 1:30.

Visiting Club Hotel: Vero Beach Inn, 4700 North A1A, Vero Beach, FL 32963. Telephone: (561) 231-1600.

WEST PALM BEACH
EXPOS

Office Address: 715 Hank Aaron Drive, West Palm Beach, FL 33401. **Mailing Address:** P.O. Box 3566, West Palm Beach, FL 33402. **Telephone:** (561) 684-6801. **FAX:** (561) 681-4880.

Affiliation (first year): Montreal Expos (1969). **Years in League:** 1955-56, 1965-.

Ownership, Management

Operated by: Montreal Expos Baseball Club.

Principal Owner/President: Claude Brochu.

General Manager: Chris Hammond. **Director of Business Operations:**. Kevin Whalen. **Director of Stadium Operations:** Budgie Clark. **Director of Sales/Marketing:** Kelley Burke. **Senior Account Representatives:** Bryan Monteleone, Jennifer Chalhub. **Ticket Manager:** Mike Stubin. **Clubhouse Operations:** Chris Westmoreland. **Office Manager:** Natalie Hargett. **Account Assistants:** Ashley Brown, Ian Olson.

Field Staff

Manager: Doug Sisson. **Coach:** Rodney McCray. **Pitching Coach:** Dennis Burtt. **Trainer:** Marty Miller.

Game Information

Radio: None.

PA Announcer: Dick Sanford. **Official Scorer:** Ted Leshinski.

Stadium Name (year opened): Municipal Stadium (1962). **Location:** I-95 to exit 53, east ½ mile on Palm Beach Lakes Blvd. Stadium at corner of Palm Beach Lakes Blvd. and Congress Ave. **Standard Game Times:** 7:05 p.m., Sun. 2:05.

Visiting Club Hotel: Wellesley Inn, 1910 Palm Beach Lakes Blvd., West Palm Beach, FL 33409. Telephone: (561) 689-8540.

MIDWEST LEAGUE

Class A

George Spelius

Office Address: 1118 Cranston Road, Beloit, WI 53511. **Mailing Address:** P.O. Box 936, Beloit, WI 53512. **Telephone:** (608) 364-1188. **FAX:** (608) 364-1913.

Years League Active: 1947-.

President/Treasurer: George Spelius.

Vice President: Ed Larson. **Legal Counsel/Secretary:** Richard Nussbaum.

Directors: Lew Chamberlin (West Michigan), William Collins III (Michigan), Dennis Conerton (Beloit), Tom Dickson (Lansing), Erik Haag (South Bend), Richard Holtzman (Quad City), Wally Krouse (Cedar Rapids), Eric Margenau (Fort Wayne), Mark McGuire (Rockford), Wally Schilling (Clinton), Pete Vonachen (Peoria), Dave Walker (Burlington), Mike Woleben (Kane County), John Wollner (Wisconsin).

League Administrator: George Spelius Jr. **Administrative Assistants:** Jim Herbison, Eric Siudzinski.

1997 Opening Date: April 4. **Closing Date:** Aug. 31.

Regular Season: 140 games (split-schedule).

Division Structure: Central—Beloit, Kane County, Peoria, Rockford, Wisconsin. **Eastern**—Fort Wayne, Lansing, Michigan, South Bend, West Michigan. **Western**—Burlington, Cedar Rapids, Clinton, Quad City.

Playoff Format: Eight teams qualify. First-half and second-half division champions, and two wild-card teams, meet in best-of-3 quarterfinal series. Winners advance to best-of-3 semifinals. Winners advance to best-of-5 final for league championship.

All-Star Game: June 17 at Lansing, Mich.

Roster Limit: 25 active. **Player Eligibility Rule:** No age limit. No more than two players and one player-coach on active list may have more than five years experience.

Brand of Baseball: Rawlings ROM-MID.

Statistician: Howe Sportsdata International, Boston Fish Pier, West Bldg. #2—Suite 306, Boston MA 02210.

1996 Standings (Overall)

Club (Affiliate)	W	L	Pct.	GB	'96 Manager
#Peoria (Cardinals)	79	57	.581	—	Roy Silver
#Wisconsin (Mariners)	77	58	.570	1½	Mike Goff
*#West Michigan (Athletics)	77	61	.558	3	Mike Quade
#Quad City (Astros)	70	61	.534	6½	Jim Pankovits
Rockford (Cubs)	70	65	.519	8½	Steve Roadcap
Fort Wayne (Twins)	69	67	.507	10	Dan Rohn
Beloit (Brewers)	69	67	.507	10	Luis Salazar
Lansing (Royals)	68	71	.489	12½	Brian Poldberg
Kane County (Marlins)	65	68	.489	12½	Lynn Jones
Clinton (Padres)	64	70	.478	14	Mike Ramsey
Burlington (Giants)	65	73	.471	15	Glenn Tufts
Cedar Rapids (Angels)	63	72	.467	15½	Tom Lawless
Michigan (Red Sox)	60	78	.435	20	Tommy Barrett
South Bend (White Sox)	54	82	.397	25	Dave Keller

*Won playoffs #Won split-season pennant

Stadium Information

Club	Stadium	Dimensions LF	CF	RF	Capacity	'96 Att.
Beloit	Pohlman Field	325	380	325	3,501	73,552
Burlington	Community Field	338	403	315	3,502	52,726
Cedar Rapids	Veterans Memorial	325	385	325	6,000	127,379
Clinton	Riverview	335	390	325	3,000	57,120
Fort Wayne	Memorial	330	400	330	6,316	226,740
Kane County	Philip B. Elfstrom	335	400	335	5,900	436,076
Lansing	Oldsmobile Park	305	412	305	11,000	538,326
Michigan	C.O. Brown	323	401	336	6,600	161,520
Peoria	Pete Vonachen	335	383	335	5,200	187,283
Quad City	John O'Donnell	340	390	340	6,500	209,513
Rockford	Marinelli Field	335	405	335	4,500	102,479
South Bend	Coveleski Regional	336	410	336	5,000	214,721
West Michigan	Old Kent Park	327	402	327	10,700	547,401
Wisconsin	Fox Cities	325	405	325	5,500	233,797

BELOIT
SNAPPERS

Office Address: 2301 Skyline Drive, Beloit, WI 53511. **Mailing Address:** P.O. Box 855, Beloit, WI 53512. **Telephone:** (608) 362-2272. **FAX:** (608) 362-0418.

Affiliation (first year): Milwaukee Brewers (1982). **Years in League:** 1982-.

Ownership, Management

Operated by: Beloit Professional Baseball Association, Inc.

Chairman of the Board: Dennis Conerton. **President:** Tom Smith.

General Manager: Jeff Nelson. **Assistant General Manager:** Matt Harris. **Director of Media/Public Relations:** Brett Dolan. **Director of Group Sales:** Scott Bucholtz. **Director of Community Relations:** Hugh Jass. **Director of Merchandising/Food Services:** Kyle Rogers. **Clubhouse Operations:** Ron Buzzell. **Administrative Assistants:** Jeff Brazzale, Corey Roberts.

Field Staff

Manager: Luis Salazar. **Coach:** John Mallee. **Pitching Coach:** Jaime Garcia. **Trainer:** Jeff Paxson.

Game Information

Radio Announcer: Brett Dolan. **No. of Games Broadcast:** Home-70, Away-70. **Flagship Station:** WGEZ 1490-AM.

PA Announcer: Al Fagerli. **Official Scorers:** Dave Sennett, Brett Dolan.

Stadium Name (year opened): Harry Pohlman Field (1982). **Location:** I-90 to exit 185-A, west to Cranston Road, right 1½ miles to park. **Standard Game Times:** 7 p.m.; Sat. (April-May) 5, (June-Sept.) 7; Sun. 2.

Visiting Club Hotel: Comfort Inn, 2786 Milwaukee Rd., Beloit, WI 53511. Telephone: (608) 362-2666.

BURLINGTON
BEES

Office Address: 2712 Mt. Pleasant St., Burlington, IA 52601. **Mailing Address:** P.O. Box 824, Burlington, IA 52601. **Telephone:** (319) 754-5705. **FAX:** (319) 754-5882. **E-Mail Address:** beesball@aol.com.

Affiliation (first year): Cincinnati Reds (1997). **Years In League:** 1962-.

Ownership, Management

Operated by: Burlington Baseball Association, Inc.

President: David Walker.

General Manager: Chuck Heeman. **Assistant General Manager:** Kent Harman. **Director of Business Operations:** John Wagner. **Director of Media/Public Relations:** Jim Nolan. **Director of Broadcasting:** Doug Greenwald. **Head Groundskeeper:** Chuck Cannon.

Field Staff

Manager: Phillip Wellman. **Pitching Coach:** Derek Botelho. **Trainer:** Billy Maxwell.

Game Information

Radio Announcers: Doug Greenwald, Jim Nolan. **No. of Games Broadcast:** Home-70, Away-70. **Flagship Station:** KCPS 1150-AM.

PA Announcer: Jim Nolan. **Official Scorer:** Scott Logas.

Stadium Name (year opened): Community Field (1973). **Location:** From U.S. 34, take U.S. 61 North to Mt. Pleasant Street, east ⅛ mile. **Standard Game Times:** 7 p.m.; Sat. (April) 2; Sun. (April-May) 2, (June-Aug.) 6.

Visiting Club Hotel: Best Western-Pzazz, 3001 Winegard Drive, Burlington, IA 52601. Telephone: (319) 753-2223.

CEDAR RAPIDS *KERNELS*

Office Address: 950 Rockford Rd. SW, Cedar Rapids, IA 52404. **Mailing Address:** P.O. Box 2001, Cedar Rapids, IA 52406. **Telephone:** (319) 363-3887. **FAX:** (319) 363-5631.

Affiliation (first year): Anaheim Angels (1993). **Years in League:** 1962-.

Ownership, Management

Operated by: Cedar Rapids Baseball Club, Inc.

President: Wally Krouse.

General Manager: Jack Roeder. **Assistant General Manager:** Andrew Graykowski. **Head Groundskeeper:** Guy Curran. **Office Manager:** Nancy Cram. **Director of Media Relations/Broadcasting:** John Rodgers.

Field Staff

Manager: Mario Mendoza. **Coach:** Todd Claus. **Pitching Coach:** Rick Wise. **Trainer:** Jaime Macias.

Game Information

Radio Announcer: John Rodgers. **No. of Games Broadcast:** Home-70, Away-70. **Flagship Station:** KCRG 1600-AM.

PA Announcer/Official Scorer: Dale Brodt.

Stadium Name (year opened): Veterans Memorial Stadium (1949). **Location:** I-380 to Wilson Ave., west to Rockford Rd., right to corner of 8th Ave. and 15th St. SW. **Standard Game Times:** 7 p.m. (6 April); Sat. (April-May) 2, (June-Aug.) 7; Sun. 2.

Visiting Club Hotel: Village Inn, 100 F Ave. NW, Cedar Rapids, IA 52405. Telephone (319) 363-8161.

CLINTON *LUMBER KINGS*

Office Address: Riverview Stadium, 6th Ave. North and 1st Street, Clinton, IA 52732. **Mailing Address:** P.O. Box 1295, Clinton, IA 52733. **Telephone:** (319) 242-0727. **FAX:** (319) 242-1433.

Affiliation (first year): San Diego Padres (1995). **Years in League:** 1956-.

Ownership, Management

Operated by: Clinton Baseball Club, Inc.

Chairman of the Board: Ed Kross. **President:** Wally Schilling.

General Manager: Alfredo Portela. **Director of Business Operations/ Assistant General Manager:** Mike Lieberman. **Director of Sales/Assistant General Manager:** Mark Sluban. **Director of Promotions:** Chris Agnitsch. **Director of Ticket Sales:** Kelly Harvey. **Office Manager:** Terri Portela.

Field Staff

Manager: Tom LeVasseur. **Coach:** Dan Simonds. **Pitching Coach:** Darrel Akerfelds. **Trainer:** Jason Haeussinger.

Game Information

Radio Announcer: Unavailable. **No. of Games Broadcast:** Home-70, Away-70. **Flagship Station:** KCLN 97.7-FM.

PA Announcer: Brad Seward. **Official Scorer:** Unavailable.

Stadium Name (year opened): Riverview Stadium (1937). **Location:** Highway 30 East to 6th Avenue North, right on 6th, cross railroad tracks, stadium on right. **Standard Game Times:** 7:05 p.m., Sun. 6.

Visiting Club Hotel: Travelodge, 302 6th Ave. S., Clinton, IA 52732. Telephone: (319) 243-4730.

FORT WAYNE *WIZARDS*

Office Address: 4000 Parnell Ave., Fort Wayne, IN 46805. **Telephone:** (219) 482-6400. **FAX:** (219) 471-4678.

Affiliation (first year): Minnesota Twins (1993). **Years in League:** 1993-.

Ownership, Management

Operated by: United Sports, Inc.

Principal Owner: Eric Margenau. **Vice President:** Mike Tatoian

General Manager: Bret Staehling. **Director of Business Operations:** Jeff Hyde. **Director of Corporate Sales:** Nina Zirille. **Director of Group Sales:** Vince Slack. **Director of Broadcasting/Media Relations:** Alan Garrett. **Director of Marketing/Promotions:** Jason Hartlund. **Secretary:** Nancy Murphy. **Group Sales Assistants:** Neil Gustafson, Jeffrey Young. **Marketing Assistant:** Doug Johnson. **Ticket Sales Representatives:** Ray Grabowski, Mark Hammond, Kevin Ulwelling.

Field Staff

Manager: Mike Boulanger. **Coach:** Jeff Carter. **Pitching Coach:** Stu Cliburn. **Trainer:** Chad Floyd.

Game Information

Radio Announcer: Alan Garrett. **No. of Games Broadcast:** Home-70, Away-70. **Flagship Station:** WHWD 1380-AM.

PA Announcer: Jim Amstutz. **Official Scorer:** Rich Tavierne, Mark Lazzer.

Stadium Name (year opened): Memorial Stadium (1993). **Location:** Exit 112A (Coldwater Road) off I-69 to Coliseum Blvd., left on Coliseum Blvd. to stadium. **Standard Game Times:** 7 p.m.; Sun. 2, 6.

Visiting Club Hotel: Budgetel Inn, 1005 West Washington Center Rd., Fort Wayne, IN 46805. Telephone: (219) 489-2220.

KANE COUNTY *COUGARS*

Office Address: 34W002 Cherry Lane, Geneva, IL 60134. **Telephone:** (630) 232-8811. **FAX:** (630) 232-8815.

Affiliation (first year): Florida Marlins (1993). **Years In League:** 1991-.

Ownership, Management

Operated by: Cougars Baseball Partners.

Principal Owners: Al Gordon (president), Mike Murtaugh (vice president), Mike Woleben (secretary/treasurer).

General Manager: Bill Larsen. **Assistant General Manager:** Jeff Sedivy. **Business Manager:** Mary Almlie. **Director of Media Relations/ Publications:** Marty Cusack. **Director of Ticket Operations:** Burke Masters. **Director of Merchandising:** Curtis Haug. **Promotions Coordinator:** Jeff Ney. **Office Manager:** Patti Savage. **Graphic Design/Computer Operations:** Kevin Gilsdorf. **Group Sales Coordinators:** Sue Lesters, Amy Mason. **Ticket Office Coordinator:** Jennifer Plesa. **Account Executive:** John Knechtges. **Facilities Management:** Mike Fik, Mike Kurns. **Concessions Operations:** Victor Alcazar. **Head Groundskeeper:** Mason Lyall. **Clubhouse:** Jose Torres.

Field Staff

Manager: Lynn Jones. **Coach:** Matt Winters. **Pitching Coach:** Brian Peterson. **Trainer:** Harold Williams.

Game Information

Radio Announcer: Unavailable. **No. of Games Broadcast:** Home-70, Away-70. **Flagship Station:** WKKD 95.9-FM.

PA Announcer: Unavailable. **Official Scorer:** Unavailable.

Stadium Name (year opened): Philip B. Elfstrom Stadium (1991). **Location:** I-88 (East-West Tollway) to Farnsworth Road North exit, 5 miles north to Cherry Lane, left to stadium. **Standard Game Times:** 7 p.m.; Sat. 6; Sun. 2.

Visiting Club Hotel: Travelodge, 1617 Naperville Road, Naperville, IL 60563. Telephone: (630) 505-0200.

LANSING
LUGNUTS

Office Address: 505 E. Michigan Ave., Lansing MI 48912. **Telephone:** (517) 485-4500. **FAX:** (517) 485-4518.

Affiliation (first year): Kansas City Royals (1996). **Years In League:** 1996-.

Ownership, Management

Principal Owners: Tom Dickson, Sherrie Myers.

Vice President/General Manager: Jim Weigel. **Assistant General Manager/Sales:** Tom Glick. **Marketing Director:** Linda Frederickson. **Marketing Manager:** Michael Baird. **Customer Service Director:** Darla Bowen. **Retail Director:** Mary Kay Schultz. **Retail Assistant Manager:** Cherie Hargitt. **Ticket Manager:** Greg Rauch. **Assistant Ticket Manager:** Rory Weber. **Sponsorship Account Executive:** Elizabeth Panich. **Sponsorship Service Manager:** Megan Frazer. **Customer Service Representative:** Jennifer Burigana. **Corporate Sales Representatives:** Matthew Felton, Tom Murphy. **Group Sales Manager:** Max Bisschop. **Group Sales Representative:** Bob Studley. **Business Manager:** Kimberly Hengsbach. **Head Groundskeeper:** Tom Preslar.

Field Staff

Manager: Bob Herold. **Coach:** Curtis Wilkerson. **Pitching Coach:** Mike Mason. **Trainer:** Jeff Stevenson.

Game Information

Radio Announcer: Mike Vander Wood. **No. of Games Broadcast:** Home-70, Away-70. **Flagship Station:** WJIM 1240-AM.

PA Announcer: J.J. Wright. **Official Scorer:** Michael Clark.

Stadium Name (year opened): Oldsmobile Park (1996). **Location:** U.S. 496 to Cedar/Larch exit, 2 blocks north on Larch, stadium on corner of Larch and Michigan. **Standard Game Times:** 7:05 p.m., Sun. (April 13-July 13) 2, (July 27-Aug. 17) 6.

Visiting Club Hotel: Holiday Inn South, 6820 S. Cedar St., Lansing, MI 48911. Telephone: (517) 627-3211.

MICHIGAN
BATTLE CATS

Office Address: 1392 Capital Ave. NE, Battle Creek, MI 49017. **Telephone:** (616) 660-2287. **FAX:** (616) 660-2288.

Affiliation (first year): Boston Red Sox (1995). **Years in League:** 1995-.

Ownership, Management

Operated by: American Baseball Capital, Inc.

Principal Owner/Chairman: William Collins III.

General Manager: Jerry Burkot. **Controller:** T.J. Egan. **Director of Media Relations:** Danielle Disch. **Director of Corporate Sales:** Steve Ventura. **Account Representative:** Anthony Errico. **Director of Community Relations:** Tonya Fenderbosch. **Director of Ticket Sales:** Ben Young. **Director of Merchandising:** Billy Krumb. **Head Groundskeeper:** Mike Varner. **Business Manager:** Sheena Weir.

Field Staff

Manager: Billy Gardner Jr. **Coach:** Gerald Perry. **Pitching Coach:** Dan Gakeler. **Trainer:** Scott Hagland.

Game Information

Radio Announcers: Terry Newton, Ken Ervin. **No. of Games Broadcast:** Home-70; Away-70. **Flagship Station:** WBCK 930-AM.

PA Announcer: Unavailable. **Official Scorer:** Chuck Ahrens.

Stadium Name (year opened): C.O. Brown Stadium (1989). **Location:** I-94 to exit 98B (downtown), to Capital Ave. NE, east to stadium. **Standard Game Times:** 7 p.m.; Sat (April-May) 2, (June-August) 7; Sun. 2.

Visiting Club Hotel: Unavailable.

PEORIA
CHIEFS

Office Address: 1524 W. Nebraska Ave., Peoria, IL 61604. **Telephone:** (309) 688-1622. **FAX:** (309) 686-4516. **E-mail Address:** peochfs@aol.com

Affiliation (first year): St. Louis Cardinals (1995). **Years in League:** 1983-.

Ownership, Management

Operated by: Peoria Chiefs Community Baseball Club, LLC.

Principal Owner/President: Pete Vonachen.

General Manager: Rocky Vonachen. **Assistant General Manager/ Director of Sales:** Dan Vonachen. **Director of Media/Public Relations:** Dave Schultz. **Account Representative:** Ralph Rashid. **Director of Group Sales:** Kevin Hill. **Director of Merchandising:** Mark Vonachen. **Head Groundskeeper:** Dennis Rothlisberger. **Office Manager:** Barbara Lindberg. **Receptionist:** Karen Patterson.

Field Staff

Manager: Joe Cunningham. **Pitching Coach:** Gary Buckels. **Trainer:** Aaron Burns.

Game Information

Radio Announcer: Dave Schultz. **No. of Games Broadcast:** Home-70, Away-70. **Flagship Station:** WEEK 98.5-FM.

PA Announcer: Unavailable. **Official Scorer:** Tom Lowey.

Stadium Name (year opened): Pete Vonachen Stadium (1984). **Location:** I-74 exit 91B (University Street North), left on Nebraska Avenue, left to ballpark. **Standard Game Times:** 7:05 p.m., Sun. 2:05.

Visiting Club Hotel: Holiday Inn City Centre, 500 Hamilton Blvd., Peoria, IL 61602. Telephone: (309) 674-2500.

QUAD CITY
RIVER BANDITS

Office Address: 209 S. Gaines St., Davenport, IA 52802. **Mailing Address:** P.O. Box 3496, Davenport, IA 52808. **Telephone:** (319) 324-2032. **FAX:** (319) 324-3109.

Affiliation (first year): Houston Astros (1993). **Years in League:** 1960-.

Ownership, Management

Operated by: Quad City Professional Baseball Club, Inc.

Principal Owner/Chairman: Richard Holtzman.

General Manager: Chris Holvoet. **Assistant General Manager:** Pat Daly. **Director of Media/Public Relations:** Mike Capps. **Director of Sales/Marketing:** Holly Morgan. **Director of Ticket Sales:** Chet Carey. **Director of Group Sales:** David Lorenz. **Office Manager:** Deb Burroughs. **Group Sales Assistant:** Keith Lucier.

Field Staff

Manager: Manny Acta. **Coach:** Jorge Orta. **Pitching Coach:** Charley Taylor. **Trainer:** Nate Lucero.

Game Information

Radio Announcer: Mike Capps. **No. of Games Broadcast:** Home-70, Away-70. **Flagship Station:** WKBE 1270-AM.

PA Announcer: Unavailable. **Official Scorer:** Jim Tappa.

Stadium Name (year opened): John O'Donnell Stadium (1931). **Location:** From I-74, south on SR 61 to corner of South Gaines Street and River Drive. **Standard Game Times:** 7 p.m.; Sun. 2.

Visiting Club Hotel: Days Inn, 3202 E. Kimberly Road, Davenport, IA 52807. Telephone: (319) 355-1190.

ROCKFORD
CUBBIES

Office Address: 101 15th Ave., Rockford, IL 61104. **Mailing Address:** P.O. Box 6748, Rockford, IL 61125. **Telephone:** (815) 962-2827. **FAX:** (815) 961-2002.

Affiliation (first year): Chicago Cubs (1995). **Years in League:** 1988-.

Ownership, Management

Operated By: Chicago Cubs.

President: Mark McGuire. **Vice President:** Connie Kowal

General Manager: Michael Holmes. **Assistant General Manager:** Andy Williams. **Director of Community/Media Relations:** Sarah Couey. **Director of Marketing/Promotions:** Gerry Clarke. **Manager, Office Administration:** Tona Eisele. **Administrative Assistant:** Chernetta Bedford. **Director of Ticket Operations:** Eric Robin.

Field Staff

Manager: Ruben Amaro. **Coach:** Moe Hill. **Pitching Coach:** Unavailable. **Trainer:** Jim O'Reilly.

Game Information

Radio: Unavailable.

PA Announcer: Lisa Fielding. **Official Scorer:** David Shultz.

Stadium Name (year opened): Marinelli Field (1988). **Location:** I-90 West to US 20 West to Hwy 2, north on Main Street to 15th Avenue.

Standard Game Times: 7 p.m.; Sat. 6, Sun. 2.

Visiting Club Hotel: Howard Johnson, 3909 11th St., Rockford, IL 61109. Telephone: (815) 397-9000.

SOUTH BEND
SILVER HAWKS

Office Address: 501 W. South St., South Bend, IN 46601. **Mailing Address:** P.O. Box 4218, South Bend, IN 46634. **Telephone:** (219) 235-9988. **FAX:** (219) 235-9950.

Affiliation (first year): Arizona Diamondbacks (1997). **Years in League:** 1988-.

Ownership, Management

Operated by: Palisades Baseball, Ltd.

Principal Owner: Alan Levin.

Vice President/General Manager: Erik Haag. **Assistant General Manager:** Jim Pool. **Director of Sales and Promotions:** Mike Foss. **Assistant Director of Sales and Promotions:** David Williams. **Director of Group Sales:** Lauren Cannon. **Assistant Director of Group Sales**: Adam Wogan. **Account Executives/Group Sales:** Sharee Brandler, Rick Delvecchio. **Director of Public Relations:** Steve Smith. **Director of Ticket Operations:** Jon Zeitz. **Director of Stadium Operations:** Tom Reed.

Field Staff

Manager: Dickie Scott. **Coach:** Jim Presley. **Pitching Coach:** Dennis Lewallyn. **Trainer:** Greg Barber.

Game Information

Radio Announcers: Unavailable. **No. of Games Broadcast:** Home-70, Away-70. **Flagship Station:** WSBT 960-AM.

PA Announcer: Unavailable. **Official Scorer:** Unavailable.

Stadium Name (year opened): Stanley Coveleski Regional Stadium (1987). **Location:** I-80/90 toll road to exit 77. Enter US 31-33 south to South Bend, to downtown (Main St.), to Western Ave., right on Western, left on Taylor. **Standard Game Times:** 7 p.m., Sat. 2 (April-May), 7 (June-August); Sun. 2.

Visiting Club Hotels: Days Inn, 52757 U.S. 31 North, South Bend, IN 46637. Telephone: (219) 277-0510.

WEST MICHIGAN
WHITECAPS

Office Address: Old Kent Park, 4500 W. River Dr., Comstock Park, MI 49321. **Mailing Address:** P.O. Box 428, Comstock Park, MI 49321. **Telephone:** (616) 784-4131. **FAX:** (616) 784-4911. **E-mail Address:** whitecap@gr.cns.net

Affiliation (first year): Detroit Tigers (1997). **Years in League:** 1994-.

Ownership, Management

Operated by: Whitecaps Professional Baseball Corp.

Principal Owners: Dennis Baxter, Lew Chamberlin.

President: Dennis Baxter. **Vice President, Managing Partner:** Lew Chamberlin.

General Manager: Scott Lane. **Director of Sales:** John Guthrie. **Director of Baseball Operations:** Jim Jarecki. **Director of Group Sales:** Greg Hill. **Media Relations/Merchandising:** Lori Clark. **Gameday Operations Manager:** Matt O'Brien. **Ticket Manager:** Bruce Radley. **Community Relations Manager:** Erin Kauth. **Account Executive:** Dan Morrison. **Promotions Coordinator:** Kris Beernink. **Ticket Assistant:** Mark Kiszka. **Concessions Assistant:** Jesse Eisenhuth. **Facility**

Maintenance Manager: Joe Eimer. **Head Groundskeeper:** Heather Nabozny. **Human Resources Coordinator:** Ellen Chamberlin. **Accountant:** Dean Haverdink. **Accounts Payable:** Kathleen Kooyers. **Accounts Receivable:** Barbara Renteria. **Receptionist:** Kim Repper.

Field Staff

Manager: Bruce Fields. **Coach:** Skeeter Barnes. **Pitching Coach:** Brian Allard. **Trainer:** Brian Goike.

Game Information

Radio Announcers: Rick Berkey, Rob Sanford. **No. of Games Broadcast:** Home-70, Away-70. **Flagship Station:** WOOD 1300-AM.

PA Announcer: Unavailable. **Official Scorers:** Don Thomas, Mike Dean.

Stadium Name (year opened): Old Kent Park (1994). **Location:** US 131 North from Grand Rapids to exit 91 (West River Drive), through intersection to stadium. **Standard Game Times:** 7 p.m.; Sun. 4.

Visiting Club Hotel: Days Inn-Downtown, 310 Pearl St. NW, Grand Rapids, MI 49504. Telephone: (616) 235-7611.

WISCONSIN
TIMBER RATTLERS

TIMBER Rattlers™

Office Address: 2400 N. Casaloma Dr., Grand Chute, WI 54915. **Mailing Address:** P.O. Box 464, Appleton, WI 54912. **Telephone:** (414) 733-4152. **FAX:** (414) 733-8032.

Affiliation (first year): Seattle Mariners (1993). **Years in League:** 1962-.

Ownership, Management

Operated by: Appleton Baseball Club, Inc.

President: John Wollner.

General Manager: Mike Birling. **Assistant General Manager:** Gary Mayse. **Team Accountant:** Cathy Spanbauer. **Head Groundskeeper:** Chad Huss. **Director of Marketing:** Gary Radke. **Senior Account Representatives:** Gerry Davis, Jim Kraft. **Director of Promotions/ Merchandising:** David Frost. **Director of Ticket Sales:** Marti Wollner. **Group Sales:** Angie Entwisle, Eric Muhlstein, Drew Niehans. **Office Manager:** Mary Robinson.

Field Staff

Manager: Gary Varsho. **Coach:** Omer Munoz. **Pitching Coach:** Pat Rice. **Trainer:** Jeff Carr.

Game Information

Radio Announcer: Tim McCord. **No. of Games Broadcast:** Home-70, Away-70. **Flagship Station:** WSGC 1050-AM.

PA Announcers: Bill Scott, Bill Schultz. **Official Scorers:** Doug Hahn, Dan Huber, Jim Youngwerth.

Stadium Name (year opened): Fox Cities Stadium (1995). **Location:** Highway 41 to Wisconsin Ave. exit, west to Casaloma Drive, right on Casaloma, stadium ½ mile on right. **Standard Game Times:** 7 p.m., Sun. 1.

Visiting Club Hotel: Fairfield Inn, 132 Mall Dr., Appleton, WI 54912. Telephone: (414) 954-0202.

SOUTH ATLANTIC LEAGUE

Class A

John Moss

Office Address: 504 Crescent Hill, Kings Mountain, NC 28086. **Mailing Address:** P.O. Box 38, Kings Mountain, NC 28086. **Telephone:** (704) 739-3466. **FAX:** (704) 739-1974.

Years League Active: 1948-1952, 1960-.

President/Secretary-Treasurer: John Moss.

First Vice President: Winston Blenckstone. **Second Vice President:** Bill Scripps.

Directors: Don Beaver (Hickory), Winston Blenckstone (Hagerstown), Chuck Boggs (Charleston, W.Va.), William Collins III (Greensboro), Marvin Goldklang (Charleston, SC), Larry Hedrick (Piedmont), Peter Kirk (Delmarva), Eric Margenau (Capital City), Ron McKee (Asheville), Chip Moore (Macon), Charles Morrow (Columbus), Charles Padgett (Cape Fear), Bill Scripps (Augusta), Ken Silver (Savannah).

Administrative Assistant: Elaine Moss.

1997 Opening Date: April 3. **Closing Date:** Aug. 31.

Regular Season: 142 games (split-schedule).

Division Structure: Central—Asheville, Capital City, Charleston SC, Greensboro, Hickory, Piedmont. **Northern**—Cape Fear, Charleston WV, Delmarva, Hagerstown. **Southern**—Augusta, Columbus, Macon, Savannah.

Playoff Format: Eight teams qualify. First-half and second-half division champions, and two wild-card teams, meet in best-of-3 quarterfinal series. Winners advance to best-of-3 semifinal series. Winners advance to best-of-3 final for league championship.

All-Star Game: June 17 at Augusta, Ga.

Roster Limit: 25 active. **Player Eligibility Rule:** No age limit. No more than two players and one player-coach on active list may have more than five years of experience.

Brand of Baseball: Rawlings.

Statistician: Howe Sportsdata International, Boston Fish Pier, West Bldg. #2—Suite 306, Boston, MA 02210.

1996 Standings (Overall)

Club (Affiliate)	W	L	Pct.	GB	'96 Manager
#Asheville (Rockies)	84	52	.618	—	P.J. Carey
#Capital City (Mets)	82	57	.590	3½	Howie Freiling
#Delmarva (Expos)	83	59	.585	4	Doug Sisson
#Columbus (Indians)	79	63	.556	8	Joel Skinner
#Fayetteville (Tigers)	76	63	.547	9½	Dwight Lowry
Piedmont (Phillies)	72	66	.522	13	Roy Majtyka
*Savannah (Dodgers)	72	69	.511	14½	John Shoemaker
#Augusta (Pirates)	71	70	.504	15½	Jay Loviglio
Hagerstown (Blue Jays)	70	71	.496	16½	J.J. Cannon
Charleston, S.C. (Rangers)	63	78	.447	23½	Gary Allenson
Macon (Braves)	61	79	.436	25	Paul Runge
Charleston, W.Va. (Reds)	58	84	.408	29	T. Thompson/D. Scott
Greensboro (Yankees)	56	86	.394	31	R. Patterson/J. Johnson
Hickory (White Sox)	55	85	.393	31	Chris Cron

*Won playoffs #Won split-season pennant

Stadium Information

Club	Stadium	Dimensions LF	CF	RF	Capacity	'96 Att.
Asheville	McCormick Field	328	406	300	4,000	145,798
Augusta	Lake Olmstead	330	400	330	4,500	157,487
Cape Fear*	J.P. Riddle	330	405	330	4,200	73,149
Capital City	Capital City	330	395	330	6,000	156,921
Charleston, SC	Riley Ballpark	306	386	336	5,908	100,428
Charleston, WV	Watt Powell Park	340	406	330	6,800	87,189
Columbus	Golden Park	330	415	330	5,000	45,110
Delmarva	Perdue	309	402	309	5,200	315,011
Greensboro	War Memorial	327	401	327	7,500	168,534
Hagerstown	Municipal	335	400	330	4,600	102,765
Hickory	L.P. Frans	335	401	335	5,100	207,069
Macon	Luther Williams	338	402	338	4,000	117,042
Piedmont	Fieldcrest Cannon	330	400	310	4,700	102,983
Savannah	Grayson	290	400	310	8,000	122,448

*Club operated as Fayetteville Generals in 1996

ASHEVILLE *TOURISTS*

Office Address: McCormick Field, 30 Buchanan Place, Asheville, NC 28801. **Mailing Address:** P.O. Box 1556, Asheville, NC 28802. **Telephone:** (704) 258-0428. **FAX:** (704) 258-0320.

Affiliation (first year): Colorado Rockies (1994). **Years In League:** 1976-.

Ownership, Management

Operated by: Tourists Baseball, Inc.

Principal Owners: Peter Kern, Ron McKee.

President: Peter Kern.

General Manager: Ron McKee. **Assistant General Manager:** R.J. Martino. **Director of Business Operations:** Carolyn McKee. **Director of Media Relations:** Chris Smith. **Director of Ticket Sales/Merchandising:** Margarita Turner. **Director of Food Services:** Jane Lentz. **Head Groundskeeper:** Grady Gardner.

Field Staff

Manager: Ron Gideon. **Coach:** Billy White. **Pitching Coach:** Jack Lamabe. **Trainer:** Bill Slosson.

Game Information

Radio: None.

PA Announcer: Sam Zurich. **Official Scorer:** Mike Gore.

Stadium Name (year opened): McCormick Field (1992). **Location:** I-240 to Charlotte Street South exit, south one mile on Charlotte, left on McCormick Place. **Standard Game Times:** 7 p.m., Sun. 2.

Visiting Club Hotel: Days Inn, 199 Tunnel Rd., Asheville, NC 28805. Telephone: (704) 254-4311.

AUGUSTA *GREENJACKETS*

Office Address: 78 Milledge Road, Augusta, GA 30904. **Mailing Address:** P.O. Box 3746, Hill Station, Augusta, GA 30904. **Telephone:** (706) 736-7889. **FAX:** (706) 736-1122.

Affiliation (first year): Pittsburgh Pirates (1988). **Years in League:** 1988-.

Ownership, Management

Operated by: Scripps Baseball Group, Inc.

Principal Owner/President: Bill Scripps.

General Manager: Chris Scheuer. **Assistant General Managers:** Scott Skadan, Marc Williamson. **Business Manager:** Nancy Crowe. **Director of Group Sales:** Jason Pellegrini. **Director of Food Services:** Brett Lowery. **Director of Media Relations:** Hollie Knudson. **Director of Promotions:** Jennifer Evans. **Assistant Director of Food Services:** Jeff Nalepa. **Head Groundskeeper:** John Packer. **Assistant Groundskeeper:** Bob Kask. **Assistant Director of Stadium Operations:** Joe Distel. **Assistant Director of Promotions:** Cate Corley. **Assistant Director of Ticket Operations:** Lou Ghetti.

Field Staff

Manager: Jeff Richardson. **Coach:** Scott Little. **Pitching Coach:** Scott Lovekamp. **Trainer:** Brian Lancaster.

Game Information

Radio: None.

PA Announcer: Tourey Hurst. **Official Scorer:** Frank Mercogliano.

Stadium Name (year opened): Lake Olmstead Stadium (1995). **Location:** I-20 to Washington Road, east to Broad Street exit, right on Milledge Road. **Standard Game Times:** 7:05 p.m; Sun. (April-May) 2:30, (June-August) 6:05.

Visiting Club Hotel: Holiday Inn West, 1075 Stevens Creek Road, Augusta, GA 30907. Telephone: (706) 738-8811.

CAPE FEAR *CROCS*

Office Address: 2823 Legion Road, Fayetteville, NC 28306. **Mailing Address:** P.O Box 64939, Fayetteville, NC 28306. **Telephone:** (910) 424-6500. **FAX:** (910) 424-4325. **E-Mail Address:** salcrocs@aol.com

Affiliation (first year): Montreal Expos (1997). **Years in League:** 1987-.

Ownership, Management

Operated by: Fayetteville Baseball Club, Inc.

Principal Owner/Chairman: Charles G. Padgett.

President: Charles E. Padgett

General Manager: Jack Swallow. **Assistant General Manager:** Brad Taylor. **Director of Business Operations/Office Manager:** Linda Bennett. **Director of Ticket Sales:** Tim Mueller. **Head Groundskeeper:** Greg Devore.

Field Staff

Manager: Phil Stephenson. **Coach:** Kash Beauchamp. **Pitching Coach:** Bryan Kelly. **Trainer:** Unavailable.

Game Information

Radio: None.

PA Announcer: Unavailable. **Official Scorer:** Unavailable.

Stadium Name (year opened): J.P. Riddle Stadium (1987). **Location:** From Route 301, west on Owen Drive, left on Legion Road. **Standard Game Times:** 7:05 p.m.; Sun. (April-May) 2:05, (June-August) 5:05.

Visiting Club Hotel: Econo Lodge, 1952 Cedar Creek Road, Fayetteville, NC 28306. Telephone: (910) 433-2100.

CAPITAL CITY *BOMBERS*

Office Address: 301 S. Assembly St., Columbia, SC 29201. **Mailing Address:** P.O. Box 7845, Columbia, SC 29202. **Telephone:** (803) 256-4110. **FAX:** (803) 256-4338.

Affiliation (first year): New York Mets (1983). **Years in League:** 1960-61, 1983-.

Ownership, Management

Operated by: United Sports Ventures, Inc.

Principal Owner/President: Eric Margenau.

Vice President: Bill Shanahan.

General Manager: Tim Swain. **Assistant General Manager, Customer and Guest Relations:** Shirley Broughton. **Assistant General Manager, Marketing and Promotions:** Nancy Behenna. **Director of Stadium Operations/Head Groundskeeper:** Bob Hook. **Director of Media/Public Relations:** Mark Bryant. **Senior Account Representatives:** Malcolm Dennis, Eddie Dowling, Brian Spencer, Heather McLean. **Director of Group Sales:** Brady Souder. **Director of Food Services:** Michael Jennings, Amy Cox, Mark Wiggins (Volume Services, Inc.). **Sales Executives:** Jesse Reese, Joe Kennedy.

Field Staff

Manager: Doug Mansolino. **Coach:** Tim Leiper. **Pitching Coach:** David Jorn. **Trainer:** Matt Deeringer.

Game Information

Radio Announcer: Mark Bryant. **No. of Games Broadcast:** Home-71, Away-71. **Flagship Station:** WISW 1320-AM.

PA Announcer: Unavailable. **Official Scorer:** Julian Gibbons.

Stadium Name (year opened): Capital City Stadium (1991). **Location:** I-26 East to Columbia, Elmwood Avenue to Assembly St., right on Assembly, 4 miles to park; I-77 South to Columbia, exit State Road 277 (Bull Street), right on Elmwood, left on Assembly. **Standard Game Times:** 7:05 p.m., Sun. 6:05.

Visiting Club Hotel: Travelodge, 2210 Bush River Road, Columbia, SC 29210. Telephone: (803) 798-9665.

CHARLESTON
RIVERDOGS

Office Address: 360 Fishburne St., Charleston, SC 29403. **Mailing Address:** P.O. Box 20849, Charleston, SC 29413. **Telephone:** (803) 965-4096. **FAX:** (803) 723-2641.

Affiliation (first year): Tampa Bay Devil Rays (1997). **Years in League:** 1973-78, 1980-.

Ownership, Management

Operated by: South Carolina Baseball Club, LP.

Principal Owner: Marvin Goldklang.

President: Mike Veeck.

Vice President/General Manager: Mark Schuster. **Vice President Ticket Sales:** Wayne Davis. **Director of Operations:** Stan Hughes. **Director of Marketing:** Carol Killough. **Senior Account Representatives:** Scott Kaufman, Stephanie Massey, David Sacchetti. **Director of Community Relations:** Melissa McCants. **Assistant Director of Group Sales:** John Leone. **Director of Merchandising:** Jason Creech. **Director of Special Projects:** Patricia Schuster. **Assistant Director of Corporate Sales:** Mark Coplea. **Director of Broadcasting:** Rob Egan. **Clubhouse Manager:** Ray Sterling.

Field Staff

Manager: Scott Fletcher. **Coach:** Unavailable. **Pitching Coach:** Dennis Rasmussen. **Trainer:** Mike Klein.

Game Information

Radio Announcer: Rob Egan. **No. of Games Broadcast:** Home-71, Away-71. **Flagship Station:** WQNT 1450-AM.

PA Announcer: Gary Towles. **Official Scorer:** Unavailable.

Stadium Name (year opened): Joseph P. Riley Jr. Ballpark (1997). **Location:** From U.S. 17, Lockwood Drive west, right on Fishburne Street. **Standard Game Times:** 7:05 p.m.; Sun. (April-May) 2:05, (June-August) 5:05.

Visiting Club Hotel: Howard Johnson, 250 Spring St., Charleston, SC 29403. Telephone: (803) 722-4000.

CHARLESTON
ALLEY CATS

Office Address: 3403 MacCorkle Ave. SE, Charleston, WV 25304. **Mailing Address:** P.O. Box 4669, Charleston, WV 25304. **Telephone:** (304) 344-2287. **FAX:** (304) 344-0083.

Affiliation (first year): Cincinnati Reds (1990). **Years in League:** 1987-.

Ownership, Management

Operated by: Wheelers Baseball, LP.

President: Mike Paterno.

General Manager: Tim Bordner. **Director of Media/Community Relations:** Rod Blackstone. **Director of Sales/Marketing:** Jay Brown. **Director of Broadcasting:** Dan Loney. **Marketing Assistant:** Leigh Ann Claywell. **Promotions Assistant:** Shannon Sharp. **Operations Assistant:** Mike Spencer. **Clubhouse Operations:** Eddie Lee. **Office Manager:** Lisa Spoor.

Field Staff

Manager: Barry Lyons. **Pitching Coach:** Andre Rabouin. **Trainer:** Dan Siegel.

Game Information

Radio Announcer: Dan Loney. **No. of Games Broadcast:** Home-71, Away-71. **Flagship Station:** WVSR 1240-AM.

PA Announcer: Rod Blackstone. **Official Scorer:** Kevin Pratt.

Stadium Name (year opened): Watt Powell Park (1947). **Location:** I-77 South/I-64 East to 35th Street Bridge exit. I-77 North/I-64 West to MacCorkle Avenue exit (Hwy. 61 North), stadium 3 miles on left. **Standard Game Times:** 7:15 p.m.; Sun. (April-May) 2:15, (June-August) 5:15.

Visiting Club Hotel: Travelodge of Dunbar, 1007 Dunbar Ave., Dunbar, WV 25064. Telephone: (304) 768-1000.

COLUMBUS
REDSTIXX

Office Address: 100 Fourth St., Columbus, GA 31901. **Mailing Address:** P.O. Box 1886, Columbus, GA 31902. **Telephone:** (706) 571-8866. **FAX:** (706) 571-9107.

Affiliation (first year): Cleveland Indians (1991). **Years in League:** 1991-.

Ownership, Management

Operated by: Columbus RedStixx and Professional Baseball, Inc.

Principal Owner/President: Charles Morrow.

General Manager: Randy Schmidt. **Director of Business Operations:** Jim White. **Director of Public/Community Relations:** Matt Musgrove. **Director of Sales/Marketing:** Rick Jacobson. **Director of Group Sales:** Tommy Fountain Sr. **Director of Food Services:** Steve Harrell. **Director of Broadcasting:** Mark Littleton. **Account Executive:** Dave Turner. **Office Manager:** Rosemary Johnson.

Field Staff

Manager: Jack Mull. **Coach:** Mike Sarbaugh. **Pitching Coach:** Fred Gladding. **Trainer:** Rick Jameyson.

Game Information

Radio Announcer: Mark Littleton. **No. of Games Broadcast:** Home-71, Away-71. **Flagship Station:** Unavailable.

PA Announcer: Steve Thiele. **Official Scorer:** Kathy Gierer.

Stadium Name (year opened): Golden Park (1951). **Location:** I-185 South to exit 1 (Victory Drive), west to 4th Street (Veterans Parkway). In South Commons Complex on left. **Standard Game Times:** 7:15 p.m.; Sun. 2:15.

Visiting Club Hotel: Holiday Inn-Airport North, 2800 Manchester Expressway, Columbus, GA 31904. Telephone: (706) 324-0231.

DELMARVA
SHOREBIRDS

Office Address: 6400 Hobbs Road, Salisbury, MD 21804. **Mailing Address:** P.O. Box 1557, Salisbury, MD 21802. **Telephone:** (410) 219-3112. **FAX:** (410) 219-9164.

Affiliation (first year): Baltimore Orioles (1997). **Years in League:** 1996-.

Ownership, Management

Operated by: Maryland Baseball Limited Partnership.

Principal Owners: John Daskalakis, Peter Kirk, Frank Perdue, Hugh Schindel, Pete Simmons.

General Manager: Keith Lupton. **Assistant General Manager:** Jim Terrill. **Director of Stadium Operations:** Charlie Shahan. **Head Groundskeeper:** Jack Hershberger. **Director of Media/Public Relations:** Lou Getman. **Director of Marketing:** Kimberly Haxter. **Account Representatives:** Chris Ouellet, Mike James. **Director of Community Relations:** Ralph Murray. **Director of Promotions:** Ray Moore. **Director of Ticket Sales:** Renee Harris. **Director of Group Sales:** Martin Ward. **Director of Merchandising:** Kevin Kulp. **Director of Food Services:** Pete Orth. **Clubhouse Operations:** Jerry Bass. **Office Manager:** Joyce Young. **Director of Client Services:** Katherine Erickson. **Director of Youth Services:** Chad Prior. **Director of Broadcasting:** Bob Socci. **Assistant Director of Ticket Sales:** Jeff Tierney. **Accounting Manager:** Gail Potts. **Receptionist:** Stephanie West.

Field Staff

Manager: Tommy Shields. **Pitching Coach:** Larry Jaster. **Trainer:** Mike Myers.

Game Information

Radio Announcer: Bob Socci. **No. of Games Broadcast:** Home-71, Away-71. **Flagship Stations:** WDNO 95.3-FM.

PA Announcer: Unavailable. **Official Scorer:** Unavailable.

Stadium Name (year opened): Arthur W. Perdue Stadium (1996). **Location:** From U.S. 50 East, exit right on Hobbs Road; From U.S. 50 West, exit left on Hobbs. **Standard Game Times:** 7 p.m., Sun. 1:05.

Visiting Club Hotel: Holiday Inn, 2625 N. Salisbury Blvd., Salisbury, MD 21801. Telephone: (410) 742-7194.

GREENSBORO
BATS

Office Address: 510 Yanceyville St., Greensboro, NC 27405. **Telephone:** (910) 333-2287. **FAX:** (910) 273-7350. **E-Mail Address:** bats@spyder.net

Affiliation (first year): New York Yankees (1990). **Years in League:** 1979-.

Ownership, Management

Operated by: Carolina Diamond Baseball Club, LP.

Principal Owners: William Collins Jr., William Collins III, John Horshok, Bill Lee.

Chairman of the Board: William Collins III. **President:** William Collins Jr. **Chief Operating Officer:** John Horshok. **Vice President, Sales:** David Mulholland. **Chief Financial Officer:** T.J. Egan.

General Manager: John Frey. **Director of Stadium Operations/Head Groundskeeper:** Mel Lanford. **Director of Promotions:** Tim Clever. **Director of Group Sales:** Shelton Grant. **Director of Merchandising:** Alan Ashkinazy. **Office Manager:** Sheila Kay Lawson. **Director of Broadcasting:** Evan Malter. **Operations Managers:** Jennifer Leung, Steve Kaufman.

Field Staff

Manager: Tom Nieto. **Coach:** Ramon Ortiz. **Pitching Coach:** Tom Filer. **Trainer:** Chris Delucia.

Game Information

Radio Announcer: Evan Malter. **No. of Games Broadcast:** Home-72, Away-70. **Flagship Station:** WKEW 1400-AM.

PA Announcer: Unavailable. **Official Scorer:** Ogi Overman.

Stadium Name (year opened): War Memorial Stadium (1926). **Location:** I-40/I-85 to Highway 29, north to Lee Street, west to Bennett Avenue, right on Bennett. **Standard Game Times:** 7:15 p.m., Sun. 6:15.

Visiting Club Hotel: Travelodge, 2112 W. Meadowview Rd., Greensboro, NC 27403. Telephone: (910) 292-2020.

HAGERSTOWN
SUNS

Office Address: 274 E. Memorial Blvd., Hagerstown, MD 21740. **Mailing Address:** P.O. Box 230, Hagerstown, MD 21740. **Telephone:** (301) 791-6266. **FAX:** (301) 791-6066.

Affiliation (first year): Toronto Blue Jays (1993). **Years in League:** 1993-.

Ownership, Management

Operated by: Norwin Corp.

Principal Owner/President: Winston Blenckstone.

General Manager: David Blenckstone. **Director of Business Operations:** Carol Gehr. **Director of Stadium Operations:** Doug Crusse. **Director of Media/Public Relations:** Kimberly Bohle. **Director of Ticket Sales:** Les Seville. **Director of Broadcasting:** David Shinsky.

Field Staff

Manager: J.J. Cannon. **Coaches:** Marty Pevey (first half), Randy Phillips (second half). **Pitching Coach:** Bruce Walton. **Trainer:** Doug Merrifield.

Game Information

Radio Announcers: David Shinsky, Matt Miller. **No. of Games Broadcast:** Home-71, Away-71. **Flagship Station:** WHAG 1410-AM.

PA Announcer: Trav Medcalf. **Official Scorer:** Jan Marcus.

Stadium Name (year opened): Municipal Stadium (1981). **Location:** Exit 32B from I-70 West, left on Cleveland Ave.; Exit 6A from I-81 South, right on Cleveland Ave; Exit 3E from I-81 North to exit 29N (Route 65), right on Memorial Blvd. **Standard Game Times:** 7:05 p.m.; Sun. (April-June 15) 2:05, (June 15-August) 5:05.

Visiting Club Hotel: Best Western Venice Inn, 431 Dual Highway, Hagerstown, MD 21740. Telephone: (800) 283-6423.

HICKORY
CRAWDADS

Office Address: 2500 Clement Blvd. NW, Hickory, NC 28601. **Mailing Address:** P.O. Box 1268, Hickory, NC 28603. **Telephone:** (704) 322-3000. **FAX:** (704) 322-6137. **E-Mail Address:** crawdad@abts.net

Affiliation (first year): Chicago White Sox (1993). **Years in League:** 1952, 1960, 1993-.

Ownership, Management

Operated by: Hickory Baseball, Inc.

Owner/President: Don Beaver.

Vice President: Marty Steele.

General Manager: David Haas. **Director of Stadium Operations:** Nick Reese. **Director of Public Relations/Broadcasting:** Matt Swierad. **Assistant Media Relations Director:** Heidi Kemery. **Director of Ticket Sales:** Scott Witherow. **Director of Ticket Services:** Mike Murray. **Director of Group Sales:** Mike Congro. **Director of Merchandising:** Melanie Zimmermann. **Office Manager:** Ronda Sigmon. **Account Representatives:** Jason Wallace, Ritchie Shuford, Jeremy Knuckman, Adam Deschenes. **Administrative Assistant:** Beverly Nichols.

Field Staff

Manager: Chris Cron. **Coach:** Dallas Williams. **Pitching Coach:** Sean Snedeker. **Trainer:** Joe Geck.

Game Information

Radio Announcer: Matt Swierad. **No. of Games Broadcast:** Home-71, Away-71. **Flagship Station:** WMNC 92.1-FM.

PA Announcer: JuJu Phillips. **Official Scorer:** Gary Olinger.

Stadium Name (year opened): L.P. Frans Stadium (1993). **Location:** I-40 to exit 123 (Lenoir North), 321 North to Clement Blvd., left for ¼ mile. **Standard Game Times:** 7 p.m.; Sun. (April-June) 2, (July-August) 6.

Visiting Club Hotel: Red Roof Inn, 1184 Lenoir-Rhyne Blvd., Hickory, NC 28602. Telephone: (704) 323-1500.

MACON
BRAVES

Office Address: Central City Park, 7th Street, Macon, GA 31201. **Mailing Address:** P.O. Box 4525, Macon, GA 31208. **Telephone:** (912) 745-8943. **FAX:** (912) 743-5559.

Affiliation (first year): Atlanta Braves (1991). **Years in League:** 1962-63, 1980-87, 1991-.

Ownership, Management

Operated by: Atlanta National League Baseball Club, Inc.

President: Stan Kasten.

General Manager: Michael Dunn. **Director of Stadium Operations:** Terry Morgan. **Head Groundskeeper:** George Stephens. **Director of Sales/Marketing:** Jim Tessmer. **Director of Ticket Sales:** Cathy James. **Director of Special Projects:** Mike Miskavech.

Field Staff

Manager: Brian Snitker. **Coach:** Glenn Hubbard. **Pitching Coach:** Mark Ross. **Trainer:** Mike Graus.

Game Information

Radio Announcers: Bobby Pope, Kevin Coulombe. **No. of Games Broadcast:** Home-20. **Flagship Station:** WMWR 940-AM.

PA Announcer: Jimmy Jones. **Official Scorer:** Kevin Coulombe.

Stadium Name (year opened): Luther Williams Field (1929). **Location:** Exit 4 off I-16, across Otis Redding Bridge to Riverside Drive, follow signs to Central City Park. **Standard Game Times:** 7 p.m., Sun. 2.

Visiting Club Hotel: Comfort Inn, 2690 Riverside Dr., Macon, GA 31204. Telephone: (912) 746-8855.

PIEDMONT
BOLL WEEVILS

Office Address: 2888 Moose Rd., Kannapolis, NC 28083. **Mailing Address:** P.O. Box 64, Kannapolis, NC 28082. **Telephone:** (704) 932-3267. **FAX:** (704) 938-7040. **E-Mail Address:** www.co.rowan.nc.us/boll

Affiliation (first year): Philadelphia Phillies (1995). **Years in League:** 1995-.

Ownership, Management

Operated by: Iredell Trading Co.

Principal Owners: Larry Hedrick, Sue Hedrick.

Vice President, Sports Division: Todd Parnell.

General Manager: Mark Viniard. **Director of Stadium Operations/ Groundskeeper:** Eric Allman. **Director of Business Development:** Patrick Coakley. **Director of Ticket Sales:** Melissa Dudek. **Director of Group Sales/Merchandise:** Jennifer Violand. **Director of Food and Beverage:** Peter Laven. **Bookkeeper:** Deb Hall. **Office Manager:** Michelle Morris.

Field Staff

Manager: Ken Oberkfell. **Coach:** Floyd Rayford. **Pitching Coach:** John Martin. **Trainer:** Unavailable.

Game Information

Radio Announcers: Woody Cain, Randy Whitley, Matt Park. **No. of Games Broadcast:** Home-59, Away-63. **Flagship Stations:** WRNA 1140-AM, WRKB 1460-AM.

PA Announcer: Allen White. **Official Scorer:** Unavailable.

Stadium Name (year opened): Fieldcrest Cannon Stadium (1995). **Location:** Exit 63 on I-85. **Standard Game Times:** 7:05 p.m.; Sun. (April-May) 2:05, (June-August) 6:05.

Visiting Club Hotel: Unavailable.

SAVANNAH
SAND GNATS

Office Address: 1401 E. Victory Drive, Savannah, GA 31404. **Mailing Address:** P.O. Box 3783, Savannah, GA 31414. **Telephone:** (912) 351-9150. **FAX:** (912) 352-9722.

Affiliation (first year): Los Angeles Dodgers (1996). **Years in League:** 1962, 1984-.

Ownership, Management

Operated by: Savannah Professional Baseball Club, Inc.

Principal Owners: Ken Silver, Ken Savin.

General Manager: Ric Sisler. **Assistant General Manager:** David Ellington. **Director of Public Relations/Merchandising:** Bruce Colgan. **Director of Sales/Marketing:** Nick Brown. **Director of Community Relations:** Julie Boggs. **Office Manager:** Reba Rogers.

Field Staff

Manager: John Shelby. **Coach:** Travis Barbary. **Pitching Coach:** Mark Brewer. **Trainer:** Alfonso Flores.

Game Information

Radio: None.

PA Announcer: T.C. Crystal. **Official Scorer:** Marcus Holland.

Stadium Name (year opened): Grayson Stadium (1941). **Location:** I-16 to 37th Street exit, left on 37th, right on Abercorn Street, left on Victory Drive. **Standard Game Times:** 7:15 p.m; Sun. (April-June 15) 2, (June 16-August) 4.

Visiting Club Hotel: Holiday Inn Midtown, 7100 Abercorn St., Savannah, GA 31406. Telephone: (912) 352-7100.

NEW YORK-PENN LEAGUE

Short-Season Class A

Mailing Address: 1629 Oneida St., Utica, NY 13501. **Telephone:** (315) 733-8036. **FAX:** (315) 797-7403.

Years League Active: 1939-.

President: Bob Julian.

Vice President: Sam Nader. **Treasurer:** Bill Gladstone. **Corporate Secretary:** Mike Schell.

Directors: Mike Ferguson (Jamestown), Rob Fowler (Utica), Barry Gordon (New Jersey), Alan Levin (Erie), Bill Gladstone (Pittsfield), Sam Nader (Oneonta), Ray Pecor (Vermont), Leo Pinckney (Auburn), Brad Rogers (Batavia), Mike Schell (Watertown), Clyde Smoll (Lowell), Greg Sorbara (St. Catharines), Paul Velte (Williamsport), Skip Weisman (Hudson Valley).

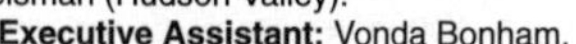

Bob Julian

Executive Assistant: Vonda Bonham.

1997 Opening Date: June 17. **Closing Date:** Sept. 3.

Regular Season: 76 games.

Division Structure: McNamara—Hudson Valley, Lowell, New Jersey, Pittsfield, Vermont. **Pinckney**—Auburn, Oneonta, Utica, Watertown, Williamsport. **Stedler**—Batavia, Erie, Jamestown, St. Catharines.

Playoff Format: Three division winners and wild-card team meet in best-of-3 semifinals. Winners meet in best-of-3 series for league championship.

All-Star Game: None.

Roster Limit: 25 active. **Player Eligibility Rule:** No more than two players who are 23 or older. No more than three players on active list may have four or more years of prior service.

Brand of Baseball: Rawlings.

Statistician: Howe Sportsdata International, Boston Fish Pier, West Bldg. #2—Suite 306, Boston MA 02210.

1996 Standings (Overall)

Club (Affiliate)	W	L	Pct.	GB	'96 Manager
*#Vermont (Expos)	48	26	.649	—	Kevin Higgins
Pittsfield (Mets)	46	29	.613	2½	Doug Davis
#Watertown (Indians)	45	30	.600	3½	Ted Kubiak
#St. Catharines (Blue Jays)	44	32	.579	5	Rocket Wheeler
Williamsport (Cubs)	43	32	.573	5½	Ruben Amaro Sr.
Batavia (Phillies)	42	33	.560	6½	Floyd Rayford
Jamestown (Tigers)	39	36	.520	9½	Bruce Fields
Auburn (Astros)	37	39	.487	12	MannyActa
Lowell (Red Sox)	33	41	.446	15	Billy Gardner Jr.
Hudson Valley (Rangers)	32	44	.421	17	Bump Wills
Oneonta (Yankees)	31	45	.408	18	Gary Tuck
Erie (Pirates)	30	46	.395	19	Jeff Richardson
Utica (Marlins)	29	47	.382	20	Steve McFarland
New Jersey (Cardinals)	28	47	.373	20½	Scott Melvin

*Won playoffs #Won division title

Stadium Information

Club	Stadium	Dimensions LF	CF	RF	Capacity	'96 Att.
Auburn	Falcon Park	330	400	330	2,800	44,813
Batavia	Dwyer	325	400	325	2,600	39,062
Erie	Jerry Uht Park	312	400	328	6,000	187,794
Hudson Valley	Dutchess	325	400	325	4,320	152,626
Jamestown	College	335	410	353	3,324	60,114
Lowell	Alumni Field	325	385	286	4,000	95,986
New Jersey	Skylands Park	330	392	330	4,346	172,314
Oneonta	Damaschke Field	352	406	350	4,200	50,509
Pittsfield	Wahconah Park	334	374	333	4,500	63,533
St. Catharines	Community Park	320	400	320	2,500	56,546
Utica	Donovan	324	400	324	4,000	51,432
Vermont	Centennial Field	330	405	323	4,000	124,496
Watertown	Duffy Fairgrounds	330	405	325	3,250	40,681
Williamsport	Bowman Field	345	405	350	4,200	65,089

AUBURN
DOUBLEDAYS

Office Address: 108 N. Division St., Auburn, NY 13021. **Telephone:** (315) 255-2489. **FAX:** (315) 255-2675.

Affiliation (first year): Houston Astros (1982). **Years in League:** 1958-80, 1982-.

Ownership, Management

Operated by: Auburn Community Baseball, Inc.

Principal Owner: City of Auburn.

President: Leo Pinckney.

General Manager: Paul Taglieri. **Business Manager:** Lynn Odrzywolski. **Director of Operations:** Paul Marriott.

Field Staff

Manager: Mike Rojas. **Coach:** Sidney Holland. **Pitching Coach:** Bill Ballou. **Trainer:** Craig Yingling.

Game Information

Radio: Unavailable.

PA Announcer/Official Scorer: Bob Coogan.

Stadium Name (year opened): Falcon Park (1995). **Location:** I-90 to exit 40, right on Route 34, 8 miles to York Street, right on York, left on North Division Street. **Standard Game Times:** 7 p.m., Sun. 6.

Visiting Club Hotel: Auburn Super 8, 9 McMaster St., Auburn, NY 13021. Telephone: (315) 253-8886.

BATAVIA
CLIPPERS

Office Address: Dwyer Stadium, 299 Bank St., Batavia, NY 14020. **Telephone:** (716) 343-5454. **FAX:** (716) 343-5620.

Affiliation (first year): Philadelphia Phillies (1988). **Years in League:** 1939-53, 1957-59, 1961-.

Ownership, Management

Operated by: Genesee County Professional Baseball, Inc.

President: Larry Roth.

General Manager: Jason Smorol. **Head Groundskeeper:** Dick Rogers. **Director of Group Sales:** Joe Henderson.

Field Staff

Manager: Greg Legg. **Pitching Coach:** Ken Westray. **Trainer:** Unavailable.

Game Information

Radio Announcer: Unavailable. **No. of Games Broadcast:** Away-38. **Flagship Station:** WBTA 1490-AM.

PA Announcer/Official Scorer: Wayne Fuller.

Stadium Name (year opened): Dwyer Stadium (1996). **Location:** I-90 to exit 48, left on Rt. 98 South, left on Richmond Ave., left on Bank Street. **Standard Game Times:** 7:05 p.m.

Visiting Club Hotel: Holiday Inn Conference Center and Suites, 8250 Park Rd., Batavia, NY 14020. Telephone: (716) 344-2100.

ERIE
SEAWOLVES

Office Address: 110 E. 10th St., Erie, PA 16501. **Mailing Address:** P.O. Box 1776, Erie, PA 16507. **Telephone:** (814) 456-1300. **FAX:** (814) 456-7520. **E-Mail Address:** seawolvesbaseball.comm

Affiliation (first year): Pittsburgh Pirates (1995). **Years in League:** 1944-45, 1954-63, 1967, 1981-93, 1995-.

Ownership, Management

Operated by: Seawolves Partners.

Principal Owners: Alan Levin, Ken Silver.

General Manager: Andy Milovich. **Assistant General Manager:** Keith Hallal. **Director of Operations:** Ken Fogel. **Director of Group Sales:** Dave Smith. **Sales Assistant:** Andrew Minister.

Field Staff

Manager: Marty Brown. **Pitching Coach:** Chris Lein. **Trainer:** Unavailable.

Game Information

Radio: Unavailable.

PA Announcer: Rick Shigo. **Official Scorers:** Les Caldwell, Steve Metzler.

Stadium Name (year opened): Jerry Uht Park (1995). **Location:** U.S. 79 North to East 12th Street exit, left on State Street, right on 10th Street. **Standard Game Times:** 7 p.m., Sun. 2.

Visiting Club Hotel: Avalon Hotel, 16 W. 10th St., Erie, PA 16501. Telephone: (814) 459-2220.

HUDSON VALLEY *RENEGADES*

Office Address: Dutchess Stadium, Route 9D, Wappingers Falls, NY 12590. **Mailing Address:** P.O. Box 661, Fishkill, NY 12524. **Telephone:** (914) 838-0094. **FAX:** (914) 838-0014. **E-Mail Address:** info@hvrenegades.com

Affiliations (first year): Tampa Bay Devil Rays (1996). **Years in League:** 1994-.

Ownership, Management

Operated by: Keystone Professional Baseball Club, Inc.

Principal Owner/Chairman: Marvin Goldklang.

President/General Manager: Skip Weisman. **Assistant General Manager/Director of Merchandising:** Kathy Lumbard-Cobb. **Assistant General Manager/Director of Sales:** Steve Gliner. **Director of Business Operations:** Sharon Evans-Weisman. **Assistant Director of Sales/Marketing:** Jessica Berry. **Customer Service Coordinator:** Dottie Paponetti. **Head Groundskeeper:** Mike Francese. **Director of Ticket Operations:** Elmer LeSuer. **Media Relations and Promotions Coordinator:** Chris Puzzuoli. **Administrative Assistants:** Dave Barnes, Rob Pinschmidt. **Clubhouse Manager:** Mike Valovich. **Director of Food Services:** Mike Beadles.

Field Staff

Manager: Julio Garcia. **Coach:** Steve Livesey. **Pitching Coach:** Greg Harris. **Trainer:** Mike Libby.

Game Information

Radio Announcers: Bill Rogan, Rick Schultz. **No. of Games Broadcast:** Home-38, Away-38. **Flagship Station:** WBNR 1260-AM.

PA Announcer: Lisa Morris. **Official Scorer:** Bob Beretta.

Stadium Name (year opened): Dutchess Stadium (1994). **Location:** From east—I-84 West to Rt. 9D (exit 11), north ½ mile to stadium; From north, south and west—New York State Thruway to exit 17 in Newburgh, to I-84 East over Newburgh-Beacon Bridge to Rt. 9D (exit 11), north ½ mile to stadium. **Standard Game Times:** 7:15 p.m., Sun. 5:15.

Visiting Club Hotel: Ramada Inn-West Point, 1055 Union Ave., Newburgh, NY 12550. Telephone: (914) 564-4500.

JAMESTOWN *JAMMERS*

Office Address: 485 Falconer St., Jamestown, NY 14702. **Mailing Address:** P.O. Box 638, Jamestown, NY 14702. **Telephone:** (716) 664-0915. **FAX:** (716) 664-4175. **E-Mail Address:** jammergm@juno.com.

Affiliation (first year): Detroit Tigers (1994). **Years in League:** 1939-57, 1961-73, 1977-.

Ownership, Management

Operated by: Rich Baseball Operations.

Principal Owners: Robert Rich Jr., Melinda Rich.

Chairman of the Board: Robert Rich Sr.

General Manager: Michael Ferguson. **Controller:** John Dougherty. **Director of Public Relations:** Marnie Tyler. **Director of Group Sales:** John Spolyar. **Director of Merchandising:** Chrissie Bliss. **Director of Food Services:** Rich Rugerio. **Director of Special Projects:** Chad Chiffon. **Head Groundskeeper:** Tom Casler. **Office Manager:** Norma Maryell.

Field Staff

Manager: Dwight Lowry. **Pitching Coach:** Steve McCatty. **Trainer:** Matt Rankin.

Game Information

Radio Announcers: Greg Mayer, Bernie Walsh. **No. of Games Broadcast:** Home-38, Away-20. **Flagship Station:** WKSN 1410-AM.

PA Announcer: Todd Peterson. **Official Scorer:** Jim Riggs.

Stadium Name (year opened): College Stadium (1941). **Location:** From I-90, south on Route 60, left on Buffalo Street, left on Falconer Street. **Standard Game Times:** 7:05 p.m.

Visiting Club Hotel: Jamestown Holiday Inn, 150 W. Fourth St., Jamestown, NY 14701. Telephone: (716) 664-3400.

LOWELL
SPINNERS

Street Address: Alumni Field, Rodgers Street, Lowell, MA 01853 (in-season); 2 Merrimack St., Lowell, MA 01852 (off-season). **Mailing Address:** P.O. Box 778, Lowell, MA 01853. **Telephone:** (508) 459-1702. **FAX:** (508) 459-1674.

Affiliation (first year): Boston Red Sox (1996). **Years in League:** 1996-.

Ownership, Management

Operated by: Diamond Action, Inc.

Principal Owners: Clyde Smoll, Charlene Smoll.

Chairman/President: Clyde Smoll.

General Manager: Shawn Smith. **Assistant General Manager, Sales/Concessions:** Brian Lindsay. **Clubhouse Operations:** Gary Miller. **Marketing Assistant:** Dan Hoffman.

Field Staff

Manager: Dick Berardino. **Coach:** Rafael Santana. **Pitching Coach:** Larry Pierson. **Trainer:** Stan Skolfield.

Game Information

Radio Announcer: Bob Ellis. **No. of Games Broadcast:** Home-13, Away-33. **Flagship Station:** WLLH 1400-AM.

PA Announcer: Unavailable. **Official Scorer:** Unavailable.

Stadium Name (year opened): Alumni Field (1996). **Location:** Route 495 to Route 38 exit, park ¼ mile north. **Standard Game Times:** 7 p.m., Sun. 5.

Visiting Club Hotel: Sheraton Inn, 50 Warren St., Lowell, MA 01853. Telephone: (508) 452-1200.

NEW JERSEY
CARDINALS

Office Address: 94 Championship Place, Suite 2, Augusta, NJ 07822. **Telephone:** (201) 579-7500. **FAX:** (201) 579-7502. **E-Mail Address:** office@njcards.com

Affiliation (first year): St. Louis Cardinals (1994). **Years in League:** 1994-.

Ownership, Management

Operated by: Minor League Heroes, LP.

Chairman, Chief Executive Officer: Barry Gordon. **President:** Marc Klee.

Vice President/General Manager: Tony Torre. **Director, Finance:** Warren Brown. **Head Groundskeeper:** Ralph Naiffe. **Director, Media Relations:** Herm Sorcher. **Director, Community Relations:** Christine Sutton. **Director, Promotions:** John Martin. **Director, Sales:** Brett Springer. **Director, Group Sales:** Bob Commentucci. **Director, Merchandising:** Don Wilson. **Director, Ticketing:** Brian Eggers.

Field Staff

Manager: Jeff Shireman. **Pitching Coach:** Mark Grater. **Trainer:** Unavailable.

Game Information

Radio Announcer: Phil Pepe. **No. of Games Broadcast:** Home-38, Away-4. **Flagship Station:** WNNJ 1360-AM.

PA Announcer: Unavailable. **Official Scorers:** Ken Hand, L.A. Foot.

Stadium Name (year opened): Skylands Park (1994). **Location:** I-80 exit 34B (Rt. 15 North) to Rt. 565 East; I-84 to Rt. 6 (Matamoras) to Rt. 209 to Rt. 206, south to Rt. 565; Route 206 north to junction of 565 and 15, then 565 east. **Standard Game Times:** 7:15 p.m.; Sat. 5; Sun. 1.

Visiting Club Hotel: Best Western at Hunt's Landing, 900 Rts. 6 and 209, Matamoras, PA 18336. Telephone: (800) 308-2378.

ONEONTA
YANKEES

Office Address: 95 River St., Oneonta, NY 13820. **Telephone:** (607) 432-6326. **FAX:** (607) 432-1965.

Affiliation (first year): New York Yankees (1967). **Years in League:** 1966-.

Ownership, Management

Operated by: Oneonta Athletic Corp., Inc.

Principal Owners: Sam Nader, Sidney Levine, John Nader.

President/General Manager: Sam Nader.

Assistant General Manager/Director of Operations: John Nader. **Controller:** Sidney Levine. **Head Groundskeeper:** Ted Christman. **Director of Media/Public Relations:** Suzanne Longo. **Director of Sales/Marketing:** Alice O'Conner. **Director of Ticket Sales:** Bob Zeh. **Director of Special Projects:** Mark Nader. **Director of Food Services:** Brad Zeh.

Field Staff

Manager: Gary Tuck. **Coach:** Bobby DeJardin. **Pitching Coach:** Steve Webber. **Trainer:** Russ Orr.

Game Information

Radio: None.

PA Announcer: Doug Decker. **Official Scorer:** Dave Bishop.

Stadium Name (year opened): Damaschke Field (1940). **Location:** Exit 13 off I-88. **Standard Game Times:** 7:15 p.m., Sun. 6.

Visiting Club Hotel: Town House Motor Inn, 318 Main St., Oneonta, NY 13820. Telephone: (607) 432-1313.

PITTSFIELD
METS

Office Address: 136 South St., Pittsfield, MA 01201. **Mailing Address:** P.O. Box 328, Pittsfield, MA 01201. **Telephone:** (413) 499-6387. **FAX:** (413) 443-7144. **E-Mail Address:** pittmets@berkshire.net

Affiliation (first year): New York Mets (1989). **Years in League:** 1989-.

Ownership, Management

Operated by: National Pastime Corporation.

Principal Owners: William Gladstone, Martin Barr, John Burton, Alfred Roberts, Stephen Siegel.

President: William Gladstone.

General Manager: Richard Murphy. **Assistant General Manager:** Richard Lenfest. **Director of Media/Public Relations:** Ethan Wilson. **Director of Ticket Sales:** Vin Buffone. **Director of Merchandising:** Craig Hyatt. **Head Groundskeeper:** Jason Mancivalano.

Field Staff

Manager: Doug Davis. **Coach:** Juan Lopez. **Pitching Coach:** Bob Stanley. **Trainer:** Unavailable.

Game Information

Radio Announcer: Unavailable. **No. of Games Broadcast:** Home-38, Away-38. **Flagship Station:** WBRK 1340-AM.

PA Announcer: Unavailable. **Official Scorer:** Ethan Wilson.

Stadium Name (year opened): Wahconah Park (1950). **Location:** From east—Mass Pike exit 2 to Route 7 North to Pittsfield, right on North Street, left on Wahconah Street; From west—Route 295E to 41 North to 20E into Pittsfield, left on Route 7, right on North Street, left on Wahconah. **Standard Game Times:** 7 p.m.; Sun. 6.

Visiting Club Hotels: Berkshire Hilton, Berkshire Common, Pittsfield, MA 01201. Telephone: (413) 499-2000. Holiday Inn of the Berkshires, 40 Main St., North Adams, MA 01247. Telephone: (413) 663-6500.

ST. CATHARINES
STOMPERS

Office Address: 426 Merritt St., St. Catharines, Ontario L2P 1P3. **Telephone:** (905) 641-5297. **FAX:** (905) 641-3007. **E-Mail Address:** stompers@vaxxine.com.

Affiliation (first year): Toronto Blue Jays (1986). **Years in League:** 1986-.

Ownership, Management

Operated by: St. Catharines Baseball Club, Ltd.

Principal Owners: Home Innings, Inc.; Leadoff Investments, Ltd.; Ernie Whitt.

President: Greg Sorbara.

General Manager: John Belford. **Assistant General Manager/Sales and Marketing:** Colin Bannister. **Senior Account Representative:** Warren Luciani. **Office Manager:** Eleanor Bowman.

Field Staff

Manager: Rocket Wheeler. **Coach:** Lloyd Moseby. **Pitching Coach:** Bill Monbouquette. **Trainer:** Mike Brady.

Game Information

Radio Announcer: Unavailable. **No. of Games Broadcast:** Home-38, Away-38. **Flagship Station:** CHSC 1220-AM.

PA Announcer: Rod Mawhood. **Official Scorers:** Ann Rudge, Marcel Landry.

Stadium Name (year opened): Community Park (1987). **Location:** From east—Queen Elizabeth Expressway to Glendale exit, turn left then right on Merritt Street, right on Seymour Ave.; From west—Queen Elizabeth Expressway to 406 South, left at Glendale Ave. exit, left on Merritt Street, right on Seymour Ave. **Standard Game Times:** 7:05 p.m., Sun: 6:05.

Visiting Club Hotel: Howard Johnson, 89 Meadowvale Dr., St. Catharines, ON L2N 3Z8. Telephone: (905) 934-5400.

UTICA
BLUE SOX

Office Address: 1700 Sunset Ave., Utica, NY 13502. **Mailing Address:** P.O. Box 751, Utica, NY 13503. **Telephone:** (315) 738-0999. **FAX:** (315) 738-0992.

Affiliation (first year): Florida Marlins (1996). **Years in League:** 1977-.

Ownership, Management

Operated by: Utica Baseball Club, Ltd.

Principal Owner/President: Bob Fowler.

General Manager: Rob Fowler. **Director of Stadium Operations:** Jim Griffiths. **Head Groundskeeper:** Carmen Russo. **Clubhouse Operations:** Robert Bill.

Field Staff

Manager: Juan Bustabad. **Coach:** Ken Joyce. **Pitching Coach:** Larry Pardo. **Trainer:** Unavailable.

Game Information

Radio: None.

PA Announcer: Unavailable. **Official Scorer:** Drew Washburn.

Stadium Name (year opened): Donovan Stadium (1976). **Location:** New York State Thruway to exit 31 (Genesee Street), south to Burrstone Rd., right to stadium. **Standard Game Times:** 7 p.m.

Visiting Club Hotel: Horizon Hotel, Oneida County Airport, 5920 Airport Rd., Oriskany, NY 13424. Telephone: (315) 736-3377.

VERMONT
EXPOS

Office Address: 1 Main Street, Box 4, Winooski, VT 05404. **Telephone:** (802) 655-4200. **FAX:** (802) 655-5660. **E-Mail Address:** vtexpos@together.net

Affiliation (first year): Montreal Expos (1994). **Years in League:** 1994-.

Ownership, Management

Operated by: Vermont Expos, Inc.

Principal Owner/President: Ray Pecor.

General Manager: Kyle Bostwick. **Assistant General Manager:** Jim O'Brien. **Director of Business Operations:** Mia Ouellette. **Head Groundskeeper:** Lee Keller. **Director of Public Relations:** Paul Stanfield. **Director of Sales/Marketing:** Chris Corley. **Director of Ticket Sales:** Mike Simpson. **Director of Merchandising:** Maggie Green. **Director of Food Services:** Steve Bernard. **Director of Special Projects:** Ron Citorik. **Clubhouse Operations:** Phil Schelzo. **Administrative Assistant:** Jessica Vachereau.

Field Staff

Manager: Kevin Higgins. **Pitching Coach:** Unavailable. **Trainer:** Unavailable.

Game Information

Radio Announcer: George Commo. **No. of Games Broadcast:** Home-20, Away-20. **Flagship Station:** WVMT 620-AM.

PA Announcer: Rich Haskell. **Official Scorer:** Ev Smith.

Stadium Name (year opened): Centennial Field (1922). **Location:** I-89 to exit 14W, right on East Ave for one mile, right at light onto Colchester Avenue. **Standard Game Times:** 7:05 p.m., Sun. 2:05.

Visiting Club Hotel: Econo Lodge, 1076 Williston Rd., South Burlington, VT 05403. Telephone: (802) 863-1125.

Watertown Indians

WATERTOWN
INDIANS

Office Address: Duffy Fairgrounds, 900 Coffeen St., Watertown, NY 13601. **Mailing Address:** P.O. Box 802, Watertown, NY 13601. **Telephone:** (315) 788-8747. **FAX:** (315) 788-8841.

Affiliation (first year): Cleveland Indians (1989). **Years in League:** 1983-.

Ownership, Management

Operated by: Sandlot Sports, Inc.

Principal Owners: Stanley Getzler (president), Joshua Getzler (vice president, secretary), Phyllis Getzler (treasurer).

General Manager: Jack Tracz. **Assistant General Manager:** Jeff Dumas. **Director of Stadium Operations:** Ed Montani. **Director of Sales/Marketing:** Shannon Upchurch. **Director of Food Services:** Tim Mosher. **Clubhouse Operations:** Ken Baker.

Field Staff

Manager: Ted Kubiak. **Coach:** Billy Williams. **Pitching Coach:** Carl Willis. **Trainer:** Nick Paparesta.

Game Information

Radio: None.

PA Announcer: Brian Hunzicker. **Official Scorer:** Dave Shampine.

Stadium Name (year opened): Alex T. Duffy Fairgrounds (1983). **Location:** I-81 to exit 46, east on Coffeen Street, left on Duffy Drive. **Standard Game Times:** 7 p.m, Sun. 6.

Visiting Club Hotel: Days Inn, 1142 Arsenal St., Watertown, NY 13601. Telephone: (315) 782-2700.

Williamsport

WILLIAMSPORT
CUBS

Office Address: Bowman Field, 1700 W. 4th St., Williamsport, PA 17701. **Mailing Address:** P.O. Box 3173, Williamsport, PA 17701. **Telephone:** (717) 326-3389. **FAX:** (717) 326-3494. **E-Mail Address:** wmsptcub@mail.csrlink.net

Affiliation (first year): Chicago Cubs (1994). **Years in League:** 1923-37, 1968-72, 1994-.

Ownership, Management

Operated by: Geneva Cubs Baseball, Inc.

Principal Owner/President: Paul Velte.

General Manager: Doug Estes. **Director of Marketing/Public Relations:** Gabe Sinicropi. **Director of Stadium Operations:** Scott Stevenson. **Head Groundskeeper:** Matt Duncan.

Field Staff

Manager: Bobby Ralston. **Coach:** Tack Wilson. **Pitching Coach:** Charlie Greene. **Trainer:** Unavailable.

Game Information

Radio Announcer: Matt Park. **No. of Games Broadcast:** Home-15, Away-15. **Flagship Stations:** WMYL 95.5-FM, WRAK 1400-AM.

PA Announcer: Unavailable. **Official Scorer:** Ken Myers.

Stadium Name (year opened): Bowman Field (1926). **Location:** From south—Rt. 15 to Maynard Street, right on Maynard, left on 4th St. for one mile; From north—Rt. 15 to 4th St., left on 4th, ballpark on left. **Standard Game Times:** 7:05 p.m.

Visiting Club Hotel: Holiday Inn, 1840 E. 3rd St., Williamsport, PA 17701. Telephone: (717) 326-1981.

NORTHWEST LEAGUE

Short-Season Class A

Office Address: 5900 N. Granite Reef Rd., Suite105, Scottsdale, AZ 85250. **Mailing Address:** P.O. Box 4941, Scottsdale, AZ 85261. **Telephone:** (602) 483-8224. **FAX:** (602) 443-3450.

Years League Active: 1901-1922, 1937-1942, 1946-.

President/Treasurer: Bob Richmond.

Vice President: Bill Pereira. **Corporate Secretary:** Tom Leip.

Directors: Bob Bavasi (Everett), Bob Beban (Eugene), Bobby Brett (Spokane), Jack Cain (Portland), Dave Connell (Yakima), Fred Herrmann (Southern Oregon), Bill Pereira (Boise), Jerry Walker (Salem-Keizer).

Administrative Assistant: Rob Richmond.

Bob Richmond

1997 Opening Date: June 17. **Closing Date:** Sept. 3.

Regular Season: 76 games.

Division Structure: North—Boise, Everett, Spokane, Yakima. **South**—Eugene, Portland, Salem-Keizer, Southern Oregon.

Playoff Format: Division winners play best-of-5 series for league championship.

All-Star Game: None.

Roster Limit: 25 active, 35 under control. **Player Eligibility Rule:** No more than four players who are 23 or older. No more than three players on active list may have four or more years of prior service.

Brand of Baseball: Rawlings.

Statistician: Howe Sportsdata International, Boston Fish Pier, West Bldg. #2—Suite 306, Boston MA 02210.

1996 Standings (Overall)

Club (Affiliate)	W	L	Pct.	GB	'96 Manager
*#Eugene (Braves)	49	27	.645	—	Jim Saul
Boise (Angels)	43	33	.566	6	Tom Kotchman
#Yakima (Dodgers)	40	36	.526	9	Joe Vavra
Bellingham (Giants)	39	36	.520	9½	O. Virgil/S. Turner
Spokane (Royals)	37	39	.487	12	Bob Herold
Everett (Mariners)	33	42	.440	15½	Roger Hansen
Portland (Rockies)	33	43	.434	16	Ron Gideon
Southern Oregon (Athletics)	29	47	.382	20	Tony DeFrancesco

*Won playoffs #Won division title

Stadium Information

		Dimensions				
Club	Stadium	LF	CF	RF	Capacity	'96 Att.
Boise	Memorial	335	400	335	4,500	164,231
Eugene	Civic	335	400	328	6,800	148,282
Everett	Everett Memorial	330	395	335	2,285	87,846
Portland	Civic	309	407	348	23,100	249,995
Salem-Keizer*	Keizer	325	400	325	4,100	—
Southern Oregon	Miles Field	332	384	344	2,900	77,437
Spokane	Seafirst	335	398	335	7,100	180,903
Yakima	Yakima County	295	406	295	3,000	82,313

*Franchise operated in Bellingham, Wash., in 1996

BOISE
HAWKS

Office Address: 5600 Glenwood St., Boise, ID 83714. **Telephone:** (208) 322-5000. **FAX:** (208) 322-7432.

Affiliation (first year): Anaheim Angels (1989). **Years in League:** 1975-76, 1978, 1985-.

Ownership, Management

Operated by: Diamond Sports, Inc.

Principal Owner: Bill Pereira.

Chairman of the Board: Peter Gray. **President:** Cord Pereira. **Executive Vice President:** Eric Trapp.

General Manager: John Cunningham. **Controller:** Lee Ryan. **Head Groundskeeper:** Joe Kelly. **Director of Media/Public Relations:** Jack Carnefix. **Director of Sales/Marketing:** Dennis Burbank. **Director of Ticket Sales:** Denise Jones. **Ticket Manager:** Ryan Rowedder. **Creative Director:** Troy Custer. **Marketing Account Executive:** Gerry Eickhoff. **Ticket Account Executive:** Jake Hines. **Group Ticket Account Executive:** Ryan Brach.

Field Staff

Manager: Tom Kotchman. **Pitching Coach:** Zeke Zimmerman. **Trainer:** Todd Hine.

Game Information

Radio Announcers: Rob Simpson, Tommy Smith. **No. of Games Broadcast:** Home-38, Away-38. **Flagship Stations:** KTIK 1340-AM.

PA Announcers: Jack Armstrong, Greg Culver, Tom Scott. **Official Scorer:** Danny Ward.

Stadium Name (year opened): Memorial Stadium (1989). **Location:** Route 84 to Cole Road, north to Western Idaho Fairgrounds. **Standard Game Times:** 7:05 p.m.

Visiting Club Hotel: Reston Hotel, 1025 S. Capitol Blvd., Boise, ID 83706. Telephone: (208) 344-7971.

EUGENE
EMERALDS

Office Address: 2077 Willamette St., Eugene, OR 97405. **Mailing Address:** P.O. Box 5566, Eugene, OR 97405. **Telephone:** (541) 342-5367. **FAX:** (541) 342-6089. **E-Mail Address:** ems@continet.com.

Affiliation (first year): Atlanta Braves (1995). **Years in League:** 1955-68, 1974-.

Ownership, Management

Operated by: Eugene Baseball, Inc.

Principal Owner: David Elmore.

President/General Manager: Bob Beban. **Assistant General Managers:** Todd Rahr, Jere Hanks. **Director of Business Operations:** Eileen Beban. **Director of Media Relations/Ticket Sales:** Chris Metz. **Special Events Coordinator:** Mike Brown. **Director of Ticket Operations:** Brian Rogers. **Assistant Director of Marketing:** Jeff Wood. **Director of Stadium Operations:** Vern Haag. **Grounds Superintendent:** Tom Nielsen.

Field Staff

Manager: Jim Saul. **Coach:** Bobby Moore. **Pitching Coach:** Jerry Nyman. **Trainer:** Keith Abrams.

Game Information

Radio Announcer: Dave Hahn. **No. of Games Broadcast:** Home-38, Away-38. **Flagship Station:** KPNW 1120-AM.

PA Announcer: Ray Martin. **Official Scorer:** David Williford.

Stadium Name (year opened): Civic Stadium (1938). **Location:** From I-5, take Hwy. 126 to downtown, west to Pearl Street, south to 20th Ave. **Standard Game Times:** 7:05 p.m; Sun. 2:05, 6:05.

Visiting Club Hotel: Red Lion Inn, 3280 Gateway Rd., Springfield, OR 97477. Telephone: (541) 726-8181.

EVERETT
AQUASOX

Office Address: 3802 Broadway, Everett, WA 98201. **Mailing Address:** P.O. Box 7893, Everett, WA 98201. **Telephone:** (206) 258-3673. **FAX:** (206) 258-3675. **E-Mail Address:** aquasox@aol.com.

Affiliation (first year): Seattle Mariners (1995). **Years in League:** 1984-.

Ownership, Management

Operated by: Farm Club Sports, Inc.

Principal Owners: Bob Bavasi, Margaret Bavasi.

President: Bob Bavasi. **Vice President:** Margaret Bavasi.

Controller: Don Anderson. **Director of Corporate Sales:** Aimee Bavasi. **Director of Client Services:** Brian Sloan. **Director of Operations:** Robb Stanton. **Director of Food Services:** Daniel Owens. **Director of Ballpark Operations:** Gary Farwell. **Director of Ticket Services:** Kim Echols. **Operations Assistant:** Nikolas Griffith. **Media Relations:** Pat Castro, Dave Juran.

Field Staff

Manager: Orlando Gomez. **Coach:** Andy Bottin. **Pitching Coach:** Steve Peck. **Trainer:** Spyder Webb.

Game Information

Radio Announcer: Chris Hester. **No. of Games Broadcast:** Home-38, Away-38. **Flagship Station:** KWYZ 1230-AM.

PA Announcer: Tom Lafferty. **Official Scorer:** John VanSandt.

Stadium Name (year opened): Everett Memorial Stadium (1984). **Location:** Exit 192 off I-5 to corner of 39th and Broadway. **Game Times:** 7:05 p.m.; Sat., Sun. 6:05.

Visiting Club Hotel: Holiday Inn Hotel and Conference Center, 101 128th St. SE, Everett, WA 98208. Telephone: (206) 337-2900.

PORTLAND
ROCKIES

Office Address: 1844 SW Morrison, Portland, OR 97205. **Mailing Address:** P.O. Box 998, Portland, OR 97207. **Telephone:** (503) 223-2837. **FAX:** (503) 223-2948. **E-Mail Address:** rockies@teleport.com

Affiliation (first year): Colorado Rockies (1995). **Years in League:** 1973-77, 1995-.

Ownership, Management

Operated by: Portland Baseball, Inc.

Principal Owners: Jack Cain, Mary Cain.

President/Chief Executive Officer: Jack Cain. **Vice President/ Secretary:** Mary Cain.

Vice President/General Manager: Mark Helminiak. **Vice President/Marketing:** Tom Leip. **Merchandise Manager:** Bob Cain. **Office Manager:** Katie Reeder. **Administrative Assistant:** Sarah Keaney. **Director of Broadcasting:** Rich Burk. **Group Sales Coordinator:** Corey Kearsley. **Account Executives:** Ben Smith, Jeff Robbins, Hank Sadorus, Dick Johnson, Peter Danner, Jill Layport, Chad Lundervold, Tom Shepherd, Annie Sumpter, Sean Burns, Aaron Jones, Rebecca Morgan.

Field Staff

Manager: Jim Eppard. **Coach:** Al Bleser. **Pitching Coach:** Tom Edens. **Trainer:** Unavailable.

Game Information

Radio Announcer: Rich Burk. **No. of Games Broadcast:** Home-38, Away-38. **Flagship Station:** KKSN 910-AM.

PA Announcer: Dan Folwick. **Official Scorers:** Chuck Charnquist, John Hilsenteger.

Stadium Name (year opened): Civic Stadium (1926). **Location:** I-405 to West Burnside exit, SW 20th Street to stadium. **Standard Game Times:** 7:05 p.m.; Sun. 2:05.

Visiting Club Hotel: Red Lion Coliseum, 1225 N. Thunderbird Way, Portland, OR 97227. Telephone: (503) 235-8311.

SALEM-KEIZER
VOLCANOES

(Franchise operated in Bellingham in 1996)

Mailing Address: P.O. Box 20936, Keizer, OR 97307. **Telephone:** (503) 390-2225. **FAX:** (503) 390-2227. **E-Mail Address:** probasebal@aol.com

Affiliation (first year): San Francisco Giants (1995). **Years in League:** 1955-65, 1977-89, 1997.

Ownership, Management

Principal Owners: Jerry Walker, Lisa Walker, Bill Tucker.

President/General Manager: Jerry Walker.

Vice President of Corporate Sales: Lisa Walker. **Vice President of Business Operations:** Rick Nelson. **Director of Ticket Services:** Thomas Buckley. **Marketing Director:** Ken Wilson. **Account Representatives:** Pat Dillon, Tony Brown, Kasey Flicker.

Field Staff

Manager: Shane Turner. **Coach:** Joe Strain. **Pitching Coach:** Shawn Barton. **Trainer:** Eric Reisinger.

Game Information

Radio Announcers: Pat Dillon, Pat Lafferty. **No. of Games Broadcast:** Home-38, Away-38. **Flagship Station:** KYKN 1430-AM.

PA Announcer: Ivan Walker. **Official Scorer:** Unavailable.

Stadium Name (year opened): Keizer Stadium (1997). **Location:** I-5 exit 260, west one block to Radiant Drive, north six blocks to stadium. **Standard Game Times:** 7:05 p.m.; Sun. 6:05, 2:05.

Visiting Club Hotel: Unavailable.

SOUTHERN OREGON
TIMBERJACKS

TIMBERJACKS™

Office Address: 1801 S. Pacific Highway, Medford, OR 97501. **Mailing Address:** P.O. Box 1457, Medford, OR 97501. **Telephone:** (541) 770-5364. **FAX:** (541) 772-4466. **E-Mail Address:** athletic@mind.net.

Affiliation (first year): Oakland Athletics (1979). **Years in League:** 1967-71, 1979-.

Ownership, Management

Operated by: National Sports Organization, Inc.

Principal Owners: Fred Herrmann, Bud Kaufman, John LeCompte, Patsy Smullin, Dwain Cross.

Chairman/President: Fred Herrmann.

General Manager: Suzanne Daniel. **Assistant General Manager:** Dan Kilgras. **Director of Business Operations:** Michael Bauer. **Head Groundskeeper:** Richard Steinmuller. **Assistant Groundskeeper:** George Hasha. **Director of Sales and Marketing:** Bryan Herrmann. **Director of Broadcasting:** Dominic Capuano. **Director of Group Sales:** Andrew Stuebner.

Field Staff

Manager: John Kuehl. **Coach:** Randy Elliott. **Pitching Coach:** Steve Bowden. **Trainer:** Blake Bowers.

Game Information

Radio Announcer: Dominic Capuano. **No. of Games Broadcast:** Home-38, Away-38. **Flagship Station:** KYJC 610-AM.

PA Announcer: Unavailable. **Official Scorer:** B.G. Gould.

Stadium Name (year opened): Miles Field (1951). **Location:** Exit 27 on I-5, west for ½ mile, left on South Pacific Highway, south one mile, stadium on left. **Standard Game Times:** 7:05 p.m.; Sun. 6:05.

Visiting Club Hotel: Horizon Motor Inn, 1150 Barnett Road, Medford, OR 97504. Telephone: (541) 779-5085.

SPOKANE
INDIANS

Office Address: 602 N. Havana, Spokane, WA 99202. **Mailing Address:** P.O. Box 4758, Spokane, WA 99202. **Telephone:** (509) 535-2922. **FAX:** (509) 534-5368.

Affiliation (first year): Kansas City Royals (1995). **Years in League:** 1972, 1983-.

Ownership, Management

Operated by: Longball, Inc.

Principal Owners: Bobby Brett, George Brett, Ken Brett, J.B. Brett.

Chairman of the Board: Bobby Brett.

President: Andrew Billig.

General Manager: Ripper Hatch. **Assistant General Manager/ Tickets:** Paul Barbeau. **Executive Director/Sponsorships:** Otto Klein. **Controller:** Carol Dell. **Director of Stadium Operations:** Chad Smith. **Head Groundskeeper:** Chad Mulholland. **Assistant Groundskeeper:** Larry Blumer. **Director of Media/Public Relations:** Margaret Fatta. **Account Executives:** Rick Barr, Eric Marglous. **Administrative Assistant:** Barbara Klante. **Director of Promotions:** Kyle McFarlane. **Ticket Office Manager:** Brent Miles. **Assistant Ticket Manager:** Jesse Uribe. **Group Sales Coordinator:** Jeremy Hadley. **Director of Merchandising:** Darren Garrity. **Director of Food Services:** Bryon Orr. **Director of Special Projects:** Dave Pier.

Field Staff

Manager: Jeff Garber. **Coach:** Greg Smith. **Pitching Coach:** Steve Crawford. **Trainer:** Unavailable.

Game Information

Radio Announcer: Craig West. **No. of Games Broadcast:** Home-38, Away-38. **Flagship Stations:** KJRB 790-AM, KVNI 1080-AM.

PA Announcer: Mike Lindskog. **Official Scorer:** Dave Edwards.

Stadium Name (year opened): Seafirst Stadium (1958). **Location:** I-90 to Havana exit, follow directions to Interstate Fairgrounds.

Standard Game Times: 7:05 p.m.; Sun. 6:05.

Visiting Club Hotel: Unavailable.

YAKIMA
BEARS

Office Address: 810 W. Nob Hill Blvd., Yakima, WA 98902. **Mailing Address:** P.O. Box 483, Yakima, WA 98907. **Telephone:** (509) 457-5151. **FAX:** (509) 457-9909.

Affiliation (first year): Los Angeles Dodgers (1990). **Years in League:** 1955-66, 1990-.

Ownership, Management

Operated by: Tradition Sports, Inc.

Principal Owner/President: Dave Connell.

General Manager: Bob Romero. **Assistant General Manager:** Ryan Connell. **Director of Ticket Sales:** Benjy Mogensen. **Clubhouse Operations:** Craig Hyatt. **Office Manager:** DeAnne Munson. **Administrative Assistants:** Joel Lehocky, Roy Hobbs, Matt Kelly.

Field Staff

Manager: Joe Vavra. **Coach:** Mitch Webster. **Pitching Coach:** Unavailable. **Trainer:** Jason Mahnke.

Game Information

Radio Announcer: Larry Weir. **No. of Games Broadcast:** Home-38, Away-38. **Flagship Station:** KMWX 1460-AM.

PA Announcer: Todd Lyons. **Official Scorer:** Gene Evans.

Stadium Name (year opened): Yakima County Stadium (1992). **Location:** I-82 to Nob Hill Blvd. (exit 34), west on Nob Hill to 10th Street, right on 10th, right on Pacific. **Standard Game Times:** 7:05 p.m.

Visiting Club Hotel: Days Inn, 2408 Rudkin Road, Union Gap, WA 98903. Telephone: (509) 248-9700.

APPALACHIAN LEAGUE

Rookie Advanced Classification

Mailing Address: 283 Deerchase Circle, Statesville, NC 28677. **Telephone:** (704) 873-5300. **FAX:** (704) 873-4333.

Years League Active: 1921-25, 1937-55, 1957-.

President/Treasurer: Lee Landers. **Corporate Secretary:** Dan Moushon.

Directors: Tom Foley (Princeton), Mike Jorgensen (Johnson City), Deric Ladnier (Danville), Reid Nichols (Pulaski), Steve Noworyta (Bristol), Jim Rantz (Elizabethton), Mark Shapiro (Burlington), Syd Thrift (Bluefield), Del Unser (Martinsville), Jack Zduriencik (Kingsport).

Administrative Assistant: Bobbi Landers.

Lee Landers

1997 Opening Date: June 18. **Closing Date:** Aug. 27.

Regular Season: 68 games.

Division Structure: East—Bluefield, Burlington, Danville, Martinsville, Princeton. **West**—Bristol, Elizabethton, Johnson City, Kingsport, Pulaski.

Playoff Format: Division winners meet in best-of-3 series for league championship.

All-Star Game: None.

Roster Limit: 30 active. **Player Eligibility Rule:** No more than 12 players who are 21 or older; no more than two of the 12 may be 23 or older.

Brand of Baseball: Rawlings.

Statistician: Howe Sportsdata International, Boston Fish Pier, West Bldg. #2—Suite 306, Boston, MA 02210.

1996 Standings (Overall)

Club (Affiliate)	W	L	Pct.	GB	'96 Manager
#Kingsport (Mets)	48	19	.716	—	John Stephenson
*#Bluefield (Orioles)	42	26	.618	6½	Bobby Dickerson
Johnson City (Cardinals)	42	26	.618	6½	Steve Turco
Elizabethton (Twins)	40	27	.597	8	Jose Marzan
Danville (Braves)	37	29	.561	4	Brian Snitker
Burlington (Indians)	29	38	.433	19	Harry Spilman
Princeton (Reds)	28	40	.412	20½	Mark Wagner
Martinsville (Phillies)	20	47	.299	28	Ramon Henderson
Bristol (White Sox)	17	51	.250	31½	Nick Capra

*Won playoffs #Won division title

Stadium Information

		Dimensions				
Club	Stadium	LF	CF	RF	Capacity	'96 Att.
Bluefield	Bowen Field	335	365	335	2,500	38,840
Bristol	DeVault Memorial	325	400	310	2,500	25,262
Burlington	Burlington Athletic	335	410	335	3,500	43,596
Danville	Dan Daniel Memorial	330	400	330	2,588	66,825
Elizabethton	Joe O'Brien Field	335	414	326	1,500	16,711
Johnson City	Howard Johnson	320	410	320	2,500	47,375
Kingsport	Wright	330	410	330	2,500	33,100
Martinsville	Hooker Field	330	402	330	3,200	42,153
Princeton	Hunnicutt Field	330	396	330	1,537	26,162
Pulaski	Calfee Park	335	405	310	2,000	—

BLUEFIELD
ORIOLES

Mailing Address: P.O. Box 356, Bluefield, WV 24701. **Telephone:** (540) 326-1326. **FAX:** (540) 326-1318.

Affiliation (first year): Baltimore Orioles (1957). **Years in League:** 1946-55, 1957-.

Ownership, Management

Operated by: Bluefield Baseball Club, Inc.

President/General Manager: George McGonagle. **Assistant General Manager/Director of Group Sales:** Traci Bledsoe. **Controller:** Charles Peters. **Head Groundskeeper:** Frank Kuffner. **Director of Promotions:** Robert Miller. **Directors of Special Projects:** John Duffy, Tuillio Ramella.

Field Staff

Manager: Bobby Dickerson. **Coach:** Len Johnston. **Pitching Coach:** Charlie Puleo. **Trainer:** Vince Palmer.

Game Information

Radio: Unavailable.

PA Announcer: Unavailable. **Official Scorer:** John Duffy.

Stadium Name (year opened): Bowen Field (1939). **Location:** I-77 Bluefield exit, Route 290 to Route 460 West, right onto Leatherwood Lane, then left at first light, past Chevron station and turn right, stadium ¼ mile on left. **Standard Game Times:** 7 p.m., Sun. 6.

Visiting Club Hotel: Ramada Inn-East River, 3175 E. Cumberland Road, Bluefield, WV 24701. Telephone: (304) 325-5421.

BRISTOL
SOX

Office Address: 1501 Euclid Ave., Bristol, VA 24201. **Mailing Address:** P.O. Box 1434, Bristol, VA 24203. **Telephone:** (540) 645-7275. **FAX:** (540) 645-7377.

Affiliation (first year): Chicago White Sox (1995). **Years in League:** 1921-25, 1940-55, 1969-.

Ownership, Management

Operated by: Bristol Baseball, Inc.

President: Boyce Cox.

General Manager: Robert Childress.

Field Staff

Manager: Nick Capra. **Coach:** Gregg Ritchie. **Pitching Coach:** J.R. Purdue. **Trainer:** Matt Bekkedal.

Game Information

Radio: None.

PA Announcer: Don Brown. **Official Scorer:** Allen Shepherd.

Stadium Name (year opened): DeVault Memorial Stadium (1969). **Location:** I-81 to exit 3 onto Commonwealth Ave., right on Euclid Ave. for ½ mile. **Standard Game Times:** 7 p.m.

Visiting Club Hotel: Ramada Inn, 2121 Euclid Ave., Bristol, VA 24201. Telephone: (540) 669-7171.

BURLINGTON
INDIANS

Office Address: 1450 Graham St., Burlington, NC 27215. **Mailing Address:** P.O. Box 1143, Burlington, NC 27216. **Telephone:** (910) 222-0223. **FAX:** (910) 226-2498. **E-Mail Address:** burindians@aol.com

Affiliation (first year): Cleveland Indians (1986). **Years in League:** 1986-.

Ownership, Management

Operated by: Burlington Baseball Club, Inc.

Principal Owner: Miles Wolff. **Vice President:** Dan Moushon.

General Manager: Carper Cole. **Assistant General Manager:** Mike Edwards. **Director of Stadium Operations:** Erich Sizelove

Field Staff

Manager: Harry Spilman. **Coach:** Joe Mikulik. **Pitching Coach:** Dave Miller. **Trainer:** Dave Lassiter.

Game Information

Radio Announcer: Kale Beers. **No. of Games Broadcast:** Home-34, Away-34. **Flagship Station:** WBBB 920-AM.

PA Announcer: Unavailable. **Official Scorer:** Unavailable.

Stadium Name (year opened): Burlington Athletic Stadium (1960). **Location:** I-40/85 to exit 145, north on Route 100 (Maple Avenue) for 1½ miles, right on Mebane Street for 1½ miles, right on Beaumont, left on Graham. **Standard Game Times:** 7 p.m.

Visiting Club Hotel: Holiday Inn, 2444 Maple Ave., Burlington, NC 27215. Telephone: (910) 229-5203.

DANVILLE
BRAVES

Office Address: Dan Daniel Memorial Park, 302 River Park Dr., Danville, VA 24543. **Mailing Address:** P.O. Box 3637, Danville, VA 24543. **Telephone:** (804) 791-3346. **FAX:** (804) 791-3347.

Affiliation (first year): Atlanta Braves (1993). **Years in League:** 1993-.

Ownership, Management

Operated by: Danville Braves, Inc.

Principal Owner: Tim Cahill.

General Manager: Scott Rittenhouse. **Assistant General Manager:** Brent Bartemeyer. **Director of Business Operations:** Mike Drahush. **Head Groundskeeper:** Russ Hudson. **Office Manager:** Tara Carter.

Field Staff

Manager: Rick Albert. **Coach:** Franklin Stubbs. **Pitching Coach:** Kent Willis. **Trainer:** Unavailable.

Game Information

Radio: None.

PA Announcer: Unavailable. **Official Scorer:** Danny Miller.

Stadium Name (first year): Dan Daniel Memorial Park (1993). **Location:** U.S. 58 to Rivermont Road, follow signs to park; U.S. 29 bypass to Dan Daniel Park exit (U.S. 58 East), to Rivermont Road, follow signs. **Standard Game Times:** 7 p.m.

Visiting Club Hotel: Innkeeper-West, 3020 Riverside Drive, Danville, VA 24540. Telephone: (804) 799-1202.

ELIZABETHTON
TWINS

Office Address: Holly Lane, Elizabethton, TN 37643. **Mailing Address:** 136 S. Sycamore St., Elizabethton, TN 37643. **Telephone:** (423) 543-4395. **FAX:** (423) 542-1510.

Affiliation (first year): Minnesota Twins (1974). **Years in League:** 1937-42, 1945-51, 1974-.

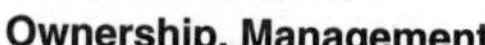

Ownership, Management

Operated by: City of Elizabethton.

Principal Owner: Minnesota Twins. **President:** Bill Crow.

General Manager: Ray Smith. **Assistant General Manager:** Harold Mains. **Director of Business Operations:** David Ornduff. **Director of Stadium Operations:** Willie Church. **Head Groundskeeper:** David McQueen. **Directors of Media/Public Relations:** Skip Hendrix, Glen McQueen. **Director of Sales/Marketing:** Shelley Cornett. **Director of Community Relations:** Jim Barker. **Director of Promotions:** Paula Bishop **Director of Ticket Sales:** Jane Crow. **Director of Group Sales:** Gertrude Bishop. **Director of Broadcasting:** Frank Santore. **Director of Merchandising:** Ray Glover. **Director of Food Services:** Jane Hardin. **Director of Special Projects:** Danny Clark. **Clubhouse Operations:** Mike Mains.

Field Staff

Manager: Jose Marzan. **Coach:** Ray Smith. **Pitching Coach:** Jim Shellenback. **Trainer:** Andrew Wilhorn.

Game Information

Radio Announcer: Frank Santore, Doug Jennett. **No. of Games Broadcast:** Home-34, Away-15. **Flagship Station:** WBEJ 1240-AM.

PA Announcer: Tom Banks. **Official Scorer:** Bill Crow.

Stadium Name (year opened): Joe O'Brien Field (1974). **Location:** Highway 321/67 to Holly Lane. **Standard Game Times:** 7 p.m.

Visiting Club Hotel: Days Inn, 505 W. Elk Ave., Elizabethton, TN 37643. Telephone: (423) 543-3344.

JOHNSON CITY
CARDINALS

Office Address: 111 Legion St., Johnson City, TN 37601. **Mailing Address:** P.O. Box 568, Johnson City, TN 37605. **Telephone:** (423) 461-4850. **FAX:** (423) 461-4864.

Affiliation (first year): St. Louis Cardinals (1975). **Years in League:** 1921-24, 1937-55, 1957-61, 1964-.

Ownership, Management

Operated By: Johnson City Cardinals Baseball Club.

Principal Owner: St. Louis Cardinals.

Chairman of the Board: Jack Chinouth. **President:** Lonnie Lowe.

General Manager/Director of Operations: Rebecca Hilbert. **Assistant General Manager/Controller:** Mary Ann Marsh. **Clubhouse Operations:** Carl Black. **Head Groundskeeper:** Mark Barker.

Field Staff

Manager: Steve Turco. **Pitching Coach:** Mike Snyder. **Trainer:** Brad Bluestone.

Game Information

Radio Announcer: Paul Overbay. **No. of Games Broadcast:** Unavailable. **Flagship Station:** WJCW 910-AM.

PA Announcer: Mike Clark. **Official Scorer:** Chris Ford.

Stadium Name (year opened): Howard Johnson Field (1956). **Location:** I-181 to exit 32, left on Commonwealth, left on State of Franklin, left on Legion Street. **Standard Game Times:** 7 p.m., Sun. 3.

Visiting Club Hotel: Ramada Inn, 2406 N. Roan St., Johnson City, TN 37601. Telephone: (423) 282-2161.

KINGSPORT
METS

Office Address: 433 E. Center St., Kingsport, TN 37662. **Mailing Address:** P.O. Box 1128, Kingsport, TN 37662. **Telephone:** (423) 378-3744. **FAX:** (423) 392-8538.

Affiliation (first year): New York Mets (1980). **Years in League:** 1921-25, 1938-52, 1957, 1960-63, 1969-82, 1984-.

Ownership, Management

Operated by: S/H Baseball.

Principal Owners: Rick Spivey, Steve Harville. **President:** Rick Spivey. **Vice President:** Steve Harville..

General Manager: Jim Arnold.

Field Staff

Manager: Ken Berry. **Coach:** Gary Ward. **Pitching Coach:** Buzz Capra. **Trainer:** Patrick Huber.

Game Information

Radio: None.

PA Announcer: Don Spivey. **Official Scorer:** Eddie Durham.

Stadium Name (year opened): Hunter Wright Stadium (1995). **Location:** Exit 57 off I-81 to I-181 North, West Stone Drive exit, left on West Stone Drive (U.S. 11W), right on Granby Road. **Standard Game Times:** 7 p.m.

Visiting Club Hotel: Ramada Inn, Highway 11W and 93 Bypass, Kingsport, TN. Telephone: (423) 245-0271.

MARTINSVILLE
PHILLIES

Office Address: Hooker Field, Commonwealth Blvd. and Chatham Heights Road, Martinsville, VA 24112. **Mailing Address:** P.O. Box 3614, Martinsville, VA 24115. **Telephone:** (540) 666-2000. **FAX:** (540) 666-2139.

Affiliation (first year): Philadelphia Phillies (1988). **Years in League:** 1988-.

Ownership, Management

Operated by: Martinsville Phillies Professional Baseball, Inc..

President/General Manager: Tim Cahill.

Assistant General Manager: Rachel Byrd. **Head Groundskeeper:** Sam Pickeral.

Field Staff

Manager: Kelly Heath. **Coach:** Tony Scott. **Pitching Coach:** Carlos Arroyo. **Trainer:** Unavailable.

Game Information

Radio: None.

PA Announcer: Unavailable. **Official Scorer:** Tim Hall.

Stadium Name (year opened): Hooker Field (1988). **Location:** U.S. 220 Business to Commonwealth Boulevard, east for three miles; or U.S. 58 to Chatham Heights Road, north two blocks. **Standard Game Times:** 7 p.m.

Visiting Club Hotel: Dutch Inn, 633 Virginia Ave., Collinsville, VA 24078. Telephone: (540) 647-3721.

PRINCETON
DEVIL RAYS

Office Address: Hunnicutt Field, Old Bluefield-Princeton Road, Princeton, WV 24740. **Mailing Address:** P.O. Box 5646, Princeton, WV 24740. **Telephone:** (304) 487-2000. **FAX:** (304) 425-6999. **E-Mail Address:** davidec@Inetone.net

Affiliation (first year): Tampa Bay Devil Rays (1997). **Years in League:** 1988-.

Ownership, Management

Operated by: Princeton Baseball Association, Inc.

Principal Owner: Tampa Bay Devil Rays.

President: Dewey Russell.

General Manager: Jim Holland. **Senior Account Representative:** Paul Lambert. **Clubhouse Operations:** Allen Fisher.

Field Staff

Manager: Charlie Montoyo. **Coach:** Mike Tosar. **Pitching Coach:** Milt Hill. **Trainer:** Unavailable.

Game Information

Radio: Unavailable.

PA Announcer: Jason Choate. **Official Scorer:** Dick Daisey.

Stadium Name (year opened): Hunnicutt Field (1988). **Location:** Exit 9 off I-77, U.S. 460 West to downtown exit, left on Stafford Drive, stadium located behind Mercer County Technical Education Center. **Standard Game Times:** 7 p.m.

Visiting Club Hotel: Days Inn, I-77 and Route 460, Princeton, WV 24740. Telephone: (304) 425-8100.

PULASKI
RANGERS

Office Address: 5th and Pierce SE, Pulaski, VA 24301. **Telephone:** (540) 980-1000. **FAX:** (540) 980-3055.

Affiliation (first year): Texas Rangers (1997). **Years in League:** 1946-50, 1952-55, 1957-58, 1969-77, 1982-92, 1997.

Ownership, Management

Operated by: Pulaski Baseball.

President: Hi Nicely.

General Manager: Tom Compton. **Controller:** Wayne Carpenter. **Director of Stadium Operations:** Dave Hart. **Head Groundskeeper:** Don Newman. **Director of Ticket Sales:** Rick Mansell. **Director of Special Projects:** Dave Edmonds.

Field Staff

Manager: Julio Cruz. **Pitching Coach:** Unavailable. **Trainer:** Gene Basham.

Game Information

Radio Announcer: Dan Callahan. **No. of Games Broadcast:** One per week. **Flagship Station:** WRAD 1460-AM.

PA Announcer: Unavailable. **Official Scorer:** Unavailable.

Stadium Name (year opened): Calfee Park (1935). **Location:** I-81 exit 89, Route 11 North to Pulaski, stadium on right off Pierce Avenue. **Standard Game Times:** 7 p.m.

Visiting Club Hotel: Comfort Inn, State Road 100, I-81 Exit 98, Newbern, VA 24126. Telephone: (540) 674-1100.

PIONEER LEAGUE

Rookie Advanced Classification

Office Address: 812 West 30th St., Spokane, WA 99203. **Mailing Address:** P.O. Box 2564, Spokane, WA 99220. **Telephone:** (509) 456-7615. **FAX:** (509) 456-0136.

Years League Active: 1939-1942, 1946-.

President/Secretary-Treasurer: Jim McCurdy.

Vice Presidents: Michael Ellis, Bill Yuill.

Directors: David Baggott (Ogden), Michael Ellis (Lethbridge), Bill Fanning (Butte), Larry Geske (Great Falls), Kevin Greene (Idaho Falls), Chris McKenna (Medicine Hat), Rob Owens (Helena), Bob Wilson (Billings).

Jim McCurdy

1997 Opening Date: June 18. **Closing Date:** Sept. 2.

Regular Season: 72 games (split-schedule).

Division Structure: North—Helena, Great Falls, Lethbridge, Medicine Hat. **South**—Butte, Billings, Idaho Falls, Ogden.

Playoff Format: First-half division winners play second-half division winners in best-of-3 series. Division playoff winners meet in best-of-3 series for league championship.

All-Star Game: None.

Roster Limit: 30 active. **Player Eligibility Rule:** No more than 17 players older than 21, provided that no more than two of the 17 are 23 or older. No player on active list may have more than three years of prior service.

Brand of Baseball: Rawlings.

Statistician: Howe Sportsdata International, Boston Fish Pier, West Bldg. #2—Suite 306, Boston, MA 02210.

1996 Standings (Overall)

Club (Affiliate)	W	L	Pct.	GB	'96 Manager
#Lethbridge (Diamondbacks)	50	22	.694	—	Chris Speier
*#Helena (Brewers)	43	29	.597	7	Alex Morales
#Ogden (Brewers)	42	30	.583	8	Bernie Moncallo
Idaho Falls (Padres)	38	34	.528	12	Don Werner
#Butte (Devil Rays)	37	35	.514	13	Tom Foley
Great Falls (Dodgers)	33	39	.458	17	Mickey Hatcher
Billings (Reds)	23	49	.319	27	Matt Martin
Medicine Hat (Blue Jays)	22	50	.306	28	Marty Pevey

*Won playoffs #Won split-season division title

Stadium Information

		Dimensions				
Club	Stadium	LF	CF	RF	Capacity	'96 Att.
Billings	Cobb Field	335	405	325	4,200	83,588
Butte	Alumni Coliseum	335	410	355	2,500	37,317
Great Falls	Legion Park	335	414	335	3,834	68,537
Helena	Kindrick Field	328	390	315	1,800	44,935
Idaho Falls	McDermott Field	350	400	340	2,800	54,475
Lethbridge	Henderson	330	400	330	2,750	49,124
Medicine Hat	Athletic Park	330	380	330	2,000	41,942
Ogden	Lindquist Field	340	390	340	5,500	62,022

BILLINGS
MUSTANGS

Office Address: Cobb Field, 901 N. 27th St., Billings, MT 59103. **Mailing Address:** P.O. Box 1553, Billings, MT 59103. **Telephone:** (406) 252-1241. **FAX:** (406) 252-2968.

Affiliation (first year): Cincinnati Reds (1974). **Years in League:** 1948-63, 1969-.

Ownership, Management

Operated by: Billings Pioneer Baseball Club, Inc.

Chairman of the Board: Ron May.

President/General Manager: Bob Wilson. **Assistant General Manager:** Gary Roller. **Head Groundskeeper:** Lowell Gorseth.

Field Staff

Manager: Derrel Thomas. **Pitching Coach:** Terry Abbott. **Trainer:** Tom Spencer.

Game Information

Radio Announcer: Chris Degnan. **No. of Games Broadcast:** Home-36, Away-36. **Flagship Station:** KCTR 970-AM.

PA Announcer: Hank Cox. **Official Scorer:** Jack Skinner.

Stadium Name (year opened): Cobb Field (1948). **Location:** I-90 to 27th Street exit, north to 9th Ave. North. **Standard Game Times:** 7 p.m.

Visiting Club Hotel: Rimrock Inn, 1203 N. 27th St., Billings, MT 59101. Telephone: (406) 252-7107.

BUTTE
COPPER KINGS

Office Address: West Park Street, Butte, MT 59701. **Mailing Address:** P.O. Box 888, Butte, MT 59703. **Telephone:** (406) 723-8206. **FAX:** (406) 723-3376.

Affiliation: Anaheim Angels (1997). **Years in League:** 1978-85, 1987-.

Ownership, Management

Operated by: Silverbow Baseball Corp.

Principal Owners: Mike Veeck, Bill Murray, Bill Fanning, Rich Taylor, Annie Huidekoper, Cynthia Gitt, Miles Wolff.

Chairman of the Board: Mike Veeck. **President:** Bill Fanning.

Vice President/General Manager: Ted Tornow. **Assistant General Manager:** Dave Meyer.

Field Staff

Manager: Bill Lachemann. **Coach:** Charlie Romero. **Pitching Coach:** Kernan Ronan. **Trainer:** Doug Baker.

Game Information

Radio Announcer: Deric Voelker. **No. of Games Broadcast:** Home-36, Away-36. **Flagship Station:** KXTL 1370-AM.

PA Announcer: Jeremy Bishop. **Official Scorer:** Jim Edgar.

Stadium Name (year opened): Alumni Coliseum (1962). **Location:** I-90 to Montana Street exit, north to Park Street, west to stadium (Montana Tech campus). **Standard Game Times:** 7 p.m., Sun. 6.

Visiting Club Hotel: War Bonnet Inn, 2100 Cornell, Butte, MT 59701. Telephone: (406) 494-7800.

GREAT FALLS
DODGERS

Office Address: 1015 25th St. North, Great Falls, MT 59401. **Mailing Address:** P.O. Box 1621, Great Falls, MT 59403. **Telephone:** (406) 452-5311. **FAX:** (406) 454-0811. **E-Mail Address:** dodgers@initco.net.

Affiliation (first year): Los Angeles Dodgers (1984). **Years in League:** 1948-63, 1969-.

Ownership, Management

Operated by: Great Falls Baseball Club, Inc.

Principal Owner: Community owned.

President: Larry Geske.

General Manager: Dave Endress. **Director of Stadium Operations:** Dick Pugh. **Head Groundskeeper:** Dan Maronick. **Director of Public Relations:** Cheyan Towne. **Director of Food Services:** Larry Lucero.

Field Staff

Manager: Mickey Hatcher. **Coach:** Tom Thomas. **Pitching Coach:** Joe Almaraz. **Trainer:** Homer Zulaica.

Game Information

Radio Announcer: Gene Black. **No. of Games Broadcast:** Home-36, Away-36. **Flagship Station:** KMSL 1450-AM.

PA Announcer: Tim Paul. **Official Scorer:** Al Audet.

Stadium Name (year opened): Legion Park (1948). **Location:** From I-15, take 10th Ave. South (exit 281) and proceed four miles to 26th Street, left to 8th Ave. North, left to 25th St. North, right to ballpark. **Standard Game Times:** 7 p.m., Sun. 5.

Visiting Club Hotel: Midtown Motel, 526 2nd Ave. N., Great Falls, MT 59401. Telephone: (406) 453-2411.

HELENA
BREWERS

Office Address: 1103 N. Main, Helena, MT 59601. **Mailing Address:** P.O. Box 4606, Helena, MT 59604. **Telephone:** (406) 449-7616. **FAX:** (406) 449-6979. **E-Mail Address:** helbrewers@aol.com

Affiliation (first year): Milwaukee Brewers (1985). **Years in League:** 1978-.

Ownership, Management

Operated by: Never Say Never, Inc.

Principal Owners: Stanley Owens (chairman), Rob Owens (president), Linda Gach Ray (vice president).

General Manager: Stephanie Taylor. **Head Groundskeeper:** Jeff Curey.

Field Staff

Manager: Alex Morales. **Coach:** Javier Gonzalez. **Pitching Coach:** Jim Merrick. **Trainer:** Mark Schoen.

Game Information

Radio Announcer: John Emmett. **No. of Games Broadcast:** Home-36, Away-36. **Flagship Station:** KBLL 1240-AM.

PA Announcer: Unavailable. **Official Scorer:** John Emmett.

Stadium Name (year opened): Kindrick Legion Field (1939). **Location:** Cedar Street exit off I-15, west to Main Street, left at Memorial Park. **Standard Game Times:** 7:05 p.m.

Visiting Club Hotel: Super 8, 2201 11th Ave., Helena, MT 59601. Telephone: (406) 443-2450.

IDAHO FALLS
BRAVES

Office Address: 568 W. Elva, Idaho Falls, ID 83402. **Mailing Address:** P.O. Box 2183, Idaho Falls, ID 83403. **Telephone:** (208) 522-8363. **FAX:** (208) 522-9858.

Affiliation (first year): San Diego Padres (1995). **Years in League:** 1940-42, 1946-.

Ownership, Management

Operated by: Elmore Sports Group.

Principal Owner: Dave Elmore.

President/General Manager: Kevin Greene.

Vice President/Director of Administration: Paul Fetz. **Director of Stadium Operations/Merchandising:** Jeff Bertrand. **Director of Media/Public Relations:** Geoff Flynn. **Director of Promotions/Ticket Sales:** David Sandler.

Field Staff

Manager: Don Werner. **Coach:** Mark Wasinger. **Pitching Coach:** Rick Sutcliffe. **Trainer:** John Maxwell.

Game Information

Radio Announcers: Jim Garshow, John Balginy, Geoff Flynn. **No. of Games Broadcast:** Home-36, Away-36. **Flagship Station:** KUPI 980-AM.

PA Announcer: Kelly Beckstead. **Official Scorer:** John Balginy.

Stadium Name (year opened): McDermott Field (1976). **Location:** I-15 to West Broadway exit, left onto Memorial Drive to Mound Ave., right ¼ mile to stadium. **Standard Game Times:** 7:15 p.m., Sun. 5.

Visiting Club Hotel: Motel West, 1540 W. Broadway, Idaho Falls, ID 83402. Telephone: (208) 522-1112.

LETHBRIDGE
BLACK DIAMONDS

Office Address: 2425 N. Parkside Drive S., Lethbridge, Alberta T1J 3Y2. **Mailing Address:** P.O. Box 1986, Lethbridge, Alberta T1J 4K5. **Telephone:** (403) 327-7975. **FAX:** (403) 327-8085.

Affiliation (first year): Arizona Diamondbacks (1996). **Years in League:** 1975-83, 1992-.

Ownership, Management

Operated by: Home Plate, Ltd.

Principal Owner/President: Michael Ellis.

General Manager: Doug Kryzanowski. **Assistant General Manager:** Rob Virginillo.

Field Staff

Manager: Rod Allen. **Coach:** Ty Van Burkleo. **Pitching Coach:** Mike Parrott. **Trainer:** Gord Watt.

Game Information

Radio Announcer: Shawn McCart. **No. of Games Broadcast:** Home-15, Away-15. **Flagship Station:** CJOC 1220-AM.

PA Announcer: Merv Caven. **Official Scorers:** Mary Oikawa, Dan Perry.

Stadium Name (year opened): Henderson Stadium (1975). **Location:** Hwy. 314 to Mayor Magrath Drive, to North Parkside Drive South. **Standard Game Times:** 7:05 p.m., Sun. 5:05.

Visiting Club Hotel: The Sandman Hotel, 421 Mayor Magrath Drive S., Lethbridge, Alberta T1J 3Y2. Telephone: (403) 328-1111.

MEDICINE HAT
BLUE JAYS

Office Address: 1 Birch Ave. SE, Medicine Hat, Alberta T1A 7G2. **Mailing Address:** P.O. Box 465, Medicine Hat, Alberta T1A 7G2. **Telephone:** (403) 526-0404. **FAX:** (403) 526-4000.

Affiliation (first year): Toronto Blue Jays (1978). **Years in League:** 1977-.

Ownership, Management

Operated By: Medicine Hat Blue Jays.

Principal Owners: Bill Yuill, Chris McKenna.

Chairman/President: Bill Yuill.

General Manager: Chris McKenna. **Head Groundskeeper/Operations Manager:** Trevor Johnson. **Administrative Assistant:** Raymonde Christensen. **Secretary:** Sandy Heidrich.

Field Staff

Manager: Marty Pevey. **Coach:** Rolando Pino. **Pitching Coach:** Neil Allen. **Trainer:** Mike Frostad.

Game Information

Radio: None.

PA Announcer: Mark Austen, Eric Bonsgaurd. **Official Scorer:** Sheldon Jobbe.

Stadium Name: Athletic Park (1976). **Location:** First Street SW exit off Trans Canada Highway, left on River Road. **Standard Game Times:** 7:05 p.m.

Visiting Club Hotel: Medicine Hat Inn, 530 4th St. SE, Medicine Hat, AB T1B 3T8. Telephone: (403) 526-1313.

OGDEN
RAPTORS

Office Address: 2330 Lincoln Ave., Ogden, UT 84401. **Telephone:** (801) 393-2400. **FAX:** (801) 393-2473.

Affiliation: Milwaukee Brewers (1996). **Years in League:** 1939-42, 1946-55, 1966-74, 1994-.

Ownership, Management

Operated by: Ogden Professional Baseball, Inc.

Principal Owners: Dave Baggott, Steve Buechele, Doug Foxley, Phil Johnson, John Lindquist, Jennifer Marshall, Ed Mattes, Jim O'Hara, John Stein, Ron Yengich.

Chairman/President: Dave Baggott.

General Manager: John Stein. **Assistant General Manager/Director of Group Sales:** Eric Hellstrom. **Head Groundskeeper:** Ken Kopinski. **Director of Media/Public/Community Relations:** Pete Diamond. **Office Manager:** Melinda Martinez.

Field Staff

Manager: Bernie Moncallo. **Coach:** Tom Houk. **Pitching Coach:** Steve Cline. **Trainer:** Keith Sayers.

Game Information

Radio Announcer: Unavailable. **No. of Games Broadcast:** Home-36, Away-36. **Flagship Station:** KSOS 800-AM.

PA Announcer: Pete Diamond. **Official Scorer:** Unavailable.

Stadium Name: Lindquist Field (1997). **Location:** From south, I-15/84 to 24th Street exit, right to Lincoln, left to park. From north, I-15/84 to 21st Street exit, left to Lincoln, right to park. **Standard Game Times:** 7 p.m.; Sun. 4.

Visiting Club Hotel: Ogden Park Hotel, 247 24th St., Odgen, UT 84401. Telephone: (801) 627-1190.

ARIZONA LEAGUE

Rookie Classification

Street Address: 5900 N. Granite Reef Road, Suite 105, Scottsdale, AZ 85250. **Mailing Address:** P.O. Box 4941, Scottsdale, AZ 85261. **Telephone:** (602) 483-8224. **FAX:** (602) 443-3450.

Years League Active: 1988-.

President/Treasurer: Bob Richmond.

Vice President: Tommy Jones. **Corporate Secretary:** Ted Polakowski. **Administrative Assistant:** Rob Richmond.

Member Clubs (Managers): Athletics (Juan Navarrete), Cubs (Terry Kennedy), Diamondbacks (Brian Butterfield), Mariners (Darrin Garner), Padres (Randy Whisler), Rockies (Tim Blackwell).

Division Structure: None.

Playing Sites: Athletics—Papago Park Sports Complex, Phoenix. **Cubs**—Fitch Park, Mesa. **Diamondbacks**—Peoria Sports Complex, Peoria. **Mariners**—Peoria Sports Complex, Peoria. **Padres**—Peoria Sports Complex, Peoria. **Rockies**—Fitch Park, Mesa, or Chandler Complex, Chandler.

1997 Opening Date: June 24. **Closing Date:** Aug. 31.

Regular Season: 56 games.

All-Star Game: None.

Playoff Format: None.

Roster Limit: 30 active, 35 under control. **Player Eligibility Rule:** No more than eight players 20 or older, and no more than two players 21 or older. At least 10 pitchers. No more than two years of prior service, excluding Rookie leagues outside the United States and Canada.

Brand of Baseball: Rawlings.

Statistician: Howe Sportsdata International, Boston Fish Pier, West Bldg. #2—Suite 306, Boston, MA 02210.

1996 Standings

	W	L	Pct.	GB	'96 Manager
Padres	36	20	.643	—	Larry See
Athletics	33	23	.589	3	Juan Navarrete
Mariners	29	27	.518	7	Tom LeVasseur
Rockies	26	30	.464	10	Jim Eppard
*Angels	24	32	.429	12	Bruce Hines
Diamondbacks	20	36	.357	16	Dwayne Murphy

*Cubs replace Angels in 1997.

GULF COAST LEAGUE

Rookie Classification

Mailing Address: 1503 Clower Creek Dr., Suite H-262, Sarasota, FL 34231. **Telephone:** (941) 966-6407. **FAX:** (941) 966-6872.

Years League Active: 1964-.

President/Treasurer: Thomas Saffell. **First Vice President:** Steve Noworyta. **Second Vice President:** John Boles. **Executive Secretary:** Anne Doyle.

Member Clubs (Managers), Division Structure: Eastern—Braves (Frank Howard), Expos (Luis Dorante), Marlins (Jon Deeble), Mets (John Stephenson). **Northern**—Astros (Julio Linares), Devil Rays (Bobby Ramos), Tigers (Kevin Bradshaw), Yankees (Ken Dominguez). **Western**—Orioles (Butch Davis), Pirates (Woody Huyke), Rangers (James Byrd), Red Sox (Luis Aguayo), Royals (Al Pedrique), Twins (Steve Liddle), White Sox (Roly de Armas).

Playing Sites: Astros—Osceola County Stadium, Kissimmee. **Braves**—Disney World, Orlando. **Devil Rays**—Huggins-Stengel Field, St. Petersburg. **Expos**—Municipal Stadium, West Palm Beach. **Marlins**—Carl Barger Baseball Complex, Melbourne. **Mets**—St. Lucie County Sports Complex, Port St. Lucie. **Orioles**—Twin Lakes Park, Sarasota. **Pirates**—Pirate City Complex, Bradenton. **Rangers**—Charlotte County Stadium, Port Charlotte. **Red Sox**—Red Sox minor league complex, Fort Myers. **Royals**—Lee County Stadium, Fort Myers. **Tigers**—Tigertown, Lakeland. **Twins**—Lee County Stadium, Fort Myers. **Yankees**—Yankee Complex, Tampa. **White Sox**—Ed Smith Stadium/Complex, Sarasota.

1997 Opening Date: June 20. **Closing Date:** Aug. 26.

Regualar Season: 60 games.

All-Star Game: None.

Playoff Format: Northern and Eastern Division winners play one game. Top two teams in Western Division play one game. Winners advance to best-of-3 series for league championship.

Roster Limit: 30 active. **Player Eligibility Rule:** No more than eight players 20 or older, and no more than two players 21 or older. No more than two years of prior service, excluding Rookie leagues outside the U.S. and Canada.

Brand of Baseball: Rawlings.

Statistician: Howe Sportsdata International, Boston Fish Pier, West Bldg. #2—Suite 306, Boston, MA 02210.

1996 Standings (Overall)

	W	L	Pct.	GB	'96 Manager
#Expos	41	18	.695	—	Jim Gabella
*#Yankees	37	21	.638	3½	Ken Dominguez
#Rangers	37	23	.617	4½	James Byrd
Orioles	36	24	600	5½	Tommy Shields
Marlins	34	25	.576	7	Juan Bustabad
#Cubs	34	26	.567	7½	Sandy Alomar Sr.
Astros	31	28	.525	10	Bobby Ramos
Royals	30	29	.508	11	Al Pedrique
Twins	30	30	.500	11½	Mike Boulanger
Mets	29	30	.492	12	Mickey Brantley
Pirates	28	31	.475	13	Woody Huyke
Tigers	26	34	.433	15½	Kevin Bradshaw
Devil Rays	24	35	.407	17	Bill Evers
Red Sox	24	36	.400	17½	Bob Geren
White Sox	20	40	.333	21½	Hector Rincones
Braves	14	45	.237	27	R. Lucas/C. Cadahia

*Won playoffs #Won division title

DOMINICAN SUMMER LEAGUE

Rookie Classification

Mailing Address: Av. John F. Kennedy, No. 3, Santo Domingo, Dominican Republic. **Telephone:** (809) 563-3233, ext. 5020. **FAX:** (809) 563-2455.

Years League Active: 1985-.

President: Freddy Jana.

Administrative Assistant: Orlando Diaz.

Member Clubs, 1997: Unavailable. **Member Clubs, 1996: Cibao Division**—Co-op, Indians, Phillies, Rockies/Royals (shared). **Santo Domingo East Division**—Cardinals, Dodgers I, Expos, Mariners, Marlins, Tigers, Yankees. **Santo Domingo West Division**—Athletics, Brewers/White Sox (shared), Cubs/Padres (shared), Diamondbacks, Mets, Pirates, Rangers. **San Pedro de Macoris Division**—Astros/Red Sox (shared), Blue Jays, Braves, Devil Rays/Angels (shared), Dodgers II, Giants, Orioles.

1997 Opening Date: June 1. **Closing Date:** Aug. 27.

Playoff Format: Four division winners meet in best-of-three semifinals. Winners meet in best-of-three series for league championship.

Roster Limit: 30 active. **Player Eligibility Rule:** No more than three years of minor league service.

MINOR LEAGUE SCHEDULES

CLASS AAA

American Association

Buffalo

APRIL

4-5-6 .... Nashville
8-9-10 .... Indianapolis
19-20-20 .... Omaha
22-23 .... Iowa
29-30 .... Louisville

MAY

1 .... Louisville
2-3 .... New Orleans
4-5 .... Oklahoma City
14-15 .... Nashville
16-17-18 .... Indianapolis
20-21-22 .... Louisville

JUNE

2-3 .... Indianapolis
4-5 .... Omaha
6-7-8-8 .... Iowa
19-20-21-21 New Orleans
22-23-24-25 ... Okla. City

JULY

1-2-3 .... Louisville
10-11-12-13 .... Omaha
14-15-16 .... Iowa
25-26-27 .... Nashville
28-29-30 ... New Orleans
31 .... Oklahoma City

AUGUST

1-2 .... Oklahoma City
14-15-16-17. Indianapolis
18-19-20 .... Louisville
21-22-23-24 .... Nashville

Indianapolis

APRIL

11-12-13 .... Louisville
14-15-16-17 .... Nashville
24-25 .... New Orleans
26-27-28 Oklahoma City

MAY

8-9-10-11 .... Omaha
12-13-14-15 .... Iowa
26-27-28-29 .... Buffalo
30-31 .... Nashville

JUNE

1 .... Nashville
5-6-7 .... New Orleans
8-9-10-11 .... Okla. City
17-18-19 .... Louisville
20-21-22 .... Omaha
23-24-25 .... Iowa

JULY

4-5-6-7 .... Buffalo
10-11-12-13 New Orleans
14-15 ..... Oklahoma City
28-29 .... Omaha
30-31 .... Iowa

AUGUST

8-9-10-11-12 ... Nashville
21-22-23-24 .... Louisville
25-26-27-28 .... Buffalo
29-30 .... Louisville

Iowa

APRIL

11-12-13 .... Omaha
14-15 ..... Oklahoma City
16-17 .... New Orleans
24-25 .... Nashville
26-27 .... Buffalo

MAY

2-3-4 .... Louisville
5-6-7 .... Indianapolis
19-20-21-22 ... Okla. City
23-24-25 ... New Orleans
27-28-29 .... Omaha

JUNE

9-10-11-12 ...... Nashville
13-14-15 .... Buffalo
26-27 .... Louisville
28-29-30 .... Indianapolis

JULY

1-2-3 ...... Oklahoma City
18-19-20 .... Nashville
21-22-23-24 .... Buffalo
25-26-27 .... Omaha

AUGUST

1-2-3-4 .... Louisville
5-6-7 .... Indianapolis
12-13-14 ... New Orleans
15-16-17 Oklahoma City
26-27-28 .... Omaha
29-30-31 ... New Orleans

SEPTEMBER

1 .... New Orleans

Louisville

APRIL

3-4-5-6 .... Indianapolis
14-15-16-17 .... Buffalo
24-25 ..... Oklahoma City
26-27-28 ... New Orleans

MAY

8-9-10-11 .... Iowa
12-13-14-15 .... Omaha
23-24-25 .... Indianapolis
26-27-28-29 .... Nashville
30-31 .... Buffalo

JUNE

1 .... Buffalo
5-6-7 ...... Oklahoma City
8-9-10-11 .. New Orleans
20-21-22 .... Iowa
23-24-25 .... Omaha

JULY

4-5-5-6-7 .... Nashville
10-11-12-13 .... Okla.City
14-15 .... New Orleans
25-26-27 .... Indianapolis
28-29 .... Iowa
30-31 .... Omaha

AUGUST

8-9-10-11-12 ...... Buffalo
25-26-27 .... Nashville
31 .... Indianapolis

SEPTEMBER

1 .... Indianapolis

Nashville

APRIL

8-9-10 .... Louisville
11-12-13 .... Buffalo
18-19-20 .... Iowa
21-22 .... Omaha
29-30 .... Indianapolis

MAY

1 .... Indianapolis
2-3 .... Oklahoma City
4-5 .... New Orleans
16-17-18 .... Louisville
20-21-22 .... Indianapolis
23-24-25 .... Buffalo

JUNE

2-3 .... Louisville
4-5 .... Iowa
6-7-8 .... Omaha
16-17 .... Buffalo
19-20-21-21 .... Okla.City
22-23-24-25 New Orleans

JULY

1-2-3 .... Indianapolis
10-11-12-13 .... Iowa
14-15-16-17 .... Omaha
28-29-30 Oklahoma City
31 .... New Orleans

AUGUST

1-2 .... New Orleans
14-15-16-17 .... Louisville
18-19-20 .... Indianapolis
29-30-31 .... Buffalo

SEPTEMBER

1 .... Buffalo

New Orleans

APRIL

11-12-13 Oklahoma City
14-15-15 .... Omaha
18-19-20 .... Indianapolis
21-22-23 .... Louisville
29-30 .... Iowa

MAY

1 .... Iowa
6-7-8-9 .... Buffalo
10-11-12-13 .... Nashville
15-16-17-18 ... Okla. City
30-31 .... Omaha

JUNE

1 .... Omaha
2-3 .... Iowa
13-14 .... Louisville
15-16 .... Indianapolis
17-18 ..... Oklahoma City
26-27 .... Buffalo
28-29-30 .... Nashville

JULY

4-5-6-7 .... Iowa
17-18-19-20 Indianapolis
21-22-23-24 .... Louisville

AUGUST

3-4-5 .... Buffalo
6-7 .... Nashville
8-9-10 .... Omaha
18-19 ..... Oklahoma City
20-21-22 .... Iowa
23-24-25 .... Omaha

Oklahoma City

APRIL

3-4-5-6 ...... New Orleans
8-9-10 .... Iowa
18-19-20 .... Louisville
21-22-23 .... Indianapolis
29-30 .... Omaha

MAY

1 .... Omaha
6-7-8-9 .... Nashville
10-11-12-13 .... Buffalo
27-28-29 ... New Orleans
30-31 .... Iowa

JUNE

1 .... Iowa
2-3 .... Omaha
13-14 .... Indianapolis
15-16 .... Louisville
26-27 .... Nashville
28-29-30 .... Buffalo

JULY

4-5-6-7 .... Omaha
17-18-19-20 .... Louisville
21-22-23-24. Indianapolis
25-26-27 ... New Orleans

AUGUST

3-4-5 .... Nashville
6-7 .... Buffalo
8-9-10 .... Iowa
20-21-22 .... Omaha
23-24-25 .... Iowa
26-27-28 ... New Orleans

Omaha

APRIL

3-4-5-6 .... Iowa
8-9 .... New Orleans
16-17 ..... Oklahoma City
24-25 .... Buffalo
26-27 .... Nashville

MAY
2-3-4 .... Indianapolis
5-6-7 .... Louisville
16-17-18 .... Iowa
19-20-21-22 New Orleans
23-24-25 Oklahoma City
JUNE
9-10-11-12 .... Buffalo
13-14-15 .... Nashville
17-18-19 .... Iowa
26-27 .... Indianapolis
28-29-30 .... Louisville
JULY
1-2-3 .... New Orleans
18-19-20 .... Buffalo
21-22-23-24 .... Nashville
AUGUST
1-2-3-4 ...... Indianapolis
5-6-7 .... Louisville
12-13-14 Oklahoma City
15-16-17 ... New Orleans
18-19 .... Iowa
29-30-31 Oklahoma City
SEPTEMBER
1 .... Oklahoma City

International League

Charlotte

APRIL
3-4-5-6 .... Pawtucket
14-15 .... Toledo
17-18-19-20 .. Columbus
28-29-30 .... Richmond
MAY
2-3-4 .... Scranton
12-13-14 .... Ottawa
21-22 .... Richmond
26-27-28 .... Norfolk
JUNE
6-7-8 .... Norfolk
13-14-15 .... Rochester
16-17-18-19 ... Syracuse
26-27-28-29 .... Ottawa
30 .... Toledo
JULY
1-2-3 .... Toledo
14-15-16 .... Pawtucket
17-18-19-20 .. Rochester
29-30-31 .... Syracuse
AUGUST
1-2-3 .... Norfolk
8-9-10 .... Columbus
11-12-13 .... Toledo
22-23-24-25 .... Scranton
26-27 .... Columbus
29-30-31 .... Richmond
SEPTEMBER
1 .... Richmond

Columbus

APRIL
3-4-5-6 .... Rochester
7-8-9 .... Ottawa
21-22-23 .... Pawtucket
25-26-27 .... Charlotte
28-29-30 .... Scranton
MAY
1 .... Scranton
9-10-11 .... Norfolk
13-14-15 .... Syracuse
26-27 .... Toledo
30-31 .... Richmond
JUNE
1 .... Richmond
2-3-4-5 .... Charlotte
6-7-8 .... Toledo
16-17-18 .... Scranton
19-20-21-22 .. Pawtucket
JULY
4-5-5-6 .... Toledo
10-11 .... Charlotte
12-13 .... Richmond
14-15-16-17 .... Ottawa
18-19-20 .... Norfolk
AUGUST
1-2-3 .... Rochester
4-5-6-7 .... Richmond
18-19-20 .... Norfolk
21-22-23-24 ... Syracuse

Norfolk

APRIL
11-12-13 .... Toledo
14-15-16 .... Columbus
25 .... Richmond
28-29-30 .... Rochester
MAY
2-3-4 .... Columbus
5 .... Richmond
15-16-17-18-19 Charlotte
20 .... Richmond
21-22 .... Toledo
30-31 .... Syracuse
JUNE
1 .... Syracuse
2-3-4-5 .... Scranton
16-17-18-19 .. Rochester
20-21-22 .... Ottawa
30 .... Richmond
JULY
1-2-3 .... Scranton
10-11-12-13 .. Pawtucket
21-22-23-24 .... Charlotte
25-26-27-28 ... Syracuse
29 .... Richmond
AUGUST
4-5-6-7 .... Toledo
8-9-10 .... Pawtucket
11-12-13 .... Columbus
22-23-24-25 .. Richmond
29-30-31 .... Ottawa
SEPTEMBER
1 .... Ottawa

Ottawa

APRIL
11-12-13 .... Charlotte
14-15-16 .... Richmond
17-18-19-20 .... Norfolk
28-29-30 .... Toledo
MAY
1 .... Toledo
2-3-4 .... Pawtucket
6-7 .... Syracuse
20-21-22 .... Rochester
23-24-25 .... Columbus
26-27-28 .... Scranton
JUNE
6-7-8 .... Rochester
13-14-15 .... Norfolk
16-17-18-19 .. Richmond
30 .... Syracuse
JULY
1-2 .... Syracuse
10-11 .... Syracuse
12-13 .... Scranton
21-22-23-24 .... Scranton
25-26-27 .... Pawtucket
28-29-30-31 .. Columbus
AUGUST
8-9-10 .... Rochester
16-17 .... Syracuse
18-19-20-21 .... Charlotte
22-23-24 .... Pawtucket
25-26-27 .... Toledo

Pawtucket

APRIL
11-12-13 .... Syracuse
14-15-16 .... Scranton
24-25-26-27 .... Ottawa
MAY
5-6-7 .... Charlotte
8-9-10-11 ...... Richmond
13-14-15 .... Toledo
23-24-25 .... Norfolk
26-27-28 .... Rochester
JUNE
6-7-8 .... Syracuse
9-10-11 .... Ottawa
12-13-14-15 .. Columbus
24-25-26 .... Rochester
JULY
1-2-3 .... Richmond
4-5-6-7 .... Norfolk
18-19-20 .... Syracuse
21-22-23-24 .... Toledo
31 .... Scranton
AUGUST
1-2-3 .... Scranton
4-5-6-7 .... Charlotte
14-15 .... Ottawa
16-17-18 .... Rochester
28-29-30 .... Columbus
31 .... Scranton
SEPTEMBER
1 .... Scranton

Richmond

APRIL
7-8-9-10 .... Pawtucket
11-12-13 .... Columbus
26-27 .... Norfolk
MAY
1-2-3-4 .... Rochester
6-7 .... Columbus
10-11-12 .... Charlotte
13-14 .... Norfolk
15-16-17-18 .... Ottawa
23-24-25 .... Toledo
27-28-28-29 ... Syracuse
JUNE
6-7-8 .... Scranton
20-21-22 .... Syracuse
23-24-25 .... Ottawa
27-28-29 .... Toledo
JULY
4-5-6 .... Charlotte
14-15-16 .... Rochester
25-26-27 .... Charlotte
30-31 .... Norfolk
AUGUST
1-2-3 .... Toledo
11-12-13 .... Pawtucket
14-15-16-17 .. Columbus
18-19-20-21 .... Scranton
26-27-28 .... Norfolk

Rochester

APRIL
11-12-13 .... Scranton
16 .... Syracuse
18-19-20 .... Richmond
21-22-23-24 .... Norfolk
26-27 .... Syracuse
MAY
6-7 .... Scranton
8-9-10-11 .... Charlotte
16-17-18-19 .. Pawtucket
23-24-25 .... Syracuse
29-30-31 .... Ottawa
JUNE
1 .... Ottawa
2-3-4 .... Pawtucket
10-11-11 .... Toledo
20-21-22 .... Charlotte
27-28-29 .... Norfolk
30 .... Columbus
JULY
1-2-3 .... Columbus
6-7 .... Ottawa
10-11 .... Scranton
21-22-23-24 .. Richmond
25-26-27 .... Columbus

AUGUST
4-5-6 .... Ottawa
11-12-13......... Syracuse
19-20 .... Pawtucket
21-22-23-24 .... Toledo
26-27 .... Scranton

Scranton/W-B

APRIL
3-4-5-6 .... Richmond
7-8-9-10 .... Norfolk
17-18-19-20 ... Syracuse
22-23 .... Ottawa
MAY
8-9-10-11 .... Ottawa
12-13-14-15 .. Rochester
19-20-21-22 .. Columbus
23-24-25......... Charlotte
30-31 .... Pawtucket
JUNE
1 .... Pawtucket
9-10-11 .... Columbus
13-14-15............ Toledo
24-25-26 .... Norfolk
27-28-29-30.. Pawtucket
JULY
4-5 .... Rochester
6-7..................... Syracuse
18-19-20 .... Richmond
25-26-27-28 .... Toledo
29-30 .... Pawtucket
AUGUST
4-5-6............... Syracuse
11-12-13 .... Ottawa
14-15-16-17.... Charlotte
28-29-30 .... Rochester

Syracuse

APRIL
3-4-5-6 .... Norfolk
7-8-9-10......... Charlotte
14-15 .... Rochester
21-22-23-24 .. Richmond
25.................. Rochester
29-30 .... Pawtucket
MAY
1 .... Pawtucket
2-3-4-5 .... Toledo
16-17 .... Scranton
20-21-22 .... Pawtucket
JUNE
2-3-4 .... Ottawa
10-11-12 .... Norfolk
13-14-15 .... Richmond
23-24-25 .... Charlotte
26-27-28-29 .. Columbus
JULY
3-4-5 .... Ottawa
12-13 .... Rochester
14-15-16-17.... Scranton
22-23-24 .... Columbus
AUGUST
1-2-3 .... Ottawa
8-9-10.............. Scranton
14-15 .... Rochester
25-26-27 .... Pawtucket
28-29-30............ Toledo
31.................. Rochester
SEPTEMBER
1.................... Rochester

Toledo

APRIL
3-4-5-6 .... Ottawa
7-8-9-10 .... Rochester
17-18-19-20.. Pawtucket
22-23-24 .... Charlotte
25-26-27 .... Scranton
MAY
6-7-8 .... Norfolk
9-10-11-12 ..... Syracuse
16-17-18 .... Columbus
28.................. Columbus
29-30-31 .... Charlotte
JUNE
1 .... Charlotte
2-3-4-5 .... Richmond
16-17-18....... Pawtucket
19-20-21-22.... Scranton
23-24-25 .... Columbus
JULY
10-11............ Richmond
12-13 .... Charlotte
15-16-17 .... Norfolk
18-19-20 .... Ottawa
29-30-31 .... Rochester
AUGUST
8-9-10 .... Richmond
15-16-17 .... Norfolk
18-19-20......... Syracuse
31.................. Columbus
SEPTEMBER
1.................... Columbus

Pacific Coast League

Albuquerque

APRIL
3-4-5-6 .... Salt Lake
17-18-19-20 . Vancouver
21-22-23-24 ...... Calgary
MAY
8-9-10-11 ..... Las Vegas
12-13-14-15...... Colo. Spr.
24-25-26-27 .. Edmonton
28-29-30-31 ..... Tacoma
JUNE
1-2-3-4 .... Phoenix
14-15-16-17....... Tucson
18-19-20-21...... Colo. Spr.
JULY
4-5-6-7.............. Tucson
10-11-12-13 . Las Vegas
18-19-20-21 . Vancouver
22-23-24-25 ...... Calgary
AUGUST
4-5-6-7.......... Edmonton
8-9-10-11 .... Tacoma
12-13-14-15 ... Salt Lake
29-30-31.......... Phoenix
SEPTEMBER
1 .... Phoenix

Calgary

APRIL
12-13-14-15 . Las Vegas
17-18-19-20...... Colo. Spr.
29-30 .... Albuquerque
MAY
1-2 .... Albuquerque
3-4-5-6 .... Tacoma
16-17-18-19....... Tucson
20-21-22-23 .. Edmonton
28-29-30-31 . Vancouver
JUNE
10-11-12-13 ... Salt Lake
14-15-16-17 ..... Phoenix
18-19-20-21 . Vancouver
30 .... Salt Lake
JULY
1-2-3.............. Salt Lake
10-11-12-13 .. Edmonton
14-15-16-17 ..... Tacoma
26-27-28-29...... Colo. Spr.
31 .... Phoenix
AUGUST
1-2-3.................. Phoenix
8-9-10-11........... Tucson
12-13-14-15 . Las Vegas
25-26-27-28 Albuquerque

Colo. Springs

APRIL
3-4-5-6 .... Phoenix
8-9-10-11 ...... Edmonton
25-26-27-28 ...... Calgary
29-30 .... Las Vegas
MAY
1-2................ Las Vegas
8-9-10-11 .... Salt Lake
16-17-18-19 . Vancouver
20-21-22-23 Albuquerque
JUNE
1-2-3-4.............. Tucson
10-11-12-13 ..... Tacoma
22-23-24-25....... Tucson
26-27-28-29 . Las Vegas
JULY
4-5-6-7 .... Calgary
14-15-16-17 Albuquerque
18-19-20-21 ..... Phoenix
31 .... Tacoma
AUGUST
1-2-3.................. Tacoma
16-17-18-19 ... Salt Lake
25-26-27-28 .. Edmonton
29-30-31 ...... Vancouver
SEPTEMBER
1 .... Vancouver

Edmonton

APRIL
12-13-13-14....... Tucson
17-18-19-20 . Las Vegas
21-22-23-24...... Colo. Spr.
MAY
3-4-5-6...... Albuquerque
8-9-10-11 .... Tacoma
16-17-18-19 ..... Phoenix
28-29-30-31 ... Salt Lake
JUNE
1-2-3-4 .... Calgary
14-15-16-17 . Vancouver
18-19-20-21 ..... Phoenix
26-27-28-29 ...... Calgary
30 .... Vancouver
JULY
1-2-3 .... Vancouver
14-15-16-17 ... Salt Lake
22-23-24-25...... Colo. Spr.
26-27-28-29 Albuquerque
AUGUST
12-13-14-15....... Tucson
16-17-18-19 . Las Vegas
21-22-23-24 ..... Tacoma

Las Vegas

APRIL
3-4-5-6.......... Edmonton
8-9-10-11 .... Phoenix
21-22-23-24 . Vancouver
25-26-27-28....... Tucson
MAY
3-4-5-6 .... Salt Lake
12-13-14-15 ...... Calgary
16-17-18-19 Albuquerque
28-29-30-31 ...... Colo. Spr.
JUNE
1-2-3-4 .... Tacoma
18-19-20-21....... Tucson
22-23-24-25 ..... Tacoma
30.............. Albuquerque
JULY
1-2-3 .... Albuquerque
18-19-20-21 ...... Calgary
31.................. Edmonton
AUGUST
1-2-3 .... Edmonton
4-5-6-7 .... Colo. Spr.

8-9-10-11 ..... Vancouver
21-22-23-24 ..... Phoenix
29-30-31 .... Salt Lake

SEPTEMBER

1 .... Salt Lake

Phoenix

APRIL

12-13-14-15 ..... Tacoma
17-18-19-20 ... Salt Lake
29-30 .... Tucson

MAY

1-2 .... Tucson
3-4-5-6 .... Vancouver
8-9-10-11 .... Calgary
20-21-22-23 . Las Vegas
24-25-26-27...... Colo. Spr.

JUNE

5-6-7-8 .... Edmonton
10-11-12-13 Albuquerque
22-23-24-25 Albuquerque
26-27-28-29 ..... Tacoma

JULY

4-5-6-6 .... Las Vegas
22-23-24-25 . Vancouver
26-27-28-29 ... Salt Lake

AUGUST

8-9-10-11 ...... Edmonton
12-13-14-15 ...... Colo. Spr.
16-17-18-19 ...... Calgary
25-26-27-28....... Tucson

Salt Lake

APRIL

8-9-10-11 .... Calgary
12-13-14-15 Albuquerque
25-26-27-28 ..... Phoenix
29-30................ Tacoma

MAY

1-2.................... Tacoma
12-13-14-15 .. Edmonton
20-21-22-23....... Tucson

JUNE

1-2-3-4 .... Vancouver
5-6-7-8 .... Las Vegas
14-15-16-17........ Colo. Spr.
22-23-24-25 ...... Calgary

JULY

4-5-6-7 .... Edmonton
10-11-12-13 . Vancouver
18-19-20-21....... Tucson
22-23-24-25 . Las Vegas

AUGUST

4-5-6-7 .... Phoenix
8-9-10-11........ Colo. Spr.
21-22-23-24 Albuquerque
25-26-27-28 ..... Tacoma

Tacoma

APRIL

3-4-5-6 .... Vancouver
8-9-10-11 .. Albuquerque
21-22-23-24 ..... Phoenix
25-26-27-28 .. Edmonton

MAY

12-13-14-15....... Tucson
16-17-18-19 ... Salt Lake
24-25-26-27 ...... Calgary

JUNE

5-6-7-8..... Colo. Springs
14-15-16-17 . Las Vegas
18-19-20-21 ... Salt Lake
30 .... Colo. Springs

JULY

1-2-3 .... Colo. Springs
10-11-12-13 ..... Phoenix
18-19-20-21 .. Edmonton
22-23-24-25....... Tucson
26-27-28-29 . Las Vegas

AUGUST

12-13-14-15 . Vancouver
16-17-18-19 Albuquerque
29-30-31 .... Calgary

SEPTEMBER

1........................ Calgary

Tucson

APRIL

3-4-5-6 .... Calgary
17-18-19-20 ..... Tacoma
21-22-23-24 ... Salt Lake

MAY

3-4-5-6..... Colo. Springs
8-9-10-11 ..... Vancouver
24-25-26-27 . Las Vegas
28-29-30-31 ..... Phoenix

JUNE

5-6-7-8 ...... Albuquerque
10-11-12-13 .. Edmonton
26-27-28-29 Albuquerque
30 .... Phoenix

JULY

1-2-3................. Phoenix
10-11-12-13...... Colo. Spr.
14-15-16-17 . Las Vegas
26-27-28-29 . Vancouver
31 .... Salt Lake

AUGUST

1-2-3............... Salt Lake
4-5-6-7 .... Tacoma
21-22-23-24 ...... Calgary
29-30-31 .... Edmonton

SEPTEMBER

1.................... Edmonton

Vancouver

APRIL

8-9-10-11........... Tucson
12-13-14-15...... Colo. Spr.
25-26-27-28 Albuquerque
29-30 .... Edmonton

MAY

1-2 .... Edmonton
12-13-14-15 ..... Phoenix
20-21-22-23 ..... Tacoma
24-25-26-27 ... Salt Lake

JUNE

5-6-7-8.............. Calgary
10-11-12-13 . Las Vegas
22-23-24-25 .. Edmonton
26-27-28-29 ... Salt Lake

JULY

4-5-6-7 .... Tacoma
14-15-16-17 ..... Phoenix
31.............. Albuquerque

AUGUST

1-2-3 .... Albuquerque
4-5-6-7.............. Calgary
16-17-18-19....... Tucson
21-22-23-24 ...... Colo. Spr.
25-26-27-28 . Las Vegas

CLASS AA

Eastern League

Akron

APRIL
10-11-12-13.. Harrisburg
14-15-16 .... Bowie
25-26-27 ..... New Britain
29-30 .... Trenton

MAY
9-10-11 .... Reading
12-13-14.......... Norwich
19-20-21 .... Binghamton
22-23-24-25...... Trenton

JUNE
5-6-7-8................ Bowie
9-10-11 .... New Haven
20-21-21-22..... Portland
23-24-25-26 New Britain

JULY
4-5-6 .... Reading
9-10-11 .... Portland
12-13-14....... Harrisburg
24-25-26-27 New Haven
28-29 .... Bowie
30-31 .... Harrisburg

AUGUST
4-5-6-7............. Norwich
19-20-21 .... Reading
22-23-24 .... Trenton
25-26-27-28 Binghamton

Binghamton

APRIL
11-12-13.......... Norwich
14-15-16....... Harrisburg
26-27 .... New Haven
28-29-30 .... Portland

MAY
9-10-11-12 .... Trenton
13-14 .... Reading
23-24-25-26 New Haven
27-28-29 .... Akron

JUNE
3-4-5 .... Portland
6-7-8 .... New Britain
12-13-14-15.. Harrisburg
20-21-22-23......... Bowie
24-25-26........... Norwich
30......................... Akron

JULY
1-2-3 .... Akron
15-16-17........... Norwich
18-19-20 .... Reading
30-31 .... Portland

AUGUST
1........................ Portland
2-3-4 .... New Britain
8-9-10................. Bowie
12-13-14 .... Trenton
19-20-21 ..... New Britain
22-23-24..... New Haven
29-30 .... Reading

Bowie

APRIL
4-5-6 .... Akron
7-8-9-10............ Norwich
18-19-20 .... Trenton
22-23 .... Reading

MAY
1-2 .... Reading
3-4 .... New Haven
6-7 .... Harrisburg
15-16-17-18 ..... Portland
26-27-28-29.. Harrisburg
30-31......... Binghamton

JUNE
1-2............. Binghamton
9-10-11-12 .. New Britain
13-14-15 .... Akron
24-25-26 .... Reading
27-28-29-30 ...... Trenton

JULY
4-5-6 .... New Britain
15-16-17 .... Akron
18-19-20.......... Norwich
21-22-23 .... Binghamton
30-31 .... Trenton

AUGUST
1-2-3............ Harrisburg
11-12-13-14-15 New Haven
22-23-24 .... Portland
25-26 .... Reading

Harrisburg

APRIL
3-4-5-6 .... Trenton
7-8-9 .... Reading
17-18-19-20..... Portland
21-22-23 .... Akron

MAY
2-3-4-5 ...... Binghamton
9-10-11-12 .. New Britain
13-14.................. Bowie
23-24-25 .... Reading

JUNE
2-3-4 .... Akron
6-7-8 .... New Haven
10-11................ Norwich
16-17-18 .... Portland
24-25-26 .... Trenton

JULY
4-5-6 .... Binghamton
9-10-11................ Bowie
22-23 .... New Haven
24-25-26-27......... Bowie
28-29 .... Trenton

AUGUST
8-9-10.............. Norwich
12-13-14 ..... New Britain
15-16-17 .... Akron
22-23-24 .... Reading
25-26 .... New Haven
29-30............... Norwich

New Britain

APRIL
3-4-5-6 .... Reading
7-8-9 .... New Haven
17-18-19-20 .... Akron
21-22-23 .... Binghamton

MAY
3-4 .... Portland
6-7-8................ Norwich
15-16-17-18.. Harrisburg
20-21-22 .... Bowie
30-31 .... Norwich

JUNE
1 .... Norwich
2-3-4-5........ New Haven
13-14-15 .... Trenton
16-17-18 .... Binghamton
27-28-29....... Harrisburg

JULY
1-2-3 .... Portland
15-16-17 .... Reading
18-19-20 .... Akron
22-23 .... Portland
28-29 .... New Haven

AUGUST
5-6-7 .... Binghamton
8-9-10-11 .... Trenton
22-23-24.......... Norwich
25-26 .... Portland
29-30-31 .... Bowie

SEPTEMBER
1 .... Bowie

New Haven

APRIL
3-4-5-6 .... Binghamton
14-15-16 .... Portland
17-18-19-20..... Reading
24-25......... Binghamton
29-30 .... Bowie

MAY
1-2 .... New Britain
6-7-8 .... Trenton
13-14 .... New Britain
15-16-17-18 ..... Norwich
27-28 .... New Britain
30-31 .... Harrisburg

JUNE
1 .... Harrisburg
13-14-15 .... Portland
16-17-18 .... Akron
27-28-29.......... Norwich
30 .... Harrisburg

JULY
1-2-3............ Harrisburg
9-10-11 .... New Britain
12-13-14 .... Binghamton
18-19-20-21...... Trenton
30-31 .... Reading

AUGUST
1....................... Reading
2-3.................... Norwich
8-9-10 .... Portland
19-20-21 .... Bowie
27-28 .... Bowie
29-30-31 .... Akron

SEPTEMBER
1.......................... Akron

Norwich

APRIL
3-4-5-6............ Portland
14-15-16 ..... New Britain
17-18-19-20 Binghamton
28-29-30....... Harrisburg

MAY
1-2-3-4 .... Akron
9-10-11 .... New Haven
19-20-21 .... Portland
23-24-25............. Bowie

JUNE
3-4-5 .... Reading
6-7-8-9 .... Trenton
16-17-18-19......... Bowie
20-21-22-23 New Haven

JULY
1-2-3 .... Trenton
9-10-11 ...... Binghamton
12-13-14 ..... New Britain
21-22-23 .... Akron
24-25 .... Portland
30-31 .... New Briatin

AUGUST
1................. New Britain
12-13-14-15..... Reading
16-17 .... New Haven
18-19-20-21.. Harrisburg
31 .... Binghamton

SEPTEMBER
1 .... Binghamton

Portland

APRIL
7-8-9 .... Binghamton
11-12-13 ..... New Britain
21-22-23 ..... New Haven
24-25-26-27.. Harrisburg

MAY
5-6-7 .... Akron
9-10-11-12........... Bowie

23-24-25-26 New Britain
27-28-29........... Norwich

JUNE

6-7-8-9............. Reading
10-11-12........... Trenton
24-25-26..... New Haven
27-28-29 .... Binghamton

JULY

4-5-6................. Norwich
15-16-17..... New Haven
18-19-20....... Harrisburg
26-27-28........... Norwich

AUGUST

2-3-4 .... Reading
5-6-7.................... Bowie
11-12-13-14......... Akron
15-16-17 .... Binghamton
27-28 .... New Britain
29-30-31 .... Trenton

SEPTEMBER

1........................ Trenton

Reading

APRIL

11-12-13............. Bowie
14-15 .... Trenton
25-26-27........... Norwich
28-29-30 ..... New Britain

MAY

6-7-8 .... Binghamton
16-17-18 .... Akron
19-20-21-22 New Haven
26-27-28-29...... Trenton
30-31 .... Portland

JUNE

1-2 .... Portland
10-11.......... Binghamton
12-13-14-15 ..... Norwich
19-20-21-22-23 Harrisburg
27-28-29 .... Akron

JULY

1-2-3.................... Bowie
9-10-11 .... Trenton
12-13-14 .... Portland
24-25-26-27 New Britain
28-29.......... Binghamton

AUGUST

5-6-7........... New Haven
8-9-10 .... Akron
16-17-18............. Bowie
27-28........... Harrisburg
31 .... Harrisburg

SEPTEMBER

1 .... Harrisburg

Trenton

APRIL

7-8-9 .... Akron
10-11-12-13 New Haven
21..................... Reading
22-23-24........... Norwich
25-26-27-28......... Bowie

MAY

1-2 .... Portland
3-4-5 .... Reading
13-14 .... Portland
16-17-18 .... Binghamton
19-20-21....... Harrisburg
30-31 .... Akron

JUNE

1.......................... Akron
3-4 .... Bowie
16-17-18 ....Re ading
19-20-21-22 New Britain

JULY

4-5-6 .... New Haven
12-13-14............. Bowie
15-16 .... Harrisburg
22-23 .... Reading
24-25-26-27 Binghamton

AUGUST

1-2-3 .... Akron
4-5-6-7.......... Harrisburg
15-16-17 ..... New Britain
19-20-21 .... Portland
25-26-27-28 ..... Norwich

Southern League

Birmingham

APRIL

3-4-5-6........... Knoxville.
12-13-14-15..... Carolina
25-26-27........ Huntsville

MAY

8-9-10-11 ...... Greenville
12-13-14-15........ Mobile
24-25-26-27.... Memphis
29-30-31........... Orlando

JUNE

1 .... Orlando
7-8-9-10.... Chattanooga
15-16-17-18 Jacksonville
23-24-25-26........ Mobile

JULY

4-5-6 .... Jacksonville
17-18-19-20..... Carolina
22-23-24-25 Chattanooga
31 .... Huntsville

AUGUST

1-2-3 .... Huntsville
4-5-6-7............ Memphis
8-9-10-11.......... Orlando
21-22-23-24 .. Greenville
29-30-31 .... Knoxville

SEPTEMBER

1...................... Knoxville

Carolina

APRIL

3-4-5-6................ Mobile
17-18-19-20...... Orlando
21-22-23......... Memphis

MAY

8-9-10-11 ... Jacksonville
12-13-14-15... Huntsville
29-30-31 .... Greenville

JUNE

1.................... Greenville
3-4-5-6 .... Birmingham
11-12-13-14 Chatanooga
15-16-17-18.... Knoxville
27-28-29-30 Jacksonville

JULY

1-2-3 .... Knoxville
9-10-11-12 .... Greenville
13-14-15-16... Huntsville
31 .... Mobile

AUGUST

1-2-3.................. Mobile
4-5-6-7...... Chattanooga
16-17-18-19 Birmingham
21-22-23-24.... Memphis
29-30-31........... Orlando

SEPTEMBER

1 .... Orlando

Chattanooga

APRIL

3-4-5-6............. Orlando
8-9-10-11 .... Knoxville
21-22-23 .... Birmingham

MAY

3-4-5-6 .... Carolina
8-9-10-11............ Mobile
12-13-14-15 Jacksonville
24-25-26-27 .. Greenville
29-30-31 .... Huntsville

JUNE

1 .... Huntsville
15-16-17-18.... Memphis
19-20-21-22.... Knoxville

JULY

1-2-3 .... Huntsville
9-10-11-12 . Birmingham
26-27-28-29 .. Greenville
31 .... Orlando

AUGUST

1-2-3................. Orlando
12-13-14-15..... Carolina
16-17-18-19 Jacksonville
21-22-23-24........ Mobile
29-30-31 .... Memphis

SEPTEMBER

1 .... Memphis

Greenville

APRIL

3-4-5-6........... Memphis
8-9-10-11 ... Birmingham
17-18-19-19 Jacksonville
25-26-27 .... Carolina

MAY

3-4-5-6........... Knoxville
16-17-18-19... Huntsville
20-21-22-23........ Mobile

JUNE

3-4-5-6...... Chattanooga
15-16-17-18...... Orlando
23-24-25-26... Huntsville
27-28-29-30.... Memphis

JULY

1-2-3........... Birmingham
13-14-15-16 Jacksonville
18-19-20-21........ Mobile
31.................... Knoxville

AUGUST

1-2-2 .... Knoxville
8-9-10-11.......... Carolina
16-17-18-19...... Orlando
25-26-27-28 Chattanooga

Huntsville

APRIL

12-13-14-15 Jacksonville
17-18-19-20 Chattanooga
21-22-23 .... Knoxville
29-30............ Greenville

MAY

1-2................. Greenville
3-4-5-6 .... Birmingham
20-21-22-23.... Memphis
24-25-26-27........ Mobile

JUNE

7-8-9-10........... Carolina
11-12-13-14 ..... Orlando
19-20-21-22 Birmingham
27-28-29-30........ Mobile

JULY

4-5-6 .... Carolina
18-19-20-21 Chattanooga
22-23-24-25 . Greenville

AUGUST

4-5-6-7....... Jacksonville
8-9-10-11........ Memphis
12-13-14-15...... Orlando
21-22-23-24.... Knoxville

Jacksonville

APRIL

3-4-5-6........... Huntsville
8-9-10-11 .... Mobile
21-22-23........... Orlando
29-30 .... Chattanooga

MAY
1-2 .... Chattanooga
3-4-5-6 .... Memphis
16-17-18-19 ..... Carolina
20-21-22-23 Birmingham

JUNE
7-8-9-10 .... Knoxville
11-12-13-14 .. Greenville
19-20-21-22 ..... Carolina
23-24-25-26 Chattanooga

JULY
1-2-3 .... Orlando
9-10-11-12 ..... Huntsville
20-21 .... Knoxville
22-23-24-25 .... Memphis
26-27-28-29 .... Knoxville

AUGUST
8-9-10-11 .... Mobile
12-13-14-15 Birmingham
29-30-31 .... Greenville

SEPTEMBER
1 .... Greenville

Knoxville

APRIL
12-13-14-15 .. Greenville
17-18-19-20 .... Memphis
25-26-27 .... Jacksonville
29-30 .... Birmingham

MAY
1-2 .... Birmingham
8-9-10-11 .... Huntsville
12-13-14-15 ...... Orlando
20-21-22-23 Chattanooga
24-25-26-27 ..... Carolina

JUNE
11-12-13-14 .... Mobile
23-24-25-26 .... Memphis
27-28-29-30. Birmingham

JULY
4-5-6 .... Greenville
14-14-15-16 ...... Orlando
17-18-19-20 Jacksonville

AUGUST
4-5-6-7 .... Mobile
8-9-10-11 .. Chattanooga
16-17-18-19 ... Huntsville
25-26-27-28 ..... Carolina

Memphis

APRIL
8-9-10-11 .... Carolina
12-13-14-15 Chattanooga
25-26-27 .... Mobile

MAY
8-8-9-10 .... Orlando
12-13-14-15 .. Greenville
16-16-17-18 .... Knoxville
29-30-31 .... Jacksonville

JUNE
1 .... Jacksonville
3-4-5-6 .... Huntsville
11-12-13-14 Birmingham
19-20-21-22 .. Greenville

JULY
4-4-5 .... Chattanooga
9-10-11-12 .... Orlando
13-14-15-16 Birmingham
26-27-28-29 ..... Carolina
31 .... Jacksonville

AUGUST
1-2-3 .... Jacksonville
12-13-14-15 .... Knoxville
16-17-18-19 .... Mobile
26-26-27-28 ... Huntsville

Mobile

APRIL
17-18-19-20 Birmingham
21-22-23 .... Greenville
29-30 .... Carolina

MAY
1-2 .... Carolina
3-4-5-6 .... Orlando
16-17-18-19 Chattanooga
29-30-31 .... Knoxville

JUNE
1 .... Knoxville
3-4-5-6 .... Jacksonville
7-8-9-10 .... Memphis
15-16-17-18 ... Huntsville
19-20-21-22 ...... Orlando

JULY
1-2-3 .... Memphis
9-10-11-12 ...... Knoxville
13-14-15-16 Chattanooga
22-23-24-25 ..... Carolina
26-27-28-29. Birmingham

AUGUST
12-13-14-15 .. Greenville
25-26-27-28 Jacksonville
29-30-31 .... Huntsville

SEPTEMBER
1 .... Huntsville

Orlando

APRIL
8-9-10-11 .... Huntsville
12-13-14-15 .... Mobile
25-26-27 ... Chattanooga
29-30 .... Memphis

MAY
1-2 .... Memphis
16-17-18-19 Birmingham
20-21-22-23 ..... Carolina
24-25-26-27 Jacksonville

JUNE
3-4-5-6 .... Knoxville
7-8-9-10 .... Greenville
23-24-25-26 ..... Carolina
27-28-29-30 Chattanooga

JULY
4-5-6 .... Mobile
18-19-20-21 .... Memphis
22-23-24-25 .... Knoxville
26-27-28-29 ... Huntsville

AUGUST
4-5-6-7 .... Greenville
21-22-23-24 Jacksonsville
25-26-27-28 Birmingham

Texas League

Arkansas

APRIL
3-4-5-5-7 ...... Shreveport
19-19-21-22-23 .... Tulsa
24-25-26-26-28 Jackson

MAY
5-6-7-8-9 .... Midland
10-10-12-13-14. El Paso
27-28-29-30-31-31 . Shr..

JUNE
9-10-11-12-13-14.. Jack.
27-28-28-30 .... Tulsa

JULY
1-2 .... Tulsa
17-18-19-19-21-22 Wich.
23-24-25-26-26-28 .... S.A.

AUGUST
5-6-7-8-9 .... Tulsa
11-12-13-14-15 Jackson
26-27-28-29-30-31 .. Shr.

El Paso

APRIL
8-9-10-11-12 ..... Midland
14-15-16-17-18 . Wichita
29-30 .... San Antonio

MAY
1-2-3 .... San Antonio
16-17-18-19-20 Jackson
21-22-23-24-25 Arkansas

JUNE
2-3-4-5-6-7 .... Midland
9-10-11-12-13-14 .. Wich.
27-28-29-30 .... S.A.

JULY
1-2 .... San Antonio
17-18-19-20-21-22 Shreve.
23-24-25-26-27-28. Tulsa

AUGUST
6-7-8-9-10 .... Midland
11-12-13-14-15 . Wichita
26-27-28-29-30 ...... S.A.

Jackson

APRIL
3-4-5-6-7 .... Tulsa
14-15-16-17-18 Arkansas
19-20-21-22-23 .. Shreve.

MAY
5-6-7-8-9 .... El Paso
10-11-12-13-14. Midland
26-27-28-29-30-31 Tulsa

JUNE
15-16-17-18-19-20.. Ark.
27-28-29-30. Shreveport

JULY
1-2 .... Shreveport
10-11-12-13-14-15. Wich.
16-17-18-19-20-21 ... S.A.

AUGUST
5-6-7-8-9...... Shreveport
21-22-23-24-25 .... Ark.
26-27-28-29-30 .... Tulsa

Midland

APRIL
14-15-16-17-18 ...... S.A.
24-25-26-27-28.. El Paso
29-30 .... Wichita

MAY
1-2-3 .... Wichita
16-17-18-19-20 .... Ark.
21-22-23-24-25 . Jackson

JUNE
9-10-11-12-13-14 ... S.A.
15-16-17-18-19-20 El Paso
27-28-29-30 .... Wichita

JULY
1-2 .... Wichita
17-18-19-20-21-22 Tulsa
23-24-25-26-27-28 Shreve.
31 .... Wichita

AUGUST
1-2-3-4 .... Wichita
11-12-13-14-15 ...... S.A.
16-17-18-19-20. El Paso

San Antonio

APRIL
3-4-5-6-7 .... Midland
19-20-21-22-23. El Paso
24-25-26-27-28 . Wichita

MAY
5-6-7-8-9 .... Tulsa
10-11-12-13-14... Shreve.
27-28-29-30-31. Midland

JUNE
1 .... Midland
15-16-17-18-19-20 Wich.
21-22-23-24-25-26 . El Paso

JULY
3-4-5-5-8-9 .... Jackson
10-11-12-13-14-15.. Ark.
31 .... El Paso

AUGUST
1-2-3-4 .... El Paso
5-6-7-8-9 .... Wichita
21-22-23-24-25. Midland

Shreveport

APRIL
8-9-10-11-12.... Jackson
24-25-26-27-28 .... Tulsa
29-30............. Arkansas

MAY
1-2-3............... Arkansas
16-17-18-19-20 . Wichita
21-22-23-24-25 ...... S.A.

JUNE
2-3-4-5-6-7....... Jackson
9-10-11-12-13-14 . Tulsa
21-22-23-24-25-26.. Ark.

JULY
3-4-5-6-8-9........ El Paso
10-11-12-13-14-15 .. Mid.
31 .... Arkansas

AUGUST
1-2-3-4 .... Arkansas
16-17-18-19-20 Jackson
21-22-23-24-25 .... Tulsa

Tulsa

APRIL
9-10-11-12-13 Arkansas
14-15-16-17-18. Shreve.
30..................... Jackson

MAY
1-2-3-4 .... Jackson
16-17-18-19-20 ...... S.A.
21-22-23-24-25 . Wichita

JUNE
3-4-5-6-7-8..... Arkansas
15-16-17-18-19-20 Shreve.
21-22-23-24-25-26 .. Jack.

JULY
3-4-5-6-8-9........ Midland
10-11-12-13-14-15 El Paso
31..................... Jackson

AUGUST
1-2-3-4 .... Jackson
11-12-13-14-15 .. Shreve.
16-17-18-19-20....... Ark.

Wichita

APRIL
3-4-5-6-7........... El Paso
8-9-10-11-12 San Antonio
19-20-21-22-23. Midland

MAY
5-6-7-8-9...... Shreveport
10-11-12-13-14 .... Tulsa
27-28-29-30-31 . El Paso

JUNE
1......................... El Paso
3-4-5-6-7-8 San Antonio
21-22-23-24-25-26 .. Mid.

JULY
3-4-4-5-6-8..... Arkansas
24-25-26-27-28 . Jackson

AUGUST
16-17-18-19-20 ...... S.A.
21-22-23-24-25. El Paso
26-27-28-29-30. Midland

CLASS A

California League

Bakersfield

APRIL

3-4-5 .... Modesto
6-7 .... High Desert
8 .... Lancaster
23-24-25 .... Visalia
26-27-28 R. Cucamonga

MAY

2-3-4-5 .... Stockton
13-14 .... Lancaster
15 .... High Desert
21-22-23 .. Lake Elsinore
24-25-26 .... San Bern.
30-31 .... Visalia

JUNE

1 .... Visalia
6-7-8 .... Modesto
9-10-11-12 ..... San Jose
19-20-21 R. Cucamonga
22-23-24 .... San Jose

JULY

2-3-4 .... Lake Elsinore
8-9-10 .... High Desert
16-17-18 .... Stockton
23-24-25 .... San Jose
26-27-28 .... San Bern.

AUGUST

1-2-3-4 .... Modesto
12-13-14 .... Stockton
15-16-17-18 .... Visalia
23-24-25 .... Lancaster

High Desert

APRIL

8 .... Stockton
9-10-11 .. R. Cucamonga
12-13-14 .... Visalia
18-19-20-21 Lake Elsinore
29-30 .... San Bern.

MAY

1 .... San Bern.
7-8-9 .... Bakersfield
10-11-11 .... San Jose
13-14 .... Stockton
21-22-23 R. Cucamonga
24-25-26-26 ... Lancaster
30-31 .... Modesto

JUNE

1 .... Modesto
3*-4*-5 .... San Bern.
19-20-21 .... San Jose
22-23-24 .... Modesto

JULY

5-6-7 .... Lancaster
16-17-18 .. Lake Elsinore
19-20 ..... R. Cucamonga
26-27-28 .... Stockton
29-30-31 .. Lake Elsinore

AUGUST

1-2-3 .... Lancaster
9-10-11 .... Bakersfield
12-13 ..... R. Cucamonga
15-16-17-18 .. San Bern.
26-27-28 .... Visalia

*At Phoenix

Lake Elsinore

APRIL

9-10-11 .... Visalia
12-13-14 .... Lancaster
15-16-17 ...... Bakersfield
23-24-25 .... San Jose
26-27-28 .... Stockton

MAY

2-3-4-5 ....San Bern.
13-14-15 .... Modesto
27-28-29 ..... High Desert
30-31 .... Lancaster

JUNE

1 .... Lancaster
9-10-11-12 ...... R. Cuca.
13-14-15 ..... High Desert
23-24 .... San Bern.
25-26-27 .... Stockton
28-29-30 R. Cucamonga

JULY

5-6-7 .... San Jose
14 .... San Bern.
19-20-21-22 ... Lancaster
26-27-28 R. Cucamonga

AUGUST

1-2-3-4 .... Visalia
6-7-8 .... High Desert
9-10-11 .... Modesto
26-27-28 ...... Bakersfield
29-30-31 .... San Bern.

Lancaster

APRIL

3-4-5 .... High Desert
6-7 .... Stockton
9-10-11 .... San Bern.
18 .... San Bern.
23-24-25 R. Cucamonga
26-27-28 .... San Jose
29-30 .... Bakersfield

MAY

1 .... Bakersfield
15 .... Stockton
16-17-18-19 .... L.E.
21-22-23 .... Modesto
27-28-29 .... Visalia

JUNE

6-7-8 ...... R. Cucamonga
10-11-12 ..... High Desert
19-20-21 .. Lake Elsinore
22-23-24 .... Visalia
28-29-30 ...... Bakersfield

JULY

2-3-4 .... Modesto
8-9-10 ...... Lake Elsinore
11-12-13-14 .... R. Cuca.
16-17-18 .... San Bern.
26-27-28 .... San Jose

AUGUST

4 .... High Desert
9-10-11 .... Stockton
12-13-14 .... San Bern.
20-21-22 ..... High Desert

Modesto

APRIL

9-10-11 .... San Jose
12-13-14 .... San Bern.
15-16-17 .... Stockton
23-24-25 ..... High Desert
26-27-28 .... Visalia

MAY

7-8-9 ...... R. Cucamonga
10-11-12 .... Lancaster
16-17-18-19. Bakersfield
24-25-26 .... San Jose

JUNE

3-4-5 .... Lake Elsinore
12 .... Stockton
13-14-15 .... Visalia
25-26-27 ...... Bakersfield
28-29-30 .... Stockton

JULY

5-6-7 .... San Bern.
11-12-13-14... High Des.
16-17-18 R. Cucamonga
23-24-25 .. Lake Elsinore
26-27-28 .... Visalia

AUGUST

15-16-17-18 ... San Jose
20-21-22 ...... Bakersfield
26-27-28 .... Lancaster
29-30-31 .... Stockton

R. Cucamonga

APRIL

3-4-5 .... San Jose
6-7-8 .... Modesto
15-16-17 .... San Bern.
18-19-20-21. Bakersfield
29-30 .... Lake Elsinore

MAY

1 .... Lake Elsinore
2-3-4-5 .... High Desert
10-11-12 .... Visalia
24-25-26 .. Lake Elsinore
27-28-29 .... Stockton
30-31 .... San Bern.

JUNE

1 .... San Bern.
13-14-15 .... Lancaster
25-26-27 .... Lancaster

JULY

5-6-7 .... Stockton
8-9-10 .... Modesto
21-22 .... High Desert
23-24-25 .... Lancaster
29-30-31 .... Visalia

AUGUST

2-3-4 .... San Bern.
6-7-8 .... Bakersfield
14 .... High Desert
15-16-17-18 .... L.E.
20-21-22 .... San Jose
28 .... San Bern.
29-30-31 ..... High Desert

San Bernardino

APRIL

3-4-5 .... Lake Elsinore
6-7-8 .... San Jose
19-20-21 .... Lancaster
23-24-25 .... Stockton
26-27-28 ..... High Desert

MAY

7-8-9 .... Lancaster
10-11-12 .. Lake Elsinore
16-17-18-19 .... R. Cuca.
27-28-29 .... Modesto

JUNE

9-10-11-12 .... Visalia
13-14-15 ...... Bakersfield
19-20-21 .... Modesto
22 .... Lake Elsinore

JULY

2-3-4 ..... R. Cucamonga
8-9-10 .... Visalia
11-12-13 .. Lake Elsinore
19-20-21-22. Bakersfield
23-24-25 ..... High Desert
29-30-31 .... Lancaster

AUGUST

1 .... R. Cucamonga
6-7-8 .... Stockton
9-10-11 .... San Jose
23-24-25 ..... High Desert
26-27 ..... R. Cucamonga

San Jose

APRIL

12-13-14 ...... Bakersfield
15-16-17 .... Lancaster
21 .... Stockton

MAY

2-3-4-5 .... Modesto
7-8-9 .... Visalia

13-14-15........ San Bern.
16-17-18-19... High Des.
27-28-29...... Bakersfield
30-31 .... Stockton

JUNE

3-4-5...... R. Cucamonga
6-7-8........ Lake Elsinore
13-14-15.......... Stockton
25-26-27..... High Desert
28-29-30........ San Bern.

JULY

2-3-4 .... Visalia
11-12-13-14. Bakersfield
16-17-18 .... Visalia
29-30-31.......... Modesto

AUGUST

1 .... Stockton
6-7-8................ Modesto
12-13-14 . Lake Elsinore
23-24-25 R. Cucamonga
26-27-28.......... Stockton
29-30-31........ Lancaster

Stockton

APRIL

9-10-11........ Bakersfield
12-13-14 R. Cucamonga
18-19-20......... San Jose
29-30 .... Modesto

MAY

1 .... Modesto
7-8-9........ Lake Elsinore
10-11-12...... Bakersfield
16-17-18-19........ Visalia
21-22-23........ San Bern.

JUNE

1 .... San Jose
3-4-5.............. Lancaster
6-7-8........... High Desert
9-10-11............ Modesto
19-20-21 .... Visalia
22-23-24 R. Cucamonga

JULY

2-3-4........... High Desert
8-9-10............. San Jose
19-20-21-22..... Modesto
23-24-25 .... Visalia
29-30-31...... Bakersfield

AUGUST

2-3-4.............. San Jose
15-16-17-18... Lancaster
20-21-22........ San Bern.
23-24-25.. Lake Elsinore

Visalia

APRIL

3-4-5............... Stockton
6-7-8........ Lake Elsinore
15-16-17..... High Desert
18-19-20-21..... Modesto
29-30............. San Jose

MAY

1 .... San Jose
2-3-4-5........... Lancaster
13-14-15 R. Cucamonga
21-22-23......... San Jose
24-25-26.......... Stockton

JUNE

3-4-5........... Bakersfield
6-7-8............. San Bern.
25-26-27........ San Bern.
28-29-30..... High Desert

JULY

5-6-7........... Bakersfield
11-12-13-14 .... Stockton
19-20-21-22 ... San Jose

AUGUST

6-7-8............. Lancaster
9-10-11.. R. Cucamonga
12-13-14.......... Modesto
20-21-22.. Lake Elsinore
23-24-25.......... Modesto
29-30-31...... Bakersfield

Carolina League

Durham

APRIL

8-9-10................ Kinston
11-12-13...... Wilmington
21-22-23-24 ... Frederick
25-26-27 .... Salem

MAY

5-6-7-8.... Prince William
9-10-11......... Lynchburg
19-20-21................. W-S
26-27-28-29 ...... Kinston
30-31 .... Wilmington

JUNE

1 .... Wilmington
10-11-12......... Frederick
13-14-15....... Lynchburg
25-26-27. Prince William

JULY

5-6-7 .... Salem
9-10-11 . Winston-Salem
15-16-17............ Kinston
18-19-20-21. Wilmington
28-29-30......... Frederick

AUGUST

1-2-3-4.......... Lynchburg
12-13-14. Prince William
23-24-25-26 .... Salem
27-28-29-30 .... W-S

Frederick

APRIL

11-12-13 .... Salem
15-16-17....... Lynchburg
25-26-27...... Wilmington
28-29-30........... Durham

MAY

1 .... Durham
5-6-7-8.. Winston-Salem
16-17-18............ Kinston
19-20-21. Prince William
26-27-28-29 .... Salem
30-31 .... Lynchburg

JUNE

1 .... Lynchburg
13-14-15...... Wilmington
19-20-21........... Durham
25-26-27................ W-S

JULY

5-6-7................. Kinston
9-10-11... Prince William
18-19-20-21.. Lynchburg
22-23-24 .... Salem

AUGUST

1-2-3-4.... Prince William
5-6-7................ Durham
12-13-14................. W-S
23-24-25-26 ...... Kinston
27-28-29-30. Wilmington

Kinston

APRIL

11-12-13................. W-S
14-15-16-17...... Durham
25-26-27. Prince William
28-29-30....... Lynchburg

MAY

1 .... Lynchburg
5-6-7-8 .... Salem
9-10-11............. Kinston
19-20-21 ...... Wilmington
30-31 .... Winston-Salem

JUNE

1........... Winston-Salem
3-4-5................ Durham
13-14-15. Prince William
19-20-21 .... Salem
25-26-27....... Lynchburg
28-29-30......... Frederick

JULY

1 .... Frederick
9-10-11........ Wilmington
18-19-20-21 .... W-S
22-23-24........... Durham

AUGUST

1-2-3-4......... Wilmington
5-6-7 .... Salem
12-13-14....... Lynchburg
15-16-17......... Frederick
27-28-29-30 . Pr. William

Lynchburg

APRIL

8-9-10............ Frederick
11-12-13. Prince William
21-22-23-24 ...... Kinston
25-26-27................ W-S

MAY

5-6-7-8......... Wilmington
14-15................... Salem
16-17-18........... Durham
21 .... Salem
22-23-24-25...... Durham
27-28-29...... Wilmington

JUNE

6-7-8................. Kinston
9-10-11-12 .... W-S
22-23-24......... Frederick
28-29-30. Prince William

JULY

1 .... Prince William
3-4...................... Salem
9-10-11 .... Salem
12-13-14........... Durham
15-16-17...... Wilmington
25-26-27........... Kinston
29-30-31................ W-S

AUGUST

8-9-10-11 .... Frederick
15-16-17. Prince-William
21-22.................... Salem

Prince William

APRIL

4-5-6.................. Kinston
8-9-10 ... Winston-Salem
18-19-20......... Frederick
21-22-23-24. Wilmington

MAY

2-3-4............ Lynchburg
13-14-15........... Durham
16-17-18 .... Salem
22-23-24-25 .... Salem
26-27-28-29 .... W-S

JUNE

6-7-8-9............. Durham
10-11-12...... Wilmington
22-23-24............ Kinston

JULY

2-3-4............... Frederick
5-6-7............ Lynchburg
12-13-14 .... Salem
15-16-17................. W-S
25-26-27........... Durham
29-30-31...... Wilmington

AUGUST

8-9-10-11 .... Kinston
19-20-21-22 ... Frederick
23-24-25-26.. Lynchburg

Salem

APRIL

4-5-6................. Durham

7-8-9-10....... Wilmington
18-19-20............ Kinston
22-23-24................. W-S

MAY

2-3-4............... Frederick
9-10-11 ... Prince William
13 .... Lynchburg
19-20 .... Lynchburg
30-31 ...... Prince William

JUNE

1 .... Prince William
2-3-4-5........... Frederick
9-10-11-12 .... Kinston
13-14-15................ W-S
25-26-27...... Wilmington
28-29-30........... Durham

JULY

1 .... Durham
2 .... Lynchburg
15-16-17......... Frederick
18-19-20-21 .. Pr. William
28-29-30............ Kinston

AUGUST

1-2-3-4 .. Winston-Salem
12-13-14...... Wilmington
15-16-17........... Durham
19-20 .... Lynchburg
27-28-29-30.. Lynchburg

Wilmington

APRIL

4-5-6.............. Frederick
14-15-16-17 .... Salem
18-19-20....... Lynchburg
28-29-30. Prince William

MAY

1 .... Prince William
2-3-4................ Durham
13-14-15........... Kinston
16-17-18................ W-S
22-23-24-25 ... Frederick

JUNE

2-3-4-5......... Lynchburg
6-7-8 .... Salem
19-20-21 ..Prince William
22-23-24.......... Durham
28-29-30................ W-S

JULY

1........... Winston-Salem
2-3-4................. Kinston
12-13-14......... Frederick
22-23-24....... Lynchburg
25- 26-27 .... Salem

AUGUST

5-6-7....... Prince William
8-9-10-11......... Durham
15-16-17................ W-S
19-20-21-22 ...... Kinston

Winston-Salem

APRIL

4-5-6-7......... Lynchburg
14-15-16-17... Pr. William
18-19-20........... Durham
29-30.................. Salem

MAY

1 .... Salem
2-3-4................. Kinston
9-10-11 .... Wilmington
12-13-14-15 ... Frederick
22-23-24-25 ....Kinston

JUNE

3-4-5....... Prince William
6-7-8.............. Frederick
19-20-21 .... Lynchburg
22-23-24 .... Salem

JULY

2-3-4................ Durham
5-6-7........... Wilmington
12-13-14............ Kinston
22-23-24. Prince William
25-26-27......... Frederick

AUGUST

5-6-7............ Lynchburg
8-9-10-11 .... Salem
19-20-21-22...... Durham
23-24-25-26. Wilmington

Florida State League

Brevard County

APRIL

3.................. West Palm
5 .... Vero Beach
8-9.................. St. Lucie
11-12-13-14 .... Tampa
15-16-17-18. Clearwater
26 .... Vero Beach
28-29 .... Kissimmee

MAY

2 .... Kissimmee
4-5 .... Daytona
14-15-16-17 St. Petersburg
19-20-21-22..... Dunedin
24................ West Palm
25 .... Kissimmee
29 .... Vero Beach
31..................... Daytona

JUNE

1...................... Daytona
3-4 .... Vero Beach
5-6 .... West Palm
15 .... Kissimmee
18-19 .... West Palm
23.....................St. Lucie
25-26-27-28.... Lakeland
30.................... Daytona

JULY

4-5 .... Daytona
6-7 .... West Palm
9-10 .... Kissimmee
14-15-16-17.... Charlotte
18-19-20-21 .... Sarasota
30-31........... Fort Myers

AUGUST

1-2............... Fort Myers
4...................... St. Lucie
14 .... Vero Beach
16-17 .... Vero Beach
21 .... Kissimmee
25.................... Daytona
26..................... St. Lucie
30 .... St. Lucie

Charlotte

APRIL

4.................. Fort Myers
7-8-9-10............ Daytona
11-12-13-14. Kissimmee
22-23...... St. Petersburg
24-25-26-27 ..... Dunedin

MAY

2-3-4-5 .... Tampa
15-16 .... Lakeland
19-20 .... Clearwater
21-22 .... Sarasota
26.......... St. Petersburg
31 .... Lakeland

JUNE

1 .... Lakeland
3-4 .... Sarasota
9-10............ Fort Myers
11-12-13-14...... Brevard
18.................... Sarasota
19 .... Lakeland
24 .... Lakeland

JULY

2-3...................... Tampa
9.................. Fort Myers
10-11 .... Lakeland
18-19-20-21 .... St. Lucie
22-23-24-25. West Palm

AUGUST

4.................. Fort Myers
6-7-8-9........ Vero Beach
11-12-13. St. Petersburg
15-16........... Fort Myers
18.................... Sarasota
22-23 .... Dunedin
25-26-27-28. Clearwater
31 .... Fort Myers

Clearwater

APRIL

4...................... Dunedin
6............ St. Petersburg
11-12-13-14 Vero Beach
19.................... Dunedin
22-23-24-25 .... St. Lucie
26......................... Tampa
28-29 .... Lakeland
30 .... Charlotte

MAY

1 .... Charlotte
2-3-4-5 .... West Palm
7............ St. Petersburg
9............ St. Petersburg
11..................... Dunedin
13..................... Dunedin
21-22........... Fort Myers
23-24 .... Charlotte
26........................ Tampa
30-31 .... Sarasota

JUNE

1...................... Sarasota
3.......................... Tampa
4 .... St. Petersburg
5...................... Sarasota
15-16 .... Dunedin
19........... St. Petersburg
23-24.................... Tampa
25-26-27-28 . Fort Myers

JULY

1-2-3....... St. Petersburg
6-7 .... Lakeland
12..................... Dunedin
22-23-24-25..... Daytona
26 .... Lakeland
29 .... Lakeland
30.................... Sarasota

AUGUST

2...................... Sarasota
10-11-12-13...... Brevard
14-15-16-17. Kissimmee
20-21 .... Charlotte
22......................... Tampa
31..................... Dunedin

Daytona

APRIL

5-6 .... Kissimmee
15-16-17-18 .... Tampa
19-20.... Brevard County
30......... Brevard County

MAY

1 .... Brevard County
2-3.................. St. Lucie
6-7-8-9............. Dunedin
10-12-13. St. Petersburg
19-20-21-22 Vero Beach
25-26-27-28. West Palm
29-30.............. St. Lucie

JUNE

11-12-13-14. Clearwater
18-19 .... Vero Beach
23-24 .... West Palm
26-27-28...... Kissimmee

JULY

1-2........ Brevard County
9-10-11-12 ..... St. Lucie

14-15-16-17 ... Sarasota
26-27-28-29 . Fort Myers
30-31 .... Charlotte

AUGUST

1-2 .... Charlotte
4 .... Kissimmee
9 .... Kissimmee
18-19-20-21 .... Lakeland
22-23.... Brevard County
28-29 .... Vero Beach

Dunedin

APRIL

3.................. Clearwater
5-6 .... Charlotte
7-8-9-10 .... West Palm
13-14 .... Lakeland
17-18...... St. Petersburg
20................ Clearwater
23................... Sarasota

MAY

3............ St. Petersburg
4-5 .... Lakeland
10................ Clearwater
14................ Clearwater
23-24................. Tampa
25-26-27-28 . Fort Myers
29................... Sarasota

JUNE

4-5...................... Tampa
7-8-9-10...... Vero Beach
11-12-13-14 .... St. Lucie
17-18 .... Clearwater
23-24........... Fort Myers
25-26-27-28-30 Sarasota

JULY

1 .... Charlotte
5-6.......... St. Petersburg
11................ Clearwater
18-19-20-21 ..... Daytona
22-23-24-25...... Brevard

AUGUST

4.................. Clearwater
5........................ Tampa
6............ St. Petersburg
8-9.................. Lakeland
10-11-12-13. Kissimmee
14....................... Tampa
16....................... Tampa
25....................... Tampa
29-30 .... Charlotte

Fort Myers

APRIL

3 .... Charlotte
5-6...................... Tampa
7-8 .... Sarasota
11-12-13-14..... Daytona
15-16-17-18. Kissimmee
26-27 .... Lakeland
28-29 .... Dunedin
30.......... St. Petersburg

MAY

1............ St. Petersburg
10-11-12-13...... Brevard
15-16-17-18. Clearwater
19-20 .... Sarasota
29-30 .... Charlotte
31.......... St. Petersburg

JUNE

1............ St. Petersburg
7-8 .... Charlotte
15-16-17-18.... Lakeland
19................... Sarasota

JULY

3..................... Sarasota
4-5-6-7 .... Tampa
10................... Sarasota
18-19-20-21 . West Palm
22-23-24-25 .... St. Lucie

AUGUST

5 .... Charlotte
9...................... Sarasota
10-11-12-13 Vero Beach
14 .... Charlotte

17 .... Charlotte
18-19-20-21 ..... Dunedin
22-23...... St. Petersburg
29-30 .... Clearwater

Kissimmee

APRIL

3-4 .... Daytona
7-8-9-10 . St. Petersburg
19-20.......... Vero Beach
21-22.... Brevard County
24-25-26-27 . West Palm

MAY

3.......... Brevard County
4-5.................. St. Lucie
15-16-17-18..... Dunedin
21-22............... St. Lucie
23-24 .... Daytona
26......... Brevard County

JUNE

3-4 .... Daytona
7-8-9-10....... Clearwater
11-12-13-14 .... Tampa
16-17.......... Vero Beach
25..................... Daytona
30................ West Palm

JULY

1.................. West Palm
4-5-6-7 .... St. Lucie
14-15-16-17 . Fort Myers
26-27-28-29.... Charlotte
30-31 .... Lakeland

AUGUST

1-2 .... Lakeland
5-6-7-8............ Sarasota
18-19-20........... Brevard
22-23.......... Vero Beach
25-26 .... West Palm
27......... Brevard County
30.................... Daytona

Lakeland

APRIL

4............ St. Petersburg
7-8-9-10....... Clearwater
11-12 .... Dunedin
20 .... St. Petersburg
22-23-24-25..... Daytona
30...................... Tampa

MAY

1........................ Tampa
2..................... Sarasota
6-7-8-9......... Kissimmee
17-18 .... Charlotte
27-28 .... Charlotte
29-30...... St. Petersburg

JUNE

3-4-5-6 .... Fort Myers
7-8-9-10............ Brevard
13-14 .... Sarasota
23 .... Charlotte
30................... Sarasota

JULY

2-3 .... Dunedin
4-5 .... Charlotte
9..................... Dunedin
12 .... Charlotte
14-15...... St. Petersburg
20-21.................. Tampa
22-23-24-25 Vero Beach
27-28 .... Clearwater

AUGUST

4..................... Sarasota
6-7............... Fort Myers
10-11-12-13 . West Palm
14-15-16-17 .... St. Lucie
22.................... Sarasota
26-27 .... Tampa
28..................... Dunedin
29-30 .... Sarasota

St. Lucie

APRIL

3 .... Vero Beach
5................. West Palm

7.......... Brevard County
10......... Brevard County
11-12-13-14.... Sarasota
15-16-17-18.... Charlotte
30 .... Kissimmee

MAY

1 .... Kissimmee
6-7-8-9 ....Fort Myers
10-11 ....Vero Beach
15................. West Palm
17-18 .... Daytona
19-20 ....Kissimmee
23-24-25-26.....Lakeland
27-28.... Brevard County
31 .... Vero Beach

JUNE

3.................. West Palm
5-6 .... Daytona
15-16-17 .... Daytona
18-19 .... Kissimmee
24......... Brevard County
27-28 .... West Palm
30 .... Vero Beach

JULY

1-2 .... Vero Beach
3....................... Daytona
14-15-16-17..... Dunedin
26-27-28-29 .... Tampa
30-31.......St. Petersburg

AUGUST

1-2.......... St. Petersburg
5-6-7-8......... Clearwater
9.................. West Palm
18 .... Vero Beach
22-23 .... West Palm
28-29.... Brevard County
31 .... Brevard County

St. Petersburg

APRIL

3 .... Lakeland
5.................. Clearwater
11-12-13-14. West Palm
15-16 .... Dunedin
19 .... Lakeland
26-27-28-29 .... St. Lucie

MAY

2...................... Dunedin
4-5 .... Sarasota
6.................. Clearwater
8.................. Clearwater
19-20-21-22 .... Tampa
23-24........... Fort Myers
25 .... Charlotte

JUNE

3...................... Dunedin
5-6 .... Charlotte
9-10 .... Sarasota
11-12-13-14 Vero Beach
16-17 .... Charlotte
18....................... Tampa
30................ Clearwater

JULY

4...................... Dunedin
7...................... Dunedin
9.................. Clearwater
10.................... Dunedin
12...................... Tampa
13 .... Lakeland
17 .... Lakeland
18-19-20-21 . Kissimmee
23-24 .... Sarasota
26-27-28-29...... Brevard

AUGUST

5 .... Lakeland
7...................... Dunedin
8................. Fort Myers
9.................. Clearwater
10 .... Charlotte
14-15-16-17 ..... Daytona
25-26-27 ...... Fort Myers
28...................... Tampa
30...................... Tampa
31 .... Lakeland

Sarasota

APRIL

3 .... Tampa
5-6 .... Lakeland
9-10 .... Fort Myers
19-20 .... Charlotte
22 .... Dunedin
24-25 .... Fort Myers
26-27-28-29 .... Daytona
30 .... Dunedin

MAY

1 .... Dunedin
3 .... Lakeland
6-7-8-9 . Brevard County
10-11-12-13. Kissimmee
16-17-18 .... Tampa
27-28 .... Clearwater

JUNE

6 .... Dunedin
7-8 .... St. Petersburg
11-12 .... Lakeland
15 .... Charlotte
23-24 .... St. Petersburg

JULY

1 .... Lakeland
2 .... Fort Myers
4-5 .... Clearwater
6-7 .... Charlotte
9 .... Tampa
11-12 .... Fort Myers
22 .... St. Petersburg
25 .... St. Petersburg
26-27-28-29 Vero Beach
31 .... Clearwater

AUGUST

1 .... Clearwater
10-11-12-13 .... St. Lucie
14-15-16-17 . West Palm
19 .... Charlotte
21 .... Tampa
23 .... Lakeland
25 .... Lakeland
26-27 .... Dunedin
28 .... Fort Myers

Tampa

APRIL

4 .... Sarasota
7-8-9-10 .... Vero Beach
19-20-21-22 . Fort Myers
24-25 .... St. Petersburg
27 .... Clearwater
28-29 .... Charlotte

MAY

6-7-8-9 .... West Palm
10-11 .... Lakeland
13-14 .... Lakeland
15 .... Sarasota
25 .... Clearwater
27-28 .... St. Petersburg
29 .... Clearwater
30-31 .... Dunedin

JUNE

1 .... Dunedin
6 .... Clearwater
7-8-9-10 .... St. Lucie
15 .... St. Petersburg
16-17 .... Sarasota
19 .... Dunedin
25-26-27-28 .... Charlotte
29-30 .... Fort Myers

JULY

10 .... Clearwater
11 .... St. Petersburg
18-19 .... Lakeland
22-23-24-25. Kissimmee

AUGUST

4 .... St. Petersburg
6-7-8-9 . Brevard County
10-11-12-13 .... Daytona
15 .... Dunedin
17 .... Dunedin
18-19 .... Clearwater
20 .... Sarasota
23 .... Clearwater
29 .... St. Petersburg
31 .... Sarasota

Vero Beach

APRIL

4 .... St. Lucie
6 .... Brevard County
15-16-17-18 .... Lakeland
22-23 .... West Palm
24-25 .... Brevard County
27 .... Brevard County
28 .... West Palm

MAY

2-3-4-5 .... Fort Myers
6-7-8-9 .... Charlotte
13-14 .... St. Lucie
15-16 .... Daytona
18 .... West Palm
23-24-24-25 .... Sarasota
27-28 .... Kissimmee
30 .... Brevard County

JUNE

1 .... St. Lucie
5-6 .... Kissimmee
15 .... West Palm
23-24 .... Kissimmee
25-26-27-28 St. Petersburg

JULY

3 .... Brevard County
6-7 .... Daytona
9 .... West Palm
11-12 .... Kissimmee
14-15-16-17 .... Tampa
18-19-20-21 . Clearwater
30-31 .... Dunedin

AUGUST

1-2 .... Dunedin
4 .... West Palm
5 .... Brevard County
15 .... Brevard County
19-20-21 .... St. Lucie
25 .... St. Lucie
26-27 .... Daytona
30 .... West Palm

W. Palm Beach

APRIL

4 .... Brevard County
6 .... St. Lucie
15-16-17-18 .... Sarasota
19-20 .... St. Lucie
29-30 .... Vero Beach

MAY

1 .... Vero Beach
10-11-12-13 ... Charlotte
16 .... St. Lucie
17 .... Vero Beach
19-20-21-22 .... Lakeland
23 .... Brevard County
29-30-31 .... Kissimmee

JUNE

1 .... Kissimmee
4 .... St. Lucie
7-8-9-10 .... Daytona
11-12-13-14 . Fort Myers
16-17 .... Brevard County
25-26 .... St. Lucie

JULY

2-3 .... Kissimmee
4-5 .... Vero Beach
10 .... Vero Beach
11-12 .... Brevard County
14-15-16-17 . Clearwater
26-27-28-29 .... Dunedin
30-31 .... Tampa

AUGUST

1-2 .... Tampa
5-6-7-8 .... Daytona
18-19-20-21 St. Petersburg
27 .... St. Lucie
28-29 .... Kissimmee
31 .... Vero Beach

Midwest League

Beloit

APRIL

4-5-6-7 .... Quad City
12-13 .... Michigan
14-15-16-16 South Bend
22-23-24-25 .... Lansing

MAY

3-4 .... Peoria
5-6 .... Kane County
9-10-11-12 Cedar Rapids
20-21 .... Rockford
22-23 .... Wisconsin
24-26 .... Rockford

JUNE

3 .... Kane County
4-5 .... Peoria
8-9 .... Kane County
13 .... Kane County
14-15 .... Wisconsin
23-24-25-26... Kane Cty.
29-30 .... Rockford

JULY

4 .... Rockford
5-6-7 .... Peoria
9-10-11-12 .... Clinton
17-18-19-20 .. Burlington
31 .... Rockford

AUGUST

8-9-10-11 .... Wisconsin
16-17-18-19 Fort Wayne
25-26-27-28 .... Michigan
29-30 .... West Michigan
31 .... Peoria

Burlington

APRIL

4-5-6-7 .... Michigan
12-13 .... Quad City
14-15-16-17... Kane Cty.
22-23-24-25 .... Peoria

MAY

2 .... Cedar Rapids
3-4-5-6 .... Fort Wayne
7-8 .... Clinton
15-16-17-18 .... Beloit
22 .... Quad City
25 .... Clinton
28 .... Cedar Rapids
31 .... Cedar Rapids

JUNE

3 .... Quad City
4-5 .... Clinton
6-7 .... Cedar Rapids
9 .... Quad City
19-20-21-22. West Mich.
27-28-29-30 South Bend

JULY

6-7 .... Cedar Rapids
13-14-15-16 .. Wisconsin
22-23-24-25 .... Rockford
30-31 .... Lansing

AUGUST

1-2 .... Lansing
6-7 .... Clinton
13-14 .... Quad City
15-16-17 .... Clinton
19-20-21 .. Cedar Rapids
29-30-31 .... Quad City

Cedar Rapids

APRIL
4-5-6-7........ South Bend
12-13................. Clinton
18.................. Quad City
21.................. Quad City
22-23-24-25... Kane Cty.

MAY
1.................... Burlington
3-4-5-6... West Michigan
13.................. Quad City
15-16-17-18.... Rockford
21.................. Quad City
26-27................. Clinton
29-30............ Burlington

JUNE
1......................... Clinton
5.................... Quad City
10-11-12-13.... Michigan
14-15............ Burlington
19-20-21-22...... Lansing
27-28-29-30 Fort Wayne

JULY
5.................... Burlington
13-14-15-16........ Peoria
22-23-24-25.. Wisconsin
26-27-28-29......... Beloit

AUGUST
3-5................. Quad City
8-9-10........... Burlington
13-14................. Clinton
22-23-24............ Clinton
25-26-27........ Quad City
28.................. Burlington

Clinton

APRIL
8-9-10-11.... Fort Wayne
14-15-16-17...... Lansing
22-23-24-25 South Bend
26-27....... Cedar Rapids

MAY
3-4-5-6.......... Wisconsin
15-16............ Quad City
20-21............ Burlington
24.................. Burlington
28-29............ Quad City
30-31.................... Beloit

JUNE
3............. Cedar Rapids
6-7........................ Beloit
8-9........... Cedar Rapids
10-11............ Burlington
13.................. Quad City
19-20-21-22.... Michigan
27-28-29-30. West Mich.

JULY
6..................... Quad City
13-14-15-16.... Rockford
22-23-24-25........ Peoria
26-27-28-29... Kane Cty.

AUGUST
3-4................ Burlington
8-9-10............ Quad City
11-12....... Cedar Rapids
19.................. Quad City
25-26-27....... Burlington
29-30-31.. Cedar Rapids

Fort Wayne

APRIL
4-5-6-7...... Kane County
14-15-16-17 Cedar Rap.
24-25..... West Michigan
27.................... Michigan
29-30.................... Beloit

MAY
1-2........................ Beloit
7-8................. Quad City
9-10-11-12........ Lansing
18............... South Bend
22-23..... West Michigan
29.................... Michigan
30-31............ Quad City

JUNE
4-5............. South Bend
11-12-13..... South Bend
14.................... Michigan
23-24-25-26.. Burlington

JULY
1-2-3-4............... Peoria
6-7.................. Michigan
9-10-11-12.... Wisconsin
13.................... Michigan
19-20..... West Michigan
22-23.......... South Bend
28-29..... West Michigan
30-31................. Clinton

AUGUST
1-2...................... Clinton
6-7............. South Bend
8-9-10-11........ Rockford
14-15............. Michigan
21-22-23-24...... Lansing

Kane County

APRIL
8-9.................. Rockford
12-13................. Peoria
18-19-20-21. West Mich.
26-27.................... Beloit
29-30............. Quad City

MAY
1-2............ South Bend
3........................ Rockford
12................. Wisconsin
13-14................ Clinton
15-16................. Peoria
20-21.......... South Bend
22-23................ Clinton
24-25.............. Michigan
26-27................. Peoria

JUNE
1.......................... Beloit
5-6-7............ Wisconsin
10-11........... Quad City
12........................ Beloit
15.................... Rockford
21-22................. Peoria
27-28-29-30...... Lansing

JULY
1-2................. Rockford
9-10-11-12... Burlington
17-18-19-20 Cedar Rap.
30-31........... Wisconsin

AUGUST
1-2-3-5................ Beloit
7....................... Rockford
12-13........... Wisconsin
15.................... Rockford
19-20.............. Michigan
23-24................. Peoria
25-26-27-28 Fort Wayne

Lansing

APRIL
8-9-10-11...... Burlington
12-13............. Michigan
18-19-20-21 Fort Wayne
29-30............. Michigan

MAY
7-8............. South Bend
13-14............. Michigan
16-17-18-19.. Wisconsin
22-23-24-25 Cedar Rap.
28-29-30-31... Kane Cty.

JUNE
4-5-7...... West Michigan
8-9............. South Bend
10.......... West Michigan
23-24-25-26....... Clinton

JULY
1-2-3-4.......... Quad City
5-6......... West Michigan
9-11................ Michigan
13-14.......... South Bend
15-16.......... Fort Wayne
22-23-24-25......... Beloit
26-27-28-29.... Rockford

AUGUST
8-9-10-11........... Peoria
12-13.......... Fort Wayne
15......... West Michigan
16-17.......... South Bend
19.......... West Michigan
29-30.............. Michigan

Michigan

APRIL
8-9-10-11............. Beloit
14-15-16-17........ Peoria
22-23-24-25.. Quad City
26.............. Fort Wayne

MAY
1-2.................. Lansing
3-4............ South Bend
9-10-11-12......... Clinton
15-16.......... Fort Wayne
18.......... West Michigan
20-21.......... Fort Wayne
26-27............... Lansing
28.............. Fort Wayne
31.......... West Michigan

JUNE
6-7............. South Bend
8-9......... West Michigan
15.............. Fort Wayne
23-24-25-26.. Wisconsin

JULY
1-2-3-4.......... Burlington
5.............. Fort Wayne
10-12............... Lansing
14.............. Fort Wayne
15-16.......... South Bend
22-23-25 West Michigan
26-27.......... South Bend
30-31....... Cedar Rapids

AUGUST
1-2.......... Cedar Rapids
6-7.................. Lansing
8-9-10-11.. Kane County
12......... West Michigan
21-22-23-24.... Rockford
31.............. Fort Wayne

Peoria

APRIL
4-5-6-7.............. Clinton
10-11........ Kane County
18-19-20-21......... Beloit
26-27............... Lansing
29-30....... Cedar Rapids

MAY
5-6................. Rockford
7-8.......... Cedar Rapids
13-14..... West Michigan
17-18........ Kane County
20-21........... Wisconsin
22-23............. Rockford
28-29............. Rockford

JUNE
1-2............... Wisconsin
6-7-8-9........ Fort Wayne
14-15..... West Michigan
19-20................... Beloit
23-24............. Rockford
27-28-29-30.. Wisconsin

JULY
9-10-11-12.... Quad City
17-18-19-20.... Michigan
26-27-28-29.. Burlington

AUGUST
3-4................... Lansing
6-7....................... Beloit
12-13............. Rockford
21-22........ Kane County
25-26-27-28 South Bend
29-30........ Kane County

Quad City

APRIL
8-9-10-11..... West Mich.
14-15-16-17.. Wisconsin
19-20....... Cedar Rapids

26-27 .... Rockford

MAY

1-2 .... Peoria
3-4-5-6............. Lansing
14........... Cedar Rapids
17-18................ Clinton
20........... Cedar Rapids
23................. Burlington
24-25 .... Peoria
26-27............ Burlington

JUNE

1.................... Burlington
4............. Cedar Rapids
6-7 .... Rockford
8..................... Burlington
12-14-15 .... Clinton
19-20-21-22 Fort Wayne
27-28-29-30 .... Michigan

JULY

5-7.................. Clinton
13-14-15-16 .... Beloit
22-23-24-25... Kane Cty.
30-31 .... South Bend

AUGUST

1-2............. South Bend
6-7........... Cedar Rapids
11-12............. Burlington
15-16-17.. Cedar Rapids
20-21................. Clinton
22-23-24 .... Burlington
28....................... Clinton

Rockford

APRIL

4-5-6-7............. Lansing
12-13 .... Fort Wayne
18-19-20-21 .... Clinton
22-23-24-25 .. Wisconsin

MAY

1-2 .... Wisconsin
4 .... Kane County
7-8............ Kane County
9-10-11-12.......... Peoria
13-14............ Burlington
25-27.................... Beloit

JUNE

2-3-4-5............ Michigan
10-11..................... Beloit
12-13............ Burlington
14 .... Kane County
19-20-21-22 South Bend
25-26 .... Peoria
27-28..................... Beloit

JULY

3.......................... Beloit
6-7 .... Wisconsin
9-10-11-12.. Cedar Rap.
17-18-19-20 .. Quad City

30 .... Beloit

AUGUST

1-2 .... Wisconsin
3-4 .... Fort Wayne
6 .... Kane County
14-16-17... Kane County
18-19 .... Peoria
25-26-27-28. West Mich.

South Bend

APRIL

8-9 .... Peoria
10-11 .... Rockford
18-19-20-21 .. Burlington
26-27 ..... West Michigan
29-30 .... Rockford

MAY

5-6 .... Michigan
9-10-11-12 .... Quad City
13-14 .... Fort Wayne
17 .... Fort Wayne
22-23 .... Michigan
26-27-28-29. West Mich.
30-31 .... Peoria

JUNE

1-2 .... Lansing
10 .... Fort Wayne
14-15 .... Lansing
23-24-25-26 Cedar Rap.

JULY

1-2-3-4 .... Clinton
5-6-7........ Kane County
9-10 ...... West Michigan
17-18-19-20...... Lansing
24-25 .... Fort Wayne
28-29 .... Michigan

AUGUST

4-5 .... Michigan
9-10 ...... West Michigan
12-13-14-15 .... Beloit
21-22-23-24 .. Wisconsin
29-30 .... Fort Wayne
31 .... Kane County

West Michigan

APRIL

4-5-6-7 .... Wisconsin
14-15-16-17 .... Rockford
23 .... Fort Wayne
29-30.................. Clinton

MAY

1-2..................... Clinton
7-8 .... Michigan
9-10-11-12 .... Burlington
15-16 .... South Bend
17.................... Michigan
20-21 .... Lansing
24-25 .... South Bend

30.................. Michigan

JUNE

1-2-3.......... Fort Wayne
6 .... Lansing
11-12-13 .... Lansing
23-24-25-26 .. Quad City

JULY

1-2-3-4 .... Cedar Rapids
7 .... Lansing
11-12 .... South Bend
13-14-15-16... Kane Cty.
17-18 .... Fort Wayne
24................... Michigan
26-27 .... Fort Wayne
30-31 .... Peoria

AUGUST

1-2 .... Peoria
8 .... South Bend
11 .... South Bend
13................... Michigan
14 .... Lansing
16-17 .... Michigan
20 .... Lansing
21-22-23-24 .... Beloit
31 .... Lansing

Wisconsin

APRIL

8-9-10-11 Cedar Rapids
12-13......... South Bend
18-19-20-21 .... Michigan
26-27-28-29 .. Burlington

MAY

7-8........................ Beloit
9-10-11..... Kane County
13-14...................... Beloit
24-25-26-27 Fort Wayne
28-29........................Beloit
30-31 .... Rockford

JUNE

4 .... Kane County
8-9 .... Rockford
10-11-12-13........ Peoria
19-20 .... Kane County
21-22..................... Beloit

JULY

1-2........................ Beloit
3-4........... Kane County
5...................... Rockford
17-18-19-20 .... Clinton
26-27-28-29 .. Quad City

AUGUST

4-5-6-7... West Michigan
14-15-16-17 .... Peoria
19-20 .... South Bend
25-26-27-28...... Lansing
29-30-31 .... Rockford

South Atlantic League

Asheville

APRIL

9-10............... Piedmont
11-12-13-14 .. Columbus
19-20-21-22........... Hag.
24-25-26-27 Capital City
28-29-30 .... Augusta

MAY

1........................ Augusta
6-7-8-9............... Hickory
15-16-17-18 ... Piedmont
19-20-21-22 ... Delmarva
27-28-29-30....Char., SC
31 ....Greensboro

JUNE

1-2-3.......... Greensboro
19-20-21-22 . Cape Fear
27-28-29........ Char., SC
30 .... Macon

JULY

1-2-3.................. Macon
15-16-17-18 ...... Hickory

19-20-21-22 .. Savannah
30-31............. Piedmont

AUGUST

1-2-3-4.......... Char., WV
5-6............. Greensboro
18-19.......... Greensboro
28-29-30-31 Capital City

Augusta

APRIL

3-4-5-6 .... Cape Fear
8-8................. Savannah
19-20 .... Macon

MAY

2-3-4-5........... Char., SC
12-13-14 .... Savannah
15-16............ Columbus
17-18.................. Macon
19-20-21-22 ... Piedmont
27-28-29-30 .. Columbus

JUNE

4-5-6-7.............. Hickory

23-24-25-26 .... Asheville
30 .... Columbus

JULY

1-2-3 .... Columbus
9-10............... Savannah
11-12 .... Macon
15-16-17-18 .. Savannah
19-20-21-22........ G'boro

AUGUST

1-2-3-4 .... Delmarva
5-6-7.................... Macon
8-9-10 .... Columbus
18-19-20-21 Capital City
22-23............. Savannah
28-29-30-31........ Macon

Cape Fear

APRIL

11-12-13-14 ...... Hickory
15-16-17-18 .... Asheville
24-25-26-27 .. Columbus
28-29-30 .... Char., WV

SOUTH ATLANTIC LEAGUE/1997 SCHEDULE

MAY
1 .... Char., WV
6-7-8 .... Hagerstown
9-10 .... Delmarva
12-13 .... Char., WV
19-20-21-22 .... Hag.
31 .... Piedmont
JUNE
1-2-3 .... Piedmont
12-13-14-15 ... Delmarva
27-28-29 .... Char., WV
JULY
4-5-6-7 .... Capital City
15-16-17-18 ... Delmarva
19-20-21-22 .. Char., WV
23-24-25-26 .. Savannah
AUGUST
5-6-7-8 .... Hagerstown
9-10-11-12 ..... Char., SC
15-16-17 .... Delmarva
22-23-24-25 .... G'boro
28-29 .... Hagerstown

Capital City
APRIL
3-4-5-5 .... Asheville
7-8-9-10 .... Char., WV
19-20-21-22 . Cape Fear
MAY
6-7-8-9 .... Char., SC
10-11-12-13 ... Piedmont
27-28-29-30 .... G'boro
31 .... Augusta
JUNE
1-2-3 .... Augusta
4-5-6-7 .... Columbus
12-13-14-15 ...... Hickory
27-28-29 .... Hickory
30 .... Delmarva
JULY
1-2-3 .... Delmarva
9-10 .... Char., SC
15-16-17-18 .... Hag.
19-20-21-22 .... Macon
23-24-25-26 .... Asheville
AUGUST
1-2-3-4 .... Savannah
9-10-11-12 . Greensboro
14-15-16-17 ... Piedmont
26-27 .... Char., SC

Charleston, SC
APRIL
7-8-9-10 .... Cape Fear
15-16-17-18 .... Macon
19-20-21-22 .. Savannah
MAY
10-11-12-13 .... Asheville
15-16-17 ..... Greensboro
19-20-21-22 .Capital City
23-24-25-26 ...... Hickory
JUNE
12-13-14-15 .. Char., WV
19-20-21-22 ..... Augusta
23-24-25-26 Capital City
JULY
4-5-6-7 .... Hickory
15-16-17-18 .. Columbus
19-20-21-22 ... Piedmont
28-29-30-31 ... Delmarva
AUGUST
1-2-3-4 .... Hagerstown
14-15-16-17 .... Asheville
18-19-20-21 ... Piedmont
28-29-30-31 .... G'boro

Charleston, WV
APRIL
11-12-13-14 .... Hag.
15-16-17-18 ... Piedmont
24-25-26-27 .... Macon
MAY
2-3-4-5 .... Asheville
6-7-8 .... Delmarva
9-10 .... Hagerstown
19-20-21-22 .... G'boro
23-24-25-26 . Cape Fear
27-28-29-30 ... Delmarva
JUNE
9-10-11 .... Cape Fear
19-20-21-22 .... Hag.
23-24-25-26 ...... Hickory
30 .... Char., SC
JULY
1-2-3 .... Char., SC
9-10 .... Delmarva
11-12-13-14 . Cape Fear
23-24-25-26 ...... Augusta
AUGUST
5-6-7-8 .... Delmarva
13-14 .... Cape Fear
15-16-17 .... Hagerstown
22-23-24-25 Capital City

Columbus
APRIL
3-4-5-6 .... Delmarva
9-10 .... Macon
15-16 .... Savannah
19-20-21-22 .... G'boro
28-29-30 .... Char., SC
MAY
1 .... Char., SC
2-3 .... Macon
6-7-8 .... Augusta
9-10 .... Macon
19-20-21-22 ...... Hickory
23-24-25-26 ... Piedmont
31 .... Savannah
JUNE
1 .... Savannah
9-10-11 .... Savannah
12-13-14-15 ..... Augusta
19-20 .... Macon
25-26 .... Savannah
27-28-29 .... Macon
JULY
4-5-6-7 .... Asheville
11-12-13-14 Capital City
28-29-30-31 .. Char., WV
AUGUST
11-12 .... Savannah
14-15-16-17 ..... Augusta
18-19 .... Macon
26-27 .... Augusta
30-31 .... Savannah

Delmarva
APRIL
11-12-13-14 Capital City
15-16-17-18 ...... Hickory
24-25-26-27 .. Savannah
MAY
2-3-4-5 .... Cape Fear
14-15 .... Char., WV
16-17-18 .... Cape Fear
23-24-25-26 .... Hag.
31 .... Char., SC
JUNE
1-2-3 .... Char., SC
4-5-6-7 .... Char., WV
9-10-11 ...... Hagerstown
19-20-21-22 ... Piedmont
23-24-25-26 . Cape Fear
JULY
4-5-6-7 .... Greensboro
19-20-21-22 .... Hag.
23-24-25-26 .... Macon
AUGUST
9-10-11-12 ...... Asheville
13-14 .... Hagerstown
19-20-21 .... Char., WV
26-27 .... Cape Fear
28-29-30-31 .. Char., WV

Greensboro
APRIL
3-4 .... Piedmont
7-8-9-10 .... Delmarva
15-16-17-18 ..... Augusta
24-25-26-27 ... Char., SC
28-29-30 .... Macon
MAY
1 .... Macon
2-3-4-5 .... Hickory
8-9 .... Piedmont
23-24-25-26 .... Asheville
JUNE
4-5-6-7 .... Cape Fear
9-10-11 .... Capital City
19-20-21-22 .. Savannah
30 .... Hagerstown
JULY
1-2-3 .... Hagerstown
9-10 .... Piedmont
15-16-17-18 .. Char., WV
23-24-25-26-27 Char., SC
28-29-30-31 Capital City
AUGUST
1-2-3-4 .... Columbus
7-8 .... Asheville
14-15-16-17 ...... Hickory
20-21 .... Asheville
26-27 .... Piedmont

Hagerstown
APRIL
15-16-17-18 Capital City
24-25-26-27 ..... Augusta
28-29-30 .... Delmarva
MAY
1 .... Delmarva
12-13 ....Delmarva
14-15 .... Cape Fear
16-17-18 .... Char., WV
27-28-29-30 . Cape Fear
31 .... Char., WV
JUNE
1-2-3 .... Char., WV
4-5-6-7 .... Char., SC
12-13-14-15 .... G'boro
23-24-25-26 ... Piedmont
27-28-29 .... Delmarva
JULY
4-5-6-7 .... Char., WV
9-10 .... Cape Fear
11-12-13-14 ... Delmarva
23-24-25-26 .. Columbus
AUGUST
9-10-11-12 ....Hickory
19-20-21 .... Cape Fear
22-23-24-25 .... Asheville
26-27 .... Char., WV
30-31 .... Cape Fear

Hickory
APRIL
3-4-5-6 .... Char., SC
7-8-9-10 ..... Hagerstown
19-20-21-22 .. Char., WV
24-25-26-27 ... Piedmont
MAY
10-11-12-13 .... G'boro
15-16-17-18 Capital City
31 .... Macon
JUNE
1-2-3 .... Macon
9-10-11 .... Asheville
19-20-21-22 Capital City
30 ....Cape Fear
JULY
1-2-3 .... Cape Fear
9-10 .... Asheville
11-12-13-14 .... G'boro
19-20-21-22 .. Columbus
25-26 .... Piedmont
28-29-30-31 ..... Augusta
AUGUST
5-6-7-8 .... Char., SC
18-19-20-21 .. Savannah
22-23-24-25 ... Delmarva
26-27 .... Asheville
28-29 .... Piedmont

Macon

APRIL

3-4-5-6 .... Hagerstown
7-8 .... Columbus
11-12-13-14 ..... Augusta
21-22 .... Augusta

MAY

4-5 .... Columbus
12-13-14 .... Columbus
15-16 .... Savannah
19-20-21-22 .. Savannah
23-24-25-26 Capital City

JUNE

4-5-6-7 .... Asheville
9-10-11 .... Augusta
12-13-14-15 ... Piedmont
21-22 .... Columbus
23-24-25-26 .... G'boro

JULY

4-5-6-7 .... Savannah
9-10 .... Columbus
13-14 .... Augusta
28-29-30-31 . Cape Fear

AUGUST

1-2-3-4 .... Hickory
8-9-10 .... Savannah
11-12 .... Augusta
20-21 .... Columbus
22-23-24-25... Char., SC

Piedmont

APRIL

5-6 .... Greensboro
7-8 .... Asheville
11-12-13-14... Char., SC
19-20-21-22 ... Delmarva
28-29-30 ..... Capital City

MAY

1 .... Capital City
2-3-4-5 .... Hagerstown
6-7 .... Greensboro
27-28-29-30 ...... Hickory

JUNE

4-5-6-7 .... Savannah
9-10-11 .... Char., SC
27-28-29..... Greensboro

JULY

4-5-6-7 .... Augusta
11-12-13-14 .... Asheville
15-16-17-18........ Macon
23-24 .... Hickory
28-29 .... Asheville

AUGUST

1-2-3-4 .... Cape Fear
5-6-7-8 .... Capital City
9-10-11-12.... Char., WV
22-23-24-25 .. Columbus
30-31 .... Hickory

Savannah

APRIL

3-4-5-6 .... Char., WV
9-10 .... Augusta
11-12-13-14........ G'boro
17-18............ Columbus
29-29-30........... Hickory

MAY

1 .... Hickory
2-3-4-5 .... Capital City
6-7-8 .... Macon
9-10 .... Augusta
17-18............ Columbus
23-24-25-26 ..... Augusta
27-28-29-30........ Macon

JUNE

2-3 .... Columbus
12-13-14-15 .... Asheville
23-24............ Columbus
27-28-29 .... Augusta
30 .... Piedmont

JULY

1-2-3 .... Piedmont
11-12-13-14... Char., SC
28-29-30-31 .... Hag.

AUGUST

5-6-7 .... Columbus
14-15-16-17........ Macon
24-25 .... Augusta
26-27 .... Macon
28-29............ Columbus

Short Season Class A

New York-Penn League

Auburn

JUNE

17 .... Utica
19-20.......... Jamestown
27-28 .... Pittsfield
29-30 .... Oneonta

JULY

1-2 .... Oneonta
4 .... Utica
7-8 .... Williamsport
12-13 .... Oneonta
14-15...... Hudson Valley
22 .... Batavia
24 .... Batavia
26 .... Watertown
31 .... Vermont

AUGUST

1 .... Vermont
4 .... Utica
6 .... Utica
8-9 .... Williamsport
12-13-14-15 St. Catharines
18 .... Watertown
21-22 .... Williamsport
23 .... Watertown
25 .... Watertown
28 .... Utica
30 .... Utica

SEPTEMBER

2-3 .... New Jersey

Batavia

JUNE

18 .... St. Catharines
21-22..................... Utica
27-28-29-30..... Vermont

JULY

3-4 .... Erie
6 .... St. Catharines
10 .... Jamestown
12-13-14-15 .... Lowell
18-19-20-21 Williamsport
23 .... Auburn
25 .... Auburn
27 .... St. Catharines
29-30 .... Erie

AUGUST

3 .... Jamestown
4-5 .... Erie
16 .... St. Catharines
21-22...................... Utica
24................. Jamestown
25-26 .... Pittsfield
27-28 .... Oneonta
30 .... Jamestown
31 .... St. Catharines

SEPTEMBER

2 .... St. Catharines

Erie

JUNE

17 .... Jamestown
19-20 ...... St. Catharines
23-24-25-26....... Auburn
27-28-29-30 . Watertown

JULY

1-2 .... Batavia
5-6 .... Jamestown
10-11 .... Oneonta
16-17 .... Batavia
18-19-20-21 New Jersey
31 .... Batavia

AUGUST

1 .... Batavia
2-3 .... St. Catharines
10-11 .... Jamestown
21-22 ...... St. Catharines
23-24-25-26 . Hud.Valley
29-30 .... Pittsfield

SEPTEMBER

3 .... Jamestown

Hudson Valley

JUNE

17 .... New Jersey
23-24-25-26 St. Catharines

JULY

1 .... New Jersey
3-4 .... Lowell
8-9 .... Vermont
10-11 .... Pittsfield
16-17 .... Pittsfield
18-19 .... Oneonta
20-21 .... Utica
22-23 .... Lowell
25 .... New Jersey
31 .... New Jersey

AUGUST

2 .... New Jersey
6 .... New Jersey
8-9-10-11 .... Batavia
12-13 .... Williamsport
16-17 .... Pittsfield
27-28-29-30..... Vermont
31 .... Lowell

SEPTEMBER

1 .... Lowell

Jamestown

JUNE

18 .... Erie
21-22 .... Auburn

JULY

1-2-3-4 .... Watertown
8-9 .... Batavia
11 .... Batavia
14-15-16-17 New Jersey
18-19 ...... St. Catharines
29-30 ...... St. Catharines

AUGUST

2 .... Batavia
4-5 .... St. Catharines
6-7 .... Batavia
8-9 .... Erie
19-20-21-22 Hud. Valley
23 .... Batavia
25-26 .... Oneonta
27-28 .... Erie
29 .... Batavia
31 .... Pittsfield

SEPTEMBER

1 .... Pittsfield
2 .... Erie

Lowell

JUNE
17-18 .... Vermont
23-24-25-26..... Pittsfield
27-28-29-30 Hud. Valley

JULY
5-6 .... New Jersey
16-17.................... Utica
18-19 .... Auburn
20-21........... Watertown
24-25-26-27 Jamestown
29-30...... Hudson Valley

AUGUST
2-3 .... Pittsfield
10-11 .... Vermont
14-15-16-17 .... Erie
19-20 .... Vermont
21-22 .... New Jersey
27-28 .... New Jersey

New Jersey

JUNE
18.......... Hudson Valley
19-20-21-22 .... Lowell
27-28-29-30 St. Catharines

JULY
2............ Hudson Valley
8-9 .... Pittsfield
10-11-12-13..... Vermont
22-23 .... Oneonta
24.......... Hudson Valley
26-27-28-29..... Pittsfield

AUGUST
1............ Hudson Valley
3............ Hudson Valley
7............ Hudson Valley
8-9............... Watertown
12-13-14-15 ...... Batavia
25-26 .... Williamsport
29-30.................. Lowell
31 .... Vermont

SEPTEMBER
1 .... Vermont

Oneonta

JUNE
19.......................... Utica
23-24-25-26 Jamestown
27.......................... Utica

JULY
3-4 .... Williamsport
5........................... Utica
8-9 .... Erie
14.......................... Utica
20-21 .... Auburn
25.......................... Utica
26-27...... Hudson Valley
29-30 .... Vermont

AUGUST
2-3 .... Auburn
4-5............... Watertown
6-7 ....Williamsport
8-9............................ Lowell
16.......................... Utica
19-20 .... Auburn
21-22........... Watertown
23-24 .... Williamsport
31........................... Erie

SEPTEMBER
1............................. Erie
2-3.............. Watertown

Pittsfield

JUNE
19-20................ Batavia
21-22 .... Oneonta

JULY
1-2....................... Lowell
3-4............. New Jersey
5-6.......... Hudson Valley
12-13.................... Utica
14-15 .... Vermont
20-21 .... Vermont
22-23.......... Jamestown
24-25.......... Watertown
31 .... Lowell

AUGUST
1 .... Lowell
4-5 .... New Jersey
8-9 .... Vermont
10-11 ...... St. Catharines
12-13 .... Erie
14-15...... Hudson Valley
19-20 .... New Jersey
23-24.................. Lowell

SEPTEMBER
2-3......... Hudson Valley

St. Catharines

JUNE
17...................... Batavia
21-22 .... Erie

JULY
1-2-3-4............ Vermont
5....................... Batavia
8-9-10-11 .... Lowell
12-13.......... Jamestown
20-21.......... Jamestown
22-23-24-25 Williamsport
26...................... Batavia
31............... Jamestown

AUGUST
1................ Jamestown
6-7 .... Erie
17...................... Batavia
19-20 .... Erie
23-24-25-26 .... Utica
27-28 .... Pittsfield
29-30 .... Oneonta

SEPTEMBER
1....................... Batavia
3....................... Batavia

Utica

JUNE
18 .... Auburn
20 .... Oneonta
23-24-25-26 Williamsport
28 .... Oneonta
29-30 .... Pittsfield

JULY
3 .... Auburn
6 ....Oneonta
7.................. Watertown
15 ....Oneonta
18................ Watertown
22-23 .... Erie
24 .... Oneonta
29................ Watertown
31................ Watertown

AUGUST
2-3 .... Vermont
5 .... Auburn
7 .... Auburn
8-9 .... St. Catharines
10-11 .... New Jersey
12-13.......... Jamestown
14................ Watertown
17 .... Oneonta
19-20................. Batavia
27 .... Auburn
29 .... Auburn

SEPTEMBER
1 .... Watertown
2-3 .... Williamsport

Vermont

JUNE
19-20-21-22 Hud. Valley
23-24-25-26 New Jersey

JULY
5-6 .... Williamsport
16-17 .... Auburn
18-19 .... Pittsfield
22-23........... Watertown
24-25-26-27 .... Erie

AUGUST
4-5.......... Hudson Valley
6-7 .... Pittsfield
12-13.................. Lowell
14-15-16-17 Jamestown
21-22 .... Pittsfield
23-24 .... New Jersey
25-26.................. Lowell

SEPTEMBER
2-3...................... Lowell

Watertown

JUNE
17-18 .... Oneonta
19-20-21-22 Williamsport
23-24-25-26 ...... Batavia

JULY
5-6 .... Auburn
8............................ Utica
10-11 .... Auburn
12-13..... Hudson Valley
14-15-16-17 St. Catharines
19.......................... Utica
28 .... Auburn
30.......................... Utica

AUGUST
1............................ Utica
6-7.......................... Lowell
10-11-12-13..... Oneonta
15.......................... Utica
16 .... Auburn
19-20 .... Williamsport
24 .... Auburn
26 .... Auburn
31.......................... Utica

Williamsport

JUNE
17-18 .... Pittsfield
27-28-29-30 Jamestown

JULY
1-2......................... Utica
10-11...................... Utica
12-13-14-15 .... Erie
16-17 .... Oneonta
26-27...................... Utica
29-30 .... Auburn
31 .... Oneonta

AUGUST
1 .... Oneonta
2-3............ Watertown
4-5....................... Lowell
10-11 .... Auburn
14-15 .... Oneonta
16-17 .... New Jersey
27-28-29-30 . Watertown
31 .... Auburn

SEPTEMBER
1 .... Auburn

Northwest League

Boise

JUNE

22-23-24-25-26. Eugene
27-28-29............ Yakima

JULY

3-4-5-6-7.......... Portland
9-10-11 .... Everett
15-16-17............ Yakima
23-24-25-26-27... Salem

AUGUST

1-2-3 .... Spokane
9-10-11-12-13 S. Oregon
26-27-28 .... Spokane

SEPTEMBER

1-2-3 .... Everett

Eugene

JUNE

17-18-19-20-21.. Everett
27-28-29 .... Salem

JULY

3-4-5-6-7 .... Yakima
15-16-17 .... S. Oregon
24-25-26-27-28 Spokane

AUGUST

1-2-3 .... Portland
4-5-6-7-8 .... Boise
18-19-20 .... S. Oregon
26-27-28 .... Salem

SEPTEMBER

1-2-3 .... Portland

Everett

JUNE

22-23-24-25-26 S. Oregon
30.................... Spokane

JULY

1-2................... Spokane
3-4-5-6-7............. Salem
15-16-17 .... Spokane
23-24-25-26-27 Portland

AUGUST

1-2-3.................. Yakima
9-10-11-12-13... Eugene
20-21-22-23-24-25 Boise
26-27-28........... Yakima

Portland

JUNE

22-23-24-25-26 Spokane
30...................... Eugene

JULY

1-2 .... Eugene
9-10-11 .... S. Oregon
12-13-14 .... Salem
18-19-20-21-22 .... Boise
29-30-31 .... Eugene

AUGUST

4-5-6-7-8 .... Yakima
15-16-17-18-19.. Everett
23-24-25 .... Salem
29-30-31 .... S. Oregon

Salem

JUNE

22-23-24-25-26 . Yakima
30.................. S. Oregon

JULY

1-2 .... S. Oregon
9-10-11 .... Eugene
15-16-17 .... Portland
18-19-20-21-22.. Everett
29-30-31 .... S. Oregon

AUGUST

4-5-6-7-8......... Spokane
15-16-17-18-19 .... Boise
20-21-22 .... Portland
29-30-31 .... Eugene

So. Oregon

JUNE

17-18-19-20-21 .... Boise
27-28-29 .... Portland

JULY

3-4-5-6-7......... Spokane
12-13-14 .... Eugene
24-25-26-27-28 . Yakima

AUGUST

1-2-3 .... Salem
4-5-6-7-8............ Everett
15-16-17 .... Eugene
26-27-28 .... Portland

SEPTEMBER

1-2-3 .... Salem

Spokane

JUNE

17-18-19-20-21 ... Salem
27-28-29 .... Everett

JULY

9-10-11.............. Yakima
12-13-14............... Boise
18-19-20-21-22 S. Oregon
29-30-31............... Boise

AUGUST

9-10-11-12-13.. Portland
18-19-20............ Yakima
21-22-23-24-25. Eugene
29-30-31 .... Everett

Yakima

JUNE

17-18-19-20-21 Portland
30......................... Boise

JULY

1-2........................ Boise
12-13-14 .... Everett
18-19-20-21-22. Eugene
29-30-31 .... Everett

AUGUST

9-10-11-12-13..... Salem
15-16-17 .... Spokane
21-22-23-24-25 S. Oregon
29-30-31............... Boise

SEPTEMBER

1-2-3 .... Spokane

ROOKIE LEAGUES
Appalachian League

Bluefield
JUNE
18 .... Princeton
23-24 .... Princeton
25-26 .... Danville
29-30 .... Elizabethton
JULY
1 .... Elizabethton
3-4-5 .... Pulaski
12-13-14 .... Danville
21-22-23 ...... Martinsville
25-26-27 ... Johnson City
30 .... Princeton
AUGUST
7-8 .... Princeton
9-10-11 .... Burlington
15-16-17 .... Kingsport
21-22-23 .... Bristol
26-27 .... Pulaski

Bristol
JUNE
19 .... Kingsport
20-21 ....Elizabethton
23 .... Johnson City
27-28 .... Kingsport
JULY
1 .... Johnson City
3 .... Kingsport
6-7-8 .... Martinsville
9-10-11 ....Burlington
15-16-17 .... Princeton
18-19-20 .... Pulaski
28-29-30 .... Danville
AUGUST
3-4-5 .... Johnson City
9-10 .... Kingsport
13-14 .... Elizabethton
18-19-20 .... Bluefield
26 .... Elizabethton

Burlington
JUNE
19 .... Danville
20-21-22 .... Bluefield
23-24 .... Danville
JULY
3-4-5 .... Princeton
12-13-14 ... Johnson City
18-19-20 .... Kingsport
21-22-23 .... Elizabethton
31 .... Bristol
AUGUST
1-2 .... Bristol
3-4-5 .... Pulaski
15-16-17 ...... Martinsville
18-19-20 .... Danville
24-25 .... Martinsville
26-27 .... Princeton

Danville
JUNE
18 .... Burlington
21-22 .... Martinsville
27-28 .... Martinsville
29-30 .... Burlington
JULY
1 .... Burlington
9-10-11 .... Princeton
15-16-17 .... Kingsport
18-19-20 .... Elizabethton
31 .... Pulaski
AUGUST
1-2 .... Pulaski
3-4-5 .... Bluefield
7-8 .... Burlington
14 .... Martinsville
15-16-17 .... Bristol
21-22-23 ... Johnson City
24-25 .... Bluefield

Elizabethton
JUNE
18 .... Johnson City
22 .... Bristol
25-26 .... Bristol
27-28 .... Johnson City
JULY
6-7-8 .... Princeton
9 .... Johnson City
11 .... Johnson City
12-13 .... Kingsport
15-16-17 .... Bluefield
25-26-27 .... Danville
28-29-30 .... Burlington
AUGUST
5 .... Kingsport
7 .... Johnson City
9-10-11 .... Martinsville
12 .... Bristol
15-16-17 .... Pulaski
24-25 .... Kingsport
27 .... Bristol

Johnson City
JUNE
19 .... Elizabethton
24 .... Bristol
25-26 .... Kingsport
29-30 .... Bristol
JULY
3-4-5 .... Danville
6-7-8 .... Burlington
10 .... Elizabethton
15-16-17 .... Pulaski
18-19-20 ...... Martinsville
28-29-30 .... Kingsport
31 .... Elizabethton
AUGUST
1-2 .... Elizabethton
8 .... Elizabethton
12-13-14 .... Bluefield
15-16-17 .... Princeton
24-25 .... Bristol

Kingsport
JUNE
18 ....Bristol
20-21-22 ... Johnson City
23-24 .... Elizabethton
JULY
4-5 .... Bristol
6-7-8 .... Bluefield
9-10-11 .... Martinsville
14 .... Elizabethton
22-23-24 .... Danville
25-26-27 .... Burington
AUGUST
3-4 .... Elizabethton
7-8 .... Bristol
11 .... Bristol
12-13-14 .... Pulaski
18-19-20 .... Princeton
26-27 .... Johnson City

Martinsville
JUNE
19 .... Pulaski
20 .... Danville
23-24 .... Pulaski
25-26 .... Burlington
JULY
3-4-5 .... Elizabethton
12-13-14 .... Pulaski
15-16-17 .... Burlington
25-26-27 .... Bristol
31 .... Bluefield
AUGUST
1-2 .... Bluefield
3-4-5 .... Princeton
12-13 .... Danville
18-19-20 ... Johnson City
21-22-23 .... Kingsport
26-27 .... Danville

Pulaski
JUNE
18 .... Martinsville
25-26 .... Princeton
27-28 .... Bluefield
29-30 .... Kingsport
JULY
1 .... Kingsport
6-7-8 .... Danville
9-10-11 .... Bluefield
21-22-23 .... Bristol
25-26-27 ....Princeton
28-29-30 ...... Martinsville
AUGUST
7-8 .... Martinsville
9-10-11 ..... Johnson City
18-19-20 .... Elizabethton
21-22-23 .... Burlington

Princeton
JUNE
19 .... Bluefield
20-21-22 .... Pulaski
27-28 .... Burlington
29-30 .... Martinsville
JULY
1 .... Martinsville
12-13-14 .... Bristol
18-19-20 .... Bluefield
22-23-24 ... Johnson City
28-29 .... Bluefield
31 .... Kingsport
AUGUST
1-2 .... Kingsport
9-10-11 .... Danville
12-13-14 .... Burlington
21-22-23 .... Elizabethton
24-25 .... Pulaski

Pioneer League

Billings

JUNE

18-19-20-21........ Ogden
22-23 .... Butte

JULY

2-3 .... Idaho Falls
4-5 .... Butte
13-14-15-16. Great Falls
18-19 .... Helena
26-27-28 .... Butte
29-30 .... Helena

AUGUST

7-8-9-10 .... Lethbridge
11-12-13-14.... Med. Hat
21-22-23...... Idaho Falls
27-28................. Ogden
29-30 .... Idaho Falls

Butte

JUNE

18-19-20-21. Idaho Falls
24-25 .... Billings

JULY

2-3...................... Ogden
6-7 .... Billings
9-10-11-12... Great Falls
22-23-24-25....... Helena
30-31........ Medicine Hat

AUGUST

1-2........... Medicine Hat
3-4-5-6 .... Lethbridge
16-17 .... Idaho Falls
20-21-22............ Ogden
29-30................. Ogden
31....................... Billings

SEPTEMBER

1-2 .... Billings

Great Falls

JUNE

18-19 .... Helena
21-22 .... Helena
24-25-26... Medicine Hat

JULY

4-5-6-7 .... Lethbridge
17-18-19-20........ Ogden
22-23-24-25. Idaho Falls
26-27-28 .... Helena

AUGUST

3-4-5-6............... Billings
12-13-14-15.......... Butte
16....................... Helena
28-29-30... Medicine Hat
31 .... Lethbridge

SEPTEMBER

1-2............... Lethbridge

Helena

JUNE

20 .... Great Falls
23 .... Great Falls
24-25-26....... Lethbridge
27-28-29-30.... Med. Hat

JULY

9-10-11-12... Idaho Falls
13-14-15-16........ Ogden
20-21 .... Billings
31....................... Billings

AUGUST

1......................... Billings
7-8-9-10 .... Butte
17-18-19-20. Great Falls
21-22-23....... Lethbridge
31 .... Medicine Hat

SEPTEMBER

1-2............ Medicine Hat

Idaho Falls

JUNE

22-23.................. Ogden
26-27-28 .... Butte
29-30 .... Billings

JULY

1.......................... Billings
4-5...................... Ogden
13-14-15-16.... Med. Hat
18-19-20-21 . Lethbridge
26-27-28............. Ogden

AUGUST

8-9-10-11..... Great Falls
12-13-14-15....... Helena
18-19 .... Butte
24-25-26 .... Billings
27-28 ....Butte

Lethbridge

JUNE

20-21........ Medicine Hat
27-28-29-30. Great Falls

JULY

1-2-3 .... Helena
9-10-11-12......... Billings
14-15-16-17.......... Butte
27-28-29... Medicine Hat
30-31 .... Idaho Falls

AUGUST

1-2 .... Idaho Falls
11-12-13-14........ Ogden
19-20........ Medicine Hat
25-26 .... Great Falls
27-28-29-30....... Helena

Medicine Hat

JUNE

18-19........... Lethbridge
22-23........... Lethbridge

JULY

1-2-3........... Great Falls
4-5-6-7 .... Helena
18-19-20-21 .... Butte
22-23-24-25 .... Billings

AUGUST

3-4-5-6......... Idaho Falls
7-8-9-10............. Ogden
15-16-17....... Lethbridge
21-22-23-24. Great Falls
25-26 .... Helena

Ogden

JUNE

24-25 .... Idaho Falls
26-27-28 .... Billings
29-30 .... Butte

JULY

1............................ Butte
6-7 .... Idaho Falls
9-10-11-12...... Med. Hat
22-23-24-25 . Lethbridge
29-30-31 ...... Great Falls

AUGUST

1 .... Great Falls
2-3-4-5 .... Helena
16-17-18-19....... Billings
24-25-26 .... Butte
31 .... Idaho Falls

SEPTEMBER

1-2 .... Idaho Falls

INDEPENDENT LEAGUES

INDEPENDENT LEAGUES

ATLANTIC LEAGUE

(Scheduled to Begin Play in 1998)

Mailing Address: 227 Fourth Ave., Bayshore, NY 11706. **Telephone:** (516) 665-5655. **FAX:** (516) 665-7277.

Chairman: Frank Boulton. **President:** Bud Harrelson.

BIG SOUTH LEAGUE

Mailing Address: 4300 N. State St., Jackson, MS 39206. **Telephone:** (601) 982-5544. **FAX:** (601) 982-8166. **E-Mail Address:** striker@teclink.net.

Year Founded: 1996.

President: Jim Caldwell. **Chief Executive Officer:** Tom Coats. **Commissioner:** Dick King. **Deputy Commissioner:** Norb Ecksl.

1997 Opening Date: May 29. **Closing Date:** Aug. 20.

Regular Season: 70 games.

Member Clubs: Greenville (Miss.), LaGrange (Ga.), Meridian (Miss.), Tupelo (Miss.).

Roster Limit: 21. **Eligibility Rule:** Maximum of five players with four years of professional experience; minimum of four first-year players.

FRONTIER LEAGUE

Mailing Address: P.O. Box 2662, Zanesville, OH 43702. **Telephone:** (614) 452-7400. **FAX:** (614) 452-2999.

Year Founded: 1993.

Commissioner: Bill Lee. **President:** Chris Hanners. **Vice President:** Doug James. **Treasurer:** Bob Wolfe.

Administrative Assistant: Kathy Lee.

1997 Opening Date: June 5. **Closing Date:** Sept. 7.

Regular Season: 80 games (split-schedule).

Division Structure: East—Canton, Chillicothe, Johnstown, Ohio Valley. **West**—Evansville, Kalamazoo, Richmond, Springfield.

Playoff Format: First-half division winners play second-half division winners in best-of-3 division playoff series. Winners meet in best-of-3 league championship series.

All-Star Game: July 23 at Chillicothe, OH.

Roster Limit: 20 minimum, 24 maximum. **Eligibility Rule:** Minimum of 11 first-year players; maximum of eight players with one year professional experience; maximum of three with unlimited experience. No player who will be 27 before June 1, 1997.

CANTON CROCODILES

(Franchise operated in Zanesville in 1996)

Office Address: 2501 Allen Ave. SE, Canton, OH 44707. **Telephone:** (330) 454-4631. **FAX:** (330) 454-4835.

Operated by: Canton Frontier League Baseball, LLC

Principal Owner: Matt Perry, Perry Heitman, Richard Ehrenreich.

General Manager: Joe Scrivner. **Director of Business Operations:** Amber Scrivner. **Director of Operations:** Dave Maloney. **Director of Sales/Marketing:** Bob Jones. **Director of Promotions:** Ben Rochester.

Manager: Unavailable.

Stadium Name: Thurman Munson Memorial Stadium. **Standard Game Times:** 7:05 p.m.

CHILLICOTHE PAINTS

Office Address: 59 North Paint St., Chillicothe, OH 45601. **Telephone:** (614) 773-8326. **FAX:** (614) 773-8338.

Principal Owner/President: Chris Hanners.

General Manager: Shirley Bandy. **Assistant General Manager:** Bryan Wickline. **Head Groundskeeper:** Derrick Mankin. **Director of Ticket Sales:** Jennifer Montgomery. **Director of Marketing/Promotions:** Heidi Simpson. **Director of Community Relations:** Harry Chenault. **Director of Concessions:** George Davis. **Clubhouse Operations:** Butch Atteberry. **Office Manager:** Carol Hopkins.

Manager/Director of Baseball Operations: Roger Hanners. **Coaches:** Steve Dawes, Marty Dunn. **Trainer:** Jamie French.

Stadium Name: V.A. Memorial Field. **Standard Game Times:** 7:05 p.m.; Sun. 6:05.

EVANSVILLE OTTERS

Office Address: 1701 North Main St., Evansville, IN 47711. **Telephone:** (812) 435-8686. **FAX:** (812) 435-8688.

Operated by: Old Time Sports I, LLC.

Principal Owner: Charles Jacey Jr.

Executive Vice President, Chief Operating Officer: Curt Jacey.

General Manager: Jim Miller. **Director, Stadium Operations:** Corey Fritz. **Assistant General Manager:** Pam Miller. **Head Groundskeeper:** Jim Mercer. **Director of Public Relations/Sales:** Brian Chattin. **Director, Ticket Sales:** Jack Wetherholt. **Director of Merchandising:** Angie Embrey. **Office Manager:** Katy Nimnicht.

Manager: Greg Tagert.

Stadium Name: Bosse Field. **Standard Game Time:** 7 p.m.; Sun. 5.

JOHNSTOWN STEAL

Office Address: 211 Main St., Johnstown, PA 15901. **Telephone:** (814) 536-8326. **FAX:** (814) 539-0056.

Operated By: Johnstown Professional Baseball, Inc.

Chairman of the Board: Tom Sullivan. **President:** Tom Lindemuth.

Vice President, General Manager: Buck Koontz. **Director of Sales/Marketing:** Patty Sladki. **Director of Community Relations:** Mike Hudek. **Director of Ticket Sales:** Barb Bailey. **Director of Merchandising:** Mark McCall. **Director of Special Projects:** Steve Tanzilli. **Clubhouse Operations:** Dana Heinze.

Manager: Brad Komminsk. **Coach:** Mike Moore. **Director of Player Procurement:** Charlie Sullivan.

Stadium Name: Point Stadium. **Standard Game Times:** 7:05 p.m.; Sun. 6:05.

KALAMAZOO KODIAKS

Office Address: 251 Mills St., Kalamazoo, MI 49003. **Telephone:** (616) 383-4487. **FAX:** (616) 383-4492.

Principal Owners: Doug James.

General Manager: Steve Hill. **Director of Sales/Marketing:** Kevin James. **Director of Public Relations/Promotions:** Neil Himelhoch. **Box Office Manager:** Stephanie John.

Manager: John Pacella. **Coach:** Tom Woelchli.

Stadium Name: Sutherland Field. **Standard Game Times:** 7:05 p.m.; Sun. 6:05.

OHIO VALLEY REDCOATS

Mailing Address: P.O. Box 1583, Parkersburg, WV 26102. **Telephone:** (304) 422-0426. **FAX:** (304) 422-2791.

Owner: Jim Nelson, Mike Hayes, Phil Ullom.

Manager: Pete Berrios.

Stadium Name: Bennett Stump Field. **Standard Game Time:** 7:05 p.m.; Sun. 6:05.

RICHMOND ROOSTERS

Mailing Address: 201 NW 13th St., Richmond, IN 47374. **Telephone:** (317) 935-7529. **FAX:** (317) 962-7047.

Operated by: Richmond Baseball, LLC.

President: John Cate.

General Manager: Gary Kitchel. **Assistant General Manager:** Scott Brumfiel. **Director of Business Operations:** Kyle Ingram.

Manager: John Cate. **Coach:** Kevin Kinnison. **Pitching Coach:** Bill Richardson.

Stadium Name: Don McBride Stadium. **Standard Game Times:** 7:05 p.m.; Sun. 6:05.

SPRINGFIELD CAPITALS

Office Address: 1351 N. Grand Ave. East, Springfield, IL 62702. **Telephone:** (217) 525-5500. **FAX:** (217) 525-5508.

Operated By: Springfield Professional Baseball, LP.

General Manager: Jim Barletto. **Assistant General Manager:** Linda Campbell. **Director of Stadium Operations:** Robert Westbrook. **Head Groundskeeper:** Larry Rockford. **Director of Media Relations:** Dan Szohr. **Director of Sales/Marketing:** Linda Campbell. **Director of Merchandising:** Kevin Ringgenberg.

Manager: Mal Fichman.

Stadium Name: Robin Roberts Stadium. **Standard Game Times:** 6:35 p.m.; Sun. 5:05.

HEARTLAND LEAGUE

Mailing Address: 3582 Canterbury Dr., Lafayette, IN 47905. **Telephone:** (317) 474-5341. **FAX:** (317) 474-6462.

Year Founded: 1995.

President: David Arch. **Vice President:** Jeff Bibb. **Treasurer:** Jeff Gamble.

Commissioner: Allen Wolf.

1997 Opeing Date: May 29. **Closing Date:** Aug. 18.

Regular Season: 72 games (split-season).

Division Structure: North—Anderson (Ind.) Lawmen, Lafayette (Ind.) Leopards, Green Bay (Wis.) Sultans, Will County (Ill.) Cheetahs. **South**—Clarksville (Tenn.) Coyotes, Columbia (Tenn.) Mules, Dubois County (Ind.) Dragons, Tennessee Tomahawks.

Playoff Format: First-half division winners play second-half winners in best-of-3 playoff series. Winners meet in best-of-5 championship series.

Roster Limit: 23. **Eligibility Rule:** None.

NORTH ATLANTIC LEAGUE

Office Address: 823-C North Highway, Southampton, NY 11968. **Telephone:** (516) 287-0557. **FAX:** (516) 283-2252.

Year Founded: 1995.

President: Ed Broidy. **Vice President:** Ken Boglia. **Commissioner:** Robert Dicey. **Operations Director:** Barbra Broidy. **Player Development:** Ellis Williams.

Member Clubs: Altoona (Pa.) Rail Kings, Catskill (N.Y.) Cougars, Massachusetts Mad Dogs, Nashua (N.H.) Hawks, Newark (N.Y.) Barge Bandits, Niagara Falls (N.Y.) Mallards.

1997 Opening Date: May 29. **Closing Date:** Aug. 24.

Regular Season: 80 games.

Roster Limit: 24.

Playoff Format: Top two regular-season finishers meet in best-of-5 championship series.

NORTHEAST LEAGUE

Mailing Address: 1306 Davos Pointe, Woodbridge, NY 12789. **Telephone:** (914) 434-7262. **FAX:** (914) 434-4806.

Year Founded: 1995.

President: Thomas Sullivan. **Vice President:** Dean Gyorgy. **Treasurer:** Charles Jacey. **Executive Director:** Michael McGuire.

Member Clubs: Adirondack (N.Y.) Lumberjacks, Albany (N.Y.) Diamond Dogs, Allentown (Pa.) Ambassadors, Bangor (Maine) Blue Ox, Elmira (N.Y.) Pioneers, Waterbury (Conn.) Wizards.

1997 Opening Date: May 30. **Closing Date:** Aug. 28.

Regular Season: 82 games (split-season).

Roster Limit: 22.

Playoff Format: Two half-season winners meet in best-of-5 championship series.

NORTHERN LEAGUE

Office Address: 524 South Duke St., Durham, NC 27701. **Mailing Address:** P.O. Box 1282, Durham, NC 27702. **Telephone:** (919) 956-8150. **FAX:** (919) 683-2693.

Year Founded: 1993.

Board of Directors: Marvin Goldklang (St. Paul), Sam Katz (Winnipeg), Bill Pereira (Sioux City), Harry Stavrenos (Sioux Falls), Pat Sweeney (Madison), Bill Terlecky (Thunder Bay), Bruce Thom (Fargo-Moorhead), Jim Wadley (Duluth-Superior).

President/Commissioner: Miles Wolff. **Executive Director:** Dan Moushon. **Recruiting Coordinator:** Van Schley.

Director of Baseball Operations: Nick Belmonte, 16395 Malibu Drive, Ft. Lauderdale, FL, 33326. Telephone: (954) 389-5286. FAX: (954) 389-5128.

Supervisor of Umpires: Butch Fisher.

1997 Opening Date: May 30. **Closing Date:** Sept. 1.

Regular Season: 84 games (split-season).

All-Star Game: Aug. 4 at St. Paul.

Division Structure: East—Duluth-Superior, Madison, St. Paul, Thunder Bay. **West**—Fargo-Moorhead, Sioux City, Sioux Falls, Winnipeg.

Playoff Format: First-half division winners play second-half division winners in best-of-5 division playoff series. Winners meet in best-of-5 league championship series.

Roster Limit: 22. **Eligibility Rule:** Minimum of six first-year players; maximum of four veterans (at least four professional seasons).

DULUTH-SUPERIOR DUKES

Office Address: Holiday Center, 207 West Superior St., Suite 206, Duluth, MN 55802. **Mailing Address:** P.O. Box 205, Duluth, MN 55801. **Telephone:** (218) 727-4525. **FAX:** (218) 727-4533.

Years in League: 1993-

Ownership, Management

Operated By: Dukes Baseball, Inc.

Principal Owners: Ted Cushmore, Jim Wadley.

President: Jim Wadley.

General Manager: Bob Gustafson. **Director of Media/Public Relations:** Dave McMillan. **Head Groundskeeper:** Ray Adameak. **Manager:** George Mitterwald. **Coach:** Pete Kuld. **Pitching Coach:** Mike Cuellar. **Trainer:** Chris Gebeck.

Game Information

Radio Announcer: Mark Fleischer. **No. of Games Broadcast:** Home—42, Away—42. **Flagship Station:** WDSM 710-AM.

Stadium Name: Wade Stadium. **Location:** I-35 to 40th Ave. West exit, three blocks west to Grand Ave., right six blocks to 34th Ave., right two blocks to park. **Standard Game Times:** 7:05 p.m.; Sun. 2:05.

Visiting Club Hotel: Black Bear Hotel, 1789 Hwy. 210, Carlton, MN 55718. Telephone: (218) 878-7400.

FARGO-MOORHEAD REDHAWKS

Office Address: 1515 15th Ave. North, Fargo, ND 58105. **Mailing Address:** P.O. Box 5258, Fargo, ND 58105. **Telephone:** (701) 235-6161. **FAX:** (701) 297-9247.

Years in League: 1996-

Ownership, Management

Operated by: Fargo Baseball, LLC.

Principal Owners: Mid-States Development Corp., Gene Allen.

Chairman of the Board, President: Bruce Thom.

Vice President/General Manager: John Dittrich. **Assistant General Manager:** Tim Flakoll. **Accounting Manager:** Trish Wiste. **Assistant Accounting Manager:** Mike Hashbarger. **Controller:** Kevin Moug. **Director of Ticket Sales/Office Manager:** Lois Dittrich. **Director of Promotions:** Kris Breuer. **Assistant Director, Promotions:** Steve Carroll. **Director, Media Relations:** Kyle Richardson. **Assistant Director, Media Relations:** Shannon Clark. **Director of Advertising:** Jan Plaude. **Director of Community Relations:** Julie Opgrande. **Director of Merchandising:** Leah Haberman. **Director of Food Services:** Trish Heitkamp. **Administrative Assistant:** Jeremy Lewis.

Manager/Director of Player Procurement: Doug Simunic. **Coach:** Andy McCauley. **Pitching Coach:** Jeff Bittiger. **Trainer:** Duane Bartley.

Game Information

Radio Announcer: Jack Michaels. **No. of Games Broadcast:** Home—42, Away—42. **Flagship Station:** KVOX 1280-AM.

Stadium Name: Fargo Baseball Stadium. **Location:** I-29 North to 19th Ave. North (exit 67), east on 19th to FargoDome, right at Albrecht Blvd., two blocks to stadium. **Standard Game Times:** 7:05 p.m.; Sun. 2:05, 6:05.

Visiting Club Hotel: Comfort Inn West, 3825 9th Ave. SW, Fargo, ND 58103. Telephone: (701) 282-9596.

MADISON BLACK WOLF

Office Address: 2920 North Sherman Ave., Madison, WI 53704. **Telephone:** (608) 244-5666. **FAX:** (608) 244-6996.

Years in League: 1996-

Ownership, Management

Operated by: Madison Baseball, LLC.

Principal Owners: Patrick Sweeney, Tom Shipley, Jimmy Buffett.

President/Chief Executive Officer: Patrick Sweeney.

General Manager: Ryan Richeal. **Director of Stadium Operations:** Jeff Desens. **Director of Community/Media Relations:** Monica Toppen. **Director of Sales/Promotions:** John Kuhn. **Director of Group Sales:** Tony Miller.

Manager: Wayne Krenchicki. **Coach:** Greg O'Brien.

Game Information

Stadium Name: Warner Park. **Location:** From south, I-90 North to Route 30, exit onto Northport Drive, left on Sherman Ave. From north, I-90 South to Route 151 south, exit onto Aberg Ave., to Northport Drive, left on Sherman Ave. **Standard Game Times:** 7:05 p.m.; Sun. 1:05.

Visiting Club Hotel: Unavailable.

ST. PAUL SAINTS

Office Address: 1771 Energy Park Dr., St. Paul, MN 55108. **Telephone:** (612) 644-3517. **FAX:** (612) 644-1627.

Years in League: 1993-

Ownership, Management

Operated by: St. Paul Saints Baseball Club Inc.

Principal Owners: Marvin Goldklang (chairman), Mike Veeck, Bill Murray.

President: Mike Veeck.

General Manager: Bill Fanning. **Director of Operations:** Tom Whaley. **Controller:** Wayne Engel. **Stadium Operations:** Bob Klepperich. **Head Groundskeeper:** Connie Rudolph. **Director of Media Relations:** Dave Wright. **Director of Advertising/Sales:** Bob St. Pierre. **Director of Community Relations:** Jody Beaulieu. **Director of Group Sales:** Peter Orme. **Director of Merchandise:** Bill Fisher. **Director of Food Services:** John Marso, Steven Marso. **Clubhouse Operations:** Brent Proulx. **Bookkeping:** Pat Cunningham.

Manager: Marty Scott. **Pitching Coach:** Ray Korn. **Infield Coach:** Wayne Terwilliger. **Trainer:** Tom Tisdale.

Game Information

Radio Announcers: Jim Lucas, Don Wardlow. **No. of Games Broadcast:** Home—42, Away—42. **Flagship Station:** KKMS-980 AM.

Stadium Name: Midway Stadium. **Location:** From I-94, north on Snelling Ave., west on Energy Park Drive to stadium. **Standard Game Times:** 7:05 p.m.; Sun. 2:05.

Visiting Club Hotel: Unavailable.

SIOUX CITY EXPLORERS

Office Address: 3400 Line Dr., Sioux City, IA 51106. **Telephone:** (712) 277-9467. **FAX:** (712) 277-9406.

Year in League: 1993-

Ownership, Management

Operated by: Diamond Sports Inc.

Principal Owner: Bill Pereira. **President:** Cord Pereira. **Vice President:** Eric Trapp.

General Manager: Tim Utrup. **Assistant General Manager:** Andrew Wheeler. **Controller:** Sue Peterson. **Director of Marketing:** Jim Frevola. **Senior Account Representative:** Kevin Farlow. **Director of Communications:** Jack Carnefix. **Director of Group Sales:** Jay Boldacci. **Director of Merchandising:** Brett Pollock. **Head Groundskeeper:** Eugene Carlson. **Administrative Assistant:** Shad Adams.

Manager/Director of Player Procurement: Ed Nottle. **Coach:** Dan McDermott. **Pitching Coach:** Lee Stange. **Trainer:** Mark Wright.

Game Information

Radio Announcers: Jim Frevola, Brett Pollock. **No. of Games Broadcast:** Home—42, Away—42. **Flagship Station:** KSCJ 1360-AM.

Stadium Name: Lewis and Clark Park. **Location:** I-29 to Industrial Road North, right at Line Drive. **Standard Game Times:** 7:05 p.m.; Sun. 6:05.

Visiting Club Hotel: Best Western, 130 Nebraska St., Sioux City, IA 51101. Telephone: (712) 277-1550.

SIOUX FALLS CANARIES

Office Address: 119 S. Main Ave., Sioux Falls, SD 57104. **Mailing Address:** P.O. Box 84412, Sioux Falls, SD 57118. **Telephone:** (605) 333-0179. **FAX:** (605) 333-0139.

Years in League: 1993-

Ownership, Management

Operated By: Sioux Falls Canaries, LP.

Principal Owner, President: Harry Stavrenos.

General Manager: Travis Lee. **Assistant General Managers:** Larry McKinney, George Stavrenos. **Director of Ticket Sales:** Brad Seymour. **Director of Community Relations:** Larry Helgeson.

Manager: Tommy Thompson.

Game Information

Radio Announcer: Brian Burkett. **No. of Games Broadcast:** Home—42, Away—42. **Flagship Station:** WSN 1230-AM.

Stadium Name: Sioux Falls Stadium. **Location:** I-29 to Russell Street exit. **Standard Game Times:** 7:05 p.m.; Sun. 2:05.

THUNDER BAY WHISKEY JACKS

Office Address: 425 Winnipeg Ave., Thunder Bay, Ontario P7B 6B7. **Mailing Address:** P.O. Box 864, Station F, Thunder Bay, Ontario P7C 4X7. **Telephone:** (807) 344-5225. **FAX:** (807) 343-4611.

Years in League: 1993-

Ownership, Management

Principal Owner: Whiskey Jack Partners LP.

Operated By: Sports Capital Management Inc.

President: Bill Terlecky.

General Manager: Rob Trippe. **Assistant General Manager:** Dan Wingold. **Director of Public Relations:** Jason Young. **Director of Promotions:** Thomas Ruttan. **Director of Ticket Sales:** Jennifer Bilous. **Director of Baseball Administration:** Pat Tilmon.

Manager: Jay Ward. **Pitching Coach:** Mike Browning.

Game Information

Stadium Name: Port Arthur Stadium. **Location:** Highway 61 North, right onto Harbour Expressway, left on Memorial Ave, ballpark one mile north on left. **Standard Game Times:** 7:05 p.m.; Sun. 6:05.

Visiting Club Hotel: Prince Arthur Hotel, 17 North Cumberland St., Thunder Bay, Ontario P7A 4K8. Telephone: (807) 345-5411.

WINNIPEG GOLDEYES

Office Address: 1430 Maroons Road, Winnipeg, Manitoba R3G 0L5. **Telephone:** (204) 982-2273. **FAX:** (204) 982-2274.

Years in League: 1994-

Ownership, Management

President, Principal Owner: Sam Katz.

General Manager: John Hindle. **Assistant to General Manager:** Barb McTavish. **Vice President, Finance:** Andrew Collier. **Director of Sales/Marketing:** Devon Kashton. **Senior Account Representatives:** Brent Borbridge, Wendy Fuerst, Dennis McLean. **Group Sales Manager:** Jo-Anne St. Goddard. **Receptionist:** Lisa Major. **Bookkeeper:** Michelle Adams.

Manager: Hal Lanier. **Pitching Coach:** Bob Kipper.

Game Information

Radio Announcer: Paul Edmonds. **No. of Games Broadcast:** Home—23, Away—23. **Flagship Station:** CJOB 680-AM

Stadium Name: Winnipeg Stadium. **Location:** Pembina Highway to Route 155, left to Route 90, right to Ness Avenue, left to St. James Street, right to stadium. **Standard Game Times:** 7:00 p.m.; Sun. 2.

PRAIRIE LEAGUE

Office Address: 427 Lark Bay North, Regina, Saskatchewan S4Y 1H7. **Telephone:** (306) 522-7575. **FAX:** (306) 522-7539.

Year Founded: 1995.

Vice President: David Ferguson. **Director of Player Personnel:** Rye Pothakos.

Member Clubs: Brandon (Manitoba) Grey Owls, Grand Forks (N.D.) Varmints, Minot (N.D.) Mallards, Moose Jaw (Sask.) Diamond Dogs, Regina (Sask.) Cyclones, Saskatoon (Sask.) Stallions, Southern Minny Stars (Austin, Minn.).

1997 Opening Date: June 13. **Closing Date:** Aug. 30..

Regular Season: 72 games.

Playoff Format: First-half division winners play second-half division winners in best-of-3 division playoff series. Winners meet in best-of-5 league championship series.

Roster Limit: 21.

TEXAS-LOUISIANA LEAGUE

Mailing Address: 401 Cypress St., Suite 300, Abilene, TX 79601. Telephone: (915) 677-4501. FAX: (915) 677-4215.

Year Founded: 1994.

Board of Directors: John Curtis, Alexander Earls, Andrew Earls, Greg Earls, Byron Pierce (all teams operated by Texas Professional Baseball Inc.).

President: Byron Pierce. **Vice President/Chief Executive Officer:** Rick Ivey. **Vice President/Director of Team Marketing:** Bruce Unrue.

Vice President/Baseball Operations: Bob Miller. **Administrative Assistant:** Mindy Cheek.

1997 Opening Date: May 22. **Closing Date:** Aug. 23.

Regular Season: 88 games (split-season).

All-Star Game: July 6-8 , Lubbock, TX.

Playoff Format: Top four teams overall, including half-season winners, meet in best-of-3 series. Winners meet in best-of-5 league championship series.

Roster Limit: 22. **Player Eligibility Rule:** Minimum of two first-year professionals; minimum of eight veterans (at least five professional seasons).

ABILENE PRAIRIE DOGS

Office Address: 401 Cypress St., Suite 300, Abilene, TX 79601. **Telephone:** (915) 673-7364. **FAX:** (915) 677-3294.

General Manager: Byron Pierce. **Assistant General Manager:** David Gardner. **Director of Business Operations:** Jay Hansen. **Director of Media/Public Relations:** Steven Solomon. **Director of Clubhouse Operations:** Blake Burton. **Director of Group Sales:** Karen Baker. **Director of Merchandising:** Charlotte Ely. **Director of Food Services:** Becca Sellers. **Office Manager:** Mindy Cheek.

Manager: Barry Jones. **Pitching Coach:** Troy Dean Conkle.

Stadium Name: Crutcher-Scott Field. **Standard Game Time:** 7:05 p.m.

ALEXANDRIA ACES

Office Address: 1 Babe Ruth Dr., Alexandria, LA 71301. **Mailing Address:** P.O. Box 6005, Alexandria, LA 71309. **Telephone:** (318) 473-2237. **FAX:** (318) 473-2229.

General Manager: Craig Brasfield. **Assistant General Manager/Media, Group Sales:** Rick Warner. **Assistant General Manager/Operations:** Reldon Owens. **Assistant General Manager/ Sales, Marketing:** Ryan Gribble. **Group Sales Assistant:** Frank Turco. **Assistant, Media Relations:** Alex Leithner. **Head Groundskeeper:** John Hickman. **Clubhouse Operations:** Paul Bencivengo. **Office Manager:** Carrie Crawford.

Manager: Stan Cliburn. **Trainer:** Mike Palumbo.

Stadium Name: Bringhurst Field. **Standard Game Times:** 6:35 p.m.; Sun. 6:05.

AMARILLO DILLAS

Mailing Address: P.O. Box 31241, Amarillo, TX 79120. **Telephone:** (806) 342-3455. **FAX:** (806) 374-2269.

General Manager: David Baur. **Director of Business Operations:** Dena Lambert. **Director of Stadium Operations:** Greg Levitt. **Head Groundskeeper:** Jackie Busby. **Director of Sales/Marketing:** Sam Schein. **Director of Group Sales:** Mike Cohen. **Clubhouse Operations:** George Escamilla. **Assistant, Sales/Marketing:** Daren Brown.

Manager: Glenn Wilson. **Trainer:** Todd Bowman.

Stadium Name: Potter County Memorial Stadium. **Standard Game Times:** 7:05 p.m.; Sun. 6:05.

LUBBOCK CRICKETS

Office Address: 1605 Broadway, Lubbock, TX 79401. **Mailing**

Address: P.O. Box 2608, Lubbock, TX 79408. **Telephone:** (806) 749-2255. **FAX:** (806) 749-6625.

General Manager: Jason Bogle. **Director of Business Operations:** Debbie Lynn. **Director of Operations:** Clay Powell. **Director of Sales/Marketing:** Darrin Cook. **Director of Ticket Sales:** Ryan Ferguson. **Account Representative:** Mike Hardge.

Manager: Glenn Sullivan. **Trainer:** Dean Easter.

Stadium Name: Dan Law Field. **Standard Game Times:** 7:05 p.m.; Sun. 5:05.

RIO GRANDE VALLEY WHITEWINGS

Office Address: 1216 Fair Park Blvd., Harlingen, TX 78550. **Mailing Address:** P.O. Box 530007, Harlingen, TX 78553. **Telephone:** (210) 412-9464. **FAX:** (210) 412-9479.

General Manager: Brian Borchardt. **Assistant General Manager/Operations:** Joseph Hart. **Assistant General Manager/Sales:** Brian Heller. **Director of Public Relations:** Ben McMann. **Public Relations/Operations Assistant:** Brian Hommel. **Office Manager:** Marilyn Farley. **Head Groundskeeper:** Omar Benevidas.

Manager: Unavailable. **Trainers:** Shawn Spanihel, Lisa Spanihel.

Stadium Name: Harlingen Field. **Standard Game Time:** 7:05 p.m.

TYLER WILDCATTERS

Office Address: 717 Fair Park Dr., Tyler, TX 75701. **Telephone:** (903) 597-9453. **FAX:** (903) 597-6464.

General Manager: Mark O'Brien. **Assistant General Manager:** Charles Witt. **Director of Operations:** Scott Sokolowski. **Director of Sales:** Mickey Smith. **Director of Community Relations:** Pamela Monday. **Office Administrator:** Karen Swindell. **Clubhouse Operations:** Melvin Tilley.

Manager: Darrell Evans. **Pitching Coach:** Larry Carter. **Trainer:** Dan Fuller.

Stadium Name: Mike Carter Field. **Standard Game Time:** 7:05 p.m.

WESTERN LEAGUE

Mailing Address: P.O. Box 80381, Portland, OR 97280. **Telephone:** (503) 203-8557. **FAX:** (503) 203-8438.

Year Founded: 1995.

President: Bruce Engel. **Treasurer:** Bob Linscheid. **Executive Director:** Tom Kowitz.

1997 Opening Date: May 23. **Closing Date:** Aug. 31.

Regular Season: 90 games (split-season).

Division Structure: Northern—Bend, Grays Harbor, Reno, Tri-Cities. **Southern**—Chico, Mission Viejo, Salinas, Sonoma County.

Playoff Format: First-half division winners meet second-half winners in best-of-3 division playoffs. Winners meet in best-of-5 league championship series.

Roster Limit: 22. **Player Eligibility Rule:** Minimum of five first-year players; maximum of six veterans (four or more years experience).

BEND BANDITS

Office Address: 1012 NW Wall St., Suite 250, Bend, OR 97701. **Mailing Address:** P.O. Box 1027, Bend, OR 97709. **Telephone:** (541) 383-1983. **FAX:** (541) 383-2004.

Operated by: Central Oregon Professional Baseball Co., Inc.

President/General Manager: Ed Zschau. **Head Groundskeeper:** Ken Zack. **Director of Media/Public Relations:** Tom Hamilton. **Director of Sales/Marketing:** Mike Smith. **Director of Group Sales:** Dean Shies. **Director of Merchandising:** Jeff Miller. **Office Manager:** Linda Longwell. **Group Services Representative:** Judi Quilter. **Promotions Manager:** Melanie Miller.

Manager/Director of Player Procurement: Alan Gallagher. **Coach:** Chip Miller. **Pitching Coach:** Derek Stroud.

Stadium Name: Vince Genna Stadium. **Standard Game Times:** 6:35 p.m.; Sun. 5:05.

CHICO HEAT

(Franchise operated in Palm Springs in 1996)

Office Address: 25 Main St., Suite 101, Chico, CA 95928. **Mailing Address:** P.O. Box 5362, Chico, CA 95927. **Telephone:** (916) 343-4328. **FAX:** (916) 894-1799.

Operated by: Chico Heat Baseball Club, LLC.

President: Steve Nettleton.

Vice-President, Operations: Bob Linscheid. **Vice-President, Sales and Marketing:** Jeff Kragel. **Customer Service Coordinator:** Gina Gestri. **Director of Group Sales:** Rory Miller. **Director of Merchandising:** Royal Courtain. **Director of Food Services:** John Milano. **Office Manager:** Tracey Perotti. **Marketing Assistant:** David Clink. **Head Groundskeeper:** Bob Miles.

Manager: Bill Plummer. **Pitching Coach:** Jeff Pico.

Stadium Name: Nettleton Stadium. **Standard Game Time:** 7:05 p.m; Sun. 5:05.

GRAYS HARBOR GULLS

Office Address: 101 28th St., Hoquiam WA 98550. **Telephone:** (360) 532-4488. **FAX:** (360) 533-8762

Operated by: Home Town Baseball, LLC.

President: Dale Giles.

Vice-President/General Manager: Patrick Brown. **Director of Media/Public Relations:** Mike Warchol. **Director of Sales/Marketing:** Sandy Ralls. **Director of Community Relations:** Chris Grubb. **Director of Merchandising:** Keith Worsham. **Office Manager:** Toni Marchie.

Manager: Charley Kerfeld. **Coach:** Dan Madsen. **Pitching Coach:** Mike Voelkel.

Stadium Name: Olympic Stadium. **Standard Game Times:** 7:05 p.m.; Sun. 2:05.

MISSION VIEJO VIGILANTES

(Franchise operated in Long Beach in 1996)

Office Address: 27301 La Paz Rd. at World Cup Center, Mission Viejo, CA 92692. **Telephone:** (714) 699-1616. **FAX:** (714) 699-1620.

Operated by: P & P Sports.

President: Patrick Elster.

General Manager: Paula Pyers. **Assistant General Manager:** Bobby Grich. **Director of Media/Public Relations:** David Ayers. **Director of Sales/Marketing:** Bill Smith.

Manager: Jeff Burroughs. **Pitching Coach:** Brad Lesley.

Stadium Name: Unavailable. **Standard Game Times:** 7:05 p.m.; Sun. 1:05.

RENO CHUKARS

Office Address: 240 W. Moana Lane, Reno, NV 89509. **Telephone:** (702) 829-7890. **FAX:** (702) 829-7895.

Operated By: Reno Professional Baseball Inc.

President: Bruce Engel.

General Manager: Dewey Stroud. **Assistant General Manager/ Promotions:** Mike Nelson. **Assistant General Manager/Group Sales:**Wendy Roberts. **Director of Business Operations, Ticket Sales:** Al Raiche. **Head Groundskeeper:** Ron Malcolm. **Director of Community Relations:** Maryann Hughes. **Director of Clubhouse Operations:** Roy Davis.

Manager/Director of Player Procurement: Butch Hughes. **Coaches:** Jacques Bolton, Randy Wiens. **Pitching Coach:** Dale Mead. **Trainer:** Pete Hoffman.

Stadium Name: Moana Stadium. **Standard Game Times:** 6:35 p.m.; Sun. 5:05.

SALINAS PEPPERS

Office Address: 175 Maryal Drive, Salinas, CA 93906. **Telephone:** (408) 758-8662. **FAX:** (408) 758-8524.

General Manager: Steve Carlson. **Assistant General Manager:** Bill Ritz. **Head Groundskeeper:** Ken Stevens. **Director of Ticket Sales, Office Manager:** Renee Moran.

Manager, Director of Player Procurement: Steve Hendricks.

Stadium Name: Salinas Municipal Stadium. **Standard Game Times:** 6:35 p.m.; Sat. 5:05; Sun. 2:05.

SONOMA COUNTY CRUSHERS

Office Address: 5900 Labath Ave., Rohnert Park, CA 94928. **Telephone:** (707) 588-8300. **FAX:** (707) 588-8721.

Operated by: Sonoma County Professional Baseball, Inc.

President/General Manager: Robert Fletcher. **Director of Business Operations:** Susan Fletcher. **Director of Public Relations:** David Raymond. **Director of Sales/Marketing:** Kevin Wolski. **Director of Group Sales:** Jessica Frey. **Box Office Manager:** Marianne Sacco.

Manager: Dick Dietz. **Coach:** Bob Barton. **Pitching Coach:** Dolf Hes. **Trainer:** Brian Powelson.

Stadium Name: Rohnert Park Stadium. **Standard Game Times:** 7:05 p.m.; Wed. 1:30; Sat. 5:05; Sun. 1:30.

TRI-CITY POSSE

Office Address: 6200 Burden Rd., Pasco, WA 99301. **Telephone:** (509) 547-6773. **FAX:** (509) 547-4008.

Operated By: Tri-City Posse Baseball Inc.

PresidentDirector, Baseball Operations: John Montero. **Vice President/General Manager:** Sean Kelly. **Assistant General Manager:** Janelle Eiscleman. **Director, Community Relations:** Rich Buel. **Office Manager:** Mary Stedman. **Ticket Manager:** Rick Marple. **Head Groundskeeper:** Bruce Schnabel.

Manager: Jamie Nelson. **Trainer:** Tressa Perkins.

Stadium Name: Tri-Cities Stadium. **Standard Game Times:** 7:05 p.m.; Thur. 1:05; Sun. 5:05.

INDEPENDENT SCHEDULES

Frontier League

Canton

JUNE
10-11-12-13 Ohio Valley
18-19-20-21.. Evansville
27-28-29-30.. Richmond

JULY
5-6-7-8......... Johnstown
13-14-15-16 . Chillicothe
18-19.......... Ohio Valley
28-29-30-31 . Chillicothe

AUGUST
5-6-7-8......... Springfield
9-10-11-12.. Kalamazoo
13-14.......... Ohio Valley
22-23-24-25. Johnstown

Chillicothe

JUNE
6-7-8-9 .... Canton
14-15-16-17 Ohio Valley
22-23-24-25 Kalamazoo

JULY
1-2-3-4.......... Richmond
9-10-11-12... Johnstown
24-25-26-27 Ohio Valley

AUGUST
1-2-3-4......... Springfield
13-14-15-16. Johnstown
18-19-20-21.. Evansville
26-27-28-29 ...... Canton

Evansville

JUNE
10-11-12-13 Kalamazoo
14-15-16-17.. Richmond
27-28-29-30 . Chillicothe

JULY
1-2-3-4 .... Ohio Valley
13-14-15-16. Springfield
18-19-20-21 Kalamazoo

AUGUST
1-2-3-4 .... Canton
5-6-7-8......... Johnstown
13-14-15-16.. Richmond
22-23-24-25. Springfield

Johnstown

JUNE
10-11-12-13 . Chillicothe
14-15-16-17 ...... Canton
22-23-24-25.. Evansville

JULY
1-2-3-4......... Springfield
13-14-15-16 Ohio Valley
18-19-20-21 . Chillicothe
24-25-26-27 ...... Canton

AUGUST
1-2-3-4.......... Richmond
18-19-20-21 Kalamazoo
26-27-28-29 Ohio Valley

Kalamazoo

JUNE
6-7-8-9.......... Richmond
14-15-16-17. Springfield
27-28-29-30. Johnstown

JULY
1-2-3-4 .... Canton
9-10-11-12....... Evansville
24-25-26-27.. Richmond

AUGUST
1-2-3-4 .... Ohio Valley
5-6-7-8 .... Chillicothe
13-14-15-16. Springfield
26-27-28-29.. Evansville

Ohio Valley

JUNE
6-7-8-9......... Johnstown
18-19-20-21 Kalamazoo
27-28-29-30. Springfield

JULY
5-6-7-8 .... Chillicothe
9-10-11-12 .... Canton
20-21................. Canton
28-29-30-31. Johnstown

AUGUST
5-6-7-8.......... Richmond
9-10-11-12.... Evansville
15-16................ Canton
22-23-24-25 . Chillicothe

Richmond

JUNE
10-11-12-13. Springfield
18-19-20-21. Johnstown
22-23-24-25 Ohio Valley

JULY
5-6-7-8.......... Evansville
13-14-15-16 Kalamazoo
18-19-20-21. Springfield
28-29-30-31.. Evansville

AUGUST
9-10-11-12 ... Chillicothe
18-19-20-21 ...... Canton
22-23-24-25 Kalamazoo

Springfield

JUNE
5-6-8-9.......... Evansville
18-19-20-21 . Chillicothe
22-23-24-25 ...... Canton

JULY
5-6-7-8........ Kalamazoo
9-10-11-12.... Richmond
24-25-26-27.. Evansville
28-29-30-31 Kalamazoo

AUGUST
9-10-11-12... Johnstown
18-19-20-21 Ohio Valley
26-27-28-29.. Richmond

Northern League

Duluth

MAY
30-31.................. Fargo

JUNE
1.......................... Fargo
9-10-11 .... Winnipeg
13-14-15 .... St. Paul
23-24-25 ..... Sioux Falls
27-28-29 .. Thunder Bay

JULY
4-5-6 .... Madison
8-9-10........... Sioux City
18-19-20 .... St. Paul
28-29-30 ..... Sioux Falls

AUGUST
1-2-3............ Sioux City
11-12-13........ Winnipeg
15-16-17 .. Thunder Bay
24-25-26.............. Fargo
27-28-29 .... Madison

Fargo-Moorhead

JUNE
6-7-8 .... Madison
10-11-12 .. Thunder Bay
20-21-22............. Duluth
24-25-26....... Sioux City

JULY
1-2-3 .... Sioux Falls
4-5-6 .... St. Paul
14-15-16 .... Winnipeg
25-26-27 .... Madison
29-30-31 .... St. Paul

AUGUST
8-9-10................ Duluth
11-12-13....... Sioux City
18-19-20 ..... Sioux Falls
21-22-23 .. Thunder Bay
30-31 .... Winnipeg

SEPTEMBER
1 .... Winnipeg

Madison

MAY
30-31........ Thunder Bay

JUNE
1 .... Thunder Bay
9-10-11 .... Sioux Falls
12-13-14....... Sioux City
23-24-25 .... Winnipeg
27-28-29 .... St. Paul

JULY
8-9-10.................. Fargo
11-12-13............ Duluth
18-19-20............. Fargo
28-29-30........ Winnipeg

AUGUST
1-2-3 .... Thunder Bay
11-12-13 ..... Sioux Falls
15-16-17 .... St. Paul
21-22-23............. Duluth
24-25-26....... Sioux City

St. Paul

JUNE
6-7-8 .... Sioux Falls
9-10-11......... Sioux City
20-21-22........ Winnipeg
24-25-26 .. Thunder Bay

JULY
1-2-3.................. Duluth
11-12-13............. Fargo
14-15-16 .... Madison
21-22-23............. Fargo
25-26-27 .... Winnipeg

AUGUST
5-6-7 .... Thunder Bay
8-9-10 .... Sioux Falls
18-19-20............. Duluth
21-22-23....... Sioux City
30-31............... Madison

SEPTEMBER
1...................... Madison

Sioux City

JUNE
2-3-4 .... St. Paul
6-7-8.................. Duluth
16-17-18.............. Fargo
20-21-22 .... Madison

JULY
1-2-3 .... Winnipeg
4-5-6 .... Thunder Bay
14-15-16 ..... Sioux Falls
21-22-23 .. Thunder Bay
25-26-27 .... Duluth
AUGUST
5-6-7 .... Fargo
8-9-10 .... Madison
16 .... Sioux Falls
18-19-20 .... Winnipeg
27-28-29 .... St. Paul
30-31 .... Sioux Falls

Sioux Falls

MAY
30-31 .... St. Paul
JUNE
1 .... St. Paul
3-4-5 .... Duluth
13-14-15 .... Fargo
17-18-19 .... Madison
27-28-29 .... Sioux City
JULY
7-8-9 .... Thunder Bay
11-12-13 .... Winnipeg
18-19-20 .. Thunder Bay
22-23-24 .... Duluth
AUGUST
1-2-3 .... Fargo
5-6-7 .... Madison
15 .... Sioux City
21-22-23 .... Winnipeg
24-25-26 .... St. Paul
31 .... Sioux City
SEPTEMBER
1 .... Sioux City

Thunder Bay

JUNE
2-3-4 .... Fargo
6-7-8 .... Winnipeg
16-17-18 .... St. Paul
20-21-22 ..... Sioux Falls
JULY
1-2-3 .... Madison
11-12-13 .... Sioux City
14-15-16 .... Duluth
25-26-27 ..... Sioux Falls
29-30-31 .... Sioux City
AUGUST
8-9-10 .... Winnipeg
11-12-13 .... St. Paul
18-19-20 .... Madison
27-28-29 .... Fargo
30-31 .... Duluth
SEPTEMBER
1 .... Duluth

Winnipeg

MAY
30-31 .... Sioux City
JUNE
1 .... Sioux City
3-4-5 .... Madison
14-15-16 .. Thunder Bay
17-18-19 .... Duluth
27-28-29 .... Fargo
JULY
4-5-6 .... Sioux Falls
7-8-9 .... St. Paul
18-19-20 .... Sioux City
22-23-24 .... Madison
AUGUST
1-2-3 .... St. Paul
5-6-7 .... Duluth
15-16-17 .... Fargo
24-25-26 .. Thunder Bay
27-28-29 ..... Sioux Falls

Texas-Louisiana League

Abilene

MAY
29-30-31 ...... Alexandria
JUNE
1-2-3 .... Amarillo
11-12-13 ...... Alexandria
20-21-22 .... Tyler
23-24-24-25 Rio Grande
30 .... Amarillo
JULY
1-2 .... Amarillo
3-4-5 .... Lubbock
9-10-11 .... Alexandria
22-23-24 .... Lubbock
29-30-31 .... Tyler
AUGUST
1-2-3 .... Amarillo
8-9-10 .... Tyler
14-15-16 .... Lubbock
17-17-18-19 Rio Grande

Alexandria

MAY
22-23-24 ..... Rio Grande
JUNE
1-2-3 .... Rio Grande
4-5-5-6 .... Abilene
14-15-16 .... Tyler
23-24-25 .... Lubbock
26-27-28 .... Tyler
29 .... Lubbock
JULY
1-2 .... Lubbock
12-13-14 .... Amarillo
19-19-20-21 ...... Abilene
29-30-31 .... Amarillo
AUGUST
8-9-10 .... Lubbock
11-12-13 .... Amarillo
14-15-16 .... Tyler
21-22-23 ..... Rio Grande

Amarillo

MAY
22-23-24 .... Lubbock
25-26-27 ...... Alexandria
JUNE
4-5-5-6 .... Tyler
7-8-9 .... Rio Grande
14-15-16 .... Lubbock
26-27-28 ..... Rio Grande
JULY
3-4-5 .... Alexandria
16-17-18 .... Abilene
19-20-21 .... Lubbock
22-23-23-24 .... Tyler
AUGUST
4-5-6 .... Abilene
14-15-16 ..... Rio Grande
17-18-19 ...... Alexandria
21-22-23 .... Abilene

Lubbock

MAY
29-30-31 .... Amarillo
JUNE
1-2-3 .... Tyler
7-8-9 .... Abilene
11-12-13 ..... Rio Grande
17-18-19 .... Amarillo
20-21-21-22. Alexandria
26-27-28 .... Abilene
JULY
12-13-14 .... Abilene
16-17-18 ..... Rio Grande
25-25-26-27 ..... Amarillo
29-30-31 ..... Rio Grande
AUGUST
1-2-3 .... Alexandria
4-5-6 .... Tyler
17-18-19 .... Tyler

Rio Grande Valley

MAY
25-26-27 .... Abilene
29-30-31 .... Tyler
JUNE
4-5-6 .... Lubbock
14-15-16 .... Abilene
17-18-19 ...... Alexandria
20-20-21-22 ..... Amarillo
JULY
3-4-5 .... Tyler
9-10-11 .... Lubbock
19-20-21 .... Tyler
22-23-24 ...... Alexandria
25-26-27 .... Abilene
AUGUST
4-5-6 .... Alexandria
8-8-9-10 .... Amarillo
11-12-13 .... Lubbock

Tyler

MAY
22-23-24 .... Abilene
25-26-27-27 .... Lubbock
JUNE
7-8-9 .... Alexandria
11-12-13 .... Amarillo
17-18-19 .... Abilene
23-24-25 .... Amarillo
30 .... Rio Grande
JULY
1-2 .... Rio Grande
9-10-11 .... Amarillo
12-13-14 ..... Rio Grande
16-17-18 ...... Alexandria
25-26-27 ...... Alexandria
AUGUST
1-2-3 .... Rio Grande
11-12-13 .... Abilene
21-22-22-23 .... Lubbock

Western League

Bend

MAY
23-24-25 .... Tri-City
26-27-28 . Grays Harbor
JUNE
3-4-5 .... Mission Viejo
6-7-8 .... Salinas
17-18-19 .... Chico
20-21-22 Sonoma County
JULY
5-6-7 .... Reno
14-15-16-17 Grays Harbor
18-19-20.. Mission Viejo
21-22-23 .... Salinas
AUGUST
5-6-7 ... Sonoma County
8-9-10 .... Chico
21-22-23-24 ...... Tri-City
25-26-27-28 .... Reno

Chico

MAY
30-31 .... Mission Viejo
JUNE
1 .... Mission Viejo
10-11-12 .... Reno
13-14-15 .... Bend
24-25-26 . Grays Harbor
27-28-29 .... Tri-City

JULY
1-2-3-4 .... Salinas
9-10-11-12 ...... Sonoma
25-26-27......... Sonoma
29-30-31 .... Reno
AUGUST
1-2-3..................... Bend
12-13-14 .... Tri-City
15-16-17 . Grays Harbor
21-22-23 .... Salinas
24-25-26-27 Mission Viejo

Grays Harbor

MAY
30-31 .... Reno
JUNE
1-2........................ Reno
3-4-5 ... Sonoma County
6-7-8 .... Chico
17-18-19 .... Salinas
20-21-22.. Mission Viejo
JULY
1-2-3-4 .... Tri-City
9-10-11-12 .... Bend
18-19-20.......... Sonoma
21-22-23............. Chico
25-26-27 .... Reno
AUGUST
5-6-7 .... Salinas
8-9-10...... Mission Viejo
18-19-20............... Bend
29-30-31 .... Tri-City

Mission Viejo

MAY
23-24-25-26......... Chico
27-28-29 .... Salinas
JUNE
10-11-12 . Grays Harbor
13-14-15 .... Tri-City
24-25-26.............. Bend
27-28-29 .... Reno
JULY
5-6-7 ... Sonoma County
13-14-15-16...... Salinas
29-30-31 . Grays Harbor
AUGUST
1-2-3 .... Tri-City
12-13-14 .... Reno
15-16-17............... Bend
18-19-20............. Chico
29-30-31-31 .... Sonoma

Reno

MAY
23-24-25 . Grays Harbor
26-27-28 .... Tri-City
JUNE
3-4-5 .... Salinas
6-7-8........ Mission Viejo
17-18-19.......... Sonoma
20-21-22............. Chico
JULY
1-2-3-4 .... Bend
14-15-16-17 ...... Tri-City
18-19-20 .... Salinas
21-22-23.. Mission Viejo
AUGUST
5-6-7.................... Chico
8-9-10 . Sonoma County
21-22-23-24 Grays Harbor
29-30-31............... Bend

Salinas

MAY
30-31 .. Sonoma County
JUNE
1-2 ...... Sonoma County
10-11-12 .... Tri-City
13-14-15 . Grays Harbor
24-25-26 .... Reno
27-28-29............... Bend
JULY
5-6-7.................... Chico
9-10-11-12........ Mission Viejo
25-26-27.. Mission Viejo
29-30-31 .... Tri-City
AUGUST
1-2-3 .... Grays Harbor
12-13-14............... Bend
15-16-17 .... Reno
18-19-20.......... Sonoma
28-29-30-31......... Chico

Sonoma County

MAY
23-24-25 .... Salinas
27-28-29.............. Chico
JUNE
10-11-12............... Bend
13-14-15 .... Reno
24-25-26 .... Tri-City
27-28-29 . Grays Harbor
JULY
1-2-3-4..... Mission Viejo
13-14-15-16......... Chico
29-30-31............... Bend
AUGUST
1-2-3 .... Reno
12-13-14 . Grays Harbor
15-16-17 .... Tri-City
21-22-23.. Mission Viejo
24-25-26-27...... Salinas

Tri-City

MAY
30-31 .... Bend
JUNE
1-2........................ Bend
3-4-5.................... Chico
6-7-8 ... Sonoma County
17-18-19.. Mission Viejo
20-21-22 .... Salinas
JULY
5-6-7 .... Grays Harbor
9-10-11-12 .... Reno
18-19-20............. Chico
21-22-23.......... Sonoma
25-26-27............... Bend
AUGUST
5-6-7........ Mission Viejo
8-9-10 .... Salinas
18-19-20 .... Reno
25-26-27-28 Grays Harbor

FOREIGN/WINTER

MEXICAN LEAGUE

Class AAA

NOTE: The Mexican League is a member of the National Association of Professional Baseball Leagues and has a Triple-A classification. However, its member clubs operate largely independent of the 30 major league teams, and for that reason the league is listed in the international and winter league section.

Mailing Address: Angel Pola #16, Col. Periodista, Mexico, D.F. CP 11220. **Telephone:** 011-525-557-2454. **FAX:** 011-525-395-2454.

Year Founded: 1955.

President: Pedro Treto Cisneros.

Vice President: Roberto Mansur Galan.

Assistant to the President/Public Relations: Nestor Alva Brito. **Treasurer:** Salvador Velazquez Andrade. **Secretaries:** Socorro Becerra, Irene Garcia.

1997 Opening Date: March 19. **Closing Date:** Aug. 6.

Regular Season: 122 games.

Division Structure: Central—Aguascalientes, Mexico City Red Devils, Mexico City Tigers, Oaxaca, Poza Rica. **North**—Monclova, Monterrey, Nuevo Laredo, Reynosa, Saltillo, Union Laguna. **South**—Campeche, Minatitlan, Quintana Roo, Tabasco, Yucatan.

Playoff Format: Three-tier playoffs involving top two teams in each zone, plus two wild-card teams. Two finalists play a best-of-7 series for league championship.

All-Star Game: June 2 at Monclova.

Roster Limit: 25. **Roster Limit, Imports:** 5.

Brand of Baseball: Rawlings.

Statistician: Ana Luisa Perea Talarico, Angel Pola #16, Col. Periodista, CP 11220 Mexico, D.F.

1996 Standings

Central Zone	W	L	Pct.	GB
Mexico City Reds	70	43	.619	—
Mexico City Tigers	68	45	.602	2
Poza Rica	63	50	.558	7
Aguascalientes	58	57	.504	13
Oaxaca	46	64	.418	22½

North Zone	W	L	Pct.	GB
Monterrey*	82	33	.713	—
Monclova	58	56	.509	23½
Reynosa	56	56	.500	24½

South Zone	W	L	Pct.	GB
Yucatan	58	56	.509	—
Quintana Roo	55	55	.500	1
Campeche	53	59	.473	4
Tabasco	48	63	.432	8½
Minatitlan	45	65	.409	11

North Zone	W	L	Pct.	GB
Union Laguna	50	62	.446	30½
Nuevo Laredo	48	65	.424	33
Saltillo	41	70	.369	39

*Won playoffs

AGUASCALIENTES RAILROADMEN

Office Address: General Manuel Madrigal 110, Col. Heroes, CP 20190, Aguascalientes, Aguascalientes. **Telephone:** (49) 15-84-22. **FAX:** (49) 18-77-78.

President: Oscar Lomelin Ibarra. **General Manager:** Ernesto Rios Gonzalez.

Manager: Juan Francisco Rodriguez.

CAMPECHE PIRATES

Office Address: Unidad Deportiva 20 de Noviembre, Local 4, CP 24000, Col. Centro, Campeche, Campeche. **Telephone:** (981) 6-60-71. **FAX:** (981) 6-38-07.

President: Gustavo Ortiz Avila. **General Manager:** Maria del Socorro Morales.

Manager: Bernardo Calvo.

MEXICO CITY RED DEVILS

Office Address: Av. Cuauhtemoc No. 451-101, Col. Piedad Narvarte, CP 03030, Mexico, D.F. **Telephone:** (5) 639-87-22 or 639-97-22.

Co-Presidents: Roberto Mansur Galan, Alfredo Harp Helu. **General Manager:** Pedro Mayorquin Aguilar.

Manager: Marco Antonio Vazquez.

MEXICO CITY TIGERS

Office Address: Tuxpan No. 45-A, Sto. Piso Col. Roma Sur, CP 06760, Mexico, D.F. **Telephone:** (5) 584-02-16. **FAX:** (5) 564-48-75.

President: Carlos Peralta. **General Manager:** Alfonso Lopez.

Manager: Jorge Calvo.

MINATITLAN COLTS

Office Address: Avila Camacho Esq. Ninos Heroes S/N, Col. Los Maestros, CP 90849, Minatitlan, Veracruz. **Telephone:** (922) 3-50-03.

President: Javier Rios Lopez.

Manager: Eddy Castro.

MONCLOVA STEELERS

Office Address: Cuauhtemoc #1002, Col. Ciudad Deportiva, CP 25700, Monclova, Coahuila. **Telephone:** (86) 34-21-72. **FAX:** (86) 34-21-76.

President: Alonso Ancira Gonzalez. **General Manager:** Carlos de la Garza Barajas.

Manager: Fernando Villaescusa.

MONTERREY SULTANS

Office Address: Av. Manuel L. Barragan S/N, Estadio Monterrey, CP 64400, Monterrey, Nuevo Leon. **Telephone:** (83) 51-02-09. **FAX:** (83) 51-80-22.

President: Jose Maiz Garcia. **General Manager:** Roberto Magdaleno Ramirez.

Manager: Derek Bryant.

NUEVO LAREDO OWLS

Office Address: Porfirio Diaz No. 2210, Col. San Jose, CP 88230, Nuevo Laredo, Tamaulipas. **Telephone:** (87) 19-12-35. **FAX:** (87) 19-12-36.

President: Manuel Canales Escamilla. **General Manager:** Samuel Lozano Molina.

Manager: Andres Mora.

OAXACA WARRIORS

Office Address: Privada del Chopo No. 105, Fraccionamiento El Chopo, CP 68000, Oaxaca, Oaxaca. **Telephone:** (951) 555-22. **FAX:** (951) 549-66.

President: Edgar Nehme Slim. **General Manager:** Roberto Castellon Yuen.

Manager: Lionel Carrion.

POZA RICA OILERS

Office Address: Privada 16 Norte, No. 111, Col. Obrera, CP 93200, Poza Rica, Veracruz. **Telephone:** (782) 2-35-50.

President: Vicente Perez Avella. **General Manager:** Raul Cano.

Manager: Jesus Sommers.

QUINTANA ROO LOBSTERERS

Office Address: Av. Kabah Super Manzana 31, Lote 25, Manzana 6, Altos, Cancun, Quintana Roo. **Telephone:** (98) 87-40-11 or 84-98-46.

President: Ariel Magara Carrillo. **General Manager:** Ricardo Argueta Maranon.

Manager: Francisco Estrada.

REYNOSA BRONCOS

Office Address: Blvd. Hidalgo 102, Col. Del Parque, CP 88650, Reynosa, Tamaulipas. **Telephone:** (89) 24-17-50. **FAX:** (89) 24-26-95.

President: Eduardo Trevino. **General Manager:** Jose Manuel Ortiz.

Manager: Aurelio Rodriguez.

SALTILLO SARAPE MAKERS

Office Address: Blvd. Nazario S. Ortiz Garza esq. con Blvd. Jesus Valdez Sanchez, CP 25280, Saltillo, Coahuila. **Telephone:** (84) 16-94-55.

President: Javier Cabello Siller.

Manager: Unavailable.

TABASCO OLMECAS

Office Address: Explanada de la Ciudad Deportiva, Estadio de Beisbol Centenario del 27 de Febrero, Col. Atasta de Serra, CP 86100, Villahermosa, Tabasco. **Telephone:** (93) 15-32-37.

President: Diego Rosique Palavicini. **General Manager:** Carlos Elias Dagdug Martinez.

Manager: Carlos Paz.

UNION LAGUNA COTTON PICKERS

Office Address: Calle Juan Gutemberg, S/N, Estadio de la Revolucion, CP 27000, Torreon, Coahuila. **Telephone:** (17) 17-43-35. **FAX:** (17) 18-55-15.

President: Jorge Duenes Zurita.

Manager: Zacatillo Guerrero.

YUCATAN LIONS

Office Address: Calle 50 #406-B, Col. Jesus Carranza, CP 97109, Merida, Yucatan. **Telephone:** (99) 26-30-22. **FAX:** (99) 26-36-31.

President: Gustavo Ricalde Duran. **General Manager:** Jose Rivero Ancona.

Manager: Javier Martinez.

JAPANESE LEAGUES

Mailing Address: Imperial Tower, 7F, 1-1-1 Uchisaiwai-cho, Chiyoda-ku, Tokyo 100, Japan. **Telephone:** 011-03-3502-0022. **FAX:** 011-03-3502-0140.

Commissioner: Ichiro Yoshikuni.

Executive Secretary: Yoshiaki Kanai. **Assistant Director of International Affairs:** Nobuhisa "Nobby" Ito.

Japan Series: Best-of-7 series between Central and Pacific League champions, begins Oct. 18 at home of Pacific League club.

All-Star Series: July 23 at Osaka, July 24 at Tokyo.

Roster Limit: 70 per organization. Major league club is permitted to register 28 players at a time, though only 25 may be available for each game. **Roster Limit, Imports:** 4.

PACIFIC LEAGUE

Mailing Address: Asahi Bldg. 9F, 6-6-7 Ginza, Chuo-ku, Tokyo 104. **Telephone:** 03-3573-1551. **FAX:** 03-3572-5843.

Years League Active: 1950-.

President: Kazuo Harano.

Secretary General: Shigeru Murata. **Public Relations:** Hiroshi Yoshimura.

1997 Opening Date: April 5. **Closing Date:** Sept. 28.

Regular Season: 135 games. **Playoff Format:** None.

1996 Standings, 1997 Stadiums

Club	W	L	T	Pct.	GB		Cap.
Orix Blue Wave	74	50	6	.597	—	Kobe Green	35,000
Nippon Ham Fighters	68	58	4	.540	7	Tokyo Dome	55,000
Seibu Lions	62	64	4	.492	13	Seibu Lions	37,008
Kintetsu Buffaloes	62	67	1	.481	14½	Osaka Dome	50,000
Chiba Lotte Marines	60	67	3	.472	15½	Chiba Marine	30,000
Fukuoka Daiei Hawks	54	74	2	.422	22	Fukuoka Dome	48,000

CHIBA LOTTE MARINES

Mailing Address: WBG Marive West 25F, 2-6 Nakase, Mihama-ku, Chiba-shi, Chiba-ken 261-71. **Telephone:** 043-297-2101. **FAX:** 043-297-2181.

Chairman of the Board: Takeo Shigemitsu. **General Manager:** Mitsumasa Mitsuno.

Field Manager: Akihito Kondo. **Foreign Coach:** Lenn Sakata.

1996 Attendance: 1,064,000.

1997 Foreign Players: Mark Carreon, Shane Dennis, Mike Fyhrie, Jason Thompson.

FUKUOKA DAIEI HAWKS

Mailing Address: Fukuoka Dome 6F, 2-2-2 Jigyohama, Chuo-ku, Fukuoka 810. **Telephone:** 092-844-1189. **FAX:** 092-844-4600.

Chairman of the Board: Isao Nakauchi. **President:** Hiroshi Murakami. **General Manager:** Ryuzo Setoyama.

Field Manager: Sadaharu Oh.

1996 Attendance: 2,207,000.

1997 Foreign Players: Rod Nichols, Jose Nunez, Greg Pirkl, David West.

KINTETSU BUFFALOES

Mailing Address: Midosuji Grand Bldg. 5F, 2-2-3 Namba, Chuo-ku, Osaka 542. **Telephone:** 06-212-9744. **FAX:** 06-212-6834.

Chairman of the Board: Yoshinori Ueyama. **President:** Hironobu Chikuma. **General Manager:** Yoshio Ikoma.

Field Manager: Kyosuke Sasaki.

1996 Attendance: 915,000.

1997 Foreign Players: Phil Clark, Bob Milacki, Tuffy Rhodes.

NIPPON HAM FIGHTERS

Mailing Address: Roppongi Denki Bldg. 6F, 6-1-20 Roppongi, Minato-ku, Tokyo 106. **Telephone:** 03-3403-9131. **FAX:** 03-3403-9143.

Chairman of the Board: Yoshinori Okoso. **President:** Saburo Mochida. **General Manager:** Takeshi Kojima.

Field Manager: Toshiharu Ueda.

1996 Attendance: 1,600,000.

1997 Foreign Players: Jerry Brooks, Kip Gross, Billy Ray Munoz, Nigel Wilson.

ORIX BLUE WAVE

Mailing Address: Kanri Center, 2F, Midoridai, Suma-ku, Kobe 654-01. **Telephone:** 078-795-1001. **FAX:** 078-795-1005.

Chairman of the Board: Yoshihiko Miyauchi. **President:** Yasushi Iwai. **General Manager:** Steve Ino.

Field Manager: Akira Ogi.

1996 Attendance: 1,796,000.

1997 Foreign Players: Willie Fraser, Doug Jennings, Troy Neel.

SEIBU LIONS

Mailing Address: Seibu Lions Stadium, 2135 Kami-Yamaguchi, Tokorozawa-shi, Saitama-ken 359. **Telephone:** 0429-24-1155. **FAX:** 0429-28-1919.

Chairman of the Board: Yoshiaki Tsutsumi. **President:** Iwao Nisugi. **General Manager:** Kenji Ono.

Field Manager: Osamu Higashio.

1996 Attendance: 1,295,000.

1997 Foreign Players: Brian Givens, Taigen Kaku (Taiwan), Domingo Martinez, Rob Wishnevski.

CENTRAL LEAGUE

Mailing Address: Asahi Bldg. 3F, 6-6-7 Ginza, Chuo-ku, Tokyo 104. **Telephone:** 03-3572-1673. **FAX:** 03-3571-4545.

President: Hiromori Kawashima.

Secretary General: Ryoichi Shibusawa. **Planning Department:** Masaaki Nagino.

Years League Active: 1950-.

1997 Opening Date: April 4. **Closing Date:** Sept. 28.

Regular Season: 135 games. **Playoff Format:** None.

1996 Standings, 1997 Stadiums

Club	W	L	T	Pct.	GB	Stadium	Cap.
Yomiuri Giants	77	53	0	.592	—	Tokyo Dome	55,000
Chunichi Dragons	72	58	0	.554	5	Nagoya Dome	40,500
Hiroshima Carp	71	59	0	.546	6	Hiroshima	32,000
Yakult Swallows	61	69	0	.469	16	Meiji Jingu	48,000
Yokohama BayStars	55	75	0	.423	22	Yokohama	30,000
Hanshin Tigers	54	76	0	.415	23	Koshien	55,000

CHUNICHI DRAGONS

Mailing Address: Chunichi Bldg. 9F, 4-1-1 Sakae, Naka-ku, Nagoya 460. **Telephone:** 052-252-5226. **FAX:** 052-251-8649.

Chairman of the Board: Hirohiko Oshima. **President:** Tsuyoshi Sato. **General Manager:** Osamu Ito.

Field Manager: Senichi Hoshino.

1996 Attendance: 2,079,000.

1997 Foreign Players: Leo Gomez, Alonzo Powell, Jimmy Williams, Sun Dong Yol (Korea).

HANSHIN TIGERS

Mailing Address: 1-47 Koshien-cho, Nishinomiya-shi, Hyogo-ken 663. **Telephone:** 0798-46-1515. **FAX:** 0798-40-0934.

Chairman of the Board: Shunjiro Kuma. **President:** Kazuhiko Miyoshi. **General Manager:** Katsuyoshi Nozaki.

Field Manager: Yoshio Yoshida.

1996 Attendance: 1,860,000.

1997 Foreign Players: Mike Greenwell, Phil Hiatt, Tateo Kaku-ri (Taiwan).

HIROSHIMA TOYO CARP

Mailing Address: 5-25 Motomachi, Naka-ku, Hiroshima 730. **Telephone:** 082-221-2040. **FAX:** 082-228-5013.

Chairman of the Board: Kohei Matsuda. **General Manager:** Chitomi Takahashi.

Field Manager: Toshiyuki Mimura.

1996 Attendance: 1,294,000.

1997 Foreign Players: Luis Lopez, Felix Perdomo, Timoniel Perez, Alfonso Soriano.

YAKULT SWALLOWS

Mailing Address: Yakult Bldg. 7F, 1-1-19 Higashi Shimbashi, Minato-ku, Tokyo 105. **Telephone:** 03-3574-0671. **FAX:** 03-3574-6764.

Chairman of the Board: Jun Kuwahara. **President:** Kiyoto Sakai. **General Manager:** Itaru Taguchi.

Field Manager: Katsuya Nomura.

1996 Attendance: 1,963,000.

1997 Foreign Players: Terry Bross, Dwayne Hosey, Luis Ortiz.

YOKOHAMA BAYSTARS

Mailing Address: Nihon Seimei Yokohama Hon-machi Bldg., 6F, 2-22 Hon-machi, Naka-ku, Yokohama 231. **Telephone:** 045-681-0811. **FAX:** 045-661-2500.

Chairman of the Board: Keijiro Nakabe. **President:** Takashi Ohori. **General Manager:** Kaoru Sakurai.

Field Manager: Akihiko Oya.

1996 Attendance: 1,533,000.

1997 Foreign Players: Mike Campbell, Bobby Rose, Bill Selby.

YOMIURI GIANTS

Mailing Address: Takebashi 3-3 Bldg., 3-3 Kanda Nishiki-cho, Chiyoda-ku, Tokyo 101. **Telephone:** 03-3295-7711. **FAX:** 03-3295-7731.

Chairman of the Board: Tsuneo Watanabe. **General Manager:** Yoshinori Fukaya.

Field Manager: Shigeo Nagashima.

1996 Attendance: 3,494,000.

1997 Foreign Players: Balvino Galvez, Eric Hillman, Cho Sung Min (Korea), Luis de los Santos.

Other Professional Leagues

CHINESE PROFESSIONAL BASEBALL LEAGUE

(Taiwan)

Mailing Address: 14F, No. 126, Sec. 4, Nanking East Road, Taipei, Taiwan. **Telephone:** 886-2-577-6992. **FAX:** 886-2-577-2606.

Year Founded: 1990.

Commissioner: C.K. Chen.

Member Clubs: Brother Elephants (Taipei), China Times Eagles (Taipei), Jungo Bears (Taichung), Mercury Tigers (Taipei), President Lions (Tainan), Weichuan Dragons (Taipei).

Regular Season: 100 games.

KOREAN BASEBALL ORGANIZATION

(South Korea)

Mailing Address: 946-16 Dokok-Dong, Kangnam-Gu, Seoul, South Korea. **Telephone:** 011-82-2-557-7887~9. **FAX:** 011-82-2-557-7800.

Year Founded: 1982.

Commissioner: Jae-Hyong Hong. **Secretary General:** Jong-Hwan Park.

Member Clubs: Haitai Tigers (Kwangju), Hanhwa Eagles (Taejun), Hyundai Unicorns (Inchon), LG Twins (Seoul), Lotte Giants (Pusan), OB Bears (Seoul), Samsung Lions (Taegu), Ssangbangwool Raiders (Cheonju).

Regular Season: 126 games.

WINTER BASEBALL

CARIBBEAN BASEBALL CONFEDERATION

Mailing Address: Frank Feliz Miranda No. 1 Naco, P.O. Box 21070 y 21416, Santo Domingo, Dominican Republic. **Telephone:** (809) 562-4737 or 562-4715. **FAX:** (809) 565-4654.

Commissioner: Juan Fco. Puello Herrera (Dominican Republic).

Member Leagues: Dominican Republic, Mexican Pacific, Puerto Rican, Venezuelan.

1998 Caribbean World Series: Feb. 3-8 at Puerto la Cruz, Venezuela.

DOMINICAN LEAGUE

Mailing Address: Estadio Quisqueya, Santo Domingo, Dominican Republic. **Telephone:** (809) 567-6371. **FAX:** (809) 567-5720.

Year Founded: 1951.

President: Dr. Leonardo Matos. **Vice President/Treasurer:** Marcos Rodriguez. **Secretary:** Dr. Francisco Pellerano. **Public Relations Director:** Felix Decena.

1996-97 Opening Date: Oct. 25, 1996. **Closing Date:** Dec. 30, 1996.

Regular Season: 48 games.

Playoff Format: Top four teams meet in an 18-game round-robin tournament. Top two finishers meet in a best-of-7 series for league championship. Winner advances to Caribbean World Series.

Roster Limit: 30. **Roster Limit, Imports:** 7.

1996-97 Standings

	W	L	Pct.	GB
*Aguilas	32	16	.667	—
Escogido	28	21	.571	4½
Azucareros	28	22	.560	5
Licey	25	23	.521	7
Northeast	20	28	.417	12
Estrellas	13	36	.265	19½

*Won playoffs

AGUILAS

Street Address: Estadio Cibao, Ave. Imbert, Santiago, Dom. Rep. **Mailing Address:** EPS B-225, P.O. Box 02-5360, Miami, FL 33102. **Telephone:** (809) 575-4310, 575-1810. **FAX:** (809) 575-0865.

Primary Working Agreement: None.

President: Ricardo Hernandez. **General Manager:** Quilvio Hernandez.

1996-97 Manager: Mike Quade.

AZUCAREROS

Mailing Address: Estadio Francisco Micheli, La Romana, Dom. Rep. **Telephone:** (809) 556-6188. **FAX:** (809) 550-1550.

Primary Working Agreement: Los Angeles Dodgers.

President: Arturo Gil. **General Manager:** Ralph Avila.

1996-97 Manager: Del Crandall.

ESCOGIDO LIONS

Mailing Address: P.O. Box 1287, Santo Domingo, Dom. Rep. **Telephone:** (809) 565-1910. **FAX:** (809) 567-7643.

Primary Working Agreement: None.

General Manager: Freddy Jana.

1996-97 Managers: Ozzie Virgil Sr., Rick Down, Junior Noboa, Sammy Mejias.

ESTRELLAS

Mailing Address: Av. Lopez de Vega, No. 46 Altos, Ens. Piantini, San Pedro de Macoris, Dom. Rep. **Telephone:** (809) 476-0080. **FAX:** (809) 476-0084.

Primary Working Agreement: None.

President: Federico Antun. **General Manager:** Manuel Antun.

1996-97 Managers: Pete Mackanin, Art DeFreites.

LICEY TIGERS

Mailing Address: Estadio Quisqueya, Santo Domingo, Dom. Rep. **Telephone:** (809) 567-3090. **FAX:** (809) 542-7714.

Primary Working Agreement: New York Mets.

President: Jose Manuel Fernandez. **General Manager:** Eddy Toledo.

1996-97 Manager: Sal Rende.

NORTHEAST GIANTS

Mailing Address: Calle Castillo No. 14, Esq. Gaspar Hernandez, San Francisco de Macoris, Dominican Republic. **Telephone:** (809) 588-3714, (809) 588-8882. **FAX:** (809) 588-8733.

Primary Working Agreement: None.
President: Siquio Ng de la Rosa. **General Manager:** Luis Silverio.
1996-97 Manager: Julian Javier.

MEXICAN PACIFIC LEAGUE

Mailing Address: Pesqueira No. 401-R, Navojoa, Sonora, Mexico. **Telephone:** (52-642) 2-3100. **FAX:** (52-642) 2-7250.

Year Founded: 1958.

President: Dr. Arturo Leon Lerma. **Vice President:** Victor Cuevas. **General Manager:** Obiel Denis.

1996-97 Opening Date: Oct. 19, 1996. **Closing Date:** Dec. 30, 1996.

Regular Season: 62 games.

Playoff Format: Six teams advance to best-of-seven quarterfinals. Three winners and losing team with best regular-season record advance to best-of-seven semifinals. Winners meet in best-of-seven series for league championship. Winner advances to Caribbean World Series.

Roster Limit: 27. **Roster Limit, Imports:** 5.

1996-97 Standings

	W	L	Pct.	GB
Culiacan*#	38	24	.613	—
Hermosillo#	34	28	.548	4
Los Mochis	31	31	.500	7
Mexicali	31	31	.500	7
Obregon	31	31	.500	7
Guasave	28	34	.452	10
Navojoa	28	34	.452	10
Mazatlan	27	35	.435	11

*Won playoff. #Won half-season championship.

CULIACAN TOMATOGROWERS

Mailing Address: Ave. Obregon 348 Sur, Culiacan, Sinaloa, Mexico, CP 820. **Telephone, FAX:** (67) 52-04-48 or 12-24-46 or 13-39-69

President: Juan Manuel Ley Lopez. **General Manager:** Jaime Blancarte.

1996-97 Managers: Paquin Estrada.

GUASAVE COTTONEERS

Mailing Address: Ave. Obregon #43, Guasave, Sinaloa, Mexico. **Telephone:** (68) 72-14-31. **FAX:** (68) 72-29-98.

President: Reynaldo Valencia Amador. **General Manager:** Narciso Orona de los Palos.

1996-97 Manager: Fernando Villaescusa.

HERMOSILLO ORANGEGROWERS

Mailing Address: Nayarit 130, Local 4, Hermosillo, Sonora, Mexico. **Telephone:** (62) 14-07-80, (62) 14-21-23. **FAX:** (62) 15-57-31.

President: Enrique Mazon. **General Manager:** Marco Antonio Manzo.

1996-97 Manager: Derek Bryant.

LOS MOCHIS SUGARCANE GROWERS

Mailing Address: Angel Flores #532 Sur, Los Mochis, Sinaloa, Mexico CP 81200. **Telephone:** (68) 18-25-05. **FAX:** (68) 15-00-45.

President: Mario Lopez Valdez. **General Manager:** Antonio Castro.

1996-97 Manager: Juan Navarrete.

MAZATLAN DEER

Mailing Address: Av. Gutierrez Navera No. 821 Centro, CP 82000, Mazatlan, Sinaloa, Mexico. **Telephone:** (69) 81-17-10. **FAX:** (69) 81-17-11.

President: Hermilo Diaz Bringas. **General Manager:** Alejandro Vega Reyna.

1996-97 Manager: Marco Antonio Vazquez.

MEXICALI EAGLES

Mailing Address: Estadio de Beisbol de la Ciudad Deportiva, Calzada Ex-Avacion, Mexicali, Baja California. **Telephone:** (65) 67-00-40, (65) 67-00-10. **FAX:** (65) 67-00-95.

President: Mario Hernandez. **General Manager:** Raul Cano.

1996-97 Manager: Mario Mendoza.

NAVOJOA MAYOS

Mailing Address: Allende #208, Dpto. 2, Novojoa, Sonora, Mexico, CP 85800. **Telephone:** (64) 22-14-33, (64) 22-37-64. **FAX:** (64) 22-89-97.

President: Victor Cuevas Garibay. **General Manager:** Lauro Villalobos.

1996-97 Manager: Buddy Bailey.

OBREGON YAQUIS

Mailing Address: Yucatan y Nainari #294 North, Ciudad Obregon, Sonora, Mexico, CP 85000. **Telephone:** (64) 14-11-56. **FAX:** (64) 14-11-56.

President: Luis Felipe Garcia DeLeon. **General Manager:** Miguel Sitten.

1996-97 Managers: Aurelio Rodriguez.

PUERTO RICAN LEAGUE

Mailing Address: P.O. Box 1852, Hato Rey, PR 00919. **Telephone:** (787) 765-6285, 765-7285. **FAX:** (787) 767-3028.

Year Founded: 1938.

President: Joaquin Monserrate. **Executive Director/Administrator:** Benny Agosto.

1996-97 Opening Date: Nov. 7, 1996. **Closing Date:** Jan. 9, 1997.

Regular Season: 50 games.

Playoff Format: Top four teams meet in two best-of-7 semifinal series. Winners meet in a best-of-9 series for league championship. Winner advances to Caribbean World Series.

Roster Limit: 26. **Roster Limit, Imports:** 4. Up to six more may be used to replace native players who are injured or are major leaguers who elect not to play.

1996-97 Standings

	W	L	Pct.	GB
Santurce	28	22	.560	—
*Mayaguez	28	22	.560	—
Caguas	27	23	.540	1
San Juan	26	25	.510	2½
Arecibo	25	26	.490	3½
Ponce	17	33	.340	11

*Won playoffs

ARECIBO WOLVES

Mailing Address: P.O. Box 1633, Arecibo, PR 00613. **Telephone:** (787) 880-1800. **FAX:** (787) 880-1800.

Primary Working Agreement: None.

President: Josue Vega. **General Manager:** Jose "Che" Conde.

1996-97 Manager: Luis Melendez, Ramon Aviles.

CAGUAS CRIOLLOS

Mailing Address: P.O. Box 1415, Caguas, PR 00726. **Telephone:** (787) 258-2222. **FAX:** (787) 743-0545.

Primary Working Agreement: None.

President: Jaime Rullan Jr. **General Manager:** David Hersh.

1996-97 Manager: Ed Romero.

MAYAGUEZ INDIANS

Mailing Address: 6 Zamora Ave., Villa Lydia, Aguadilla, PR 00603. **Telephone:** (787) 891-3398. **FAX:** (787) 834-7480.

Primary Working Agreement: None.

President/General Manager: Luis Mendez.

1996-97 Manager: Tom Gamboa.

PONCE LIONS

Mailing Address: Box 363148, San Juan, PR 00936. **Telephone:** (787) 841-7521. **FAX:** (787) 848-7947.

Primary Working Agreement: Florida Marlins.

Owner: Antonio Muniz Sr. **President:** Antonio Muniz Jr.

1996-97 Managers: Fredi Gonzalez, Orlando Gomez.

SAN JUAN SENATORS

Street Address: Estadio Hiram Bithorn, Ave. Roosevelt, Hato Rey, PR 00959. **Mailing Address:** P.O. Box 366246, San Juan, PR 00936. **Telephone:** (787) 754-1300. **FAX:** (787) 763-2217.

Primary Working Agreement: Kansas City Royals.

President: Benjamin Rivera. **Special Assistant to the President:** Mako Oliveras.

1996-97 Manager: Sandy Alomar Sr.

SANTURCE CRABBERS

Mailing Address: P.O. Box 1077, Hato Rey, PR 00919. **Telephone:** (787) 274-0240, 274-0241. **FAX:** (787) 765-0410.

Primary Working Agreement: Houston Astros.

President: Reinaldo Paniagua Diaz. **General Manager:** Frankie Thon.

1996-97 Manager: Matt Galante.

VENEZUELAN LEAGUE

Mailing Address: Avenida Sorbona, Edif. Marta Piso 2 No. 25, Urbanizacion Colinas de Bello Monte, Caracas, Venezuela. **Telephone:** (011-58-2) 751-2079 or 752-6897. **FAX:** (011-58-2) 751-0891.

Year Founded: 1946.

President: Carlos Cordido. **Vice President:** Jaime Benitez. **Vice President/General Manager:** Domingo Alvarez. **Public Relations Director:** Yocoima Mata.

Division Structure: East—Caracas, La Guaira, Magallanes, Oriente. **West**—Aragua, Lara, Occidente, Zulia.

1996-97 Opening Date: Oct. 23, 1996. **Closing Date:** Dec. 29, 1996.

Regular Season: 60 games.

Playoff Format: Top two teams in each division, plus a wild-card team, meet in a 16-game round-robin series. Top two finishers meet in a best-of-7 series for league championship. Winner advances to Caribbean World Series.

Roster Limit: 27. **Roster Limit, Imports:** 7.

1996-97 Standings

	W	L	Pct.	GB
*Magallanes	33	17	.660	—
Caracas	32	18	.640	1
Lara	31	21	.596	3
Aragua	26	24	.520	7
Oriente	25	28	.472	9½
Zulia	24	29	.453	10½
Occidente	18	34	.346	16
La Guaira	16	34	.320	17

*Won playoffs

ARAGUA TIGERS

Street Address: Campo Elias, Barrio la Democracia, Maracay, Aragua, Venezuela. **Mailing Address:** Stadium Jose Perez Colmenares, Maracay, Aragua, Venezuela. **Telephone:** (58-43) 54-4632. **FAX:** (58-43) 54-4134.

Primary Working Agreement: New York Yankees.

President: Jose Maria Pages. **General Manager:** Carlos Isava.

1996-97 Manager: Alfredo Ortiz.

CARACAS LIONS

Street Address: Av. Francisco de Miranda, Centro Seguros La Paz, Caracas, Venezuela. **Mailing Address:** Piso 4 Oficina N42-C, Caracas, Venezuela 1070. **Telephone:** (58-2) 238-7733. **FAX:** (58-2) 238-0691.

Primary Working Agreement: None.

President: Pablo Morales. **Vice President/General Manger:** Oscar Prieto.

1996-97 Manager: Phil Regan.

La GUAIRA TIBURONES

Mailing Address: 1a Avenida Urbanizacion, Detras del Periferico de Pariata, Maiquetia, Venezuela. **Telephone:** (58-31) 25-579. **FAX:** (58-31) 23-116.

Primary Working Agreement: Atlanta Braves.

President/General Manager: Pedro Padron Panza.

1996-97 Manager: Jeff Cox.

LARA CARDINALS

Mailing Address: Av. Rotaria, Estadio Barquisimeto, Barquisimeto, Venezuela 3001. **Telephone:** (58-51) 42-8321. **FAX:** (58-51) 42-1921.

Primary Working Agreement: Toronto Blue Jays.

President: Adolfo Alvarez. **General Manager:** Humberto Oropeza.

1996-97 Manager: Omar Malave.

MAGALLANES NAVIGATORS

Mailing Address: Centro Comercial Caribbean Plaza, Modulo 8, Piso 1, Local 173, Planta Alta, Valencia, Venezuela. **Telephone:** (58-41) 24-0321. **FAX:** (58-41) 24-0705.

Primary Working Agreement: New York Mets.

President/General Manager: Alfredo Guadarrama.

1996-97 Manager: John Tamargo.

OCCIDENTE PASTORA

Mailing Address: Circunvalacion No. 2, Casa Paris, Zona Industrial, Maracaibo, Zulia, Venezuela. **Telephone:** (58-61) 35-8236. **FAX:** (58-61) 35-8730.

President: Andres Finol. **Vice President/General Manager:** Enrique Finol.

Primary Working Agreement: None.

1996-97 Manager: Domingo Carrasquel.

ORIENTE CARIBBEANS

Mailing Address: Ave. Stadium, Centro Comercial Novocentro, Piso 2, Local 2-4, Puerto la Cruz, Sucre, Venezuela. **Telephone, FAX:** (58-81) 66-7054.

Primary Working Agreement: Cleveland Indians.

President: Gioconda de Marquez. **General Manager:** Luis Aponte.

1996-97 Manager: Pompeyo Davalillo.

ZULIA EAGLES

Mailing Address: Ave. 8 Antes Santa Rita, Edificio las Carolinas Mezanina, Local M-10, Maracaibo, Zulia, Venezuela. **Telephone:** (58-61) 97-9834. **FAX:** (58-61) 98-0210.

Primary Working Agreement: None.

President: Lucas Rincon. **General Manager:** Luis Rodolfo Machado Silva.

1996-97 Managers: Ruben Amaro Sr, Noe Maduro.

OTHER WINTER LEAGUES

ARIZONA FALL LEAGUE

Mailing Address: 10201 S. 51st St., Suite 230, Phoenix, AZ 85044. **Telephone:** (602) 496-6700. **FAX:** (602) 496-6384.

Year Founded: 1992.

Executive Vice President: Steve Cobb. **Director of Marketing:** Todd Woodford. **Administrative Assistant:** Joan McGrath.

Division Structure: North—Peoria, Scottsdale, Sun Cities. **South**—Mesa, Phoenix, Tempe.

1996 Opening Date: Oct. 10. **Closing Date:** Dec. 5.

Regular Season: 51 games.

Playoff Format: Division champions meet in best-of-3 series for league championship.

Roster Limit: 28. No players from Puerto Rico, Dominican Republic or

Venezuela. Players with less than one year of major league service are eligible.

1996-97 Standings

	W	L	Pct.	GB
Mesa	28	22	.560	—
Scottsdale*	25	24	.510	2½
Peoria	25	25	.500	3
Phoenix	25	25	.500	3
Sun Cites	24	25	.490	3½
Tempe	22	28	.440	6

*Won playoffs

MESA SAGUAROS

Mailing Address: See league address.

Working Agreements: Boston Red Sox, Chicago Cubs, Montreal Expos, New York Yankees, Pittsburgh Pirates.

1996 Manager: Trent Jewett (Pirates).

PEORIA JAVELINAS

Mailing Address: See league address.

Working Agreements: Colorado Rockies, Detroit Tigers, New York Mets, Philadelphis Phillies, Seattle Mariners.

1996 Manager: Brad Mills (Rockies).

PHOENIX DESERT DOGS

Mailing Address: See league address.

Working Agreements: Baltimore Orioles, Cincinnati Reds, Houston Astros, Oakland Athletics, Toronto Blue Jays.

1996 Manager: Gary Jones (Athletics).

SCOTTSDALE SCORPIONS

Mailing Address: See league address.

Working Agreements: Arizona Diamondbacks, Cincinnati Reds, Cleveland Indians, Minnesota Twins, St. Louis Cardinals, San Francisco Giants.

1996 Manager: George Hendrick (Cardinals).

SUN CITIES SOLAR SOX

Mailing Address: See league address.

Working Agreements: Atlanta Braves, Kansas City Royals, Los Angeles Dodgers, Milwaukee Brewers, San Diego Padres.

1996 Manager: Davey Lopes (Padres).

TEMPE RAFTERS

Mailing Address: See league address.

Working Agreement: Anaheim Angels, Atlanta Braves, Chicago White Sox, Florida Marlins, Tampa Bay Devil Rays, Texas Rangers.

1996 Manager: Jeff Pentland (Marlins).

AUSTRALIAN BASEBALL LEAGUE

Mailing Address: Level 2, 48 Atchison St., St. Leonards, NSW 2065 Australia. **Telephone:** (011-61-2) 9437-4622. **FAX:** (011-61-2) 9437-4155.

Chairman: Rod Byrne. **General Manager:** Don Knapp. **Administration Manager:** Jane Taylor.

1996-97 Opening Date: Oct. 18, 1996. **Closing Date:** Feb. 2, 1997.

No. of Regular-Season Games: 60.

Playoff Format: Top four teams meet in best-of-3 semifinals. Winners meet in best-of-3 final for league championship.

1996-97 Standings

	W	L	Pct.	GB
Perth	40	20	.666	—
Adelaide	36	23	.610	3½
Brisbane	33	27	.550	7
Sydney	32	27	.542	7½
Gold Coast	31	28	.525	8½
Mel. Monarchs	28	29	.491	10½
Hunter	18	40	.310	21
Melbourne Reds	17	41	.293	22

ADELAIDE GIANTS

Mailing Address: Unit 4/83-85 Fullarton Rd., Kent Town, SA 5067 Australia. **Telephone:** (8) 8364-3231. **FAX:** (8) 8364-1730.

Primary Working Agreement: Los Angeles Dodgers.

Chairman of the Board: Darryl Stanton. **General Manager:** Geoff Hosking.

1996-97 Manager: Tony Harris.

BRISBANE BANDITS

Street Address: 28 Mayne Road, Bowen Hills, QLD 4006 Australia. **Mailing Address:** Locked Bag 8912, Brisbane, QLD 4006 Australia.

Telephone: (7) 3842-8001. **FAX:** (7) 3842-8098.

Primary Working Agreements: Detroit Tigers, San Diego Padres.

General Manager: Peter Wood.

1996-97 Manager: David Nilsson.

GOLD COAST COUGARS

Mailing Address: P.O. Box 2343, Nerang MDC, QLD 4211 Australia. **Telephone:** (75) 57-99972. **FAX:** (75) 57-99983.

Primary Working Agreement: Boston Red Sox.

General Manager: Glen Partridge.
1996-97 Manager: Billy Gardner Jr.

HUNTER EAGLES

Mailing Address: P.O. Box 134, Lambton, NSW 2299 Australia. **Telephone:** (49) 52-3344. **FAX:** (49) 52-3365.
Primary Working Agreement: New York Mets.
General Manager: Ian Lewis.
1996-97 Manager: Shane Barclay.

MELBOURNE MONARCHS

Mailing Address: 86 High St., Suites 6 and 7, Berwick, VIC 3806 Australia. **Telephone:** (3) 9769-5328. **FAX:** (3) 9769-5544.
Primary Working Agreement: Atlanta Braves.
General Manager: Phil Dale.
1996-97 Manager: Jon Deeble.

MELBOURNE REDS

Mailing Address: P.O. Box 501, Moorabbin, VIC 3189 Australia. **Telephone:** (3) 9553-3202. **FAX:** (3) 9553-3257.
Primary Working Agreement: New York Yankees.
Director of Operations: Andy Karetsky.
1996-97 Manager: Tom Nieto.

PERTH HEAT

Street Address: Suite 12, The Russell Centre, 159 Adelaide Terrace, Perth, WA 6000 Australia. **Mailing Address:** P.O. Box 6008, East Perth, WA 6892 Australia. **Telephone:** (9) 221-9799. **FAX:** (9) 221-9798.
Primary Working Agreement: Baltimore Orioles.
General Manager: Douglas Mateljan.
1996-97 Manager: Joe Ferguson.

SYDNEY BLUES

Mailing Address: 48 Atchison St., Level 1, St. Leonards, NSW 2065 Australia. **Telephone:** (2) 9437-5500. **FAX:** (2) 9437-5834.
Primary Working Agreement: Toronto Blue Jays.
Chairman: Trevor Jarrett.
1996-97 Manager: Paul Elliott.

HAWAII WINTER BASEBALL

Mailing Address: 905 Makahiki Way, Unit C, Honolulu, HI 96826. **Telephone:** (808) 973-7247. **FAX:** (808) 973-7117.
Year Founded: 1993.
President: Frank Kudo. **Administrative Assistant:** Lynn Hirashima.
1997 Opening Date: Oct. 3. **Closing Date:** Dec. 5.
Regular Season: 54 games.
Division Structure: Outrigger: Honolulu, West Oahu. **Volcano:** Hilo, Maui.
Playoff Format: One-game championship between two division winners.
Roster Limit: 26.

1996-97 Standings

	W	L	Pct.	GB
Honolulu	36	16	.692	—
Maui*	25	24	.510	9½

	W	L	Pct.	GB
West Oahu	20	30	.400	15
Hilo	19	30	.388	15½

*Won playoffs

HILO STARS

Mailing Address: P.O. Box 1051, Hilo, HI 96720. **Telephone:** (808) 969-9033. **FAX:** (808) 961-6053.
General Manager: Clyde Nekoba. **1996 Manager:** DeMarlo Hale.

HONOLULU SHARKS

Mailing Address: 905 Makahiki Way, Unit C, Honolulu, HI 96826. **Telephone:** (808) 973-1935. **FAX:** (808) 973-7122.
General Manager: Russell Park. **1996 Manager:** Jeff Banister.

MAUI STINGRAYS

Mailing Address: P.O. Box 1193, Wailuku, HI 96793. **Telephone:** (808) 242-2950. **FAX:** (808) 244-1059.
General Manager: Lane Fujii. **1996 Manager:** P.J. Carey.

WEST OAHU CANEFIRES

Mailing Address: 905 Makahiki Way, Unit C, Honolulu, HI 96826. **Telephone:** (808) 973-7121. **FAX:** (808) 973-7122.
General Manager: Mark Nishiyama. **1996 Manager:** Jeff Datz.

COLLEGE BASEBALL

COLLEGE BASEBALL

NATIONAL COLLEGIATE ATHLETIC ASSOCIATION

Mailing Address: 6201 College Blvd., Overland Park, KS 66211. **Telephone:** (913) 339-1906. **FAX:** (913) 339-0026.

Executive Director: Cedric Dempsey. **Director of Championships:** Dennis Poppe. **College World Series Contact:** Jim Wright. **Statistics Contact:** John Painter.

Chairman, Baseball Committee: Ron Maestri (athletic director, University of New Orleans). **Baseball Committee:** Rich Alday (baseball coach, New Mexico), Joe Castiglione (athletic director, Missouri), John Easterbrook (athletic director, Cal State Fullerton), Paul Fernandes (associate athletic director, Columbia), Dick Rockwell (athletic director, LeMoyne), John Skeeters (baseball coach, Sam Houston State), Tim Weiser (athletic director, Eastern Michigan), Ron Wellman (athletic director, Wake Forest).

1998 National Convention: Jan. 10-14 at Atlanta.

1997 Championship Tournaments

NCAA Division I

College World Series .... Omaha, NE, May 30-June 7
Regionals .... Campus sites, May 22-25
Play-ins .... Campus sites, May 15-17

NCAA Division II

World Series .... Montgomery, AL, May 24-31

NCAA Division III

World Series .... Salem, VA, May 24-28

NATIONAL ASSOCIATION OF INTERCOLLEGIATE ATHLETICS

Mailing Address: 6120 South Yale Ave., Suite 1450, Tulsa, OK 74136. **Telephone:** (918) 494-8828. **FAX:** (918) 494-8841.

Interim Chief Executive Officer: Bill Patterson. **Director of Championship Events:** Tim Kramer. **Baseball Event Coordinator:** John Mark Adkison.

1997 Championship Tournament

NAIA World Series .... Sioux City, IA, May 23-29

NATIONAL JUNIOR COLLEGE ATHLETIC ASSOCIATION

Mailing Address: P.O. Box 7305, Colorado Springs, CO 80933. **Telephone:** (719) 590-9788. **FAX:** (719) 590-7324.

Executive Director: George Killian. **Division I Baseball Tournament Director:** Sam Suplizio. **Division II Tournament Director:** John Daigle. **Division III Tournament Director:** Barry Bower.

1997 Championship Tournaments

Division I

Junior College World Series .... Grand Junction, CO, May 24-31

Division II

World Series .... Millington, TN, May 17-23

Division III

World Series .... Batavia, NY, May 18-21

COMMUNITY COLLEGE LEAGUE OF CALIFORNIA

Mailing Address: 2017 O St., Sacramento, CA 95814. **Telephone:** (916) 444-1600. **FAX:** (916) 444-2616.

Commissioner of Athletics: Joanne Fortunato. **Associate Commissioner of Athletics:** Paul Lanning.

1997 Championship Tournament

State Championships .... Fresno City College, May 23-26

AMERICAN BASEBALL COACHES ASSOCIATION

Office Address: 108 South University Ave., Suite 3, Mt. Pleasant, MI 48858. **Telephone:** (517) 775-3300. **FAX:** (517) 775-3600.

Executive Director: Dave Keilitz. **Assistant to the Executive Director:** Betty Rulong. **Administrative Assistant:** Nick Williams.

President: Bob Warn (Indiana State University).

1998 National Convention: Jan. 2-5 at San Diego.

NCAA DIVISION I CONFERENCES

AMERICA EAST CONFERENCE

(Known as North Atlantic Conference in 1996)

Mailing Address: 28 Main St., Orono, ME 04473. **Telephone:** (207) 866-2383. **FAX:** (207) 866-7524.

Baseball Members (First Year): Delaware (1991), Drexel (1991), Hartford (1985), Hofstra (1994), Maine (1979), New Hampshire (1979), Northeastern (1979), Towson State (1996), Vermont (1979).

Staff Associate: Len Harlow.

1997 Tournament: Six teams, double-elimination. May 8-11 at Wilmington, Del.

ATLANTIC COAST CONFERENCE

Office Address: 4512 Weybridge Lane, Greensboro, NC 27407. **Mailing Address:** P.O. Drawer ACC, Greensboro, NC 27417. **Telephone:** (910) 854-6062. **FAX:** (910) 854-8797.

Baseball Members (First Year): Clemson (1953), Duke (1953), Florida State (1992), Georgia Tech (1979), Maryland (1953), North Carolina (1953), North Carolina State (1953), Virginia (1953), Wake Forest (1953).

Director of Media Relations: Brian Morrison. **Media Relations Intern:** Joanna Sparkman.

1997 Tournament: Nine teams, double-elimination. May 13-18 at St. Petersburg, FL.

ATLANTIC 10 CONFERENCE

Mailing Address: 2 Penn Center Plaza, Suite 1410, Philadelphia, PA 19102. **Telephone:** (215) 751-0500. **FAX:** (215) 751-0770.

Baseball Members (First Year): East—Fordham (1996), Massachusetts (1977), Rhode Island (1981), St. Bonaventure (1980), St. Joseph's (1983), Temple (1983). **West**—Dayton (1996), Duquesne (1977), George Washington (1977), LaSalle (1996), Virginia Tech (1996), Xavier (1996).

Director of Communications: Ray Cella.

1997 Tournament: Four teams, double-elimination. May 15-17 at Boyertown, PA.

BIG EAST CONFERENCE

Mailing Address: 56 Exchange Terrace, Providence, RI 02903. **Telephone:** (401) 453-0660. **FAX:** (401) 751-8540.

Baseball Members (First Year): American—Boston College (1985), Connecticut (1985), Pittsburgh (1985), Providence (1985), St. John's (1985), West Virginia (1996). **National**—Georgetown (1985), Notre Dame (1996), Rutgers (1996), Seton Hall (1985), Villanova (1985).

Assistant Director of Public Relations: Rob Carolla.

1997 Tournament: Six teams, double-elimination. May 13-16 at Norwich, CT.

BIG SOUTH CONFERENCE

Mailing Address: Winthrop Coliseum, Eden Terrace, Rock Hill, SC 29733. **Telephone:** (803) 817-6340. **FAX:** (803) 817-6578.

Baseball Members (First Year): Charleston Southern (1983), Coastal Carolina (1983), Liberty (1991), Maryland-Baltimore County (1992), UNC Asheville (1985), UNC Greensboro (1992), Radford (1983), Winthrop (1983).

Public Relations Director: Angela Phelps.

1997 Tournament: None.

BIG TEN CONFERENCE

Mailing Address: 1500 West Higgins Rd., Park Ridge, IL 60068. **Telephone:** (847) 696-1010. **FAX:** (847) 696-1110.

Baseball Members (First Year): Illinois (1896), Indiana (1899), Iowa (1899), Michigan (1896), Michigan State (1950), Minnesota (1896), Northwestern (1896), Ohio State (1912), Penn State (1990), Purdue (1896).

Information Services Director: Dennis LaBissoniere.

1997 Tournament: Four teams, double-elimination. May 15-18 at regular-season champion.

BIG 12 CONFERENCE

Mailing Address: 2201 Stemmons Freeway, 28th Floor, Dallas, TX 75207. **Telephone:** (214) 742-1212. **FAX:** (214) 742-2046.

Baseball Members (First Year): Baylor (1997), Iowa State (1997), Kansas (1997), Kansas State (1997), Missouri (1997), Nebraska (1997), Oklahoma (1997), Oklahoma State (1997), Texas (1997), Texas A&M (1997), Texas Tech (1997).

Director of Service Bureau: Bo Carter.

1997 Tournament: Six teams, double-elimination. May 15-18 at Oklahoma City, OK.

BIG WEST CONFERENCE

Mailing Address: 2 Corporate Park, Suite 206, Irvine, CA 92606. **Telephone:** (714) 261-2525. **FAX:** (714) 261-2528.

Baseball Members (First Year): Cal Poly San Luis Obispo (1996), UC Santa Barbara (1969), Cal State Fullerton (1975), Cal State Sacramento

(1996), Long Beach State (1970), Nevada (1992), New Mexico State (1992), Pacific (1969).

Assistant Information Director: Mike Villamor.

1997 Tournament: Four teams, double-elimination. May 15-18 at Long Beach State and Cal State Fullerton (co-hosts).

COLONIAL ATHLETIC ASSOCIATION

Mailing Address: 8625 Patterson Ave., Richmond, VA 23229. **Telephone:** (804) 754-1616. **FAX:** (804) 754-1830.

Baseball Members (First Year): East Carolina (1985), George Mason (1985), James Madison (1985), UNC Wilmington (1985), Old Dominion (1992), Richmond (1985), Virginia Commonwealth (1996), William & Mary (1985).

Sports Information Director: Steve Vehorn.

1997 Tournament: Eight teams, double-elimination. May 13-17 at Kinston, NC.

CONFERENCE USA

Mailing Address: 35 East Wacker Dr., Suite 650, Chicago, IL 60601. **Telephone:** (312) 553-0483. **FAX:** (312) 553-0495.

Baseball Members (First Year): Alabama-Birmingham (1996), Cincinnati (1996), Houston (1997), Louisville (1996), Memphis (1996), UNC Charlotte (1996), Saint Louis (1996), South Florida (1996), Southern Mississippi (1996), Tulane (1996).

Assistant Director of Communications: Russ Anderson.

1997 Tournament: Ten teams, double-elimination. May 13-18 at New Orleans, LA.

IVY LEAGUE

Mailing Address: 120 Alexander St., Princeton, NJ 08544. **Telephone:** (609) 258-6426. **FAX:** (609) 258-1690.

Baseball Members (First Year): Rolfe—Brown (1993), Dartmouth (1993), Harvard (1993), Yale (1993). **Gehrig**—Columbia (1993), Cornell (1993), Pennsylvania (1993), Princeton (1993).

Associate Director of Public Information: Chuck Yrigoyen.

1997 Tournament: Best-of-3 series between division champions. May 10-11 at Rolfe Division champion.

METRO ATLANTIC ATHLETIC CONFERENCE

Mailing Address: 1090 Amboy Ave., Edison, NJ 08837. **Telephone:** (908) 225-0202. **FAX:** (908) 225-5440.

Baseball Members (First Year): North—Canisius (1989), LeMoyne (1990), Niagara (1989), Siena (1989). **South**—Fairfield (1980), Iona (1980), Manhattan (1980), St. Peter's (1980).

Director of Media Relations: Mike Scala.

1997 Tournament: Four teams, double-elimination. May 9-11 at Albany, NY.

MID-AMERICAN CONFERENCE

Mailing Address: Four SeaGate, Suite 102, Toledo, OH 43604. **Telephone:** (419) 249-7177. **FAX:** (419) 249-7199.

Baseball Members (First Year): Akron (1992), Ball State (1973), Bowling Green State (1952), Central Michigan (1971), Eastern Michigan (1971), Kent (1951), Miami (1947), Ohio (1946), Toledo (1950), Western Michigan (1947).

Assistant Director of Communications: Mike Cihon.

1997 Tournament: Four teams, double-elimination. May 15-17 at regular-season champion.

MID-CONTINENT CONFERENCE

Mailing Address: 40 Shuman Blvd., Suite 118, Naperville, IL 60563. **Telephone:** (630) 416-7560. **FAX:** (630) 416-7564.

Baseball Members (First Year): East—Central Connecticut State (1994), C.W. Post (1995), New York Tech (1995), Pace (1995), Troy State (1994), Youngstown State (1992). **West**—Chicago State (1994), Eastern Illinois (1983), Northeastern Illinois (1994), Valparaiso (1982), Western Illinois (1982).

Director of Media Relations: Mark Simpson.

1997 Tournament: Four teams, double-elimination. May 9-11 at Western Division champion.

MID-EASTERN ATHLETIC CONFERENCE

Mailing Address: 102 North Elm St., Suite 401, Greensboro, NC 27420. **Telephone:** (910) 275-9961. **FAX:** (910) 275-9964.

Baseball Members (First Year): North—Coppin State (1985), Delaware State (1972), Howard (1972), Maryland-Eastern Shore (1972). **South**—Bethune-Cookman (1979), Florida A&M (1979), North Carolina A&T (1972).

Publicity Director: Larry Barber.

1997 Tournament: Four teams, double-elimination. May 2-5 at Tallahassee, FL.

MIDWESTERN COLLEGIATE CONFERENCE

Mailing Address: 201 South Capitol Ave., Suite 500, Indianapolis, IN

46225. **Telephone:** (317) 237-5622. **FAX:** (317) 237-5620.

Baseball Members (First Year): Butler (1979), Cleveland State (1994), Detroit (1980), Illinois-Chicago (1994), Northern Illinois (1994), Wisconsin-Milwaukee (1994), Wright State (1994).

Director of Communications: Unavailable.

1997 Tournament: Four teams, double-elimination. May 15-16 at regular-season champion.

MISSOURI VALLEY CONFERENCE

Mailing Address: 1000 Union Station, Suite 105, St. Louis, MO 63103. **Telephone:** (314) 421-0339. **FAX:** (314) 421-3505.

Baseball Members (First Year): Bradley (1949), Creighton (1929), Evansville (1995), Illinois State (1981), Indiana State (1976), Northern Iowa (1992), Southern Illinois (1975), Southwest Missouri State (1991), Wichita State (1946).

Assistant Commissioner, Communications: Jack Watkins.

1997 Tournament: Six teams, double-elimination. May 14-17 at Wichita, KS.

NORTHEAST CONFERENCE

Mailing Address: 900 Route 9, Woodbridge, NJ 07095. **Telephone:** (908) 636-9119. **FAX:** (908) 636-6496.

Baseball Members (First Year): Fairleigh Dickinson (1981), Long Island (1981), Marist (1981), Monmouth (1985), Mount St. Mary's (1989), Rider (1992), St. Francis, N.Y. (1981), Wagner (1981).

Assistant Commissioner: David Siroty.

1997 Tournament: Four teams, double-elimination. May 9-11 at Sussex, NJ.

OHIO VALLEY CONFERENCE

Mailing Address: 278 Franklin Road, Suite 103, Brentwood, TN 37027. **Telephone:** (615) 371-1698. **FAX:** (615) 371-1788.

Baseball Members (First Year): Austin Peay State (1963), Eastern Illinois (1996), Eastern Kentucky (1948), Middle Tennessee State (1952), Morehead State (1948), Murray State (1948), Southeast Missouri State (1991), Tennessee-Martin (1992), Tennessee Tech (1949).

Information Director: Rob Washburn.

1997 Tournament: Six teams, double-elimination. May 15-17 at undetermined site.

PACIFIC-10 CONFERENCE

Mailing Address: 800 South Broadway, Suite 400, Walnut Creek, CA 94596. **Telephone:** (510) 932-4411. **FAX:** (510) 932-4601.

Baseball Members (First Year): North—Oregon State (1915), Portland State (1982), Washington (1915), Washington State (1916). **South**—Arizona (1978), Arizona State (1978), California (1915), UCLA (1927), Southern California (1921), Stanford (1916).

Public Relations Assistant: Kevin Grigg.

1997 Tournament: Best-of-3 series between division champions. May 15-17 at Northern Division champion.

PATRIOT LEAGUE

Mailing Address: 3897 Adler Place, Suite C-310, Bethlehem, PA 18017. **Telephone:** (610) 691-2414. **FAX:** (610) 691-8414.

Baseball Members (First Year): Army (1993), Bucknell (1991), Holy Cross (1991), Lafayette (1991), Lehigh (1991), Navy (1993).

Director of Media Relations: Todd Newcomb.

1997 Tournament: Three teams. Winner of one-game playoff between Nos. 2-3 seeds meets No. 1 seed in best-of-3 series. May 4-5 at home of No. 1 seed.

SOUTHEASTERN CONFERENCE

Mailing Address: 2201 Civic Center Blvd., Birmingham, AL 35203. **Telephone:** (205) 458-3010. **FAX:** (205) 458-3030.

Baseball Members (First Year): East—Florida (1933), Georgia (1933), Kentucky (1933), South Carolina (1991), Tennessee (1933), Vanderbilt (1933). **West**—Alabama (1933), Arkansas (1991), Auburn (1933), Louisiana State (1933), Mississippi (1933), Mississippi State (1933).

Director of Media Services: Charles Bloom.

1997 Tournament: Eight teams, modified double-elimination. May 14-18 at Columbus, GA.

SOUTHERN CONFERENCE

Mailing Address: One West Pack Square, Suite 1508, Asheville, NC 28801. **Telephone:** (704) 255-7872. **FAX:** (704) 251-5006.

Baseball Members (First Year): Appalachian State (1971), The Citadel (1936), Davidson (1936), East Tennessee State (1978), Furman (1936), Georgia Southern (1991), Marshall (1976), Virginia Military Institute (1924), Western Carolina (1976).

Assistant Commisioner/Media Relations: Heather Czeczok.

1997 Tournament: Eight teams, double-elimination. April 24-27 at Charleston, SC.

SOUTHLAND CONFERENCE

Mailing Address: 8150 North Central Expressway, Suite 930, Dallas, TX 75206. **Telephone:** (214) 750-7522. **FAX:** (214) 750-8077.

Baseball Members (First Year): Louisiana—McNeese State (1973), Nicholls State (1992), Northeast Louisiana (1983), Northwestern State (1988). **Texas**—Sam Houston State (1988), Southwest Texas State (1988), Texas-Arlington (1971), Texas-San Antonio (1993).

Publicity Director: Tommy Newsom.

1997 Tournament: Four teams, double-elimination. May 14-18 at Monroe, LA.

SOUTHWESTERN ATHLETIC CONFERENCE

Mailing Address: Louisiana Superdome, 1500 Sugar Bowl Drive, New Orleans, LA 70112. **Telephone:** (504) 523-7574. **FAX:** (504) 523-7513.

Baseball Members (First Year): East—Alabama State, Alcorn State, Jackson State, Mississippi Valley State. **West**—Grambling State, Prairie View A&M, Southern, Texas Southern.

Assistant Commissioner/Director of Publicity: Lonza Hardy.

1997 Tournament: Four teams, double-elimination. April 18-20 at New Orleans, LA.

SUN BELT CONFERENCE

Mailing Address: One Galleria Blvd., Suite 2115, Metairie, LA 70001. **Telephone:** (504) 834-6600. **FAX:** (504) 834-6806.

Baseball Members (First Year): Arkansas-Little Rock (1991), Arkansas State (1991), Jacksonville (1976), Lamar (1991), Louisiana Tech (1991), New Orleans (1976), South Alabama (1976), Southwestern Louisiana (1991), Texas-Pan American (1991), Western Kentucky (1982).

Director of Media Services: Dayna Wells.

1997 Tournament: Six teams, double-elimination. May 14-17 at Jacksonville, FL.

TRANSAMERICA ATHLETIC CONFERENCE

Mailing Address: The Commons, 3370 Vineville Ave., Suite 108-B, Macon, GA 31204. **Telephone:** (912) 474-3394. **FAX:** (912) 474-4272.

Baseball Members (First Year): East—Campbell (1994), Charleston (1991), Georgia State (1983), Mercer (1978). **South**—Central Florida (1992), Florida Atlantic (1993), Florida International (1990), Stetson (1985). **West**—Centenary (1978), Jacksonville State (1996), Samford (1978), Southeastern Louisiana (1991).

Director of Information: Tom Snyder.

1997 Tournament: Six teams, double-elimination. May 14-17 at DeLand, FL.

WEST COAST CONFERENCE

Mailing Address: 400 Oyster Point Blvd., Suite 221, South San Francisco, CA 94080. **Telephone:** (415) 873-8622. **FAX:** (415) 873-7846.

Baseball Members (First Year): Gonzaga (1996), Loyola Marymount (1955), Pepperdine (1955), Portland (1976), St. Mary's (1952), San Diego (1979), San Francisco (1952), Santa Clara (1952).

Assistant Commissioner: Don Ott.

1997 Tournament: None.

WESTERN ATHLETIC CONFERENCE

Mailing Address: 9250 East Costilla Ave., Englewood, CO 80112. **Telephone:** (303) 799-9221. **FAX:** (303) 799-3888.

Baseball Members (First Year): North—Air Force (1980), Brigham Young (1962), Grand Canyon (1994), Utah (1962). **South**—Nevada (1997), New Mexico (1962), Rice (1997), Texas Christian (1997). **West**—Fresno State (1992), Hawaii (1979), San Diego State (1979), San Jose State (1997).

Associate Commissioner: Jeff Hurd.

1997 Tournament: Six teams, double-elimination. May 14-17 at San Diego, CA.

NCAA DIVISION I TEAMS

AIR FORCE ACADEMY Falcons

Conference: Western Athletic/North.

Mailing Address: Building 2169, Room 100D, Colorado Springs, CO 80840.

Head Coach: Eric Campbell. **Assistant Coaches:** Mike Barbato, Capt. Manny Robinson. **Telephone:** (719) 333-2057. **Baseball SID:** Dave Toller. **Telephone:** (719) 333-2313. **FAX:** (719) 333-3798.

Home Field: Falcon Field. **Seating Capacity:** 1,000. **Outfield Dimensions:** LF—349, CF—410, RF—316. **Press Box Telephone:** (719) 333-3472.

AKRON Zips

Conference: Mid-American.

Mailing Address: JAR Arena, Carroll Street, Akron, OH 44325.

Head Coach: Dave Fross. **Assistant Coaches:** Tim Berenyi, Jeff Fisher. **Telephone:** (330) 972-7277. **Baseball SID:** Tom Liggett. **Telephone:** (330) 972-7468. **FAX:** (330) 374-8844.

Home Field: Lee R. Jackson Field. **Seating Capacity:** 2,500. **Outfield Dimensions:** LF—330, CF—405, RF—330. **Press Box Telephone:** (330) 972-8896.

ALABAMA Crimson Tide

Conference: Southeastern/West.

Mailing Address: P.O. Box K, Tuscaloosa, AL 35487.

Head Coach: Jim Wells. **Assistant Coaches:** Kirk Blount, Todd Butler, Mitch Gaspard. **Telephone:** (205) 348-6161. **Baseball SID:** Barry Allen. **Telephone:** (205) 348-6084. **FAX:** (205) 348-8840, 8841.

Home Field: Sewell-Thomas Stadium. **Seating Capacity:** 4,300. **Outfield Dimensions:** LF—325, CF—405, RF—325. **Press Box Telephone:** (205) 348-4927.

ALABAMA-BIRMINGHAM Blazers

Conference: Conference USA.

Mailing Address: 617 13th St. S., Birmingham, AL 35294.

Head Coach: Pete Rancont. **Assistant Coaches:** Jim Case, Steve Gillispie. **Telephone:** (205) 934-5181. **Baseball SID:** Brent Hollingsworth. **Telephone:** (205) 934-0722. **FAX:** (205) 934-7505.

Home Field: Young Field. **Seating Capacity:** 1,000. **Outfield Dimensions:** LF—337, CF—390, RF—330. **Press Box Telephone:** (205) 934-4163.

ALABAMA STATE Hornets

Conference: Southwestern Athletic/East.

Mailing Address: P.O. Box 271, Montgomery, AL 36101.

Head Coach: Larry Watkins. **Assistant Coaches:** John Broom, James Graham. **Telephone:** (334) 293-4507, ext. 4228. **Baseball SID:** Peter Forest. **Telephone:** (334) 229-4511. **FAX:** (334) 262-2971.

ALCORN STATE Braves

Conference: Southwestern Athletic/East.

Mailing Address: 1000 ASU Drive, No. 510, Lorman, MS 39096.

Head Coach: Willie McGowan. **Assistant Coach:** David Robinson. **Telephone:** (601) 877-6279. **Baseball SID:** Derick Hackett. **Telephone:** (601) 877-6466. **FAX:** (601) 877-3821.

APPALACHIAN STATE Mountaineers

Conference: Southern.

Mailing Address: Broome-Kirk Gymnasium, Boone, NC 28608.

Head Coach: Jim Morris. **Assistant Coach:** Troy Heustess. **Telephone:** (704) 262-6097. **Baseball SID:** Will Prewitt. **Telephone:** (704) 262-2268. **FAX:** (704) 262-6106.

ARIZONA Wildcats

Conference: Pacific-10/South.

Mailing Address: 229 McKale Center, Tucson, AZ 85721.

Head Coach: Jerry Stitt. **Assistant Coaches:** Bill Kinneberg, Victor Solis. **Telephone:** (520) 621-2063. **Baseball SID:** David Hardee. **Telephone:** (520) 621-4163. **FAX:** (520) 621-2681.

Home Field: Frank Sancet Field. **Seating Capacity:** 6,700. **Outfield Dimensions:** LF—340, CF—400, RF—340. **Press Box Telephone:** (520) 621-4440.

ARIZONA STATE Sun Devils

Conference: Pacific-10/South.

Mailing Address: P.O. Box 872505, Tempe, AZ 85287.

Head Coach: Pat Murphy. **Assistant Coaches:** Nino Giarratano, Doug Schreiber, Dave Sinnes. **Telephone:** (602) 965-6085. **Baseball SID:** Aimee Dombrowski. **Telephone:** (602) 965-6592. **FAX:** (602) 965-5408.

Home Field: Packard Stadium. **Seating Capacity:** 7,875. **Outfield Dimensions:** LF—340, CF—395, RF—340. **Press Box Telephone:** (602) 965-1509, 7397.

ARKANSAS Razorbacks

Conference: Southeastern/West

Mailing Address: Broyles Athletic Complex, Fayetteville, AR 72701.

Head Coach: Norm DeBriyn. **Assistant Coaches:** Doug Clark, Chris Durham, Jay Eddings. **Telephone:** (501) 575-3655. **Baseball SID:** Kevin Trainor. **Telephone:** (501) 575-2751. **FAX:** (501) 575-7481.

Home Field: George Cole Field at Baum Stadium. **Seating Capacity:** 3,300. **Outfield Dimensions:** LF—320, CF—400, RF—320. **Press Box Telephone:** (501) 444-0031.

ARKANSAS-LITTLE ROCK Trojans

Conference: Sun Belt.

Mailing Address: 2801 S. University, Little Rock, AR 72204.

Head Coach: Brian Rhees. **Assistant Coaches:** Bo Bundrick, Mark Coca, Karl Kuhn. **Telephone:** (501) 663-8095. **Baseball SID:** Mike Garrity. **Telephone:** (501) 569-3449. **FAX:** (501) 569-3030.

ARKANSAS STATE Indians

Conference: Sun Belt.

Mailing Address: P.O. Box 1000, State University, AR 72467.

Head Coach: Bill Bethea. **Assistant Coaches:** Skip Blythe, David Grimes, David Kenley. **Telephone:** (501) 972-2700. **Baseball SID:** Scott Costello. **Telephone:** (501) 972-2541. **FAX:** (501) 972-3367.

Home Field: Tomlinson Stadium at Kell Field. **Seating Capacity:** 1,000. **Outfield Dimensions:** LF—335, CF—400, RF—335. **Press Box Telephone:** (501) 972-3383.

ARMY Cadets

Conference: Patriot.

Mailing Address: Howard Road, Building 639, West Point, NY 10996.

Head Coach: Dan Roberts. **Assistant Coaches:** Robert Nadal, Joe Sottolano. **Telephone:** (914) 938-3712. **Baseball SID:** Bob Beretta. **Telephone:** (914) 938-3303. **FAX:** (914) 446-2556.

AUBURN Tigers

Conference: Southeastern/West.

Mailing Address: P.O. Box 351, Auburn University, AL 36831.

Head Coach: Hal Baird. **Assistant Coaches:** Steve Renfroe, Tom Slater. **Telephone:** (334) 844-9767. **Baseball SID:** Scott Stricklin. **Telephone:** (334) 844-9800. **FAX:** (334) 844-9807.

Home Field: Plainsman Park. **Seating Capacity:** 3,186. **Outfield Dimensions:** LF—315, CF—385, RF—331. **Press Box Telephone:** (334) 844-4138.

AUSTIN PEAY STATE Governors

Conference: Ohio Valley.

Mailing Address: P.O. Box 4515, Clarksville, TN 37044.

Head Coach: Gary McClure. **Assistant Coaches:** Steve Cornelison, Kris Runk. **Telephone:** (615) 648-7903. **Baseball SID:** Ken Golner. **Telephone:** (615) 648-7561. **FAX:** (615) 648-7562.

BALL STATE Cardinals

Conference: Mid-American.

Mailing Address: 2000 University Ave., Muncie, IN 47306.

Head Coach: Rich Maloney. **Assistant Coaches:** Rob Gamble, Ken Jones, John Lowery. **Telephone:** (317) 285-8226. **Baseball SID:** Bob Moore. **Telephone:** (317) 285-8242. **FAX:** (317) 285-8929.

Home Field: Ball Diamond. **Seating Capacity:** 1,700. **Outfield Dimensions:** LF—330, CF—400, RF—330. **Press Box Telephone:** (317) 285-8932.

BAYLOR Bears

Conference: Big 12.

Mailing Address: 3031 Dutton Ave., Waco, TX 76711.

Head Coach: Steve Smith. **Assistant Coaches:** Steve Johnigan, Tommy Pharr. **Telephone:** (817) 755-3029. **Baseball SID:** Jason Archinal. **Telephone:** (817) 755-3066. **FAX:** (817) 755-1369.

Home Field: Ferrell Field. **Seating Capacity:** 1,700. **Outfield Dimensions:** LF—330, CF—400, RF—330. **Press Box Telephone:** (817) 754-5546.

BETHUNE-COOKMAN Wildcats

Conference: Mid-Eastern Athletic/South.

Mailing Address: 640 Second Ave., Daytona Beach, FL 32114.

Head Coach: Richard Skeel. **Assistant Coaches:** Willie Brown, Mervyl Melendez. **Telephone:** (904) 255-1401, ext. 349. **Baseball SID:** Earl Kitchings. **Telephone:** (904) 255-1401. **FAX:** (904) 253-4231.

BOSTON COLLEGE Eagles

Conference: Big East/American.

Mailing Address: 321 Conte Forum, Chestnut Hill, MA 02167.

Head Coach: Moe Maloney. **Assistant Coaches:** David Burnes, Matt Hyde, Michael Martin. **Telephone:** (617) 552-3092. **Baseball SID:** Dick Kelley. **Telephone:** (617) 552-3039. **FAX:** (617) 552-4930.

Home Field: Commander Shea Field. **Seating Capacity:** 1,000. **Outfield Dimensions:** LF—315, CF—390, RF—310. **Press Box Telephone:** None.

BOWLING GREEN STATE Falcons

Conference: Mid-American.

Mailing Address: Perry Stadium, Bowling Green, OH 43403.

Head Coach: Danny Schmitz. **Assistant Coaches:** L.J. Archambeau, Mark Nell. **Telephone:** (419) 372-7065. **Baseball SID:** Mark Kunstmann. **Telephone:** (419) 372-7076. **FAX:** (419) 372-6015.

Home Field: Warren E. Steller Field. **Seating Capacity:** 2,500. **Outfield Dimensions:** LF—340, CF—400, RF—340. **Press Box Telephone:** (419) 372-2069.

BRADLEY Braves

Conference: Missouri Valley.

Mailing Address: 1501 W. Bradley Ave., Peoria, IL 61625.

Head Coach: Dewey Kalmer. **Assistant Coaches:** John Dyke, John Young. **Telephone:** (309) 677-2684. **Baseball SID:** Joe Dalfonso. **Telephone:** (309) 677-2624. **FAX:** (309) 677-2626.

Home Field: Pete Vonachen Stadium. **Seating Capacity:** 6,200. **Outfield Dimensions:** LF—335, CF—383, RF—335. **Press Box Telephone:** (309) 688-2653.

BRIGHAM YOUNG Cougars

Conference: Western Athletic/North.

Mailing Address: 30 SFH, Provo, UT 84602.

Head Coach: Gary Pullins. **Assistant Coach:** Bob Noel. **Telephone:** (801) 378-5049. **Baseball SID:** Ralph Zobell. **Telephone:** (801) 378-4911. **FAX:** (801) 378-3520.

Home Field: Cougar Field. **Seating Capacity:** 4,000. **Outfield Dimensions:** LF—345, CF—390, RF—345. **Press Box Telephone:** (801) 378-4041.

BROWN Bears

Conference: Ivy League/Rolfe.

Mailing Address: Box 1932, Providence, RI 02912.

Head Coach: Marek Drabinski. **Assistant Coaches:** Ken Coffee, Dennis Dwyer. **Telephone:** (401) 863-3090. **Baseball SID:** Gordon Marton. **Telephone:** (401) 863-2219. **FAX:** (401) 863-1436.

BUCKNELL Bison

Conference: Patriot.

Mailing Address: Davis Gym, Lewisburg, PA 17837.

Head Coach: Gene Depew. **Assistant Coach:** Brian Hoyt. **Telephone:** (717) 524-3715. **Baseball SID:** Bob Behler. **Telephone:** (717) 524-1227. **FAX:** (717) 524-1660.

BUTLER Bulldogs

Conference: Midwestern Collegiate.

Mailing Address: 4600 Sunset Ave., Indianapolis, IN 46208.

Head Coach: Steve Farley. **Assistant Coaches:** Tony Baldwin, Matt Tyner. **Telephone:** (317) 940-9375. **Baseball SID:** Jim McGrath. **Telephone:** (317) 940-9671. **FAX:** (317) 940-9808.

C.W. POST Pioneers

Conference: Mid-Continent/East.

Mailing Address: Northern Boulevard, Brookville, NY 11548.

Head Coach: Dick Vining. **Assistant Coaches:** Jamie Apicella, Dan Mascia, Pete Timmes. **Telephone:** (516) 299-2288. **Baseball SID:** Jeremy Kniffin. **Telephone:** (516) 299-4156. **FAX:** (516) 299-3155.

CALIFORNIA Golden Bears

Conference: Pacific-10/South.

Mailing Address: 210 Memorial Stadium, Berkeley, CA 94720.

Head Coach: Bob Milano. **Assistant Coaches:** David Lawn, Scott Murray. **Telephone:** (510) 643-6006. **Baseball SID:** Scott Ball. **Telephone:** (510) 643-1741. **FAX:** (510) 643-7778.

Home Field: Evans Diamond. **Seating Capacity:** 4,000. **Outfield Dimensions:** LF—325, CF—395, RF—325. **Press Box Telephone:** (510) 642-3098.

UCLA Bruins

Conference: Pacific-10/South.

Mailing Address: 405 Hilgard Ave., Los Angeles, CA 90024.

Head Coach: Gary Adams. **Assistant Coaches:** Vince Beringhele, Brian Criss, Tim Leary. **Telephone:** (310) 794-8210. **Baseball SID:** Jeff Blank. **Telephone:** (310) 206-7870. **FAX:** (310) 825-8664.

Home Field: Jackie Robinson Stadium. **Seating Capacity:** 1,250. **Outfield Dimensions:** LF—330, CF—390, RF—330. **Press Box Telephone:** (310) 794-8213.

UC SANTA BARBARA Gauchos

Conference: Big West/South.

Mailing Address: Robertson Gym, No. 302B, Santa Barbara, CA 93106.

Head Coach: Bob Brontsema. **Assistant Coach:** John Kirkgard. **Telephone:** (805) 893-3690. **Baseball SID:** David Sobel. **Telephone:** (805) 893-3428. **FAX:** (805) 893-4537.

Home Field: Caesar Uyesaka Stadium. **Seating Capacity:** 1,000. **Outfield Dimensions:** LF—335, CF—400, RF—335. **Press Box Telephone:** (805) 893-4671.

CAL POLY SAN LUIS OBISPO Mustangs

Conference: Big West/South.

Mailing Address: One Grand Ave., San Luis Obispo, CA 93407.

Head Coach: Ritch Price. **Assistant Coaches:** Tom Kunis, Mark O'Brien. **Telephone:** (805) 756-1201. **Baseball SID:** Eric McDowell. **Telephone:** (805) 756-6531. **FAX:** (805) 756-2650.

Home Field: San Luis Obispo Stadium. **Seating Capacity:** 2,500. **Outfield Dimensions:** LF—333, CF—410, RF—333. **Press Box Telephone:** (805) 756-2410.

CAL STATE FULLERTON Titans

Conference: Big West/South.

Mailing Address: 800 N. State College Blvd., PE 133C, Fullerton, CA 92634.

Head Coach: George Horton. **Assistant Coaches:** Mike Kirby, Dave Serrano, Rick Vanderhook. **Telephone:** (714) 773-3789. **Baseball SID:** Jason Pommier. **Telephone:** (714) 773-3970. **FAX:** (714) 773-3141.

Home Field: Titan Field. **Seating Capacity:** 1,750. **Outfield Dimensions:** LF—330, CF—400, RF—330. **Press Box Telephone:** (714) 449-5327.

CAL STATE NORTHRIDGE Matadors

Conference: Independent.

Mailing Address: 18111 Nordhoff St., Northridge, CA 91330.

Head Coach: Mike Batesole. **Assistant Coaches:** Grant Hohman, Tim Montez. **Telephone:** (818) 677-7055. **Baseball SID:** Daniel Lathey. **Telephone:** (818) 677-3243. **FAX:** (818) 677-4762.

Home Field: Matador Field. **Seating Capacity:** 1,200. **Outfield Dimensions:** LF—325, CF—400, RF—330. **Press Box Telephone:** (818) 677-4502.

CAMPBELL Fighting Camels

Conference: TransAmerica Athletic/East.

Mailing Address: 215 Pope St., Buies Creek, NC 27506.

Head Coach: Chip Smith. **Assistant Coaches:** Doug Clark, Randy Hood. **Telephone:** (910) 893-1354. **Baseball SID:** Stan Cole. **Telephone:** (910) 893-1331. **FAX:** (910) 893-1330.

CANISIUS Golden Griffins

Conference: Metro Atlantic/North.

Mailing Address: 2001 Main St., Buffalo, NY 14208.

Head Coach: Don Colpoys. **Assistant Coach:** Ray Hennessy. **Telephone:** (716) 858-2977. **Baseball SID:** John Maddock. **Telephone:** (716) 888-2977. **FAX:** (716) 888-2980.

CENTENARY Gents

Conference: Trans America Athletic/West.

Mailing Address: Box 41188, Shreveport, LA 71134.

Head Coach: Mark Linden. **Assistant Coaches:** Harold Christensen, Ed McCann, Bill Ostermeyer, Matt Prysock. **Telephone:** (318) 869-5095. **Baseball SID:** Charlie Cavell. **Telephone:** (318) 869-5092. **FAX:** (318) 869-5145.

CENTRAL CONNECTICUT STATE Blue Devils

Conference: Mid-Continent/East.

Mailing Address: Kaiser Hall, 1615 Stanley St., New Britain, CT 06050.

Head Coach: George Redman. **Assistant Coaches:** Mike Church, Craig Schmitt. **Telephone:** (860) 832-3074. **Baseball SID:** Shamus Mcknight. **Telephone:** (860) 832-3059. **FAX:** (860) 832-3084.

CENTRAL FLORIDA Golden Knights

Conference: Trans America Athletic/South.

Mailing Address: Building 39, Room 109, Orlando, FL 32816.

Head Coach: Jay Bergman. **Assistant Coaches:** Greg Frady, Jim Newlin. **Telephone:** (407) 823-0140. **Baseball SID:** Stephanie Burchill. **Telephone:** (407) 823-2464. **FAX:** (407) 823-5266.

Home Field: UCF Baseball Complex. **Seating Capacity:** 2,000. **Outfield Dimensions:** LF—330, CF—400, RF—330. **Press Box Telephone:** (407) 823-5002.

CENTRAL MICHIGAN Chippewas

Conference: Mid-American.

Mailing Address: 108 West Hall, Mount Pleasant, MI 48858.

Head Coach: Dean Kreiner. **Assistant Coaches:** Jim Fuller, Tom Tresh. **Telephone:** (517) 774-6670. **Baseball SID:** Fred Stabley Jr. **Telephone:** (517) 774-3277. **FAX:** (517) 774-7324.

Home Field: Theunissen Stadium. **Seating Capacity:** 4,100. **Outfield Dimensions:** LF—335, CF—395, RF—335. **Press Box Telephone:** (517) 774-3579, 3594.

CHARLESTON Cougars

Conference: Trans America Athletic/East.

Mailing Address: 26 George St., Charleston, SC 29424.

Head Coach: Ralph Ciabattari. **Assistant Coaches:** Scott Foxhall, R.J. Kackley. **Telephone:** (803) 953-5916. **Baseball SID:** Tony Ciuffo. **Telephone:** (803) 953-5465. **FAX:** (803) 953-6534.

CHARLESTON SOUTHERN Buccaneers

Conference: Big South.

Mailing Address: P.O. Box 10087, Charleston, SC 29411.

Head Coach: Gary Murphy. **Assistant Coach:** Jeff Kinne. **Telephone:** (803) 863-7591. **Baseball SID:** Mike Hoffman. **Telephone:** (803) 863-7688. **FAX:** (803) 863-7676.

CHICAGO STATE Cougars

Conference: Mid-Continent/West.

Mailing Address: 9500 South King Drive, Chicago, IL 60628.

Head Coach: Kevin McCray. **Assistant Coaches:** Terrence Jackson, Steve Spielman. **Telephone:** (773) 995-3655. **Baseball SID:** Terrence Jackson. **Telephone:** (773) 995-2217. **FAX:** (773) 995-3656.

CINCINNATI Bearcats

Conference: Conference USA.

Mailing Address: Mail Location 21, Cincinnati, OH 45221.

Head Coach: Brian Cleary. **Assistant Coach:** Erik Hagen. **Telephone:** (513) 556-0566. **Baseball SID:** Dan McCormick. **Telephone:** (513) 556-5191. **FAX:** (513) 556-0619.

Home Field: Johnny Bench Field. **Seating Capacity:** 500. **Outfield Dimensions:** LF—327, CF—385, RF—330. **Press Box Telephone:** (513) 556-0818.

THE CITADEL Bulldogs

Conference: Southern.

Mailing Address: P.O. Box 7, Citadel Station, Charleston, SC 29409.

Head Coach: Fred Jordan. **Assistant Coaches:** Chris Lemonis, Dan

McDonnell. **Telephone:** (803) 953-5070. **Baseball SID:** Katie Frazier. **Telephone:** (803) 953-5120. **FAX:** (803) 953-5058.

CLEMSON Tigers

Conference: Atlantic Coast.

Mailing Address: P.O. Box 31, Clemson, SC 29633.

Head Coach: Jack Leggett. **Assistant Coaches:** Tim Corbin, Kevin Erminio, John Pawlowski. **Telephone:** (864) 656-1940. **Baseball SIDs:** Bob Bradley, Brian Hennessy. **Telephone:** (864) 656-2114. **FAX:** (864) 656-0299.

Home Field: Tiger Field. **Seating Capacity:** 5,000. **Outfield Dimensions:** LF—328, CF—400, RF—338. **Press Box Telephone:** (864) 654-3326.

CLEVELAND STATE Vikings

Conference: Midwestern Collegiate.

Mailing Address: CSU Convocation Center, 2000 Prospect, Cleveland, OH 44115.

Head Coach: Jay Murphy. **Assistant Coach:** Dennis Healy, Dave Sprochi. **Telephone:** (216) 687-4822. **Baseball SID:** Paulette Welch. **Telephone:** (216) 687-5288. **FAX:** (216) 523-7257.

COASTAL CAROLINA Chanticleers

Conference: Big South.

Mailing Address: P.O. Box 1954, Conway, SC 29526.

Head Coach: Gary Gilmore. **Assistant Coaches:** Bill Jarmen, Matt Schilling, Mac Smith. **Telephone:** (803) 349-2816. **Baseball SID:** Kevin Hadsell. **Telephone:** (803) 349-2809. **FAX:** (803) 349-2819.

COLUMBIA Lions

Conference: Ivy League/Gehrig.

Mailing Address: Dodge Physical Fitness Center, 3030 Broadway, New York, NY 10027.

Head Coach: Paul Fernandes. **Assistant Coach:** Derek England. **Telephone:** (212) 854-2543. **Baseball SID:** Heather Croze. **Telephone:** (212) 854-2534. **FAX:** (212) 854-8168.

CONNECTICUT Huskies

Conference: Big East/American.

Mailing Address: U-78, 2095 Hillside Road, Storrs, CT 06269.

Head Coach: Andy Baylock. **Assistant Coaches:** Jerry Lapenta, Jim Penders. **Telephone:** (860) 486-2458. **Baseball SID:** Kyle Muncy. **Telephone:** (860) 486-3531. **FAX:** (860) 486-5085.

Home Field: J.O. Christian Field. **Seating Capacity:** 2,000. **Outfield Dimensions:** LF—340, CF—405, RF—340. **Press Box Telephone:** (860) 486-2018.

COPPIN STATE Eagles

Conference: Mid-Eastern Athletic/North.

Mailing Address: 2500 W. North Ave., Baltimore, MD 21216.

Head Coach: Jason Booker. **Assistant Coaches:** Raymond Hale, Reggie Smith. **Telephone:** (410) 383-5981. **Baseball SID:** David Popham. **Telephone:** (410) 383-5981. **FAX:** (410) 669-2511.

CORNELL Big Red

Conference: Ivy League/Rolfe.

Mailing Address: Schoellkopf House, Campus Road, Ithaca, NY 14851.

Head Coach: Tom Ford. **Assistant Coaches:** Carmen Carcone, Tom Fisher. **Telephone:** (607) 255-6604. **Baseball SID:** Dave Wohlhueter. **Telephone:** (607) 255-3753. **FAX:** (607) 255-9791.

CREIGHTON Blue Jays

Conference: Missouri Valley.

Mailing Address: Vinardi Athletic Center, 2500 Burt St., Omaha, NE 68178.

Head Coach: Jack Dahm. **Assistant Coaches:** Elvis Dominguez, Mike Filipowicz. **Telephone:** (402) 280-5545. **Baseball SID:** Bobby Parker. **Telephone:** (402) 280-2488. **FAX:** (402) 280-2495.

Home Field: Creighton University Sports Complex. **Seating Capacity:** 2,000. **Outfield Dimensions:** LF—330, CF—405, RF—330. **Press Box Telephone:** TBA.

DARTMOUTH Big Green

Conference: Ivy League/Rolfe.

Mailing Address: 6083 Alumni Gym, Hanover, NH 03755.

Head Coach: Bob Whalen. **Assistant Coach:** Mik Aoki, Chris Dotolo. **Telephone:** (603) 646-2477. **Baseball SID:** Mike Mahoney. **Telephone:** (603) 646-2468. **FAX:** (603) 646-1286.

DAVIDSON Wildcats

Conference: Southern.

Mailing Address: P.O. Box 1750, Davidson, NC 28036.

Head Coach: Dick Cooke. **Assistant Coaches:** Rick Bender, Brett Boretti, Chris Pollard. **Telephone:** (704) 892-2368. **Baseball SID:** Rick Bender. **Telephone:** (704) 892-2123. **FAX:** (704) 892-2636.

DAYTON Flyers

Conference: Atlantic 10/West.

Mailing Address: Box 1238, 300 College Park, Dayton, OH 45469.

Head Coach: Chris Sorrell. **Assistant Coaches:** Terry Bell, Johnny Campbell, Mickey Martin. **Telephone:** (513) 229-4456. **Baseball SID:** Kent McElhinney. **Telephone:** (513) 229-4460. **FAX:** (513) 229-4461.

DELAWARE Fightin' Blue Hens

Conference: America East.

Mailing Address: Bob Carpenter Center, Newark, DE 19716.

Head Coach: Bob Hannah. **Assistant Coaches:** Dan Hammer, Bruce Hannah, Jim Sherman. **Telephone:** (302) 831-8596. **Baseball SID:** Jim Miller. **Telephone:** (302) 831-2186. **FAX:** (302) 831-8653.

DELAWARE STATE Hornets

Conference: Mid-Eastern Athletic/North.

Mailing Address: 1200 N. DuPont Highway, Dover, DE 19901.

Head Coach: Harry Van Sant. **Assistant Coach:** Robert Probst. **Telephone:** (302) 739-4928. **Baseball SID:** Craig Cotton. **Telephone:** (302) 739-4926. **FAX:** (302) 739-5241.

DETROIT MERCY Titans

Conference: Midwestern Collegiate.

Mailing Address: 4001 W. McNichols Road, Detroit, MI 48219.

Head Coach: Bob Miller. **Assistant Coaches:** Lee Bjerke, Don Sikora. **Telephone:** (313) 993-1725. **Baseball SID:** Ken Lasky. **Telephone:** (313) 993-1745. **FAX:** (313) 993-1765.

DREXEL Dragons

Conference: America East.

Mailing Address: 32nd and Chestnut Streets, Building 14-312, Philadelphia, PA 19104.

Head Coach: Don Maines. **Assistant Coaches:** Chris Calciano, Darren Munns. **Telephone:** (215) 590-8931. **Baseball SID:** Chris Beckett. **Telephone:** (215) 590-8946. **FAX:** (215) 590-8668.

DUKE Blue Devils

Conference: Atlantic Coast.

Mailing Address: 115 Cameron Indoor Stadium, Durham, NC 27706.

Head Coach: Steve Traylor. **Assistant Coaches:** Dave Koblentz, Chris McMullan. **Telephone:** (919) 684-2358. **Baseball SID:** Sean Moore. **Telephone:** (919) 684-2633. **FAX:** (919) 684-2489.

Home Field: Jack Coombs Field. **Seating Capacity:** 2,000. **Outfield Dimensions:** LF—330, CF—400, RF—331. **Press Box Telephone:** (919) 684-6074.

DUQUESNE Dukes

Conference: Atlantic 10/West.

Mailing Address: A.J. Palumbo Center, Pittsburgh, PA 15282.

Head Coach: Mike Wilson. **Assistant Coaches:** Norm Frey, Bob Shearer, Jay Stoner. **Telephone:** (412) 396-5245. **Baseball SID:** George Nieman. **Telephone:** (412) 396-6560. **FAX:** (412) 396-6210.

EAST CAROLINA Pirates

Conference: Colonial Athletic.

Mailing Address: Third Floor, Sports Medicine Building, Greenville, NC 27858.

Head Coach: Gary Overton. **Assistant Coach:** Charlie Smith. **Telephone:** (919) 328-4604. **Baseball SID:** Tammy Wison. **Telephone:** (919) 328-4522. **FAX:** (919) 328-4528.

EAST TENNESSEE STATE Buccaneers

Conference: Southern.

Mailing Address: P.O. Box 70641, Johnson City, TN 37614.

Head Coach: Ken Campbell. **Assistant Coaches:** Johnny Cloud, Burke McKinney. **Telephone:** (423) 929-4496. **Baseball SID:** Sanford Rogers. **Telephone:** (423) 929-5612. **FAX:** (423) 929-6138.

EASTERN ILLINOIS Panthers

Conference: Ohio Valley.

Mailing Address: Lantz Gym, Charleston, IL 61920.

Head Coach: Jim Schmitz. **Assistant Coaches:** Melesio Salazar, Brad Walsh. **Telephone:** (217) 581-2522. **Baseball SID:** Dave Kidwell. **Telephone:** (217) 581-6408. **FAX:** (217) 581-6434.

EASTERN KENTUCKY Colonels

Conference: Ohio Valley.

Mailing Address: 205 Begley Building, Kit Carson Drive, Richmond, KY 40475.

Head Coach: Jim Ward. **Assistant Coaches:** Deskaheh Bombery, Steve Roof, Jason Stein, Jon Wiggins. **Telephone:** (606) 622-2128. **Baseball SID:** Karl Park. **Telephone:** (606) 622-1253. **FAX:** (606) 622-1230.

EASTERN MICHIGAN Eagles

Conference: Mid-American.

Mailing Address: 200 Bowen Fieldhouse, Ypsilanti, MI 48197.

Head Coach: Roger Coryell. **Assistant Coach:** David Martin. **Telephone:** (313) 487-0315. **Baseball SID:** Emily Griffin. **Telephone:** (313) 487-0317. **FAX:** (313) 485-3840.

Home Field: Oestrike Stadium. **Seating Capacity:** 2,500. **Outfield Dimensions:** LF—330, CF—390, RF—330. **Press Box Telephone:** (313) 484-1396.

EVANSVILLE Purple Aces

Conference: Missouri Valley.

Mailing Address: 1800 Lincoln Ave., Evansville, IN 47722.

Head Coach: Jim Brownlee. **Assistant Coaches:** Tim Brownlee, Jeff Leyestra, Denny Potts. **Telephone:** (812) 479-2059. **Baseball SID:** Jay Jameson. **Telephone:** (812) 479-2350. **FAX:** (812) 479-2199.

FAIRFIELD Stags

Conference: Metro Atlantic/South.

Mailing Address: N. Benson Road, Fairfield, CT 06430.

Head Coach: John Slosar. **Assistant Coach:** Aaron Quinn. **Telephone:** (203) 254-4000, ext. 2605. **Baseball SID:** Drew Brown. **Telephone:** (203) 254-4000, ext. 2878. **FAX:** (203) 254-4117.

FAIRLEIGH DICKINSON Knights

Conference: Northeast.

Mailing Address: Temple Avenue, Rothman Center, Hackensack, NJ 07601.

Head Coach: Dennis Sasso. **Assistant Coaches:** Jerry DeFabbia, John Evans. **Telephone:** (201) 692-2245. **Baseball SID:** Cecilia Skraastad. **Telephone:** (201) 692-2204. **FAX:** (201) 692-9361.

FLORIDA Gators

Conference: Southeastern/East.

Mailing Address: Box 14485, Gainesville, FL 32604.

Head Coach: Andy Lopez. **Assistant Coaches:** Rick Eckstein, Gary Henderson, Steve Kling. **Telephone:** (352) 375-4683, ext. 4457. **Baseball SID:** Steve Shaff. **Telephone:** (352) 375-4683, ext. 6100. **FAX:** (352) 375-4809.

Home Field: McKethan Stadium at Perry Field. **Seating Capacity:** 4,500. **Outfield Dimensions:** LF—329, CF—400, RF—325. **Press Box Telephone:** (352) 375-4683, ext. 4355.

FLORIDA A&M Rattlers

Conference: Mid-Eastern Athletic/Southern.

Mailing Address: Room 204-D, Gaither Athletic Center, Tallahassee, FL 32307.

Head Coach: Joe Durant. **Assistant Coach:** Willie Brown, Curtis George, Sean Gilliam, Harry Sapp. **Telephone:** (904) 599-3202. **Baseball SID:** Jabari Glapion. **Telephone:** (904) 599-3200. **FAX:** (904) 599-3206.

FLORIDA ATLANTIC Owls

Conference: TransAmerica Athletic/South.

Mailing Address: 500 NW 20th St., Boca Raton, FL 33431.

Head Coach: Kevin Cooney. **Assistant Coaches:** Kerwin Belle, John McCormack, Steve Whitaker. **Telephone:** (407) 367-3956. **Baseball SID:** Katrina McCormack. **Telephone:** (407) 367-3163. **FAX:** (407) 361-3963.

FLORIDA INTERNATIONAL Golden Panthers

Conference: TransAmerica Athletic/South.

Mailing Address: University Park Campus, Miami, FL 33199.

Head Coach: Danny Price. **Assistant Coaches:** Marc Calvi, Rolando Casanova, Ken Foster. **Telephone:** (305) 348-3166. **Baseball SID:** Rich Kelch. **Telephone:** (305) 348-3166. **FAX:** (305) 348-2963.

Home Field: University Park. **Seating Capacity:** 1,000. **Outfield Dimensions:** LF—325, CF—400, RF—325. **Press Box Telephone:** (305) 554-8694.

FLORIDA STATE Seminoles

Conference: Atlantic Coast.

Mailing Address: P.O. Drawer 2195, Tallahassee, FL 32316.

Head Coach: Mike Martin. **Assistant Coaches:** Chip Baker, Jack Niles, Jamey Shouppe. **Telephone:** (904) 644-1073. **Baseball SID:** Amy Farnum. **Telephone:** (904) 644-0615. **FAX:** (904) 644-3820.

Home Field: Dick Howser Stadium. **Seating Capacity:** 5,000. **Outfield Dimensions:** LF—340, CF—400, RF—320. **Press Box Telephone:** (904) 644-1553.

FORDHAM Rams

Conference: Atlantic 10/East.

Mailing Address: 441 E. Fordham Road, Bronx, NY 10458.

Head Coach: Dan Gallagher. **Assistant Coaches:** Charles Aliano, John Ceprini, Tony Mellaci. **Telephone:** (718) 817-4292. **Baseball SID:** Joe DiBari. **Telephone:** (718) 817-4240. **FAX:** (718) 817-4244.

FRESNO STATE Bulldogs

Conference: Western Athletic/West.

Mailing Address: 5305 N. Campus Drive, Room 153, Fresno, CA 93740.

Head Coach: Bob Bennett. **Assistant Coaches:** Steve Pearse, Mike Rupcich. **Telephone:** (209) 278-2178. **Baseball SID:** Dave Haglund. **Telephone:** (209) 278-2509. **FAX:** (209) 278-4689.

Home Field: Beiden Field. **Seating Capacity:** 4,575. **Outfield Dimensions:** LF—330, CF—400, RF—330. **Press Box Telephone:** (209) 278-7678.

FURMAN Paladins

Conference: Southern.

Mailing Address: 3300 Poinsett Highway, Greenville, SC 29613.

Head Coach: Ron Smith. **Assistant Coaches:** David Lancaster, Jeff Massey, Aaron Stults. **Telephone:** (864) 294-2146. **Baseball SID:** Julie Prince. **Telephone:** (864) 294-3062. **FAX:** (864) 294-3061.

GEORGE MASON Patriots

Conference: Colonial Athletic.

Mailing Address: 4400 University Drive, Fairfax, VA 22030.

Head Coach: Bill Brown. **Assistant Coaches:** Chris Burr, Chris Murphy, J.J. Picollo, Mike Sylvester. **Telephone:** (703) 993-3282. **Baseball SID:** Ben Trittipoe. **Telephone:** (703) 993-3263. **FAX:** (703) 993-3259.

GEORGE WASHINGTON Colonials

Conference: Atlantic 10/West.

Mailing Address: 600 22nd St. NW, Washington, DC 20052.

Head Coach: Tom Walter. **Assistant Coaches:** Joe Raccuia, Terry Rooney.

Telephone: (202) 994-7399. **Baseball SID:** Jason Guy. **Telephone:** (202) 994-0339. **FAX:** (202) 994-2713.

GEORGETOWN Hoyas

Conference: Big East/National.

Mailing Address: 37th & O Streets NW, Washington, DC 20057.

Head Coach: Kirk Mason. **Assistant Coaches:** Dan Nellum. **Telephone:** (202) 687-2462. **Baseball SID:** Bill Hurd. **Telephone:** (202) 687-2492. **FAX:** (202) 687-2491.

Home Field: Georgetown Baseball Field. **Seating Capacity:** 2,000. **Outfield Dimensions:** LF—300, CF—425, RF—310. **Press Box Telephone:** None.

GEORGIA Bulldogs

Conference: Southeastern/East.

Mailing Address: P.O. Box 1472, Athens, GA 30613.

Head Coach: Robert Sapp. **Assistant Coaches:** Randy Mazey, Allen Osborne, David Perno. **Telephone:** (706) 542-7971. **Baseball SID:** Christopher Lakos. **Telephone:** (706) 542-1621. **FAX:** (706) 542-9339.

Home Field: Foley Field. **Seating Capacity:** 3,200. **Outfield Dimensions:** LF—350, CF—410, RF—320. **Press Box Telephone:** (706) 542-6162.

GEORGIA SOUTHERN Eagles

Conference: Southern.

Mailing Address: Landrum Box 8085, Statesboro, GA 30460.

Head Coach: Jack Stallings. **Assistant Coaches:** Scott Baker, Garth Spendiff, Darin Van Tassell. **Telephone:** (912) 681-5187. **Baseball SID:** Tom McClellan. **Telephone:** (912) 681-5239. **FAX:** (912) 681-0046.

Home Field: J.I. Clements Stadium. **Seating Capacity:** 2,000. **Outfield Dimensions:** LF—330, CF—380, RF—320. **Press Box Telephone:** (912) 681-2508.

GEORGIA STATE Panthers

Conference: TransAmerica Athletic/East.

Mailing Address: University Plaza, Atlanta, GA 30303.

Head Coach: Mike Hurst. **Assistant Coaches:** David Hartley, Bob Keller. **Telephone:** (404) 651-1198. **Baseball SID:** Peter O'Reilly. **Telephone:** (404) 651-3168. **FAX:** (404) 651-3204.

GEORGIA TECH Yellow Jackets

Conference: Atlantic Coast.

Mailing Address: 150 Bobby Dodd Way NW, Atlanta, GA 30332.

Head Coach: Danny Hall. **Assistant Coaches:** Jeff Guy, Mike Trapasso. **Telephone:** (404) 894-5471. **Baseball SID:** Mike Stamus. **Telephone:** (404) 894-5445. **FAX:** (404) 853-1248.

Home Field: Russ Chandler Stadium. **Seating Capacity:** 2,500. **Outfield Dimensions:** LF—320, CF—400, RF—330. **Press Box Telephone:** (404) 894-3167.

GONZAGA Bulldogs

Conference: West Coast.

Mailing Address: E. 502 Boone Ave, Spokane, WA 99258.

Head Coach: Steve Hertz. **Assistant Coaches:** Greg Gores, Mark Machtolf, Scott Rogers. **Telephone:** (509) 328-4220, ext. 4226. **Baseball SID:** Oliver Pierce. **Telephone:** (509) 328-4220, ext. 6373. **FAX:** (509) 324-5730.

GRAMBLING STATE Tigers

Conference: Southwestern Athletic/West.

Mailing Address: P.O. Box N, Grambling, LA 71245.

Head Coach: Wilbert Ellis. **Assistant Coach:** James Randall. **Telephone:** (318) 274-6121. **Baseball SID:** Scott Boatwright. **Telephone:** (318) 274-6199. **FAX:** (318) 274-6281.

GRAND CANYON Antelopes

Conference: Western Athletic/North.

Mailing Address: 3300 W. Camelback Road, Phoenix, AZ 85061.

Head Coach: Gil Stafford. **Assistant Coaches:** Dave Stapleton, Ed Wolfe. **Telephone:** (602) 589-2805. **Baseball SID:** Deron Filip. **Telephone:** (602) 589-2795. **FAX:** (602) 589-2529.

Home Field: Brazell Stadium. **Seating Capacity:** 2,500. **Outfield Dimensions:** LF—325, CF—390, RF—325. **Press Box Telephone:** (602) 589-2719.

HARTFORD Hawks

Conference: America East.

Mailing Address: 200 Bloomfield Ave., West Hartford, CT 06117.

Head Coach: Jim Bretz. **Assistant Coaches:** Mike Morhardt, Bob Nenna. **Telephone:** (860) 768-4656. **Baseball SIDs:** Mike Falkowitz, James Keener. **Telephone:** (860) 768-4620. **FAX:** (860) 768-4068.

HARVARD Crimson

Conference: Ivy League/Rolfe.

Mailing Address: Department of Athletics, 60 John F. Kennedy St., Cambridge, MA 02138.

Head Coach: Joe Walsh. **Assistant Coaches:** Gary Donovan, Ed Gallagher, Marty Nastasia. **Telephone:** (617) 495-2629. **Baseball SID:** Paul McNeely. **Telephone:** (617) 495-2206. **FAX:** (617) 495-2130.

HAWAII Rainbows

Conference: Western Athletic/West.

Mailing Address: 1337 Lower Campus Road, Honolulu, HI 96822.

Head Coach: Les Murakami. **Assistant Coaches:** Carl Furutani, Dave Murakami, Les Nakama. **Telephone:** (808) 956-6247. **Baseball SID:** Markus

Owens. **Telephone:** (808) 956-7523. **FAX:** (808) 956-4470.

Home Field: Rainbow Stadium. **Seating Capacity:** 4,312. **Outfield Dimensions:** LF—340, CF—400, RF—340. **Press Box Telephone:** (808) 956-6253.

HAWAII-HILO Vulcans

Conference: Independent.

Mailing Address: 200 W. Kawili St., Hilo, HI 96720.

Head Coach: Joey Estrella. **Assistant Coaches:** Richard DeSa, Kallen Miyataki, Lyle Tamaribuchi. **Telephone:** (808) 974-7700. **Baseball SID:** Kelly Leong. **Telephone:** (808) 974-7606. **FAX:** (808) 974-7711.

HOFSTRA Flying Dutchmen

Conference: America East.

Mailing Address: 1000 Hempstead Turnpike, PFC 240, Hempstead, NY 11550.

Head Coach: Reggie Jackson. **Assistant Coaches:** Kevin Delaney, Larry Minor. **Telephone:** (516) 463-5065. **Baseball SID:** Jim Sheehan. **Telephone:** (516) 463-6764. **FAX:** (516) 463-5033.

HOLY CROSS Crusaders

Conference: Patriot.

Mailing Address: One College Street, Worcester, MA 01610.

Head Coach: Jack Whalen. **Assistant Coach:** Tim Whalen. **Telephone:** (508) 793-3628. **Baseball SID:** Tracy King. **Telephone:** (508) 793-2583. **FAX:** (508) 793-2309.

HOUSTON Cougars

Conference: Conference USA.

Mailing Address: Room 155, 3855 Holman, Houston, TX 77204.

Head Coach: Rayner Noble. **Assistant Coaches:** Trip Couch, Todd Whitting. **Telephone:** (713) 743-9396. **Baseball SID:** John Sullivan. **Telephone:** (713) 743-9410. **FAX:** (713) 743-9411.

Home Field: Cougar Field. **Seating Capacity:** 5,000. **Outfield Dimensions:** LF—330, CF—390, RF—330. **Press Box Telephone:** (713) 743-0841.

HOWARD Bison

Conference: Mid-Eastern Athletic/North.

Mailing Address: 511 Gresham Place NW, Drew Hall, Washington, DC 20059.

Head Coach: Chuck Hinton. **Assistant Coaches:** Chico Hinton, Eric Johnson. **Telephone:** (202) 806-5162. **Baseball SID:** Martin Lewis. **Telephone:** (202) 806-7188. **FAX:** (202) 806-9595.

ILLINOIS Fighting Illini

Conference: Big Ten.

Mailing Address: Bielfeldt Athletic Administration Building, 1700 S. Fourth Street, Champaign, IL 61820.

Head Coach: Itch Jones. **Assistant Coaches:** Dan Hartleb, Todd Murphy. **Telephone:** (217) 244-8138. **Baseball SID:** Mike Mandujano. **Telephone:** (217) 244-3707. **FAX:** (217) 333-5540.

Home Field: Illinois Field. **Seating Capacity:** 2,500. **Outfield Dimensions:** LF—330, CF—400, RF—330. **Press Box Telephone:** (217) 333-1227.

ILLINOIS-CHICAGO Flames

Conference: Midwestern Collegiate.

Mailing Address: Box 4348, Chicago, IL 60680.

Head Coach: Dean Refakes. **Assistant Coaches:** Wally Berhns, Arnie Hartoch, Tony Hubbard, Dan Kusinski. **Telephone:** (312) 996-8645. **Baseball SID:** Anne Schoenherr. **Telephone:** (312) 996-5880. **FAX:** (312) 996-5882.

ILLINOIS STATE Redbirds

Conference: Missouri Valley.

Mailing Address: 123 Horton Field House, Normal, IL 61761.

Head Coach: Jeff Stewart. **Assistant Coaches:** Dan Drdak, Stephen Gadlage, Tim Johnson. **Telephone:** (309) 438-5151. **Baseball SID:** Todd Kober, Julie Thompson. **Telephone:** (309) 438-3825. **FAX:** (309) 438-5634.

INDIANA Hoosiers

Conference: Big Ten.

Mailing Address: 17th & Fee Lane, Assembly Hall, Bloomington, IN 47405.

Head Coach: Bob Morgan. **Assistant Coaches:** Jeff Calcaterra, Scott Googins, Bill Mueller. **Telephone:** (812) 855-9790. **Baseball SID:** Perry Mann. **Telephone:** (812) 855-9399. **FAX:** (812) 855-9401.

Home Field: Sembower Field. **Seating Capacity:** 3,000. **Outfield Dimensions:** LF—333, CF—380, RF—333. **Press Box Telephone:** (812) 855-2754.

INDIANA STATE Sycamores

Conference: Missouri Valley.

Mailing Address: Room 118, Indiana State Arena, Terre Haute, IN 47809.

Head Coach: Bob Warn. **Assistant Coaches:** Bob Doty, Mitch Hannahs. **Telephone:** (812) 237-4051. **Baseball SID:** Tim O'Brien. **Telephone:** (812) 237-4160. **FAX:** (812) 237-4157.

Home Field: Sycamore Field. **Seating Capacity:** 2,500. **Outfield Dimensions:** LF—340, CF—402, RF—340. **Press Box Telephone:** (812) 237-4187.

IONA Gaels

Conference: Metro Atlantic/South.

Mailing Address: Mulcahy Center, 715 North Ave., New Rochelle, NY 10801.

Head Coach: Al Zoccolillo. **Assistant Coaches:** J.B. Buono, Lou Persiani. **Telephone:** (914) 633-2319. **Baseball SID:** Dave Cagianello. **Telephone:** (914) 633-2057. **FAX:** (914) 633-2072.

IOWA Hawkeyes

Conference: Big Ten.

Mailing Address: 340 Carver-Hawkeye Arena, Iowa City, IA 52242.

Head Coach: Duane Banks. **Assistant Coaches:** Scott Broghamer, Ken Charipar. **Telephone:** (319) 335-9389. **Baseball SID:** Kristy Fick. **Telephone:** (319) 335-9411. **FAX:** (319) 335-9417.

Home Field: Iowa Field. **Seating Capacity:** 3,000. **Outfield Dimensions:** LF—330, CF—370, RF—330. **Press Box Telephone:** (319) 335-9520.

IOWA STATE Cyclones

Conference: Big 12.

Mailing Address: Jacobson Athletic Building, 1800 S. Fourth St., Ames, IA 50011.

Head Coach: Lyle Smith. **Assistant Coaches:** Jerry McNertney, Ed Servais. **Telephone:** (515) 294-4201. **Baseball SID:** Stacie Michaud. **Telephone:** (515) 294-3372. **FAX:** (515) 294-0558.

Home Field: Cap Timm Field. **Seating Capacity:** 3,000. **Outfield Dimensions:** LF—330, CF—400, RF—330. **Press Box Telephone:** TBA.

JACKSON STATE Tigers

Conference: Southwestern Athletic/East.

Mailing Address: 1325 West Lynch St., Jackson, MS 39217.

Head Coach: Robert Braddy. **Assistant Coaches:** Lewis Braddy, Stanley Stubbs. **Telephone:** (601) 968-2425. **Baseball SID:** Samuel Jefferson. **Telephone:** (601) 968-2273. **FAX:** (601) 968-2000.

JACKSONVILLE Dolphins

Conference: Sun Belt.

Mailing Address: 2800 University Blvd. N., Jacksonville, FL 32211.

Head Coach: Terry Alexander. **Assistant Coaches:** Rusty Green, Johnny Wiggs. **Telephone:** (904) 745-7410. **Baseball SID:** Brian Fremund. **Telephone:** (904) 745-7402. **FAX:** (904) 743-0067.

Home Field: Brest Field. **Seating Capacity:** 2,300. **Outfield Dimensions:** LF—340, CF—405, RF—340. **Press Box Telephone:** TBA.

JACKSONVILLE STATE Gamecocks

Conference: TransAmerica Athletic/West.

Mailing Address: Gamecock Fieldhouse, 700 Pelham Road N., Jacksonville, AL 36265.

Head Coach: Rudy Abbott. **Assistant Coach:** Skipper Jones. **Telephone:** (205) 782-5367. **Baseball SID:** Greg Seitz. **Telephone:** (205) 782-5279. **FAX:** (205) 782-5958.

JAMES MADISON Dukes

Conference: Colonial Athletic.

Mailing Address: South Main, Harrisonburg, VA 22807.

Head Coach: Kevin Anderson. **Assistant Coaches:** Barry Given, Todd Raleigh. **Telephone:** (540) 568-6467. **Baseball SID:** Curt Dudley. **Telephone:** (540) 568-6154. **FAX:** (540) 568-3703.

Home Field: Mauck Stadium at Long Field. **Seating Capacity:** 1,200. **Outfield Dimensions:** LF—340, CF—400, RF—320. **Press Box Telephone:** (703) 568-6545.

KANSAS Jayhawks

Conference: Big 12.

Mailing Address: 202 Allen Fieldhouse, Lawrence, KS 66045.

Head Coach: Bobby Randall. **Assistant Coaches:** Mike Bard, Wilson Kilmer. **Telephone:** (913) 864-7907. **Baseball SID:** Craig Pinkerton. **Telephone:** (913) 864-3417. **FAX:** (913) 864-7944.

Home Field: Hoglund-Maupin Stadium. **Seating Capacity:** 1,320. **Outfield Dimensions:** LF—350, CF—380, RF—350. **Press Box Telephone:** (913) 864-4037.

KANSAS STATE Wildcats

Conference: Big 12.

Mailing Address: Suite 144, Bramlage Coliseum, 1800 College Ave., Manhattan, KS 66502.

Head Coach: Mike Clark. **Assistant Coaches:** Mike Hensley, Robbie Moen. **Telephone:** (913) 532-5723. **Baseball SID:** Dan Wallenberg. **Telephone:** (913) 532-6735. **FAX:** (913) 532-6093.

Home Field: Frank Myers. **Seating Capacity:** 5,000. **Outfield Dimensions:** LF—340, CF—400, RF—325. **Press Box Telephone:** (913) 532-6926.

KENT Golden Flashes

Conference: Mid-American.

Mailing Address: P.O. Box 5190, 154 Memorial Gym, Kent, OH 44242.

Head Coach: Rick Rembielak. **Assistant Coach:** Greg Beals. **Telephone:** (330) 672-3696. **Baseball SID:** Will Roleson. **Telephone:** (330) 672-2110. **FAX:** (330) 672-2112.

Home Field: Gene Michael Field. **Seating Capacity:** 2,000. **Outfield Dimensions:** LF—330, CF—400, RF—330. **Press Box Telephone:** (330) 672-2036.

KENTUCKY Wildcats

Conference: Southeastern/East.

Mailing Address: Room 23, Memorial Coliseum, Lexington, KY 40506.

Head Coach: Keith Madison. **Assistant Coaches:** Chuck Bartlett, Jan Weisberg, Jeff Young. **Telephone:** (606) 257-6500. **Baseball SID:** Shawn Robinson. **Telephone:** (606) 257-3838. **FAX:** (606) 323-4310.

Home Field: Cliff Hagan Stadium. **Seating Capacity:** 2,500. **Outfield Dimensions:** LF—340, CF—390, RF—310. **Press Box Telephone:** (606) 257-8027.

LAFAYETTE Leopards

Conference: Patriot.

Mailing Address: Room 17, Watson Hall, High Street, Easton, PA 18042.

Head Coach: Greg Vogel. **Assistant Coaches:** Lloyd Brewer, Clayton Gum. **Telephone:** (610) 250-5476. **Baseball SID:** Michael Forcucci. **Telephone:** (610) 250-5122. **FAX:** (610) 250-5519.

LAMAR Cardinals

Conference: Sun Belt.

Mailing Address: Box 10066, LU Station, Beaumont, TX 77710.

Head Coach: Jim Gilligan. **Assistant Coaches:** Brian Biggers, Matt Blando, Rick Hirtensteiner. **Telephone:** (409) 880-8974. **Baseball SID:** Davey Crizer. **Telephone:** (409) 880-8329. **FAX:** (409) 880-2338.

Home Field: Vincent-Beck Stadium. **Seating Capacity:** 3,500. **Outfield Dimensions:** LF—325, CF—380, RF—325. **Press Box Telephone:** (409) 880-8327.

LA SALLE Explorers

Conference: Atlantic 10/West.

Mailing Address: 1900 W. Olney Ave., Box 805, Philadelphia, PA 19141.

Head Coach: Frank DiMichele. **Assistant Coach:** Bob Hemphill. **Telephone:** (215) 951-1995. **Baseball SID:** Kevin Currie. **Telephone:** (215) 951-1605. **FAX:** (215) 951-1694.

LEHIGH Engineers

Conference: Patriot.

Mailing Address: Taylor Gym, 641 Taylor St., Bethlehem, PA 18015.

Head Coach: Sean Leary. **Assistant Coaches:** Craig Anderson, Jerry Mack. **Telephone:** (610) 758-4315. **Baseball SID:** Glenn Hofmann. **Telephone:** (610) 758-3174. **FAX:** (610) 758-4407.

LE MOYNE Dolphins

Conference: Metro Atlantic/North.

Mailing Address: Springfield Road, Syracuse, NY 13214.

Head Coach: John King. **Assistant Coaches:** Teddy Klamm, Brock Matlock, Bobby Nandin. **Telephone:** (315) 445-4415. **Baseball SID:** Mike Tuberosa. **Telephone:** (315) 445-4412. **FAX:** (315) 445-4678.

LIBERTY Flames

Conference: Big South.

Mailing Address: Box 20000, Lynchburg, VA 24506.

Head Coach: Johnny Hunton. **Assistant Coach:** Dave Pastors. **Telephone:** (804) 582-2100. **Baseball SID:** Trevor Price. **Telephone:** (804) 582-2292. **FAX:** (804) 582-2076.

LONG BEACH STATE 49ers

Conference: Big West.

Mailing Address: 1250 Bellflower Blvd., Long Beach, CA 90840.

Head Coach: Dave Snow. **Assistant Coaches:** Mike Stembridge, Jon Strauss, Mike Weathers, Jim Yogi. **Telephone:** (562) 987-0457. **Baseball SID:** Randy Franz. **Telephone:** (562) 985-7977. **FAX:** (562) 985-8197.

Home Field: Blair Field. **Seating Capacity:** 3,000. **Outfield Dimensions:** LF—348, CF—400, RF—348. **Press Box Telephone:** (562) 930-0714.

LONG ISLAND Blackbirds

Conference: Northeast.

Mailing Address: University Plaza, Brooklyn, NY 11201.

Head Coach: Frank Giannone. **Assistant Coaches:** Chris Bagley, Nick Doscher, Mike Ryan. **Telephone:** (718) 488-1538. **Baseball SIDs:** Greg Fox, Steven Torres. **Telephone:** (718) 488-1420. **FAX:** (718) 780-4046.

LOUISIANA STATE Tigers

Conference: Southeastern/West.

Mailing Address: P.O. Box 25095, Baton Rouge, LA 70894.

Head Coach: Skip Bertman. **Assistant Coaches:** Mike Bianco, Dan Canevari, Jim Schwanke, Daniel Tomlin. **Telephone:** (504) 388-4148. **Baseball SID:** Bill Franques. **Telephone:** (504) 388-8226. **FAX:** (504) 388-1861.

Home Field: Alex Box Stadium. **Seating Capacity:** 7,006. **Outfield Dimensions:** LF—330, CF—405, RF—330. **Press Box Telephone:** (504) 388-4149.

LOUISIANA TECH Bulldogs

Conference: Sun Belt.

Mailing Address: P.O. Box 3166, Ruston, LA 71272.

Head Coach: Randy Davis. **Assistant Coaches:** Brian Rountree, Sean Teague. **Telephone:** (318) 257-4111. **Baseball SID:** Larry Little. **Telephone:** (318) 257-3144. **FAX:** (318) 257-3757.

LOUISVILLE Cardinals

Conference: Conference USA.

Mailing Address: Floyd & Brandeis Streets, Louisville, KY 40292.

Head Coach: Lelo Prado. **Assistant Coaches:** Keith Chester, Brian Mundorf, Larry Owens. **Telephone:** (502) 852-0103. **Baseball SID:** Nancy Smith. **Telephone:** (502) 852-6581. **FAX:** (502) 367-5000.

Home Field: Cardinal Stadium. **Seating Capacity:** 20,000. **Outfield Dimensions:** LF—360, CF—410, RF—320. **Press Box Telephone:** (502) 852-1444.

LOYOLA MARYMOUNT Lions

Conference: West Coast.

Mailing Address: Loyola Boulevard and W. 80th, Los Angeles, CA 90045.

Head Coach: Frank Cruz. **Assistant Coaches:** Ron Hauczinger, David Ravitz, John Verhoeven. **Telephone:** (310) 338-2765. **Baseball SID:** Bruce Meyers. **Telephone:** (310) 338-7643. **FAX:** (310) 338-2703.

MAINE Black Bears

Conference: America East.

Mailing Address: 186 Memorial Gym, Orono, ME 04469.

Head Coach: Paul Kostacopoulos. **Assistant Coaches:** Mike Coutts, Jay Kemble, Ted Novio. **Telephone:** (207) 581-1090. **Baseball SID:** Joe Roberts. **Telephone:** (207) 581-3646. **FAX:** (207) 581-3297.

Home Field: Mahaney Diamond. **Seating Capacity:** 4,000. **Outfield Dimensions:** LF—330, CF—400, RF—330. **Press Box Telephone:** (207) 581-1049.

MANHATTAN Jaspers

Conference: Metro Atlantic/South.

Mailing Address: Manhattan College Parkway, Riverdale, NY 10471.

Head Coach: Gary Puccio. **Assistant Coach:** Anthony Fallacaro. **Telephone:** (718) 862-7486. **Baseball SID:** Jeff Bernstein. **Telephone:** (718) 862-0228. **FAX:** (718) 862-8020.

MARIST Red Foxes

Conference: Northeast.

Mailing Address: McCann Center, North Road, Poughkeepsie, NY 12601.

Head Coach: John Szefc. **Assistant Coaches:** Al Hammell, Mike Mancuso. **Telephone:** (914) 575-3000, ext. 2570. **Baseball SID:** Sean Morrison. **Telephone:** (914) 575-3000, ext. 2322. **FAX:** (914) 471-0466.

MARSHALL Thundering Herd

Conference: Southern.

Mailing Address: P.O. Box 1360, Huntington, WV 25715.

Head Coach: Craig Antush. **Assistant Coaches:** Mike Fagan, Dave Piepenbrink. **Telephone:** (304) 696-6454. **Baseball SID:** Archie Gleason. **Telephone:** (304) 696-4662. **FAX:** (304) 696-2325.

MARYLAND Terrapins

Conference: Atlantic Coast.

Mailing Address: P.O. Box 295, College Park, MD 20741.

Head Coach: Tom Bradley. **Assistant Coaches:** Jim Flack, Don Fontana, Kelly Kulina. **Telephone:** (301) 314-7122. **Baseball SID:** Mark Ragonese, Jeff Stauffer. **Telephone:** (301) 314-7062. **FAX:** (301) 314-9094.

Home Field: Shipley Field. **Seating Capacity:** 2,200. **Outfield Dimensions:** LF—320, CF—360, RF—320. **Press Box Telephone:** None.

MARYLAND-BALTIMORE COUNTY Retrievers

Conference: Big South.

Mailing Address: 5401 Wilkens Ave., Baltimore, MD 21228.

Head Coach: John Jancuska. **Assistant Coaches:** Larry Freer, Bob Mumma. **Telephone:** (410) 455-2239. **Baseball SID:** Jerry Milani. **Telephone:** (410) 455-2639. **FAX:** (410) 455-3994.

MARYLAND-EASTERN SHORE Hawks

Conference: Mid-Eastern Athletic/North.

Mailing Address: Tawes Gymnasium, Backbone Road, Princess Anne, MD 21853.

Head Coach: Kaye Pinhey. **Assistant Coach:** Brian Holliman, Mike Shockley. **Telephone:** (410) 651-6539. **Baseball SID:** Unavailable. **Telephone:** (410) 651-6499. **FAX:** (410) 651-7600.

MASSACHUSETTS Minutemen

Conference: Atlantic 10/East.

Mailing Address: 255A Boyden Building, Amherst, MA 01003.

Head Coach: Mike Stone. **Assistant Coaches:** Brian Bright, Julie Croteau, Jay Murphy. **Telephone:** (413) 545-3120. **Baseball SID:** Charlie Bare. **Telephone:** (413) 545-2439. **FAX:** (413) 545-1556.

McNEESE STATE Cowboys

Conference: Southland/Louisiana.

Mailing Address: P.O. Box 92735, Lake Charles, LA 70609.

Head Coach: Jim Ricklefsen. **Assistant Coaches:** Brad Holland, Ron Riley. **Telephone:** (318) 475-5484. **Baseball SID:** Louis Bonnette. **Telephone:** (318) 475-5207. **FAX:** (318) 475-5202.

MEMPHIS Tigers

Conference: Conference USA.

Mailing Address: 205 Athletic Office Building, 570 Normal, Memphis, TN 38152.

Head Coach: Jeff Hopkins. **Assistant Coaches:** Rob McDonald, Eric Page. **Telephone:** (901) 678-2452. **Baseball SID:** Brian Eaton. **Telephone:** (901) 678-2337. **FAX:** (901) 678-4134.

Home Field: Nat Buring Stadium. **Seating Capacity:** 2,000. **Outfield Dimensions:** LF—320, CF—380, RF—320. **Press Box Telephone:** (901) 678-2862.

MERCER Bears

Conference: TransAmerica Athletic/East.

Mailing Address: 1400 Coleman Ave., Macon, GA 31207.

Head Coach: Barry Myers. **Assistant Coaches:** Jim Cole, Craig Gibson **Telephone:** (912) 752-2738. **Baseball SID:** Kevin Coulombe. **Telephone:** (912) 752-2735. **FAX:** (912) 752-5350.

MIAMI Hurricanes

Conference: Independent.

Mailing Address: Box 248167, Coral Gables, FL 33124.

Head Coach: Jim Morris. **Assistant Coaches:** Lazaro Collazo, Gino DiMare, Turtle Thomas. **Telephone:** (305) 284-4171. **Baseball SID:** Phil deMontmollin. **Telephone:** (305) 284-3244. **FAX:** (305) 284-2807.

Home Field: Mark Light Stadium. **Seating Capacity:** 5,000. **Outfield Dimensions:** LF—330, CF—400, RF—330. **Press Box Telephone:** (305) 284-4512.

MIAMI Redskins

Conference: Mid-American.

Mailing Address: 230 Millett Hall, Oxford, OH 45056.

Head Coach: Tracy Smith. **Assistant Coaches:** Bill Doran, Tom Kinkelaar, Greg McVey. **Telephone:** (513) 529-6631. **Baseball SID:** Sean Palchick. **Telephone:** (513) 529-4327. **FAX:** (513) 529-6729.

Home Field: Stanley G. McKie Field. **Seating Capacity:** 1,500. **Outfield Dimensions:** LF—325, CF—400, RF—325. **Press Box Telephone:** (513) 529-4331.

MICHIGAN Wolverines

Conference: Big Ten.

Mailing Address: 1000 S. State St., Ann Arbor, MI 48109.

Head Coach: Geoff Zahn. **Assistant Coaches:** Ace Adams, Tom Dodge, Chris Harrison. **Telephone:** (313) 647-4550. **Baseball SID:** Jim Schneider. **Telephone:** (313) 763-1381. **FAX:** (313) 747-1188.

Home Field: Ray Fisher Stadium. **Seating Capacity:** 4,000. **Outfield Dimensions:** LF—330, CF—400, RF—330. **Press Box Telephone:** (313) 647-1283.

MICHIGAN STATE Spartans

Conference: Big Ten.

Mailing Address: 401 Olds Hall, East Lansing, MI 48824.

Head Coach: Ted Mahan. **Assistant Coaches:** Jason Baker, Greg Gunderson, Eddie Turek. **Telephone:** (517) 355-4486. **Baseball SID:** Brenda McGuire. **Telephone:** (517) 355-2271. **FAX:** (517) 353-9636.

Home Field: Kobs Field and Oldsmobile Park. **Seating Capacity:** 4,000 (Kobs); 6,000 (Oldsmobile). **Outfield Dimensions:** LF—340, CF—400, RF—301 (Kobs); LF—330, CF—412 , LF—337 (Oldsmobile). **Press Box Telephone:** (517) 353-3009 (Kobs), (517) 485-2616/267-0583 (Oldsmobile).

MIDDLE TENNESSEE STATE Blue Raiders

Conference: Ohio Valley.

Mailing Address: MTSU Box 20, Murfreesboro, TN 37132.

Head Coach: Steve Peterson. **Assistant Coaches:** Buddy Custer, Jim McGuire. **Telephone:** (615) 898-2120. **Baseball SID:** Ed Given. **Telephone:** (615) 898-2450. **FAX:** (615) 898-5626.

MINNESOTA Golden Gophers

Conference: Big Ten.

Mailing Address: 516 15th Ave. SE, Bierman Building, Room 208, Minneapolis, MN 55455.

Head Coach: John Anderson. **Assistant Coaches:** Mike Dee, Robert Fornasiere, Herb Isakson. **Telephone:** (612) 625-1060. **Baseball SID:** Jim Christman. **Telephone:** (612) 625-0854. **FAX:** (612) 625-0359.

Home Field: Siebert Field. **Seating Capacity:** 2,500. **Outfield Dimensions:** LF—330, CF—380, RF—330. **Press Box Telephone:** (612) 625-4031.

MISSISSIPPI Rebels

Conference: Southeastern/West.

Mailing Address: P.O. Box 217, University, MS 38677.

Head Coach: Pat Harrison. **Assistant Coaches:** Darby Carmichael, Tom Fleenor, Keith Kessinger. **Telephone:** (601) 232-7538. **Baseball SID:** Joel Weems. **Telephone:** (601) 232-7522. **FAX:** (601) 232-7006.

Home Field: Oxford University Stadium. **Seating Capacity:** 3,000. **Outfield Dimensions:** LF—330, CF—400, RF—330. **Press Box Telephone:** (601) 236-1931.

MISSISSIPPI STATE Bulldogs

Conference: Southeastern/West.

Mailing Address: P.O. Box 5308, Mississippi State, MS 39762.

Head Coach: Ron Polk. **Assistant Coaches:** Pat McMahon, Tim Parenton, Tommy Raffo. **Telephone:** (601) 325-2805. **Baseball SID:** Joe Dier. **Telephone:** (601) 325-8040. **FAX:** (601) 325-3654.

Home Field: Dudy Noble Field. **Seating Capacity:** 6,700.

Outfield Dimensions: LF—325, CF—390, RF—325. **Press Box Telephone:** (601) 325-3776.

MISSISSIPPI VALLEY STATE Delta Devils

Conference: Southwestern Athletic/East.

Mailing Address: 14000 Highway 82, P.O. Box 7246, Itta Bena, MS 38941.

Head Coach: Cleotha Wilson. **Assistant Coach:** James Shores. **Telephone:** (601) 254-3398. **Baseball SID:** Chuck Prophet. **Telephone:** (601) 254-3550, 3551. **FAX:** (601) 254-3639.

MISSOURI Tigers

Conference: Big 12.

Mailing Address: Hearnes Center, Columbia, MO 65211.

Head Coach: Tim Jamieson. **Assistant Coaches:** John Cohen, Chal Fanning. **Telephone:** (314) 882-0731. **Baseball SID:** Jeremy McNeive. **Telephone:** (314) 882-3241. **FAX:** (314) 882-4720.

Home Field: Simmons Field. **Seating Capacity:** 2,500. **Outfield Dimensions:** LF—340, CF—400, RF—340. **Press Box Telephone:** (314) 882-2112.

MONMOUTH Hawks

Conference: Northeast.

Mailing Address: Cedar Avenue, West Long Branch, NJ 07764.

Head Coach: Dean Ehehalt. **Assistant Coaches:** Jeff Barbalinardo, Joe Litterio. **Telephone:** (908) 263-5186. **Baseball SID:** Chris Risden. **Telephone:** (908) 263-5180. **FAX:** (908) 571-3535.

MOREHEAD STATE Eagles

Conference: Ohio Valley.

Mailing Address: UPO 1023, Morehead, KY 40351.

Head Coach: John Jarnagin. **Assistant Coach:** Larry Lipker. **Telephone:** (606) 783-2882. **Baseball SID:** Randy Stacy. **Telephone:** (606) 783-2500. **FAX:** (606) 783-2550.

MOUNT ST. MARY'S Mountaineers

Conference: Northeast.

Mailing Address: Route 15, Emmitsburg, MD 21727.

Head Coach: Ray Ruffing. **Assistant Coach:** Bob Hampton. **Telephone:** (301) 447-5296. **Baseball SID:** Eric Kloiber. **Telephone:** (301) 447-5384. **FAX:** (301) 447-5300.

MURRAY STATE Racers

Conference: Ohio Valley.

Mailing Address: Murray State Athletics, P.O. Box 9, Stewart Stadium, Murray, KY 42071.

Head Coach: Mike Thieke. **Assistant Coaches:** Dave Jarvis, Chris Moddelmog. **Telephone:** (502) 762-4892. **Baseball SID:** Brian Morgan. **Telephone:** (502) 762-4270. **FAX:** (502) 762-6814.

NAVY Midshipmen

Conference: Patriot.

Mailing Address: Ricketts Hall, 566 Brownson Road, Annapolis, MD 21402.

Head Coach: Bob MacDonald. **Assistant Coaches:** Glenn Davis, Joe Kinney. **Telephone:** (410) 293-5571. **Baseball SID:** Scott Strasemeier. **Telephone:** (410) 293-4517. **FAX:** (410) 269-6779.

NEBRASKA Cornhuskers

Conference: Big 12.

Mailing Address: 116 S. Stadium, Lincoln, NE 68588.

Head Coach: John Sanders. **Assistant Coaches:** Mike Anderson, Dave Crain, Phil Harrison. **Telephone:** (402) 472-2269. **Baseball SID:** Hank Largin. **Telephone:** (402) 472-2263. **FAX:** (402) 472-2005.

Home Field: Buck Beltzer Stadium. **Seating Capacity:** 1,500. **Outfield Dimensions:** LF—330, CF—400, RF—330. **Press Box Telephone:** (402) 472-2279.

NEVADA Wolf Pack

Conference: Big West.

Mailing Address: Mail Stop 232, Reno, NV 89557.

Head Coach: Gary Powers. **Assistant Coaches:** Jason Gill, Stan Stolte. **Telephone:** (702) 784-4180. **Baseball SID:** Paul Stuart. **Telephone:** (702) 784-4600. **FAX:** (702) 784-4386.

Home Field: Peccole Park. **Seating Capacity:** 1,500. **Outfield Dimensions:** LF—340, CF—401, RF—340. **Press Box Telephone:** (702) 784-1585.

NEVADA-LAS VEGAS Rebels

Conference: Western Athletic/South.

Mailing Address: 4505 Maryland Parkway, Las Vegas, NV 89154.

Head Coach: Rod Soesbe. **Assistant Coaches:** Kurt Mattson, Jim Pace, Jon Polson. **Telephone:** (702) 895-3499. **Baseball SID:** Jim Gemma. **Telephone:** (702) 895-3995. **FAX:** (702) 895-0989.

Home Field: Earl E. Wilson Stadium. **Seating Capacity:** 3,000. **Outfield Dimensions:** LF—335, CF—400, RF—335. **Press Box Telephone:** (702) 895-1595.

NEW HAMPSHIRE Wildcats

Conference: America East.

Mailing Address: 224 Field House, Durham, NH 03824.

Head Coach: Rob Carpentier. **Assistant Coaches:** Leo Grabell, Tony Lachowetz. **Telephone:** (603) 862-3902. **Baseball SID:** Scott Flanders. **Telephone:** (603) 862-0717. **FAX:** (603) 862-3839.

NEW MEXICO Lobos

Conference: Western Athletic/South.

Mailing Address: South Campus, Albuquerque, NM 87131.

Head Coach: Rich Alday. **Assistant Coaches:** Joe Coleman, Paul Huitt, Mark Martinez. **Telephone:** (505) 925-5720. **Baseball SID:** Bryan Satter. **Telephone:** (505) 925-5528. **FAX:** (505) 925-5529.

Home Field: Lobo Field. **Seating Capacity:** 500. **Outfield Dimensions:** LF—340, CF—405, RF—340. **Press Box Telephone:** (505) 925-5722.

NEW MEXICO STATE Aggies

Conference: Big West.

Mailing Address: Box 3145, Las Cruces, NM 88003.

Head Coach: Rocky Ward. **Assistant Coaches:** Fred Ocasio, Earl Wheeler. **Telephone:** (505) 646-5813. **Baseball SID:** John Gilger. **Telephone:** (505) 646-3929. **FAX:** (505) 646-2425.

Home Field: Presley Askew Field. **Seating Capacity:** 1,000. **Outfield Dimensions:** LF—330, CF—400, RF—370. **Press Box Telephone:** (505) 646-5700.

NEW ORLEANS Privateers

Conference: Sun Belt.

Mailing Address: Lakefront Arena, New Orleans, LA 70148.

Head Coach: Tom Schwaner. **Assistant Coaches:** Jim Boehne, Jeff Twitty. **Telephone:** (504) 280-7021. **Baseball SID:** Ed Cassiere. **Telephone:** (504) 280-6284. **FAX:** (504) 280-7240.

Home Field: Privateer Park. **Seating Capacity:** 5,225. **Outfield Dimensions:** LF—330, CF—405, RF—330. **Press Box Telephone:** (504) 280-7027.

NEW YORK TECH Bears

Conference: Mid-Continent/East.

Mailing Address: Northern Boulevard, Old Westbury, NY 11568.

Head Coach: Bob Hirschfield. **Assistant Coach:** Scott Hatten, Bill Timmes. **Telephone:** (516) 686-7513. **Baseball SID:** Tom Riordan. **Telephone:** (516) 686-7626. **FAX:** (516) 626-0750.

NIAGARA Purple Eagles

Conference: Metro Atlantic/North.

Mailing Address: O'Shea Hall, Niagara University, NY 14109.

Head Coach: Jim Mauro. **Assistant Coaches:** Mark Gabriele, Bob Kowalski, Mike McRae. **Telephone:** (716) 286-8602. **Baseball SID:** Mark Vandergrift. **Telephone:** (716) 286-8602. **FAX:** (716) 286-8609.

NICHOLLS STATE Colonels

Conference: Southland/Louisiana.

Mailing Address: P.O. Box 2032, Thibodaux, LA 70310.

Head Coach: Jim Pizzolatto. **Assistant Coaches:** Gerald Cassard, Rocke Musgraves, Everett Russell. **Telephone:** (504) 448-4808. **Baseball SID:** Jack Duggan. **Telephone:** (504) 448-4281. **FAX:** (504) 448-4924.

NORTH CAROLINA Tar Heels

Conference: Atlantic Coast.

Mailing Address: P.O. Box 2126, Chapel Hill, NC 27514.

Head Coach: Mike Roberts. **Assistant Coaches:** Chad Holbrook, Roger Williams. **Telephone:** (919) 962-2351. **Baseball SID:** Matt Bowers. **Telephone:** (919) 962-2123. **FAX:** (919) 962-0612.

Home Field: Boshamer Stadium. **Seating Capacity:** 3,500. **Outfield Dimensions:** LF—335, CF—400, RF—335. **Press Box Telephone:** (919) 962-1607.

UNC ASHEVILLE Bulldogs

Conference: Big South.

Mailing Address: One University Heights, Asheville, NC 28804.

Head Coach: Bill Hillier. **Assistant Coach:** Eric Filipek. **Telephone:** (704) 251-6920. **Baseball SID:** Mike Gore. **Telephone:** (704) 251-6923. **FAX:** (704) 251-6386.

UNC CHARLOTTE 49ers

Conference: Conference USA.

Mailing Address: Highway 49, Charlotte, NC 28223.

Head Coach: Loren Hibbs. **Assistant Coaches:** Joey Anderson, Matt Criss, Jay Matthews, Mike Shildt, Matt McWilliams. **Telephone:** (704) 547-3935. **Baseball SID:** James McCoy. **Telephone:** (704) 510-6313. **FAX:** (704) 547-4918.

Home Field: Tom and Lib Phillips Field. **Seating Capacity:** 2,000. **Outfield Dimensions:** LF—335, CF—390, RF—335. **Press Box Telephone:** (704) 547-3148.

UNC GREENSBORO Spartans

Conference: Big South.

Mailing Address: 337 HHP Building, Greensboro, NC 27412.

Head Coach: Mike Gaski. **Assistant Coaches:** Neil Avent, Matt Faulkner, Tonka Maynor. **Telephone:** (910) 334-3247. **Baseball SID:** Chris Militello. **Telephone:** (910) 334-5615. **FAX:** (910) 334-3182.

UNC WILMINGTON Seahawks

Conference: Colonial Athletic.

Mailing Address: 601 S. College Road, Wilmington, NC 28403.

Head Coach: Mark Scalf. **Assistant Coach:** Todd Wilkinson. **Telephone:** (910) 962-3570. **Baseball SID:** Joe Browning. **Telephone:** (910) 962-3236. **FAX:** (910) 962-3686.

NORTH CAROLINA A&T Aggies

Conference: Mid-Eastern Athletic/South.

Mailing Address: 108 Memorial Union, Greensboro, NC 27411.

Head Coach: Keith Shumate. **Assistant Coach:** Ric Chandgie. **Telephone:** (910) 334-7371. **Baseball SID:** B.J. Evans. **Telephone:** (910) 334-7371. **FAX:** (910) 334-7272.

NORTH CAROLINA STATE Wolfpack

Conference: Atlantic Coast.

Mailing Address: P.O. Box 8501, Raleigh, NC 27695.

Head Coach: Elliott Avent. **Assistant Coaches:** Billy Best, Mark Bockelman, Matt Donahue. **Telephone:** (919) 515-3613. **Baseball SID:** Bruce Winkworth. **Telephone:** (919) 515-1182. **FAX:** (919) 515-2898.

Home Field: Doak Field. **Seating Capacity:** 3,000. **Outfield Dimensions:** LF—340, CF—400, RF—340. **Press Box Telephone:** (919) 515-7213.

NORTHEAST LOUISIANA Indians

Conference: Southland/Louisiana.

Mailing Address: 308 Stadium Drive, Monroe, LA 71209.

Head Coach: Smoke Laval. **Assistant Coaches:** Gary Aucoin, Allen Chance. **Telephone:** (318) 342-5395. **Baseball SID:** Troy Mitchell. **Telephone:** (318) 342-5467. **FAX:** (318) 342-5464.

NORTHEASTERN Huskies

Conference: America East.

Mailing Address: 360 Huntington Ave., Boston, MA 02115.

Head Coach: Neil McPhee. **Assistant Coach:** Matt Noone. **Telephone:** (617) 373-3657. **Baseball SID:** Patrick Paolantonio. **Telephone:** (617) 373-2691. **FAX:** (617) 373-3152.

NORTHEASTERN ILLINOIS Golden Eagles

Conference: Mid-Continent/West.

Mailing Address: 5500 N. St. Louis Ave., Chicago, IL 60625.

Head Coach: Jim Hawrysko. **Assistant Coaches:** Pete Farapia, Bob Koopmann, Issie Sopena. **Telephone:** (773) 794-2884. **Baseball SID:** Damion Jones. **Telephone:** (773) 794-6241. **FAX:** (773) 794-6244.

NORTHERN ILLINOIS Huskies

Conference: Midwestern Collegiate.

Mailing Address: 112 Evans Field House, Dekalb, IL 60115.

Head Coach: Spanky McFarland. **Assistant Coaches:** Frank Del Medico, Tony Dello. **Telephone:** (815) 753-0147. **Baseball SID:** Robert Hester. **Telephone:** (815) 753-1706. **FAX:** (815) 753-9540.

NORTHERN IOWA Panthers

Conference: Missouri Valley.

Mailing Address: 23rd and College, Cedar Falls, IA 50614.

Head Coach: Dave Schrage. **Assistant Coaches:** Ken Misfeldt, Randy Wee. **Telephone:** (319) 273-6323. **Baseball SID:** Dave Moll. **Telephone:** (319) 273-3642. **FAX:** (319) 273-3602.

NORTHWESTERN Wildcats

Conference: Big Ten.

Mailing Address: 1501 Central St., Evanston, IL 60208.

Head Coach: Paul Stevens. **Assistant Coaches:** Joe Keenan, Ron Klein, Tim Stoddard. **Telephone:** (847) 491-4652. **Baseball SID:** Chris Hughes. **Telephone:** (847) 491-7503. **FAX:** (847) 491-8818.

Home Field: Rocky Miller Park. **Seating Capacity:** 1,000. **Outfield Dimensions:** LF—340, CF—400, RF—340. **Press Box Telephone:** (847) 491-4200.

NORTHWESTERN STATE Demons

Conference: Southland/Louisiana.

Mailing Address: 112 Prather Coliseum, Natchitoches, LA 71497.

Head Coach: Dave Van Horn. **Assistant Coach:** Rob Childress. **Telephone:** (318) 357-4139. **Baseball SID:** Dart Volz. **Telephone:** (318) 357-6467. **FAX:** (318) 357-4515.

NOTRE DAME Fighting Irish

Conference: Big East/National.

Mailing Address: Joyce Center, Notre Dame, IN 46556.

Head Coach: Paul Mainieri. **Assistant Coaches:** Cory Mee, Brian O'Connor. **Telephone:** (219) 631-6366. **Baseball SID:** Pete LaFleur. **Telephone:** (219) 631-7516. **FAX:** (219) 631-7941.

Home Field: Frank Eck Stadium. **Seating Capacity:** 2,500. **Outfield Dimensions:** LF—331, CF—401, RF—331. **Press Box Telephone:** (219) 631-9018/9476.

OHIO Bobcats

Conference: Mid-American.

Mailing Address: 105 Convocation Center, Athens, OH 45701.

Head Coach: Joe Carbone. **Assistant Coaches:** Jose Sorge, Bill Toadvine. **Telephone:** (614) 593-1180. **Baseball SID:** Ken Dewey. **Telephone:** (614) 593-1298. **FAX:** (614) 593-2420.

Home Field: Trautwein Field. **Seating Capacity:** 2,500. **Outfield Dimensions:** LF—330, CF—400, RF—330. **Press Box Telephone:** (614) 593-0501.

OHIO STATE Buckeyes

Conference: Big Ten.

Mailing Address: 124 St. John Arena, 410 Woody Hayes Drive, Columbus, OH 43210.

Head Coach: Bob Todd. **Assistant Coaches:** Pat Bangston, Greg Cypret. **Telephone:** (614) 292-1075. **Baseball SID:** Gerry Emig. **Telephone:** (614) 292-6861. **FAX:** (614) 292-8547.

Home Field: Bill Davis Stadium. **Seating Capacity:** 3,000. **Outfield Dimensions:** LF—330, CF—400, RF—330. **Press Box Telephone:** (614) 292-0623.

OKLAHOMA Sooners

Conference: Big12.

Mailing Address: Memorial Stadium, Norman, OK 73019.

Head Coach: Larry Cochell. **Assistant Coaches:** Bill Mosiello, Aric Thomas, Jackson Todd. **Telephone:** (405) 325-8354. **Baseball SID:** Mike Treps. **Telephone:** (405) 325-8225. **FAX:** (405) 325-7623.

Home Field: L. Dale Mitchell Park. **Seating Capacity:** 2,300. **Outfield Dimensions:** LF—340, CF—411, RF—340. **Press Box Telephone:** (405) 325-8363.

OKLAHOMA STATE Cowboys

Conference: Big 12.

Mailing Address: 202 Gallagher-Iba Arena, Stillwater, OK 74078.

Head Coach: Tom Holliday. **Assistant Coaches:** John Farrell, Robbie Wine. **Telephone:** (405) 744-5849. **Baseball SID:** Chad Grubbs. **Telephone:** (405) 744-5749. **FAX:** (405) 744-7754.

Home Field: Allie P. Reynolds Stadium. **Seating Capacity:** 4,000. **Outfield Dimensions:** LF—330, CF—398, RF—330. **Press Box Telephone:** (405) 744-5757.

OLD DOMINION Monarchs

Conference: Colonial Athletic.

Mailing Address: Building 136, Athletic Administration, Norfolk, VA 23529.

Head Coach: Tony Guzzo. **Assistant Coaches:** Dexter Harris, Jayson Nave, Rick Robinson. **Telephone:** (757) 683-4230. **Baseball SID:** Carol Hudson. **Telephone:** (757) 683-3372. **FAX:** (757) 683-3119.

Home Field: Bud Metheny. **Seating Capacity:** 3,000. **Outfield Dimensions:** LF—375, CF—395, RF—375. **Press Box Telephone:** (757) 683-5036.

ORAL ROBERTS Golden Eagles

Conference: Independent.

Mailing Address: 7777 S. Lewis, Tulsa, OK 74171.

Head Coach: Sunny Golloway. **Assistant Coaches:** Jim Freeman, Scott Marr, Bob Miller. **Telephone:** (918) 495-7131. **Baseball SID:** Todd Addington. **Telephone:** (918) 495-7102. **FAX:** (918) 495-7142.

OREGON STATE Beavers

Conference: Pacific-10/North.

Mailing Address: 209 Gill Coliseum, Corvallis, OR 97331.

Head Coach: Pat Casey. **Assistant Coaches:** Ron Northcutt, Dan Spencer. **Telephone:** (541) 737-2825. **Baseball SID:** Kip Carlson. **Telephone:** (541) 737-3720. **FAX:** (541) 737-3072.

Home Field: Coleman Field. **Seating Capacity:** 2,310. **Outfield Dimensions:** LF—330, CF—400, RF—330. **Press Box Telephone:** (541) 737-7475.

PACE Setters

Conference: Mid-Continent/East.

Mailing Address: 861 Bedford Road, New York, NY 10570.

Head Coach: Fred Calaicone. **Assistant Coaches:** Tim Kelly. **Telephone:** (914) 773-3411. **Baseball SID:** Nick Renda. **Telephone:** (914) 773-3411. **FAX:** (914) 773-3491.

PACIFIC Tigers

Conference: Big West.

Mailing Address: 3601 Pacific Ave., Stockton, CA 95211.

Head Coach: Quincey Noble. **Assistant Coaches:** Joe Moreno, Jim Yanko, Curt Zimmerman. **Telephone:** (209) 946-2512. **Baseball SID:** Scott Spencer. **Telephone:** (209) 946-2289. **FAX:** (209) 946-2757.

Home Field: Billy Hebert Field. **Seating Capacity:** 3,500. **Outfield Dimensions:** LF—325, CF—392, RF—330. **Press Box Telephone:** (209) 944-5951.

PENNSYLVANIA Quakers

Conference: Ivy League/Gehrig.

Mailing Address: Weightman Hall South, 235 S. 33rd St., Philadelphia, PA 19104.

Head Coach: Bob Seddon. **Assistant Coaches:** John Nace, Bill Wagner, Dan Young. **Telephone:** (215) 898-6282. **Baseball SID:** Carla Shultzberg. **Telephone:** (215) 898-9232. **FAX:** (215) 898-1747.

PENN STATE Nittany Lions

Conference: Big Ten.

Mailing Address: 234 Recreation Building, University Park, PA 16802.

Head Coach: Joe Hindelang. **Assistant Coaches:** Jeff Ditch, Randy Ford, Mike Nesbit. **Telephone:** (814) 863-0239. **Baseball SID:** Alan Ashby. **Telephone:** (814) 865-1757. **FAX:** (814) 863-3165.

Home Field: Beaver Field. **Seating Capacity:** 1,000. **Outfield Dimensions:** LF—350, CF—400, RF—350. **Press Box Telephone:** None.

PEPPERDINE Waves

Conference: West Coast.

Mailing Address: 24255 Pacific Coast Highway, Malibu, CA 90263.

Head Coach: Frank Sanchez. **Assistant Coaches:** Kevin Brockway, Dave Esquer, David Rhoades. **Telephone:** (310) 456-4199. **Baseball SID:** Michael Zapolski. **Telephone:** (310) 456-4333. **FAX:** (310) 456-4322.

Home Field: Eddy D. Field Stadium. **Seating Capacity:** 2,200. **Outfield Dimensions:** LF—330, CF—400, RF—330. **Press Box Telephone:** (310) 456-4598.

PITTSBURGH Panthers

Conference: Big East/American.

Mailing Address: P.O. Box 7436, Pittsburgh, PA 15213.

Head Coach: Mark Jackson. **Assistant Coaches:** Joe Hill, Jeff Minick. **Telephone:** (412) 648-8208. **Baseball SID:** Harry Ennis. **Telephone:** (412) 648-8240. **FAX:** (412) 648-8248.

Home Field: Trees Field. **Seating Capacity:** 500. **Outfield Dimensions:** LF—328, CF—380, RF—335. **Press Box Telephone:** None.

PORTLAND Pilots

Conference: West Coast.

Mailing Address: 5000 N. Willamette Blvd., Portland, OR 97203.

Head Coach: Terry Pollreisz. **Assistant Coaches:** Ed Gustafson, Bill Wallin. **Telephone:** (503) 283-7707. **Baseball SID:** Steve Walker. **Telephone:** (503) 283-7439. **FAX:** (503) 283-7242.

PORTLAND STATE Vikings

Conference: Pacific-10/North.

Mailing Address: P.O. Box 751, Portland, OR 97207.

Head Coach: Dave Dangler. **Assistant Coaches:** Hal DeBarry, Reed Rainey. **Telephone:** (503) 725-3852. **Baseball SID:** Larry Sellers. **Telephone:** (503) 725-2525. **FAX:** (503) 725-5610.

Home Field: Civic Stadium. **Seating Capacity:** 23,100. **Outfield Dimensions:** LF—309, CF—407, RF—348. **Press Box Telephone:** (503) 294-2942.

PRAIRIE VIEW A&M Panthers

Conference: Southwestern Athletic/West.

Mailing Address: P.O. Box 97, Prairie View, TX 77446.

Head Coach: John Tankersley. **Assistant Coach:** Matt Berly, Raymond Burgess, Royal Hammond, Scipio Johnson. **Telephone:** (409) 857-4290. **Baseball SID:** Harlan Robinson. **Telephone:** (409) 857-2114. **FAX:** (409) 857-2408.

PRINCETON Tigers

Conference: Ivy League/Gehrig.

Mailing Address: P.O. Box 71, Room Nine, Jadwin Gym, Princeton, NJ 08544.

Head Coach: Tom O'Connell. **Assistant Coaches:** Jason Garman, Hank Kraft, Ken Silber. **Telephone:** (609) 258-5059. **Baseball SID:** Erin Melody. **Telephone:** (609) 258-5701. **FAX:** (609) 258-2339.

PROVIDENCE Friars

Conference: Big East/American.

Mailing Address: River Avenue, Providence, RI 02918.

Head Coach: Charles Hickey. **Assistant Coaches:** John Garside, John Navilliat. **Telephone:** (401) 865-2273. **Baseball SID:** Tim Connor. **Telephone:** (401) 865-2272. **FAX:** (401) 865-2583.

Home Field: Hendricken Field. **Seating Capacity:** 1,000. **Outfield Dimensions:** LF—330, CF—405, RF—301. **Press Box Telephone:** None.

PURDUE Boilermakers

Conference: Big Ten.

Mailing Address: 1790 Mackey Arena, West Lafayette, IN 47907.

Head Coach: Steve Green. **Assistant Coaches:** Mark Kingston, Brian McDonald, Bob Sheperd. **Telephone:** (317) 494-3998. **Baseball SID:** Joseph Jones. **Telephone:** (317) 494-3202. **FAX:** (317) 494-5447.

Home Field: Lambert Field. **Seating Capacity:** 1,100. **Outfield Dimensions:** LF—343, CF—400, RF—342. **Press Box Telephone:** (317) 494-1522.

RADFORD Highlanders

Conference: Big South.

Mailing Address: P.O. Box 6916, Radford, VA 24142.

Head Coach: Lew Kent. **Assistant Coach:** Wayne Smith. **Telephone:** (540) 831-5881. **Baseball SID:** Marty Smith. **Telephone:** (540) 831-5211. **FAX:** (540) 831-5036.

RHODE ISLAND Rams

Conference: Atlantic 10/East.

Mailing Address: 3 Keaney Road., Suite 1, Kingston, RI 02881.

Head Coach: Frank Leoni. **Assistant Coaches:** Raphael Cerrato, John LaRose. **Telephone:** (401) 874-4550. **Baseball SID:** Bryan Morry. **Telephone:** (401) 874-2409. **FAX:** (401) 874-5354.

RICE Owls

Conference: Western Athletic/South.

Mailing Address: P.O. Box 1892, Houston, TX 77251.

Head Coach: Wayne Graham. **Assistant Coaches:** Chris Feris, Jon Prather. **Telephone:** (713) 527-6022. **Baseball SID:** Bill Cousins. **Telephone:** (713) 737-5775. **FAX:** (713) 527-6019.

Home Field: Cameron Field. **Seating Capacity:** 2,000. **Outfield Dimensions:** LF—330, CF—400, RF—330. **Press Box Telephone:** (713) 527-4931.

RICHMOND Spiders

Conference: Colonial Athletic.

Mailing Address: Robins Center, Richmond, VA 23173.

Head Coach: Ron Atkins. **Assistant Coaches:** Braxton Bell, Mark McQueen. **Telephone:** (804) 289-8391. **Baseball SID:** Phil Stanton. **Telephone:** (804) 289-8320. **FAX:** (804) 289-8820.

RIDER Broncs

Conference: Northeast.

Mailing Address: 2083 Lawrenceville Road, Lawrenceville, NJ 08648.

Head Coach: Sonny Pittaro. **Assistant Coach:** Tom Petroff, Jeff Plunkett. **Telephone:** (609) 896-5055. **Baseball SID:** Bud Focht. **Telephone:** (609) 896-5138. **FAX:** (609) 896-0341.

RUTGERS Scarlet Knights

Conference: Big East/National.

Mailing Address: Louis Brown Athletic Center, P.O. Box 1149, Piscataway, NJ 08855.

Head Coach: Fred Hill. **Assistant Coaches:** Tom Baxter, Scott Bradley, Glen Gardner. **Telephone:** (908) 445-3553. **Baseball SID:** Scott Novak. **Telephone:** (908) 445-4200. **FAX:** (908) 445-3063.

Home Field: Class of '53 Baseball Complex. **Seating Capacity:** 1,500. **Outfield Dimensions:** LF—330, CF—400, RF—320. **Press Box Telephone:** Unavailable.

SACRAMENTO STATE Hornets

Conference: Western Athletic/West.

Mailing Address: 6000 J St., Sacramento, CA 95819.

Head Coach: John Smith. **Assistant Coaches:** Jim Barr, Brian Hewitt. **Telephone:** (916) 278-7225. **Baseball SID:** Holly Caldwell. **Telephone:** (916) 278-6896. **FAX:** (916) 278-5429.

Home Field: Hornet Field. **Seating Capacity:** 600. **Outfield Dimensions:** LF—333, CF—400, RF—333. **Press Box Telephone:** None.

ST. BONAVENTURE Bonnies

Conference: Atlantic 10/East.

Mailing Address: Department of Athletics, St. Bonaventure, NY 14778.

Head Coach: Larry Sudbrook. **Assistant Coaches:** Jon Phillips, Tom Tegeler. **Telephone:** (716) 375-2641. **Baseball SID:** Jeremy Hartigan. **Telephone:** (716) 375-2575. **FAX:** (716) 375-2383.

ST. FRANCIS Terriers

Conference: Northeast.

Mailing Address: 180 Remsen St., Brooklyn, NY 11201.

Head Coach: Frank Del George. **Assistant Coaches:** Tony Barone, Mike Lopiparo, Frank Salzone. **Telephone:** (718) 522-2300. **Baseball SID:** Jim Hoffman. **Telephone:** (718) 522-2300. **FAX:** (718) 797-2140.

ST. JOHN'S Red Storm

Conference: Big East/American.

Mailing Address: Grand Central & Utopia Parkways, Jamaica, NY 11439.

Head Coach: Ed Blankmeyer. **Assistant Coaches:** Mike Maerten, Kevin McMullan, Bob Pertsas. **Telephone:** (718) 990-6148. **Baseball SID:** Chris DeLorenzo. **Telephone:** (718) 990-1521. **FAX:** (718) 969-8468.

Home Field: McCallen Field. **Seating Capacity:** 1,000. **Outfield Dimensions:** LF—375, CF—390, RF—375. **Press Box Telephone:** (718) 969-1521.

ST. JOSEPH'S Hawks

Conference: Atlantic 10/East.

Mailing Address: 5600 City Ave., Philadelphia, PA 19131.

Head Coach: Jim Ertel. **Assistant Coaches:** Jed Johnson, Ken Krsolovic, Jack Stanzak. **Telephone:** (610) 660-1718. **Baseball SID:** Ken Krsolovic. **Telephone:** (610) 660-1704. **FAX:** (610) 660-1724.

SAINT LOUIS Billikens

Conference: Conference USA.

Mailing Address: Room 39, DeBourg Hall, 221 N. Grand Blvd., St. Louis, MO 63103.

Head Coach: Bob Hughes. **Assistant Coaches:** Frank Mormino, Dan Nicholson. **Telephone:** (314) 977-3172. **Baseball SID:** Chris Cook. **Telephone:** (314) 977-3463. **FAX:** (314) 977-7193.

Home Field: Billiken Sports Center. **Seating Capacity:** 1,000. **Outfield Dimensions:** LF—330, CF—395, RF—330. **Press Box Telephone:** None.

ST. MARY'S Gaels

Conference: West Coast.

Mailing Address: P.O. Box 5100, Moraga, CA 94575.

Head Coach: Rod Ingram. **Assistant Coaches:** John Baptista, Bill Ferrari, Sean Kenny. **Telephone:** (510) 631-4400. **Baseball SID:** Andy McDowell. **Telephone:** (510) 631-4402. **FAX:** (510) 631-4405.

ST. PETER'S Peacocks

Conference: Metro Atlantic/South.

Mailing Address: 2641 Kennedy Blvd., Jersey City, NJ 07306.

Head Coach: Bruce Sabatini. **Assistant Coach:** Steve Russo. **Telephone:** (201) 915-9459. **Baseball SID:** Brian Callahan. **Telephone:** (201) 915-9101. **FAX:** (201) 915-9102.

SAM HOUSTON STATE Bearkats

Conference: Southland/Texas.

Mailing Address: P.O. Box 2268, Huntsville, TX 77341.

Head Coach: John Skeeters. **Assistant Coach:** Carlo Gott. **Telephone:** (409) 294-1731. **Baseball SID:** Paul Ridings. **Telephone:** (409) 294-1764. **FAX:** (409) 294-3538.

SAMFORD Bulldogs

Conference: TransAmerica Athletic/West.

Mailing Address: 800 Lakeshore Drive, Birmingham, AL 35229.

Head Coach: Tommy Walker. **Telephone:** (205) 870-2134. **Baseball SID:** Riley Adair. **Telephone:** (205) 870-2966. **FAX:** (205) 870-2132.

SAN DIEGO Toreros

Conference: West Coast.

Mailing Address: Alcala Park, San Diego, CA 92110.

Head Coach: John Cunningham. **Assistant Coaches:** Chad Boyd, Glenn Godwin, Jake Molina. **Telephone:** (619) 260-8894. **Baseball SID:** Mike Daniels. **Telephone:** (619) 260-4745. **FAX:** (619) 292-0388.

SAN DIEGO STATE Aztecs

Conference: Western Athletic/West.

Mailing Address: Department of Athletics, SDSU, San Diego, CA 92182.

Head Coach: Jim Dietz. **Assistant Coaches:** Rusty Filter, Pat Oliverio, Jim Warner. **Telephone:** (619) 594-6889. **Baseball SID:** Dave Kuhn. **Telephone:** (619) 594-5547. **FAX:** (619) 582-6541.

Home Field: Tony Gwynn Stadium. **Seating Capacity:** 1,000. **Outfield Dimensions:** LF—336, CF—412, RF—340. **Press Box Telephone:** Unavailable.

SAN FRANCISCO Dons

Conference: West Coast.

Mailing Address: 2130 Fulton St., San Francisco, CA 94117.

Head Coach: Rich Hill. **Assistant Coaches:** Chad Konishi, Nate Rodriquez, Ted Turkington. **Telephone:** (415) 422-2934. **Baseball SID:** Kyle McRae. **Telephone:** (415) 422-6161. **FAX:** (415) 422-2929.

SAN JOSE STATE Spartans

Conference: Western Athletic/West.

Mailing Address: One Washington Square, San Jose, CA 95192.

Head Coach: Sam Piraro. **Assistant Coaches:** Juan Batula, Scott Hertler, Doug Thurmond. **Telephone:** (408) 924-1255. **Baseball SID:** Phil Simon. **Telephone:** (408) 924-1217. **FAX:** (408) 924-1291.

Home Field: Municipal Stadium. **Seating Capacity:** 5,200. **Outfield Dimensions:** LF—340, CF—400, RF—340. **Press Box Telephone:** (408) 924-7276.

SANTA CLARA Broncos

Conference: West Coast.

Mailing Address: Toso Pavillion, Santa Clara, CA 95053.

Head Coach: John Oldham. **Assistant Coaches:** Mike Cummins, Matt Marks, Billy Smith. **Telephone:** (408) 554-4680. **Baseball SID:** Jim Young. **Telephone:** (408) 554-4661. **FAX:** (408) 554-6942.

Home Field: Buck Shaw Stadium. **Seating Capacity:** 6,800. **Outfield Dimensions:** LF—350, CF—400, RF—330. **Press Box Telephone:** (408) 554-4752.

SETON HALL Pirates

Conference: Big East/National.

Mailing Address: 400 S. Orange Ave., South Orange, NJ 07079.

Head Coach: Mike Sheppard. **Assistant Coaches:** Fred Hopke, Ed Lyons, Rob Sheppard. **Telephone:** (201) 761-9557, 9563. **Baseball SID:** Dwayne Harrison. **Telephone:** (201) 761-9493. **FAX:** (201) 761-9061.

Home Field: Owen T. Carroll Field. **Seating Capacity:** 1,500. **Outfield Dimensions:** LF—330, CF—410, RF—312. **Press Box Telephone:** None.

SIENA Saints

Conference: Metro Atlantic/North.

Mailing Address: 515 Loudon Road, Loudonville, NY 12211.

Head Coach: Tony Rossi. **Assistant Coaches:** Tony Curro, Dave Perry, Paul Thompson. **Telephone:** (518) 786-5044. **Baseball SID:** Mike Hogan. **Telephone:** (518) 783-2411. **FAX:** (518) 783-2992.

SOUTH ALABAMA Jaguars

Conference: Sun Belt.

Mailing Address: 1107 HPELS Building, Mobile, AL 36688.

Head Coach: Steve Kittrell. **Assistant Coaches:** Joel Erdmann, Ron Pelletier, Ronnie Powell. **Telephone:** (334) 460-6876. **Baseball SID:** Matt Smith. **Telephone:** (334) 460-7035. **FAX:** (334) 460-7297.

Home Field: Stanky Field. **Seating Capacity:** 5,000. **Outfield Dimensions:** LF—330, CF—400, RF—330. **Press Box Telephone:** (334) 460-7126.

SOUTH CAROLINA Gamecocks

Conference: Southeastern/East.

Mailing Address: Rosewood Drive, Columbia, SC 29208.

Head Coach: Ray Tanner. **Assistant Coaches:** Tripp Keister, Jerry Meyers, Jim Toman. **Telephone:** (803) 777-7913. **Baseball SID:** Bob Balut, Tom Price. **Telephone:** (803) 777-5204. **FAX:** (803) 777-2967.

Home Field: Sarge Frye Field. **Seating Capacity:** 4,000. **Outfield Dimensions:** LF—330, CF—390, RF—320. **Press Box Telephone:** (803) 777-6648.

SOUTH FLORIDA Bulls

Conference: Conference USA.

Mailing Address: 4202 E. Fowler Ave., Tampa, FL 33620.

Head Coach: Eddie Cardieri. **Assistant Coaches:** Mark Rose, Ed Stabile. **Telephone:** (813) 974-2504. **Baseball SID:** Fred Huff. **Telephone:** (813) 974-4087. **FAX:** (813) 974-5328.

Home Field: Red McEwen Field. **Seating Capacity:** 1,500. Outfield **Dimensions:** LF—340, CF—400, RF—340. **Press Box Telephone:** (813) 974-3604.

SOUTHEAST MISSOURI STATE Indians

Conference: Ohio Valley.

Mailing Address: One University Plaza, Cape Girardeau, MO 63701.

Head Coach: Mark Hogan. **Assistant Coaches:** Bart Osborne, Brian Schaefer, Mark Wasikowski. **Telephone:** (314) 651-2645. **Baseball SID:** Ron Hines. **Telephone:** (314) 651-2294. **FAX:** (314) 651-2810.

SOUTHEASTERN LOUISIANA Lions

Conference: TransAmerica Athletic/West.

Mailing Address: P.O. Drawer 880, SLU Station, Hammond, LA 70402.

Head Coach: Greg Marten. **Assistant Coaches:** Johnny Brechtel, Mark Gosnell, Mark Willoughby. **Telephone:** (504) 549-2253. **Baseball SID:** Bary Niemeyer. **Telephone:** (504) 549-2253. **FAX:** (504) 549-3495.

SOUTHERN Jaguars

Conference: Southwestern Athletic/West.

Mailing Address: P.O. Box 9942, Baton Rouge, LA 70813.

Head Coach: Roger Cador. **Assistant Coach:** Richard Gaines. **Telephone:** (504) 771-2513. **Baseball SID:** Errol Domingue. **Telephone:** (504) 771-4142. **FAX:** (504) 771-4400.

SOUTHERN CALIFORNIA Trojans

Conference: Pacific-10/South.

Mailing Address: HER-103, University Park, Los Angeles, CA 90089.

Head Coach: Mike Gillespie. **Assistant Coaches:** Rob Klein, Andy Nieto, John Savage. **Telephone:** (213) 740-5762. **Baseball SID:** Nancy Mazmanian. **Telephone:** (213) 740-8480. **FAX:** (213) 740-7584.

Home Field: Dedeaux Field. **Seating Capacity:** 1,800. **Outfield Dimensions:** LF—335, CF—395, RF—335. **Press Box Telephone:** (213) 748-3449.

SOUTHERN ILLINOIS Salukis

Conference: Missouri Valley.

Mailing Address: SIU Arena, Carbondale, IL 62901.

Head Coach: Dan Callahan. **Assistant Coaches:** Ken Henderson, Derek Johnson. **Telephone:** (618) 453-2802. **Baseball SID:** Gene Green. **Telephone:** (618) 453-5470. **FAX:** (618) 536-2152.

SOUTHERN MISSISSIPPI Golden Eagles

Conference: Conference USA.

Mailing Address: Southern Station, Box 5161, Hattiesburg, MS 39406.

Head Coach: Hill Denson. **Assistant Coaches:** Corky Palmer, Dan Wagner, Scott Wagner. **Telephone:** (601) 266-5017. **Baseball SID:** Ricky Hazel. **Telephone:** (601) 266-4503. **FAX:** (601) 266-4507.

Home Field: Pete Taylor Park. **Seating Capacity:** 3,678. **Outfield Dimensions:** LF—340, CF—400, RF—340. **Press Box Telephone:** (601) 266-5684.

SOUTHERN UTAH Thunderbirds

Conference: Independent.

Mailing Address: 350 W. Center St., Cedar City, UT 84720.

Head Coach: Jeff Scholzen. **Assistant Coaches:** DeLynn Corry, Kevin Howard. **Telephone:** (801) 586-7932. **Baseball SID:** Neil Gardner. **Telephone:** (801) 586-7753. **FAX:** (801) 865-8037.

SOUTHWEST MISSOURI STATE Bears

Conference: Missouri Valley.

Mailing Address: 901 S. National, Springfield, MO 65804.

Head Coach: Keith Guttin. **Assistant Coaches:** Paul Evans, Evan Pratte, Brent Thomas. **Telephone:** (417) 836-5242.

Baseball SIDs: Mark Stillwell. **Telephone:** (417) 836-5402. **FAX:** (417) 836-4868.

SOUTHWEST TEXAS STATE Bobcats

Conference: Southland/Texas.

Mailing Address: 136 Jowers Center, San Marcos, TX 78666.

Head Coach: Howard Bushong. **Assistant Coaches:** Monte Cain, Tim Doherty. **Telephone:** (512) 245-3586. **Baseball SID:** Corey Bobo. **Telephone:** (512) 245-3586. **FAX:** (512) 245-2967.

SOUTHWESTERN LOUISIANA Ragin' Cajuns

Conference: Sun Belt.

Mailing Address: 201 Reinhardt Drive, Lafayette, LA 70506.

Head Coach: Tony Robichaux. **Assistant Coaches:** Anthony Babineaux, Troy May, John McClure, Wade Simoneaux. **Telephone:** (318) 482-6189. **Baseball SID:** Chad Schexnayder. **Telephone:** (318) 482-6331. **FAX:** (318) 482-6649.

Home Field: M.L. "Tigue" Moore Field. **Seating Capacity:** 7,000. **Outfield Dimensions:** LF—330, CF—404, RF—330. **Press Box Telephone:** (318) 482-6331.

STANFORD Cardinal

Conference: Pacific-10/South.

Mailing Address: Department of Athletics, Stanford, CA 94305.

Head Coach: Mark Marquess. **Assistant Coaches:** Ton Dunton, Dave Nakama, Dean Stotz. **Telephone:** (415) 723-4528. **Baseball SID:** Scott Leykam. **Telephone:** (415) 723-4418. **FAX:** (415) 725-2957.

Home Field: Sunken Diamond. **Seating Capacity:** 4,000. **Outfield Dimensions:** LF—335, CF—400, RF—335. **Press Box Telephone:** (415) 723-4629.

STETSON Hatters

Conference: TransAmerica Athletic/South.

Mailing Address: Campus Box 8317, DeLand, FL 32720.

Head Coach: Pete Dunn. **Assistant Coaches:** Rick Hall, Larry Jones. **Telephone:** (904) 822-8106. **Baseball SID:** Tom McClellan. **Telephone:** (904) 822-8131. **FAX:** (904) 822-8132.

Home Field: Conrad Field. **Seating Capacity:** 1,500. **Outfield Dimensions:** LF—350, CF—410, RF—350. **Press Box Telephone:** (904) 736-7360.

TEMPLE Owls

Conference: Atlantic 10/East.

Mailing Address: McGonigle Hall 101, Philadelphia, PA 19122.

Head Coach: Skip Wilson. **Assistant Coach:** Shawn Dawds, Dan Kusters, Joseph McNally. **Telephone:** (215) 204-7447. **Baseball SID:** Brian Kirschner. **Telephone:** (215) 204-4824. **FAX:** (215) 204-7499.

TENNESSEE Volunteers

Conference: Southeastern/East.

Mailing Address: P.O. Box 47, Knoxville, TN 37901.

Head Coach: Rod Delmonico. **Assistant Coaches:** Mike Maack, Larry Simcox. **Telephone:** (423) 974-2057. **Baseball SID:** Jeff Muir. **Telephone:** (423) 974-1212. **FAX:** (423) 974-1269.

Home Field: Lindsey Nelson Stadium. **Seating Capacity:** 5,500. **Outfield Dimensions:** LF—335, CF—404, RF—330. **Press Box Telephone:** (423) 974-3376.

TENNESSEE-MARTIN Skyhawks

Conference: Ohio Valley.

Mailing Address: 40 Skyhawk Fieldhouse, Martin, TN 38238.

Head Coach: Vernon Prather. **Assistant Coach:** Mitch Dunn. **Telephone:** (901) 587-7667. **Baseball SID:** Lee Wilmot. **Telephone:** (901) 587-7632/7630. **FAX:** (901) 587-7624.

TENNESSEE TECH Golden Eagles

Conference: Ohio Valley.

Mailing Address: Department of Athletics, P.O. Box 5057, Cookeville, TN 38501.

Head Coach: David Mays. **Assistant Coach:** Donley Canary. **Telephone:** (615) 372-3925. **Baseball SID:** Rob Schabert. **Telephone:** (615) 372-3088. **FAX:** (615) 372-6139.

TEXAS Longhorns

Conference: Big 12.

Mailing Address: P.O. Box 7399, Austin, TX 78713.

Head Coach: Augie Garrido. **Assistant Coaches:** Tommy Harmon, Marcus Hendry, Burt Hooton. **Telephone:** (512) 471-5732. **Baseball SID:** Amy Hirschman. **Telephone:** (512) 471-6039. **FAX:** (512) 471-6040.

Home Field: Disch-Falk Field. **Seating Capacity:** 6,649. **Outfield Dimensions:** LF—340, CF—400, RF—325. **Press Box Telephone:** (512) 471-1146.

TEXAS-ARLINGTON Mavericks

Conference: Southland/Texas.

Mailing Address: P.O. Box 19079, Arlington, TX 76019.

Head Coach: Butch McBroom. **Assistant Coaches:** Clay Gould, Ron Liggett. **Telephone:** (817) 272-2261. **Baseball SID:** Steve Weller. **Telephone:** (817) 273-2239. **FAX:** (817) 272-2254.

Home Field: Allan Saxe Field. **Seating Capacity:** 1,200. **Outfield Dimensions:** LF—330, CF—400, RF—330. **Press Box Telephone:** (817) 460-3522.

TEXAS-PAN AMERICAN Broncos

Conference: Sun Belt.

Mailing Address: 1201 W. University Drive, Edinburg, TX 78539.

Head Coach: Al Ogletree. **Assistant Coaches:** Mike Brown, Reggie Tredaway. **Telephone:** (210) 381-2234. **Baseball SID:** Jim McKone. **Telephone:** (210) 381-2240. **FAX:** (210) 381-2398.

TEXAS-SAN ANTONIO Roadrunners

Conference: Southland/Texas.

Mailing Address: 6900 Loop 1604 W., San Antonio, TX 78249.

Head Coach: Mickey Lashley. **Assistant Coach:** David Coleman, Daryl Renfrow. **Telephone:** (210) 458-4805. **Baseball SID:** Rick Nixon. **Telephone:** (210) 458-4551. **FAX:** (210) 458-4569.

TEXAS A&M Aggies

Conference: Big 12.

Mailing Address: Joe Routt Boulevard, College Station, TX 77843.

Head Coach: Mark Johnson. **Assistant Coaches:** Bill Hickey, Jim Lawler. **Telephone:** (409) 845-9534. **Baseball SID:** Alan Cannon. **Telephone:** (409) 845-5725. **FAX:** (409) 845-0564.

Home Field: Olsen Field. **Seating Capacity:** 7,053. **Outfield Dimensions:** LF—330, CF—400, RF—330. **Press Box Telephone:** (409) 845-4810.

TEXAS CHRISTIAN Horned Frogs

Conference: Western Athletic/South.

Mailing Address: P.O.Box 32924, Fort Worth, TX 76129.

Head Coach: Lance Brown. **Assistant Coaches:** J.J. Gottsch, Nolan Ryan, Donnie Watson. **Telephone:** (817) 921-7985. **Baseball SID:** Trey Carmichael. **Telephone:** (817) 921-7969. **FAX:** (817) 921-7964.

Home Field: TCU Diamond. **Seating Capacity:** 1,500. **Outfield Dimensions:** LF—330, CF—390, RF—320. **Press Box Telephone:** (817) 921-7966.

TEXAS SOUTHERN Tigers

Conference: Southwestern Athletic/West.

Mailing Address: 3100 Cleburne St., Houston, TX 77004.

Head Coach: Candy Robinson. **Assistant Coach:** Arthur Jenkins, Brian White. **Telephone:** (713) 313-7993. **Baseball SID:** Gary Abernathy. **Telephone:** (713) 313-7271. **FAX:** (713) 313-7270.

TEXAS TECH Red Raiders

Conference: Big 12.

Mailing Address: P.O. Box 43021, Lubbock, TX 79409.

Head Coach: Larry Hays. **Assistant Coaches:** Frank Anderson, Marty Lamb, Brian Wilson. **Telephone:** (806) 742-3344. **Baseball SID:** Walt McAlexander. **Telephone:** (806) 742-2770. **FAX:** (806) 742-1970.

Home Field: Dan Law Field. **Seating Capacity:** 5,614. **Outfield Dimensions:** LF—330, CF—405, RF—330. **Press Box Telephone:** (806) 742-3688.

TOLEDO Rockets

Conference: Mid-American.

Mailing Address: 2801 W. Bancroft St., Toledo, OH 43606.

Head Coach: Joe Kruzel. **Assistant Coaches:** Dusty Lepper, Steve Parrill. **Telephone:** (419) 530-2526. **Baseball SID:** Stacie O'Kane. **Telephone:** (419) 530-3791. **FAX:** (419) 530-3795.

TOWSON STATE Tigers

Conference: America East.

Mailing Address: Towson Center, Towson, MD 21204.

Head Coach: Mike Gottlieb. **Assistant Coaches:** Todd Buczek, John Matheis,

Tony Viglucci. **Telephone:** (410) 830-3775. **Baseball SID:** Dan O'Connell. **Telephone:** (410) 830-2232. **FAX:** (410) 830-3861.

TROY STATE Trojans

Conference: Mid-Continent/East.

Mailing Address: Davis Field House, Troy State University, Troy, AL 36082.

Head Coach: John Mayotte. **Assistant Coaches:** Barry Hightower, Rod McWhorter. **Telephone:** (334) 670-3480. **Baseball SID:** Brad Grice. **Telephone:** (334) 670-3229. **FAX:** (334) 670-3278.

TULANE Green Wave

Conference: Conference USA.

Mailing Address: James W. Wilson Jr. Center, New Orleans, LA 70118.

Head Coach: Rick Jones. **Assistant Coaches:** Rob Cooper, Bryan Ferree. **Telephone:** (504) 865-8239. **Baseball SID:** Gregory Blackwell. **Telephone:** (504) 865-5506. **FAX:** (504) 865-5512.

Home Field: Turchin Stadium. **Seating Capacity:** 3,000. **Outfield Dimensions:** LF—325, CF—400, RF—325. **Press Box Telephone:** (504) 862-8224.

UTAH Utes

Conference: Western Athletic/North.

Mailing Address: John Huntsman Center, Salt Lake City, UT 84112.

Head Coach: Tim Eamay. **Assistant Coaches:** David Cassidy, Todd Delnoce, John Flores. **Telephone:** (801) 581-3526. **Baseball SID:** Mickelle Marston. **Telephone:** (801) 581-3511. **FAX:** (801) 581-4358.

Home Field: Franklin Quest Field. **Seating Capacity:** 15,500. **Outfield Dimensions:** LF—345, CF—420, RF—315. **Press Box Telephone:** (801) 464-6938.

VALPARAISO Crusaders

Conference: Mid-Continent/West.

Mailing Address: Recreation Center, Valparaiso, IN 46383.

Head Coach: Paul Twenge. **Assistant Coaches:** Jeff Brooks, Tim Holmes, John Olson, Chip Petit. **Telephone:** (219) 464-5239. **Baseball SID:** Bill Rogers. **Telephone:** (219) 464-5232. **FAX:** (219) 464-5762.

VANDERBILT Commodores

Conference: Southeastern/East.

Mailing Address: Box 120158, 2601 Jess Neely Drive, Nashville, TN 37212.

Head Coach: Roy Mewbourne. **Assistant Coaches:** John Barlowe, Ross Jones, Mike Lockhart. **Telephone:** (615) 322-4127. **Baseball SID:** Tom Weber. **Telephone:** (615) 322-4121. **FAX:** (615) 343-7064.

Home Field: McGugin Field. **Seating Capacity:** 1,000. **Outfield Dimensions:** LF—328, CF—362, RF—316. **Press Box Telephone:** (615) 320-0436.

VERMONT Catamounts

Conference: America East.

Mailing Address: 86 S. Williams St., Burlington, VT 05401.

Head Coach: Bill Currier. **Assistant Coaches:** Ed Hockenbury, Steve Trimper. **Telephone:** (802) 656-7701. **Baseball SID:** Paul Stanfield. **Telephone:** (802) 656-1109. **FAX:** (802) 656-8328.

VILLANOVA Wildcats

Conference: Big East/National.

Mailing Address: Lancaster & Ithan Avenues, Villanova, PA 19085.

Head Coach: George Bennett. **Assistant Coaches:** Joe Calfapietra, Lou Soscia. **Telephone:** (610) 519-4529. **Baseball SID:** Dean Kenefick. **Telephone:** (610) 519-4120. **FAX:** (610) 519-7323.

Home Field: McGeehan Field. **Seating Capacity:** 2,000. **Outfield Dimensions:** LF—332, CF—392, RF—332. **Press Box Telephone:** None.

VIRGINIA Cavaliers

Conference: Atlantic Coast.

Mailing Address: P.O. Box 3785, University Hall, Charlottesville, VA 22903.

Head Coach: Dennis Womack. **Assistant Coaches:** Tommy Crowley, Steve Heon, Kevin O'Sullivan. **Telephone:** (804) 982-5775. **Baseball SID:** Charlie Bare. **Telephone:** (804) 982-5500. **FAX:** (804) 982-5525.

Home Field: Virginia Baseball Field. **Seating Capacity:** 2,300. **Outfield Dimensions:** LF—347, CF—400, RF—347. **Press Box Telephone:** (804) 295-9262.

VIRGINIA COMMONWEALTH Rams

Conference: Colonial Athletic.

Mailing Address: 819 W. Franklin St., Richmond, VA 23284.

Head Coach: Paul Keyes. **Assistant Coaches:** Chris Finwood, Paul O'Neil. **Telephone:** (804) 828-4820. **Baseball SID:** Eric Morton. **Telephone:** (804) 828-7000. **FAX:** (804) 828-9428.

VIRGINIA MILITARY INSTITUTE Keydets

Conference: Southern.

Mailing Address: Cameron Hall, Lexington, VA 24450.

Head Coach: Scott Gines. **Assistant Coaches:** Chris Chernisky, Mike Parker. **Telephone:** (540) 464-7605. **Baseball SID:** Chris King. **Telephone:** (540) 464-7253. **FAX:** (540) 464-7583.

VIRGINIA TECH Hokies

Conference: Atlantic 10/West.

Mailing Address: 364 Jamerson Center, Blacksburg, VA 24061.

Head Coach: Chuck Hartman. **Assistant Coaches:** Jon Hartness, Trey McCoy, Jay Phillips. **Telephone:** (540) 231-3671. **Baseball SID:** Dave Smith. **Telephone:** (540) 231-6726. **FAX:** (540) 231-6984.

WAGNER Seahawks

Conference: Northeast.

Mailing Address: 631 Howard Ave., Staten Island, NY 10301.

Head Coach: Rich Vitaliano. **Assistant Coaches:** Mike Arsenuk, Don Croce. **Telephone:** (718) 390-3483. **Baseball SID:** James Speciale. **Telephone:** (718) 390-3209. **FAX:** (718) 390-3347.

WAKE FOREST Demon Deacons

Conference: Atlantic Coast.

Mailing Address: P.O. Box 7426, Winston-Salem, NC 27109.

Head Coach: George Greer. **Assistant Coaches:** Bobby Moranda, Mike Rikard. **Telephone:** (910) 759-5570. **Baseball SID:** Dan Zacharias. **Telephone:** (910) 759-5640. **FAX:** (910) 759-5140.

Home Field: Hooks Stadium. **Seating Capacity:** 2,500. **Outfield Dimensions:** LF—355, CF—400, RF—315. **Press Box Telephone:** (910) 759-9711.

WASHINGTON Huskies

Conference: Pacific-10/North.

Mailing Address: 202 Graves Building, Seattle, WA 98195.

Head Coach: Ken Knutson. **Assistant Coaches:** Kevin Johnston, Joe Ross, Joe Weis. **Telephone:** (206) 543-9365. **Baseball SID:** Jeff Bechthold. **Telephone:** (206) 543-2230. **FAX:** (206) 543-5000.

Home Field: Graves Field. **Seating Capacity:** 1,500. **Outfield Dimensions:** LF—341, CF—397, RF—341. **Press Box Telephone:** (206) 685-1994.

WASHINGTON STATE Cougars

Conference: Pacific-10/North.

Mailing Address: M-8 Bohler Gym, Pullman, WA 99164.

Head Coach: Steve Farrington. **Assistant Coaches:** Tom Chamberlain, Corky Franklin, Buzzy Verduzco. **Telephone:** (509) 335-0331. **Baseball SID:** Rod Commons. **Telephone:** (509) 335-0270. **FAX:** (509) 335-0267.

Home Field: Bailey Field. **Seating Capacity:** 3,500. **Outfield Dimensions:** LF—330, CF—400, RF—335. **Press Box Telephone:** (509) 335-2684.

WEST VIRGINIA Mountaineers

Conference: Big East/American.

Mailing Address: Box 877, Morgantown, WV 26507.

Head Coach: Greg Van Zant. **Assistant Coaches:** Doug Little, Jon Szynal. **Telephone:** (304) 293-2308. **Baseball SID:** John Antonik. **Telephone:** (304) 293-2821. **FAX:** (304) 293-4105.

Home Field: Hawley Field. **Seating Capacity:** 1,500. **Outfield Dimensions:** LF—325, CF—390, RF—325. **Press Box Telephone:** (304) 293-5988.

WESTERN CAROLINA Catamounts

Conference: Southern.

Mailing Address: 2517 Ramsey Center, Cullowhee, NC 28723.

Head Coach: Keith LeClair. **Assistant Coaches:** Rodney Hennon, Mike Martin. **Telephone:** (704) 227-7373. **Baseball SID:** Steve White. **Telephone:** (704) 227-7171. **FAX:** (704) 227-7688.

Home Field: Hennon Stadium at Childress Field. **Seating Capacity:** 1,500. **Outfield Dimensions:** LF—325, CF—390, RF—325. **Press Box Telephone:** (704) 293-9315.

WESTERN ILLINOIS Leathernecks

Conference: Mid-Continent/West.

Mailing Address: Western Hall 213, Macomb, IL 61455.

Head Coach: Dick Pawlow. **Assistant Coaches:** Chris Lachapell, Tony Trumm. **Telephone:** (309) 298-1521. **Baseball SID:** Greg Seiler. **Telephone:** (309) 298-1133. **FAX:** (309) 298-3366.

WESTERN KENTUCKY Hilltoppers

Conference: Sun Belt.

Mailing Address: Wetherby Administration Building, 1526 Russellville Road, Bowling Green, KY 42101.

Head Coach: Joel Murrie. **Assistant Coaches:** Jerry Martinez, Dan Mosier. **Telephone:** (502) 745-6023. **Baseball SID:** Jeff Reynolds. **Telephone:** (502) 745-4298. **FAX:** (502) 745-3444.

WESTERN MICHIGAN Broncos

Conference: Mid-American.

Mailing Address: B-205 Ellsworth Hall, Kalamazoo, MI 49008.

Head Coach: Fred Decker. **Assistant Coaches:** Rich Morales, Brian Saltzgaber. **Telephone:** (616) 387-8149. **Baseball SID:** John Beatty. **Telephone:** (616) 387-4138. **FAX:** (616) 387-4139.

Home Field: Hyames Field. **Seating Capacity:** 4,000. **Outfield Dimensions:** LF—320, CF—390, RF—325. **Press Box Telephone:** (616) 387-8630.

WICHITA STATE Shockers

Conference: Missouri Valley.

Mailing Address: Campus Box 18, Wichita, KS 67208.

Head Coach: Gene Stephenson. **Assistant Coaches:** Brent Kemnitz, Jim Thomas. **Telephone:** (316) 978-3636. **Baseball SID:** Larry Rankin. **Telephone:** (316) 978-3265. **FAX:** (316) 978-3336.

Home Field: Eck Stadium. **Seating Capacity:** 5,665. **Outfield Dimensions:** LF—330, CF—390, RF—330. **Press Box Telephone:** (316) 978-3390.

WILLIAM & MARY Tribe

Conference: Colonial Athletic.

Mailing Address: P.O. Box 399, Williamsburg, VA 23187.

Head Coach: Jim Farr. **Assistant Coaches:** John Cole, Scott Kelly, Ryan Wheeler. **Telephone:** (757) 221-3399. **Baseball SID:** Bob Rothwell. **Telephone:** (757) 221-3344. **FAX:** (804) 221-3412.

WINTHROP Eagles

Conference: Big South.

Mailing Address: Winthrop Coliseum, Rock Hill, SC 29733.

Head Coach: Joe Hudak. **Assistant Coaches:** Dwight Hottle, Mike McGuire. **Telephone:** (803) 323-2129. **Baseball SID:** Jack Frost. **Telephone**: (803) 323-2129. FAX: (803) 323-2433.

WISCONSIN-MILWAUKEE Panthers

Conference: Midwestern Collegiate.

Mailing Address: P.O. Box 413, Milwaukee, WI 53201.

Head Coach: Jerry Augustine. **Assistant Coaches:** Scott Doffek, Jim Rosen. **Telephone:** (414) 229-5670. **Baseball SID:** Greg Bromberg. **Telephone:** (414) 229-4593. **FAX:** (414) 229-6759.

WOFFORD Terriers

Conference: Independent.

Mailing Address: Athletic Office, 429 N. Church St., Spartanburg, SC 29303.

Head Coach: Ernie May. **Assistant Coach:** Andy Kiah. **Telephone:** (864) 597-4100. **Baseball SID:** Melanie Dillingham. **Telephone:** (864) 597-4093. **FAX:** (864) 597-4129.

WRIGHT STATE Raiders

Conference: Midwestern Collegiate.

Mailing Address: P.O. Box 516, Dayton, OH 45435.

Head Coach: Ron Nischwitz. **Assistant Coach:** Bo Bilinski. **Telephone:** (513) 873-2771. **Baseball SID:** Mindy Bishop. **Telephone:** (513) 873-3666. **FAX:** (513) 873-2368.

XAVIER Musketeers

Conference: Atlantic 10/West.

Mailing Address: 3800 Victory Parkway, Cincinnati, OH 45207.

Head Coach: John Morrey. **Assistant Coaches:** Ryan McGinnis, Joe Regruth. **Telephone:** (513) 745-2890. **Baseball SID:** Courtney Morrison. **Telephone:** (513) 745-2058. **FAX:** (513) 745-2825.

YALE Bulldogs

Conference: Ivy League/Rolfe.

Mailing Address: 402-A Yale Station, New Haven, CT 06520.

Head Coach: John Stuper. **Assistant Coaches:** Dick Jeynes, Dan Scarpa. **Telephone:** (203) 432-1466. **Baseball SID:** Steve Conn. **Telephone:** (203) 432-1455. **FAX:** (203) 432-1454.

YOUNGSTOWN STATE Penguins

Conference: Mid-Continent/East.

Mailing Address: 410 Wick Ave., Youngstown, OH 44555.

Head Coach: Dan Kubacki. **Assistant Coach:** Jeff Davenport. **Telephone:** (216) 742-3485. **Baseball SID:** Greg Gulas. **Telephone:** (216) 742-3190. **FAX:** (216) 742-3191.

AMATEUR BASEBALL
HIGH SCHOOL BASEBALL
YOUTH BASEBALL

HIGH SCHOOL BASEBALL

NATIONAL FEDERATION OF STATE HIGH SCHOOL ASSOCIATIONS

Office Address: 11724 NW Plaza Circle, Kansas City, MO 64153. **Mailing Address:** P.O. Box 20626, Kansas City, MO 64195. **Telephone:** (816) 464-5400. **FAX:** (816) 464-5571.

Executive Director: Robert Kanaby. **Associate Director:** Fritz McGinness. **Assistant Director/Baseball Rules Editor:** Brad Rumble. **Director of Public Relations:** Bruce Howard.

NATIONAL HIGH SCHOOL BASEBALL COACHES ASSOCIATION

Mailing Address: P.O. Box 12354, Omaha, NE 68112. **Telephone/FAX:** (402) 457-1962.

Executive Director: Jerry Miles. **Administrative Assistant:** Elaine Miles. **President:** Ron Davini (Tempe, AZ).

1997 National Convention: Dec. 5-7 at Louisville.

NATIONAL CLASSIC HIGH SCHOOL TOURNAMENT

Mailing Address: El Dorado High School, 1651 North Valencia Ave., Placentia, CA 92870. **Telephone:** (714) 993-5350. **FAX:** (714) 524-2458.

Tournament Director: Iran Novick.

1997 Tournament: March 31-April 3 in Orange County, CA (16 teams). **1998 Tournament:** April 13-16.

SUNBELT BASEBALL CLASSIC SERIES

Mailing Address: 505 North Boulevard, Edmond, OK 73034. **Telephone:** (405) 348-3839.

Chairman: Gordon Morgan. **Director:** John Schwartz.

1997 Series: Shawnee and Tecumseh, OK, June 24-28 (eight states: Arizona, California, Florida, Georgia, Maryland, Ohio, Oklahoma, Texas).

NATIONAL SHOWCASE EVENTS

(For High School Players)

ADIDAS AREA CODE GAMES

Mailing Address: P.O. Box 213, Santa Rosa, CA 95402. **Telephone:** (707) 525-0498. **FAX:** (707) 525-0214.

President, Goodwill Series, Inc.: Bob Williams.

1997 Area Code Games: Aug. 11-17, Tony Gwynn Stadium, San Diego, CA.

Goodwill Series XIII: Dec. 21-28, Adelaide, Australia.

TEAM ONE NATIONAL SHOWCASE

Mailing Address: P.O. Box 8943, Cincinnati, OH 45208. **Telephone/FAX:** (606) 291-4463.

President, Team One Sports: Jeff Spelman.

1997 Team One National Showcase: June 26-29, Ed Smith Stadium, Sarasota, FL. **Regional Showcases:** July 18-20, Clemson, SC (Clemson University); Aug. 10-12, Lexington, KY (University of Kentucky).

EASTERN U.S. BASEBALL SHOWCASE

Mailing Address: P.O. Box 2126, Chapel Hill, NC 27514. **Telephone:** (919) 962-2351.

Facility Director: Roger Williams.

1997 Showcase: Aug. 6-9, Chapel Hill, NC (University of North Carolina).

NATIONAL AMATEUR ALL-STAR BASEBALL TOURNAMENT

Mailing Address: 400 North Michigan Ave., Suite 1016, Chicago, IL 60611. **Telephone:** (800) 622-2877. **FAX:** (312) 245-8088.

Operated by: Amateur All-Star Baseball, Inc.

Chairman: Allan Cox. **President:** Ron Berryman.

League Members: American Amateur Baseball Congress, Babe Ruth League, Dixie Baseball, National Amateur Baseball Federation, PONY Baseball.

1997 Tournament: June 26-July 1 at unavailable site.

AMATEUR BASEBALL

Organizations

INTERNATIONAL OLYMPIC COMMITTEE

Mailing Address: Chateau de Vidy, 1000 Lausanne, Switzerland. **Telephone:** 41-21-621-61-11. **FAX:** 41-21-621-62-16.

President: Juan Antonio Samaranch.

U.S. OLYMPIC COMMITTEE

Mailing Address: One Olympic Plaza, Colorado Springs, CO 80909. **Telephone:** (719) 632-5551. **FAX:** (719) 578-4654.

President: William Hybl. **Executive Director:** Dick Schultz. **Director of Public Relations:** Mike Moran.

Olympics, 2000: Sept. 16-Oct. 1, 2000 at Sydney, Australia.

GOODWILL GAMES ORGANIZING COMMITTEE

Mailing Address: One CNN Center, P.O. Box 105366, Atlanta, GA 30348. **Telephone:** (404) 827-3400. **FAX:** (404) 827-1394.

President: Mike Plant. **Vice President, Sports:** David Raith. **Director of Publicity:** Leslie King.

Goodwill Games, 1998: July 19-Aug. 2, 1998 at New York.

PAN AMERICAN GAMES ORGANIZING COMMITTEE

Mailing Address: 1999 Pan American Games Society, 500 Shaftesbury Blvd., Winnipeg, Manitoba, R3P 0M1 Canada. **Telephone:** (204) 985-1999. **FAX:** (204) 985-1993.

President: Don MacKenzie. **Coordinator of Media/Broadcasting:** Ernie Naim.

Pan American Games, 1999: July 24-Aug. 8, 1999 at Winnipeg.

SYDNEY OLYMPIC ORGANIZING COMMITTEE

Mailing Address: Level 14, The Maritime Centre, 207 Kent St., Sydney, New South Wales 2000 Australia. **Telephone:** 011 (61-2) 931-2000. **FAX:** 011 (61-2) 931-2020.

Executive President: Gary Pemberton. **Director General:** Bob Elphinston.

Games of the XXVIIth Olympiad: Sept. 16-Oct. 1, 2000.

INTERNATIONAL BASEBALL ASSOCIATION

Mailing Address: Avenue de Mon-Repos 24, Case Postale 131, 1000 Lausanne 5, Switzerland. **Telephone:** 41-21-311-18-63. **FAX:** 41-21-311-18-64.

President: Aldo Notari (Italy). **Secretary General:** Richard Case (United States). **Executive Director:** Miquel Ortin.

1997 Events

Asian Senior Championship* .... Chinese Taipei, May 20-June 1
AAA Pan American Championship* ...... Londrina, Brazil, May 23-June 1
AA Pan American Championship .... Cartagena, Colombia, June 19-29
AA World Youth Championship .... Chinese Taipei, July 12-20
AA European Championship* .. Chozen, Czech Republic, July 28-Aug. 3
XIII Intercontinental Cup .... Barcelona, Spain, Aug. 1-10
World Children Baseball Fair .... Nagasaki, Japan, Aug. 1-8
AAA World Youth Championship ...... Moncton, N.B., Canada, Aug. 8-16
European Senior A Championship* .... Paris, France, Aug. 15-23

*Qualifying tournament for 1998 World Championship

USA BASEBALL

Mailing Address, Corporate Headquarters: 2160 Greenwood Ave., Trenton, NJ 08609. **Telephone:** (609) 586-2381. **FAX:** (609) 587-1818.

Chairman of the Board: Cliff Lothery. **President:** Mark Marquess. **Executive Vice President:** Neil Lantz. **Secretary:** Tom Hicks. **Treasurer:** Gale Montgomery.

Executive Director/Chief Executive Officer: Dan O'Brien. **Associate Director/USA Team General Manager:** Mike Fiore. **Deputy Director:** Wanda Rutledge.

Controller: Barbara Case. **Operations Director:** Pam Case.

Special Projects Manager: Paul Seiler. **Marketing and Licensing Director:** Derek Bradley. **Media Relations Director:** George Doig.

National Members: Amateur Athletic Union, American Amateur Baseball Congress, American Baseball Coaches Association, American Legion Baseball, Dixie Baseball, Little League Baseball, National Amateur Baseball Federation, National Baseball Congress, National Collegiate Athletic Association, National Association of Intercollegiate Athletics,

National High School Baseball Coaches Association, National Junior College Athletic Association, National Federation of State High School Athletic Associations, Police Athletic League, PONY Baseball, YMCA of the USA.

1997 Events

Training Camp, Senior Team .... Site unavailable, June 10-25
USA Junior Olympic Championship .... Fort Myers, FL, June 20-29
AA World Youth Championship .... Chinese Taipei, Taiwan, July 12-20
XIII Intercontinental Cup .... Barcelona, Spain, Aug. 1-10
AAA World Youth Championship ...... Moncton, N.B., Canada, Aug. 8-16
World University Games .... Palermo, Italy, Aug. 20-31

BASEBALL CANADA

Mailing Address: 1600 James Naismith Dr., Suite 712, Ottawa, Ontario K1B 5N4. **Telephone:** (613) 748-5606. **FAX:** (613) 748-5767.

Director General: Duncan Grant.

NATIONAL BASEBALL CONGRESS

Mailing Address: P.O. Box 1420, Wichita, KS 67201. **Telephone:** (316) 267-3372. **FAX:** (316) 267-3382.

Year Founded: 1931.

President: Robert Rich Jr. **Executive Vice President:** Melinda Rich.

Vice President: Steven Shaad. **National Commissioner/Tournament Director:** Larry Davis. **General Manager:** Lance Deckinger. **Director of Administration:** Dian Overaker. **National Coordinator:** Mark Chiarucci. **Stadium Manager:** Rich Zizek. **Marketing and Public Relations Coordinator:** Todd Rutledge.

1997 NBC National Tournament (non-professional, ex-professional): Aug. 1-15, Lawrence-Dumont Stadium, Wichita, KS.

INTERNATIONAL BASEBALL FOUNDATION

Mailing Address: 1313 13th St. South, Birmingham, AL 35205. **Telephone:** (205) 558-4235. **FAX:** (205) 918-0800.

Executive Director: David Osinski.

Summer College Leagues

NCAA Summer Baseball

Office Address: 6201 College Blvd., Overland Park, KS 66211. **Telephone:** (913) 339-1906. **FAX:** (913) 339-0026.

NCAA Compliance Representative: Dave Brunk.

NCAA Certified Leagues: Atlantic Collegiate League, Cape Cod League, Central Illinois Collegiate League, Great Lakes League, New England Collegiate League, Northeastern League, Northwest Collegiate League, San Diego Collegiate League, Shenandoah Valley League.

ALASKA LEAGUE

Mailing Address: 1625 Old Steese Highway, Fairbanks, AK 99701. **Telephone:** (907) 451-0095.

Year Founded: 1974.

Publicity Director: Don Dennis.

1997 Opening Date: June 13. **Closing Date:** Aug. 10.

Regular Season: 16 league games.

Roster Limit: 21, plus exemption for Alaska residents.

ALASKA GOLDPANNERS

Mailing Address: P.O. Box 71154, Fairbanks, AK 99707. **Telephone:** (907) 451-0095. **FAX:** (907) 452-2714

President: Bill Stroecker. **General Manager:** Don Dennis. **Head Coach:** Stacy Parker (Orange Coast, Calif., CC).

ANCHORAGE BUCS

Mailing Address: 903 W. 29th Ave., Anchorage, AK 99503. **Telephone:** (907) 561-2827. **FAX:** (907) 561-2920.

President: Patricia Kennedy. **General Manager:** Dennis Mattingly. **Head Coach:** Mark O'Brien (Cal Poly San Luis Obispo).

HAWAII ISLAND MOVERS

Mailing Address: P.O. Box 17865, Honolulu, HI 96817. **Telephone:** (808) 848-5203. **FAX:** (808) 841-2321.

President/General Manager: Donald Takaki. **Head Coach:** Tom Gushiken (Waipahu HS, Waipahu, HI). **Assistant Coach:** David Nakama (Mission, Calif., JC).

ALASKA CENTRAL LEAGUE

Mailing Address: P.O. Box 318, Kenai, AK 99611. **Telephone:** (907) 283-7133. **FAX:** (907) 283-3390.

Year Founded: 1990.

President: Lou Sinnett. **Vice President:** Stan Zaborac. **Treasurer:** Coral Seymour. **Executive Director:** Jack Slama.

1997 Opening Date: June 8. **Closing Date:** July 29.

Regular Season: 41 games.

Playoff Format: None. Regular-season champion advances to National Baseball Congress World Series.

Roster Limit: 22.

ANCHORAGE GLACIER PILOTS

Mailing Address: P.O. Box 100895, Anchorage, AK 99510. **Telephone:** (907) 274-3627. **FAX:** (907) 274-3628.

General Manager: Ron Okerlund. **Head Coach:** Kevin Smallcomb. (Mendocino, Calif., CC).

MAT-SU MINERS

Mailing Address: P.O. Box 1633, Palmer, AK 99645. **Telephone:** (907) 745-4901. **FAX:** (907) 745-7275.

General Manager: Stan Zaborac Jr. **Head Coach:** Dave Ravitz (Loyola Marymount U.)

PENINSULA OILERS

Office Address: 601 S. Main, Kenai, AK 99611. **Mailing Address:** P.O. Box 318, Kenai, AK 99611. **Telephone:** (907) 283-7133. **FAX:** (907) 283-3390.

President: Dave Machado. **Baseball Operations Manager:** Mike Baxter. **Head Coach:** Scott Marr (Oral Roberts U.).

ARIZONA COLLEGIATE LEAGUE

Mailing Address: 995 E. Baseline Rd., Suite 1024, Tempe, AZ 85283. **Telephone/FAX:** (602) 949-4225.

Year Founded: 1989.

Commissioner/President: Jeff Antoon. **Student-Athlete Liaison:** Jaymie Bane.

Member Clubs: Angels, Athletics, Braves, Giants, Marlins, Royals, Yankees.

1997 Opening Date: July 1. **Closing Date:** Aug. 5.

Regular Season: 30 games.

Playoff Format: Top two teams meet in best-of-3 championship series.

Roster Limit: 22 (college-eligible players only).

ATLANTIC COLLEGIATE LEAGUE

Mailing Address: 26 Eric Trail, Sussex, NJ 07461. **Telephone:** (201) 702-1755. **FAX:** (201) 702-1898.

Commissioner: Bob Pertsas. **President:** Henry Burke. **Executive Vice President:** Tom Bonekemper.

Member Clubs: Jersey Pilots, Metro New York Cadets, Nassau (N.Y.) Collegians, Quakertown (Pa.) Blazers, Scranton/Wilkes-Barre (Pa.) Twins, Sussex (N.Y.) Colonels, West Deptford (N.J.) Storm.

1997 Opening Date: June 1. **Closing Date:** Aug. 15.

No. of Games, Regular Season: Unavailable.

Playoff Format: Unavailable.

Roster Limit: 21 (college-eligible players only).

CAPE COD LEAGUE

Mailing Address: Tabor Academy, Marion, MA 02738. **Telephone:** (508) 748-0337. **FAX:** (508) 748-0552.

Year Founded: 1885.

Commissioner: Richard Marr. **President:** Judy Scarafile.

Vice Presidents: Jim Higgins, Don Tullie, Howard Wayne.

Publicity Director: Missy Alaimo. **Assistant, Publicity:** Cathie Nichols.

Member Clubs, Division Structure: East—Brewster, Chatham, Harwich, Orleans, Yarmouth-Dennis. **West**—Bourne, Cotuit, Falmouth, Hyannis, Wareham.

1997 Opening Date: June 12. **Closing Date:** Aug. 13.

Regular Season: 44 games.

All-Star Game: July 26, site unavailable.

Playoff Format: Top two teams in each division meet in best-of-3 semifinals. Winners meet in best-of-3 series for league championship.

Roster Limit: 23 (college-eligible players only).

BOURNE BRAVES

Mailing Address: P.O. Box 895, Monument Beach, MA 02553 **Telephone:** (508) 564-6484. **FAX:** (508) 563-6921.

President: Edward Ladetto. **General Manager:** Francis Howland. **Head Coach:** Kevin O'Sullivan (U. of Virginia).

BREWSTER WHITECAPS

Mailing Address: P.O. Box 1319, Brewster, MA 02631. **Telephone:** (617) 720-7870. **FAX:** (617) 720-7877.

President: Robert Hecker. **General Managers:** Howard Wayne, Sol Yas, Barry Souder. **Head Coach:** Bill Mosiello (Oklahoma U.).

CHATHAM A's

Mailing Address: 61 Whidah Dr., East Harwich, MA 02645. **Telephone:** (508) 432-4228.

General Manager: Jeff McGuire. **Head Coach:** John Schiffner (Plainville, Conn., HS).

COTUIT KETTLEERS

Mailing Address: P.O. Box 411, Cotuit, MA 02635. **Telephone/FAX:** (508) 428-9075.

President: Bruce Murphy. **General Manager:** George Streeter. **Head Coach:** Tom Walter (George Washington U.).

FALMOUTH COMMODORES

Mailing Address: 33 Wintergreen Rd., Mashpee, MA 02649. **Telephone:** (508) 548-5800. **FAX:** (508) 540-3835.

President: Bob Weiss. **General Manager:** Chuck Sturtevant. **Head Coach:** Harvey Shapiro (Bowdoin, Me., College).

HARWICH MARINERS

Mailing Address: P.O. Box 201, Harwich Port, MA 02646. **Telephone:** (508) 432-8515.

President: Mary Henderson. **General Manager:** Ken Keenan. **Head Coach:** Chad Holbrook (U. of North Carolina).

HYANNIS METS

Mailing Address: 59 Blueberry Hill Rd., Hyannis, MA 02601. **Telephone:** (508) 778-0275.

President, General Manager: Steve Norton. **Head Coach:** Steve Mrowka (Georgia College).

ORLEANS CARDINALS

Mailing Address: P.O. Box 516, East Orleans, MA 02643. **Telephone:** (508) 240-5867. **FAX:** (508) 240-5871.

General Manager: David Reed. **Head Coach:** Don Norris (Georgia College).

WAREHAM GATEMEN

Mailing Address: 71 Towhee Rd., Wareham, MA 02571. **Telephone:** (508) 295-3956. **FAX:** (508) 295-8821.

President: Donna Joseph. **General Manager:** John Wylde. **Head Coach:** Don Reed.

YARMOUTH-DENNIS RED SOX

Mailing Address: P.O. Box 814, South Yarmouth, MA 02664. **Telephone:** (508) 398-0165.

President: Robert Beauchemin. **General Manager:** Jim Hagemeister. **Head Coach:** Steve Cohen (North Hennepin, Minn., CC). **Assistant Coach:** Doug Wabeke (Grand Rapids, Mich., CC).

CENTRAL ILLINOIS COLLEGIATE LEAGUE

Mailing Address: RR 13, Box 369, Bloomington, IL 61704. **Telephone/FAX:** (309) 828-4429.

Year Founded: 1963.

President: Duffy Bass. **Commissioner:** Mike Woods. **Publicity Director:** Jim Bowers.

Member Clubs: Danville Dans, Decatur Blues, Quincy Gems, Springfield Rifles, Twin City Stars.

1997 Opening Date: June 5. **Closing Date:** July 31.

Regular Season: 40 games.

All-Star Game: July 1 at Danville, July 3 at Quincy.

Playoff Format: Five teams, single-elimination tournament.

Roster Limit: 23 (college-eligible players only).

CLARK GRIFFITH COLLEGIATE LEAGUE

Mailing Address: 4917 North 30th St., Arlington, VA 22207. **Telephone:** (703) 536-3252. **FAX:** (703) 536-1729.

Year Founded: 1945.

President/Commissioner: John Depenbrock. **Executive Vice President:** Frank Fannan. **Director, Publicity:** Ben Trittipoe.

Member Clubs: Arlington (Va.) Senators, Herndon (Va.) Optimists, Prince William (Va.) Gators, Reston (Va.) Hawks, Southern Maryland Cats.

1997 Opening Date: May 30. **Closing Date:** July 31.

Regular Season: 40 games (split-schedule).

All-Star Game: July 3 at Reston.

Playoff Format: First-half winner meets second-half winner in best-of-3 final for league championship.

Roster Limit: 24 (players 20 and under).

COASTAL PLAIN LEAGUE

Mailing Address: 4900 Waters Edge Dr., Suite 201, Raleigh, NC 27606. **Telephone:** (919) 852-1960. **FAX:** (919) 852-1973.

Year Founded: 1997.

Chairman/Chief Executive Officer: Jerry Petitt. **President:** Pete Bock. **Director, Media Relations:** Steve McDonald.

Member Clubs (all teams in North Carolina)**:** Durham Braves, Outer Banks Dare Devils, Raleigh Red Wolves, Rocky Mount Rockfish, Wilmington Sharks, Wilson Tobs.

1997 Opening Date: May 30. **Closing Date:** Aug. 9.

Regular Season: 50 games (split schedule).

Playoff Format: First-half winner meets second-half winner in best-of-3 series.

Roster Limit: 20 (college-eligible players only).

GREAT LAKES LEAGUE

Office Address: 24700 Center Ridge Rd., Suite 10, Westlake, OH 44145.

Mailing Address: P.O. Box 16679, Cleveland, OH 44116. **Telephone:** (216) 871-8100. **FAX:** (216) 871-4221.

Year Founded: 1986.

Commissioner: Brian Sullivan. **President:** Barry Ruben. **Vice-Presidents:** Ron Miller, Rob Piscetta.

Member Clubs (all teams located in Ohio)**:** Bexley, Columbus All-Americans, Euclid Admirals, Grand Lake Mariners, Lima Locos, Sandusky Bay Stars.

1997 Opening Date: June 10. **Closing Date:** August 3.

Regular Season: 40 games.

All-Star Game: July 27 at Lima.

Playoff Format: Top four teams meet in best-of-3 series. Winners meet in best-of-3 final for league championship.

Roster Limit: 25 (college-eligible players only).

JAYHAWK LEAGUE

Mailing Address: 5 Adams Place, Halstead, KS 67056. **Telephone:** (316) 755-2361, (316) 835-2589. **FAX:** (316) 755-1285.

Year Founded: 1976.

Commissioner: Bob Considine. **President:** Don Carlile. **Public Relations Director:** Pat Chambers. **Statistician:** Gary Karr.

Member Clubs: El Dorado (Kan.) Broncos, Elkhart (Kan.) Dusters, Hays (Kan.) Larks, Liberal (Kan.) Bee Jays, Nevada (Mo.) Griffons, Topeka (Kan.) Capitols.

1997 Opening Date: May 30. **Closing Date:** July 16.

Regular Season: 40 games.

Playoff Format: Six teams, single-elimination tournament.

Roster Limit: 25.

NEW ENGLAND COLLEGIATE LEAGUE

Mailing Address: 57 Steuben St., Meriden, CT 06451. **Telephone/FAX:** (203) 238-4111.

Year Founded: 1993.

President: Joel Cooney. **Vice President:** Richard Rossiter.

Member Clubs: Central Mass Collegians (Sterling, MA), Danbury (Conn.) Westerners, Eastern Tides (Willimantic, CT), Middletown (Conn.) Giants, Rhode Island Reds (West Warwick, RI), Torrington (Conn.) Twisters.

1997 Opening Date: May 31. **Closing Date:** July 31.

Regular Season: 40 games.

All-Star Game: July 19 at Norwich, CT.

Playoff Format: Four teams, round-robin.

Roster Limit: 23 (college-eligible players only).

NORTHEASTERN COLLEGIATE LEAGUE

Mailing Address: 3148 Riverside Dr., Wellsville NY 14895. **Telephone/FAX:** (716) 593-3923..

Year Founded: 1986.

Commissioner: Dave Chamberlain. **Chairman:** Bob Bellizzi. **Vice Chairman:** Jim Burke. **Publicity Director:** Dick Cuykendall.

Member Clubs, Division Structure (all teams located in New York)**:** **East**—Binghamton Triple Cities, Little Falls Knickerbockers, Schenectady Mohawks, Utica Indians, Utica Six-Guns. **West**—Cohocton Red Wings, Cortland Apples, Geneva Knights, Hornell Dodgers, Ithaca Lakers.

1997 Opening Date: June 2. **Closing Date:** July 26.

Regular Season: 40 games.

All-Star Game: July 7 at Hornell, NY.

Playoff Format: Top three teams in each division, single-elimination tournament.

Roster Limit: 24 (college-eligible players only).

NORTHWEST COLLEGIATE LEAGUE

Mailing Address: 16077 Bales Way, Sherwood, OR 97140. **Telephone:** (503) 725-5634. **FAX:** (503) 725-5610.

Year Founded: 1992.

Commissioner: Reed Rainey. **Vice President:** Hal DeBerry.

Member Clubs (all teams located in Oregon)**:** Bucks, Dukes, Lobos, Ports, Stars, Toros.

1997 Opening Date: June 2. **Closing Date:** Aug. 10.

Regular Season: 30 games (split schedule).

Playoff Format: First-half winner meets second-half winner in best-of-3 series for league championship.

Roster Limit: 19 (college-eligible players only).

NORTHWOODS LEAGUE

Mailing Address: 5145 Colbert Rd., Lakeland, FL 33813. **Telephone:** (941) 644-4022. **FAX:** (941) 644-1238.

Year Founded: 1994.

President: George MacDonald Jr. **Vice Presidents:** Dick Radatz Jr., William McKee, John Wendel.

Member Clubs: Kenosha (Wis.) Kroakers, Manitowoc (Wis.) Skunks, Rochester (Minn.) Honkers, St. Cloud (Minn) River Bats, Waterloo (Iowa) Bucks, Wausau (Wis.) Woodchucks.

1997 Opening Date: June 6. **Closing Date:** Aug. 12.

Regular Season: 64 games.

All-Star Game: July 19 at Rochester, MN.

Playoff Format: First-half winner meets second-half winner in best-of-3 series for league championship.

Roster Limit: 22 (college-eligible players only).

PACIFIC INTERNATIONAL LEAGUE

Mailing Address: 504 Yale Ave. North, Seattle, WA 98109. **Telephone:** (206) 623-8844. **FAX:** (602) 623-8361.

Year Founded: 1992.

Commissioner: Seth Dawson. **President:** Steve Konek. **Secretary/ Statistician:** Beth Griffin. **Director, Marketing/Public Relations:** Mickie Schmith.

Member Clubs, Division Structure: Mountain—Kelowna (B.C.) Grizzlies, Ontario Orchard (Ore.) Meadowlarks, Penticton (B.C.) Bats, Yakima (Wash.) Chiefs. **Pacific**—Coquitlam (B.C.) Athletics, Everett (Wash.) Merchants, Richmond (B.C.) Budgies, Seattle (Wash.) Cruisers, Seattle (Wash.) Studs, Tacoma (Wash.) Timbers.

1997 Opening Date: June 1. **Closing Date:** Aug. 1.

Regular Season: 32 games.

Roster Limit: 25.

SAN DIEGO COLLEGIATE LEAGUE

Mailing Address: 948 Jasmine Ct., Carlsbad, CA 92009. **Telephone:** (619) 438-0347.

Year Founded: 1984.

Commissioner: Gerald Clements. **Vice Commissioner:** John Verdusco. **Publicity Director:** Dave Kuhn.

Member Clubs, Division Structure: National—Beach City Cubs, El Cajon Padres, North County Mets. **American**—East County Orioles, San Diego Royals, South Bay Indians.

1997 Opening Date: June 2. **Closing Date:** Aug. 10.

Regular Season: 30 games (split schedule).

Playoff Format: First-half division winners meet second-half division winners in best-of-3 series. Winners meet in best-of-3 series for league championship.

Roster Limit: 18 to 21 (college-eligible players only).

SHENANDOAH VALLEY LEAGUE

Mailing Address: Route 1, Box 189J, Staunton, VA 24401. **Telephone:** (540) 886-1748. **FAX:** (540) 885-7612.

Commissioner/President: David Biery. **Executive Vice President:** James Weissenborn. **Vice President/Public Relations:** Curt Dudley.

Member Clubs: Front Royal, Harrisonburg, New Market, Staunton, Waynesboro, Winchester.

1997 Opening Date: May 30. **Closing Date:** Aug. 3.

Regular Season: 40 games.

Playoff Format: Six teams, round robin. Top two teams meet in best-of-5 series for league championship.

Roster Limit: 25 (college-eligible players only).

FRONT ROYAL CARDINALS

Mailing Address: P.O. Box 995, Front Royal, VA 22630. **Telephone:** (540) 636-2716.

Majority Owner: Darryl Windham. **President:** Linda Keen. **General Manager:** Danny Wood. **Head Coach:** Gilbert Payne.

HARRISONBURG TURKS

Mailing Address: 1489 South Main St., Harrisonburg, VA 22801. **Telephone/FAX:** (540) 434-5919.

President, General Manager: Bob Wease. **Head Coach:** Tom Carr (Quincy, Ill., U.).

NEW MARKET REBELS

Mailing Address: P.O. Box 902, New Market, VA 22844. **Telephone:** (540) 740-8727. **FAX:** (540) 740-4186.

General Manager: Tom Linski. **Head Coach:** Mike Rikard (Wake Forest U.).

STAUNTON BRAVES

Mailing Address: P.O. Box 621, Staunton, VA 24402. **Telephone:** (540) 885-2598. **FAX:** (540) 886-7601.

President: Garland Eutslev. **General Manager:** Tom Chrisman. **Head Coach:** Mike Bocock.

WAYNESBORO GENERALS

Mailing Address: P.O. Box 243, Waynesboro, VA 22980. **Telephone:** (540) 949-6949. **FAX:** (540) 943-9645.

Owner/General Manager: Warren Shand. **Head Coach:** Kevin Erminio (Clemson U.).

WINCHESTER ROYALS

Mailing Address: P.O. Box 2485, Winchester, VA 22601. **Telephone:** (540) 662-4466. **FAX:** (540) 662-3299.

President: Todd Thompson. **Recruiting Coordinator/Head Coach:** Paul O'Neil (Shenandoah, Va., U.).

YOUTH BASEBALL

ALL AMERICAN AMATEUR BASEBALL ASSOCIATION

Mailing Address: 331 Parkway Drive, Zanesville, OH 43701. **Telephone:** (614) 453-8531. **FAX:** (614) 453-3978.

Year Founded: 1944.

President: James McElroy Jr. **Executive Director:** Bob Wolfe.

1997 National Tournament (21 and under): Aug. 9-16 at Johnstown, PA.

AMATEUR ATHLETIC UNION

Mailing Address: The Walt Disney World Resort, P.O. Box 10000, Lake Buena Vista, FL 32830. **Telephone:** (407) 363-6170. **FAX:** (407) 363-6171.

Year Founded: 1982.

Vice President, Baseball: Pam Marshall.

Age Classifications, World Series

9 and under .... Sherwood, AR, July 25-Aug. 2
10 and under .... Kansas City, MO, August 2-9
11 and under .... Walt Disney Sports Complex, Aug. 1-9
12 and under .... Burnsville, MN, Aug. 1-8
13 and under (90 foot) .... Chickasha, OK, July 25-Aug. 2
13 and under (80 foot) .... Riverside, CA, Aug. 8-15
14 and under .... Cocoa, FL, Aug. 1-9
15 and under .... Millington, TN, Aug. 1-9
16 and under .... Charlotte, NC, July 31-Aug. 9
17 and under .... Norman, OK, July 25-Aug. 2
18 and under .... Walt Disney Sports Complex, July 18-26
20 and under .... Fort Myers, FL, July 26-Aug. 2

National Invitation Championships

10 and under .... Moore, OK, July 25-Aug. 1
11 and under .... Akron/Talmadge, OH, Aug. 9-16
12 and under .... Walt Disney Sports Complex, July 25-Aug. 1
13 and under .... Bakersfield, CA, July 25-Aug. 3
14 and under .... Walt Disney Sports Complex, July 25-Aug. 2
15 and under .... Sarasota, FL, Aug. 1-9

AMERICAN AMATEUR BASEBALL CONGRESS

National Headquarters: 118-119 Redfield Plaza, P.O. Box 467, Marshall, MI 49068. **Telephone:** (616) 781-2002. **FAX:** (616) 781-2060.

Year Founded: 1935.

President: Joe Cooper.

Age Classifications, World Series

Roberto Clemente (8 and under) .... Wheatridge, CO, July 31-Aug. 3
Willie Mays (10 and under) .... Site unavailable, July 31-Aug. 3
Pee Wee Reese (12 and under) .... Toa Baja, PR, July 30-Aug. 4
Sandy Koufax (14 and under) .... Jersey City, NJ, Aug. 6-10
Mickey Mantle (16 and under) .... McKinney, TX, Aug. 7-10
Connie Mack (18 and under) .... Farmington, NM, Aug. 8-15
Stan Musial (unlimited) .... Battle Creek, MI, Aug. 14-18

AMERICAN LEGION BASEBALL

National Headquarters: National Americanism Commission, P.O. Box 1055, Indianapolis, IN 46206. **Telephone:** (317) 630-1213. **FAX:** (317) 630-1369.

Year Founded: 1926.

Program Coordinator: Jim Quinlan.

1997 World Series (19 and under): Aug. 21-26 at Rapid City, SD.

BABE RUTH BASEBALL

International Headquarters: 1770 Brunswick Pike, P.O. Box 5000, Trenton, NJ 08638. **Telephone:** (609) 695-1434. **FAX:** (609) 695-2505.

Year Founded: 1951.

President/Chief Executive Officer: Ron Tellefsen.

Vice President/Chief Financial Officer: Rosemary Schoellkopf. **Commissioners:** Robert Faherty, Jimmy Stewart. **Marketing Manager:** Joe Smiegocki.

Age Classifications, World Series

Bambino (11-12) .... Altamonte Springs, FL, Aug. 9-16
13-Prep .... Clifton Park, NY, Aug. 16-23
13-15 .... Longview, WA, Aug. 16-23
16 .... Springdale, AR, Aug. 16-23
16-18 .... Jamestown, NY, Aug. 9-16

CONTINENTAL AMATEUR BASEBALL ASSOCIATION

Mailing Address: 82 University St., Westerville, OH 43081. **Telephone:** (614) 899-2103. **FAX:** (614) 899-2103.

Year Founded: 1984.

President: Carl Williams. **Executive Director:** Roger Tremaine. **Commissioner:** John Mocny. **Franchise Director:** Tanya Wilkinson.

Age Classifications, World Series

9 and under .... Charles City, IA, Aug. 7-17
10 and under .... Aurelia/Cherokee, IA, July 31-Aug. 10
11 and under .... Tarkio, MO, July 31-Aug. 11
12 and under .... Omaha, NE, Aug. 7-18
13 and under .... Broken Arrow, OK, Aug. 7-18
14 and under .... Dublin, OH, Aug. 7-18
15 and under .... Crystal Lake, IL, Aug. 3-14
16 and under .... Arlington, TX, Aug. 3-14
High school age .... Cleveland, OH, July 24-Aug. 4
18 and under .... Homestead, FL, Aug. 7-18
College age .... Glen Ellyn, IL, July 29-Aug. 4
Unlimited age .... Eau Claire, WI, Aug. 12-18

DIXIE BASEBALL, INC.

Mailing Address: P.O. Box 193, Montgomery, AL 36101. **Telephone:** (334) 241-2300. **FAX:** (334) 241-2301.

Year Founded: 1956.

Executive Director: Jimmy Brown.

Age Classifications, World Series

Dixie Youth (13 and under) .... Bossier City, LA, Aug. 2-7
Dixie Boys (13-14) .... Covington, GA, Aug. 2-7
Dixie Pre-Majors (15-16) .... Enterprise, AL, Aug. 2-7
Dixie Majors (15-18) .... Lufkin, TX, Aug. 2-7

DIZZY DEAN BASEBALL, INC.

Mailing Address: 902 Highway 9 North, Eupora, MS 39744. **Telephone:** (601) 258-7626, (904) 455-8827.

Year Founded: 1962.

Commissioner: Billy Powell. **Assistant to Commissioner:** Don Stuart.

Age Classifications, World Series

Minor League (9-10) .... Athens, TN, July 26-31
Freshman (11-12) .... Eastridge, TN, July 26-31
Sophomore (13-14) .... Baton Rouge, LA, July 26-31
Junior (15-16) .... Boynton, GA, July 25-30
Senior (17-18) .... Boynton, GA, Aug. 2-7

HAP DUMONT YOUTH BASEBALL

Mailing Address: P.O. Box 17455, Wichita, KS 67217. **Telephone:** (316) 721-1779. **FAX:** (316) 721-8054.

Year Founded: 1978.

National Chairman: Jerry Crowell. **National Vice Chairman:** Virgil Coley.

Age Classifications, World Series

10 and under .... Houston, TX, Aug. 1-6
11 and under .... Harrison, AR, Aug. 8-13
12 and under .... Casper, WY, Aug. 1-6
14 and under .... Harrison, AR, Aug. 1-6
16 and under .... Brainerd, MN, Aug. 1-6

JUNIOR PAN AM and WORLD BASEBALL PROGRAM

Mailing Address: P.O. Box 72711, Roselle, IL 60172. **Telephone:** (630) 893-6273. **FAX:** (630) 893-5549.

Year Founded: 1990.

President, General Manager: Peter Caliendo. **Director of Marketing and Administration:** Jon Wolf. **Public Relations Director:** Mark Madorin. **Fund Raising Director:** Mark Kedziora.

Age Classifications, World Series

10 and under .... Mexico City, Aug. 21-31
12 and under .... Santo Domingo, D.R., July 10-20
14 and under .... Fairview Heights, IL, Aug. 1-11

LITTLE LEAGUE BASEBALL, INC.

International Headquarters: P.O. Box 3485, Williamsport, PA 17701. **Telephone:** (717) 326-1921. **FAX:** (717) 326-1074.

Year Founded: 1939.

Chairman: Dr. Luke LaPorta. **Vice Chairman:** James Whittington. **President and Chief Executive Officer:** Steve Keener.

Director of Communications: Dennis Sullivan. **Media Relations Director:** Lance Van Auken. **Director of Special Projects:** Scott Rosenberg.

Age Classifications, World Series

Little League (11-12) .... Williamsport, PA, Aug. 18-23
Junior League (13) .... Taylor, MI, Aug. 11-16
Senior League (13-15) .... Kissimmee, FL, Aug. 10-16
Big League (16-18) .... Ft. Lauderdale, FL, Aug. 8-16

NATIONAL AMATEUR BASEBALL FEDERATION

Mailing Address: P.O. Box 705, Bowie, MD 20718. **Telephone/FAX:** (301) 262-5005.

Year Founded: 1914.

Executive Director: Charles Blackburn.

Age Classifications, World Series

Freshman (12 and under) .... Sylvania, OH, July 17-20
Sophomore (14 and under).................... Miamisburg, OH, July 24-27
Junior (16 and under) .... Northville, MI, July 31-Aug. 3
High School (HS students) .... Hopkinsville, KY, July 31-Aug. 3
Senior (18 and under).................... Evansville, IN, Aug. 7-10
College (22 and under).................... Rome, GA, Aug. 7-10
Major (unlimited).................... Louisville, KY, Aug. 14-17

NATIONAL ASSOCIATION OF POLICE ATHLETIC LEAGUES

Mailing Address: 618 U.S. Highway 1, Suite 201, North Palm Beach, FL 33408. **Telephone:** (561) 844-1823. **FAX:** (561) 863-6120.

Year Founded: 1944.

Executive Director: Joseph Wilson. **General Manager:** Tina Lux. **Director of Member Services:** Nerilda Lugo.

Age Classifications, World Series

16 and Under ....Niagara Falls, NY, July 28-Aug. 2

PONY BASEBALL, INC.

National Headquarters: P.O. Box 225, Washington, PA 15301. **Telephone:** (412) 225-1060. **FAX:** (412) 225-9852.

Year Founded: 1951.

President: Abraham Key. **Director of Baseball Operations:** Don Clawson.

Age Classifications, World Series

Shetland (5-6) ....No National Tournament
Pinto (7-8) ....No National Tournament
Mustang (9-10) ....Irving, TX, Aug. 6-9
Bronco (11-12) ....Monterey, CA, Aug. 7-13
Pony (13-14) ....Washington, PA, Aug. 16-23
Colt (15-16) ....Lafayette, IN, Aug. 5-12
Palomino (17-18) ....Greensboro, NC, Aug. 13-16

REVIVING BASEBALL IN INNER CITIES (RBI)

Mailing Address: 350 Park Ave., New York, NY 10022. **Telephone:** (212) 339-7800.

Year Founded: 1989.

Founder: John Young. **Executive Director, Major League Baseball Charities:** Cathy Francis. **National Manager:** Tom Brasuell (212-339-7844).

Age Classifications, World Series

Junior League (13-15) .... Denver, CO, Aug. 10-15
Senior League (16-18) .... Denver, CO, Aug. 10-15

T-BALL USA ASSOCIATION, INC.

Office Address: 915 Broadway, Suite 1901, New York, NY 10010. **Telephone:** (212) 254-7911, (800) 741-0845. **FAX:** (212) 254-8042.

Year Founded: 1993.

President: Bing Broido. **Vice President:** Lois Richards.

U.S. AMATEUR BASEBALL ASSOCIATION

Mailing Address: 7101 Lake Ballinger Way, Edmonds, WA 98026. **Telephone/FAX:** (206) 776-7130.

Year Founded: 1969.

Executive Director: Al Rutledge.

Age Classifications, World Series

11 and under.................... San Marcos, CA, Aug. 16-23
12 and under.................... San Marcos, CA, Aug. 15-23
13 and under.................... Tumwater, WA, Aug. 8-16
14 and under.................... St. Albert, Alberta, Aug. 6-16
15 and under .... Las Vegas, NV, Aug. 16-23
16 and under .... Los Angeles, CA, Aug. 8-17
17 and under .... Spokane, WA, Aug. 9-17
18 and under.................... Site unavailable, Aug. 8-17
19 and under.................... Site unavailable, Aug. 2-9

U.S. JUNIOR OLYMPIC BASEBALL CHAMPIONSHIP

Mailing Address: 2160 Greenwood Ave., Trenton, NJ 08609. **Telephone:** (609) 586-2381. **FAX:** (609) 587-1818.

Age Classifications, Championships

16 and Under.................... Fort Myers, FL, June 20-29

YOUTH BASEBALL ATHLETIC LEAGUE

Mailing Office: 567 Alger Dr., Palo Alto, CA 94306. **Telephone:** (800) 477-9225. **FAX:** (415) 843-1316.

SERVICE DIRECTORY

ACCOUNTANTS

Azis, Jeffrey A. CPA, M Acc.
561-655-5089
Fax: 561-835-0909

APPAREL

Cape Cod Connection/The Dugout
904-243-0738
Fax: 904-243-0738

Diamond Sports
310-598-9717
Fax: 310-598-0906

Joy Athletic, Inc
3555 East 11 Avenue
Hialeah, FL 33013
305-691-7240
Fax: 305-691-7247

Minor Leagues, Major Dreams
P.O. Box 6098
Anaheim, CA 92816
800-345-2421 Fax:714-939-0655
http://www.minorleagues.com

Native Sun Sportswear
4590 62 Avenue North
Pinellas Park, FL 33781
813-528-2111
Fax: 813-528-8441

Western Athletic Supply
800-624-6637
Fax: 909-683-2444

Wilson Sporting Goods
773-714-6800
Fax: 800-642-4600

ATHLETIC TRAINING

Quic Hands
800-295-8851
Fax: 800-295-8851

AWARDS/TROPHIES

Barnstable Bat Company
40 Pleasant Pines Avenue
Centerville, MA 02632
508-362-8046
Fax: 508-362-3983

Sigma Glass Studio
2318 16th Avenue North
St. Petersburg, FL 33713
813-525-5384
Fax: 813-522-5211

BAGS

Cooper Baseball
800-268-1732
Fax: 416-533-0715

Louisville Slugger
800-282-2287 502-585-5226
Fax: 502-585-1179

Markwort Sporting Goods
4300 Forest Park Avenue
St. Louis, MO 63108
314-652-3757
Fax: 314-652-6241

Triple-M
909-624-0359
Fax: 909-624-3031

Western Athletic Supply
800-624-6637
Fax: 909-683-2444

Wilson Sporting Goods
773-714-6800
Fax: 800-642-4600

BASEBALL CARDS

FOTOBALL USA, Inc.
800-325-3686
Fax: 619-467-9900

GrandStand Cards
818-992-5642
Fax: 818-348-9122

Minford's Minors
704-733-1145
Fax: 704-733-1145

Wild Pitch
908-549-8984

BASEBALLS

The Jugs Company
11885 S.W. Herman Road
Tualatin, OR 97062
800-547-6843
Fax: 503-691-1100

Markwort Sporting Goods
4300 Forest Park Avenue
St. Louis, MO 63108
314-652-3757
Fax: 314-652-6241

Master Pitching Machine, Inc.
800-878-8228
Fax: 816-452-7581

SSK America
800-421-2674
Fax: 310-549-2904

Western Athletic Supply
800-624-6637
Fax: 909-683-2444

Wilson Sporting Goods
773-714-6800
Fax: 800-642-4600

BASES

Adams USA/Neumann Gloves
610 South Jefferson Avenue
Cookeville, TN 38501
615-526-2109
Fax: 615-372-8510

Beacon Ballfields/Lodestar L.L.C.
P.O. Box 45557
Madison, WI 53744-5557
800-747-5985
Fax: 608-274-6072

Markwort Sporting Goods
4300 Forest Park Avenue
St. Louis, MO 63108
314-652-3757
Fax: 314-652-6241

Western Athletic Supply
800-624-6637
Fax: 909-683-2444

BATS

Barnstable Bat Company
40 Pleasant Pines Avenue
Centerville, MA 02632
508-362-8046
Fax: 508-362-3983

Cooper Baseball
800-268-1732
Fax: 416-533-0715

Easton Sports, Inc.
800-347-3901
415-347-3900

Glomar Enterprises
116 W. Walnut Avenue
Fullerton, CA 92832
714-871-5956
Fax: 714-871-5958

Grover Products Company
3504 E. Olympic Blvd.
Los Angeles, CA 90023
213-263-9981
Fax: 213-268-8555

Louisville Slugger
P.O. Box 35700
Louisville, KY 40232
800-282-2287 502-585-5226
Fax: 502-585-1179

Markwort Sporting Goods
4300 Forest Park Avenue
St. Louis, MO 63108
314-652-3757
Fax: 314-652-6241

The Original Maple Bat Co.
Maker of SamBat™ & S. Holman Bat
93 Bayswater Avenue
Ottawa, Ontario K1Y 2G2
613-724-2421 Fax: 613-725-3299

Professional Diamond Clubs Inc.
401 Woodsway Drive
Lexington, NC 27292-4655
910-248-5537
Fax: 910-248-5537

SSK America
800-421-2674
Fax: 310-549-2904

Stick By Stan Bat Co.
P.O. Box 703
Jeffersonville, NY 12748
914-482-3824

STIX Baseball
800-533-STIX 407-425-3360
Fax: 407-425-3560

Western Athletic Supply
P.O. Box 5407
Riverside, CA 92517-5407
800-624-6637
Fax: 909-683-2444

Wilson Sporting Goods
773-714-6800
Fax: 800-642-4600

Worth Sports Company
800-423-3714 615-455-0691
Fax: 615-454-9164

BATTING CAGES

AstroTurf Industries, Inc.
512-259-0080
Fax: 512-259-2952

Beacon Ballfields/Lodestar L.L.C.
P.O. Box 45557
Madison, WI 53744-5557
800-747-5985
Fax: 608-274-6072

C & H Baseball, Inc.
801 7th Avenue West
Bradenton, FL 34205
941-748-0011 800-248-5192
Fax: 941-748-0012

Gates Batting Cages
5280 Bainbridge Drive
Boise, ID 83703
800-838-5917 208-345-7657

The Jugs Company
11885 S.W. Herman Road
Tualatin, OR 97062
800-547-6843
Fax: 503-691-1100

Master Pitching Machine, Inc.
800-878-8228
Fax: 816-452-7581

Miller Net Company
P.O. Box 18787
Memphis, TN 38181
800-423-6603 901-744-3804
Fax: 901-743-6580

National Batting Cages
800-547-8800 503-357-6615
Fax: 503-357-3727

Omni Sports Technologies
800-529-6664
Fax: 816-734-3931

Sterling Net
800-342-0316
Fax: 800-232-6381

BOOKS/VIDEOS

All About Pitching
800-243-6851

SPORTAMERICA
800-467-7885
Fax: 801-568-3777

Sysko's Sports Books
P.O. Box 6
Benton, WI 53803
800-932-2534
Fax: 800-932-2511

CAMPS/SCHOOLS

The Baseball Academy
5500 34th Street West
Bradenton, FL 34210
941-755-1000
Fax: 941-756-6891

Mickey Owen Baseball School
P.O. Box 88, Missouri Hwy. 96
Miller, MO 65707
800-999-8369
Fax: 417-889-6978

CAPS/HEADWEAR

American Promotions of IL., Inc.
P.O. Box 4488
Skokie, IL 60076
800-426-8054
Fax: 800-426-8054

Minor Leagues, Major Dreams
P.O. Box 6098
Anaheim, CA 92816
800-345-2421 Fax:714-939-0655
http://www.minorleagues.com

Native Sun Sportswear
4590 62 Avenue North
Pinellas Park, FL 33781
813-528-2111
Fax: 813-528-8441

New ERA Cap Co. Inc.
8061 Erice Rd. Box 208
Derby, NY 14047
800-989-0445
Fax: 716-549-5424

Star Struck, Inc.
8 F.J. Clarke Circle, Box 308
Bethel, CT 06801
800-908-4637
Fax: 800-962-8345

CASES

Anvil Cases
15650 Salt Lake Avenue
City of Industry, CA 91745
800-359-2684 Matt Larson (x120)
Fax: 818-968-1703

CATCHING EQUIPMENT

Cooper Baseball
800-268-1732
Fax: 416-533-0715

Diamond Sports
310-598-9717
Fax: 310-598-0906

Markwort Sporting Goods
4300 Forest Park Avenue
St. Louis, MO 63108
314-652-3757
Fax: 314-652-6241

SSK America
800-421-2674
Fax: 310-549-2904

Western Athletic Supply
P.O. Box 5407
Riverside, CA 92517-5407
800-624-6637
Fax: 909-683-2444

Wilson Sporting Goods
8700 W. Bryn Mawr Avenue
Chicago, IL 60631
312-714-6800
Fax: 800-642-4600

COMPUTER SOFTWARE

Concession Solutions, Inc.
16022 - 26th Avenue NE
Seattle, WA 98155
206-440-9203
Fax: 206-440-9213

TicketStop, Inc.
14042 NE 8th St., Suite 108
Bellevue, WA 98007
800-961-6111 Fax: 206-641-8151
www.ticketstop.com info@ticketstop.com

ENTERTAINMENT

ACME Mascots
718-722-7900
Fax: 718-858-7833

BirdZerk!
P.O. Box 36061
Louisville, KY 40233
502-458-4020 Fax: 502-458-0867
Email: wejam@bellsouth.net

Bleacher Preacher/
Jerry Pritikin
150 Maple Street #1307
Chicago, IL 60610
312-664-3231 Fax: 630-543-1215

C.R.O.S.S.FIRE CRUSADERS
3000 Cross Country
Germantown, TN 38138
901-756-1818
Fax: 901-755-5330

Morganna c/o SRO Events
"Baseball's Kissing Bandit"
3727 E. 31st Street
Tulsa, OK 74135
918-743-8461 Fax: 918-749-6643

Stick By Stan Bat Show
914-482-3824

Total Sports Entertainment
Blz Bro, SkyyDog, Gorilla Warfare, Cajun Commotion, Elvis, TV Celebs, Cecil Clown Piano Guys~ "Original" wireless piano act 800-962-2471

FIELD CONSTRUCTION/RENOVATION

Alpine Services, Inc.
5313 Brookeville Road
Gaithersburg, MD 20882
800-292-8420
Fax: 301-963-7901

FOOD SERVICE

Concession Solutions, Inc.
16022 - 26th Avenue NE
Seattle, WA 98155
206-440-9203
Fax: 206-440-9213

DiGiovanni's Food Service
4773 Hunter's Run
Sarasota, FL 34241
941-922-0092
Fax: 941-922-8122

"Houston's" Peanuts
P.O. Box 160
Dublin, NC 28332
910-862-2136 800-334-8383
Fax: 910-862-8076

The Peanut Roaster
919-469-1676 800-445-1404
Fax: 919-467-7444

Slush Puppie Brands
800-543-0860 513-244-2400
Fax: 513-251-3458

Sportservice Corporation
438 Main Street
Buffalo, NY 14202
716-858-5000

Vinnie's Hot Soft Pretzels
P.O. Box 59
Durham, NC 27702
919-477-3715 954-989-7594
Fax: 919-477-3093 954-989-0229

FOOTWEAR ACCESSORIES

SecondWind Products, Inc.
P.O. Box 93447
Paso Robles, CA 93447
800-248-0425 (x120)
Fax: 805-239-2555

Tuff Toe
1571 S. Sunkist Street #E
Anaheim, CA 92806
800-888-0802
Fax: 714-935-2838

GAME CARDS/CHARTS

Allegheny Publishing Company
5943 Graybrooke Drive
Export, PA 15632-8941
800-733-0543
Fax: 412-733-5445

GLOVE CARE/REPAIR

DC Enterprises/Glove Guard
916-257-5844

Hot Glove Treatment
800-869-0021
Fax: 770-916-1217

Louisville Slugger
800-282-2287 502-585-5226
Fax: 502-585-1179

GLOVES

Adams USA/Neumann Gloves
610 South Jefferson Avenue
Cookeville, TN 38501
615-526-2109
Fax: 615-372-8510

Cooper Baseball
800-268-1732
Fax: 416-533-0715

Diamond Sports
310-598-9717
Fax: 310-598-0906

Guerrero/Diamond King Sports
800-826-1464
Fax: 517-321-1756

Hot Glove Treatment
800-869-0021
Fax: 770-916-1217

Louisville Slugger
P.O. Box 35700
Louisville, KY 40232
800-282-2287 502-585-5226
Fax: 502-585-1179

Markwort Sporting Goods
4300 Forest Park Avenue
St. Louis, MO 63108
314-652-3757
Fax: 314-652-6241

Professional Diamond Clubs Inc.
401 Woodsway Drive
Lexington, NC 27292-4655
910-248-5537
Fax: 910-248-5537

Rawlings
800-729-7770

SSK America
800-421-2674
Fax: 310-549-2904

STIX Baseball
800-533-STIX 407-425-3360
Fax: 407-425-3560

Western Athletic Supply
P.O. Box 5407
Riverside, CA 92517-5407
800-624-6637
Fax: 909-683-2444

Wilson Sporting Goods
8700 W. Bryn Mawr Avenue
Chicago, IL 60631
773-714-6800
Fax: 800-642-4600

GRAPHIC DESIGN

Low & Inside Creative
612-797-0777
Fax: 612-797-7441
E-Mail: baseball@bitstream.net

HELMETS

Diamond Sports
310-598-9717
310-598-0906

HITTING GLOVES

TurboSlot Sports, Inc.
P.O. Box 2190
Advance, NC 27006
800-726-3568
Fax: 910-998-0694

HITTING MACHINES

Quic Hands
800-295-8851
Fax: 800-295-8851

INSURANCE

American Hole 'n One
800-822-2257
770-271-4006

Azis, Jeffrey A. CPA, M Acc.
561-655-5089
Fax: 561-835-0909

K & K Insurance Group, Inc.
219-459-5604
Fax: 219-459-5120

LIGHTING

Universal Sports Lighting
800-962-2068
Fax: 217-648-5209

LOGO DESIGN

Silverman Group, Inc.
700 State Street
New Haven, CT 06511
203-562-6418
Fax: 203-777-9637

MASCOT COSTUMES

Carol Flemming
Costume Design Studio
209-795-7074

Olympus Flag & Banner
Mascot Division
8939 N 55th Street
Milwaukee, WI 53229
800-558-9620 Fax: 414-355-1931

MEMORABILIA

Adelson Sports
602-596-1913
Fax: 602-596-1914

Stan's Sports Memorabilia
201-228-5257
Fax: 201-228-5257

MERCHANDISING SERVICES

Feron's Merchandising Services
203-221-3580
Fax: 203-221-3583

MESSAGE CENTERS

Daktronics, Inc.
888-325-8766
Fax: 605-697-4700

Display Solutions, Inc.
6301 Best Friend Road
Norcross, GA 30071
770-662-5400
Fax: 770-263-8353

Spectrum Scoreboards
10048 Easthaven
Houston, TX 77075
800-392-5050
Fax: 713-944-1290

MUSIC/SOUND EFFECTS

Sound Creations
2820 Azalea Place
Nashville, TN 37204
615-460-7330
Fax: 615-460-7331

NATIONAL SHOWCASE EVENTS

Baseball Factory, Inc.
5537 Twin Knolls Rd., Suite 440
Columbia, MD 21045
800-641-4487
Fax: 410-730-7701

NETTING/POSTS

ATEC
10 Greg Street
Sparks, NV 89431
800-755-5100
Fax: 702-352-2822

Beacon Ballfields/Lodestar L.L.C.
P.O. Box 45557
Madison, WI 53744-5557
800-747-5985
Fax: 608-274-6072

C & H Baseball, Inc.
801 7th Avenue West
Bradenton, FL 34205
941-748-0011 800-248-5192
Fax: 941-748-0012

Master Pitching Machine, Inc.
800-878-8228
Fax: 816-452-7581

Miller Net Company
P.O. Box 18787
Memphis, TN 38181
800-423-6603 901-744-3804
Fax: 901-743-6580

National Batting Cages
800-547-8800 503-357-6615
Fax: 503-357-3727

Omni Sports Technologies
800-529-6664
Fax: 816-734-3931

Saleen Sportnet
800-382-5399

Sterling Net
800-342-0316
Fax: 800-232-6381

ON DECK CIRCLES

AstroTurf Industries, Inc.
512-259-0080
Fax: 512-259-2952

PITCHING MACHINES

ATEC
10 Greg Street
Sparks, NV 89431
800-755-5100
Fax: 702-352-2822

The Jugs Company
11885 S.W. Herman Road
Tualatin, OR 97062
800-547-6843
Fax: 502-691-1100

Master Pitching Machine, Inc.
4200 NE Birmingham Road
Kansas City, MO 64117
800-878-8228
Fax: 816-452-7581

Omni Sports Technologies
800-529-6664
Fax: 816-734-3931

PLAYING FIELD PRODUCTS

AstroTurf Industries, Inc.
512-259-0080
Fax: 512-259-2952

Beacon Ballfields/Lodestar L.L.C.
P.O. Box 45557
Madison, WI 53744
800-747-5985
Fax: 608-274-6072

C & H Baseball, Inc.
801 7th Avenue West
Bradenton, FL 34205
941-748-0011 800-248-5192
Fax: 941-748-0012

Cooper Baseball
800-268-1732
Fax:416-533-0715

Diamond-Dry
800-962-2068
Fax: 217-648-5209

Diamond Pro
1341 W. Mockingbird Lane
Dallas, TX 75247
800-228-2987
Fax: 800-640-6735

National Batting Cages
800-547-8800 503-357-6615
Fax: 503-357-3727

Partac Peat/Beam Clay
Kelsey Park
Great Meadows, NJ 07838
800-247-BEAM
Fax: 908-637-8421

Promats, Inc.
P.O. Box 508
Fort Collins, CO 80522
800-678-6287
Fax: 970-482-7740

Stabilizer, Inc.
2218 E. Magnolia Street
Phoenix, AZ 85034
602-225-5900
Fax: 602-225-5902

Western Athletic Supply
P.O. Box 5407
Riverside, CA 92517-5407
800-624-6637
Fax: 909-683-2444

PRINTING

TradeMark Printing
415-592-9130
Fax: 415-592-2776

Triple-M
2801 N. Towne Avenue
Pomona, CA 91767
909-624-0359
Fax: 909-624-3031

PRIZE INDEMNITY INSURANCE

American Hole 'n One
800-822-2257
Fax: 770-271-4006

SCA Promotions, Inc.
8300 Douglas Ave., Suite 625
Dallas, TX 75225
888-860-3700
Fax: 214-860-3740

PROFESSIONAL SERVICES

Baseball Opportunities
602-483-8224

Heery International
999 Peachtree Street N.E.
Atlanta, GA 30367-5401
404-881-9880 Fax: 404-875-1283
http:/www.heery.com

PROMOTIONAL ITEMS

American Promotions of IL., Inc.
P.O. Box 4488
Skokie, IL 60076
800-426-8054
Fax: 800-426-8054

Caddy Products
800-845-0591
Fax: 612-829-0166

Conder Company
216-241-6052
Fax: 216-241-6065

Creative Craze, L.L.C.
888-506-0929
Fax: 972-506-7197

Fotoball USA, Inc.
800-325-3686
Fax: 619-467-9900

K R Industries, Inc.
708-863-1200 (ext.13)
Fax: 708-222-1400

Louisville Slugger
800-282-2287 502-585-5226
Fax: 502-585-1179

Native Sun sportswear
4590 62 Avenue North
Pinellas Park, FL 33781
813-528-2111
Fax: 813-528-8441

PROTECTIVE FIELDWALL PADDING

Promats, Inc.
P.O. Box 508
Fort Collins, CO 80522
800-678-6287
Fax: 970-482-7740

PUBLICATIONS

All About Pitching
800-243-6851

Baseball Information Network
800-381-3351
Fax: 770-565-9632

The Baseball Scout Newsletter
508-753-8387
Fax: 508-753-8387

Braunstein's Met/Yankee Minor League Reporter
117 West 74th Street #4C
New York, NY 10023
212-258-0026 Fax: 212-307-9518

Low & Inside
612-797-0777
Fax: 612-797-7441
E-Mail: baseball@bitstream.net

South Central Minor Leaguer
915-735-2278
Fax: 915-735-2230

RADAR EQUIPMENT

ATEC
10 Greg Street
Sparks, NV 83431
800-755-5100
Fax: 702-352-2822

Decatur Electronics, Inc.
800-428-4315
Fax: 217-428-5302

The Jugs Company
11885 S.W. Herman Road
Tualatin, OR 97062
800-547-6843
Fax: 503-691-1100

Omni Sports Technologies
800-529-6664
Fax: 816-734-3931

Radar Sales
5640 International Parkway
Minneapolis, MN 55428
612-533-1100 888-782-5537
Fax: 612-533-1400

SCOREBOARD ANIMATION

JAMINATION
1384 Grandview Ave. Suite. 205
Columbus, OH 43212
614-481-0524
Fax: 614-481-0452

SCOREBOARDS

Daktronics, Inc.
888-325-8766
Fax: 605-697-4700

Display Solutions, Inc.
6301 Best Friend Road
Norcross, GA 30071
770-662-5400
Fax: 770-263-8353

Markwort Sporting Goods
4300 Forest Park Avenue
St. Louis, MO 63108
314-652-3757
Fax: 314-652-6241

Spectrum Scoreboards
10048 Easthaven
Houston, TX 77075
800-392-5050
Fax: 713-944-1290

SHIPPING/CARRYING CASES

Anvil Cases
15650 Salt Lake Avenue
City of Industry, CA 91745
800-359-2684 (ext 120)
Fax: 818-968-1703

SIGN SYSTEMS/TRI-ACTION

Action Graphix
P.O. Box 2337
Jonesboro, AR 72402
501-931-7440
Fax: 501-931-7528

STADIUM ARCHITECTS

Design Exchange Architects, Inc.
Polly Drummond Office Park
Building. 3, Suite 3205
Newark, DE 19711
302-366-1611 Fax: 302-366-1657

Devine deFlon Yaeger Architects
The Uptown Bldg., Suite 300
3700 Broadway
Kansas City, MO 64111
816-561-2761 Fax: 816-561-9222

Ellerbe Becket
Two Arizona Center
400 North 5th St., Suite 1100
Phoenix, AZ 85004
602-514-8585 Fax: 602-514-8590

Heery International
999 Peachtree Street N.E.
Atlanta, GA 30367-5401
404-881-9880 Fax: 404-875-1283
http:/www.heery.com

HNTB Sports Architecture
1201 Walnut, Suite 700
Kansas City, MO 64106
816-472-1201
Fax: 816-472-4060

HOK Sports Facilities Group
323 W. 8th St. Suite 700
Kansas City, MO 64105
816-221-1576
Fax: 816-221-5816

L.D. Astorino & Associates
227 Fort Pitt Blvd.
Pittsburgh, PA 15222
412-765-1700
Fax: 412-765-1711

Lescher & Mahony Sports
601 West Swann Avenue
Tampa, FL 33606
813-254-9811
Fax: 813-254-4230

M. C. Smith Associates & Architectural Group, Inc.
529 Greenwood Avenue S.E..
East Grand Rapids, MI 49506
616-451-3346 Fax: 616-451-1935

STADIUM SEATING

Caddy Products
7667 Cahill Road
Minneapolis, MN 55439-2749
800-845-0591
Fax: 612-829-0166

Coasters
198 East Blithedale Avenue
Mill Valley, CA 94941
415-389-8322
Fax: 415-389-5452

Hill Arts & Entertainment Systems
37 Soundview Road
Guilford, CT 06457
800-899-8086 203-453-1718
Fax: 203-458-2465

Interkal/ Gas Seating
616-349-1521
Fax: 616-349-5888

K R Industries, Inc.
708-863-1200 (ext 13)
Fax: 708-222-1400

Seating Services, Inc.
800-552-9470
Fax: 716-549-9011

Southern Bleacher
P.O. Box One
Graham, TX 76450
800-433-0912
Fax: 817-549-1365

Sturdisteel Company /div. of Schultz Industries, Inc.
P.O. Box 2655
Waco, TX 76710
800-433-3116 Fax: 817-666-4472

TAXES

Azis, Jeffrey A. CPA, M Acc.
561-655-5089
Fax: 561-835-0909

TRAINING SYSTEMS

Set Pro
800-890-8803

TICKETS

Easy Computer Systems
417-335-3279
Fax: 417-335-5246

Select Ticketing Systems
315-479-6663 800-944-7277
Fax: 315-471-2715

Sport Productions, Inc.
216-591-2400
Fax: 216-591-2424

TicketStop, Inc.
14042 NE 8th St., Suite 108
Bellevue, WA 98007
800-961-6111 Fax: 206-641-8151
www.ticketstop.com info@ticketstop.com

TRAVEL

Broach Baseball Tours
2727 Selwyn Avenue, Suite C
Charlotte, N.C. 28209
800-849-6345
Fax: 704-333-1978

KenSport
106 Electra Drive
Cary, NC 27513
919-380-7476

Sports Tours, Inc.
The Sporting News FanTrips
195 Main Street, Suite 2B
Northampton, MA 01060
800-722-7701 Fax: 413-584-0424

TURNSTILE ADS

Entry Media, Inc.
407-678-4446
Fax: 407-679-3590

UNIFORMS

DeLong
515-236-3106
Fax: 515-236-4891

Markwort Sporting Goods
4300 Forest Park Avenue
St. Louis, MO 63108
314-652-3757
Fax: 314-652-6241

Rawlings
800-729-7770
Fax: 314-349-3576

Russell Athletic
205-329-5089

Wilson Sporting Goods
8700 W. Bryn Mawr Avenue
Chicago, IL 60631
773-714-6800
Fax: 800-642-4600

Western Athletic
800-624-6637
Fax: 909-683-2444

1997 DIRECTORY INDEX

MAJOR LEAGUE TEAMS

American League

Page	Club	Phone	FAX
18	Anaheim Angels	714-940-2000	714-940-2205
20	Baltimore Orioles	410-685-9800	410-547-6272
22	Boston Red Sox	617-267-9440	617-236-6797
24	Chicago White Sox	312-674-1000	312-674-5116
26	Cleveland Indians	216-420-4200	216-420-4396
28	Detroit Tigers	313-962-4000	313-962-2138
30	Kansas City Royals	816-921-2200	816-921-5775
32	Milwaukee Brewers	414-933-4114	414-933-7323
34	Minnesota Twins	612-375-1366	612-375-7473
36	New York Yankees	718-293-4300	718-293-8431
38	Oakland Athletics	510-638-4900	510-568-3770
40	Seattle Mariners	206-628-3555	206-628-3340
42	Tampa Bay Devil Rays	813-825-3137	813-825-3300
44	Texas Rangers	817-273-5222	817-273-5206
46	Toronto Blue Jays	416-341-1000	416-341-1245

National League

Page	Club	Phone	FAX
50	Arizona Diamondbacks	602-514-8500	602-514-8599
52	Atlanta Braves	404-522-7630	404-614-1391
54	Chicago Cubs	773-404-2827	773-404-4129
56	Cincinnati Reds	513-421-4510	513-421-7342
58	Colorado Rockies	303-292-0200	303-312-2319
60	Florida Marlins	305-626-7400	305-626-7428
62	Houston Astros	713-799-9500	713-799-9562
64	Los Angeles Dodgers	213-224-1500	213-224-1269
66	Montreal Expos	514-253-3434	514-253-8282
68	New York Mets	718-507-6387	718-565-6395
70	Philadelphia Phillies	215-463-6000	215-389-3050
72	Pittsburgh Pirates	412-323-5000	412-323-9133
74	St. Louis Cardinals	314-421-3060	314-425-0640
76	San Diego Padres	619-881-6500	619-497-5454
78	San Francisco Giants	415-468-3700	415-467-0485

MINOR LEAGUE TEAMS

Page	Club	League	Phone	FAX
125	Akron	Eastern	330-253-5151	330-253-3300
111	Albuquerque	PCL	505-243-1791	505-842-0561
137	Arkansas	Texas	501-664-1555	501-664-1834
168	Asheville	SAL	704-258-0428	704-258-0320
176	Auburn	NYP	315-255-2489	315-255-2675
168	Augusta	SAL	706-736-7889	706-736-1122
142	Bakersfield	Cal	805-322-1363	805-322-6199
176	Batavia	NYP	716-343-5454	716-343-5620
160	Beloit	Midwest	608-362-2272	608-362-0418
193	Billings	Pioneer	406-252-1241	406-252-2968
125	Binghamton	Eastern	607-723-6387	607-723-7779
131	Birmingham	Southern	205-988-3200	205-988-9698
188	Bluefield	Appy	540-326-1326	540-326-1318
183	Boise	Northwest	208-322-5000	208-322-7432
126	Bowie	Eastern	301-805-6007	301-805-6008
153	Brevard County	FSL	407-633-9200	407-633-9210
188	Bristol	Appy	540-645-7275	540-645-7377
108	Buffalo	Am. Assoc.	716-846-2000	716-852-6530
160	Burlington, IA	Midwest	319-754-5705	319-754-5882
188	Burlington, NC	Appy	910-222-0223	910-226-2498
193	Butte	Pioneer	406-723-8206	406-723-3376
119	Calgary	PCL	403-284-1111	403-284-4343
169	Cape Fear	SAL	910-424-6500	910-424-4325
169	Capital City	SAL	803-256-4110	803-256-4338
131	Carolina	Southern	919-269-2287	919-269-4910
161	Cedar Rapids	Midwest	319-363-3887	319-363-5631
170	Charleston, SC	SAL	803-965-4096	803-723-2641
170	Charleston, WV	SAL	304-344-2287	304-344-0083
153	Charlotte, FL	FSL	941-625-9500	941-624-5168
113	Charlotte, NC	IL	704-357-8071	803-548-8055
132	Chattanooga	Southern	423-267-2208	423-267-4258
153	Clearwater	FSL	813-441-8638	813-447-3924
161	Clinton	Midwest	319-242-0727	319-242-1433
120	Colorado Springs	PCL	719-597-1449	719-597-2491
171	Columbus, GA	SAL	706-571-8866	706-571-9107

113	Columbus, OH	IL	614-462-5250	614-462-3271
189	Danville	Appy	804-791-3346	804-791-3347
154	Daytona	FSL	904-257-3172	904-257-3382
171	Delmarva	SAL	410-219-3112	410-219-9164
154	Dunedin	FSL	813-733-9302	813-734-7661
148	Durham	Carolina	919-687-6500	919-687-6560
120	Edmonton	PCL	403-429-2934	403-426-5640
189	Elizabethton	Appy	423-543-4395	423-542-1510
137	El Paso	Texas	915-755-2000	915-757-0671
176	Erie	NYP	814-456-1300	814-456-7520
183	Eugene	Northwest	541-342-5367	541-342-6089
184	Everett	Northwest	206-258-3673	206-258-3675
155	Fort Myers	FSL	941-768-4210	941-768-4211
162	Fort Wayne	Midwest	219-482-6400	219-471-4678
148	Frederick	Carolina	301-662-0013	301-662-0018
193	Great Falls	Pioneer	406-452-5311	406-454-0811
172	Greensboro	SAL	910-333-2287	910-273-7350
132	Greenville	Southern	864-299-3456	864-277-7369
172	Hagerstown	SAL	301-791-6266	301-791-6066
126	Harrisburg	Eastern	717-231-4444	717-231-4445
194	Helena	Pioneer	406-449-7616	406-449-6979
173	Hickory	SAL	704-322-3000	704-322-6137
142	High Desert	Cal	619-246-6287	619-246-3197
177	Hudson Valley	NYP	914-838-0094	914-838-0014
133	Huntsville	Southern	205-882-2562	205-880-0801
194	Idaho Falls	Pioneer	208-522-8363	208-522-9858
108	Indianapolis	Am. Assoc.	317-269-3545	317-269-3541
109	Iowa	Am. Assoc.	515-243-6111	515-243-5152
138	Jackson	Texas	601-981-4664	601-981-4669
133	Jacksonville	Southern	904-358-2846	904-358-2845
177	Jamestown	NYP	716-664-0915	716-664-4175
190	Johnson City	Appy	423-461-4850	423-461-4864
162	Kane County	Midwest	630-232-8811	630-232-8815
190	Kingsport	Appy	423-378-3744	423-392-8538
149	Kinston	Carolina	919-527-9111	919-527-2328
155	Kissimmee	FSL	407-933-5500	407-847-6237
134	Knoxville	Southern	423-637-9494	423-523-9913
143	Lake Elsinore	Cal	909-245-4487	909-245-0305
156	Lakeland	FSL	941-688-7911	941-688-9589
143	Lancaster	Cal	805-726-5400	805-726-5406
163	Lansing	Midwest	517-485-4500	517-485-4518
121	Las Vegas	PCL	702-386-7200	702-386-7214
195	Lethbridge	Pioneer	403-327-7975	403-327-8085
109	Louisville	Am. Assoc.	502-367-9121	502-368-5120
178	Lowell	NYP	508-459-1702	508-459-1674
149	Lynchburg	Carolina	804-528-1144	804-846-0768
173	Macon	SAL	912-745-8943	912-743-5559
190	Martinsville	Appy	540-666-2000	540-666-2139
195	Medicine Hat	Pioneer	403-526-0404	403-526-4000
134	Memphis	Southern	901-272-1687	901-278-3354
163	Michigan	Midwest	616-660-2287	616-660-2288
138	Midland	Texas	915-683-4251	915-683-0994
135	Mobile	Southern	334-479-2327	334-476-1147
144	Modesto	Cal	209-572-4487	209-572-4490
110	Nashville	Am. Assoc.	615-242-4371	615-256-5684
127	New Britain	Eastern	860-224-8383	203-225-6267
127	New Haven	Eastern	203-782-3140	203-782-3150
178	New Jersey	NYP	201-579-7500	201-579-7502
110	New Orleans	Am. Assoc.	504-734-5155	504-734-5118
114	Norfolk	IL	757-622-2222	757-624-9090
128	Norwich	Eastern	860-887-7962	860-886-5996
196	Ogden	Pioneer	801-393-2400	801-393-2473
111	Oklahoma City	Am. Assoc.	405-946-8989	405-942-4198
111	Omaha	Am. Assoc.	402-734-2550	402-734-7166
179	Oneonta	NYP	607-432-6326	607-432-1965
134	Orlando	Southern	407-649-7297	407-649-1637
114	Ottawa	IL	613-747-5969	613-747-0003
115	Pawtucket	IL	401-724-7300	401-724-2140
164	Peoria	Midwest	309-688-1622	309-686-4516
121	Phoenix	PCL	602-275-0500	602-990-8987
174	Piedmont	SAL	704-932-3267	704-938-7040
179	Pittsfield	NYP	413-499-6387	413-443-7144
128	Portland, ME	Eastern	207-874-9300	207-780-0317
184	Portland, OR	Northwest	503-223-2837	503-223-2948
149	Prince William	Carolina	703-590-2311	703-590-5716
191	Princeton	Appy	304-487-2000	304-425-6999
191	Pulaski	Appy	540-980-1000	540-980-3055
164	Quad City	Midwest	319-324-2032	319-324-3109
144	Rancho Cuca.	Cal	909-481-5000	909-481-5005
129	Reading	Eastern	610-375-8469	610-373-5868
115	Richmond	IL	804-359-4444	804-359-0731

116	Rochester	IL	716-454-1001	716-454-1056
164	Rockford	Midwest	815-962-2827	815-961-2002
179	St. Catharines	NYP	905-641-5297	905-641-3007
156	St. Lucie	FSL	561-871-2100	561-878-9802
156	St. Petersburg	FSL	813-822-3384	813-895-1556
150	Salem	Carolina	540-389-3333	540-389-9710
185	Salem-Keizer	Northwest	503-390-2225	503-390-2227
122	Salt Lake	PCL	801-485-3800	801-485-6818
139	San Antonio	Texas	210-675-7275	210-670-0001
145	San Bernardino	Cal	909-888-9922	909-888-5251
145	San Jose	Cal	408-297-1435	408-297-1453
157	Sarasota	FSL	941-365-4460	941-365-4217
174	Savannah	SAL	912-351-9150	912-352-9722
116	Scranton/W-B	IL	717-969-2255	717-963-6564
139	Shreveport	Texas	318-636-5555	318-636-5670
165	South Bend	Midwest	219-235-9988	219-235-9950
185	So. Oregon	Northwest	541-770-5364	541-772-4466
186	Spokane	Northwest	509-535-2922	509-534-5368
146	Stockton	Cal	209-944-5943	209-463-4937
117	Syracuse	IL	315-474-7833	315-474-2658
122	Tacoma	PCL	206-752-7707	206-752-7135
157	Tampa	FSL	813-875-7753	813-673-3174
117	Toledo	IL	419-893-9483	419-893-5847
129	Trenton	Eastern	609-394-3300	609-394-9666
123	Tucson	PCL	520-325-2621	520-327-2371
140	Tulsa	Texas	918-744-5998	918-747-3267
180	Utica	NYP	315-738-0999	315-738-0992
123	Vancouver	PCL	604-872-5232	604-872-1714
180	Vermont	NYP	802-655-4200	802-655-5660
158	Vero Beach	FSL	561-569-4900	561-567-0819
146	Visalia	Cal	209-625-0480	209-739-7732
181	Watertown	NYP	315-788-8747	315-788-8841
165	West Michigan	Midwest	616-784-4131	616-784-4911
158	West Palm Beach	FSL	561-684-6801	561-681-4880
140	Wichita	Texas	316-267-3372	316-267-3382
181	Williamsport	NYP	717-326-3389	717-326-3494
150	Wilmington	Carolina	302-888-2015	302-888-2032
151	Winston-Salem	Carolina	910-759-2233	910-759-2042
166	Wisconsin	Midwest	414-733-4152	414-733-8032
186	Yakima	Northwest	509-457-5151	509-457-9909

Phone and FAX numbers for minor league offices can be found on page 106.

OTHER ORGANIZATIONS

Page	Organization	Phone	FAX
285	AAABA	614-453-8531	614-453-3978
279	Alaska Central League	907-283-7133	907-283-3390
279	Alaska League	907-451-0095	—
285	Amateur Athletic Union	407-363-6170	407-363-6171
285	American Amateur BB Congress	616-781-2002	616-781-2060
246	American BB Coaches Assoc.	517-775-3300	517-775-3600
17	American League	212-339-7600	212-593-7138
285	American Legion Baseball	317-630-1213	317-630-1369
277	Area Code Games	707-525-0498	707-525-0214
242	Arizona Fall League	602-496-6700	602-496-6384
280	Arizona Collegiate League	602-949-4225	602-949-4225
101	Associated Press	212-621-1630	212-621-1639
98	Assoc. of Prof. BB Players	714-892-9900	714-897-0233
104	Athletes In Action	813-968-7400	813-968-7515
280	Atlantic Collegiate League	201-702-1755	201-702-1898
243	Australian Baseball League	61-2-9437-4622	61-2-9437-4155
285	Babe Ruth Baseball	609-695-1434	609-695-2505
99	Baseball Assistance Team	212-339-7884	212-888-8632
279	Baseball Canada	613-748-5606	613-748-5767
99	Baseball Chapel	847-438-0978	847-438-6554
102	Baseball Digest	847-491-6440	847-491-0867
104	Baseball Trade Show	813-822-6937	813-821-5819
101	BB Writers Assoc. of America	516-981-7938	516-585-4669
103	Beckett Publications	972-991-6657	972-991-8930
222	Big South League	601-483-7245	601-483-9040
101	CBS Radio	212-975-4321	212-975-3515
101	Canadian Press	416-594-2154	—
280	Cape Cod League	508-748-0337	508-748-0552
239	Caribbean BB Confederation	809-562-4737	809-565-4654
281	Central Illinois Collegiate League	309-828-4429	309-828-4429
281	Clark Griffith League	703-536-3252	703-536-1729
281	Coastal Plain League	919-852-1960	919-852-1973
104	Colorado Silver Bullets	404-636-8200	404-636-0530
246	CC League of California	916-444-1600	916-444-2616
103	Coman Publishing	919-688-0218	919-682-1532
286	Continental Amateur BB Assoc.	614-899-2103	614-899-2103
286	Dixie Baseball, Inc.	334-241-2300	334-241-2301

286	Dizzy Dean Baseball	601-258-7626	—
239	Dominican League	809-567-6371	809-567-5720
101	ESPN Radio	860-585-2661	860-589-5523
99	ESPN-TV	860-585-2000	860-585-2400
99	Elias Sports Bureau	212-869-1530	212-354-0980
100	FOX-TV	213-856-1234	213-462-5931
222	Frontier League	614-452-7400	614-452-2999
278	Goodwill Games	404-827-3400	404-827-1394
282	Great Lakes League	216-871-8100	216-871-4221
98	Hall of Fame	607-547-7200	607-547-2044
286	Hap Dumont Youth Baseball	316-721-1779	316-721-8054
244	Hawaii Winter Baseball	808-973-7247	808-973-7117
223	Heartland League	317-474-5341	317-474-6462
99	Howe Sportsdata International	617-951-0070	617-737-9960
102	Inside Sports	847-491-6440	847-491-0867
278	International Baseball Assoc.	41-21-311-1863	41-21-311-1864
102	International Baseball Rundown	630-790-3087	630-790-3182
278	International Olympic Committee	41-21-621-61-11	41-21-621-62-16
236	Japanese Baseball	03-3502-0022	03-3502-0140
282	Jayhawk League	316-835-2589	316-755-1285
103	Krause Publications	715-445-2214	715-445-4087
286	Little League Baseball, Inc.	717-326-1921	717-326-1074
15	MLB International	212-350-8300	212-826-2230
98	MLB Players Alumni Association	813-822-3399	813-822-6300
15	MLB Player Relations Comm.	212-339-7400	212-371-2242
97	MLB Productions	201-807-0888	201-807-0272
15	MLB Properties	212-339-7900	212-339-7628
97	MLB Umpire Dev. Program	813-823-1286	813-823-7212
97	Major League Players Assoc.	212-826-0808	212-752-3649
97	Major League Scouting Bureau	714-458-7600	714-458-9454
97	Major League Umpires Assoc.	215-979-3200	215-979-3201
234	Mexican League	525-557-2454	525-395-2454
240	Mexican Pacific League	52-642-2-3100	52-642-2-7250
246	NAIA	918-494-8828	918-494-8841
100	NBC-TV	212-664-4444	212-664-3602
246	NCAA	913-339-1906	913-339-0026
279	NCAA Summer Baseball	913-339-1906	913-339-0026
246	NJCAA	719-590-9788	719-590-7324
287	National Amateur Baseball Fed.	301-262-5005	301-262-5005
106	National Association	813-822-6937	813-821-5819
287	National Association/PAL	561-844-1823	561-863-6120
279	National Baseball Congress	316-267-3372	316-267-3382
277	Nat'l Classic HS Tournament	714-993-5350	714-524-2458
101	National Collegiate BB Writers	312-553-0483	312-553-0495
277	Nat'l Fed. of State HS Assoc.	816-464-5400	816-464-5571
277	Nat'l HS Baseball Coaches Assoc.	402-457-1962	402-457-1962
49	National League	212-339-7700	212-935-5069
282	New England Collegiate League	203-238-4111	203-238-4111
224	North Atlantic League	516-287-0557	516-283-2252
224	Northeast League	914-434-7262	914-434-4806
282	Northeastern Collegiate League	716-593-3923	716-593-3923
224	Northern League	919-956-8150	919-683-2693
283	Northwest Collegiate League	503-725-5634	503-725-5610
283	Northwoods League	941-644-4022	941-644-1238
15	Office of the Commissioner	212-339-7800	212-355-0007
283	Pacific International League	206-623-8844	602-623-8361
278	Pan American Games	204-985-1999	204-985-1993
287	PONY Baseball, Inc.	412-225-1060	412-225-9852
227	Prairie League	306-522-7575	306-522-7539
240	Puerto Rican League	787-765-6285	787-767-3028
287	RBI	212-339-7800	—
99	SABR	216-575-0500	216-575-0502
283	San Diego Collegiate League	619-438-0347	—
283	Shenandoah Valley League	540-886-1748	540-885-7612
102	The Sporting News	314-997-7111	314-997-0765
102	Sports Illustrated	212-522-1212	212-522-4543
100	The Sports Network	416-494-1212	416-490-7010
101	SportsTicker	201-309-1200	201-860-9742
102	Spring Training BB Yearbook	919-967-2420	919-967-6294
99	STATS, Inc.	847-676-3322	847-676-0821
102	Street and Smith's Baseball	212-880-8698	212-880-4347
278	Sydney Olympic Org. Committee	61-2-931-2000	61-2-931-2020
277	Team One/HS Baseball USA	606-291-4463	606-291-4463
227	Texas-Louisiana League	915-677-4501	915-677-4215
102	Total Baseball	203-454-2451	203-454-8761
287	US Amateur Baseball Association	206-776-7130	206-776-7130
278	USA Baseball	609-586-2381	609-587-1818
278	US Olympic Committee	719-632-5551	719-578-4654
102	USA Today	703-276-3731	703-558-3988
102	USA Today Baseball Weekly	703-558-5630	703-558-4678
241	Venezuelan League	58-2-751-2079	58-2-751-0891
228	Western League	503-203-8557	503-203-8438